"We've embarked on the beginning of the Last Days of the Age of Oil. Nations of the world that are striving to modernize will make choices different from the ones we have made. They will have to. And even today's industrial powers will shift energy use patterns....[T]he market share for carbon-rich fuels will diminish, as the demand for other forms of energy grows. And energy companies have a choice: to embrace the future and recognize the growing demand for a wide array of fuels; or ignore reality, and slowly—but surely—be left behind."

> —Mike Bowlin, Chairman and CEO, ARCO,
> and Chairman, American Petroleum Institute,
> 9 Feb. 1999 [1]

"My personal opinion is that we are at the peak of the oil age and at the same time the beginning of the hydrogen age. Anything else is an interim solution in my view. The transition will be very messy, and will take many and diverse competing technological paths, but the long-term future will be in hydrogen and fuel cells."

> —Herman Kuipers, Business Team Manager,
> Innovation & Research, Shell Global Solutions,
> 21 Nov. 2000 [2]

"The days of the traditional oil company are numbered, in part because of emerging technologies such as fuel cells...."

> —Peter I. Bijur, Chairman and CEO, Texaco, Inc.,
> late 1990s [3]

"Market forces, greenery, and innovation are shaping the future of our industry and propelling us inexorably towards hydrogen energy. Those who don't pursue it...will rue it."

> —Frank Ingriselli, President, Texaco Technology
> Ventures, 23 April 2001 [4]

"...[W]e'll evolve from a world of hydrocarbon dependency to a mixture of hydrocarbon and alternative energies use. Vast quantities of liquid hydrocarbons (oil and gas) will be left behind in the ground, just as solid hydrocarbons (coal) are being left behind today."

> —Chris Gibson-Smith, Managing Director, BP,
> 25 Sept. 1998 [5]

"Thirty years from now there will be a huge amount of oil—and no buyers. Oil will be left in the ground. The Stone Age came to an end, not because we had a lack of stones, and the Oil Age will come to an end not because we have a lack of oil....[Fuel cell technology] is coming before the end of the decade and will cut gasoline consumption by almost 100 per cent....On the supply side it is easy to find oil and produce it, and on the demand side there are so many new technologies, especially when it comes to automobiles."

> —Sheikh Zaki Yamani,
> Oil Minister of Saudi Arabia (1962–86), June 2000 [6]

1. Bowlin 1999.

2. Kuipers 2000.

3. Bijur, undated.

4. Ingriselli 2001.

5. Gibson-Smith 1998.

6. Fagan 2000.

"So why is Sheikh Yamani predicting the end of the Oil Age? Because he believes that something fundamental has shifted since…[1973]—and, sadly for countries like Saudi Arabia, he is quite right. Finally, advances in technology are beginning to offer a way for economies…to diversify their supplies of energy and reduce their demand for petroleum, thus loosening the grip of oil and the countries that produce it.…The only long-term solution…is to reduce the world's reliance on oil. Achieving this once seemed pie-in-the-sky. No longer. Hydrogen fuel cells are at last becoming a viable alternative.…One day, these new energy technologies will toss the OPEC cartel in the dustbin of history. It cannot happen soon enough."

—"The End of the Oil Age," editorial,
The Economist, 25 Oct. 2003

"The markets for renewable energy are the fastest growing energy markets in the world today. ***[S]uccessfully promoting renewables over the period to 2030 will prove less expensive than …'business as usual'…within any realistic range of real discount rates.***[T]he G8 should give priority to efforts to trigger a step change in renewable energy markets."

—G8 Renewable Energy Task Force, July 2001 [7]

"We…need to make great strides in transport efficiency.…We need to engage the consumer, not force him or her into public transport. A European Environment minister once asked me how to get people off their love affair with the motor car. I believe we should not even try and interfere with that love. It is deeply imbedded, and interfering in other people's love affairs is seldom productive. But the love is with personal movement and space and the freedom that it brings, not the internal combustion engine *per se*. We have to make eco-efficiency as fashionable as 4-wheel-drive vehicles. We need to use the powers of social pressure and the attraction of beautiful engineering. This is not hairshirt stuff—it should be eco-hedonism—taking pleasure from comfort, operating performance as well as eco-efficiency."

—Sir Mark Moody-Stuart, Chairman,
AngloAmerican, and former Chairman,
Royal Dutch/Shell Group, May 2002 [8]

"…I believe fuel cells will finally end the 100-year reign of the internal combustion engine.… Fuel cells could be the predominant automotive power source in 25 years."

—William Clay Ford, Jr., Chairman and CEO,
Ford Motor Company, 5 Oct. 2000 [9]

"There have already been two oil crises; we are obligated to prevent a third one. The fuel cell offers a realistic opportunity to supplement the 'petroleum monoculture' over the long term. All over the world, the auto industry is working in high gear on the fuel cell. We intend to be the market leader in this field. Then we will have the technology, the secured patents and the jobs on our side. In this manner, we will optimize conditions for profitable growth."

—Jürgen Schrempp, Chairman of the Board of
Management, DaimlerChrysler, Nov. 2000 [10]

"General Motors absolutely sees the long-term future of the world being based on a hydrogen economy.***Forty-five percent of *Fortune* 50 companies will be affected, impacting almost two trillion dollars in revenue."

—Larry Burns, VP R&D and Planning, General Motors
Corporation, undated and 10–11 Feb. 2003 [11]

7. Clini & Moody-Stuart 2001, pp. 5, 15, 9, and 7.

8. Moody-Stuart 2002.

9. Ford, Jr. 2000.

10. Berlin event with Chancellor Schröder, quoted in Autoweb.com.au 2000.

11. First part verified but not dated or specifically cited by speaker (personal communication, 25 January 2004); second part from Burns 2003, percentage written out.

Winning the **Oil** Endgame

Innovation for Profits, Jobs,
and Security

Amory B. Lovins,

E. Kyle Datta, Odd-Even Bustnes, Jonathan G. Koomey, and Nathan J. Glasgow

with

Jeff Bannon, Lena Hansen, Joshua Haacker, Jamie Fergusson, Joel Swisher PE,

Joanie Henderson, Jason Denner, James Newcomb, Ginny Yang, and Brett Farmery

RMI Published by Rocky Mountain Institute

1739 Snowmass Creek Road

Snowmass, Colorado 81654-9199, USA

phone: 1.970.927.3851

fax 1.970.927.4510

www.rmi.org

This document and its detailed *Technical Annex* are posted at www.oilendgame.com for free public download (for individual use).
Please send **corrections and comments** to oilendgamecomments@rmi.org.
Errata will be posted at www.oilendgame.com.

Cover art: The cover art, commissioned from Ian Naylor (www.aircrew.co.uk) on a concept by Amory Lovins and incorporated into the cover design by RMI's Ben Emerson, stylizes the 13th game of the 1972 world title match between Bobby Fischer (USA) and Boris Spassky (USSR). It shows the endgame position after 61. Be7-f8, kindly provided by Academician R.Z. Sagdeev and reproduced at the right. Fischer, playing Black (but shown as White in our stylized artwork), won with a trapped rook and five passed pawns against rook, bishop, and pawn.

Acknowledgments:
This study was made possible by many people and organizations to whom the authors and publishers are deeply grateful. Our debt to these researchers, in-kind supporters, informants, peer-reviewers, and funders is acknowledged on pp. 266–267.

Disclaimers: This work does not express the opinion or official position of the United States Government or the U.S. Department of Defense. Only the authors and publisher—not the sponsors, Foreword authors, or reviewers—are responsible for the views expressed. In expressing those personal opinions and ideas, the authors and publisher are not engaged in rendering professional services. Readers wishing personal assistance or advice should consult a competent professional. No patent liability is assumed with respect to the use of the information contained herein. Hypercar® and Body-in-Black™ are trademarks owned by Hypercar, Inc. Power by the Hour™ is a trademark owned by Rolls-Royce. Scotch™ Brand Tape is a trademark of 3M. Spectra® is a trademark of Honeywell. Chap Stick™ is a trademark owned by Wyeth Consumer Healthcare. All other trademarks, service marks, registered names, and images are the property of their respective owners. Most product images belong to their respective manufacturers and are downloaded from their public websites. The authors have sought to obtain permission from all image owners, and apologize to any who could not be traced for permission and acknowledgement. Although normal scholarly care has been taken in the preparation of this study, the authors, publisher, Foreword authors, and reviewers assume no responsibility for any errors or omissions, nor any liability for damages resulting from the use of or reliance on information contained herein, and they specifically disclaim any responsibility for any liability, loss, or risk, personal or otherwise, which is incurred as a consequence, directly or indirectly, of the use or application of any of the contents of this work. We accept no responsibility or liability for the contents of pages accessible through links to our webpages. This report is unclassified and contains no confidential or proprietary data.

The publisher and authors The publisher and authors are described on pp. 282–285.
The senior author's and publisher's interest is declared on pages 61 and 63.

Units of measure are customary U.S. units with some metric supplements; see also p. 39.

Production Credits
Editor: *Beatrice Aranow*
Art Director, Graphic Designer: *Ben Emerson*
Production Assistants: *Jenny Constable, Vinay Gupta, Anne Jakle, Tyler Lindsay, Morley McBride, Ann Mason, Christina Page*
Webmaster (www.oilendgame.com): *William Simon*
Type: Centaur (primary), Palatino (main text) and Univers (supporting text elements)
Paper: New Leaf Reincarnation® matte 95#, 100% recycled, 50% PCW, PCF (cover) and Envirographic® 100, 100% recycled, 100%PCW, PCF (text)
Printed with vegetable-based ink in the United States of America

First Edition, Third printing
Incorporating revised back cover and typographic corrections posted at www.oilendgame.com

1 November 2005

ISBN 1-881071-10-3

Overview Contents

www.oilendgame.com

Detailed Contents . . . . *iv*

Abstract . . . . *vii*

Executive Summary . . . . *ix*

Forewords . . . . *xv*
      George P. Shultz *xv*
      Sir Mark Moody-Stuart *xviii*

Frontispiece . . . . *xxiii*

Oil Dependence I

This Report 33

Saving Oil 43

Substituting for Oil 103

Combined Conventional Potential 123

Implementation 127

Implications and Conclusions 243

Image credits 276

Table of figures and tables 277

Acknowledgments 278

About the publisher and authors 282

References 286

Other RMI publications 307

Detailed Contents

Winning the Oil Endgame: Innovation for Profits, Jobs, and Security

Oil Dependence I

Boxes

Oil is the lifeblood of modern industrial economies—but not forever 1

Even an important industry can be displaced by competitors 4

1: An example of domestic
energy vulnerability (p. 12)

America can replace oil quickly—and already has 7

2: Oil is fungible (p. 14)

Oil supplies are becoming more concentrated and less secure 8
   Domestic oil is limited 12

3: The uncounted economic
cost of oil-price volatility
(p. 16)

Counting the direct cost of oil dependence 15

Oil dependence's hidden costs may well exceed its direct costs 17
   Petrodollars tend to destabilize 18

4: Hedging the risk of oil
depletion (p. 24)

   Sociopolitical instability drives military costs 19
   Nonmilitary societal costs 21
   Adding up the hidden costs 22

Could less oil dependence be not only worthy but also profitable? 26
   Beliefs that hold us back 26

Whatever exists is possible 29

This Report 33

5: Conventions (p. 39)

Structure and methodology 33
Conservatisms and conventions 37

Saving Oil 43

Option 1. Efficient use of oil 43
  Transportation 44
   Light vehicles 44
    The conventional view 49

6: How do light vehicles
use fuel, and how can they
save fuel? (p. 46)

    Advanced automotive technologies: lightweight, low-drag, highly integrated 52
     Drag and rolling resistance 52

7: Superefficient but
uncompromised (p. 62)

     Lightweighting: the emerging revolution 53
     Ultralight but ultrastrong 57
     Applying ultralight materials 61

8: Analyzing an ultralight
hybrid's efficiency (p. 68)

     Lighter-but-safer vehicles dramatically extend cheap oil savings 64
   Heavy trucks 73

9: Analyzing and extending
ultralight vehicle costs
(p. 69)

   Medium trucks 77
   Intelligent highway systems (IHS) 78
   Other civilian highway and off-road vehicles 79

10: Comparing light-vehicle
prices (p. 72)

   Trains 79
   Ships 79
   Airplanes 79

11: Saving oil in existing
military platforms (p. 86)

   Military vehicles 84
    The fuel logistics burden 84
    Military efficiency potential 85

  Feedstocks and other nonfuel uses of oil 93
  Industrial fuel 97
  Buildings 97
  Electricity generation 98
  Combined efficiency potential 99

Substituting for Oil 103

Option 2. Substituting biofuels and biomaterials   103
  The input side: biomass feedstocks and rural economies   107
  Biomaterials   110

Option 3. Substituting saved natural gas   111
  Overview   111
  Saving natural gas   112
    Electric utilities   113
    Buildings   115
    Industrial fuel   115
  Substituting saved gas for oil   117

Boxes (continued)

12: Replacing one-third of remaining non-transportation oil use with saved natural gas (p. 118)

Combined Conventional Potential 123

Implementation 127

Strategic vision   127
  The prize   127
  Vaulting the barriers   128

The endangered automotive sector—why it's important to act now   130
  Four competitive threats   132
  China and India   135
  Suppressing the signals   136

Crafting an effective energy strategy: transformative business innovation   137
  The creative destruction dilemma   138
  Business challenges: market, business, and customer realities   139
    Most U.S. light-vehicle buyers scarcely value fuel economy   139
    Most firms underinvest in energy efficiency too   141
    The risk of being risk-averse   143
  Business opportunities: competitive strategy for profitable transformation in the transportation sector   145
    Lowering light vehicles' manufacturing risk   146
      Manufacturing investment and variable cost   146
      Market adoption   149
    Restoring profitability in the trucking sector   150
    Revitalizing the airline and airplane industries   154
      Getting generation-after-next planes off the ground   157
  Creating a new high-technology industrial cluster   159
  Restoring farming, ranching, and forest economies   162

If we don't act soon, the invisible hand will become the invisible fist   166

13: Guilt-free driving: hybrid cars enter the market (p. 131)

14: Opening moves: Boeing's bet on fuel efficiency as the future for commercial aircraft (p. 133)

15: Radically simpler automaking with advanced composites (p. 147)

16: Flying high: fuel savings arbitrage (p. 156)

(Implementation continued next page)

(Implementation continued from previous page)

Crafting coherent supportive policies   169
  Government's role in implementation   169
    Fuel taxes   173
    Standards, mandates, and quotas   175
  Federal policy recommendations for light vehicles   178
    Feebates   186
    Low-income scrap-and-replace program   191
    Smart government fleet procurement   197
    "Golden Carrots" and technology procurement   199
    "Platinum Carrot" advanced-technology contest   201
    Supporting automotive retooling and retraining   203
    R&D and early military procurement   204
    Automotive efficiency and safety regulation: first, do no harm   206
  Other federal policy recommendations   208
    Supporting investment in domestic energy supply infrastructure   208
    Heavy-vehicle policy   211
    Aircraft policy   212
    Other transportation policy   212
      Shifting taxation from fuel to roads and driving   212
      Integrating transportation systems   214
      Is this trip necessary (and desired)?   214
    Non-transportation federal policy   215
  States: incubators and accelerators   216
    Transportation   216
    Electricity and natural-gas pricing   219
    Renewable energy   220
  Military policy: fuel efficiency for mission effectiveness   221
  Civil preparedness: evolving toward resilience   222
  Civil society: the sum of all choices   223
  Beyond gridlock: changing politics   225

Option 4. Substituting hydrogen   227
  Beyond mobilization to a basic shift in primary energy supply   227
  Hydrogen: practical after all   230
  Eight basic questions   233
    Why is hydrogen important, and is it safe?   233
    How would a light vehicle safely and affordably store enough hydrogen
    to drive 300+ miles?   233
    Under what conditions is hydrogen a cheaper light-vehicle fuel than oil?   234
    What's the cheapest way to produce and deliver hydrogen to meet the economic
    conditions required for adoption?   236
    Are there enough primary energy sources for this transition?   238
    What technologies are required to enable the hydrogen transition?   241
    How can the U.S. profitably make the transition from oil to hydrogen?   241
    When could this transition occur?   242

Boxes (continued)

17: *Gridlock as Usual*
according to Thucycides,
ca. 431–404 BCE (p. 170)

18: Modeling the effects
of policy on light vehicle
sales and stocks (p. 182)

19: How feebates work
(p. 186)

20: More antidotes to
regressivity (p. 196)

21: Golden Carrots: theme
and variations (p. 200)

22: Realigning auto-safety
policy with modern
engineering (p. 207)

23: Pay-at-the-Pump
car insurance (p. 218)

Implications and Conclusions 243

Implications 243

    Employment 243

    Allies and trading partners 244

    Developing countries 245

        Leapfrog development 245

        Climate change and development 246

        The global economy, oil savings, and development 247

    Oil-exporting countries 248

    The creative destruction challenge for oil companies 250

    Other energy industries 257

    U.S. military force structure, posture, and doctrine 261

        Toward a new strategic doctrine 262

    U.S. federal budget 265

    Environment, public health, and quality of life 268

Conclusions 271

Boxes (continued)

24: Shell's visionary energy futures (p. 252)

25: What about nuclear power? (p. 258)

Abstract:

This independent, peer-reviewed synthesis for American business and military leaders charts a roadmap for getting the United States completely, attractively, and profitably off oil. Our strategy integrates four technological ways to displace oil: using oil twice as efficiently, then substituting biofuels, saved natural gas, and, optionally, hydrogen. Fully applying today's best efficiency technologies in a doubled-GDP 2025 economy would save half the projected U.S. oil use at half its forecast cost per barrel. Non-oil substitutes for the remaining consumption would also cost less than oil. These comparisons conservatively assign zero value to avoiding oil's many "externalized" costs, including the costs incurred by military insecurity, rivalry with developing countries, pollution, and depletion. The vehicle improvements and other savings required needn't be as fast as those achieved after the 1979 oil shock.

The route we suggest for the transition beyond oil will expand customer choice and wealth, and will be led by business for profit. We propose novel public policies to accelerate this transition that are market-oriented without taxes and innovation-driven without mandates. A $180-billion investment over the next decade will yield $130-billion *annual* savings by 2025; revitalize the automotive, truck, aviation, and hydrocarbon industries; create a million jobs in both industrial and rural areas; rebalance trade; make the United States more secure, prosperous, equitable, and environmentally healthy; encourage other countries to get off oil too; and make the world more developed, fair, and peaceful.

Executive Summary

Winning the Oil Endgame offers a coherent strategy for ending oil dependence, starting with the United States but applicable worldwide. There are many analyses of the oil problem. This synthesis is the first roadmap of the oil *solution*—one led by business for profit, not dictated by government for reasons of ideology. This roadmap is independent, peer-reviewed, written for business and military leaders, and co-funded by the Pentagon. It combines innovative technologies and new business models with uncommon public policies: market-oriented without taxes, innovation-driven without mandates, not dependent on major (if any) national legislation, and designed to support, not distort, business logic.

Two centuries ago, the first industrial revolution made people a hundred times more productive, harnessed fossil energy for transport and production, and nurtured the young U.S. economy. Then, over the past 145 years, the Age of Oil brought unprecedented mobility, globe-spanning military power, and amazing synthetic products.

But at what cost? Oil, which created the sinews of our strength, is now becoming an even greater source of weakness: its volatile price erodes prosperity; its vulnerabilities undermine security; its emissions destabilize climate. Moreover the quest to attain oil creates dangerous new rivalries and tarnishes America's moral standing. All these costs are rising. And their root causes—most of all, inefficient light trucks and cars—also threaten the competitiveness of U.S. automaking and other key industrial sectors.

The cornerstone of the next industrial revolution is therefore winning the Oil Endgame. And surprisingly, it will cost *less* to displace all of the oil that the United States now uses than it will cost to *buy* that oil. Oil's current market price leaves out its true costs to the economy, national security, and the environment. But even without including these now "externalized" costs, it would still be profitable to displace oil completely over the next few decades. In fact, by 2025, the *annual* economic benefit of that displacement would be $130 billion gross (or $70 billion net of the displacement's costs). To achieve this does not require a revolution, but merely consolidating and accelerating trends already in place: the amount of oil the economy uses for each dollar of GDP produced, and the fuel efficiency of light vehicles, would need only to improve about three-fifths as quickly as they did in response to previous oil shocks.

Saving half the oil America uses, and substituting cheaper alternatives for the other half, requires four integrated steps:

- **Double the efficiency of using oil**. The U.S. today wrings twice as much work from each barrel of oil as it did in 1975; with the latest proven efficiency technologies, it can double oil efficiency all over again. The investments needed to save *each* barrel of oil will cost only $12 (in 2000 $), less than half the officially forecast $26 price of that barrel in the world oil market. The most important enabling technology is ultralight vehicle design. Advanced composite or lightweight-steel materials can nearly double the efficiency of today's popular hybrid-electric cars and light trucks while improving safety and performance. The vehicle's total extra cost is repaid from fuel savings in about three years; the ultralighting is approximately free. Through emerging manufacturing techniques, such vehicles are becoming practical and profitable; the factories to produce them will also be cheaper and smaller.

- **Apply creative business models and public policies** to speed the profitable adoption of superefficient light vehicles, heavy trucks, and airplanes. Combined with more efficient buildings and factories, these efficient vehicles can cut the official forecast of oil use by 29% in 2025 and another 23% soon thereafter—52% in all. Enabled by a new industrial cluster focusing on lightweight materials, such as carbon-fiber composites, such advanced-technology vehicles can revitalize these three strategic sectors and create important new industries.

- **Provide another one-fourth of U.S. oil needs by a major domestic biofuels industry**. Recent advances in biotechnology and cellulose-to-ethanol conversion can double previous techniques' yield, yet cost less in both capital and energy. Replacing fossil-fuel hydrocarbons with plant-derived carbohydrates will strengthen rural America, boost net farm income by tens of billions of dollars a year, and create more than 750,000 new jobs. Convergence between the energy, chemical, and agricultural value chains will also let versatile new classes of biomaterials replace petrochemicals.

- Use well established, highly profitable efficiency techniques to **save half the projected 2025 use of natural gas**, making it again abundant and affordable, then substitute part of the saved gas for oil. If desired, the leftover saved natural gas could be used even more profitably and effectively by converting it to hydrogen, displacing most of the remaining oil use—and all of the oil use if modestly augmented by competitive renewable energy.

These four shifts are fundamentally disruptive to current business models. They are what economist Joseph Schumpeter called "creative destruction," where innovations destroy obsolete technologies, only to be overthrown in turn by ever newer, more efficient rivals. In *The Innovator's Dilemma*, Harvard Business School professor Clayton Christensen explained why industry leaders often get blindsided by disruptive innovations—technological gamechangers—because they focus too much on today's most profitable customers and businesses, ignoring the needs of the future. Firms that are quick to adopt innovative technologies and business models will be the winners of the 21st century; those that deny and resist change will join the dead from the last millennium. In the 108-year history of the Dow Jones Industrial Average, only one of 12 original companies remains a corporate entity today—General Electric. The others perished or became fodder for their competitors.

What policies are needed? American companies can be among the quick leaders in the 21st century, but it will take a cohesive strategy-based transformation, bold business and military leadership, and supportive government policies at a federal or at least a state level. *Winning the Oil Endgame* charts these practical steppingstones to an oil-free America:

- Most importantly, revenue- and size-neutral "feebates" can shift customer choice by combining fees on inefficient vehicles with rebates to efficient vehicles. The feebates apply separately within each vehicle-size class, so freedom of choice is unaffected. Indeed, choice is enhanced as customers start to count fuel savings over the vehicle's life, not just the first few years, and this new pattern of demand pulls superefficient but uncompromised vehicles from the drawing-board into the showroom.

- A scrap-and-replace program can lease or sell super-efficient cars to low-income Americans—on terms and with fuel bills they can afford—while scrapping clunkers. This makes personal mobility affordable to all, creates a new million-car-a-year market for the new efficiency technologies, and helps clean our cities' air.

- Military needs for agility, rapid deployment, and streamlined logistics can drive Pentagon leadership in developing key technologies.

- Implementing smart government procurement and targeted technology acquisition (the "Golden Carrot") for aggregated buyers will accelerate manufacturers' conversion, while a government-sponsored $1-billion prize for success in the marketplace, the "Platinum Carrot," will speed development of even more advanced vehicles.

- To support U.S. automakers' and suppliers' need to invest about $70 billion to make advanced technology vehicles, federal loan guarantees can help finance initial retooling where needed; the investments should earn a handsome return, with big spin-off benefits.

- Similar but simpler policies—loan guarantees for buying efficient new airplanes (while scrapping inefficient parked ones), and better information for heavy truck buyers to spur market demand for doubled-efficiency trucks—can speed these oil-saving innovations from concept to market.

- Other policies can hasten competitive evolution of next-generation biofuels and biomaterials industries, substituting durable revenues for dwindling agricultural subsidies, and encouraging practices that protect both topsoil and climate.

What happens to the oil industry? The transition beyond oil is already starting to transform oil companies like Shell and BP into energy companies. Done right, this shift can profitably redeploy their skills and assets rather than lose market share. Biofuels are already becoming a new product line that leverages existing retail and distribution infrastructure and can attract another $90 billion in biofuels and biorefining investments. By following this roadmap, the U.S. would set the stage by 2025 for the checkmate move in the Oil Endgame—the optional but advantageous transition to a hydrogen economy and the complete and permanent displacement of oil as a direct fuel. Oil may, however, retain or even gain value as one of the competing sources of hydrogen.

How big is the prize? Investing $180 billion over the next decade to eliminate oil dependence and revitalize strategic industries can save $130 billion gross, or $70 billion net, *every year* by 2025. This saving, equivalent to a large tax cut, can replace today's $10-billion-a-month oil imports with reinvestments in ourselves: $40 billion would pay farmers for biofuels, while the rest could return to our communities, businesses, and children. Several million automotive and other transportation-equipment jobs now at risk can be saved, and one million net new jobs can be added across all sectors. U.S. automotive, trucking, and aircraft production can again lead the world, underpinned by 21st century advanced-materials and fuel-cell industries. A more efficient and deployable military could refocus on its core mission— protecting American citizens rather than foreign supply lines—while supporting and deploying the innovations that eliminate oil as a cause of conflict. Carbon dioxide emissions will shrink by one-fourth with no additional cost or effort. The rich-poor divide can be drastically narrowed at home by increased access to affordable personal mobility, shrinking the welfare rolls, and abroad by leapfrogging over oil-dependent development patterns. The U.S. could treat oil-rich countries the same as countries with no oil. Being no longer suspected of seeking oil in all that it does in the world would help to restore U.S. moral leadership and clarity of purpose.

While the $180-billion investment needed is significant, the United States' economy already pays that much, with zero return, every time the oil price spikes up as it has done in 2004. (And that money goes into OPEC's coffers instead of building infrastructure at home.) Just by 2015, the early steps in this proposed transition will have saved as much oil as the U.S. gets from the Persian Gulf. By 2040, oil imports could be gone. By 2050, the U.S. economy should be flourishing with no oil at all.

How do we get started? Every sector of society can contribute to this national project. Astute business leaders will align their corporate strategies and reorganize their firms and processes to turn innovation from a threat to a friend. Military leaders will speed military transformation by promptly laying its foundation in superefficient platforms and lean logistics. Political leaders will craft policies that stimulate demand for efficient vehicles, reduce R&D and manufacturing investment risks, support the creation of secure domestic fuel supplies, and eliminate perverse subsidies and regulatory obstacles. Lastly, we, the people, must play a role—a big role—because our individual choices guide the markets, enforce accountability, and create social innovation.

Our energy future is choice, not fate. Oil dependence is a problem we need no longer have—and it's cheaper not to. U.S. oil dependence can be eliminated by proven and attractive technologies that create wealth, enhance choice, and strengthen common security. This could be achieved only about as far in the future as the 1973 Arab oil embargo is in the past. When the U.S. last paid attention to oil, in 1977–85, it cut its oil use 17% while GDP grew 27%. Oil imports fell 50%, and imports from the Persian Gulf by 87%, in just eight years. That exercise of dominant market power—from the demand side—broke OPEC's ability to set world oil prices for a decade. Today we can rerun that play, only better. The obstacles are less important than the opportunities if we replace ignorance with insight, inattention with foresight, and inaction with mobilization. American business can lead the nation and the world into the post-petroleum era, a vibrant economy, and lasting security—if we just realize that we are the people we have been waiting for.

Together we can end oil dependence forever.

Foreword

Crude prices are rising, uncertainty about developments in the Middle East roils markets and, well, as Ronald Reagan might say, "Here we go again."

Once more we face the vulnerability of our oil supply to political disturbances. Three times in the past thirty years (1973, 1978, and 1990) oil price spikes caused by Middle East crises helped throw the U.S. economy into recession. Coincident disruption in Venezuela and Russia adds to unease, let alone prices, in 2004. And the surging economies of China and India are contributing significantly to demand. But the problem far transcends economics and involves our national security. How many more times must we be hit on the head by a two-by-four before we do something decisive about this acute problem?

In 1969, when I was Secretary of Labor, President Nixon made me the chairman of a cabinet task force to examine the oil import quota system, in place since 1954. Back then, President Eisenhower considered too much dependence on imported oil to be a threat to national security. He thought anything over 20 percent was a real problem. No doubt he was nudged by his friends in the Texas and Louisiana oil patches, but Ike was no stranger to issues of national security and foreign policy.

The task force was not prescient or unanimous but, smelling trouble, the majority could see that imports would rise and they recommended a new monitoring system to keep track of the many uncertainties we could see ahead, and a new system for regulating imports. Advocates for even greater restrictions on imports argued that low-cost oil from the Middle East would flood our market if not restricted.

By now, the quota argument has been stood on its head as imports make up an increasing majority, now almost 60 percent and heading higher, of the oil we consume. And we worry not about issues of letting imports in but that they might be cut off. Nevertheless, the point about the importance of relative cost is as pertinent today as back then and applies to the competitive pressures on any alternative to oil. And the low-cost producers of oil are almost all in the Middle East.

That is an area where the population is exploding out of control, where youth is by far the largest group, and where these young people have little or nothing to do. The reason is that governance in these areas has failed them. In many countries, oil has produced wealth without the effort that connects people to reality, a problem reinforced in some of them by the fact that the hard physical work is often done by imported labor. The submissive role forced on women has led to this population explosion. A disproportionate share of the world's many violent conflicts is in this area. So the Middle

A native of New York, George P. Shultz graduated from Princeton University in 1942. After serving in the Marine Corps (1942–45), he earned a PhD at MIT. Mr. Shultz taught at MIT and the University of Chicago Graduate School of Business, where he became dean in 1962. He was appointed Secretary of Labor in 1969, Director of the Office of Management and Budget in 1970, and Secretary of the Treasury in 1972. From 1974 to 1982, he was President of Bechtel Group, Inc. Mr. Shultz served as Chairman of the President's Economic Policy Advisory Board (1981–82) and Secretary of State (1982–89). He is chairman of the J.P. Morgan Chase International Council and the Accenture Energy Advisory Board. Since 1989, he has been a Distinguished Fellow at the Hoover Institution, Stanford University.

East remains one of the most unstable parts of the world. Only a dedicated optimist could believe that this assessment will change sharply in the near future. What would be the impact on the world economy of terrorist sabotage of key elements of the Saudi pipeline infrastructure?

I believe that, three decades after the Nixon task force effort, it is long past time to take serious steps to alter this picture dramatically. Yes, important progress has been made, with each administration announcing initiatives to move us away from oil. Advances in technology and switches from oil to natural gas and coal have caused our oil use per dollar of GDP to fall in half since 1973. That helps reduce the potential damage from supply problems. But potential damage is increased by the rise of imports from 28 percent to almost 60 percent of all the oil we use. The big growth sector is transportation, up by 50 percent. Present trends are unfavorable; if continued, they mean that we are likely to consume—and import—several million barrels a day more by 2010.

Beyond U.S. consumption, supply and demand in the world's oil market has become tight again, leading to many new possibilities of soaring oil prices and massive macroeconomic losses from oil disruptions. We also have environmental problems to concern us. And, most significantly, our national security and its supporting diplomacy are left vulnerable to fears of major disruptions in the market for oil, let alone the reality of sharp price spikes. These costs are not reflected in the market price of oil, but they are substantial.

What more can we do? Lots, if we are ready for a real effort. I remember when, as Secretary of the Treasury, I reviewed proposals for alternatives to oil from the time of the first big oil crisis in 1973. Pie in the sky, I thought. But now the situation is different. We can, as Amory Lovins and his colleagues show vividly, win the oil endgame.

How do we go about this? A baseball analogy may be applicable. Fans often have the image in their minds of a big hitter coming up with the bases loaded, two outs, and the home team three runs behind. The big hitter wins the game with a home run. We are addicted to home runs, but the outcome of a baseball game is usually determined by a combination of walks, stolen bases, errors, hit batsmen, and, yes, some doubles, triples, and home runs. There's also good pitching and solid fielding, so ball games are won by a wide array of events, each contributing to the result. Lovins and his coauthors show us that the same approach can work in winning the oil endgame. There are some potential big hits here, but the big point is that there are a great variety of measures that can be taken that each will contribute to the end result. The point is to muster the will power and drive to pursue these possibilities.

How do we bring that about? Let's not wait for a catastrophe to do the job. Competitive information is key. Our marketplace is finely tuned to the desire of the consumer to have real choices. We live in a real information age, so producers have to be ready for the competition that can come out of nowhere. Lovins and his colleagues provide a huge amount of information about potential competitive approaches. There are home run balls here, the ultimate one being the hydrogen economy. But we don't have to wait for the arrival of that day. There are many things that can be done now, and this book is full of them. Hybrid technology is on the road and currently increases gas mileage by 50 percent or more. The technology is scaleable. This report suggests many ways to reduce weight and drag, thereby improving performance. A big point in this report is evidence that new, ultralight-but-safe materials can nearly redouble fuel economy at little or no extra cost.

Sequestration of effluent from use of coal may be possible on an economic and comfortable basis, making coal a potentially benign source of hydrogen. Maybe hydrogen could be economically split out of water by electrolysis, perhaps using renewables such as windpower; or it could certainly be made, as nearly all of it is now, by natural gas saved from currently wasteful practices, an intriguingly lucrative option often overlooked in discussions of today's gas shortages. An economy with a major hydrogen component would do wonders for both our security and our environment. With evident improvements in fuel cells, that combination could amount to a very big deal. Applications include stationary as well as mobile possibilities, and other ideas are in the air. Real progress has been made in the use of solar systems for heat and electricity. Scientists, technologists, and commercial organizations in many countries are hard at work on these issues.

Sometimes the best way to get points across is to be provocative, to be a bull in a china closet. Amory Lovins loves to be a bull in a china closet—anybody's china closet. With this book, the china closet he's bursting into is ours and we should welcome him because he is showing us how to put the closet back together again in far more satisfactory form. In fact, Lovins and his team make an intriguing case that is important enough to merit careful attention by all of us, private citizens and business and political leaders alike.

— George P. Shultz

Foreword

Born in Antigua, Mark Moody-Stuart earned a doctorate in geology in 1966 at Cambridge, then worked for Shell starting as an exploration geologist, living in the Netherlands, Spain, Oman, Brunei, Australia, Nigeria, Turkey, Malaysia, and the UK, and retiring as Chairman of the Royal Dutch/Shell Group in 2001. He is Chairman of Anglo American plc, a Director of HSBC and of Accenture, a Governor of Nuffield Hospitals, President of the Liverpool School of Tropical Medicine, and on the board of the Global Reporting Initiative and the International Institute for Sustainable Development. He is Chairman of the Global Business Coalition for HIV/AIDS and Co-Chair of the Singapore British Business Council. He was Co-Chair of the G8 Task Force on Renewable Energy (2000–01) and Chairman of Business Action for Sustainable Development, an initiative of the ICC and the World Business Council for Sustainable Development before and during the 2002 World Summit on Sustainable Development in Johannesburg. During 2001–04 he served on the UN Secretary General's Advisory Council for the Global Compact. He was knighted in 2000. With his wife Judy, he drives a Toyota *Prius* and is an investor in Hypercar, Inc.

In this compelling synthesis, Amory Lovins and his colleagues at Rocky Mountain Institute provide a clear and penetrating view of one of the critical challenges facing the world today: the use of energy, especially oil, in transportation, industry, buildings, and the military. This report demonstrates that innovative technologies can achieve spectacular savings in all of these areas with no loss of utility, convenience and function. It makes the business case for how a profitable transition for the automotive, truck, aviation, and oil sectors can be achieved, and why they should embrace technological innovation rather than be destroyed by it. We are not short of energy in this world of ours; we have large resources of the convenient hydrocarbons on which our economies are based, and even greater resources of the coal on which our economies were originally built. But there are two serious issues relating to its supply and use.

First, some three fourths of the reserves sit in a few countries of the Middle East, subject to actual and potential political turmoil. Second, there are the long-term climatic effects of the burning of increasing amounts of fossil fuels. While the normal rate of change of technology is likely to mean that we will be on one of the lower impact scenarios of climate change and not at the apocalyptic end favoured by doom mongers, it is reasonably certain that our world will have to adapt to significant climate change over the next century. These two factors mean that, unless there is a change of approach, the United States will inexorably become increasingly dependent on imported energy—be it oil or natural gas. At the same time, on the international scene, the United States will be criticised by the rest of the world for profligate use of energy, albeit to fuel an economy on whose dynamism and success the rest of the world is also manifestly dependent. Furthermore, thoughtful people wonder what we will do if the booming economies and creative people of China and India have energy demands which are on the same development curve as the United States.

The RMI team has approached this economic and strategic dilemma with technical rigour, good humour, and common sense, while addressing two key requirements often overlooked by energy policy advocates.

First, we have to deliver the utility, reliability and convenience that the consumer has come to expect. As business people we recognise this. It is no good expecting people in the United States to suddenly drive smaller, less convenient or less safe vehicles. We have to supply the same comfort and utility at radically increased levels of energy efficiency. Most consumers, who are also voters, have only a limited philosophical interest in energy efficiency, security of supply, and climate change. Most of us have a very intense interest in personal convenience and safety—we expect governments and business to handle those other issues on our behalf. There is a very small market in this world for hair shirts. Similarly, we cannot expect the citizens of China and India to continue to ride bicycles in the interests of the global environment. They have exactly the same aspirations to comfort and convenience as we do. This book demonstrates how by applying existing technologies to lightweight vehicles with the use of composites, by the use of hybrid powertrains already in production, and with the rapid evolution to new technologies, we can deliver the high levels of convenience and reliability we are used to at radically increased levels of energy efficiency, while also maintaining cost efficiency.

The second critical requirement is that the process of transition should be fundamentally economic. We know in business that while one may be prepared to make limited pathfinding investments at nil or low return in order to develop new products and markets, this can not be done at a larger scale, nor indefinitely. What we can do, and have seen done repeatedly, is to transform markets by delivering greater utility at the same cost or the same utility at a lower cost, often by combining more advanced technologies with better business models. When this happens, the rate of change of markets normally exceeds our wildest forecasts and within a space of a few years a whole new technology has evolved.

A good example of the rapid development and waning of technology is the fax machine. With astonishing rapidity, because of its functional advantages over surface mail, the fax machine became globally ubiquitous. The smallest businesses around the world had one and so did numerous homes. The fax has now become almost obsolete because of e-mail, the e-mail attachment and finally the scanned e-mail attachment. The connectivity of the Internet, of which e-mail is an example, has transformed the way we do business. What this book shows is that the delivery of radically more energy-efficient technologies has dramatic cost implications and therefore has the potential for a similarly economically driven transition.

The refreshingly creative government policies suggested here to smooth and speed that transition are a welcome departure from traditional approaches that often overlook or even reject the scope of enterprise to be an important part of the solution. These innovative policies, too, merit serious attention, especially as an integrated package, and I suspect they could win support across the political spectrum.

The technological, let alone policy, revolution has not been quick in coming to the United States. Yet as has happened before in the automobile industry, others are aware of the potential of the technology. Perhaps because of Japan's obsession with energy security, Toyota and Honda began some years ago to hone the electric-hybrid technology that is likely to be an important part of the energy efficiency revolution. As a result, U.S. automobile manufacturers who now see the market opportunities of these technologies are turning to the proven Japanese technology to deliver it rapidly.

I believe that we may see a similar leapfrogging of technology from China. China is fully aware of the consequences on energy demand, energy imports, and security of supply of its impressive economic growth. Already China is using regulation to channel development into more energy-efficient forms. The burgeoning Chinese automobile industry is likely to be guided down this route—delivering the function and convenience, but at greatly increased levels of efficiency. And it is not just in the automobile industry—by clearly stated national policy it applies to all areas of industrial activity. This has great implications both for the participation by U.S. firms in investment in China, and also in the impact of future Chinese manufactures on a global market that is likely to be paying much greater attention to energy efficiency.

As a businessman, I am attracted by the commercial logic and keen insight that this report brings to the marketplace struggle between oil and its formidable competitors on both the demand and the supply sides. Indeed, during my time in both Shell and AngloAmerican, RMI's engineers have helped ours to confirm unexpectedly rich deposits of mineable "negawatts" and "negabarrels" in our own operations—an exploration effort we're keen to intensify to the benefit of both our shareholders and the environment.

As a lifelong oil man and exploration geologist, I am especially excited to learn about the Saudi Arabia-size riches that Amory Lovins and RMI's explorers have discovered in what they term the Detroit Formation—through breakthrough vehicle design that can save vast amounts of oil more cheaply than it can be supplied. And as a citizen and grandparent, I am pleased that RMI proposes new business models to span the mobility divide that separates rich and poor, not just in the United States, but in many places in the world. Concern about such opportunity divides is increasingly at the core not just of international morality but also of stability and peace.

This book points the way to an economically driven energy transformation. And its subtitle "Innovation for Profit, Jobs, and Security" is both a prospectus for positive change and a reminder that both the United States and other countries can be rapid adapters of innovative technologies, with equally transformative economic consequences. As someone who has spent a lifetime involved in energy and changes in energy patterns, I find the choice an easy one to make. The global economy is very much dependent on the health of the U.S. economy, so I hope that the U.S. indeed makes the right choice.

This report will help to launch, inspire, and inform a new and necessary conversation about energy and security, economy and environment. Its outcome is vital for us all.

— Sir Mark Moody-Stuart

Winning the Oil Endgame:
Innovation for Profits, Jobs, and Security

"On our present course, America 20 years from now will import nearly two of every three barrels of oil—a condition of increased dependency on foreign powers that do not always have America's interests at heart.***But it is not beyond our power to correct. America leads the world in scientific achievement, technical skill, and entrepreneurial drive. Within our country are abundant natural resources, unrivaled technology, and unlimited human creativity. With forward-looking leadership and sensible policies, we can meet our future energy demands and promote energy [efficiency]…and do so in environmentally responsible ways that set a standard for the world.***Per capita oil consumption, which reached a peak in 1978, has fallen 20 percent from that level.***Today's automobiles…use about 60 percent of the gasoline [per mile] they did in 1972, while new refrigerators require just one-third the electricity they did 30 years ago. As a result, since 1973, the U.S. economy has grown by 126 percent, while energy use has increased by only 30 percent. In the 1990s alone, manufacturing output expanded by 41 percent, while industrial electricity consumption grew by only 11 percent. We must build on this progress and strengthen America's commitment to energy efficiency***[which] helps the United States reduce energy imports, the likelihood of energy shortages, emissions, and the volatility of energy prices.***Our country has met many great tests. Some have imposed extreme hardship and sacrifice. Others have demanded only resolve, ingenuity, and clarity of purpose. Such is the case with energy today."

— **National Energy Policy Development Group**;
Reliable, Affordable, and Environmentally Sound Energy for America's Future; 2001[12]

"If you want to build a ship, don't drum up the men to gather wood, divide the work and give orders. Instead, teach them to yearn for the vast and endless sea."

"As for the future, your task is not to foresee it, but to enable it."

— Antoine de Saint-Exupéry [13]

12. National Energy Policy Development Group 2001, pp. x, viii–ix, 1–10, xi–xii, 1–4, and xv.

13. de Saint-Exupéry 1948.

Oil Dependence

How can America—all Americans together—win the oil endgame?
Is a world beyond oil imaginable? Practical? Profitable?
Why might it be prudent to get there sooner rather than later?
How could we get there if we wanted to?
How could this build a stronger country and a safer world?

At the start of World War II, Detroit switched in six months from making four million cars a year to making the tanks and aircraft that won the war.[14] Today, even absent the urgency of those dark days, American industry could advantageously launch a transition to different cars and other tools for making oil use stabilize, dwindle, and in a few generations become but a memory in museums. Some farsighted oil and car companies already envisage such a future (see inside front cover). Some are striving to create it before their rivals discover how major asset redeployments can yield more profit and less risk. These business leaders see that if government steers, not rows, then competitive enterprise, supported by judicious policy and vibrant civil society, can turn the insoluble oil puzzle into an unprecedented opportunity for wealth creation and common security.

That opportunity rests on a startling fact proven in the next 101 pages: *most of the oil now used in the United States (and the world) is being wasted, and can be saved more cheaply than buying it*. To assess that solution, let's start with a common understanding of the problem.

Oil is the lifeblood of modern industrial economies—but not forever

The United States of America has the mightiest economy and the most mobile society in the history of the world. Its mobility is 96%[15] fueled by oil costing a quarter-trillion dollars a year[16] and consuming seven of every ten barrels the nation uses. Oil provides 40–43% of all energy used by the United States, Europe, Asia, Africa, and the world. Oil dependence[17] varies—30% in China, 50% in Japan, 59% in Central and South America—but it's high everywhere. The whole world is happily hooked on convenient, transportable, versatile, ubiquitous, cheap oil.

> Cheap oil, the world's seemingly irreplaceable addiction, is no longer the only or even the cheapest way to do its vital and ubiquitous tasks.

14. Wrynn (1993) states at p. 52 that by war's end, "the automobile industry was responsible for 20 percent of the nation's war production by dollar volume." He shows striking examples (pp. 30, 54, 75, 76) of automakers' ads emphasizing fuel economy to help the war effort and to help civilians stretch rationed gasoline. And in 1943, GM (p. 39) advertised not just "Victory Through Progress" but also "Progress Through Victory": "…from what is learned in the stern test of war are being gathered many lessons to make more bountiful the blessings of the coming peace."

15. Measured by energy content, not volume; excluding energy (nearly all natural gas) used to run pipelines (2.7% of transportation energy); excluding here (contrary to the "Hydrocarbon definitions" convention on p. 40, otherwise used throughout this report) the portion of gasoline-blended oxygenates (1.3% of total oil use) that don't actually come from petroleum; and excluding the negligible miscellaneous transportation fuels in note 202, p. 36.

16. The U.S. energy statistics in this section and throughout this report are drawn, unless otherwise noted, from U.S. Energy Information Administration (EIA) 2003c, and forecasts from EIA 2004. Primary sources are often documented in Lovins 2003.

17. The fraction of total primary energy use that is provided by oil. Oil *import* dependence is how much of the oil used has been imported (usually net of oil exports, unless specified as "gross" imports).

The average U.S. light vehicle each day burns 100 times its weight in ancient plants in the form of gasoline.

Only an eighth of that fuel energy even reaches the wheels, a sixteenth accelerates the car, and less than one percent ends up moving the driver.

The oil we're burning in two centuries took hundreds of millions of years to form. When the Russian chemist D.I. Mendelyeev figured out what it was, he exclaimed it was far too precious to burn. We've been burning it ever since—ten thousand gallons a second in America alone. Each gallon of gasoline took eons to form (very inefficiently) from a quarter-million pounds of primeval plants. Thus the average U.S. light vehicle[18] each day burns 100 times its weight in ancient plants in the form of gasoline.[19] Only an eighth of that fuel energy even reaches the wheels, a sixteenth accelerates the car, and less than one percent ends up moving the driver.[20]

A 20-mile round trip in an average two-ton[21] new light vehicle to buy a gallon of milk burns a gallon of gasoline at about half the milk's cost.[22] The extraordinary global oil industry has made U.S. gasoline abundant, cheaper than bottled water, a half to a fourth of Europe's or Japan's gasoline price.[23] We use it accordingly. A comedian's acid remark, even if it touches a sensitive nerve today, could as well have been made under at least six of the past seven Administrations:[24]

> Two dollars a gallon to go ten miles is too much, but five to the parking valet to go ten feet is okay. The irony is [that] what we love most about our cars—the feeling of freedom they provide —has made us slaves. Slaves to cheap oil, which has corrupted our politics, threatened our environment, funded our enemies….Faced with our addiction to oil, what does our leadership say? Get more of it! Strange when you consider their answer to drug dependence is to cut off the supply.

The world consumes a cubic mile of oil per year. This is growing by just over one percent per year and is forecast to accelerate. A third of the growth supplies number two user China,[25] whose car sales soared 56% in 2003.[26] By 2025 its cars could need another Saudi Arabia or two. Just one-

18. "Light vehicles," sometimes called "light-duty vehicles," comprise cars, light trucks (sport-utility vehicles [SUVs], pickup trucks, and vans), and "crossover vehicles" (a new category combining SUV with sedan attributes), with a gross vehicle weight not exceeding 10,000 pounds (4,537 kg).

19. Dukes (2003), adjusted from his assumed 0.67 refinery yield of gasoline to the actual 2000 U.S. average of 0.462 (EIA 2001a, Table 19) and using EIA's 2.46 kgC/gal for gasoline and carbon contents of 0.855 for crude oil and 0.866 for gasoline (EIA 2002a, p. B-8, Table B-6). The average U.S. light vehicle in 2000 burned 591 U.S. gallons (2,238 L) of gasoline (ORNL 2002, Tables 7.1, 7.2) made from ~65,000 metric tonnes of ancient plants, using the adjusted Dukes coefficient of 111 T/gal. The average new light vehicle sold in 2000 weighed 3,821 lb (EPA 2003). Annual ancient-plant consumption is thus ~37,000× its curb weight, because, as Dukes explains, only a tiny fraction of the plants ends up in oil that's then geologically trapped and ultimately recovered.

20. See Box 5 on pp. 39–42.

21. The average Model Year 2003 light vehicle, at 4,021 pounds, "broke the two-ton barrier for the first time since the mid-1970's": Hakim 2004a.

22. Michael Lewis, head of Deutsche Bank's commodity research in London, notes that if Safeway shoppers in Maryland bought a barrel of milk, it'd cost $138; orange juice, $192; Evian mineral water, $246. By comparison, $40 oil looks cheap. The *Wall Street Journal*'s M.R. Sesit (2004) neatly concludes, however: "But oranges grow on trees; oil doesn't. SUVs don't run on mineral water. And, Mr. Lewis acknowledges, 'Nobody's blowing up cows.'"

23. In 2000, 22 countries sold gasoline at below a nominal benchmark of retail cost, 25 at between cost and U.S. prices, and 111 at higher-than-U.S. prices. Post-tax prices varied from Turkmenistan's 8¢/gal to Hong Kong's $5.53/gal (including $4.31 tax, vs. U.S. tax of 57¢). The U.S. tax rate of 32% of post-tax retail price was half the OECD average of 67%; in absolute terms, the U.S. tax, pretax price, and post-tax price were respectively 26%, 128%, and 56% of the OECD average. Diesel fuel was generally taxed substantially less per gallon than gasoline (Bacon 2004). See also Metshies 1999.

24. Maher 2002, pp. 29–30.

25. IEA 2003a, p. 13; average of 2001 through projected 2004 global demand growth; updated by Mallet 2004. China's ascendancy to number two was seven years earlier than forecast. In the first four months of 2004, China imported 33% more oil than a year earlier (CNN 2004).

26. *People's Daily* (Beijing) 2004; Auffhammer 2004; NAS/NRC/CAE 2003; cf. Wonacott, White, & Shirazou 2004 (~80% growth 2002, 36% 2003).

eighth of the world's people own cars; more want one. Africa and China have only the car ownership America enjoyed around 1915.[27]

Yet it's the superaffluent United States whose growing call on a fourth of the world's oil is the mainspring of global demand. During 2000–25, oil use is officially forecast to grow by 44% in the United States and 57% in the world.[28] A fifth of that global increase is to fuel the U.S., which by 2025 would use as much oil as Canada, Western and Eastern Europe, Japan, Australia, and New Zealand combined. As the richest nation on earth, we can afford it. But five, soon seven, billion people in poor countries, whose economies average more than twice as oil-intensive,[29] want the same oil to fuel their own development. The forecast 2000–25 *increase* in U.S. oil imports exceeds the 2001 oil *use* of China and India (plus South Korea). Competing with those emerging giants can't be good for their vital development, for fostering their hoped-for friendship and cooperation, or for the prospects of a peaceful and prosperous world community.

Oil, the world's biggest business, bestrides the world like a colossus.[30] Surely such a stupendous source of energy is indispensable, its cost a necessity of sustaining modernity and prosperity. Surely its possible substitutes are too small, slow, immature, unattractive, or costly to offer realistic alternatives to rising oil consumption—unless, perhaps, forced down our throats by draconian taxes or intrusive regulation. And surely it's premature to speculate about life after oil:[31] let our grandchildren, or someone else's grandchildren, do that.

This study tests all these comfortable assumptions and finds them unsound. On the contrary, rigorously applying orthodox market economics and modern technologies, it proves that *the services Americans get from oil could be more cheaply provided by wringing more work from the oil we use and substituting non-oil sources for the rest.* And because the alternatives to oil generally cost less and work better, they can be implemented quickly in the marketplace, with all its free choice, dynamism, and innovation. If guided more by profit and less by regulation and subsidy, this approach could even help to make government leaner, more flexible, and more valuable.

The services Americans get from oil could be more cheaply provided by wringing more work from the oil we use and substituting non-oil sources for the rest.

27. Greene 2004. Demand growth for personal mobility becomes obvious in the vast world market only for big countries with a burgeoning middle class. But for countries at the bottom of the development ladder, oil is for most people an unimaginable luxury: destitute Chad's nine million people, with just 80 miles of paved roads, use oil at only the rate of two jumbo jets making a daily transatlantic round-trip. ("A *747-400* [the newest, most efficient jumbo] that flies 3,500 statute miles [5,630 km] and carries 126,000 pounds [56,700 kg] of fuel will consume an average of five gallons [19 L] per mile." [Boeing, undated] The nominal flight distance New York to London is 3,461 statute miles, so a round trip uses ~824 barrels, unadjusted for refining. Chad used ~1,500 bbl/d in 2002 [www.theodora.com 2003]). If rich countries use too much oil, Chad can scarcely afford any. But all this could change now that Chad has discovered oil—and signed a pathfinding transparency agreement guiding its development.

28. EIA 2004b.

29. IEA 2003, p. 74. The IEA's May 2004 update (IEA 2004b) finds that oil price rises are twice as damaging to the Asian economy as to OECD's, four times in "very poor highly indebted countries," and at least eight times in sub-Saharan African countries.

30. Oil economist and World Bank consultant Mamdouh G. Salameh (2004) summarizes: "One could not imagine modern societies existing without oil….Oil makes the difference between war and peace. The importance of oil cannot be compared with any other commodity because of its versatility and dimensions, namely, economic, military, social, and political. The free enterprise system…and modern business owe their rise and development to the discovery of oil. Oil is the world's largest and most pervasive business….Of the top 20 companies in the world, 7 are oil companies."

31. Roberts 2004.

Just as whale oil was outcompeted before it was depleted, ← powerful technologies and implementation methods could make oil uncompetitive even at low prices before it becomes unavailable even at high prices.

Even an important industry can be displaced by competitors

Discovering such a startling, unseen, seemingly radical possibility right under our noses is not a pipe dream; it's a normal event in the history of technology, as Figure 1 illustrates.

In whaling's 1835–45 heyday, millions of homes used the clean, warm, even light of sperm-oil lamps and candles. As sperm whales got scarcer, the fleet hunted more plentiful but less oil-rich species whose inferior oil fetched half the price. But meanwhile, whale-based illumination's price had stayed high enough for long enough to elicit two fatal coal-based competitors (*Technical Annex*, Ch. 1): "town gas" and "coal-oil" kerosene.[33] As both steadily spread, whaling peaked in 1847. Ten years later, Michael Dietz's clean, safe, smokeless, odorless kerosene lantern was imported and promptly entered cheap U.S. production. In just three more years, whale oil's disdained competitors became dominant: the whalers lost their customers before they ran out of whales, as the "public abandoned

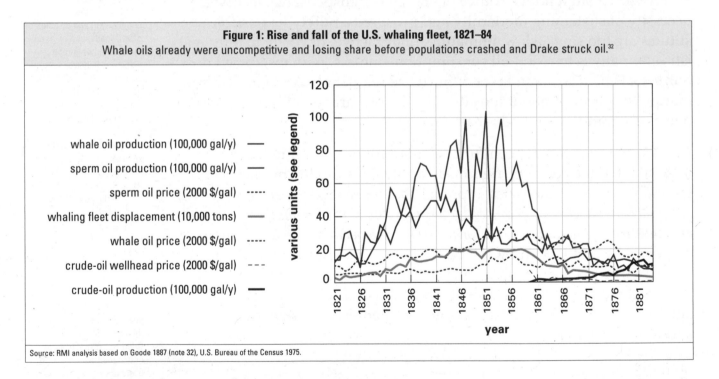

Figure 1: Rise and fall of the U.S. whaling fleet, 1821–84
Whale oils already were uncompetitive and losing share before populations crashed and Drake struck oil.[32]

whale oil production (100,000 gal/y) —
sperm oil production (100,000 gal/y) —
sperm oil price (2000 $/gal) -----
whaling fleet displacement (10,000 tons) —
whale oil price (2000 $/gal) -----
crude-oil wellhead price (2000 $/gal) ---
crude-oil production (100,000 gal/y) —

Source: RMI analysis based on Goode 1887 (note 32), U.S. Bureau of the Census 1975.

32. Goode 1887, pp. 168–173. CPI (Consumer Price Index) deflator from McCusker 1991, completed for 1999–2000 using CPI–U (CPI for All Urban Consumers) of the U.S. Department of Commerce, Bureau of Economic Statistics. A GDP implicit price deflator was also kindly provided by Dr. Philip Crowson, calculated from U.S. Bureau of Mines 1993 at pp. 51–52 (copper) and 201, but was not used here because that series goes back only to 1870, and the near-doubling of consumer prices during 1860–65 makes earlier deflators relatively unreliable. All the real prices graphed here should therefore be taken as indicative but not necessarily accurate. Petroleum data (deflated with same McCusker CPI): USCB 1975.

33. Camphene (from ethanol and turpentine), lard oil, various mixtures, and tallow candles were also lesser competitors. Camphene was the most important; it gave good light but sometimes caused accidents. It had about a tenth of the market for the main illuminants and lubricants until 1862–64, when a $2.08/gal alcohol tax to help fund the Civil War, meant to apply to beverage alcohol but written to tax all alcohol, threw the lighting market to kerosene. Davis, Gallman, & Gleiter 1997, pp. 365–366; Kovarik 1998.

whale oil almost overnight."[34] In the 1850s, whale oils lost two-thirds of their total market share (by value), even more if lubricants are factored out.[35] By the end of the decade, whale-derived illuminants sold under $3 million,[36] while coal-derived kerosene sold $5 million in 1859,[37] and 221 town-gas networks, up from 31 in 1850,[38] sold $12 million in 1860.[39] But also in 1859, Drake struck oil in Pennsylvania, making kerosene ubiquitous within a year, and by 1865, a third to a fourth the price of sperm or whale oil per unit of energy.[40] Ultimately, town gas got replaced in turn by natural gas; gas and kerosene lights, by Edison's 1879 electric lamp. But by the 1870s, the whaling industry was already nearly gone, pleading for federal subsidies on a national-security rationale.[41] The remnant whale populations had been saved by technological innovators and profit-maximizing capitalists.[42]

Around the mid-1850s, an astute investor with no gift of prophecy could have foreseen that the better and cheaper substitutes on the market and in inventors' laboratories could quickly capture whale oil's core market. Oddly, nobody at the time seems to have done a clear-eyed assessment adding up whale oil's competitors, so the industry didn't see them coming until too late.

A century and a half later, history looks set to repeat itself in the petroleum ("rock-oil") industry. Its mature provinces are in decline, more-volatile prices show new upward bias, and exploration is being driven to remote, costly, and hostile frontier provinces, just as in this 1887 comment:[43]

> The general decline of the whale-fishery, resulting partly from the scarcity of whales, has led to the abandonment of many of the once famous grounds, and cargoes of sperm oil are obtained only after the most energetic efforts in scouring the oceans.

34. San Joaquin Geological Society 2002. As Doug Koplow points out, the transition was quick because it took only individual action, not collective action like creating a town-gas network. Lamp expert Heinz Baumann (personal communication, 1 June 2004) notes that lamps designed for any fuel—whale oil, camphene, etc.—were "commonly converted" to the superior kerosene product, facilitated by *de facto* standardization to three thread sizes. Kerosene providers often offered the needed conversion kit. It cost ~$0.5–1 in nominal dollars, comparable to a gallon of kerosene ($0.59 in 1859), whale oil ($0.49 but inferior), or sperm oil ($1.36), and typically paid back in months.

35. Davis, Gallman, & Gleiter 1997, p. 362.

36. Goode (1887) shows $5.4 million in total whale-and-sperm-oil sales in 1860, of which, however, $3.2 million was sperm oil almost wholly committed to lubricant and export markets (Davis, Gallman, & Gleiter 1997, p. 345).

37. Yergin 1991, p. 23. This 1859 comparison is in nominal 1859 dollars.

38. Tarr 1999, pp. 19–37; Tarr 2004. In 1850, manufactured gas had one-fourth the value of whale, sperm, and fish oils; in 1860, twice their value (Davis, Gallman, & Gleiter 1997, pp. 353–4).

39. Davis, Gallman, & Gleiter 1997, p. 353, citing the 1865 *Eighth Census of Manufactures* for 1860.

40. Kerosene sold for $0.59/gal nominal in 1859 (Robbins 1992), or $6.20/gal in 2000 $. A gallon of sperm oil has the same energy content (~41.9 MJ/kg) as a gallon of light petroleum, or 91% that of kerosene (Hodgman, Weast, & Selby 1961, pp. 1945, 1936); we assume whale oil does too.

41. Starbuck 1878/1989, p. 113.

42. The authors have been unable to find time-series data for the production or consumption of U.S. town gas or coal-oil before 1859, but these fuels clearly won before Drake struck oil: Robbins 1992; Davis, Gallman, & Hutchins 1988; Davis, Gallman, & Gleiter 1997, pp. 342–362, 515.

43. Starbuck 1878/1989. "The increase in [human] population would have caused an increase in [whale-oil] consumption beyond the power of the fishery to supply, for even at the necessary high prices people would have had light. But…[t]he expense of procuring [whale-]oil was yearly increasing when the oil-wells of Pennsylvania were opened, and a source of illumination opened at once plentiful, cheap, and good. Its dangerous qualities at first greatly checked its general use, but, these removed, it entered into active, relentless competition with whale-oil, and it proved the more powerful of the antagonistic forces."

**Techniques for finding and lifting oil have made stunning progress too.
But innovations to save and replace oil are progressing even faster. Oil thus has dwindling resources and rising costs; its competitors have expanding resources and falling costs.**

44. Grübler, Nakićenović, & Victor 1999.

45. Abernathy 1978, pp. 18–19, 65, 183–5. The closed-body price premium fell from ~50% in 1922 to 5% in 1926 (p. 19).

46. By April 2004, more people owned cellphones in China (296 million) than there are people in the U.S. (293 million), and China was adding two subscribers per second—even though only a fifth of Chinese people yet had cellphones, vs. half in the U.S., two-thirds in Japan (Bloomberg 2004), and >100% saturation in Hong Kong and Taiwan. The world's 1.2 billion cellphones in 2001, one for every 5.2 people, are expected to become 2 billion by 2006, one for every 3.3 people. By 2002, wireless telephony was a global half-trillion-dollar-a-year business. In Germany, not traditionally a hotbed of innovative telecom providers, the fraction of the population with cellphone subscriptions doubled to nearly 60% in the single year 2000.

Fortunately, the power of today's technologies is immeasurably greater than that of 1887. The modern competitors that could capture petroleum's key markets range from doubled-efficiency hybrid-electric cars to ultra-thin heat insulation and superwindows, from windfarms and asphalt substitutes to advanced aircraft. Information systems hook up the world, streamline business operations (design, process control, freight logistics, building management), and optimize everything with cheap microchips. Laboratories are hatching such marvels as doubled-efficiency heavy trucks, competitive solar cells, liquid-hydrogen cryoplanes, and quintupled-efficiency carbon-fiber cars powered by clean hydrogen fuel cells. To be sure, techniques for finding and lifting oil have made stunning progress too. But innovations to save and replace oil are progressing even faster. Oil thus has dwindling resources and rising costs; its competitors have expanding resources and falling costs. Shrewd investors are starting to hedge bets and re-allocate assets.

Nobody knows how quickly these new oil-displacing techniques will spread, but to a great degree that speed is not fate but choice. Transitions can be swift when market logic is strong, policies are consistent, and institutions are flexible. It took the United States only 12 years to go from 10% to 90% adoption (in the capital stock, not new sales) in switching from horses to cars, from uncontrolled automotive emissions to catalytic converters, and from steam to diesel/electric locomotives; 15 years from vacuum-tube to transistor radios and from black-and-white to color televisions. Even such a big infrastructure shift as intercity rail to air travel took just 26 years.[44] U.S. autobody manufacturing went from 85% open and made of wood in 1920 to more than 70% closed and made of steel just six years later.[45] Techniques available to any individual, like cellphones, tend to spread fastest.[46]

The powerful portfolio of ways to accelerate oil efficiency and non-oil supplies isn't only technological: innovations in implementation are equally rapid and important, and they all reinforce each other. Nations can speed up spontaneous market transitions by turning purpose into policy. Creative, common-sense frameworks can clear away decades of underbrush and obstacles, solve problems at their root cause, and command wide support across ideological boundaries. Global challenges are starting to reinspire the public engagement that empowers citizens to manifest their patriotism in their everyday choices. Major sectors of the economy need the revitalization and job growth that this agenda can deliver. If Americans, with business in the vanguard, chose to mobilize their resources—and to help make markets more mindful of new profit potential—the world's premier market economy could pivot and charge through obstacles as unstoppably as football legend Walter Payton.

By combining new technologies, business strategies, marketing methods, policy instruments, and community and personal choices, we can displace more oil, faster, cheaper, than ever imagined. This report shows how. And there's a precedent.

America can replace oil quickly— and already has

The United States last paid attention to oil during 1977–85, spurred by the 1979 "second oil shock," which raised prices even more than the 1973 Arab embargo had done. In those eight years, *the United States proved it could boost its oil efficiency faster than OPEC could cut its oil sales: the U.S. had more flexibility on the demand side than OPEC had on the supply side.* While U.S. GDP rose by 27%, oil consumption *fell* by 17%, net oil imports *fell* by 50%, and net oil imports from the Persian Gulf *fell* by 87%.[47] The drop in oil use was three times 1977 imports from Saudi Arabia, nearly twice today's imports from the Gulf. Faced with suppliers' "oil sword," we drew our own and won the day as plummeting American imports took away one-seventh of OPEC's market. The entire world oil market shrank by one-tenth, OPEC's global market share was slashed from 52% to 30%, and its output fell by 48%, breaking its pricing power for a decade.[48] During 1977–85, U.S. oil intensity (barrels per dollar of real GDP) dropped by 35%. If we'd resumed that pace of oil savings—5.2% a year— starting in January 2001, the United States could have eliminated the equivalent of its 2000 Persian Gulf imports by May 2003 at constant GDP, or by 2007 with 3%/y GDP growth. And we *could* rerun that old play, only better—starting, as we did then, with our personal motor vehicles.

The cornerstone of the 1977–85 revolution in U.S. oil savings—when Washington led with coherent policy and Detroit rose to the occasion— was 7.6-mpg-better domestic cars. On average, each new car drove 1% fewer miles on 20% fewer gallons, achieving 96% of that efficiency gain from smarter design, only 4% from smaller size.[49] During 1975–84, the fuel economy of the entire light-vehicle fleet rose by 62% while vehicles became safer, far cleaner, and no less peppy.[50] Detroit then kept on innovating, but once its success had crashed the world oil price in 1985–86, ever-better powertrains were used to make cars more muscular, not more

> **In the eight years when we last paid attention to oil (1977–85), GDP grew 3% a year, yet oil use fell 2% a year. That pace of reducing oil intensity, 5.2%/y, is equivalent, at a given level of GDP, to displacing a Gulf's worth of oil every two and a half years.**

47. EIA 2003c shows gross imports from the Gulf as 2.448 Mbbl/d in 1977 and 0.311 (0.309 net) in 1985. The gross-minus-net-imports difference—exports from the U.S. *to* the Gulf—was only 0.002 Mbbl/d in 1985, averaged 0.0034 Mbbl/d (0.54%) during 1981–85, and is unpublished and apparently unavailable from EIA for all years before 1981. Plausibly applying the 1981–85 average export rate to 1977–80 yields inferred 1977 net imports of 2.448 – 0.003 = 2.445 Mbbl/d, falling 87.4% to 1985's 0.309 Mbbl/d. By mentioning Persian Gulf imports in this report, we don't mean to imply this is a critical index; more important is how much of its oil the U.S. imports and how much of world supply (and of world traded supply) comes from the Persian Gulf.

48. The U.S. contribution was vital but not unique, and was part of longer-term trends throughout the industrialized world. During 1973–2002, oil as a fraction of total primary energy fell from 80% to 48% in Japan, 64% to 33% in Europe, and 48% to 37% in the world, but only from 47% to 39% in the U.S., which in these terms did worse than the global average. Even during 1979–85, the golden age of U.S. oil savings, oil's share of primary energy fell only from 45% to 40% in the U.S., vs. 72% to 55% in Japan, 55% to 45% in Europe, and 45% to 38% in the world: Franssen 2004.

49. Patterson 1987: "If the 1976 size class shares for autos were applied to the 1987 car class fuel economies, the resulting new car MPG would be 27.7 in 1987 (just 0.4 MPG less than the actual values). Thus, if in 1987 the nation had reverted back to the 1976 new car size mix, the eleven year gain of 10.9 MPG would have been reduced by only 4 percent." This is not valid for light trucks, whose size shift was dominated by sale of smaller imports to new pickup buyers.

50. NAS/NRC 1992, Fig. 1-1; ORNL 2003; EPA 2003.

**Oil
(or more precisely,
the service provided
by oil)
makes us strong,
but oil dependence
makes us weak.**

**Which would be
worse—if Saudi
Arabia couldn't meet
huge forecast
increases in output,
or if it could?
One attack on a key
Saudi oil facility could
crash the world econ-
omy at any moment.
American business
is particularly
vulnerable to** ◄——
**oil disruptions.
Yet the rising dangers
of dependence on
the world's most
vulnerable sources,
both abroad and at
home, are a self-
inflicted problem.
We can profitably
eliminate it by
choosing the best buys
first.**

frugal. The average new U.S. light vehicle in 2003 had 24% more weight, 93% more horsepower, and 29% faster 0–60-mph time than in 1981, but only 1% more miles per gallon. If 1981 performance had instead stayed constant, light vehicles would have become 33% more efficient,[51] displac- ing more than` 2000 Persian Gulf imports. America's light-vehicle fleet today is nearly the world's most fuel-efficient per *ton*-mile, but with more tons, it uses the most fuel per mile of any advanced country. It needn't. We'll see how the same engineering prowess, harnessing a whole new set of advanced technologies, could make that fleet the world's *least* fuel- intensive[52] while continuing to offer all the sizes and features that cus- tomers want.

Similar opportunities beckon throughout the U.S. economy. To under- stand their true value, let's review how, as security scholar Michael Klare puts it, oil (or more precisely, the service provided by oil) makes us strong, but oil dependence makes us weak.

Oil supplies are becoming more concentrated and less secure

The imported fraction of U.S. oil is officially projected to rise from 53% in 2000 to 70% in 2025 (Fig. 2), vs. 66% in the E.U. and 100% in Japan. By 2025, U.S. imports are projected to rise by half, while imports from OPEC's 11 member nations and from the Persian Gulf are nearly to double.

In 2000, 2.5 million barrels per day (Mbbl/d[53]) and nearly half of world oil exports came from the Persian Gulf, an unstable region racked by violent ethnic, religious, and political conflicts.[54] The Gulf provided 24% of U.S. net imports or 13% of total oil consumption. The 1980 Carter Doctrine declared that "any attempt by an outside force to gain control of the Persian Gulf will be regarded as an assault on the vital interests of the United States of America, and…will be repelled by any means necessary, including military force." U.S. forces have since engaged in at least four

51. EPA 2003. Roberts (2004, p. 155) states that "of the nearly twenty million barrels of oil that America uses every day, more than a sixth [actually 13% in 2000] represents a direct consequence of the decision by automakers to invest the efficiency dividend in power, not fuel economy." That remains true regardless of whether automakers were passively responding to the demands of sovereign consumers or designing their marketing to influence those demands.

52. Schipper 2004: "…[A]utomobiles in the United States actually use less energy per kilometer and per unit of weight than do those in nearly every other country. By that measure, U.S. cars are efficient. But they also use more energy per kilometer because they weigh more than cars elsewhere. Thus, one can say that the U.S. car fleet is more fuel intensive than fleets in any other advanced countries. The reason is that American behavior 'favors' large cars, largely due to low car prices and low fuel prices"—and to the habit, no longer necessary (see pp. 53–67), of making them out of heavy steel.

53. Throughout this report, as noted in Box 5 ("Conventions"), "bbl" means barrel (42 U.S. gallons) and "M" is used in its scientific sense of "million" rather than in its engineering sense of "thousand." We therefore avoid the ambiguous usages (common in the energy literature) of Mbpd, MMBTU, etc.

54. More than 90 conflicts in the whole Middle East killed 2.35 million people between World War II and sometime in the early 1990s: Delucchi & Murphy 1996, p. 2, note 3, citing Cordesman 1993, pp. 5–8.

55. Protecting U.S.-reflagged Kuwaiti tankers in the Iran-Iraq war of 1980–88; the 1991 Gulf war; the subsequent containment of Saddam Hussein; and the 2003 Iraq war. This doesn't include the 2001 Afghanistan war or many other skirmishes. Klare (2004) notes that most of Central Command's casualties have been incurred in the Gulf and in its well-documented primary mission—ensuring access to Middle Eastern, chiefly Persian Gulf, oil.

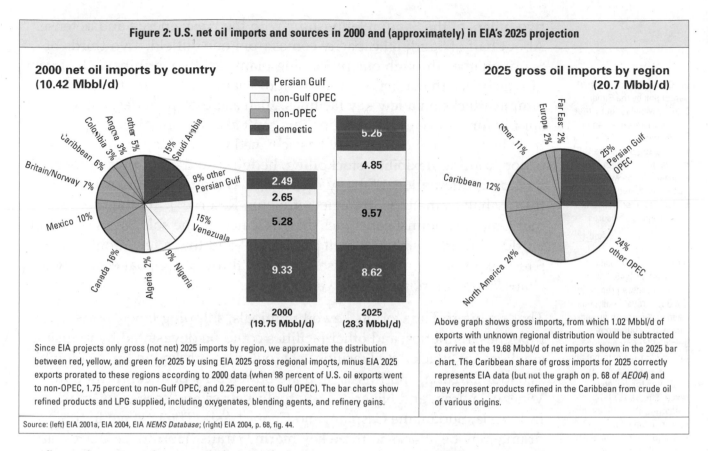

Figure 2: U.S. net oil imports and sources in 2000 and (approximately) in EIA's 2025 projection

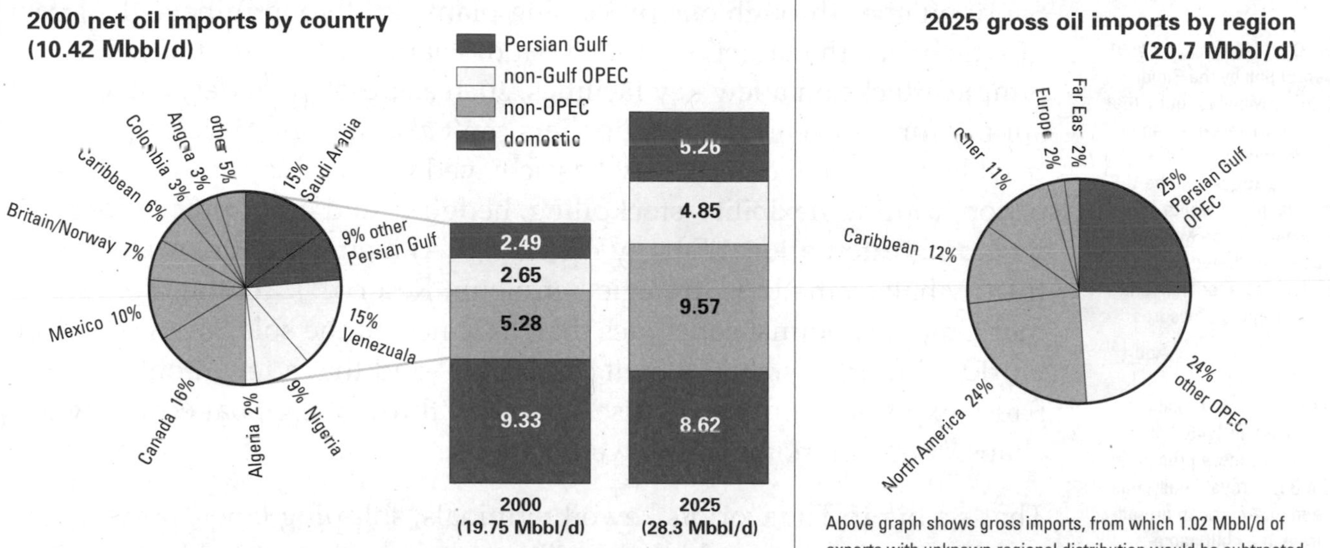
2000 net oil imports by country (10.42 Mbbl/d)
Persian Gulf
non-Gulf OPEC
non-OPEC
domestic
15% Saudi Arabia
9% other Persian Gulf
15% Venezuela
9% Nigeria
Algeria 2%
Canada 16%
Mexico 10%
Britain/Norway 7%
Caribbean 6%
Colombia 3%
Angola 3%
other 5%
2.49
2.65
5.28
9.33
5.26
4.85
9.57
8.62
2000 (19.75 Mbbl/d)
2025 (28.3 Mbbl/d)
2025 gross oil imports by region (20.7 Mbbl/d)
25% Persian Gulf OPEC
24% other OPEC
North America 24%
Caribbean 12%
other 11%
Europe 2%
Far East 2%

Since EIA projects only gross (not net) 2025 imports by region, we approximate the distribution between red, yellow, and green for 2025 by using EIA 2025 gross regional imports, minus EIA 2025 exports prorated to these regions according to 2000 data (when 98 percent of U.S. oil exports went to non-OPEC, 1.75 percent to non-Gulf OPEC, and 0.25 percent to Gulf OPEC). The bar charts show refined products and LPG supplied, including oxygenates, blending agents, and refinery gains.

Above graph shows gross imports, from which 1.02 Mbbl/d of exports with unknown regional distribution would be subtracted to arrive at the 19.68 Mbbl/d of net imports shown in the 2025 bar chart. The Caribbean share of gross imports for 2025 correctly represents EIA data (but not the graph on p. 68 of *AEO04*) and may represent products refined in the Caribbean from crude oil of various origins.

Source: (left) EIA 2001a, EIA 2004, EIA *NEMS Database*; (right) EIA 2004, p. 68, fig. 44.

conflicts there[55] without stabilizing the region. Moreover, despite intensive worldwide efforts to find alternative oil sources, the Gulf's ~65% share of declared global reserves (and even more of the *cheapest* oil) is up from 54% two decades earlier.[56] Thus the U.S. depends ever more on the region[57] that's most volatile, militarized, geopolitically challenged, and hostile to American values.

Today the U.S. imports twice as much oil as it did in 1973, when a hiccup in one-eighth of the supply doubled unemployment, slashed 1975 GDP by 3–5.5%, and quadrupled oil prices in weeks. Prolonged shortages could rip the fabric of American society, throttling everything from daily commuting and air travel to food trucking.[58] And that could actually happen.

Saudi Arabia, the world's sole "swing producer" (with spare capacity to ramp up if prices soar), holds one-fourth of global oil reserves and ~80–85% of spring 2004 spare output capacity,[59] and provided 63% of U.S. net imports from the Gulf in 2000. Saudi Arabia's fractious, fragile monarchy faces a "slow-motion insurrection"[60] and rising terrorism "focused on the

56. BP 2003, pp. 4–5.

57. Its complexities and heterogenities are surveyed by Cordesman 2004.

58. The average molecule of American food is said to travel ~1,400–1,500 miles, mainly by truck, before it's eaten. If trucking stopped (or a few bridges across the Mississippi went down), the East Coast could run short within days.

59. Bahree & McKay (2004) report that although Saudi Arabia could (barely) offset "a sharp drop in output from Iraq, which is producing an estimated 2.5 million barrels a day,...the world's oil exporters are mostly pumping flat out and, taken together, couldn't make up a loss of even a 15% reduction in output, analysts say." Russia was hoped to become a second swing producer, but this is now in doubt, and the two countries may even be increasing their cooperation more than becoming independent counterweights to each other. The ~80–85% estimate of the Saudi share of world crude-oil swing capacity is from EIA 2004c. A year earlier, most estimates were around two-thirds. Unfortunately, most Saudi crudes are too sour (high in sulfur) for many developed-country and Chinese refineries, so the 2004 shortage of sweet crudes is more acute than the aggregate supply/demand balance implies.

two pillars of the Saudi relationship[61] with the West: energy and defense."[62] About half of Saudi oil capacity comes from one oilfield. Two-thirds of Saudi oil goes through one processing plant and two terminals, the larger of which was the target of a foiled Saudi Islamist attack in mid-2002.[63] Simple attacks on a few key facilities, such as pipeline nodes, could choke supply for two years.[64] The defenders can't *always* win. Anticipating trouble, the global oil industry has achieved impressive supply diversification, routing flexibility, stockpiling, hedging, and other precautions, including International Energy Agency (IEA) member nations' stockpiles[65] (nearly half in the U.S. Strategic Petroleum Reserve[66]). Yet the IEA's former Chief Economist concludes that "reliance on the sole Saudi pillar" of world oil-market stability "will continue"—and that a few months' halt in Saudi exports "would spell disaster" and "throw the global economy into chaos,"[67] even if nothing else were harmed.[68]

That's a big if. The world's key oil terminals, shipping lanes, ports, pipelines, refineries, and other facilities could be devastated by plausible small-group attacks.[69] Oil facilities are routinely attacked in Iraq, Colombia, Ecuador, Nigeria, and Russia, and are buffeted by political turmoil in Venezuela, Iran, and Nigeria. They fuel rivalries and secessionism in Indonesia, Sudan, the Caspian, and Central Asia. The next act in this drama may be attacks in three key marine straits (Hormuz, Malacca, and Bab el-Mandab), perhaps in league with local pirates armed with rocket-propelled grenades and even ship-to-ship missiles.[70] FBI Director Mueller

60. Dyer (2004) says a 2001 secret poll by the Saudi Interior Ministry found that 95% of Saudi males aged 19–34 approved of bin Laden's attacks on the U.S., whose alliance with and presence in the Kingdom has exacerbated severe underlying economic and demographic pressures.

61. Ever since King Abd al-Aziz [Ibn Saud] struck a bargain with President Roosevelt in 1945, Saudi Arabia, or more precisely the Saudi royal family, has been an American protectorate in all but name—shielded by American military might from external and internal enemies in exchange for selling oil (except in the 1973–74 embargo). The intricate history, including a failed 1943 U.S. effort to buy the major Saudi oilfields outright through the Petroleum Reserves Corporation, is summarized by Klare 2004 and more fully reviewed by Pollack 2002.

62. Kerr (2004), quoting Kevin Rosser of Control Risks Group, referring to the 1 May 2004 attack on ABB Lummus's Yanbu office. These attacks were clearly meant to spark an exodus of the 6 million expatriates, including ~35,000 Americans, on whom the Saudi oil industry heavily relies. Many have since left. The murder of 22 people at Khobar on 29–30 May 2004 and subsequent attacks have speeded that exodus (MacFarquhar 2004).

63. Luft & Korin 2003; Bradley 2004; Arabialink.com 2002; Lumpkin 2002.

64. Hersh 2001. See also Baer 2003 and Baer 2003a.

65. Financial managers, tempted by mature spot and futures markets and wrongly believing that financial hedges and physical inventories are equivalent, have tended to wring out private buffer stocks as a carrying cost while hedging in futures and options markets. This further burdens the inadequate public stockpiles. Nonetheless, the total of all public and private stockpiles worldwide is probably around four billion barrels (Warren 2004). Some of this is required to keep oil systems operating. Stockpiles of refined products must be changed periodically to prevent spoilage.

66. This 0.7-billion-barrel-capacity underground reservoir complex in the Gulf of Mexico was 94% full in May 2004, aiming at 100% by summer 2005. Its 0.65 billion barrels, available on two weeks' notice, are equivalent to 58 days of 2003 net imports, but its maximum drawdown rate is only three-eighths as big as total net imports, and can deliver 4.3 million bbl/d, or 173% of 2003 Gulf gross imports, for an initial 90 days; the other two-fifths of its capacity has only a 1 Mbbl/d delivery rate. Its facilities and pipeline links to refineries are highly centralized and could be destroyed by a small group of saboteurs.

67. Franssen 2004.

68. Besides ~2.6 billion barrels of private stocks, not all usable due to operational constraints, IEA public emergency stocks of 1.4 billion bbl can produce 12.8 Mbbl/d for a month, or 8 Mbbl/d for three months, or 3 Mbbl/d for five months. The biggest historical supply disruption, in 1978–79, was 5.6 Mbbl/d for six months. In 2002, exports were 7 Mbbl/d from Saudi Arabia and totaled 15.5 Mbbl/d from the Persian Gulf (EIA 2003a). By May 2004, Saudi output had risen to an estimated 9.1 Mbbl/d and Saudi spare capacity had shrunk to ~1.5 Mbbl/d (both quite uncertain). China kept little stockpile but is starting to create a more robust one, with a goal of 22 million tonnes (~161 Mbbl) by 2010 (CNN 2004). Until China and other Asian nations have large stocks, IEA stocks and shortage-sharing arrangements could be badly stressed.

69. Lovins & Lovins 1982: a 1981 report to DoD, 436 pages, 1,200 references.

70. Pirates, often from international criminal syndicates, have attacked and plundered 96 ships along Africa's coast; 22% of pirate attacks on worldwide shipping in 2003 were on tankers (Hosken 2004). The coordinated 24 April 2004 attacks on Iraq's two offshore oil terminals by dhow and speedboat suicide bombers are further worrisome illustrations of the risk.

reports that "any number of attacks on ships have been thwarted,"[71] but in 2003 alone, about 100 tankers *were* attacked. Some hijacked vessels became unregistered "ghost ships."[72] The Strait of Hormuz is now targeted by anti-ship missiles emplaced by Iran's mullahs, perhaps to discourage awkward inquiries into their apparent nuclear-weapons program.

About half of Saudi oil capacity comes from one oilfield. Two-thirds of Saudi oil goes through one processing plant and two terminals, the larger of which was the target of a foiled Saudi Islamist attack in mid-2002. Al Qa'eda calls oil the "umbilical cord and lifeline of the crusader community."

Oil facilities attract terrorists, "undermining the stability of the regimes they are fighting and economically weakening foreign powers with vested interests in their region."[73] Al Qa'eda calls oil the "umbilical cord and lifeline of the crusader community,"[74] and in April 2004 specifically incited attacks on key Persian Gulf installations.[75] As those attacks began, the market, seeing Gulf oil "in the crosshairs,"[76] added a ~$5–12/bbl risk premium.[77] This may mark the start of a new level of interacting social, economic, and political instabilities that lead global oil into an unpleasant era of anxiety and chronic disruption. Saudi Arabia, spending 36% of its budget on defense,[78] might yet avoid both social upheaval[79] and external attacks on its concentrated oil facilities—for example, via aircraft that could be hijacked anywhere in the often security-lax region. Nevertheless a slow, "dripping" kind of sabotage could block the Kingdom's swing production—the mainstay of liquidity from "the world's central banker for petroleum."[80] Insider collusion in the 2003 Riyadh bombings and 2004 Yanbu shooting, Al Qa'eda efforts to assassinate Saudi security officials,[81] and weekly sabotage of Iraqi oil facilities[82] all suggest that such scenarios

A handful of people could halt three-fourths of the oil and gas supplies to the eastern states in one evening without leaving Louisiana.

71. Luft & Korin 2003.

72. The International Chamber of Commerce's International Maritime Bureau's annual piracy report for 2003 reports 469 incidents (including 100 armed attacks), 21 seafarers killed and 71 missing, 359 taken hostage, 311 ships boarded, and 19 hijacked (ICC Commercial Crime Services 2004). The Bureau recommends adding electrified anti-boarding barriers (ICC Commercial Crime Services 2004a).

73. Luft & Korin 2003.

74. Luft & Korin 2003.

75. Both the 1 May 2004 shooting spree in Yanbu and the 24 April 2004 dhow-and-speedboat-bombs attack on the Basra oil terminal (which exports ~85% of Iraq's oil) were called for in early April by Al Qa'eda (Sachs 2004). Days before the Basra attack, U.S. intelligence had warned all Gulf states of such attacks using boats, jet-skis, or explosives hidden in marine shipping containers (*Jordan Times* 2004; Agencies 2004).

76. Pope 2004. The quotation is from John Kilduff, senior VP for energy risk management at Fimat USA (Société Générale): Banerjee 2004.

77. Cummins 2004; Banerjee 2004a.

78. Karl 2004.

79. Franssen 2004; Baer 2003; Baer 2003a; UNDP 2002/3; McMillan 2001; Sciolino 2001; and Hersh 2001. Cordesman 2002–04 provides extensive background.

80. This phrase is due to Bahree & McKay (2004). Saudi prospects are also questioned because of high (>30%) and increasing water cuts in production from the immense but mature Al Ghawar field—about half of Saudi production capacity—and analogous issues in other fields: Darley (2004, pp. 16–17) summarizing the stark contrast between the 24 February 2004 Center for Strategic and International Studies presentations by Simmons (2004) and Abdul Baqi & Saleri (2004); Reed 2004; Bahree 2004. Similar issues are arising elsewhere, e.g., Gerth & Labaton 2004. The popular view that "the Middle East was poorly explored and has a huge potential" for future giant and supergiant oilfield discoveries may be geologically unsound (Laherrere 2004).

81. Jehl 2003. See also Pope 2004a.

82. Luft (2004a) notes that "an average of one to two sabotage attacks a week against Iraq's oil pipelines" cut prewar exports of 2.5 Mbbl/d to 1.5 Mbbl/d despite nearly 14,000 security guards and electronic surveillance equipment. "After more than 100 pipeline attacks in northern Iraq, terrorists last month began hitting the pipelines in the south near Basra." (Mid-June pipeline bombings then cut off all Basra exports, costing several hundred million dollars.) Saudi Arabia, with over 10,000 miles of pipelines, mostly aboveground, has over twice the network size of Iraq. In all, pipelines, "moving 40% of the world's oil across some of the world's most volatile regions,…are a real prize for terrorists." See also IAGS 2004; Lovins & Lovins 1982; Baer 2003b.

83. Bahree & McKay 2004.
84–88. See next page.

aren't fanciful.[83] Some in Washington continue to muse about seizing the Kingdom's oil-rich east if the House of Saud implodes.[84] Understanding the scope for American mobilization to stop needing that oil would seem more prudent. Executing such a contingency plan could preemptively blunt the oil weapon that America's enemies increasingly seek to wield.

Even if the United States imported no oil and its economy weren't intertwined with others that do, its own oil still wouldn't be secure. Its infrastructure is so vulnerable that a handful of people could halt three-fourths of the oil and gas supplies to the eastern states in one evening without leaving Louisiana.[85] Some is as vulnerable as the most worrisome Persian Gulf sites (Box 1).[86]

The United States produces 21% of Gross World Product and uses 26% of the world's oil, but produces only 9% and owns a mere 2–3%, so we can't ← drill our way out of depletion.

Domestic oil is limited

America's domestic output has declined for 34 years, returning in 2003 to its ~1955 level. Prolonged reversal is not a realistic or profitable option. After 145 years of exploitation, U.S. reserves are mostly played out, so new oil typically costs more at home than abroad.[87] The United States, with 4.6% of the world's people, produces 21% of Gross World Product and uses 26% of the world's oil, but produces only 9% and owns a mere 2–3% (including all off-limits areas),[88] so we can't drill our way out of depletion. Over time, other non-Mideast oil areas will follow this pattern too. But a market economy with relatively limited and costly oil of its own

The policy issue is the level of *oil*, not *import*, dependence, so more "oil independence" is not an optimal goal.

1: An example of domestic energy vulnerability

The 800-mile Trans-Alaska Pipeline System (TAPS) delivers one-sixth of U.S. refinery input and of domestic oil output. TAPS is rapidly aging, suffers from thawing permafrost, has persistent and increasingly serious maintenance and management problems (shown from the accidental destruction of a key pumping station in 1977 to repeatedly botched recent restarts), and has been shot at more than 50 times and incompetently bombed twice. It luckily escaped destruction by a competent bomber caught by chance in 1999, and by a fire averted at the Valdez terminal in 2000. It was shut down for 60 hours in 2001 by a drunk's rifle shot and for two days at New Year's 2004 by a terrorism alert. If interrupted for a midwinter week, at least the aboveground half of TAPS's 9 million barrels of hot oil would probably congeal into the world's largest Chap Stick™. TAPS is the only way to deliver potential reserves beneath the Arctic National Wildlife Refuge (ANWR), the biggest onshore U.S. oil prospect, estimated by the U.S. Geological Survey to average 3.2 billion barrels—enough to meet today's U.S. oil demand for six months starting in a decade. But if Refuge oil were exploited despite what USGS found to be dismal economics, it would double TAPS's throughput, making TAPS for several more decades an even more critical chokepoint than the famously vulnerable Strait of Hormuz.

can cut dependence on cheaper oil imports in only three basic ways, of which the first two have been officially favored so far:

- *Protectionism* taxes foreign oil or subsidizes domestic oil[89] to distort their relative prices. (In the case of subsidies, it also retards efficient use and substitution.) This approach, at the heart of present U.S. policy, sacrifices economic efficiency and competitiveness, violates market principles and free-trade rules, and illogically supposes that the solution to domestic depletion is to deplete faster—a policy of "Strength Through Exhaustion."[90]

- *Trade*, being nondiscriminatory, unsentimentally buys oil wherever it's cheapest. Such big economies as Japan and Germany import all their oil, and pay for it by exporting goods and services in which they enjoy a comparative advantage. U.S. oil imports are 24% of world oil trade, yet major U.S. allies and trading partners import an even larger fraction of their oil, and many developing countries rely still more on imports. Trade can be economically efficient, dominates world oil use, sets its price, and underpins the global economy on which the U.S. economy depends. But it exacerbates the issue of unreliable and vulnerable supplies, because for a fungible commodity (Box 2), everyone shares shortages as well as surpluses.

- *Substitution* replaces oil with more efficient use or alternative supplies wherever that's cheaper. These domestic substitutes have all the advantages of protectionism without its drawbacks, and all the advantages of trade without its vulnerabilities. Substitution offers a major opportunity to all countries, both rich and poor. It has so far received less attention and investment than it merits, but it generally turns out to have lower costs and risks than buying oil in the world market, so it forms this study's main focus.

The value of substitution depends on the costs it incurs and avoids. Besides business risks from insecure sources and brittle infrastructure, America's oil habit burdens us all with purchase price, foregone growth and competitiveness, trade and budget deficits, inflated and volatile prices, compromised public and environmental health, faster resource depletion, damage to national reputation and influence, the prospect of growing rivalry rather than friendship with countries like China and India, and erosion of the global stability and security on which all commerce depends. In 1975, 1979, 1981, 1989, 1995, and 2000, U.S. presidents indeed officially found that oil imports threaten to impair national security.[97] So what's it worth to reduce U.S. oil dependence?

84. E.g., Peters 2002; Pryce-Jones 2002; Frum & Perle 2003, p. 141; Barone 2002, p. 49; Podhoretz 2002; Henderson 2002; Murawiec 2002 (see also Ricks 2002 and Ricks 2002a); R.E. Ebel, quoted in Dreyfuss 2003; Margolis 2002; K. Adelman, quoted in Marshall 2002; cf. Buchanan 2003. The risks today would probably be far greater than envisaged in CRS 1975, or by former Ambassador Akins (Higgins 2004; see note 127).

85. Lovins & Lovins 1982.

86. Lovins & Lovins 2001, particularly the detailed annotations to the severely abridged security discussion on p. 75. See also online updates at www.rmi.org, Library, Energy, Security.

87. "The United States is a high cost producer compared to most other countries because it has already depleted its known low cost reserves": DOC/BEA 1999.

88. The lower figure is from the U.S. Energy Information Administration, the higher from the American Petroleum Institute and British Petroleum, both using the canonical *Oil and Gas Journal* denominator.

89. Foreign oil is also heavily subsidized (and its shipping lanes defended at taxpayer expense, pp. 20–21); the leading independent authority on energy subsidies (D. Koplow, personal communication, 28 May 2004) says it's uncertain whether foreign or domestic oil is now more heavily subsidized to U.S. users.

90. This phrase is due to the late conservationist and USA Tenth Mountain Division Maj. (Ret.) D.R. Brower.

91–96: See Box 2 on p. 14.

97. DOC/BEA 2001. These findings under the Trade Expansion Act of 1962 authorized the president to adjust oil imports, as was done in 1973 (licensing fees), 1975 and 1979 (tariffs), 1979 (Iran embargo), and 1982 (Libya embargo). In 1989, 1995, and 2000, the threat finding was still made, but no action beyond existing energy policy was deemed to be required.

2: Oil is fungible

Many commentators imagine that we can simply shift from hostile to friendly oil sources. But because oil is freely traded, the only path to reliable supply and stable price is to *use* less total oil, not just to *import* less oil. Although the world market trades a great variety of crudes—light and heavy, sweet and sour—crude oil is basically a fungible (interchangeable) commodity.[91] Saving 1 Mbbl/d therefore can't reduce U.S. imports from a particular country or region by 1 Mbbl/d: rather, world flows of oil will re-equilibrate at 1 Mbbl/d or ~1.3% lower supply and demand (and at a slightly lower price[92]). If a low-cost producer like Saudi Arabia chose to undercut, say, costly marginal wells in the U.S., as has happened before,[93] then unconstrained imports might not decrease at all. (The aim of the OPEC cartel is to constrain supply, and thereby force others to produce higher-cost oil first, then sell the cartel's cheap oil for that higher price—and by depleting others' oil first, make buyers even more dependent on the cartel later.)

Cutting U.S. oil use by, say, one-eighth will thus save the *equivalent* of imports from the Gulf (the sort of comparison sometimes made in this report to illustrate magnitudes), but one way or another, the same amount of oil may still flow from the Gulf to the U.S., as low-cost exporters share reduced sales. Even the 1973 Arab embargo couldn't stop large oil flows from reaching the U.S. by transshipment or by freeing up other supplies. Saving oil is vital and valuable: it saves the purchase price, helps dampen world prices, avoids indirect economic and social costs, erodes the leverage of any particular supplier, and enables any given substitute to meet a larger share of the decreased demand. But if we keep the oil habit, we'll still need a fix from the same pushers in the same market. The policy issue is the level of *oil*, not *import*, dependence, so more "oil independence" is not an optimal goal. As President George H.W. Bush's 1991 energy plan explained,[94]

> Popular opinion aside, our vulnerability to price shocks is not determined by how much oil we import. Our vulnerability to oil price shocks is more directly linked to: (1) how oil dependent our economy is; (2) our capacity for switching to alternative fuels; (3) reserve oil stocks around the world; and (4) the spare worldwide oil production[95] capacity that can be quickly brought on line.

And as President George W. Bush's energy plan rightly reiterated ten years later,[96]

> We should not…look at energy security in isolation from the rest of the world. In a global energy marketplace, U.S. energy and economic security are directly linked not only to our domestic and international energy supplies, but to those of our trading partners as well. A significant disruption in world oil supplies could adversely affect our economy and our ability to promote key foreign and economic policy objectives, regardless of the level of U.S. dependence on oil imports.***The first step toward a sound international energy policy is to use our own capability to produce, process, and transport the energy resources we need in an efficient and environmentally sustainable manner. Market solutions to limit the growth in our oil imports would reduce oil consumption for our economy and increase our economic flexibility in responding to any…disruption.…

91. This is decreasingly true of U.S. gasoline because of a proliferation of "boutique" state and regional formulas. The resulting difficulty of swapping supplies can create local shortages of gasoline meeting local regulatory requirements, even if there's plenty of total gasoline in the market.

92. Based on the Greene and Tishchishyna (2000) analysis, a 1% decrease in U.S. oil demand reduces world oil price by ~0.3–0.5%; p. 20 in NAS/NRC 2001 concurs.

93. For example, low oil prices from late 1997 to early 1999 squeezed the ~7,000 independent operators who produce two-fifths of lower-48 oil, forcing them to cut staff and exploration, increase debt, and shut in or abandon high-cost wells. Such squeezes periodically endanger nearly 1 Mbbl/d of marginal production, mainly from small "stripper" wells.

94. DOE 1991, p. 3.

95. By industry and economic convention, we use the term "production" in this report, even though people only extract the oil that geological processes have produced. We similarly use "consumption" in its economic sense; burned oil simply reacts with oxygen to form combustion products of identical total weight, plus heat.

96. National Energy Policy Development Group 2001, pp. 8-3 and 8-1.

Counting the direct cost of oil dependence

In 2000, Americans paid $362 billion for retail oil. Although that's $334 billion less than they would have spent at the 1975 oil/GDP ratio, they spent nearly as much just on transportation fuel ($285 billion[98]) as on national defense ($294 billion in FY2000[99]). Transportation's need for light refined products, especially gasoline, causes ~93% of projected growth in oil demand to 2025.[100] Worse, it propels oil imports, which met 53% of U.S. oil demand in 2000. Those imports' net cost, $109 billion, was 24% of that year's goods-and-services trade deficit, now a major economic concern that erodes the U.S. dollar's value and hence boosts dollar oil prices.[101] It's getting worse. In 2003, imports cost $10 billion a month. And the bill mounts up. During 1975–2003, Americans have sent $2.2 trillion (2000 $) abroad for net oil imports. Those high and rising imports have strengthened OPEC's ability to price oil above its fair market value. By sucking purchasing power and reinvestment out of the U.S. economy, that pricing power has incurred a total economic cost estimated at $4–14 trillion (1998 present-valued dollars) over the past three decades—about a GDP-year, rivaling total payments on the National Debt.[102]

> Sending $2 trillion abroad for oil and empowering OPEC to charge excessive prices has cost the U.S. many trillions of dollars. Volatile oil prices buffet the economy, and still would even if all our oil were domestic— to the extent we still depend on oil.

> In 2000, Americans spent nearly as much on transportation fuel as on national defense.

> In 2003, oil imports cost $10 billion a month. During 1975–2003, Americans sent $2.2 trillion (2000 $) abroad for net oil imports.

98. EIA 2003, Table A3, converting 2001 to 2000 $.

99. DoD 2001, Table 1-11.

100. EIA 2004, p. 97.

101. Leone & Wasow (2004) correctly note that from the end of February 2002 to two years later, the world oil price rose 51% in dollars but only 4% in euros, as the exchange rate plunged from 1.16 to 0.80 euros per dollar, for reasons the authors ascribe largely to loss of international confidence in U.S. tax and fiscal policy. "In this situation, it is perfectly rational for foreign suppliers of oil to charge more in dollars to make up for the falling value of our currency." On these figures, ~96% of the increase in the U.S.-dollar oil price was simply an exchange-rate adjustment relative to the euro, although OPEC spends dollars too.

102. Greene & Tishchishyna 2000. Competing, but in our view unpersuasive, theoretical arguments are presented by Bohi & Toman 1996. Kohl (2004) notes that the ORNL estimate assumes oil would compete at ~$10/bbl absent the cartel, and that opinions differ on that assumption.

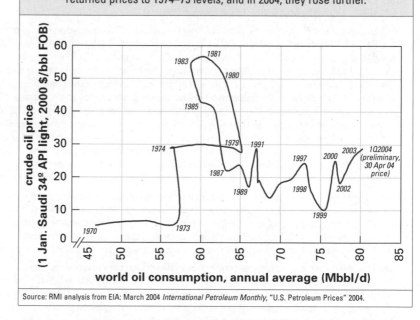

Figure 3: World oil consumption and real price, 1970–1Q2004[103]
Demand grew quickly at low prices until the 1973 "first oil shock," then slowly at high prices, until 1979's worse "second oil shock" sent demand into decline, softening price until demand began to rise again. Prices spiked in the 1991 Gulf War. In 2003, the Iraq War and OPEC discipline returned prices to 1974–79 levels, and in 2004, they rose further.

y-axis: crude oil price (1 Jan. Saudi 34° API light, 2000 $/bbl FOB)

x-axis: world oil consumption, annual average (Mbbl/d)

Source: RMI analysis from EIA: March 2004 *International Petroleum Monthly*, "U.S. Petroleum Prices" 2004.

It is indeed controversial; yet noted oil economist Phil Verleger has reportedly estimated that real GDP would be higher by about 10% in the U.S., 15% in the EU, and 20% in Japan if hydrocarbon prices had been determined by free markets over the past quarter-century.

103. Consumption data 1970–2003 from EIA 2004a, Table 46. Price data (applying implicit GDP price deflator) from EIA, undated; 2004 data are preliminary, for 1Q only, and 30 April instead of 2 January data. Prices are opening-of-year snapshots, not annual averages, for the standard Saudi light marker crude, excluding shipping costs.

3: The uncounted economic cost of oil-price volatility

Oil-price volatility (often measured by the standard deviation of log-price differences) incurs up to 11 kinds of economic costs compared to less- or nonvolatile alternatives. These costs seem not to have been well explored in the economic literature, even though oil price volatility is important, and might better explain output and unemployment than the level of oil price does.[104] RMI commissioned a review of these costs by researcher Jamie Fergusson, summarized in *Technical Annex*, Ch. 2. The uncounted costs are partly overlapping, hard to assess accurately, but large: one illustrative econometric analysis found on the order of $20b/y but was methodologically unconvincing.[105] At RMI's request, therefore, Dr. Richard Sandor, Vice Chair of the Chicago Board of Trade, discovered the volatility's value in the derivatives market using forward option pricing. As of 2 June 2004,

over a five-year time horizon, *the market valued oil-price volatility at ~$3.8/bbl, a ~10% premium.*[106] This figure, which we adopt as $3.5/bbl in 2000 $, would theoretically (not practically)[107] equate to ~$7–8b/y to hedge the portion of U.S. oil consumption traded in the market, or nearly $30b/y if notionally extended to all current U.S. oil consumption. (Volatility's value is usually higher over a shorter time horizon,[108] and varies over time according to real-time oil-price volatility itself: *Technical Annex*, Ch. 2) Displacing oil with alternatives whose prices are less volatile than oil's, or may even be nonvolatile (such as end-use efficiency, which is financially riskless[109] because once installed it has zero price fluctuation), would thus create major economic benefits. Any risk premium on oil price must be included in a properly risk-adjusted comparison of oil vs. such less risky alternatives (p. 101). The social *cost* of volatility may be higher than that risk premium implies.

104. Hooker 1996; Awerbuch & Sauter 2002.

105. EIA 2001. The same is true of the ~$6–9 billion/y estimate by the CRS (1992), updated by Moore, Behrens, & Blodgett (1997).

106. Dr. Sandor and his staff at the Chicago Climate Exchange (CCX) obtained 5-year "at-the-money" option pricing—prices for contracts to buy oil at the 2 June 2004 price of $40, using the West Texas Intermediate (WTI) U.S. marker crude. CCE economist Murali Kanakasabai (personal communications, 26 May and 11 June 2004) used a $40 spot price, a strike price of $31.70 equal to the 5-y NYMEX futures price, and the 2 June 2004 forward price volatility of 17% (from Lewis Nash, Morgan Stanley). Under these conditions, contracts on the New York Mercantile Exchange, valued using standard Black-Scholes option calculators as of 2 June 2004 with a 5% riskless interest rate, were priced at $3.31/option for a call and $0.52 for a put for 5-year Asian Options, which entitle the holder to buy oil for cash five years hence at the average price during the five-year period, thus separating secular trends from mere fluctuations. The corresponding European Options cost $15.88 call and $0.572 put; American Options, $15.89 call and $0.774 put. (An American Option costs more than the Asian Option because it entitles the holder to exercise anytime between purchase and expiration, rather than only at expiration, exposing the option seller to the most extreme price of the underlying commodity during the entire period; a European option carries the same risk but can be exercised only *on* its expiry date.) We interpret the Asian Option call-plus-put price as a broad metric of volatility's market value. (Banker's Trust's Tokyo office invented Asian Options in 1987 precisely for the purpose of laying off crude-oil price risk.) The owner of Asian Options for both a call and a put has paid the sum of these instruments' cost to eliminate price risk and be subject only to secular trend.

107. Extending the ~$4/bbl price discovered from small-quantity option quotations to the entire U.S. oil market (or at least the ~1.8 billion bbl/y traded in the market—not the bulk of oil supply that comes from vertically integrated suppliers) is theoretical, in the sense that the market couldn't stand the hedging of such a large volume, nor is there a sufficiently large and creditworthy private counterpart. (Just the 5-year maturity would require a AAA rating.) Despite this lack of a clear interpretation at large volumes, we believe the small-quantity marginal price is a helpful contribution to understanding the reality of oil-price volatility and its economic cost: as in any hedging transaction, the option seller is being compensated for a real risk.

108. This is because the market, correctly or not, assumes long-term reversion to mean. At 2 June 2004, exceptionally, the 1-year call-plus-put Asian Options cost a total of $2.98/bbl, because the oil price was so anomalously high that most or all of the upside price risk was presumed to have already occurred. However, the 90-day volatility price was higher than the 1-year, presumably because the market anticipated a greater short-term risk of Middle Eastern supply disruptions. Going in the other direction, it would be possible to obtain longer-than-5-y option pricing, say for 7 or even 10 y, but at that maturity, the market becomes quite thinly traded, and unfortunately there is no 20-y market deep enough to be validly quoted.

109. In financial economics, "riskless" means the price is known or constant, not that there are no other risks in a transaction (such as equipment breakdowns or installer malfeasance). Thus a fixed-rate mortgage and the yield of a Treasury note are riskless. Such cashflows cost more because they lack the price-fluctuation risk of an adjustable-rate mortgage or of the market value of a stock. (Treasury debt also yields less and costs more than junk bonds because it lacks their credit risk.)

But the oil problem isn't just about imports from unstable countries and from a global cartel. That's because replacing unstable suppliers with diversified, stable, friendly sources is helpful but inadequate: even if the U.S. imported *no* oil, it would still be a price-taker, its domestic markets whipsawed by the world oil market's price volatility (Fig. 3), which exceeds that of the stock market or of most commodities. Oil price shocks hurt far more than declines help, cutting the annual GDP growth rate by about half a percentage point.[110] Eight of ten postwar U.S. recessions closely followed an oil-price spike,[111] and according to Fed Chairman Alan Greenspan, "All economic downturns in the United States since 1973...have been preceded by sharp increases in the price of oil."[112] Each $1/bbl price rise amounts to a gross tax of $7 billion per year (less any return flows). For more than a century, oil prices have been random, just like other commodity prices, increasingly exposing the U.S. economy— as many key partners abroad have long been exposed—to costly short- and long-term perturbations. The market itself values oil-price volatility at several dollars per barrel (Box 3).

Oil-price volatility, let alone cutoffs, poses major risks to key industries. One American private-sector job in ten is linked to the auto industry,[113] and almost all jobs ultimately depend on mobility. The Big Three automakers earn 60% of their global profits from North American sales of light trucks, but surging oil prices in 2004 stalled those sales, swelling inventories and requiring ~$4,000 incentives to "move the metal."[114] Hard-pressed U.S. air-lines, which lose $180 million a year for every penny-per-gallon rise in fuel cost, may see their precarious gains scuttled.[115] Independent truckers can't pay both their truck loans and sky-high fuel prices. As such bellwether sectors falter, the damage reverberates through the whole economy. And that's just the tip of a giant iceberg of hidden security, fiscal, environmental, and foreign-relations costs.

Oil dependence's hidden costs may well exceed its direct costs

One-fourth of all the oil America uses comes from OPEC countries, one-seventh from Arab OPEC countries, one-eighth from Persian Gulf countries. Reliance on unstable oil sources incurs costs for both buying and defending it. Those costs are compounded by how some oil exporters respend the petrodollars. The $2.2 trillion paid for U.S. oil imports since 1975 has financed needed development by neighbors and allies, but has also paid for profligacy, polarizing inequities, weapons of mass destruc-tion, state-sponsored violence, and terrorism—perhaps indirectly and unofficially including the 9/11 attack on the American homeland.

"All economic down-turns in the United States since 1973... have been preceded by sharp increases in the price of oil."

— *Alan Greenspan*

104–109: See Box 3, p. 16.

110. This summary assess-ment by Hamilton is described and supported in Fergusson's Ch. 2 of the *Technical Annex.*

111. Kohl 2004.

112. Greenspan 2002.

113. Including multipliers from the direct employment of 1.3 million direct employ-ees of automakers and 2.2 million employees of the industry's suppliers, plus the rest of the value chain (McAlinden, Hill, & Swiecki 2003). The multiplier is large because the motor-vehicle manufacturing sector adds value of $292,000/worker, 143% above the U.S. manu-facturing average—the third-highest value-added per worker of any major sector, with wages also 60% above the average U.S. worker's. The total reaches 13.3 million if it also includes 3.9 million professional drivers.

114. Freeman, Zuckerman, & White 2004.

115. Trottman 2004.

Military, subsidy, and environmental costs could at least double oil's true price to society.

One-fourth of all the oil America uses comes from OPEC countries, one-seventh from Arab OPEC countries, one-eighth from Persian Gulf countries.

Oil dependence creates incentives and structures that make most oil-exporting countries uniquely ill-governed, unfree, unjust, unstable, militarized, and conflict-prone.

Petrodollars tend to destabilize

The costs of oil imports (broadly defined) include political ties to unstable countries. Prospects of those countries' achieving greater political stability simply by acquiring oil wealth are slim, as historic experience amply demonstrates. There are some commendable exceptions, and recent initiatives by BP and others to post on the Web the amounts and recipients of all payments to governments[116] are important and laudable blows against corruption. Oil-driven development failure is not inevitable.[116a] But more often, oil wealth has fomented power struggles among governmental, sociopolitical, and industrial factions. Such rivalries, social divisions, and developmental distortions can threaten price and supply stability, incur escalating protection costs,[117] and overstress oil reservoirs (as under Saddam Hussein). Indeed, countries often *become* unstable once they discover oil. Of the top eight non-Gulf oil prospects—Angola, Azerbaijan, Colombia, Kazhakstan, Mexico, Nigeria, Russia, and Venezuela—not one is stable.[118] In some, buying rights to a new multi-billion-dollar oilfield might mean bargaining with both the government and other sellers such as rebels, clan chieftains, warlords, or druglords.[119]

Flows of oil revenue to governments that start off neither transparent nor fair tend to create incentives and structures that then exacerbate destabilizing corruption, inequity, and repression:[120] only 9% of world oil reserves are held by countries considered "free" by Freedom House, and oil riches correlate well with Transparency International's corruption ratings.[121] An NGO report on the more than $200 billion destined for sub-Saharan African governments in the next decade from their rapidly expanding oil reserves notes:[122]

> The dramatic development failures that have characterized most other oil-dependent countries around the world…warn that petrodollars have not helped developing countries to reduce poverty; in many cases, they have actually exacerbated it.***Countries that depend upon oil exports, over time, are among the most economically troubled, the most authoritarian, and the most conflict-ridden states in the world today.

Nigeria, for example, has received more than $300 billion in oil revenues in the past quarter-century, but its per-capita income remains below $1 a day, and its economy has performed worse than that of sub-Saharan Africa as a whole, let alone other developing regions. The Center for Strategic and International Studies' energy task force found in 2000[123] that the nations now counted upon to moderate U.S. Gulf dependence often

> …share the characteristics of "petro-states," whereby their extreme dependence on income from energy exports distorts their political and economic institutions, centralizes wealth in the hands of the state, and makes each country's leaders less resilient in dealing with change but provides them with sufficient resources to hope to stave off necessary reforms indefinitely.

116. The "Publish What You Pay" campaign (www.publishwhatyoupay.org) nearly got BP expelled from Angola in 2001, but is now becoming the "gold standard" for extractive industries, especially in Africa. The World Bank Group endorsed the Extractive Industries Transparency Initiative in 2003 (www.worldbank.org/ogmc/) and is considering in 2004 the wider and more controversial recommendations of the Extractive Industries Review, which include phasing out oil-project investments within five years.

116a. Moody-Stuart 2003.

117. DoD sought funding in 2003 to train Colombian soldiers to protect assets of private U.S. oil operators there (BBC News World Edition 2003). The two main pipelines, each over 400 miles long, suffered 98 bombings in 2000 alone (Karl 2004).

118. Klare (2004) gives details.

119. Klare (2001) lists (pp. 227–231) 19 separate conflicts then underway over oil, involving an overlapping total of 49 countries.

120. Karl 2004.

121. Luft & Korin (2003), citing Freedom House 2003 and Transparency International 2003.

122. Gary & Karl 2003, pp. 77, 18; see also Karl 1997. The $200 billion, chiefly from the Gulf of Guinea, is about ten times expected Western aid flows.

123. Nunn et al. 2000.

The vicious circle of rent-seeking behavior and concentrated power also often reinforces prevalent over-militarization, which in turn is both internally and externally destabilizing:[124]

> In the decade from 1984 to 1994…OPEC members' share of annual military expenditures as a percentage of total central government expenditures was three times as much as the developed countries, and two to ten times that of the non-oil developing countries. From the perspective of poverty alleviation, the sheer waste of this military spending is staggering….Fights over oil revenues become the reason for ratcheting up the level of pre-existing conflict in a society, and oil may even become the very rationale for starting wars. This is especially true as economies move into decline. Petroleum revenues are also a central mechanism for prolonging violent conflict and only rarely a catalyst for resolution. Think, for example, of Sudan, Algeria, the Republic of Congo, Indonesia (Aceh), Nigeria, Iraq, Chechnya [a key transit point for Caspian oil pipelines] and Yemen.

Of these eight states, at least seven, not coincidentally, now harbor Islamic extremists.[125]

Sociopolitical instability drives military costs

Thus arise threats to regional stability: the wars, terrorist movements, and decaying state structures that the U.S. Central Command's forces must address in order to keep the oil flowing. But that mission presupposes that the United States needs the oil (or is willing to protect it for others' sake). Financially, net of other countries' ~$54 billion contributions, the 1991 Gulf War cost the U.S. only $7 billion—equivalent to a $1/bbl price increase for a year. Yet spending $7 billion each year to buy oil efficiency technologies then available could have permanently *eliminated* the equivalent of Gulf oil imports.[126] This comparison suggests a serious and continuing misallocation of America's capital and attention.

The United States has multiple interests in the Middle East, including its commitment to Suez Canal/Red Sea navigation and to Israel. But those interests are at best distorted and at worst overwhelmed by the vital need for oil. Three decades ago, President Nixon was even prepared as a last resort to use airborne troops to seize oilfields in Saudi Arabia, Kuwait, and Abu Dhabi—perhaps for up to a decade—if the Arab oil embargo weren't lifted, because the U.S. "could not tolerate [being]…at the mercy of a small group of unreasonable countries."[127] Historians will long debate whether the United States would have sent a half-million troops to liberate Kuwait in 1991 if Kuwait just grew broccoli and the U.S. didn't need it. Decades hence, historians may be better able to say whether an odious tyrant would have been overthrown with such alacrity in 2003 if he didn't control the world's second-largest oil reserves. But even in peacetime, without lives directly at stake, the United States has for decades routinely

---

Countries often *become* unstable once they discover oil.

Financially, the 1991 Gulf War cost the U.S. only $7 billion; spending less than this to buy oil efficiency instead could have eliminated the equivalent of Gulf oil imports.

Dependence on oil from the world's least stable region has created the largest single burden on America's military forces, their costs, and their likelihood of success.

124. Gary & Karl 2003, p. 24.

125. Their presence is obvious in all but the Republic of Congo, whose weak state structure nonetheless sustains activities that would be useful support structures for terrorism, such as money-laundering and illicit arms sales.

126. Lovins & Lovins 2001, hypertext to p. 77, "cost the United States." Today's technologies are even better (Fig. 28, p. 100 below), and the cheapest ones have negative or very low costs.

127. Frankel 2004; Alvarez 2004. According to Higgins (2004), James Akins, the U.S. Ambassador to Saudi Arabia, sent a confidential cable to Washington calling the notion of seizing Saudi oil "criminally insane," and was fired a few months later—because of that view, he says.

We pay two to three times as much to maintain military forces poised to intervene in the Gulf as we pay to buy oil from the Gulf.

maintained large forces whose stated primary mission is intervention in the Persian Gulf. In every issue of their *United States Military Posture Statement* from FY1979 to FY1989, the Joint Chiefs said this was even more important than containing Soviet ambitions in the region.[128] The 2002 U.S. national-security strategy mentioned neither oil nor the Gulf,[129] but the 18 February 1992 draft of *Defense Planning Guidance for the Fiscal Years 1994–1999* forthrightly stated America's "overall objective" in the Gulf: "to remain the predominant outside power in the region and preserve U.S. and Western access to the region's oil."[130] Big U.S. military bases now blanket the area. By 2000, prominent conservatives wrote,[131]

> The presence of American forces, along with British and French units, has become a semipermanent fact of life....In the decade since the end of the Cold War, the Persian Gulf and the surrounding region has witnessed a geometric increase in the presence of U.S. armed forces, peaking above 500,000 troops during Operation Desert Storm, but rarely falling below 20,000 in the intervening years....[R]etaining forward-based forces in the region would still be an essential element in U.S. security strategy given the longstanding American interests in the region***[where] enduring U.S. security interests argue forcefully for an enduring American military presence.

Gulf-centric forces' 1990s readiness cost, allocating DoD's non-regionally-specific costs *pro rata*, was ~\$54–86 billion per year in 2000 \$.[132] That is, *the U.S. pays two to three times as much to maintain military forces poised to intervene in the Gulf as it pays to buy oil from the Gulf.* By claiming that we'd need most of those forces anyway, and that their presence is largely altruistic, some analysts select numerators and denominators that can translate \$54–86b/y into per-barrel costs around \$2 rather than, say, \$77.[133] Econometrics[134] and calculations of military-plus-Strategic-Petroleum-Reserve costs[135] estimated just \$10/bbl before 1991. But all these figures understate the distortion of paying oil-related military costs in taxes and blood, not at the pump,[136] because they count only Central Command. The Pentagon's other unified commands are also having to set aside many of the other missions that they have trained for, as they are "slowly but surely being

128. Delucchi & Murphy 1996; extensive further evidence is marshaled by Klare (2004).

129. The White House 2002.

130. Quoted, with extensive historical analysis, in Delucchi & Murphy 1996.

131. Donnelly, Kagan, & Schmitt 2000, pp. 14, 17, 74.

132. Koplow & Martin 1998, Ch. 4; ORNL 2003, Table 1.9. The estimates are by Earl Ravenal (Cato Institute and Georgetown U. School of Foreign Service), William Kaufmann (Brookings Institution), and Milt Copulos (National Defense Council Foundation), whose detailed unit-by-unit cost assessment included no general DoD overheads, yet yielded peacetime readiness costs of \$49.1 billion (2002 \$).

133. Koplow & Martin (1998) very conservatively allocated only one-third of this military cost to oil-related missions, then divided it by all oil exports from the Gulf (mainly to Europe and Japan, which get about one-fourth and three-fourths of their oil from the Gulf, respectively, but contribute inversely to the Gulf's G7 military costs: Johnson 2000, p. 87). Accepting the rationale that U.S. consumers benefit too from resulting improvements in price stability and global economic health, the U.S. military subsidy cut the cost of Gulf exports to all countries by ~\$1.65–3.65/bbl, or 4–9¢/gal. But one might wonder whether an oil-*in*dependent United States would be quite so altruistic. If not, a different cost allocation could be warranted. If the entire nominal \$70 billion of 2000 Gulf-related military costs were allocated to the one-eighth of Gulf exports that the U.S. imports, they'd be equivalent to \$77/bbl—2.7 times the landed price of Saudi crude in 2000—and would boost the 2000 pump price to \$4.29 a gallon. The complexities of assessing the military costs of oil dependence are well discussed by Delucchi & Murphy (1996).

134. Broadman & Hogan 1988.

135. Hall 2004.

136. The belief that this distortion is large spans a wide spectrum of politics and methodology. For example, M.R. Copulos (2003) reckons that imported oil incurs U.S. economic costs of \$5.28/gal of gasoline, annually comprising (2002 \$) \$49 billion military cost, \$99 billion direct import cost, \$61 billion indirect cost of sending that money abroad, \$13 billion lost tax revenue on the wages of domestic petroleum workers assumed to supply the oil instead, and \$75–83 billion from amortizing three historic oil shocks' economic cost (totaling \$2.2–2.5 trillion) over the 30 years they spanned.

converted into a global oil-protection service"[137]—for example, Southern Command in Colombia, European Command in Africa (except the Horn) and the Republic of Georgia, Pacific Command in two oceans, and Northern Command in undisclosed places. DoD doesn't do activity-based costing, so how much of its peacetime budget relates to oil is unknown. But if you think, for example, that half might be a reasonable estimate, and should be ascribed to oil use by the United States but not by its oil-using allies, that would be equivalent to ~$25/bbl.

Nonmilitary societal costs

Oil dependence also bears other important hidden costs to U.S. society:

- Direct federal subsidies to both domestic and imported oil in 1995 added several dollars per barrel, may well have been higher for imports (disadvantaging domestic producers), and are rising.[138]

- Federal net subsidies to oil-*using* systems are probably larger still— by one reckoning, $111 billion a year just for light vehicles,[139] equivalent to $16/bbl.

- Oil's unmonetized air-pollution costs have been estimated at ~$1/bbl[140] to ~$15/bbl.[141]

- That doesn't yet count ~$2–5/bbl for oil combustion's potential contribution to climate change.[142] That may well be understated for irreversible processes that threaten to submerge some countries, starve or flood others, and export environmental refugees to others. This could in turn destabilize whole regions, raise major national-security contingencies with possibly tremendous associated costs,[143] and increase catastrophic-risk costs to the private sector.[144]

> **Subsidies and environmental costs (including climate risks), combined with oil's military costs, could easily cost society more than the oil price we pay in the market.**

> **Whatever all these hidden costs turn out to total—clearly upwards of $10/bbl, plausibly comparable to oil's market price, and perhaps much higher yet—they should hide no longer.**

137. Klare 2004, p. 7; Cummins 2004a (~30 U.S. warships now patrol in and around the Persian Gulf); Glanz 2004.

138. Subsidies are complex, arcane, and often artfully concealed (e.g., by waiving normally required payments or rules), but their net effect is to transfer government-provided goods, services, or risk-bearing to private firms that must otherwise buy them in the marketplace. In 1995, annual nonmilitary subsidies to the U.S. petroleum industries (both domestic and via imported oil, net of federal revenues from oil-industry user fees and consumer excise taxes) totaled upwards of $5.2–11.9 billion; those to domestic oil, $4.4–10.2 billion, totaled $1.2–2.8/bbl according to Koplow & Martin (1998; see also Koplow 2004). Their analysis included subsidies mainly in tax breaks, R&D support, subsidized credit, below-market resource sales, subsidized oil transport, and socialization of private-sector liabilities, but excluded subsidies to the car, aircraft, and other oil-*using* industries; subsidies from eight hard-to-analyze federal programs; effects on oil supply and demand and on employment; and leveraging of private investment into the oil sector beyond the levels attractable at fair market prices. Some other oil-subsidy estimates are much higher. For example, ICTA (1998) estimate annual subsidies to U.S. oil (1997 $, including defense) at $126–273 billion plus $0.4–1.4 trillion in externalities of *using* the oil, including all side effects of the transportation system. (For example, vehicular combustion products can be a major threat to public health, especially in the teeming cities of the developing world. Congestion, collision, and inequitable access to mobility add to the social toll.) ICTA therefore finds an order-of-magnitude underpricing of gasoline, because of externalities totaling $4.6–14.1/gal. Conversely, the American Petroleum Institute strongly disputes Koplow & Martin 1998 (Dougher 1999); they have responded (www.earthtrack.net/earthtrack/index.asp?pageID=144&catID=66).

139. Roodman 1998, Ch. 5.

140. NAS/NRC (2001, Ch. 5, summarized at p. 86), estimated gasoline's environmental externalities at ~14¢ per U.S. gallon (~$35 billion/y in 2000), or $6 per barrel, with a range from one-fifth to twice that much "not implausible" and perhaps not inclusive; 12¢ of the 14¢ was for climate change, which we show separately in the next bullet.

141. Hall 2004 and that article's journal citations.

142. NAS/NRC 2002a and Hall 2004, respectively.

143. Stipp 2004, Schwartz & Randall 2003.

144. See next page.

Whatever all these hidden costs turn out to total—clearly upwards of $10/bbl, plausibly several tens of dollars per barrel, and perhaps even higher—they should hide no longer. President Nixon got the economic principle of truthful pricing right when he told the Congress in 1971,[145]

> One reason we use energy so lavishly today is that the price of energy does not include all the social costs of producing it. The costs incurred in protecting the environment and the health and safety of workers, for example, are part of the real costs of producing energy—but they are not now all included in the price of the product.

Oil dependence compromises fundamental U.S. security and foreign-policy interests and ideals, harms global development, ← and weakens the nation's economy. And even if world oil output peaks later than some fear, it's none too early to begin an orderly transition that could capture its manifest profits sooner.

Adding up the hidden costs

To be sure, despite all of oil's direct and hidden costs, oil revenues are important drivers of national development in such places as Mexico, Russia, and potentially West Africa, the Middle East, and the Caspian region. The need to diversify economies trapped in petro-codependency, the needs of oil-dependent industries, and oil's pivotal role in today's economy must be dispassionately balanced against the benefits of oil displacement. But taken together, the costs of continuing America's current dependence on oil pose a potentially grave impediment to achieving stated national security and economic objectives. In sum, U.S. oil dependence:

U.S. oil dependence is intensifying competition over oil with all other countries, ultimately including China and India. It sets the stage for billions of people to blame their poverty and oil shortages on what demagogues could portray as America's uncaring gluttony.

- **erodes U.S. national security** by:

  ○ engaging vital national interests in far-off and unfamiliar places where intervention causes entanglement in ancient feuds and grievances, and even in oil wars;

  ○ requiring military postures—such as deployments in the midst of proud traditional societies—that reinforce Islamist arguments and Islam/West friction, arousing resentment and inciting violence among some of the world's 1.3 billion Muslims;[146]

  ○ thereby turning American citizens and assets worldwide into symbolic targets;

  ○ providing resources for legal but excessive and destabilizing arms acquisitions: as a 2000 CIA assessment dryly remarked, OPEC revenues "are not likely to be directed primarily toward core human resources and social needs"[147] despite staggering development deficits;[148]

144. As "global weirding" (in Hunter Lovins's phrase) shifts weather patterns and increases weather's volatility, the escalating costs of drought, fires, ocean temperature changes, devastating storms, crop and fishery failures, etc. could double catastrophic losses to $150 billion in ten years, including insured losses of $30–40b/y (Heck 2004). U.S. oil subsidies are equivalent to ~$7–59 per ton of carbon emitted, so they more than offset the value of CO_2 abatement discovered in emerging carbon markets (Koplow & Martin 1998).

145. Nixon 1971.

146. Johnson 2004.

147. NIC 2000, p. 5.

148. Most of all in the 280-million-person, 22-nation Arab world (UNDP 2002/3; *Economist* 2002).

If you worry that depletion may happen sooner rather than later, this study offers profitable and practical solutions; if you're a depletion skeptic, it's a negative-premium insurance policy against the chance that the depletionists might prove right.

○ giving oil-exporting states extra leverage to demand to be sold advanced weapons that may later be turned against the U.S. or its allies;[148a]

○ providing resources for state-sponsored terrorism and for rogue states' development and fielding of weapons of mass destruction;[149]

○ requiring an unusually centralized energy production and transportation system inherently vulnerable to terrorism;

- **constrains U.S. actions, principles, ideals, and diplomatic effectiveness** by:

○ distorting relationships with,[150] and appearing to apply double standards in dealing with, oil-producing states;

○ undermining the nation's moral authority by making every issue appear to be "about oil" and national policy in thrall to oil interests: this is arguably one of the most important contributors to rampant anti-American sentiment in much of the world—hostility that has itself "become a central national security concern";[151]

○ accelerating the militarization of foreign policy at the expense of the international norms, institutions, and relationships crafted by a century of diplomacy;[152]

○ injecting climate-driven irritants into relations with current partners, such as Europe and Japan, and potential ones, such as China and India, whose long-term friendship is a key to robust counter-terrorism collaborations and many other elements of global stability;

○ intensifying competition over oil with all other countries, ultimately including China and India—a likely path not to friendly relationships but to geopolitical rivalries akin to those that helped to trigger World War II;[153]

○ setting the stage for billions of people to blame their poverty and oil shortages on what demagogues could portray as America's uncaring gluttony;

- **retards global development**, perpetuating injustice and breeding unrest, by:

○ supporting unaccountable governments and undiversified economies based on resource extraction at the expense of balanced, broad-based development;

○ thereby perpetuating regimes unable to meet the growing aspirations and demands of their populations, thus heightening political tension, instability, and extremism;

○ engendering corruption, opacity, rent-seeking, and concentration of wealth, all of which can be exploited by terrorists and criminal cartels, including the drug trade, and can undermine emerging democratic institutions and norms of human dignity;

148a. Roberts (2004a) reports Chinese offers of ballistic missiles for Saudi oil.

149. Outside North Korea, most proliferation of weapons of mass destruction appears to be financed by oil revenues and motivated by oil-linked rivalries; current concerns focus on oil-funded terrorists' becoming a customer for North Korean bombs. However, oil funding is abundantly sufficient but not necessary as a revenue source for terrorists and proliferators: they could still find other funds, e.g. from the drug trade, even if their oil-derived revenues fell to zero. A world buying no oil may well sprout less terrorism, but more by trimming its roots than by cutting off its water.

150. Partly through unilateralist foreign policy, in the view of Daalder & Lindsay (2003). But probably all foreign-policy experts would agree that, as DOE's 1987 report to the president, *Energy Security*, put it, "Increased dependence on insecure foreign oil supplies reduces flexibility in the conduct of U.S. foreign policy."

151. Today, "[T]he bottom has indeed fallen out of support for the United States," and "hostility toward the United States makes achieving our policy goals far more difficult": Djerejian 2004.

152. Priest 2003.

153. From Iraq to the six-claimant Spratly (aka Spratley) Islands, from the Baku subplot of World War I to the Ploesti and East Asian oil roots of World War II to the oil-driven intrigues and tyrannies and civil wars of West Africa and Central Asia, oil's wasteful use and concentrated supply remain preeminent among causes of rivalry and conflict.

4: Hedging the risk of oil depletion

Former Shell USA chief geologist M. King Hubbert predicted in 1956 that U.S. oil production would peak in the early 1970s and then decline. It peaked in 1970. In 1974 he predicted world oil production would peak in 1995. His successors, such as noted petroleum geologists Colin Campbell and Kenneth Deffeyes, now predict that peak around 2004–2010. They warn that the resulting shift from a buyer's to a seller's market would trigger higher prices and ultimately severe economic disruption if

(continued next page)

- retards global development (continued)
  - increasing oil prices and hence the unserviceable Third World debt:[154] in 2001, low- and middle-income countries' fuel (mainly oil) imports equaled two-thirds of their new borrowings;[155] and

- **weakens the national economy** by:
  - imposing huge deficit-financed burdens on the U.S. for military forces able to protect and secure access to oil and to deter mischief in oil-related regions;[156]
  - increasing U.S. trade deficits, compromising currency reserves and the strength of the U.S. dollar, thereby straining import-dependent industries and monetary policy while encouraging exporters to raise dollar oil prices, or even redenominate oil trade in euros, and to shift their reinvestments into stronger currencies;
  - escalating price volatility and supply risks that hazard not only oil-sensitive sectors, such as automotive and aviation, but ultimately the entire economy;
  - extracting from unduly influenced legislators ever larger deficit-financed domestic oil subsidies (which distort markets by suppressing fair competition and retarding cheaper options that could reduce national costs);
  - creating major environmental liabilities both at home and abroad, increasing social and economic pressures, raising health-care costs and lost labor productivity, adding expense to development projects and reclamation efforts, and raising the risk of costly and irrevocable climate change;
  - incurring large domestic opportunity costs in jobs, education, environment, and other benefits achievable through a different allocation of national resources.

Thus even if nothing goes badly wrong in the Middle East, the routine direct and indirect costs of oil dependence, plus the rising contingent risks of serious political or terrorist disruptions of supply elsewhere, are compelling arguments for using less oil. They would remain so even if the ultimate depletion of affordable global oil resources were infinitely remote. But in fact the industry's only debate about economic depletion is timing (Box 4), and all experts predict a worrisome and inexorable rise in Gulf dependence regardless of timing.

154. The debt crisis is rooted in the dizzying 150% increase in the foreign debt of 100 developing countries during 1973–77: IMF 2002.

155. Imports of ~$147b (World Bank 2003, Table 4.6) vs. disbursements of new debt (World Bank 2003a). B. Bosquet (World Bank), personal communication, 21 January 2003.

156. For the broader resource context of such issues, see Klare 2001.

157–160. See Box 4.

4: Hedging the risk of oil depletion (cont.)

policies weren't adjusted timely and we noticed the shift too late to respond gracefully.[157] In some circles, these predictions arouse deep anxiety.[158] The depletion debate[159] is partly about geology and the integrity of and agendas behind various parties' published oil-reserve and -resource data; most key data are proprietary and opaque, many are disputed, "geological" reserves differ from "political" reserves (on which OPEC quotas depend), and many producers cheat, leaving tanker-counting scouts to estimate actual shipments. Differing units and definitions,[160] reporting cumulative discoveries as if they were remaining reserves, and not backdating reserve declarations to discovery dates, all add to the confusion. (To an economic geologist, "reserves" are resources profitably exploitable with present technology, hence varying with price and time even without new discoveries. Economic theorists, for whom reserves are simply an inventory replenished by investment, presume supply forecasts' historic understatement will continue. Geologists are increasingly split.)

Unconventional oil, such as newly competitive (though capital-, water-, and energy-intensive) Albertan tar sands, may or may not be included.

157. Sources on this view are collected at www.peakoil.net and www.peakoil.org. See also Bakhtiari 2004, pp. 19–21, and Berenson 2004.

158. For example, British Environment Minister (1997–2003) Michael Meacher (Meacher 2004) warns that "if we do not immediately plan to make the switch to renewable energy—faster, and backed by far greater investment than currently envisaged—then civilisation faces the sharpest and perhaps most violent dislocation in recent history."

159. Laherrere (2004) provides an unusually clear summary of all the key supply-side issues. Greene, Hopson, & Li (2003) provide a more optimistic non-geological overview, summarized in Greene, Hopson, & Li 2004. Yet they still find non-Middle-East oil production is likely to peak by 2025. The timing of the Middle East production peak is less certain because the key geological and reservoir-engineering data are secret and disputed.

160. For example, in 2003, differences between SEC rules (which require an accounting standard of proof) and normal industry practice based on geologically probable reserves, as well as internal assessment and reporting problems linked to decentralized management, led Shell to debook 3 billion bbl of petroleum reserves.

And should past demand growth be extrapolated, or will substitutions automatically avert scarcity? Most industry strategists say that while oil resources are finite, modern technologies for finding and extracting them at declining real cost are so powerful that barring major political disruptions—a key and sanguine assumption—oil depletion is unlikely to cause big problems for decades. Such analysts reject depletionists' concern of physical shortages unpleasantly soon. We agree. But historically, major shifts in energy supply have also required decades, so if world production will peak in (say) 2020–40, a common view among oil optimists, then starting action now would seem sensible.

If you worry that depletion may happen sooner rather than later, this study offers profitable and practical solutions; if you're a depletion skeptic, it's a negative-premium insurance policy against the chance that the depletionists might prove right. Such hedging seems prudent for three basic reasons. Peak production, whenever it occurs, will be visible only in hindsight, too late to respond. Both producers and consumers have strong market disincentives to express any concern about depletion, so farsighted public policies lack wide support. And the market inversion caused by cartel behavior—OPEC's output restrictions force others to extract costlier oil first—masks the smooth price run-up that would otherwise provide early warning of depletion. EIA, among the most optimistic resource estimators, thinks world oil output will peak sometime after 2020 or 2030—but it also projects rapidly rising oil demand in that period, implying a collision. The transitional dynamics analyzed in this study therefore suggest that it's none too soon to begin graceful adaptation—especially if postponing the displacement of oil *delays major profits* by needlessly prolonging the use of oil that costs more than its substitutes.

If, as we'll show, oil's replacements work better and cost less, then buying them instead would make sense and make money. This would be true even if oil had no hidden costs to society.

To the extent oil's replacements proved more lucrative than oil itself, even for oil companies, the option of dramatically reducing oil dependence would become an imperative.

Contrary to some economic theorists' presumption that all efficiency worth buying has already been bought, plenty of low-hanging fruit has fallen down and is in danger of mushing up around the ankles. Noticing and picking it offers enticing business opportunities.

161. Bizarrely, this is sometimes assumed even for mixed and nonmarket economies.

Could less oil dependence be not only worthy but also profitable?

In 1987–88, this report's senior author was asked by Royal Dutch/Shell Group Planning to estimate how much of the oil used by the United States in 1986 could have been saved if the most efficient oil-using technologies demonstrated in 1986 had been fully deployed in that year, and if similar savings in natural gas had been substituted for oil in the furnaces and boilers where they're interchangeable. The shocking conclusion (*Technical Annex*, Ch. 3): 80% of 1986 U.S. oil use could have been saved at an average 1986 cost of $2.5/bbl. This was said to be "very influential" in shaping Shell's thinking about how supplying more oil would have to compete with its more efficient use; where an energy company could find profits on the demand side; and what market risks its supply-side investments might face if customers bought efficient use instead.

The potential for oil saving and gas substitution, when far more closely examined, remains impressive 18 years later: the technologies have improved by even more than their potential has been used up. Moreover, other supply-side oil displacements that didn't look so attractive 15 years ago—by biofuels and waste-derived fuels, even by hydrogen—are now possible and potentially profitable. This study therefore explores for the first time the *combined* potential of *all four* ways to displace oil by domestic (or North American) resources, and hence to surmount the national-security, economic, and environmental challenges of oil dependence. And it suggests that much if not all of this diverse portfolio of opportunities for the next energy era may also enable oil companies and oil-exporting countries to make more profit at less risk than they do now (pp. 248–257).

To the extent this were true—to the extent oil's replacements proved better, cheaper, and more lucrative than oil itself, even for oil companies—the option of dramatically reducing oil dependence would become an imperative. Using less oil would not only reduce or ultimately eliminate the many risks just described; it would make money, even in the short term. But if that bonanza *were* real, why wouldn't it already have been captured?

Beliefs that hold us back

A central dogma of dimly recalled Economics 101 courses, widely sloganized by pundits (good economists know better), holds that existing markets are essentially perfect,[161] so if smarter technologies could save energy more cheaply than buying it, they'd already have been adopted. Actually, perfect markets are only a simplifying *assumption* to render theory tractable. Practitioners of energy efficiency find it utterly contrary to their experience. Every day they battle scores of "market failures"—perverse rules, habits, and perceptions that leave lucrative energy savings unbought. A huge literature documents these obstacles and explains how to turn them into business opportunities.[162] Armed with such "prospector's guides," firms like DuPont,[163] IBM, and STMicroelectronics are cutting their energy use per unit of output by 6% every year with 1–3-year paybacks. That's among the highest and safest returns in the whole economy. If markets *were* perfect—if it's not worth picking up that $20 bill lying on the ground, because if it were real, someone would have picked it up already—these and other real-world examples of big, cheap, rapid, continuing energy savings couldn't exist.[164] In fact, if markets were perfect, all profit opportunities would already have been arbitraged out and nobody could earn more than routine profits.[165] Fortunately, that's not true: the genius of the free-enterprise system lets entrepreneurs create wealth by exploiting opportunities others haven't yet noticed. This messy, squirming hubbub of innovation, even to the point of "creative destruction," is at the heart of wealth creation.

The old debate about how much energy can be saved at what cost by more productive technologies has largely ascended to the rarified plane of theology, partly because the policy priesthood includes more ordinary economists than extraordinary engineers, and the two rarely connect. We therefore alert you to this dispute up front. If you believe that economic theory is reality and physical measurement is hypothesis, you may doubt many of our findings.[166] Market competition will ultimately reveal who was right. But if you're a pragmatist who weighs the evidence of costs and savings rigorously measured by engineers in actual factories, buildings, and vehicles; if you believe that price is an important but not the sole influence on human behavior; if you consider economics a tool, not a dogma; and if you think markets make a splendid servant, a bad master, and a worse religion; then we have good news: *displacing most, probably all, of our oil not only makes sense, but also makes money, without even counting any reductions in oil's hidden costs.*

This view reflects four insights from basic economics (but not the pundits' glib and corrupted slogans):

* High energy prices are neither necessary nor sufficient for rapid energy savings. They're not necessary because modern, well-deployed energy-saving techniques yield phenomenal returns even at low prices—as the leading firms mentioned above are demonstrating quarter after quarter. Nor are high energy prices sufficient by themselves to overcome force of habit: DuPont's European chemical plants were no more efficient than its U.S. ones despite having long paid twice the energy price, because all the plants were similarly designed.[167]

Firms like DuPont, IBM, and STMicro-electronics are cutting their energy use per unit of output by 6% every year with 1–3-year paybacks. That's among the highest and safest returns anywhere.

High energy prices are neither necessary nor sufficient for rapid energy savings.

162. Lovins & Lovins 1997.

163. DuPont's goal "is to never use more energy no matter how fast we grow"; it has cut greenhouse gas emissions by 67% since 1990 without profits' suffering (Wisby 2004). Raising output 35% while cutting energy use 9% has saved ~$2 billion (A.A. Morell, personal communication, 11 June 2004).

164. Dr. Florentin Krause says each $20 bill is actually more like 2,000 pennies. As field practitioners, we prefer another simile: saving energy is like eating an Atlantic lobster. There are big, obvious chunks of tender meat in the tail and the front claws. There's also a roughly equal quantity of tasty morsels that skilled and persistent dissection can free from crannies in the body. They're all tasty, and they're worth eating—scraps, broth, and all.

165. For a critique of the foundations of many contemporary economic constructs, see DeCanio 2003. As a senior staff member of President Reagan's Council of Economic Advisors, his cogent arguments carry special weight. See also McCloskey 1996.

166. Lovins 2004.

167. See next page.

- Ability to respond to price is more important than price itself. During 1991–96, people in Seattle paid only half as much for a kilowatt-hour of electricity as did people in Chicago, but in Seattle they saved electricity far faster (by 12-fold in peak load and 3,640-fold in annual usage), because the electric utility helped them save in Seattle but tried to stop them from saving in Chicago.[168] That logical outcome is the opposite of what the bare price signals would predict.

- Energy prices are important, should be correct,[169] and are a vital way to interpret past behavior and guide future policy; yet price is only one way of getting people's attention. U.S. primary energy use per dollar of real GDP fell by nearly 3% a year[170] in 1996–2001 despite record-low and falling energy prices—evidently spurred by factors other than price.

- Some theorists, their vision perhaps strained by years of peering through econometric microscopes, suppose that the potential to save oil in the future can be inferred only from the historic ratio of percentage changes in oil consumption to percentage changes in oil price. This "price elasticity of demand" is real but small, though it gradually rises over many years. In fact, it says little about what's possible in the future, when technologies, perceptions, and policies may be very different. Supposing that the nation can never save more energy than historic price elasticities permit, and that we must interpret and influence choice only through price signals, is like insisting a car can be steered only in a straight line chosen by staring in the rear-view mirror. Such drivers, who pay dangerously little attention to what's visible through the windshield, risk getting slammed into by speeding technological changes.

We therefore take economics seriously, not literally, and we blend it with other disciplines to gain a more fully rounded picture of complex realities.

From this perspective, Americans still use so much oil mainly because they've been inattentive to alternatives and overly comfortable in the assumption that optimal progress will automagically[171] be provided by a competitive market. Americans have also been too ready to accept dismissive claims, often from those whom change might discomfit, that any improvement will be decades away, crimp lifestyles and freedoms, and require intrusive interventions and exorbitant taxation. Such gloom rejects the rich American tradition of progress led by business innovation. Consumer electronics every month get smaller, better, faster, cheaper; why can't anything else? And although cars normally last 14 years and are getting even more durable, why can't we accelerate the turnover of the fleet—thereby opening up vast new markets for earlier replacement—while revitalizing the factories and jobs that make the cars?

167. J.W. Stewart (DuPont), personal communication, 9 October 1997. All these examples are readily explicable in economic terms and described in economic literature dealing with organizational behavior, transaction costs, information costs, etc. (Lovins & Lovins 1997, pp. 11–20). Our point is rather that too many policymakers and analysts, whose economic tools may not be sharp enough, tend to treat market failures as *ad hoc* add-ons—contrived to explain supposedly minor departures from an underlying near-perfect market. In reality, market failures can be considered more important than market function, not just because they're so pervasive, but because correcting them first is the main opportunity for innovation and profit.

168. Hawken, Lovins, & Lovins 1999, p. 254.

169. For example, much of the 1979–85 energy efficiency revolution was driven by energy price decontrols long and rightly urged by economists, launched by President Carter, and accelerated by President Reagan.

170. Namely, 2.9%/y, vs. 4.6%/y at the record-high and rising energy prices of 1979–85.

171. As inventor Dean Kamen puts it.

Whatever exists is possible

Americans are starting to discover this different reality. Exhibit A is Toyota's 2004 *Prius* hybrid-electric midsize sedan (Fig. 4). Secretly developed and brought to market without government intervention, it's rated at 55 mpg, more than twice the fuel efficiency of the average 2003 car on the U.S. market,[173] yet it costs the same—between *Camry* and *Corolla* in size and price, but more value-loaded:[174] it has more features, and protects you just as well.[175] Sluggish? "Impressive performance, with unexpectedly quick acceleration," noted a tester for *Motor Trend*, which measured 0–60 mph in 9.8 seconds.[176] Unpopular? Ever since it went on sale in October 2003, the *Wall Street Journal* has listed it as the fastest-selling automobile in the United States, flying off dealers' lots in 5–6 days—after 3–12 months on a waitlist. *Car and Driver* named *Prius* among its "Best Ten."

> Today's doubled-efficiency hybrid cars illustrate how dramatic oil savings can be achieved without sacrifice, compromise, or even appreciable cost.

Figure 4: Toyota's 2004 *Prius*
The *Prius* is a 5-passenger, near-zero-emission, 55-mpg, ~$20,000[172] midsize sedan

It was *Automobile*'s Design of the Year and the Society of Automotive Engineers' magazine *Automotive Engineering International*'s Best Engineered Vehicle. At Detroit's January 2004 North American International Auto Show, the auto journalists' panel straightfacedly named the Japanese-made *Prius* North American Car of the Year.

172. When introduced in October 2003, the 2004 *Prius*'s Manufacturer's Suggested Retail Price (MSRP) before destination charges was $19,995, the same as when *Prius* first entered the U.S. market in 2001. On 3 April 2004, Toyota raised *Prius*'s MSRP to $20,295 as part of a ten-model general price increase to offset the stronger yen. The 2005 model released 14 September 2004 has a base price of $20,875—triple the increase for other models. Most dealers still report ~6–12-month waitlists.

173. At 55 adjusted EPA mpg, the 2004 *Prius* is 107% better in ton-mpg than the best midsize model or 113% better than the average of all midsize and compact models. (Based on some contractors to the Big Three/federal PNGV [Partnership for a New Generation of Vehicles] program, Congress's Office of Technology Assessment predicted in 1995 that hybrids could do this, and DOE established that as its program goal for hybrids: OTA 1995, pp. 175–176.) In size, *Prius* is toward the lower end of the midsize range, but through innovative design, it has more cargo space than many midsize sedans. Like all hybrid cars, *Prius* must be properly driven to approach or exceed its EPA-rated fuel economy; failure to do so typically yields in the low 40s of mpg (Rechtin 2003). "Pulse driving" is recommended—accelerating rather rapidly, because a brief high engine load uses less fuel than a prolonged low engine load, and braking well ahead of a stop to maximize brake regeneration. *Prius* can then reach or exceed 55 mpg (one driver got 70 mpg, albeit at <40 mph). Toyota USA's executive engineer reports that his 2004 *Prius*, driven with his expert knowledge, averages 53–55 mpg (Rechtin 2003), confirming that the issue is one not of automotive technology but of driver re-education. (It's too early for population-based data on the 2004 *Prius*, but the *Prius*-expert at (John's Stuff 2004) shows that his 2001 *Prius*, rated at 48 mpg, has averaged 45.4 over 59,827 miles—close agreement in view of his Minnesota location's predominance of cold weather, which hurts regeneration, and snow tires, which cost 1–3 mpg.) Similar variations are observed among Honda *Insight* hybrid drivers, who can fall far short of the rated 62–64 mpg if they ignore the tall gearing and upshift light. But without correcting for minor model differences or snow tires, the self-selected drivers at www.insightcentral.net report lifetime averages of 63.0 mpg for 77 owners (the senior author of this study gets 63.4) and 61.92 mpg for 295 owners. Of course, *non*-hybrid cars with average U.S. drivers also typically underperform their adjusted EPA mpg by ~5–15%; what's different with hybrid cars is the technical reasons—and the hybrids' greater ability to approach or achieve their mpg ratings if well driven.

174. Specifications, features, and options at Toyota 2004b. The fullest option package adds $5,245 and offers many features absent from the costlier top-of-the-line *Camry* option package. Hybrid cars in 2003 got a $2,000 federal tax deduction (which phases down starting in 2004), plus a tax credit in a half-dozen states (www.fueleconomy.gov, undated). Japan currently offers a ~$2,300 rebate to hybrid-buyers (originally worth ~$3,500 at the exchange rate then prevailing), and subsidized 31,000 hybrids during 1998–2001.

175. The crash "star" ratings at NHTSA 2004, frontal-crash driver/passenger and side-impact front/rear, are 5/4/4/4 (5-star is the best possible rating). *Prius* in 2003 was 4/4/3/3; the 2004 *Corolla* and *Camry* are respectively 5/5/4/4 and 4/4/3/3. All these 2004 ratings are considered excellent. The 2004 *Prius* also has a good rollover rating (4-star, 13%, no tip), matching the best-rated MY2004 SUV on the market.

176. Some initial Toyota remarks claimed 10.1 s (4.9s for 30–50 mph) with a 103-mph top speed. An & Santini (2004) and current official Toyota presentations say 10.5 s, and emphasize the 9% increase in interior volume, to 110 cubic feet, from the 2001 *Prius*.

Its coveted *Motor Trend* "Car of the Year" award came with this editorial comment:[177]

> The *Prius* is a capable, comfortable, fun-to-drive car that just happens to get spectacular fuel economy. It also provides a promising look at a future where extreme fuel-efficiency, ultra-low emissions, and exceptional performance will happily coexist. That makes it meaningful to a wide range of car buyers.

Toyota "says it'll make money on each one it builds,"[178] and "a large portion of its model lineup will offer hybrid power by 2007." President Fujio Cho plans to make 300,000 hybrids a year (about half for the North American market[179]), boosted U.S. production by 31% and has been asked for more,[180] and licensed the powertrain technology to Nissan and Ford[181] and offered it to GM and DaimlerChrysler.[182] Economic theory notwithstanding, you *can* pick up several $100 bills a year off the ground at your local gas station without extra cost. If all U.S. cars (not light trucks) were *Prius*es today, they'd save 15% more oil than the U.S. got in 2002 from the Gulf.

Toyota, whose ¥1-trillion 2003 profits and ¥2-trillion liquidity lets it place multiple technology bets, is widely considered at least three or four years ahead of Detroit with this third-generation hybrid technology. As the world's number-two automaker (it passed Ford in 2003), with market capitalization exceeding that of the Big Three combined, and as arguably the world's premier manufacturing company, Toyota can price its cutting-edge innovations aggressively and deploy them in many sizes, shapes, and segments:[183]

> "This *Prius* is an industry sputnik," says Jim SanFillippo, [executive VP] of Automotive Marketing Consultants Inc., Warren, Mich. "The question is will there be a serious response, particularly from American competitors—because there should be. It is a serious, serious piece of technology."

177. Italics added. All *Motor Trend* quotations in this paragraph are from December 2003 issue and *Motor Trend* 2003a.

178. Some commentators, including *Motor Trend*, initially speculated that the 2004 *Prius* was a loss-leader, as it probably was in its early years; Detroit experts estimate added production cost at about $2,500–4,000. But Toyota denies a loss; Executive Vice President Yoshio Ishizaka confirmed 5 January 2004 that after reducing hybrid-system costs by more than 30% since 1997, "Every *Prius* we sell, we make a profit" (Hakim 2004). Welch (2004) says *Prius* didn't turn profitable until MY2003, but Chairman Hiroshi Okuda was already saying *Prius* was profitable in a 29 September 2002 *Financial Times* story. Reuters explains how: the 2004 *Prius* is assembled at a rate of one per minute on the same Tsutsumi line as four other mass-production sedans, where every other car made is now a *Prius* (Kim 2003). The 2004 global *Prius* sales target of 76,000 was recently increased as U.S. targets were boosted by 31%; first-month global sales of the 2004 model matched 2003's total (Toyota 2003). An authoritative source confirms that in early 2004, the 2004 *Prius* was incurring an extra production cost corresponding to a ~$4,000-higher (2003–04 $) retail price, but that this marginal MSRP is intended and expected to fall to $2,000 (~2007 $): D. Greene, personal communication, 25 March 2004. Normal industry cost structure would imply marginal manufacturing costs roughly half as big, but a Toyota official has estimated they're ~$2,500–3,000, yielding a reduced but still positive factory margin, rumored to be ~$1,100 (~2003 $): Peter 2003. These figures depend on accounting conventions: Toyota probably assumes that every *Prius* is a sale it wouldn't otherwise make, and undoubtedly amortizes the powertrain R&D over many future models. It's not clear whether the attractive margins on options are included. And these *Prius* data are consistent—if adjusted for powertrain complexity and vehicle size—with current Honda *Civic Hybrid* estimates of at least $3,000 extra MSRP, intended to be reduced to ~$1,500.

179. *Nihon Keizai Shimbun* reported (AFP 2004) in March 2004 that Toyota plans a North American hybrid version of its best-selling *Camry* in 2006: M.P. Walsh 2004 (pp. 32–33; pp. 45–48) reports this as a Toyota announcement.

180. Mid-May 2004 press reports indicate a 150% rise in *Prius* sales in April 2004 vs. April 2003, and say Toyota expects to sell 50,000 *Prius* cars in 2004 vs. its original target of 34,000. Lyke (2004) reports a monthly *AutoVIBES* report from Harris Interactive and Kelley Blue Book finding that 17% of U.S. new-car buyers have already changed their minds about which vehicle to buy because of fuel prices, 21% are strongly considering models they hadn't previously considered, and 15% say they'd strongly consider more fuel-efficient vehicles if gasoline prices rose just 25¢/gal (Automotive.com 2004).

181. The license, announced (probably belatedly) in March 2004, is for 20 Toyota patents on hybrid systems and control technology, but does not include the use of hybrid powertrain components as the 2002 Nissan licensing agreement does (Toyota 2004), and may not be as advanced as the 2004 *Prius*.

182. Peter 2003.

183. Italics added. Freeman 2003.

Figure 5: Four hybrid SUVs
From L–R, they are: 2005 Ford *Escape*, 5 seats, 32 mpg in 2WD, 1,000-lb towing, ~$27,000; 2005 Lexus *RX 400h*, 5 seats, 3.3-L V-6, 270 effective hp, 0–60 mph in <8 s, range >600 miles, SULEV, AWD option, 1,000-lb towing, ≥28 mpg, ~$39,000; 2005 Toyota *Highlander*, 7 seats, similar characteristics, 3,500-lb towing option; and the 2005 Mercedes *Vision Grand Sports Tourer*, 6 seats, 314 hp, 0–62 mph/6.6 s, 155 mph, 33 mpg.

Detroit is of course striving to emulate this brilliant achievement of Japanese engineering. GM, a leader in hybrid buses, postponed its general-market hybrid cars to 2007, dismissing them as an "interesting curiosity" that does not "make sense at $1.50 a gallon,"[184] and is introducing only slightly more efficient "mild-hybrid" pickups in 2004 while focusing on longer-term fuel-cell development.[185] But Ford is launching in October 2004 the 2005 *Escape* SUV (Fig. 5a) with a hybrid powertrain like *Prius*'s.[186] It'll offer roughly three-fifths better fuel economy than the 2004 201-hp V-6 *Escape*'s 20 mpg—32 mpg with front-wheel or somewhat less with four-wheel drive—yet provide comparable acceleration with only a 2.3-L, 4-cylinder Atkinson engine. But initial production is targeted for just 20,000 a year, one-sixth of the 2004 *Prius*'s volume, and priced at a few thousand dollars' premium.[187] A fancier Mercury *Mariner* model will follow about a year later, then a midsize car after 2006.[188] Analysts differ on whether Ford can make money on these early hybrids. Clearly Detroit has a lot of catch-up to do with its four planned SUV hybrids in 2005–07— and its competitors are rapidly moving targets.

Four months after Ford's hybrid *Escape* is launched, Toyota will unleash brawnier versions of *Prius*'s powertrain: in February 2005, both the Lexus *RX 400h* luxury hybrid SUV based on the *RX 300*,[189] combining V-8-like acceleration from a V-6 with the "fuel economy of a [4-cylinder] compact car,"[190] and the Toyota *Highlander* 7-seat hybrid SUV (Fig. 5b).[191] Honda is meanwhile launching its peppy *Accord* V-6 hybrid midsize sedan in autumn 2004.[192] Hybrids' powerful torque also boosts acceleration in Honda's beefy 2003 *SU-HV1* concept SUV and *CS&S* roadster, GM's 2003 Chevy *S-10* concept pickup (which can "smoke" a Corvette[193]), and

184. Robert Lutz (GM Vice Chairman/Product Development), remarks at the Detroit auto show, 6 January 2004 (Isidore 2004).

185. Hakim 2003. Originally GM had planned to offer a hybrid option on its MY2005 Saturn *Vue* small SUV. The new plan would put it on two MY2008 full-sized SUVs, using a scalable system that fits in a 6-speed transmission envelope and is expected to boost mpg by 25–35%. Meanwhile, late in 2003 GM began offering mild-hybrid Chevrolet *Silverado* and GMC *Sierra* pickup trucks to fleet customers; these hybrid-assist models should reach other customers in the third quarter of 2004, as will a Chrysler Dodge *Ram* mild-hybrid pickup. Such heavy vehicles' fuel savings in gallons will be substantial.

186. Information from Ford Vehicles, undated.

187. Information from Ford Vehicles 2004(a); a *Prius*-like $3,500 premium was estimated by WardsAuto.com (2004). By mid-May 2004, 34,000 potential buyers had signed up for the *Escape* E-newsletter (Schneider 2004).

188. Crain 2004.

189. Information from Lexus, undated (downloaded 6 January 2004).

190. All data from Lexus, undated (downloaded 1 January 2004).

191. All data from Toyota, undated (downloaded 6 January 2004).

192. Its acceleration is expected to beat that of the 240-hp nonhybrid *Accord*.

193. GM 2003.

By the end of 2005, at least a dozen diverse models of hybrid-electric cars, pickups, and SUVs will be in American showrooms.

A self-interested melding of advanced technology with bold business strategies can present extraordinary opportunities for private enterprise to lead in making a better world.

Mercedes-Benz's six-seat diesel-hybrid *Grand Sports Tourer* (Fig. 5d), to be launched in Europe early in 2005.[194] Automakers will introduce hybrids in middle and high-end products with greater amenity and performance requirements and richer margins. But they won't stop there.
As hybrids become cheaper, they'll diffuse downmarket and become ubiquitous. At the October 2003 Tokyo Motor Show, 10 of 25 cars featured in *Car and Driver* were hybrids, by Daihatsu, Honda, Jeep, Lexus, Mazda, Mercedes-Benz, Subaru, Suzuki, and Toyota, plus Nissan.

The 2004 *Prius* shows more than the competitive challenge to U.S. auto-makers. In the global marketplace, a self-interested melding of advanced technology with bold business strategies can present extraordinary opportunities for private enterprise to lead in making a better world. Toyota didn't wait for government to tell it what to do or pay it to inno-vate; it simply led.

Likewise in America, the 1977–85 "practice run" (p. 7) shows there's nothing mysterious about saving oil quickly and massively. It takes atten-tion; leadership at all levels and in many sectors of society; a comprehen-sive and systematic but diversified and flexible approach; a spirit of adventure and experimentation; enlisting cities and states as policy labo-ratories to speed up learning; openness to other countries' technical and policy innovations; and intelligent exploitation of today's tripolar world, where the private sector and civil society increasingly collaborate to fill gaps left by government. In 1977–85 federal policy and industrial innova-tion succeeded beyond all expectations.[195] But today, not all action need await decisions by the national government. Our more dynamic society, empowered by the Internet and its self-organizing networks, has far more ways to get things done. Gridlock in Washington—captured by the bumper-sticker "Progress: Opposite of Congress"—is no longer a reason for inaction, but a spur to private-sector, civil-society, and state- and local-government experimentation and initiative. And we daresay America could mobilize to get off oil even faster by drawing on the leadership qualities and organizing skills of certain retired military personnel, who understand why displacing oil defends the values we hold dear, and how to execute that new mission decisively.

The rest of this report outlines how—by technology, business strategy, and policy innovations—the United States of America can rise together to the greatest challenge of this generation: winning the oil endgame in a way that preserves and enhances our freedoms, our prosperity, and our quest for common goals of substance and spirit, applying the problem-solving prowess that for two centuries has helped to make the nation and the world better and safer.

194. From Mercedes-Benz, undated (down-loaded 7 January 2004); Mercedes-Benz 2004; DaimlerChrysler AG 2004; Germancar-fans.com 2004.

195. Greene 1997. The 1979 oil price shock (Fig. 3, p. 15) certainly helped too.

This Report

Structure and methodology

Pages 29–126 summarize an independent, transdisciplinary analysis of four ways to displace oil:

1. Using oil more efficiently, through smarter technologies that wring more (and often better) services from less oil (pp. 29–102).

2. Substituting for petroleum fuels other liquids made from biomass or wastes (pp. 103–111).

3. Substituting saved natural gas for oil in uses where they're interchangeable, such as furnaces and boilers (pp. 111–122). Note that gas and oil, though sometimes found and thought of together, are utterly different in geology, economics, industry, and culture.

4. Replacing oil with hydrogen made from non-oil resources (postponed to pp. 228–242).

These options will be described first separately and then in integrative combination, because together they can do more than the sum of their parts. Efficiency options are presented for each end-use of oil. Each class of oil-displacing technology is presented as two different portfolios:[196]

- *Conventional Wisdom*: Expectations broadly accepted by industry and government; technologies on or soon to enter the market using thoroughly proven methods; surprisingly often already overtaken by the best technologies already on the market.

- *State of the Art*: Best technologies sufficiently developed by mid-2004, applying established principles and techniques, to be expected confidently as timely and competitive market entrants; well supported by empirical data and industry-standard simulations; require no technological breakthroughs; not all off-the-shelf, but no longer heretical.

The current public-policy approach to implementation might be described as:

- *Gridlock as Usual*: Political will, chiefly focused on national policy and driven by traditional constituency politics, can make modest, incremental advances comparable to those of the past two decades, but cannot execute gamechanging shifts in the status quo.

In contrast, pp. 127–168 present the business case, and pp. 169–226 the policy content, of:

- *Coherent Engagement*: Advanced technologies are rapidly and widely adopted via innovative business strategies and a diverse portfolio of innovative policy instruments with trans-ideological appeal, weaving a rich tapestry of experiments by diverse actors.

This study transparently and rigorously applies orthodox market economics and measured performance data to assessing how much oil can be displaced at what cost. We present two portfolios of technologies and contrast two implementation methods to highlight key choices and consequences.

Readers might expect us to outline at least three[197] internally consistent scenarios for America's path beyond oil. But the first is uninteresting:

- *Drift*: *Conventional Wisdom* technologies plus *Gridlock as Usual* implementation;

We briefly mention it on pp. 180–181 as a recalibration of the base-case forecast described below, just to clarify that some oil savings would occur even without our policy portfolio. We pay slightly more attention to what good policies can do even with incremental technologies:

- *Let's Get Started*: *Conventional Wisdom* technologies plus *Coherent Engagement* implementation;

But we focus mainly on the "best of both worlds":

- *Mobilization*: *State of the Art* technologies plus *Coherent Engagement* implementation.

None of these possible futures is a forecast, but we believe all are possible. Their divergent results show the importance of wisely choosing the future we want, then fearlessly creating it.

Our calculations can be reproduced on a hand calculator or with a simple spreadsheet. All calculations are shown and documented in the *Technical Annex*.

To ground our possible futures in policymakers' day-to-day reality, each technological option gauges potential oil displacement against the U.S. economic activity and oil consumption projected for 2025 in the Reference Case of the U.S. Energy Information Administration's *Annual Energy Outlook 2004*.[198] EIA uses the National Energy Modeling System (NEMS), which lacks the predictive power, modern technological assumptions, and structural flexibility needed for sound business planning, but is widely used by government. Our analysis uses NEMS's outputs (e.g., forecast oil use by each sector and each class of end-use device in 2025) and inputs (e.g., how briskly new light vehicles sold in 2025 will accelerate, so we can match our assumed vehicle designs to that performance). However, we have chosen not to use the NEMS model itself, nor any other large computer model of the energy system. (Econometric models, though widely used, would be especially misleading because they rely on historic coefficients that our proposed technological and policy changes are meant to transform.) Rather, our calculations have been kept so simple and scrutable that they can all be reproduced on a hand calculator or with a simple spreadsheet. All calculations are shown and documented in the *Technical Annex*, so they can be checked and so readers who prefer other assumptions can plug in their own. We believe that for modeling the long-term energy system, less is more, that it's better to be approximately right than precisely wrong, and that simplicity and transparency trump complexity and opacity.

196. We use this term in this report to mean a cluster of internally consistent assumptions that help to understand the nature and implications of choices. This differs from the meaning in scenario planning: Schwartz 1996.

197. We don't explore the off-diagonal matrix element combining *State of the Art* technologies with *Gridlock as Usual* implementation because those technologies are unlikely to be commercialized within that policy framework.

198. EIA 2004.

As a baseline for energy comparisons, we mainly use the year 2000, both because its statistics are available and stable (those for 2002 and even 2001 are still subject to revision at this writing in mid-2004[199]) and because 2000 was a broadly typical year for most energy statistics.

Though we remain mindful of market failures and the importance of correcting them, our economic analysis rests on orthodox market principles and economic methods—with one exception. To avoid using a large and opaque model, we haven't performed a general-equilibrium simulation to test how far the strong efficiency improvements we describe would undermine their own viability by reducing the prices of energy or of energy services.[200] However, our conclusions are made more robust by multiple countervailing forces, including: About half of the *State of the Art* end-use efficiency potential using 2004 technologies can compete even at the lowest oil prices (Fig. 3) that might be expected to result even from its full *global* adoption (its use just in the United States, a fourth of the world market, would cut oil prices by only one-fourth as much); wide global adoption of strong energy efficiency could take about as long as depletion of low- and intermediate-cost oil outside the Gulf, further focusing OPEC's market power; China, India, and others will meanwhile want more oil; once adopted, the efficient vehicles, boilers, insulation, and other oil-using devices are unlikely to be switched back to inefficient ones; and if oil gets too cheap, it could always be taxed. Of course, if we're wrong, a durable oil surplus would be a nice problem to have.

We test cost-competitiveness against EIA's January 2004 projections of real energy costs in 2025, which are 14% above 2002's real costs for world oil, 8% for gasoline, and 19% for retail natural gas. However, EIA's 2025 U.S. Refiner's Acquisition Cost, $26.08/bbl in 2000 $, is well *below* the ~$35–50/bbl (2004 $) world market prices prevailing in summer 2004. EIA's energy cost projections aren't market price forecasts or expected values; they assume that weather, climate, inventories, regulations, geopolitics, and other background conditions remain "normal." We use them because EIA considers them consistent with its demand projections—our base case.

Our *Conventional Wisdom* technology options rely heavily on prior studies by authoritative industry, government, and academic teams. Many of these studies are sound, available, documented, and adequate. Where such prior work is unavailable or insufficient, our own *State of the Art* analysis is documented in the *Technical Annex*. Our limited analytic resources are focused mainly on the seven biggest terms, each at least 6% of 2025 U.S. oil use (Fig. 6), treating only briefly the small terms that make up the last 6%.

For modeling the long-term energy system, less is more, it's better to be approximately right than precisely wrong, and simplicity and transparency trump complexity and opacity.

199. For example, EIA's *Annual Energy Review* showed 2000 petroleum consumption 1.2% higher in its 2002 edition (EIA 2003c) than in its 2000 edition (EIA 2001c). We prefer to wait a few years until the numbers stabilize.

200. Such a calculation would entail many assumptions and great complexity—akin to the inverse of the challenge of calculating macroeconomic effects of increases in oil price, where results vary substantially depending on model structure and assumptions (IEA 2004b, pp. 5–6), especially about exchange rates and monetary policy. Unmodeled effects, such as changes in business and consumer confidence and in gas pricing, can be important (IEA 2004b).

A doubled economy and an assumed huge shift to ineffi-cient light trucks, such as SUVs, drive the Energy Information Admin-istration's forecast of 44% more U.S. oil use in 2025 than in 2000 (shown by making the 2025 pies that much bigger in area). Light and heavy trucks cause 70% of the increase. We focus mainly on trucks, cars, airplanes, industrial fuel and feedstocks, and buildings because they use 94% of the oil in 2025.

Figure 6: The end-uses of U.S. oil in 2000 (model input, 1% above actual) **and projected for 2025**, by ener-gy content, according to the U.S. Energy Information Administration (2004, Reference Case), scaled by the area of each pie. We compare all ways to save or substitute for oil with EIA's 2025 projection.

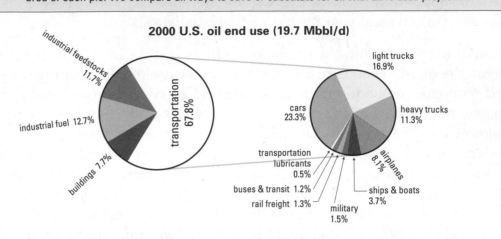

2000 U.S. oil end use (19.7 Mbbl/d)

The main 2000–25 changes are general growth and a further shift from cars to light trucks. The 2.9→1.5% of oil used to make electricity (see p. 98) is allocated here to the sectors that use the electricity. The graphed end-uses of petroleum products supplied (including LPG) conventionally include ethanol and MTBE[201] oxygenates equivalent in 2000 to 0.25 Mbbl/d crude-oil-energy-equivalent or 1.3% of oil consumption, plus biodiesel equivalent to 0.02% of diesel fuel.[202] EIA projects oxygenates to become 0.28 Mbbl/d or 1.0% of oil consumption by 2025.[203] Light trucks include here both passenger (Class 1–2) and commercial (Class 3–6, using 0.29 Mbbl/d in 2000 and 0.42 Mbbl/d in 2025); heavy trucks are Class 7–8. Of military petroleum use, 94% in FY2000 was for transportation, mainly aviation, and nearly all the rest for buildings. Construction and agricultural equipment is classified as industrial use, not transportation. Lubricants, divided equally between industrial use and transportation in 2000 and assumed likewise in 2025, use 1% of oil. Within feedstock end-use, 3.3% of total oil use in 2000 and 3.1% in 2025 is asphalt and road oil. Totals may not add exactly due to rounding.

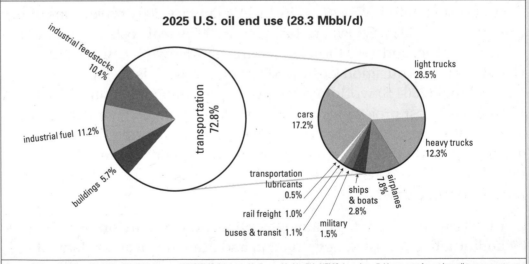

2025 U.S. oil end use (28.3 Mbbl/d)

Source: RMI analysis from EIA 2003c; EIA 2004; January 2004 NEMS database, kindly provided by EIA. NEMS doesn't explicitly account for such small terms as motorcy-cles, snowmobiles, and all-terrain vehicles, but the bottom-up composition shown here fits the transportation and all-sector totals within less than 1% cumulative error.

201. Methyl tertiary butyl ether.

202. In addition, vehicular fuel equivalent in 2000 to 0.3% of gasoline was supplied by liquefied petroleum gas (68%), compressed natural gas (27%), liquefied natural gas (0.02%), methanol (0.003%), and 85% or 95% ethanol (0.02%): EIA 2002.

203. This is because ethanol is due to replace MTBE in 17 states "over the next few years" (EIA 2004, p. 256), and ethanol is twice as effective an oxygenate per unit volume (EPA 1998).

We have also focused chiefly on the terms accounting for most of the demand growth (Fig. 7).

Our emphasis on empiricism leads us, wherever possible, to rely upon and document actual measurements rather than relying on theoretical projections. (Similarly, where results seemingly contrary to economic theory—such as expanding rather than diminishing returns to investments in energy productivity—have been solidly established by empirical practice, we don't reject them in favor of theory.) And we have followed Aristotle's counsel[205] that "it is a mark of educated people, and a proof of their culture, that in solving any problem, they seek only so much precision as its nature permits or its solution requires." Energy analysis, especially looking a quarter-century ahead, is an uncertain art, so we strive to avoid implying spurious precision.

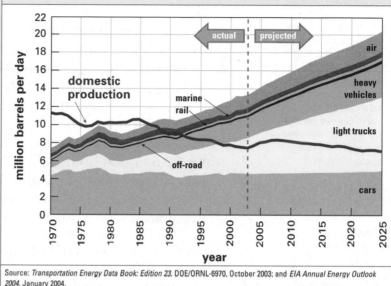

Figure 7: Transportation Petroleum Use by Mode (1970–2025)
Of the growth EIA projected in January 2004 for U.S. oil consumption during 2000–25, graphed here by the U.S. Department of Energy, 55% was for light trucks, 15% heavy vehicles, 7% aircraft, and only 3% automobiles.[204] Total oil used for transportation surpassed domestic oil production (crude oil plus lease condensate) starting in 1987, and is projected to be twice domestic production by 2010.

Source: *Transportation Energy Data Book: Edition 23*, DOE/ORNL-6970, October 2003; and *EIA Annual Energy Outlook 2004*, January 2004.

Conservatisms and conventions

We believe our findings are conservative—tending to understate the quantity and overstate the cost of oil-displacing alternatives—for four main reasons:

1. We assume little *future* technological innovation—just what's already in the commercialization pipeline. This is likely to understate future opportunities dramatically, much as if we sought to solve problems in 2004 by using only the technologies already being commercialized in 1979 (like IBM's first personal computer, which came on the market two years later). Though our broad conclusions don't depend on the biggest breakthroughs now emerging in oil-displacing technologies (such as cheap ultralight autobodies and cheap durable fuel cells), we do consider those at least as plausible as any conceivable further advances in finding and lifting oil, and probably far more so.

2. We uncritically adopt EIA's official projection that in 2025, 20% more Americans—348 million people—will use 40% more energy and 44% more oil than 289 million Americans used in 2002. This extrapolation

Our findings are conservative. We've measured potential oil displacements against the government's generous projection of demand in 2025. We haven't included technologies still to be developed nor important non-technological ways to save oil, such as not subsidizing nor mandating sprawl.

204. From EERE 2003. The car/light-truck data, which EIA's *Annual Energy Outlook* doesn't show, were confirmed from the NEMS database. Light trucks include both passenger (Class 1–2) and commercial (Class 3–6).

205. A paraphrase combined from *Nicomachean Ethics* I:3.24 (Berlin 1094b) and I:7.26 (Berlin 1098a).

Conservatism #2
(continued):

206. TTI 2003.

207. Literature summarized by Lovaas (2004) convincingly shows that continuing to expand land-use twice as fast as population is not necessary, desirable, or economic, and that more thoughtful land-use patterns can reduce cost and crime, increase social cohesion and economic vitality, reduce travel needs by tens of percent (even more with the drop in "induced travel" when fewer roads must be built), and increase real-estate values and profits.

208. Shifting from cars to, say, transit buses may or may not save fuel, depending on efficiencies and load factors: e.g., ORNL 2003, Table 2.11.

209. A Dutch pilot study suggests point-to-point flight patterns could serve the same origin-destination network with ~17% less fuel: Peeters et al. 1999, summarized in Peeters, Rietveld, & Schipper 2001.

210. Hawken, Lovins, & Lovins 1999, Ch. 14.

211. See www.cybertran.com.

212. Such as the software and hardware suite described at Trans-Decisions 2003. A further step could be applying to civilian logistics the intelligent-software-agents approach developed in the Defense Advanced Research Projects Agency's Advanced Logistics Project: Carrico 2000.

213. These are being commercialized by German (including Lufthansa) and Russian consortia: examples are at Aerospace Technology, undated and RosAeroSystems, undated.

214–9. See Box 5 on p. 39.

reflects a far from deprived future: a 96% higher GDP, 97% bigger personal disposable income, 22% larger labor force, 80% higher industrial output, 81% more freight trucking, 41% more commercial floorspace, and 25% more and 6% bigger houses. Each person will drive 33% and fly 48% more miles. Total light-vehicle miles rise 67%. Average horsepower rises 24% for new cars and 18% for new light trucks, while light-vehicle efficiency improves 3 mpg for new models and 1.2 mpg, or 6%, for the operating fleet, and light-vehicle annual sales grow 27%. EIA's forecast also assumes a 29.4% (1.5%/y) drop in primary energy intensity during 2002–25, encouraged by slightly costlier energy (except electricity, which gets 4% cheaper). Every indicator of consumer choice and material standard of living rises steeply, though one might wonder about such quality-of-life indicators as inequities, social tensions, dissatisfaction, and traffic congestion (which in 2001 wasted 3.6 billion hours and 5.7 billion gallons, worth $70 billion, in 75 U.S. urban areas[206]). We also assume that the required expansions of infrastructure (driving and flying space, refineries, pipelines, etc.) will all occur smoothly, undisturbed by any unbudgeted costs or ill effects.

3. We omit many oil-saving options that are individually often large and collectively immense, and we don't analyze some others that are individually small but collectively significant. The main transportation options we deliberately omit, many important, include:

○ Improving land-use (e.g., by not subsidizing nor mandating sprawl, or by smart-growth initiatives) so people needn't travel so much to get where they want to be, or ideally are already there;[207]

○ Telecommuting and other substitutions of telecommunications for physical mobility;

○ Shifting passenger transportation modes, e.g., from road or air to rail, car to public transit,[208] or driving to walking and biking;

○ Increasing passenger load factors, except by HOV lanes and normal airline methods;

○ Restructuring the airline industry (through authentic gate and slot competition) to permit fair competition between hub-and-spokes airlines and a Southwest-Airlines-like hubless point-to-point pattern that reduces unnecessary aircraft movements, travel time, misconnections, hub congestion, and oligopoly rents;[209]

○ Innovative public transit vehicles such as Curitiba-style[210] express buses or Cybertran®-style[211] ultralight trains;

○ Improved freight logistics,[212] and innovative vehicles such as containerized airships,[213] although we do include continued gradual expansion of road/rail freight intermodality.

4. Instead, we adopt only options that provide EIA's projected 2025 mobility "transparently" to the user, with no change of lifestyle or loss of convenience—other than those entailed by the congestion implicit in EIA's enthusiastic traffic forecasts. Similarly, beyond any changes implicit in EIA's growth forecast, we assume no shifts in where, when, or how people use buildings (just more of everything including sprawl); no savings in the materials that industry processes and fabricates (due to materials-frugal and longer-lived product design or closed materials loops, except plastics recycling); and no changes in when people choose to use electricity (even though price signals to do so, and "smart meters" and other technologies to make demand response convenient, are rapidly emerging).

> We adopt only options that provide EIA's projected 2025 mobility "transparently" to the user, with no change of lifestyle or loss of convenience.

Using the technical conventions in Box 5, we next present our analysis and findings of what each of the four oil-displacing options can do by itself in each of the two technology suites. We'll combine them successively, showing how each leaves less oil to be displaced by later options (pp. 123–125, 227–230). Having contrasted *Conventional Wisdom* and *State of the Art* technologies, each incorporating all four oil-displacing options in integrated form, we'll finally discuss their implementation, global context, and strategic implications.

5: Conventions

(details are described in the *Technical Annex*, Ch. 4)

Units and conversions: We use customary U.S. units, plus international (metric) units in parentheses where readers from countries other than the United States, Liberia, and Myanmar are most likely to want them. Year is abbreviated "y", day "d", hour "h", second "s". Tons are U.S. short tons (2,000 lb); tonnes are metric (1,000 kg). Thousand (10^3) is "k", million (10^6) is "M" (the worldwide scientific, not the U.S. engineering, convention), and billion (10^9) is "b". We use industry-standard conversion constants, including EIA's[214] for fuels. By industry and EIA convention, we express fossil-fuel prices, energy content, and efficiency at the Higher Heating Value (which includes the energy needed to evaporate water created by combustion), but we use the Lower Heating Value for hydrogen (120 MJ/kg).

Economic assumptions: Unless otherwise noted, all monetary quantities are converted to constant 2000 U.S. dollars (2000 $) using the GDP implicit price deflator.[215] All discounting—to present value or to levelize cost streams, where noted—applies a 5%/year real discount rate. Pages 189–190 discuss the spread between this conservatively high social rate and much higher implicit consumer discount rates; pp. 16 and 101, risk-adjustment. (The federal government uses 3.29%/y for most long term projects, and 3.0%/y for its own energy-efficiency investments.) Prices in our analysis exclude sales and ownership taxes on vehicles and all taxes on retail fuels, because those taxes are transfer payments, not real resource costs.

(continued on next page)

214. EIA 2003c, Appendix A.
215. BEA 2004.

5: Conventions (continued)

Data sources: U.S. energy data not otherwise cited are from the U.S. Energy Information Administration (EIA, www.eia.doe.gov), typically the *Annual Energy Review 2002*, *Annual Energy Outlook 2004*, or sectoral yearbooks. Transportation data not otherwise cited are from Oak Ridge National Laboratory's *Transportation Energy Data Book 23* (2003, ORNL-6970, www-cta.ornl.gov/data), which relies heavily on U.S. Department of Transportation data.

Road-vehicle efficiency metric: Unless otherwise stated, we measure fuel economy in the "adjusted" USEPA (combined city/highway driving cycle) miles per U.S. gallon (mpg) of gasoline or equivalent—the same figure used for sales stickers, but 10%/22% below the city/highway "laboratory" mpg measured in EPA testing and used for Corporate Average Fuel Economy (CAFE) regulation. (When calculating the corresponding oil usage or savings, we use EIA's "degradation factor" to obtain "on-road" mpg.) Fuel intensity is expressed in gal/mi or L/100 km (liters per 100 kilometers).

Hydrocarbon definitions: As in EIA statistics, "petroleum" is the sum of crude oil, lease condensate, and natural gas plant liquids. Thus liquefied petroleum gas (LPG) is "petroleum" whether it was derived from producing oil or natural gas, and whether it is used as a fuel or as a feedstock. "Oil" is used in this report to refer to "petroleum" or "refined petroleum products" or both, according to context (production or use). We include all non-fuel (feedstock) oil consump-

216. EIA's 2000 "oil" consumption includes 0.25 Mbbl/d (in crude-oil energy equivalent) of biomass-derived ethanol and natural-gas-derived MTBE. We obtain the sources of MTBE in 1996, which we assume also for 2000, from Wang 1999, who says that over 90% of MTBE's isobutylene and methanol components originate in natural-gas processing plants rather than from petroleum. EIA thus understates the degree of biomass- and natural-gas-for-oil substitution that has already occurred to produce these oxygenates.

tion. We adopt EIA's convention of accounting for oxygenate production and consumption as petroleum-based (even though most of it is not[216]), with one noted exception on p. 1 (see note 15).

Petroleum processing: U.S. statistics measure oil by volume (1 barrel $\equiv$ 1 bbl $\equiv$ 42 U.S. gallons = 159 L), but refining heavy crude oil into lighter refined products expands its volume while consuming energy and money. We convert from end-use fuel savings back to equivalent crude-oil refinery inputs not by relative volume but by using their EIA-compiled relative energy content as the best measure of utility. We don't adjust that conversion for refineries' energy use because that's counted as part of industrial energy consumption. We conservatively convert the cost of saved fuel back to 2000 Refiner's Acquisition Cost (RAC) solely on the short-run margin, i.e., by deducting only the 2000-average cash operating costs needed to refine the crude oil and deliver it to the point in the value chain where the savings occur. (These cash operating costs include EIA's estimate of incremental investment to comply with low-sulfur regulations, but aren't adjusted for any deferral or avoidance by reducing demand.) This value-chain addback thus calculates the RAC of crude oil that would have produced and delivered that saved fuel in the short run from existing industry physical assets, taking no credit for avoided future refining or delivery *capacity*. Thus an RAC of $26.08/bbl (2000 $), EIA's projected 2025 crude-oil price, breaks even against saving 76¢/gal pretax retail gasoline. The difference between 76¢ and the pretax retail price reflects all embedded costs from refinery to filling station. Our oil displacements could avoid further investment for new refineries, pipelines, delivery fleets, etc. For this reason, and because our conversion isn't risk-adjusted, it understates oil displace-

(continued on next page)

ments' implied value. Our supply-curve graphs show both RAC $/bbl and retail ¢/gal (of the fuel being displaced—gasoline, diesel fuel, or jet fuel), but due to the value-chain addback and the energy-per-unit-volume conversion, their relationship isn't simply the standard conversion factor of 42 gal/bbl.

Cost of Saved Energy: We express the cost of saving a unit of oil as a Cost of Saved Energy (CSE), calculated at the point in the value chain where it occurs, then converted (as just described) to equivalent short-run RAC per barrel of crude oil. We calculate CSE using the standard formula developed at Lawrence Berkeley National Laboratory. This divides the marginal cost of buying, installing, and maintaining the more efficient device by its discounted stream of lifetime energy savings. Using the standard annuity formula, the dollar cost of saving 1 bbl then equals $Ci/S[1-(1+i)^{-n}]$, where C is installed capital cost ($), i is annual real discount rate (assumed here to be 0.05), S is the rate at which the device saves energy (bbl/y), and n is its operating life (y). Thus a $100 device that saved 1 bbl/y and lasted 20 y would have a CSE of $8/bbl. Against a $26/bbl oil price, a 20-y device with a 1-y simple payback would have a CSE of $2.1/bbl. Engineering-oriented analysts conventionally represent efficiency "resources" as a supply curve, rather than as shifts along a demand curve (economists' convention). CSE is methodologically equivalent to the cost of *supplied* energy, such as refined petroleum

products: *the value of the energy saved isn't part of the CSE calculation*, which shows only the cost of achieving the saving. Whether that saving is cost-effective depends on whether its CSE is more or less than the cost of the energy it saves, and on what costs are counted (private internal vs. full societal). Except as noted, our CSEs are compared on the short-run margin with EIA's RAC of $26.08 (2000 $) in 2025, excluding externalities and downstream capital costs. CSEs can be negative if capital charges are more than offset by saved maintenance cost, avoided equipment, etc.

Rebound: People may drive more miles in more-efficient light vehicles because their fuel cost per mile drops. Although their decision to do so indicates that they value the increased mobility more than the cost of the fuel consumed, they will use more fuel, and we're calculating oil use, not economic welfare. Older estimates of ~10% rebound, or even up to 30% long-term, now appear overstated, and are about halved by the latest econometric evidence.[217] Variabilized insurance payment (p. 218) and the need to replace lost gasoline tax revenues by equivalent user fees (pp. 212–213) offset 73% of the ¢/mile reduction from 2025 *State of the Art*'s 69% fuel savings. This reduces the long-run driving rebound to 3.3%. Intelligent Highway Systems (p. 78) then save 1.8% of light-vehicle fuel, leaving a 1.5% net rebound.[218] We're comfortable neglecting that because of a larger unanalyzed issue with EIA's Reference Case: it assumes each driver travels 36% more miles in 2025 than in 2000, yet that extra driving time, exacerbated by congestion, will collide with other priorities in people's already-saturated time budgets—and with their 64% higher per-capita disposable incomes, they'll value time even more highly than they do today.[219]

217. Small & Van Dender 2004. The authors' findings, used here by kind permission, should not be ascribed to their research sponsors (nor should our findings). Their calculated long-run elasticity should decline further with increasing income. Even from an economic welfare perspective, net rebound effects are small enough to have been neglected by NAS/NRC 2001a, p. 89.

218. Details are in *Technical Annex*, Ch. 4. We count Intelligent Highway Systems here rather than in the supply curve of oil-saving potential because its cost is hard to determine (note 380, p. 78).

219. See next page.

(continued on next page)

Interaction between efficiency improvements: Successive energy savings don't add; they multiply. That's because each leaves less energy use to be saved by the next. We count this effect fully. Some savings incur additional costs or, more often, synergistic benefits: e.g., better aerodynamics or tires can reduce the weight and size of a vehicle's engine. We count such effects carefully for light vehicles, by relying on an archetypical design specifically optimized for that purpose, and partially (tending to understate oil savings) for heavy trucks and for aircraft.

219. Like EIA, we have not explicitly analyzed rebound for trucks or aircraft, both because they're much smaller oil-users and because of the lack of literature. However, trucking demand tends to be driven by industrial production, which doesn't go up just because trucks become more efficient. Airlines can rarely pass through higher fuel costs today, but if competition did allow them to pass through future fuel savings, that might increase flying somewhat. Meanwhile, however, there will be increased competition from efficient high-speed rail, videoconferencing, etc.; and in our view, travel hassle is likely to constrain the already-high EIA forecasts of air travel from rising further.

Turnover of capital stocks: The following analysis first presents the technical potential *as if* all the efficiency improvements and supply substitutions shown were (by magic) fully adopted by 2025. This helps readers to understand the size of the "efficiency resource" independent of how quickly it can actually be captured. Later, on pp. 178–212, we contrast actual adoption trajectories if we passively wait for capital stocks to turn over normally with those achievable under innovative policies that accelerate turnover. Thus turnover rates aren't fixed; they're a policy variable. See *Technical Annex*, Ch. 21, for a fuller discussion of stock turnover and of related issues about the degree of adoption. The simulated effects of our proposed policies to accelerate adoption of advanced technology vehicles are summarized graphically on pp. 180–181.

Saving Oil

Option 1. Efficient use of oil

American oil savings were a gusher in 1977–85, but slowed to a trickle in the mid-1980s when we closed the main valve—light-vehicle efficiency. During 1975–2003, U.S. primary energy consumption per dollar of real GDP fell by 43%[220]—in effect, creating the nation's biggest energy "source," now providing two-fifths of U.S. energy services, and equivalent to 1.9 times 2003 U.S. oil consumption, 5.1 times oil production, 3.4 times net oil imports, and 13.9 times Persian Gulf net imports. Per-capita U.S. primary energy use rose 0.6% while per-capita GDP grew 78%. And we've saved oil even faster than total energy: the black line in Fig. 8 shows that in 2003, producing a dollar of GDP took only half as much oil as it took in 1975. Yet that halved intensity was achieved despite a severe handicap: the aqua line shows that new light vehicles (which use a third of U.S. oil) have generally been getting *less* efficient for the past 23 years. The nation's oil intensity fell anyway, by 1.8% per year, during 1986–2003 as other sectors' efficiency gains offset light vehicles' efficiency losses (some shifts in the composition of economic output may have helped too). In short, after 1985, the pace of saving oil per dollar of GDP fell by two-thirds—yet the tripled speed of 1977–85, when we were paying attention, could be regained if light vehicles simply resumed the sort of rapid technological progress they were achieving two decades ago.

EIA projects, as the black line shows, that oil intensity will fall by a further 26% during 2003–25—falling only half as quickly in the next 22 years

Government forecasts assume that oil use per dollar of GDP will fall only half as fast in the next 22 years as it did in the past 15, and that cars and light trucks take nine years to regain their 1987 mpg. But continuing the sedate oil-saving pace of the past 15 years, and improving light vehicles only five-eighths as fast as we did in 1975–81, would save half of 2025 oil use.

Option 1. Full use of cost-effective, established technologies can wring twice as much work from each barrel by 2025 as the government projects, at half the cost of buying that barrel. Most of the savings, like most of the use, is in light trucks, heavy trucks, cars, and airplanes.

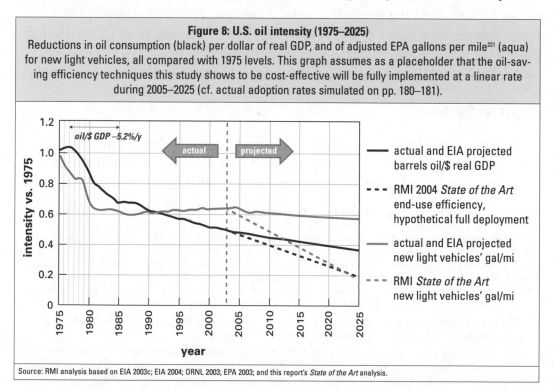

Figure 8: U.S. oil intensity (1975–2025)
Reductions in oil consumption (black) per dollar of real GDP, and of adjusted EPA gallons per mile[221] (aqua) for new light vehicles, all compared with 1975 levels. This graph assumes as a placeholder that the oil-saving efficiency techniques this study shows to be cost-effective will be fully implemented at a linear rate during 2005–2025 (cf. actual adoption rates simulated on pp. 180–181).

oil/$ GDP –5.2%/y

actual   projected

— actual and EIA projected barrels oil/$ real GDP

- - - RMI 2004 *State of the Art* end-use efficiency, hypothetical full deployment

— actual and EIA projected new light vehicles' gal/mi

- - - RMI *State of the Art* new light vehicles' gal/mi

Source: RMI analysis based on EIA 2003c; EIA 2004; ORNL 2003; EPA 2003; and this report's *State of the Art* analysis.

220–221. See next page.

After 1985, the pace of saving oil per dollar of GDP fell by two-thirds—yet the tripled speed of 1977–85, when we were paying attention, could be regained if light vehicles simply resumed the sort of rapid technological progress they were achieving two decades ago.

as it actually fell in the past 15 years, a period of moderate prices and stagnant policy. We'll show that cost-effectively efficient use of oil, using *State of the Art* technologies, could double this to another 50% cut (the same percentage as 1975–2003's), as illustrated by the dashed black line. The most important change is in light vehicles. EIA assumes their gallons per mile will fall only 9% by 2025, surpassing by only 0.5 mpg in the next 22 years the efficiency they enjoyed in 1987. In contrast, we'll find a potential drop not of 9% but of 72% in gallons per mile (to 73 mpg), as shown in the dashed aqua line.

Fig. 8 illustrates that if, hypothetically, both these improvements were made at a constant rate during 2005–25, they'd still both be much slower than the steep gains actually made in 1977–85: the overall drop in oil intensity would simply continue the sedate slope of the 1990s. Nonetheless, the dramatic savings we propose may at first sight surprise some readers. To understand why they're both practical and profitable, we must delve more deeply into each end-use of U.S. oil, starting with transportation—which uses 27% of the nation's energy but 70% of its oil.

Saving oil must focus on transportation, projected to use 74% of oil in 2025, and (as we'll see starting on p. 169) on how to reward people for buying efficient and scrapping inefficient vehicles.

Transportation

Highway transportation is a gigantic industry for which Americans pay trillions of dollars a year (mainly unmonetized[222]). Its oil use is disproportionately bigger still. As shown in Figs. 6–7, in 2000, of the 70% of U.S. oil that fueled transportation, three-fourths fueled road vehicles. Light trucks cause 55% of the total growth in oil consumption to 2025 (Fig. 7)—3.8 times the growth share of the runner-up, heavy trucks, both distantly followed by aircraft and automobiles. We therefore emphasize oil-saving opportunities in these four uses, especially light and heavy trucks.

Cars and light trucks, projected to burn 46% of U.S. oil in 2025, can save over two-thirds of their fuel by artfully combining today's best techniques—without compromise, with better safety and pep, at attractive cost, and with competitive advantage.

Light vehicles

Every two seconds, American automakers produce a new light vehicle—a marvel of engineering, manufacturing skill, business coordination, and economy, costing less per pound than a McDonald's quarter-pound ham-

220. The drop in intensity for primary energy used directly, not in power plants, was 52%. (Total gas intensity fell 54%; direct [non-electric] gas intensity fell 57%.) The 43% drop in total primary energy intensity is all the more impressive because by 2003, generating electricity used 39% of all primary energy consumption, up from 28% in 1975, and electric intensity fell by only 12% since 1975. (The modest saving, despite electricity's being the costliest form of energy, is not surprising since electricity is often priced at historic average cost; electricity is the most heavily subsidized form of energy; and importantly, 48 states reward distribution utilities for selling more electricity but penalize them for cutting customers' bills—see pp. 219–220) Indeed, 44% of all growth in primary energy consumption during 1975–2003 went to losses in generating and delivering electricity. (Fortunately, those processes also became 12% more efficient.)

221. Departing from this report's normal convention, the gal/mi values in Fig. 8 are in "laboratory" terms to conform to the EIA projections shown, but it doesn't matter because all values are indexed to 1975.

222. Delucchi 1998. Table 1-10 summarizes social costs of $2.0–3.9 trillion/y in 2000 $, less than half of it produced and priced in the private sector. Vehicle-miles have grown by more than 30% since his base year. One indicator of social cost is that U.S. passenger vehicles emit as much CO_2 as all of Japan, the world's second-largest market economy.

burger. The trillion-dollar global auto industry is the largest and most complex undertaking in the history of the world. It meets conflicting requirements with remarkable skill. As a classic mature industry,[223] it is starting to undergo fundamental innovation that will redefine the core of how vehicles are designed and built. That innovation is focusing on new ways to reconcile customer requirements (occupant safety, driving experience, functionality, durability, sticker price, total cost of ownership, and esthetics—cars are vehicles for emotions as well as for bodies) with such public concerns as third-party safety, fuel efficiency, carbon and smog-forming emissions, recyclability, fuel diversity, competitiveness, and choice.

Both Detroit and Washington have long assumed, from economic theory and incremental engineering tweaks, that fuel-thrifty vehicles must be unsafe, sluggish, squinchy, or unaffordable, so customers wouldn't buy them without government inducement or mandate. Congress has deadlocked for two decades on whether such intervention should use higher gasoline taxes or stiffer fuel-economy standards—notably the CAFE standards signed into law by President Ford in 1975 with effect from 1978, followed by analogous Department of Transportation light-truck standards effective in 1985, and widely believed to account for most of the dramatic light-vehicle fuel savings shown in Fig. 8.[224] Europe and Japan attained similar or better mpg levels (typically with smaller vehicles) via high gasoline taxes, but now find those insufficient. They and soon Canada are implementing further 25% savings by policy.[225] China's comparable or stiffer efficiency standards apply to every new car sold from July 2005, and with anticipated extensions, should save 10.7 billion barrels by 2030,[226] rivaling the oil reserves of Oman plus Angola. Most U.S. SUVs would flunk China's 2009 standards.[227] Given China's focus on building a huge auto industry as a pillar of industrial strategy (p. 167), even more dramatic efficiency or fuel leapfrogs will be needed for China to avoid full-fledged U.S.-style oil dependence, which could "undercut all of today's costly efforts by the U.S. to reform and stabilize the Middle East."[228]

Growing evidence suggests that besides fuel taxes and efficiency regulations, there's an even better way: light vehicles can become very efficient through breakthrough engineering that doesn't compromise safety, size,

Most U.S. SUVs would flunk China's 2009 efficiency standards.

223. Characterized by convergent products, fighting for shares of saturated and oversegmented core markets, at cut-throat commodity prices, with generally low returns and global overcapacity (by about one-third). For U.S. automakers, innovation of a fundamental rather than incremental nature was also stagnant until the past decade.

224. Greene 1990; although we find this paper compelling, diverse views are cited in both the 2001 and the 1992 NAS/NRC reports. Greene (1997) summarizes the arguments.

225. The European Auto Manufacturers' Association (ACEA) has voluntarily agreed to reduce new cars' fuel use by 25% by 2008. The International Energy Agency (2001) judged this feasible at low cost, although execution may be lagging. DaimlerChrysler extrapolates the improvement from an average of ~42 mpg in 2008 to 47 mpg in 2012 (Herrmann 2003, p. 2). Japan's "Top Runner" program requires all new vehicles over time to approach the efficiency of the best in each of eight weight classes (with some 50%-discounted trading allowed for over-/underperformance between classes); this has improved the overall fleet's fuel economy by about 1% a year even though vehicles have become larger (ECCJ, undated).

226. D. Ogden (Energy Foundation), personal communication, 7 April 2004. Full implementation of the new standards is expected to save a cumulative 1.6 billion bbl by 2030; with anticipated tightening, 4.8; and with expected new standards on light- and heavy-duty trucks and motorcycles, an additional 5.9, for a total of 10.7 billion barrels. The short-term reduction in fuel intensity is roughly 15%.

227. An et al. 2003; Bradsher 2003.

228. Luft 2004.　　　　　　　　　　229–43. See Box 6 on p. 46.

Light vehicles can become very efficient through breakthrough engineering that doesn't compromise safety, size, performance, cost, or comfort, but enhances them all.

performance, cost, or comfort, but enhances them all. Disruptive technology could make government intervention, though potentially still very helpful, at least less vital: customers would want such vehicles because they're *better*, not because they're efficient, much as people buy digital media instead of vinyl phonograph records. Automakers could then rely on traditional and robust business models based solely on competitive advantage in manufacturing and value to the customer, and have to worry much less about such random but potentially harsh variables as oil price, climate-change concerns, and elections.

We first present the traditional, incremental, policy-based approach to light-vehicle efficiency, adopting a widely respected industry analysis as the basis for *Conventional Wisdom* (p. 69). *State of the Art*, in contrast, uses the integrative designs and advanced technologies illustrated by some recently developed concept and market cars. Later, when discussing public policy, we'll analyze innovative ways to accelerate market adoption. To ground readers' understanding of where better car efficiency can come from, we first offer a short tutorial on the physics of light vehicles (Box 6).

6: How do light vehicles use fuel, and how can they save fuel?

A typical recent-year production car gets about 28 EPA adjusted mpg, or 8.4 liters of fuel per 100 km, on level city streets. (To convert between miles per U.S. gallon [mpg] and L/100 km, divide 235.2 by the other.) Where does the energy in that fuel go? About 85–87% is lost as heat and noise in the powertrain—engine, pollution controls, the mechanical drivetrain transmitting torque to the wheels—or in idling at 0 mpg (which wastes 17%). Only ~17% reaches the wheels in EPA testing, or ~12–13% in actual driving using accessories; ~6% accelerates the car. Since ~95% of the mass moved by that

229. Sovran & Blaser (2003) show that for a typical contemporary midsize car (Table 6), tank-to-wheels efficiency is 15.5% city and 20.2% highway, hence 17.3% combined. A standard 70-kg driver is 4.3% of the car's test mass, so 0.7% of the fuel moves the driver even with no idling. The average load factor of U.S. cars is not much above 1.0.

230. Sovran & Blaser (2003) give more exact values: for a typical contemporary midsize car, ~32% aero, 29% rolling, and 40% braking losses, all sensitive to assumptions made. An & Santini (2004) give corresponding values of 24%, 25%, and 42% for a 2000 *Taurus*, plus 8% accessory loads that are not counted in CAFE testing.

~12–13% of the fuel energy is the car, not the driver, the car uses less than 1% of its fuel to move the driver—not a very gratifying outcome from a century of devoted engineering effort.[229]

The ~12% (more or less in different models) of the fuel energy that reaches the wheels meets three kinds of "tractive load." In round numbers, nearly one-third heats the air that the car pushes aside ("aerodynamic drag"), one-third heats the tires and road ("rolling resistance"), and one-third accelerates the car, then heats the brakes when it stops ("inertia load" or "braking loss").[230] At low speed, the last two terms account for 80+% of the load, but the fuel needed to overcome aerodynamic drag rises as the *cube* of driving speed, doubling between 55 and 70 mph. Energy used to heat air, tires, and road can't be recovered, but most of the braking energy can be.

(continued on next page)

The basic physics of these loss mechanisms is straightforward. At a given speed and air density, aerodynamic drag depends on the product of the vehicle's frontal area times its drag coefficient. That number, abbreviated C_d, depends on how far back the smooth laminar flow of air around the car adheres before detaching into turbulence; this reflects shape, smoothness, and such details as wheel-well design, underbody protrusions, body seams, side-mirrors, etc. Rolling resistance depends only slightly on speed, but mainly on the product of the car's weight (how hard it presses down on the tires), times the tires' coefficient of rolling resistance, r_0 (which can be reduced by better tire designs and materials, taking care not to compromise safe handling). Both the power needed to accelerate the car and the energy dissipated in the brakes to decelerate it rise directly with the car's weight. Thus two of the three tractive loads are weight-dependent, as is any energy used for climbing hills, so as we'll see on p. 52, two-thirds to three-fourths of fuel consumption is typically weight-dependent—and we don't need weight for safety (see pp. 57–60).

Fuel can be saved either by needing to do less work or by doing it more efficiently. Automakers have traditionally focused mainly on the latter—on tank-to-wheels efficiency, especially engine efficiency—because that's where most of the losses are. (On the same logic, Willie Sutton

explained that he robbed banks because that's where the money is.)[231] Powertrain efficiency has risen by about one-third since 1975, though its benefits were reversed by faster acceleration and increased weight and features (p. 8). Further gains are still available from many mechanical and control improvements; running the engine in its most efficient ranges of speed and torque; automatically turning off the engine when idling; and cutting off fuel to cylinders whose power isn't needed. Such "Displacement on Demand," projected to reach more than two million GM vehicles by 2008, will add ~1 mpg to some 2004 V-8 midsize SUVs, and similarly for Chrysler, Honda, and others.

Internal-combustion engines—both standard Otto engines and high-compression diesel engines, named after their German inventors—are most efficient at high power. Yet they actually run mainly at low power, averaging about 11% of their full potential on the highway and 8% in the city, because most cars are more than half steel, and steel is heavy. Accelerating its weight takes so much force that the mismatch between available and actually used engine power cuts a typical Otto engine's operating efficiency about in half—worse as engines get even bigger. Continuously variable or automated transmissions and engine computer controls help, but modern power electronics and advanced electric motors permit a more fundamental solution to this mismatch.

Hybrid-electric ("hybrid") cars, invented by Ferdinand Porsche in 1900,[232] overcome the engine/tractive-load mismatch by turning the wheels with various mixtures of power transmitted directly from an engine and from one or more electric motors that decouple traction from the engine. The electricity comes from the

(continued on next page)

---

231. In a typical midsize car, the powertrain averages ~70% efficient from engine output shaft to wheels (Sovran & Blaser 2003) but the peak efficiency of an Otto engine is only about half that, and its average efficiency under varying load is about halved again.

232. In the Lohner-Porsche Chaise, which hauled cannon for the Austrian Imperial Army in World War I (von Frankenberg 1977, pp. 10, 17). Of course, a century ago, power electronics didn't exist, and both structural materials and motors were an order of magnitude inferior to today's. Efficient car designs have a long and fascinating history, ranging from Buckminster Fuller's ~30-mpg, 120-mph, 11-seat *Dymaxion* in 1933–34 to the 1,200-lb *Pertran* designed by Battelle Memorial Institute (Columbus, Ohio) in 1980 and simulated to get 80–85 mpg with an Otto or 100–105 mpg with a diesel engine.

Figure 9: Two mild hybrids competing with the full-hybrid Toyota *Prius* in the U.S. L: 2-seat Honda *Insight*, 59–64 mpg. R: The reportedly profitable 5-seat Honda *Civic Hybrid*, 49 mpg, ~10% share of *Civic* market. *Insight*'s successor might resemble the 2003 carbon-fiber concept *IMAS*— 698 kg, C_d 0.20, 94 mpg on the Japanese 10/15 cycle.

engine or from stored energy recovered from the motors when the car brakes or coasts downhill; hybrids don't plug in for recharging like battery-electric cars. Modern hybrids entered the Japanese market with the first Toyota *Prius* in 1997, a decade or two earlier than the industry expected. Honda brought hybrids to the U.S. in 1999 (Fig. 9), Toyota in 2000.

In "hybrid-assist" or "mild hybrid" designs like these Hondas, a small electric motor boosts the engine's power for acceleration and hill-climbing. The small engine, run mostly at or near its "sweet spot," can then act like a bigger one and boost efficiency by ~25% (~66% for *Insight* including mass and drag reduction).[233] In Toyota's full-hybrid 2004 *Prius* (5 seats, 55 mpg, pp. 29–30), planetary gears split the gasoline engine's shaftpower between wheelpower and generating electricity, smoothly providing a computer-choreographed mix of mechanical

and electric drive (the latter can run the car on its own at up to 42 mph for a quarter- to a half-mile). This more complex arrangement slightly more than doubles efficiency: Toyota reckons that in U.S. average-driving tests, its production models' overall efficiency in ton-mpg is about 18% for typical 2003 non-hybrid cars, 27% for the 1998 *Prius*, 31% for the incrementally refined 2003 *Prius*, and 37% for the redesigned 2004 *Prius*, which uses the Atkinson variant of an Otto engine better suited to hybrid operation, augmented by electric drive nearly as powerful.[234] Toyota now sells seven gasoline- and diesel-hybrid models in Japan, from subcompacts to delivery trucks.[235]

The 2004 *Prius* is not only ~104% more efficient in ton-mpg than a modern non-hybrid; it also gets 38% more ton-mpg than the 1998 *Prius*. That *six*-year gain beats the average new U.S. light vehicle's gain during the past *26* years (1977–2003).[236] Just from the 2003 to the 2004 *Prius*, Toyota reports that its permanent-magnet motors gained 50% in power and 30% in peak torque; its traction batteries gained 35% in power/weight;[237] its inverter became more powerful and efficient while the size of its power-switching transistors shrank 20%; its engine got 10% more power per liter; and its overall powertrain efficiency on a ton-mpg basis rose 19%

(continued on next page)

---

233. An et al. 2001; DeCicco, An, & Ross 2001. The latter paper states at p. B-12 that Honda ascribes 30% of *Insight*'s urban-cycle mpg improvement to mass and drag reduction, 30% to the efficient lean-burn engine, and 25% to the hybrid powertrain, but synergies between these probably raise hybridization's share of the mpg gain to ~40%, corresponding to ~25% higher mpg.

234. A useful technical presentation from Toyota is posted at John's Stuff 2004. The Atkinson engine is apparently made by Nissan, to which Toyota has licensed the Synergy Hybrid Drive's power electronics and transmission (both technology and actual components) so that Nissan can sell 100,000 hybrids during 2006–11 (Peter 2003).

235. Fairley 2004. Models include the *Estima* 7-seat minivan (18.6 km/L on Japan's 10/15 test mode) and the *Alphard* 8-seat 4WD minivan (17.2 km/L) with a 1.5-kW AC power outlet. At the approximate 1.37 conversion factor from these Japanese test results to EPA adjusted mpg (ORNL 2003, Table 4.26), these models would respectively get roughly 60 and 55 EPA adjusted mpg.

236. EPA 2003, Table 1.

237. They are also designed to last the life of the vehicle, partly by controls designed to prevent deep discharge (and probably overcharge). Next will come even lighter, cheaper, longer-lived ultracapacitors, as in Honda's fuel-cell *FCX*.

The conventional view

In July 2001,[244] a panel of the National Academies' National Research Council (NRC) found that under pure competition not driven by regulation, new midsize cars in 2012 could improve from 27.1 to 30.0 mpg at an extra retail price of $465, and with aggressive development of unproven but basically sound technologies, such cars could achieve 41.3 mpg by 2012–17 at an extra price of $3,175—all assuming unchanged vehicle per-

> **A National Academy panel's 2001 finding that light vehicles could achieve major fuel savings—without compromising size, comfort, safety, performance, or affordability— is already way behind the market.**

244. The report was prepublished at the end of July 2001 and formally released in mid-January 2002.

Box 6: How do light vehicles use fuel, and how can they save fuel? (continued)

(three-fifths from better software controls and regeneration, which recovers 66% of braking energy[238]). Emissions also dropped 30% and production cost fell. The hybrid powertrain's extra weight was cut to ~70–75 kg[239] or ~5%, then to ~1% (offset by reduced drag[240]) by weight savings elsewhere, so contrary to industry expectations, hybrids "can provide significant improvements in fuel economy with little or no change in [net] mass."[241] After one and a quarter centuries of maturation, modern non-hybrid powertrains offer far less scope for such impressive gains.

Automakers want to shift from Otto to ~25–30%-more-efficient[242] diesel engines, which intensive development (mainly in Europe, where they're nearing 50% market share) has lately made far cleaner and quieter than rattling and soot-belching 1970s models. Of course, *Prius* or any other hybrid could also adopt small diesel engines,

boosting its overall efficiency in proportion to that of the engine. Conservatively, this study assumes no light-vehicle diesel engines (p. 71).

Even more fundamental efficiency gains can come from making cars lighter in weight (but also safer, thanks to advanced materials and designs—pp. 55–71) and lower in aerodynamic drag and rolling resistance. These "platform physics" advances, keys to *State of the Art* designs (pp. 62–71), can then be valuably combined with hybrid powertrains and other propulsion improvements, gaining a more-than-additive (synergistic) mpg advantage[243] and manufacturing cost reduction.

Much smaller but still useful fuel savings can also come from more efficient accessories, such as metal-halide headlights, visually clear but heat-blocking windows, and more efficient air-conditioners and fans. These are applicable to all kinds of vehicles, and become more important as savings in propulsion fuel make accessory loads a larger fraction of the remaining fuel use.

238. An & Santini 2004. Even better future regenerative braking recovery could even make the vehicle more efficient than its engine (An & Santini 2004): the 2004 *Prius* and its engine are 35% efficient, while the theoretical SAE limit on an Otto engine's peak efficiency is 38%.

239. D. Hermance (Executive Engineer, Toyota USA), personal communication, 6 February 2004.

240. None of the platform's efficiency gain is attributed to improved physics (weight, aerodynamic drag, and rolling resistance), because the better drag coefficient and any tire improvements were offset by increases in weight and perhaps in frontal area.

241. An & Santini 2004.

242. The efficiency gain doesn't include diesel fuel's advantage of 15% more miles per gallon or 13% fewer gallons per mile than gasoline even if engine efficiencies are identical, simply because it's a 15% heavier distilled product. Care must be taken in comparing the efficiencies of diesel- and gasoline-fueled vehicles to ensure that the fuel difference has been properly adjusted for and the convention described, e.g., note 349, p. 71.

243. An & Santini 2004.

245. The federal/Big Three collaboration called the Partnership for a New Generation of Vehicles developed these tripled-efficiency midsize concept sedans and much significant enabling and manufacturing technology, and established valuable collaborations that moved government technology into the private sector. Its successor program, FreedomCAR, has less clear objectives and status (Lovins 2002).

246. Dunne 2001.

247. Edmunds.com 1999; Electrifyingtimes.com 2000; Moore 2000.

248. NAS/NRC 2002a at Fig. 3-14.

249. Manufacturer's Suggested Retail Price. McCraw 2000; *Automotive Intelligence*, undated.

250. NAS/NRC 2002, p. 45.

251. An et al. 2001.

252. NAS/NRC 2002, p. 53.

253. NAS/NRC 2002, p. 40.

254. U.S. hybrid sales totaled about 38,000 in 2002 and 54,000 in 2003, according to J.D. Powers and Associates. Although that's still modest in the United States' 16.7-million-light-vehicle 2003 market, hybrid sales grew by nearly 89%/y during 2000–03 according to R.L. Polk & Co. data (*Wall St. J.* 2004). J.D. Powers predicts sales of about 107,000 in 2004 and 211,000 in 2005. However, Toyota is said to project its own U.S. hybrid sales alone at 300,000 in 2005, and at May 2004 had a 6–12-month backlog of *Prius* orders (Silverstein 2004).

Figure 10: Three 2000 PNGV[245] diesel-hybrid midsize concept sedans and their gasoline-equivalent mpg L to R: GM *Precept* (1,176 kg, C_d 0.163, 80 mpg),[246] Ford *Prodigy* (1,083 kg, C_d 0.20, 70 mpg),[247] and Dodge *ESX3* (polymer body, 1,021 kg, C_d 0.22, 72 mpg). Of their efficiency gains, totaling 2.7–3.1× vs. the 26-mpg *Taurus*-class base vehicle, ~15–18% came from switching to diesel engines, 36–47% from smaller loads and engines (better platform physics, accessories, and their consequences), and 43–48% from hybridization.[248] ESX3's cost premium over a Chrysler *Concorde* at 80,000 units/y was cut from the initial 1996 *ESX*'s $60,000 to $7,500, equivalent to a ~$28,500 MSRP.[249] However, none of these concept cars has yet been turned into a market platform due to their higher production cost, which is ascribed largely to costlier light metals and greater powertrain complexity.

formance and a 3.5% efficiency penalty from heavier safety systems.[250] Oddly, the panelists excluded hybrid propulsion. They noted the Big Three's diesel-hybrid concept family sedans[251] rated at 70–80 mpg (Fig. 10), but concluded only that such advanced hybrids "would cost much more than conventional vehicles":[252] hybrids, they found, might boost fuel efficiency by 15–30% at an extra cost of $3,000–7,500+ if more than 100,000/year were made, but weren't yet realistic. Global sales of 85,000+ hybrid cars during 1997–2001 didn't make hybrid propulsion listable even among "emerging" technologies in 2001, let alone those with "production intent."[253] (Through 2003, more than 200,000 were sold.[254])

Applying traditional, modest, incremental improvements, including only minor reductions in weight and drag,[255] the panel found that mpg gains of 14–53%[256] (if weighted by the 2002 sales mix[257]) would raise prices by ~$168–217/mpg—a 6–8-y simple payback at ~$1.50/gal. Applying the larger savings instantaneously to the 2001 fleet would reduce U.S. oil use by 2.7 Mbbl/d,[258] more than imports from the Gulf. Thus the 2001 NRC study found a technical potential for major fuel savings without compromising safety, performance, or affordability. This

> …would necessitate the introduction of emerging technologies, which have the potential for major market penetration within 10 to 15 years. These emerging technologies require further development in critical aspects of the total system prior to commercial introduction. However, their thermodynamic, mechanical, electrical, and controls features are considered fundamentally sound.

255. While correcting some findings in its initial report, in NAS/NRC 2002, the panel later correctly noted that it "may have underestimated" the near-term (10–15-year) savings available from reducing vehicles' mass and drag (*Wall St. J.* 2002). Its revision made the savings bigger and cheaper.

256. Based on the revised 2002 data (NAS/NRC 2002, p. 18) the potential mpg gains in that scenario were 11–43% for small, 11–52% for midsize, and 12–58% for large cars; 11–51% for small, 20–63% for midsize, and 20–65% for large SUVs; 15–59% for minivans; and 17–58% for small and 15–59% for large pickup trucks, all at increased retail prices ranging from about one to five thousand dollars. See Fig. 11.

257. The latest stable data available at this writing: ORNL 2003, p. 4-9.

258. Applying a 35% improvement to the actual 2002 fleet's on-road efficiency of 20.2 mpg (ORNL 2003), its 2.56 trillion vehicle-miles, and a 0.94 multiplier to convert energy content per barrel from gasoline to crude oil, and assuming the panel's "Path 3" (highest-implementation) scenario.

These 2001 findings continued two historic trends (Fig. 11): savings become bigger and cheaper over time, and the NRC panel was fully as conservative as one might expect.[259]

Some found the NRC's 2001 findings implausibly optimistic, and a 2002 revision made them a tad more so.[260] But the NRC seriously underestimated the pace of private-sector innovation. Just 34 weeks after its report was released, the 2004 *Prius* came on the market. It beat the NRC's forecast for midsize sedans (27.1 mpg) by not the projected 20 but 28 mpg, not in 2012–17 but in 2003, at the predicted price increase of $2,000–4,000 but largely shaved from the manufacturer's margin, not added to the sticker price.[261] Nor was this the NRC's first such embarrassment by the market: its 1992 auto study was published only weeks before the 51-mpg 1992 Honda *VX* subcompact hatchback entered the U.S. market. It was 16% more efficient, and its 56%-in-one-year mpg gain was 32–73% cheaper, than the NRC had deemed feasible with "lower confidence" for 14 years later (model year 2006).[262] In a 1991 symposium to inform that NRC study, the Big Three had claimed that cars could be made only about 10% more efficient without making them undriveable or unmarketable—a vision framed by dividing the future into "too soon to change anything" and "too far off to speculate about," with nothing in between. Fortunately, Honda in 1992 and Toyota in 2003 felt uninhibited by this cramped vision, and market share now rewards their boldness. But even more fundamental efficiency advances are now emerging within the industry—innovations that can shift the curves in Fig. 11 even further toward the lower right.

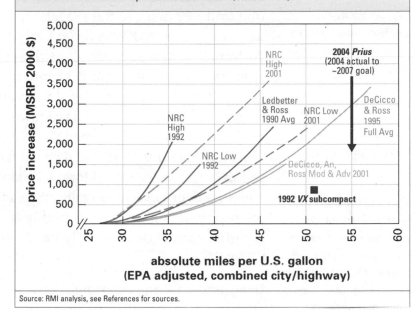

Figure 11: 1990–2004 comparison of absolute mpg vs. incremental costs for new U.S. automobiles

Smoothed automotive-efficiency supply curves from the 1992 and 2001 National Academies' National Research Council analyses, compared with a credible line of independent analysis they declined to adopt. Both sets of studies trend toward the lower right over time, and all have turned out empirically to be conservative, as shown by the 1992 Honda *VX* subcompact and the 2004 *Prius* hybrid midsize sedan (both in red).

Source: RMI analysis, see References for sources.

259. The American Council for an Energy-Efficiency Economy (ACEEE) advanced-technology analyses, graphed for comparison, were mentioned by the panel as assuming much more optimistic techniques than the panel considered, but their substance was rejected without explanation. Apparently the panel was simply unable to deal with this serious, independent, but for some members uncomfortable, analysis—which, as we'll see, also proved conservative.

260. NAS/NRC 2002; these revisions made the 2001 preliminary edition's predicted savings slightly cheaper, particularly for cars. The critiques include Sovran & Blaser 2003 and Patton et al. 2002.

261. Public data do not permit a comparison of possible differences in manufacturer's margin between the 2004 *Prius* and such benchmark vehicles as the 2004 *Camry* or *Corolla*, but as reported in note 178, *Prius* is informally said to earn a ~$1,100 manufacturer's margin. The base price (before destination charges) of the *Prius* was constant in nominal dollars, hence declining in real terms, from U.S. market in 2000 until April 2004 (Toyota 2004b).

262. NAS/NRC 1992, p. 152 (projecting as "technically achievable" a 44-mpg subcompact at a marginal retail price of $1,000–2,500 in 1990 $; average MY1990 subcompacts were EPA-rated 31.4 mpg); cf. Koomey, Schechter, & Gordon 1993. They found the 1992 U.S. (not CA) version *VX*'s adjusted EPA city/highway rating of 50.9 mpg incurred a marginal retail price, adjusted for other model differences, of $726 in 1992 $ (equivalent to $684 in 1990 $ or $845 in 2000 $), consistent with engineering estimates of the added production cost. This retail price was equivalent, at a 7%/y real discount rate, to $0.77/gal in 1992 $,

Advanced automotive technologies: lightweight, low-drag, highly integrated

The key to the next efficiency breakthrough, previously slighted, is ultralight materials now entering the market.

To catch up with and extend modern technology requires a deeper and wider view of what's possible, not just with hybrid and other advanced propulsion options, but especially in reducing light vehicles' weight and drag. Because a typical car consumes about 7–8 units of fuel to deliver one unit of power to the wheels, *every unit of tractive load saved by reducing weight and drag will save 7–8 units of fuel* (or ~3–5 units in a hybrid). Automakers traditionally consider compounding losses as energy flows from tank to wheels, but it's more fruitful to start at the wheels, save energy there, and turn those losses around backwards into compounding *savings* at the fuel tank. This requires systematic reductions in drag, rolling resistance, and especially weight, which is causally related to *two-thirds to three-fourths of the total fuel consumption* of a typical midsize sedan.[263] Contrary to folklore, *it's more important to make a car light and low-drag than to make its engine more efficient or change its fuel.* Yet this platform-physics emphasis has had less systematic attention than it deserves: weight reductions especially have been incremental, not yet radical.

Weight causes two-thirds to three-fourths of total fuel consumption. It's more important to make a car light and low-drag than to make its engine more efficient or to change its fuel.

Much of the fuel used to overcome air and rolling resistance can be routinely saved at low or no cost by careful engineering design.

Drag and rolling resistance Low aerodynamic drag needn't sacrifice styling: even a brutish pickup truck can do it. The most important step is making the underside of the vehicle (which causes about one-fourth of the air drag) as smooth as the top, since the air doesn't know which side it's on. Low drag coefficients need careful design and construction but don't cost much,[264] and may even cut total vehicle cost by downsizing the powertrain. Fleetwide C_d has thus fallen 2.5%/y for two decades.[265] It was ~0.55 for new American cars (0.6–0.7 for station wagons) and ~0.45 for new European cars in 1975, when a distinguished group of physicists concluded that "about 0.3–0.5 is probably near the minimum for a practical automobile…."[266] Today, most production cars get ~0.3; the 2004 Toyota *Prius*, Mercedes *C180*, and Opel *Calibra*, 0.26; the Opel *A2 1.2 TDI*, Lexus *LS/AVS*, and Honda *Insight*, 0.25. GM's 1999 battery-electric *EV1* got 0.19. GM's 2000 *Precept* concept sedan (Fig. 10a) cut C_d to 0.163, approaching Ford's mid-1980s laboratory records (*Probe IV*, 0.152, and

[fn 262 cont.] or 45% less than the 1992 average taxed gasoline price). Less than one-tenth of the 56 percentage points' increase in fuel economy in the 1992 *VX* (vs. the 1991 *DX*) came from reduced weight and drag, the rest from powertrain improvements.

263. An & Santini 2004, Table 5 gives data for a 2000 *Taurus* on the CAFE combined city/highway cycle augmented to break out 8% of fuel consumption due to accessory loads; without these, 73% of fuel use would be weight-related.

264. Automakers told OTA (1995, p. 76) that "current [mid-1990s] body assembly procedures and existing tolerances were adequate to manufacture vehicles with C_d levels of 0.25 or less," and provided data from which OTA estimated marginal MSRP ~$138–166 (2000 $) for C_d 0.20–0.22. Low drag also raises the fixed costs of development, but to a degree much reduced by modern computational fluid dynamics and by interaction with styling.

265. De Cicco, An, & Ross 2001, p. 10, citing 1997 Interlaboratory Working Group data.

266. American Physical Society 1975.

Probe V, 0.137).[267] Most light trucks today are still ~0.4–0.5, due largely to inattention, and have a huge frontal area—around 2.5–3.5 m², vs. ~2.0 for U.S. passenger cars accommodating the same people.[268]

Tiremakers have also developed much-lower-drag versions without compromising safety or handling. Compared to the mid-1970s r_0 norm of 0.015 or the 2001 norm of ~0.009[269] (~0.010–0.011 for SUVs), 0.006 is "not uncommon" for the best car tires even today,[270] and 0.005, tiremakers said a decade ago, "could be a realistic goal for a 'normal' [average] tire in 2015," with some therefore even lower, at a marginal price around $130 per car.[271] Test procedures and labeling requirements emerging in California will soon let buyers discover how efficient their tires are (previously a secret). The best tires, developed for battery-electric cars, are nearly twice as efficient as normal radials of a few years ago (even with self-sealing and run-flat models that can avoid the space and weight of carrying a spare tire and jack); they could save around a tenth of fuel use in a typical sedan. Rolling resistance also declines as the square root of tire pressure. And lighter wheels and tires cut rotating inertia, which is equivalent to a ~2–3% heavier car.[272]

Lightweighting: the emerging revolution Lightweighting cars is more ⟶ controversial because it can affect both cost and safety—but not in the way often assumed: both can now *improve*, markedly and simultaneously. The 2001 NRC graph of gallons per 100 ton-miles vs. weight (Fig. 12)[273] shows diverse vehicles, spanning about a threefold range in both weight and efficiency. The key point is their vertical scatter: *at a given weight* they varied in efficiency by typically ~1.6× and up to ~2.3×. This suggests, consistent with the NRC findings, that fleet efficiency could be about doubled by adopting in all cars the best powertrain and drag-reducing designs now used in some. But that doesn't count potential weight *reduction*, to which

> **Taking as much as another ton out of our vehicles was long assumed to be unsafe and unaffordable. Today, lightweighting needn't be either, thanks to advances in both metals and plastics.**

---

267. Today's best U.S. midsize and large production sedans only narrowly beat the 0.28 C_d measured by VW for a streamlined 1921 car, the Rumpler *Tropfenwagen*, and no current production vehicle yet approaches the 0.21 C_d achieved in 1935 by the Tatra *77a* (www.team.net/www/ktud/ Tatra_history_auto3.html). Perhaps the best value recorded for any enclosed vehicle—for a Swiss recumbent one-person solar-powered racecar, the 1993 *Spirit of Biel III*—is 0.088, falling to 0.05 if the airstream is 20° off-axis—but it's doubtful a real car can achieve this even with huge hypothetical advances in boundary-layer control. The theoretical minimum, for a perfect teardrop ~2.5–4 times as long as its maximum diameter, is 0.03–0.04.

268. The ~2.3 m² effective [aerodynamic] frontal area typical of new U.S. cars compares with 1.9 m² in the 2003 Honda *Insight* and *Civic*, 1.71 in the 1991 GM *Ultralite*, 1.64 in the 1987 Renault *Vesta II*, and perhaps ~1.5 possible with the rearranged packaging permitted by fuel-cell hybrids. But those figures are all for the compact size class, and people are not getting any smaller—rather the opposite. Crossover designs, providing SUV-and-sedan functionality but built like a unibody car, not a framerail truck, may help to reduce the clearly excessive frontal areas of SUVs while retaining their other customer attributes. For example, Hypercar's *Revolution* crossover design, with the functionality of a midsize SUV, has *A* 2.38 m², vs. 2.90 for a typical midsize SUV. It's 10% lower and 6% shorter than a 2000 Ford *Explorer*, but has equal or greater passenger headroom and legroom due to its better packaging.

269. Weiss et al. 2003, p. 22.

270. Sovran & Blaser 2003.

271. OTA 1995, p. 78. OTA also noted that brake drag and bearing-and-seal drag in the mid-1990s caused ~6% and ~12% of rolling resistance, respectively. The former can be virtually eliminated (as in motorcycles) and the latter much reduced, supporting reductions of rolling resistance totaling 25% in 2005 and ≤40% in 2015 (OTA 1995, p. 79).

272. Sovran & Blaser 2003.   273. NAS/NRC 2002.

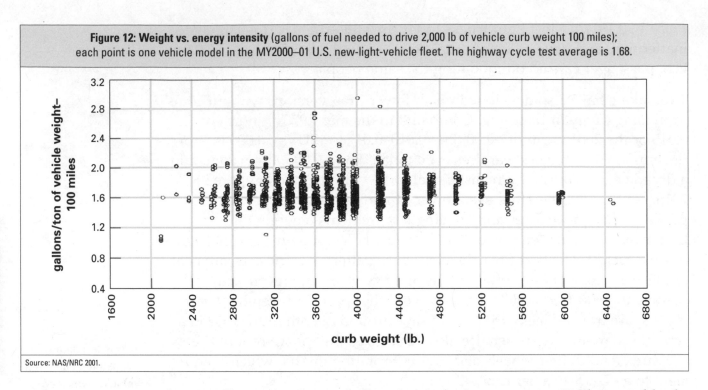

Figure 12: Weight vs. energy intensity (gallons of fuel needed to drive 2,000 lb of vehicle curb weight 100 miles); each point is one vehicle model in the MY2000–01 U.S. new-light-vehicle fleet. The highway cycle test average is 1.68.

Source: NAS/NRC 2001.

Extra-strong steel alloys and innovative structures could double automotive fuel economy and improve safety at no extra cost.

the panel's report gave only two inconclusive sentences.[274] The panel had been offered data on the potential of ultralight body materials, advanced aerodynamics, and fuel-cell propulsion, but it declined to consider them, in the unexamined beliefs that none could matter within a decade and that lightweighting would unduly compromise both cost and safety.

They had a point about cost. Most automakers' lightweighting experience was then limited to aluminum and magnesium. Saving a pound of weight via these light metals costs ~$1–3, but saves only about a gallon of gasoline every 12 years,[275] so it has long been barely cost-effective against U.S. gasoline, though it's widely done in Europe and Japan where taxes make gasoline prices ~2–4× higher.[276] European automakers typically tolerate weight savings costing up to €5/kg (~$3/lb) in light vehicles, and up to six times that in some truck applications.[277] In the mid-1980s, many European and Japanese automakers even built light-metal-dominated 4–5-seat concept cars weighing as little as 1,000 pounds, using internal-combustion engines but with 2–4× normal overall efficiencies.[278]

274. NAS/NRC 2002, p. 39. The NRC's analysis included only trivial weight and drag reductions of a few percent (pp. 3-20–3-22 in the 2001 preliminary edition), all assumed to cost more, as they would if weight were cut by the traditional means of substituting light metals for steel in a few components.

275. Greene & DeCicco (2000), quoting EEA data at p. 500, state that gal/mi in a typical 1,400-kg 1998 car is reduced by 0.54% (0.64% with engine downsizing for constant acceleration) for each 1% decrease in vehicle mass. The corresponding elasticities are –0.22 for reductions in C_d and –0.23 in rolling resistance.

276. Many production and prototype platforms in the 1980s weighed only about half as much as the U.S. MY2003 compact-car average of 1,430 kg: e.g., VW's 5-seat *Auto 2000* (779 kg), Peugeot's 5-seat *205XL* (767 kg), Volvo's 4-seat *LCP 2000* (707 kg), VW's 4-seat *E80* diesel (699 kg), British Leyland's 4-seat *ECV-3* (664 kg), Toyota's 5-seat *AXV* diesel (649 kg), Renault's 4-seat *Vesta II* (475 kg), and Peugeot's 4-seat *Eco 2000* (449 kg), among others, had all been reported by 1988. See Bleviss 1988.

277. COMPOSIT, undated.

278. Bleviss 1988; examples in note 276.

Most looked rather costly; none came to market. Since then, light-metal manufacturing has become cheaper, so it's creeping into cars part by part.[279] New processes might even halve the cost of superstrong titanium,[280] bringing it nearer practicality. But the belief that lightweight necessarily means light metals and hence high cost is deeply embedded.

Now that belief is unraveling at both ends: steels are getting stronger and light metals unnecessary. First, driven by competition from light materials and by automakers' need for light, strong, more formable, lower-cost materials, steelmakers continue to develop new products: half the steel alloys in today's GM vehicles didn't exist a decade ago. In 2002, a global consortium of 33 steel companies reported an *ULSAB-AVC* design showing that extra-strong steel alloys and innovative structures *could double automotive fuel economy and improve safety at no extra cost.*[281]

Meanwhile, an even bigger gamechanger is emerging—composites whose polymer resins (solidified by heat, chemical reaction, or other means) bind embedded glass or other strong reinforcing fibers, of which the most

Lightweighting no longer requires costly light metals, thanks to advances in lightweight steels and advanced polymer composites.

Figure 13: Four composite concept cars: From L–R, they are: *Daihatsu* 2003 2+(2)-seat *UFE-II* hybrid (569 kg, carbon-fiber, C_d 0.19, 141 mpg on Japanese 10/15 cycle, by-wire);[282] 1996 4-seat *Coupé* (1,080 kg including 320 kg/25 kWh NaNiCl batteries, pure-electric, 100-mi range with a/c on, 12–20 DC kWh/100 km, 114–190 mpg-equivalent) developed by Horlacher in Switzerland for Pantila in Thailand; BMW 1999 *Z22* (~20 body parts, ~1,100 kg [~30% weight cut] via carbon and other composites and light metals, 39 mpg, by-wire);[283] VW 2001 "Ein-Liter-Auto" 2-seat tandem 1-cylinder diesel[284] (carbon fiber, 290 kg, C_d 0.159, 8.5 hp, 74 mph, 238 mpg).[285] (A 1990 carbon/aramid 2-seat Swiss electric car weighed just 230 kg without batteries.)[286]

279. Sometimes this shifts an automaker's entire line, as with Nissan, which plans to cut all models' weight by an average of 5–10% in the next five years to tap demand for fuel efficiency (Kyodo News 2004).

280. This corrosion-resistant aerospace metal has half the weight, twice the strength, and currently 2–10 times the cost per part of steel. Nonetheless, it's starting to find selected applications, including saving ~180 pounds in the springs in the 2001 VW *Lupo FSI* (Das 2004).

281. The UltraLight Steel Auto Body-Advanced Vehicle Concept analysis assumes a high production volume of 225,000/y. The 5-seat midsize sedan's virtual design, with C_d 0.25 and curb mass (m_c) 998 kg (gasoline) or 1031 kg (diesel), was predicted to achieve respective EPA combined city/highway ratings of 52 and 68 mpg with respective production costs (apparently in 2001 $) of $9,538 and $10,328. The body would weigh 52 kg less than normal, cost $7 less, and have 81 rather than 135 parts: American Iron and Steel Institute 2002; Porsche Engineering 2002.

282. Daihatsu Motor Co. 2003; see also *Motor Trend*'s impressions at *Motor Trend* 2003. The minihybrid uses a 0.66-L 3-cylinder gasoline Atkinson engine buffered by NiMH batteries.

283. Birch 2000; Ganesh 2000.

284. Schindler 2002; Warrings 2003; Volkswagen, undated. One source (Endreß 2001) describes this concept car as the basis for a future market platform cheaper than the ~DM27,000, 78-mpg *Lupo*, but the authors understand that VW has indicated to the contrary.

285. The literature is unclear about whether the diesel vehicles' mpg ratings have been adjusted to gasoline-equivalent terms as the PNGV platforms in Fig. 8 were (using their 1.11 ratio of Lower Heating Value for the respective fuels). The Daihatsu's claimed rating is on the Japanese 10/15 cycle, and the VW 2-seater's to a European test mode, neither of which is directly comparable to the U.S. rating system. A 2001 Argonne National Laboratory estimate (ORNL 2003, p. 4-32) indicates that for a typical midsize car, a Japanese 10/15 rating will be ~73% and a New European Driving Cycle rating ~92% of an adjusted EPA rating, but that cannot be accurately extrapolated to very light and efficient cars. (If it could, the Daihatsu would get ~192 and the VW ~259 EPA mpg! These concept cars are remarkably efficient, but probably not that efficient.)

286. The carbon-and-aramid body of this *OMEKRON* concept car weighed 34 kg; its 490-kg curb mass included 260 kg of batteries. The envelope was similar to *Miata*'s. The design and fabrication were by Peter Kägi, then with ESORO (www.esoro.ch).

BMW is developing carbon fiber for use in series production cars because it's "50% lighter than steel" and "performs extremely well in vehicle crash testing."

287. *Composites World* 2004a.

288. Most cost discussions focus on cost per pound of carbon fiber. Bulk creel carbon of intermediate strength and stiffness sells in 2004 for ~$5–8/lb. This has fallen by one or two orders of magnitude in the past few decades and is coming down more with volume and with process innovations, such as the ~18%-cheaper microwave-carbonizing machine being tested at Oak Ridge National Laboratory (ORNL 2004). Price fluctuations may also soon be damped by proposed futures and options markets. But at least as important is the major scope for reducing the manufacturing cost of finished composite parts.

289. Das 2004.

290. Volkswagen AG 2002. Carbon fiber also has a marketing value prized in cosmetic trim (Patton 2004).

291. Brosius 2003, pp. 32–36. Brosius 2003a and Brosius 2003b provide helpful background on rapid advances in the wider world of automotive composites, often using reinforcing fibers weaker than carbon.

292. Diem et al. 2002.

293. Kochan 2003. Meanwhile, MG is selling a *X-Power SV* carbon-fiber roadster: although made from costly "prepreg" carbon-fiber cloth, it has solved several key manufacturing problems while reportedly cutting body-panel weight and cost by three-fourths (*JEC Composites Magazine* 2003).

promising is carbon fiber. Such "advanced" (stronger than Fiberglas®) composites, which already use more than 11 million pounds of carbon fiber per year in worldwide sporting goods, are finally starting to transition from fancy concept cars (Figs. 13, 18) and Formula One racecars to serious market platforms.

Carbon composites have long been used in aerospace because they're stronger and tougher than steel but one-fourth as dense (one-third in finished composites with 55–60% fiber content), and their strength can be directionally oriented to match load paths and save the most weight. Boeing plans ~25 tonnes of advanced composites, more than half the total structural mass, in its *7E7*; Airbus, ~30 tonnes in its superjumbo *A380*.[287] The main issue is cost. Civilian aircraft can justify paying far more than $100 to save a pound; some space missions, more than $10,000. Aerospace composites, laid up by hand like fine couture, are made of carbon tape and cloth costing up to $100 a pound.[288] Steel is ~40¢ a pound. To be sure, only ~15% of the cost of a finished steel car part is the steel, and composites can save much of the other ~85% through simpler shaping, assembly, and finishing. As VW notes, low-cost carbon-composite automotive structures could cut the weight of a car by 40% (most firms say 50–65%[289]) and body parts by 70%, making this approach "cost effective even if the manufacturing costs per part are still expected to be higher"[290]—partly because lighter cars need smaller, cheaper powertrains. But so vast was the cost-per-pound gulf that automakers—who think of cost per pound, not per car, and whose steel bodymaking skills are exquisitely evolved— long denied carbon any serious attention. Until the mid-1990s, Detroit had only a few dozen people exploring advanced composites, probably none with manufacturing experience. The industry's few high-profile experiments, like Ford's 1979 1,200-pound-lighter *LTD* sedan and GM's 1991 *Ultralite* (Fig. 18a below), were interpreted mainly as proving carbon cost far too much to compete, so it wasn't worth learning more about.

Such skepticism is now waning.[291] In 2002, *Ward's Automotive Weekly* reported that BMW "is planning to do what virtually every other major auto maker on the planet has dreamed about: mass producing significant numbers of carbon-fiber-intensive vehicles that are not only light and fast, but also fuel efficient."[292] BMW "…in the last two years…has shown several concept vehicles using considerable amounts of carbon fiber, and two projects are now in development for serial production. A major introduction with volumes as high as 100 cars per day is expected in 2005," based on the *Z22* concept car revealed in 2000 (Fig. 13c) and using 200+ pounds of carbon fiber. (BMW's *M3 CSL*'s five-layer, 13-lb carbon-fiber roof is already automatically made 5× faster than hand layup.[293]) BMW has built "the world's first highly automated production process for carbon-fiber-reinforced plastic" and with 60 full-time composites manufacturing specialists, is "going 'all out' to develop the skills…to expand use of the material from its primary domain in motorsports…to regular vehicle production."[294] BMW itself says the Z22's "tour de force," whose "success borders on the phenomenal," has "virtually launched a technological chain reaction at BMW…[which is] developing this material for use in series production cars" because it's "50% lighter than steel" and "performs extremely well in vehicle crash testing."[295]

This transition is accelerating as firms like Hypercar, Inc.[296] commercialize low-cost advanced-composite manufacturing solutions. Its illustrative patented process[297] automatically and rapidly lays carbon and/or other fibers in desired positions and orientations on a flat "tailored blank," compacting the layers, then thermopressing the blank into its final three-dimensional shape. Long discontinuous carbon fibers can flow into complex shapes and deep draws with high strength and uniformity. The goal is 80% of the performance of hand-layup aerospace composites at 20% of their cost—enough to beat aluminum for an autobody with the same attributes, and, in a whole-system solution, possibly to match steel per car (net of savings from fewer pounds, smaller powertrain and other parts, and simpler, more agile, and less capital-intensive manufacturing). By unlocking advanced composites' full manufacturing potential for ultralight autobodies, such methods' far lower capital, assembly, and parts count could decisively favor early adopters.

Ultralight but ultrastrong Even using traditional manufacturing processes, carbon fiber is showing up in 2004 hoods, roofs, and other parts from U.S., Japanese, and German automakers, including Chevrolet, Dodge, Ford, Mazda, Nissan, and BMW. Its virtues include ultralight weight, virtual immunity to fatigue and corrosion, and impressive crash absorption (Fig. 14).[298] Advanced composites' encouraging crash performance[299] is made possible by three attributes:

- Optimally shaped carbon-fiber composite structures can absorb an order of magnitude more crash energy per pound than steel or aluminum (Fig. 15).

- Such structures can crush relatively smoothly, not jerkily as metal does, because rather than accordion-folding, composite crush structures can crumble into dust from one end to the other (Fig. 16), using the crush length or stroke ~1.5–2× as efficiently as metal can.[300]

> BMW calls its carbon-fiber *Z22* concept car a "tour de force" whose "success borders on the phenomenal."

294. Including the world's largest Resin Transfer Molding press (1,800 tonnes): Ponticel 2003.

295. BMW Group 2001/2002.

296. Hypercar, Inc. (www.hypercar.com). Please see the declaration of interest on pp. 61, 63.

297. Cramer & Taggert 2002, Whitfield 2004.

> Ultrastrong carbon-fiber composite autobodies can save oil and lives at the same time, and by greatly simplifying manufacturing, can give automakers a decisive competitive advantage.

298. iafrica.com 2003.

299. In principle, the Mercedes *SLR McLaren*, at a test weight of 1,768 kg curb weight + 136 kg driver and luggage, could dissipate its crash energy against a fixed barrier at

29.3 m/s, 105 km/h, or 66 mph if its 6.8 kg of composite crush structures, reacting against a rigid member, absorbed a nominal 120 kJ/kg—half what the best carbon-thermoplastic structures can absorb (Fig. 15). However, data from Larry Evans of GM, presented by Ross & Wenzel (2001, p. 18), suggest that over 99% of U.S. vehicle crashes, and 75% of fatalities, involve a velocity change of less than 35 mph.

300. Norr & Imbsweiler (2001) give a simple empirical example of a ~50% gain in crush efficiency.

- A light but extraordinarily stiff beam can surround the passengers and prevent intrusion.[301]

These safety capabilities of advanced composites, combined with other materials like aluminum and plastic foams, solve the mystery that led a majority of the 2001 NRC panel to doubt lightweight cars' crashworthiness and hence to limit analyzed mass reductions to 5%.[302]

Bigger needn't mean heavier, lighter needn't mean smaller, and light but strong materials can improve both safety and fuel economy without tradeoff.

They assumed that autobodies will continue to be welded from stamped steel in today's designs, so future cars, like past ones, will become less protective if they're made lighter *and*—importantly—if nothing else changes.[303] But as Henry Ford said, "I cannot imagine where the delusion that weight means strength came from."[304] Cars' weight does *not* necessarily determine their size or crashworthiness as historic correlations imply.[305] Of course, physics requires

A car that's bigger but not heavier is safer for people in *both* vehicles.

Adding size without weight provides protection without hostility.

Figure 14: The strength of ultralight carbon-fiber autobodies was illustrated in November 2003 in Capetown, South Africa, when a Mercedes *SLR McLaren* was rammed by a VW *Golf* running a red light. The *SLR*—a 1,768-kg, hand-layup, 626-hp, 207-mph, 16-mpg, street-licensed supercar priced at a half-million dollars—sustained only minor damage despite being hit on the driver's-side door (the photograph shows a carbon side panel popped off). The unfortunate steel *Golf*, roughly one-fourth lighter than the *SLR*, had to be towed.

that, other things being equal, a heavier car is safer to be in but more dangerous to be struck by.[306] *But other things aren't equal.* Vehicle *size*—"the most important safety parameter that doesn't inherently conflict with greater fuel efficiency"[307]—doesn't shift risk from the projectile to the target vehicle. Rather, a car that's bigger but not heavier is safer for people in

301. Research recently assembled by senior University of Michigan physics professor Marc Ross indicates a shift in many safety experts' opinions, especially in Europe, away from momentum and towards intrusion into the passenger compartment as the major cause of death and serious injuries. He points out that although European designs that greatly improve safety, yet weigh very little, are not automatically applicable to the U.S.—where many victims weren't wearing seat belts and automakers must assume they might not be—some obvious design improvements could greatly reduce the risk and consequences of intrusion. These include very strong and intrusion-resistant passenger cells, front ends homogeneous over a large enough area to spread loads (rather than penetrating at a point, as light trucks' framerails tend to do), and stiffnesses calibrated so that vehicles absorb their own kinetic energy rather than crushing a lighter collision partner (though this requirement becomes more difficult if masses within the fleet vary widely). None of these is a current or contemplated U.S. requirement; instead, NHTSA rules now encourage stiff front ends (to resist fixed-barrier frontal collisions) and may soon disincentivize downweighting. If U.S. safety policy continues to diverge from findings and the policies that emerge from them elsewhere, U.S. cars may become increasingly unmarketable abroad.

302. Members Dr. David Greene and Maryanne Keller correctly dissented: Greene & Keller 2002.

303. Kahane 2003.   304. Ford 1923, p. 14.

305. The October 2003 NHTSA report (Kahane 2003) was prepared in support of a 2004 rulemaking in which the Administration proposes to reclassify CAFE standards by weight classes, so that heavier cars need not be as efficient as lighter ones. This would tend to perpetuate and exacerbate the "mass arms race," increase public hazard, and make American cars less marketable abroad. The *Technical Annex*'s Ch. 5 further discusses this issue and its proper resolution.

306. Evans & Frick (1993), state two "laws" fitting their data for vehicles of various types and sizes but similar materials and design: that "when other factors are equal, (1) the lighter the vehicle, the less risk to other road users, and (2) the heavier the vehicle, the less risk to its occupants."

307. O'Neill 1995. The quotation refers specifically to crush length, which O'Neill agrees can improve safety in both striking and struck vehicle if added without increasing weight, i.e., by using light-but-strong materials. (His article also correctly criticizes a ten-year-old journalistic misstatement of some safety principles of ultralight cars.)

both vehicles, because extra crush length absorbs crash energy without adding the aggressivity of weight. Since weight is hostile but size is protective,[308] adding size without weight provides protection without hostility. Lighter but stronger materials can thus decouple size from both weight and safety: bigger needn't mean heavier, lighter needn't mean smaller. Light but strong materials can improve both safety *and* fuel economy without tradeoff, offsetting ultralight vehicles' mass disadvantage.

The practical engineering reality of safe lightweighting, coordinated with sophisticated occupant protection, is well established,[312] and is advanced enough, particularly in Europe,[313] that a 2.5-meter-long *Smart* microcar's crash dummies "survived" a 32-mph 50%-offset frontal crash with a Mercedes *S*-class.[314] Similarly, open-wheel race car drivers are seldom killed by 200-plus-mph crashes in their ultralight carbon-fiber vehicles. Kinetic energy rises as the *square* of speed—it's 13 times as great at 220 mph as at 60—so just the race drivers' special padding can't save them. But Swedish driver Kenny Brack survived a horrific 220-mph crash in his carbon-fiber race car (Fig. 17).

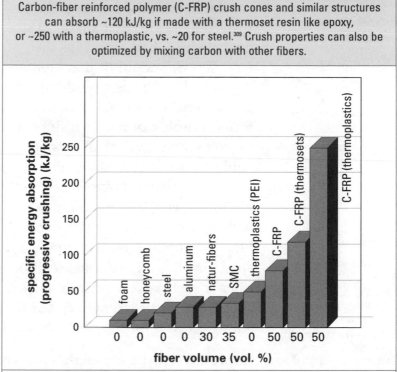

Figure 15: Advanced composites' remarkable crash energy absorption
Carbon-fiber reinforced polymer (C-FRP) crush cones and similar structures can absorb ~120 kJ/kg if made with a thermoset resin like epoxy, or ~250 with a thermoplastic, vs. ~20 for steel.[309] Crush properties can also be optimized by mixing carbon with other fibers.

Source: Herrman, Mohrdeck, & Bjekovic 2002, p. 17.

Figure 16:
Two of these 7.5-lb (3.8-kg) Mercedes *SLR McLaren* crush cones, whose cross-section varies over their two-foot length to provide constant deceleration, can absorb all of that supercar's energy in a ~65-mph fixed-barrier crash,[310] with 4–5× steel's energy absorption per pound.[311]

308. O'Neill, Haddon, & Joksch 1974. However, there are some special circumstances, such as a collision with a deformable object, where weight may protect occupants. This aim too can be achieved by suitable design without simply relying on high weight that increases hazard to struck vehicles.

309. Herrmann, Mohrdieck, & Bjekovic 2002. In practice, carbon-fiber layers in crush structures are often overlain or interwoven with tougher fibers (aramid, glass, Spectra®, polyethylene, etc.) for fracture control in extreme failures.

310. Miel 2003.

311. Mercedes-Benz 2004a.

312. For example, after quoting a 91% weight saving for a carbon-composite square-section axial tube compared with an equally energy-absorbing steel one, the Academy's Commission on Engineering and Technical Systems (CETS 1999, p. 67) concluded: "Based on these test results, the committee believes that structural concepts and analytical tools are available to design lightweight PNGV concept cars that will perform safely in collisions with heavier cars because of the excellent energy absorption characteristics of the alternate materials."

313. E.g., Frei et al. 1997; Frei et al. 1999; Muser et al. 1996; Käser et al. 1995; Moore & Lovins 1995.
See also note 301, and the extensive efforts and publications of the EU's Composit network, www.compositn.net.

314. *Auto-Motor-Sport Journal* 1999; Müller 2000; Three Point Motors Ltd. 2003.
An offset-crash video is at www.off-road.com/mbenz/videos/Sclass_Smart.avi, with a >2:1 mass ratio corresponding to a velocity far over 70 km/h; an offset-crash still photo with an E-class is at Wolfgang 1998; and a head-on is at Pistonheads.com 1998.

If safety required weight, bicycle helmets would be made of steel.

Two days after Brack's crash, nearly all major media misreported in unrelated stories that a federal statistical study had found (as the *New York Times* put it) that "reducing vehicle weights would have a deadly effect over all." It had found nothing of the sort: since it examined only old steel cars, it couldn't predict anything about *future* cars using different materials and designs.[317] If safety required weight, Brack would be dead and bicycle helmets would be made of steel. Brack is alive because carbon fiber is such a great crash-absorber. If you doubt the strength of ultralight structures, just try, without tools, eating an Atlantic lobster in its shell. Carbon composites are even stronger.

Figure 17: On 12 October 2003 at the Texas Motor Speedway's Chevy 500, 37-year-old race car driver Kenny Brack's car was hit from behind, pinwheeled into the air and into a steel-and-concrete barrier, and smashed to bits. He survived this 220-mph crash with five fractures, because his ultralight carbon-fiber Formula One racecar is extraordinarily strong and designed to fail in a controlled fashion. He recovered in six months, and by April 2004 was expecting to return to racing later in 2004.[315] He commented, "Obviously, this shows that the cars are very safe."[316]

Impressively safe ultralight composite family vehicles have already been designed. Some show promise of cost-competitiveness. National policy should encourage such decoupling of size from weight and safety, reverse the spiraling (and unsubtly marketed) "arms race" in vehicle weight,[318] and save both lives *and* oil. Nothing in the backward-looking federal study, nor in science or engineering, refutes such innovations. To make its light-vehicle fleet safer, the U.S. needs to

> …resolve the incompatibility of light trucks with cars [in weight, frontal stiffness, and height] and it needs to continue development and adoption of powerful crash mitigation and avoidance technologies. Making heavy vehicles lighter (but not smaller) and making lighter cars larger (but not heavier) would not only increase safety but also increase fuel economy…[by] over 50%….[319]

Or as GM's former head researcher on crash safety confirmed in March 2004:[320]

> Increasing the amount of light-weight materials in a vehicle can lead to lighter, larger vehicles [possessing]…all of the following concurrent characteristics: reduced risk to its occupant in two-vehicle crashes; reduced risk to occupants in other vehicles into which it crashes; reduced risk to its occupants in single-vehicle crashes; reduced fuel consumption; reduced emissions of [CO_2]….

Advanced polymer composites are especially attractive for this role, because not only do they have exceptional crash energy absorption, stiffness, and durability, but they also hold promise of simpler and cheaper manufacturing with dramatically reduced capital intensity and plant scale.

315. Cavin 2004.

316. Savage 2003.

317. Not only was the NHTSA study cited (Kahane 2003) artfully framed to invite readers to draw the erroneous conclusion that the media did—that its backward-looking correlations showed what was possible with future cars—but those correlations were deeply flawed: e.g., see Public Citizen 2003; Ross & Wenzel 2001; and Wenzel & Ross 2003. The last of these shows that Kahane's weight/risk correlation may even be artifactual, since a safety/quality correlation, measured by resale value or quality ratings, explains the data better.

318. Gladwell 2004, which notes, for example, that the subcompact VW *Jetta* has half the total fatality rate (per million car-miles driven) of popular SUVs nearly twice its weight, and protects its occupants similarly or better. See also Roberts 2001; Bradsher 2002.

319. Ross & Wenzel 2001; Wenzel & Ross 2003. These authors correctly emphasize that weight should be reduced not only via light materials but also via improved body design and styles and via high-efficiency powertrains.

320. Evans 2004, his bullets converted into semicolons.

Applying ultralight materials As automakers start to exploit this
new ability to make cars ultralight but ultrasafe—and more agile in
avoiding crashes—they're also making them superefficient and fun to
drive. Four carbon-fiber concept cars instructively combine all these
attributes (Fig. 18). GM's pioneering 1991 *Ultralite* packed the interior
space of a Chevy *Corsica* (twice its weight and half its efficiency), and
the wheelbase of a Lexus *LS-400*, into a Mazda *Miata* package, matching
the acceleration of that era's 12-cylinder BMW *750iL*, yet with an engine
smaller than a Honda *Civic*'s. In 2002, Opel's diesel *Eco-Speedster* turned
heads with 155 mph, 94 mpg, and below-Euro-4 emissions.[321] Toyota's
2004 *Alessandro Volta* is a muscular carbon-fiber hybrid supercar with
compact-car fuel economy.[322] And less widely noted but of particular technical interest is the production-costed and manufacturable virtual design
for the *Revolution* concept car (Box 7)—a midsize crossover-style upmar-
ket SUV. SUVs' share of U.S. light-vehicle sales rose from 1.8% in 1975 to
26.1% in 2004,[323] so this popular category merits especially close analysis.

> Concept cars,
> early market cars,
> and components
> presage an era of
> affordable carbon-
> fiber cars that
> combine better safety
> with sporty perform-
> ance and startling
> fuel economy.

Figure 18: Four carbon-fiber concept cars: From L–R, they are: 1991 GM 4-seat *Ultralite* (635 kg, C_d 0.192, 0–60 mph in 7.3 s, 84 mpg [2.8 L/100 km] using a nonhybrid gasoline engine); 2002 Opel 2-seat *Eco-Speedster* diesel hybrid (660 kg, C_d 0.20, max. 155 mph [250 km/h], 94 mpg [2.5 L/100 km], below-Euro-4 emissions; 2004 Toyota *Alessandro Volta*, 3 seats abreast, by-wire, 408-hp hybrid, 32 mpg, 0–60 mph in <4 s, top speed governed to 155 mph; 2000 Hypercar *Revolution* show car that mocks up a midsize SUV virtual design (857 kg, 5 seats, by-wire, C_d 0.26, 0–60 mph in 8.2 s, 114 mpg-equivalent with fuel cell).

The design of *Revolution* revealed important new information for this
study, but our discussion of it requires an explanation and a declaration
of interest. This concept car was designed in 2000 by Hypercar, Inc., a
small private technology development firm supporting the auto industry's transition (p. 57). The senior author of this report (ABL) invented
the broad concept of such vehicles in 1991 and has written and consulted
about it extensively. He is cofounder, Chairman, and a modest stock-
and option-holder of Hypercar, Inc. and is cofounder and CEO of Rocky
Mountain Institute, this report's nonprofit publisher, which became a

---

321. *Automotive Intelligence News* 2002; Car.kak.net 2003; Paris Motor Show 2002. The Euro 4 standard permits four times the particulates and ten times the NO_x allowed by the next stage of very stringent U.S. standards (Tier 2, bin 5), but technical solutions appear feasible (Schindler 2002). Starting in October 2003, Mercedes-Benz introduced additional particulate filtration, requiring no additives, to several of its European car lines. However, care must be taken in interpreting these solutions' effectiveness because the Euro 4 test does not catch or count many of the extremely fine particulates that U.S. regulators con- sider of greatest health concern—a concern that is increasing (Cavanaugh 2004). German automakers are seeking to accelerate Euro 5 standards.

322. See Toyota, undated (downloaded 12 April 2004); Serious Wheels, undated; RSportCars.com, undated. This Italdesign concept car was revealed at the Geneva Motor Show in February 2004. The midengine hybrid system, with four traction motors, is variously said to be, or to be derived from, the *Lexus RX 400h*'s powertrain. The even faster 2004 Chrysler concept *ME412* has been simulated to achieve 248 mph (0–60 mph in 2.9 s) with a carbon-fiber body and 850-hp engine (*Composites World* 2004).

323. ORNL 2003, Table 4.9.

7: Superefficient but uncompromised

The original *Revolution* concept car (Fig. 18d) was designed in 2000 by an engineering team assembled by Hypercar, Inc., including two leading European Tier One engineering companies (a noted UK design integrator with automaking and Formula One sister firms, and the German company FKA[325] for powertrain) and such industrial partners as Michelin and Sun Microsystems.[326] The goal was to demonstrate the technical feasibility and the driver, societal, and automaker benefits of holistic vehicle design focused on efficiency and lightweight composite structures. It was designed to have breakthrough (5–6×) efficiency, meet U.S. and European safety standards, and satisfy a rigorous and complete set of product requirements for a sporty and spacious five-passenger SUV crossover vehicle segment with technologies that could be in volume production at competitive cost within five years. The team developed a CAD (computer-aided design) model of the concept vehicle and performed static bending and torsion, frontal-crash, powertrain-performance, aerodynamic, thermal, and electrical analyses to validate the conceptual design, as well as midvolume manufacturing and cost analyses described below (see end of this box on p. 63, Fig. 20, and pp. 65ff).

The design combined packaging comparable to the 2000 Lexus *RX 300* (five adults in comfort, and up to 69 ft³ (1.95 m³) of cargo with the rear seats folded flat), half-ton hauling capacity up a 44% grade, and brisk acceleration (0–60 mph in 8.2 s). Its low drag and halved weight yielded a simulated EPA adjusted 114 mpg (2.06 L/100 km), or ≥99 mpg on-the-road (2.38),[327] using a fuel cell ~5 percentage points less efficient than today's norm.[328] Industry-standard simulations also showed that a 35-mph (56-km/h) crash into a wall wouldn't damage the passenger compartment—

most cars get totaled at about half that speed—and that even in a head-on collision with a steel SUV twice its weight, each at 30 mph (48 km/h), the ultralight car would protect its occupants from serious injury.[329] The highly integrated design process systematically maximized "mass decompounding"—snowballing of weight savings—by downsizing and even eliminating components and subsystems that a capable and comfortable but ultralight vehicle wouldn't need.

Revolution's direct-hydrogen fuel-cell system was simulated to achieve a 330-mile (531-km)

(continued on next page)

325. Fahrkraftwesengesellschaft Aachen mbH, www.fka.de.

326. *Revolution* development was led by D.F. Taggart, the same aerospace engineer who'd led the 1994–96 Lockheed Martin Skunk Works® team that designed a 95%-carbon advanced-tactical-fighter airframe—one-third lighter but two-thirds cheaper than its 72%-metal predecessor, due to its clean-sheet design for optimal composites manufacturing—mentioned on p. 82.

327. As is common industry practice, FKA simulated *Revolution*'s on-road efficiency in 2000 by multiplying each vector in the EPA driving cycles by 1.3. This achieves an on-road result, ~95 mpg, conservatively below the ~109 mpg obtained by successively applying the EPA's normal correction factor from "laboratory" to "adjusted" combined city/highway efficiency—a reduction in efficiency by factors of 0.9 for city and 0.78 for highway driving—*and* EPA's ~0.96 estimated adjustment to real-world driving. Before these adjustments, using unscaled driving vectors, the "laboratory" efficiency of this fuel-cell variant was 134 mpg on the EPA combined city/highway cycle.

328. The original 2000 fuel-cell *Revolution* design's peak-load efficiency was reduced from 50% to 45% in the fuel-cell one of the three variants simulated for this study. However, since peak loads seldom occur, this reduced the average adjusted EPA mpg by only 1 mpg (while reducing cost considerably), and required no mass adjustment. Acceleration was increased 12.5% over EIA 2025 projected values by scaling the front traction motors, buffer battery, and power electronics, not the fuel cell. The resulting fuel-cell system efficiency averaged 59.4% city and 58.7% highway, or tank-to-wheels, 55.0% and 46.4%, respectively. In contrast, 50% peak-load efficiency is assumed for a nominal neat-hydrogen fuel-cell system in the latest MIT Energy Lab analysis (Weiss et al. 2003). All these efficiencies are on the same accounting basis: from neat-hydrogen Lower Heating Value to fuel-cell DC bus output, net of all auxiliary power consumption.

329. Defined as meeting the same deceleration limits as the Federal Motor Vehicle Safety Standards require for a 30-mph fixed-barrier frontal crash test. The project's limited budget precluded simulation of other crash modes, let alone physical crash tests, but the quality of the simulation tools and the Tier One prime contractor's extensive Formula One experience give reasonable confidence that the design would perform well in crash modes other than the two basic ones simulated.

major stockholder on spinning off Hypercar in 1999. (Sir Mark Moody-Stuart, author of the Foreword on p. *xviii*, is also a stockholder.) Hypercar has not done automotive design since 2000, and since 2002 has focused solely on composite manufacturing processes. Normally such a history of self-interest would discourage more than passing mention of *Revolution*'s design. But in fact, that design's technical details are uniquely useful here, for four reasons: it integrates advanced technologies more fully than any market vehicle; it shows promise of competitive manufacturing cost; its technical description, unlike that of advanced automaker projects, has been rather fully published;[324] and its proprietary cost and other data, available to RMI only because of these historic connections, permit far deeper analysis than could be performed on any automaker's advanced projects. For these reasons, *Revolution* has been specially reanalyzed for this report, both by and independently of RMI, using both public and proprietary data, to produce a detailed case-study of advanced technolo-

A 35-mph crash into a wall wouldn't damage the passenger compartment and even in a head-on collision with a steel SUV twice its weight, each at 30 mph, the ultralight car would protect its occupants from serious injury.

324. Cramer & Taggart 2002; Lovins & Cramer 2004; www.hypercar.com.

Box 7: Superefficient but uncompromised (continued)

average range on 7.5 lb (3.4 kg) of safely stored compressed hydrogen in U.S.-approved 5,000-psi (350-bar) carbon-fiber tanks; newer German-approved tanks tested by GM operate at twice that pressure, which would extend the range beyond 500 miles (by 2003, 10,000 psi had become an industry design norm). *Revolution* combined a body much stiffer than a good sports sedan's[330] with all-wheel fast digital traction control, 13–20-cm variable ride height, and smart semiactive suspension, so it should be very sporty. *Revolution* may have been the first car designed from scratch to be all-digital, all-networked, with all functionality in software—a highly robust computer with wheels, not a car with chips—thus potentially offering many new kinds of aftermarket customization, wireless background tune-ups and diagnostics, remote upgrades, and other novel value propositions. Since its body wouldn't fatigue, rust, nor dent in a 6-mph collision, and the rest of the car was radically simplified, the design was consistent with a 200,000-mile warranty.

In 2000, Hypercar, Inc. analyzed detailed costs for hypothetical 2005 production of *Revolution* at a greenfield plant making 50,000 vehicles per year—about the volume of the aluminum Audi *A2*. A 499-line-item Bill of Materials, developed in close collaboration with two Tier Ones and the supply chain, accounted for 94% of manufacturing cost. It supported cost estimates based 60% on unnegotiated[331] quotations by the supply chain in response to anonymous Tier One cost-pack requests, 6% on standard parts-bin costs, 25% on consultant analyses of powertrain cost, and 9% on in-house analyses of proprietary production processes for composite components. The resulting production-cost private analysis then supported the extensions summarized in Fig. 20 on p. 65.

330. Static analyses showed bending stiffness 14,470 N/mm, torsional stiffness 38,490 N•m/deg, first bending mode 93 Hz, and first torsion mode 62 Hz. These are respectively 85%, 221%, 140%, and 141% of corresponding values for the ultra-high-strength-steel *ULSAB-AVC* midsize car design, whose 218-kg body-in-white is 17% heavier. The large-area adhesive bonding in the *Revolution*'s body would also maintain stiffness throughout the very long life of the vehicle, vs. most metal autobodies' rapid degradation of spot-welds.

331. Probably therefore overstated; *ULSAB-AVC*, for example, was assumed in its cost analysis to gain a 10% reduction in suppliers' bids via "virtual negotiation."

gies' integrated performance and cost. Similar results could be readily achieved by others, and all our calculations are shown in and replicable from *Technical Annex*, Ch. 5. Using this particular foundation for our analysis simply makes it more specific, detailed, and transparent than could otherwise be possible. That one of us has been so long engaged with it, and has advanced it in other fora, should not disqualify it from informing this report.

A specially optimized ultralight design for a superefficient midsize SUV provides an archetype for saving 69% of 2025 light-vehicle fuel at a cost of 57¢/gallon. In case the composites don't work out, lighter steel autobodies offer a worthy backstop.

Lighter-but-safer vehicles dramatically extend cheap oil savings

The important lesson of our light-vehicle analysis, summarized next, is that advanced-composite ultralight hybrids roughly double the efficiency of a normal-weight hybrid *without* materially raising its total manufacturing cost. That's partly because of simpler and cheaper manufacturing, partly because ultralighting shrinks powertrains.

The model-year-2005 hybrid SUVs shown in Fig. 5 (p. 31) use *Prius*-style hybrid powertrains to double their efficiency, but they don't yet capture the further efficiency of cutting their weight in half. This synergistic *ultralight-hybrid combination*, illustrated by the simulated *Revolution* hybrid, is the approach we adopted for all *State of the Art* light vehicles.[332]

332. Strict economic marginalists might want us to stick with a lightweight non-hybrid, saving 58% of its gasoline at 15¢ per pretax gallon, and say it's uneconomic to go to a lightweight hybrid, saving 72% of its gasoline at an *additional* cost of $2.36/gal. We bundle these together and go straight to the hybrid because its savings, as an integrated package, cost only a very profitable 56¢/gal, and it's impractical to buy a non-hybrid car and then retrofit it to a hybrid. Buying only 81% of the hybrid's potential savings would be a classic suboptimization. Energy-saving experts call it "cream-skimming"—buying only a smaller, cheaper increment of savings in a way that makes larger savings, though cost-effective when bought together, economically and practically unobtainable when bought separately.

333. For this graph, we estimate the mass effect using the method and data of An & Santini (2004) and scale it to the *Audi 2.7T* base vehicle; obtain the drag/rolling-resistance/accessories/integration term from the difference between the hybrid and internal-combustion-engine *Revolution* variants; and use the *Revolution* hybrid to obtain the last decrement of fuel use. The calculation is in *Technical Annex*, Ch. 5.

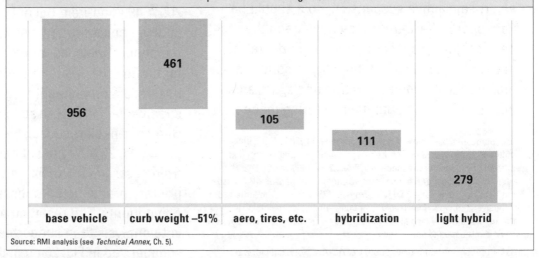

Figure 19: Two-thirds of a *State of the Art* light vehicle's fuel saving comes from its light weight
This figure charts causes of successive reductions in nominal 2025 gal/y of gasoline consumed, comparing a *Revolution* hybrid to a 2004 Audi *Allroad 2.7T* base vehicle. About 68% of our *State of the Art* hybrid's fuel saving comes from its 51% lighter curb weight.[333] The hybrid powertrain—the main focus of the better of the previous studies—contributes only ~16% of the savings, and so do the reductions in drag, rolling resistance, accessory loads, etc. that previous studies partly or mostly counted.
The exact shares will depend on the sequence assumed for these savings, but lightweighting will always dominate, and should be done (along with other tractive-load reductions) *before* hybridization in order to make the powertrain smaller, simpler, and cheaper. The key is ultralight weight; without it, two-thirds of the potential fuel savings are lost.

base vehicle	curb weight −51%	aero, tires, etc.	hybridization	light hybrid
956	461	105	111	279

Source: RMI analysis (see *Technical Annex*, Ch. 5).

Lightweight steels could also achieve much of the same oil saving more conventionally if advanced composites prove unready (p. 67).

Two-thirds of what makes ultralight hybrids so efficient *and* cost-effective is their light-but-strong construction, as shown in Fig. 19. Previous studies largely neglected this major opportunity, for three reasons: presumed high cost from using light metals, presumed loss of crashworthiness from not offsetting lighter weight with disproportionately strong and high-energy-absorption new materials, and lack of an integrated design that properly captures ultralight autobodies' snowballing weight savings and powertrain downsizing. (Previous studies also generally assumed part-by-part substitution, which largely misses these key benefits and often raises new technical complications.[334]) By avoiding all three problems, our methodology highlights an important new area of the design space—ultralight, superefficient, exceptionally safe, and cost-competitive.

Specifically analyzing and integrating this approach's breakthrough potential for each type and size of light vehicle is so daunting that

Two-thirds of what makes ultralight hybrids so efficient *and* cost-effective is their light-but-strong construction. Our analysis highlights an important new area of the design space—ultralight, superefficient, exceptionally safe, and cost-competitive.

334. Brylawski & Lovins 1995.

Figure 20: An ultralight hybrid SUV saves 72% of today's comparable model's fuel at 56¢/gal. Comparison of pretax retail price and other attributes of a 2004 *Audi Allroad 2.7T with Tiptronic* SUV and three functionally comparable *Revolution* simulated SUV/crossover vehicles—gasoline-fueled with internal-combustion-engine (ICE) and with hybrid drive, and fuel-cell-powered. Details of this RMI analysis, based on efficiencies simulated by independent consultants, are in *Technical Annex*, Ch. 5. Note that the composite autobody (dark blue) is only a small part of *Revolution*'s total vehicle cost, and the major efficiency gains of ultralighting are quite inexpensive.

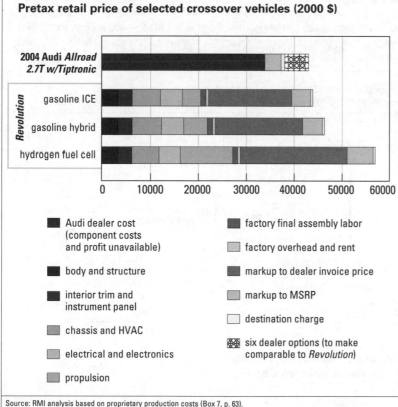

Pretax retail price of selected crossover vehicles (2000 $)

Legend:
- Audi dealer cost (component costs and profit unavailable)
- body and structure
- interior trim and instrument panel
- chassis and HVAC
- electrical and electronics
- propulsion
- factory final assembly labor
- factory overhead and rent
- markup to dealer invoice price
- markup to MSRP
- destination charge
- six dealer options (to make comparable to *Revolution*)

Three all-wheel-drive *Revolution* variants with EIA 2025 acceleration (0–60 mph in 7.1 s)

	Audi Allroad 2.7T	Revolution gasoline ICE	Revolution gasoline hybrid	Revolution hydrogen fuel cell
curb mass (kg)	1,929	878	916	892
EPA adjusted mpg	18.5	44.6	66.0	107.8
Cost of Saved Energy* (2000 $/gal) relative to:				
Audi *Allroad 2.7T*	0.	0.15	0.56	2.11
previous step	–	0.15	2.36	12.32
pretax price over Audi (%)		1.6	7.4	31.9
mpg increase over Audi (%)		140	256	481
decrease in annual fuel use @13,874 mi/y (2025 SUV) (%)		58	72	83

* 5%/y real discount rate, 14-y life, 0.10/y implicit capital recovery factor

Source: RMI analysis based on proprietary production costs (Box 7, p. 63).

Advanced-composite ultralight hybrids roughly double the efficiency of a normal-weight hybrid without materially raising its total manufacturing cost.

nobody has attempted it. One would need to create and simulate a complete virtual design separately optimized for each of about a dozen main subclasses. This would cost tens of millions of dollars, so the results would doubtless be secret. Yet we have been able to approximate such results adequately and transparently by adapting Hypercar, Inc.'s published and proprietary data on its virtual design for the *Revolution* ultralight midsize SUV fuel-cell crossover vehicle (p. 61 and Box 7). We engaged Hypercar and independent consultants to analyze that design's efficiency and cost using gasoline-engine powertrains instead (Box 8), while meeting EIA's 2025 assumed new and stock vehicle efficiency, vehicle-miles, acceleration, and other attributes. This yielded the results in Fig. 20. We then extrapolated those results to all 2025 light vehicles, by the methods in Boxes 9–10 (*Technical Annex*. Ch. 5), to obtain the fleet results shown in Fig. 21.

Based on these data for lightweight hybrids, we adopt as *State of the Art* an average light-vehicle fuel saving of 69% at $0.57/gal. Fig. 21 compares these ultralight vehicles to the conventional, small, incremental improvements shown earlier in Fig. 11. It also shows the 2000 *Revolution* design's

Figure 21: 1990–2004 comparison of absolute mpg vs. incremental costs for new U.S. light vehicles: ultralighting doubles the savings. The studies (curves) and the two market vehicles (red) shown in Fig. 11, contrasted with the *Revolution* crossover-vehicle virtual design (dark green), this report's findings (light green, 2025 sales mix), and the steel industry's virtual design (magenta). Prior studies didn't consider the potential for ultralight designs to save more fuel at lower cost. Note that the *Revolution* hybrid, and the *State of the Art* light vehicles inferred from it, all cost about the same as today's ordinary-weight *Prius* hybrid. This means that advanced composites' fuel- and life-saving advantages—opening up the new design space on the right-hand half of the graph—are roughly free. The *ULSAB-AVC* 52-mpg gasoline-internal-combustion-engine steel design (magenta) illustrates another path to saving fuel, and implies the scope for a more efficient hybrid version whose attributes RMI roughly estimates as shown. Please see text for citations.

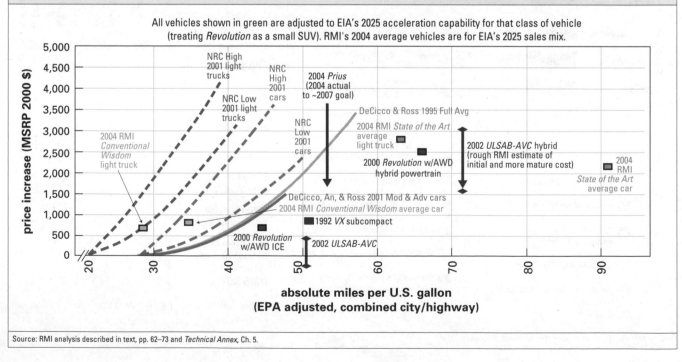

Source: RMI analysis described in text, pp. 62–73 and *Technical Annex*, Ch. 5.

underlying variants from which these fleet potentials are derived (all adjusted in 2004 to 2025 EIA acceleration), as well as the light-steel *ULSAB-AVC* virtual design.

Revolution's passenger cell's 14 self-fixturing composite parts are easily hand-liftable and snap together for gluing.
This and its colorable-in-the-mold body shell make the body shop disappear and the paint shop optional—the two costliest elements of automaking. (See Box 10, p. 73.)

This comparison reveals the dramatic advantages of lightweighting hybrids—using either advanced composites, as we assumed, or new lightweight steels, which are heavier but cheaper.

Our *Conventional Wisdom* vehicles are also shown, comfortably within the zone of the conservative NRC curves. But since they save less fuel than a non-hybrid gasoline-engine *Revolution,* and cost the same or more to build, they're not as economic a choice as *State of the Art* vehicles.

Some readers may not be comfortable with our calculations of cost based on the *Revolution* analysis (*Technical Annex,* Ch. 5), or may view differently the technological and economic risk of switching automaking to advanced composites. For those who expect automaking to remain in the Iron Age of which it is the highest achievement, the global steel industry's *ULSAB-AVC* design with Porsche Engineering (p. 55) offers a conventional-materials alternative for doubling fuel economy and improving crashworthiness at no extra cost. This conventional technological backstop for our less familiar composites route should greatly reduce the perceived technical and economic risks of achieving breakthrough efficiency at reasonable cost. Specifically, based on the 52-mpg gasoline-engine *Taurus*-class *ULSAB-AVC* design,[360] which is 21% heavier than the 45-mpg gasoline-engine crossover *Revolution* but 19% lighter than a 2004 *Prius,* one could reasonably estimate that a mature hybrid 2WD *ULSAB-AVC* would sell for a few thousand dollars more than the steel industry's projected ~$20,260 (2000 $) for its non-hybrid versions, and would get ~74 mpg,[361] approaching the same supply curve of savings vs. cost as the similar-size *State of the Art* average car. This confirms that *ULSAB-AVC* lightweight steel hybrids should be considered plausible backup candidates and worthy competitors for major oil savings in case advanced composites proved unable to fulfill their promise.

CAUTION: ENTERING CALCULATIONAL THICKET.

The next six pages summarize the analysis whose results we just presented in Fig. 21.

Box 8 shows how we analyzed the efficiency of the gasoline version of the *Revolution* ultralight SUV.

Box 9 explains how we extended its cost analysis (Fig. 20, p. 65) to all light vehicles.

Box 10 discusses light-vehicle cost comparisons more broadly.

If you don't need this level of detail—far more than this report presents for any other use of oil, because light vehicles account for 46% of 2025 oil use and three-fifths of potential oil savings— you are now finished with light vehicles and can skip to the next biggest oil use, heavy trucks, on p. 73.

335–340. See Box 8.

341–353. See Box 9.

354–359. See Box 10.

360. We assume a curb mass of 1,059 kg (Porsche Engineering 2001, Ch. 10, p. 20) rather than the apparently dry-and-bare mass of 998 kg stated elsewhere. *Prius* is 1,311 kg, the non-hybrid AWD *Revolution* 878 kg. We assume that the costs and prices in Shaw & Roth 2002 are in 2001 $.

361. For mpg, we scale 52 mpg by the 1.44 *Prius/ULSAB-AVC* ratio of ton-mpg, and subtract 1 mpg for mass compounding. We estimate a range of costs in two ways. First, we scale the $1,832 marginal cost of electrically hybridizing the AWD gasoline *Revolution* (adjusted downward somewhat for 2WD, upward slightly for mass compounding) by the 1.15 *ULSAB-AVC/Revolution* ICE test-mass ratio to get perhaps $2,000. Second, we scale the 1Q2004 (2000 $) ~$3,740 *Prius* marginal MSRP of hybridization (D. Greene, personal communication, 25 March 2004) downward by the test-mass ratio, yielding ~$3,160 but expected to fall by half in the next few years (id.). More elaborate calculations are of course possible but probably not useful without a full design exercise.

**We assumed our midsize SUV would achieve the same muscular 0–60 mph in 7.1 seconds
that EIA assumes for light trucks in 2025.**

8: Analyzing an ultralight hybrid's efficiency

The 2000 virtual design described in Box 7 (pp. 62–62) used a fuel cell, but this study requires a detailed understanding of how such an ultralight, low-drag vehicle would work with gasoline powertrains. Rocky Mountain Institute therefore commissioned independent reanalyses of what fuel economy this *Revolution* platform could achieve using a gasoline engine (*Technical Annex*, Ch. 5).[335] RMI's consultants first boosted acceleration by 12.5%, to 0–60 mph in 7.1 s, to match EIA's light-truck forecast for 2025, although comparable 2003 U.S. crossover vehicles already accelerate 20% faster than cars and 22% faster than light trucks. This made the 114-mpg 2000 fuel-cell *Revolution* 4% heavier and 4% less efficient (109 mpg). The consultants then simulated an all-wheel-drive powertrain using Honda's ~2000 *Insight* 1-L Otto engine,[336] because it's light and efficient, has a published performance map, and was designed for a car with the same curb weight and drag coefficient. (The 2000 5-seat carbon-fiber *Revolution* fuel-cell SUV weighs the same—857 kg (1,888 lb)—as the 2-seat aluminum *Insight*.) The resulting gasoline-fueled *Revolution* variants were simulated[337] to get 62.4 mpg with a hybrid powertrain, or 45 mpg with a non-hybrid automated 5-speed transmission.[338] Making the hybrid *Revolution*'s powertrain as efficient as a 2004 *Prius*'s would increase its fuel economy to 68.4 mpg,[339] which we then reduced to 66 mpg to adjust for the assumed all-wheel drive.[340]

335. The consultant on fuel economy was FKA (note 325), probably the leading Tier One engineering firm for advanced powertrain design and simulation. Mass and cost were analyzed by Whole Systems Design, Inc. (Boulder, CO), whose principal, car engineer Timothy C. Moore, had previously led RMI's and Hypercar's automotive simulations and was a key contributor to Hypercar's cost analyses during the *Revolution* project. He previously designed four cars (two by himself), built three, sold one, and won national awards for three.

336. Scaled linearly in torque. Conservatively, no adjustment was made in the efficiency map to reflect the somewhat higher efficiency that a larger engine would normally achieve.

337. Using a second-by-second proprietary model (Longitudinal Simulation model of ika/fka Rev. 2003) frequently engaged by major automaker clients of FKA, and correcting for hybrid battery state-of-charge and for the powertrain variants' weight, engine size, and other characteristics. See *Technical Annex*, Ch. 5, for details.

338. Neither powertrain was fully optimized, so the hybrid *Revolution*'s tank-to-wheels efficiency averaged 30.4%—like a 2003 *Prius*'s 31%—rather than a 2004 *Prius*'s 33.2%. Specifically the laboratory (unadjusted dynamometer) 2004 *Prius* measurements are: city (synthesized from 43% cold and 57% hot testing), 66.6 mpg, 35.0% engine efficiency, 36.2% system efficiency (tank-to-wheels); highway, 64.8 mpg, 34.6% engine efficiency, 30.1% system efficiency. System efficiency exceeds engine efficiency (An & Santini 2004) because of regenerative braking, which is 68.1% efficient on the city and 64.1% on the highway cycle. On the adjusted EPA combined city-highway cycle, which reduces laboratory city mpg by 10% and laboratory highway mpg by 22%, then combines their reciprocals, 2004 *Prius* thus gets 55.3 mpg at a system efficiency of 33.2%. These *Prius* data were generously provided by D. Hermance (Executive Engineer, Toyota USA), personal communications, 14 and 20 April 2004.

339. The reverse calculation from physics yields the same answer, as follows. If the *Revolution* hybrid design had the mass, aerodynamic drag, rolling resistance, and accessory test load of the 2004 *Prius*, it would get an adjusted EPA mpg of 50.7 mpg, vs. *Prius*'s actual 9.2%-better 55.3 mpg—reasonably close to the 9.3% greater tank-to-wheels efficiency of the tested *Prius* vs. the simulated *Revolution*. Thus a *Revolution* hybrid with a *Prius* powertrain yields the same mpg as a *Prius* with *Revolution* physics and accessory test load, as shown in *Technical Annex*, Ch. 5. (It's inappropriate to resize *Revolution*'s powertrain for increased tractive load with *Prius* physics because the *Prius* powertrain already has a higher specific power than the *Revolution* hybrid's conservative mass budget assumed: e.g., *Prius*'s battery, at 1.25 kW/kg, weighs 58% less per kW than *Revolution*'s ~1995-vintage 0.53 kW/kg, which would save the 2004 *Revolution* hybrid 27 kg.) *Prius*'s better powertrain efficiency includes both hardware and software effects, but since the incremental pretax retail price calculated below for a *Revolution* hybrid's powertrain is comparable to or below *Prius*'s actual marginal powertrain price (see note 178), any incremental powertrain hardware cost of the more efficient *Prius* over the *Revolution* hybrid can be considered negligible.

340. This 2.4-mpg reduction, from the senior author's and a consultant's engineering judgment, is believed to be very conservative because the traction is electric, the powertrain highly regenerative, and the AWD mass already included. Unlike the larger loss with mechanical drivetrains (e.g., the 2004 Audi *A6 3.0* loses 2.0 mpg or nearly 9% adjusted EPA efficiency between the 2WD and AWD versions), the *Revolution*'s AWD conversion incurs only the minor electric, inertial, and mass penalties of using four traction motors rather than two.

9: Analyzing and extending ultralight vehicle costs

To extend to other light vehicles the efficiency and cost directly simulated for our *Revolution* archetypical *State of the Art* ultralight hybrid, we combined previous work with special new analyses, and made simplifying assumptions that adequately capture the first-order effects to be characterized. Our main guide in this extension was Ashuckian et al.'s detailed 2003 efficiency and cost analysis of potential gains in light-vehicle efficiency in California, applying a consistent and well-documented framework to many different reports and vehicle classes.[341] Details are in *Technical Annex*, Ch. 5.

Ashuckian et al.'s analysis contains a detailed study by one of the most respected industry analysts, K.G. Duleep (Energy & Environmental Analysis, Inc. [EEA]), that forms the basis of our *Conventional Wisdom* light vehicles. (For that calculation we start with EIA's projected mpg by vehicle class in 2025; scale each mpg figure by the ratio of EEA's policy case to EEA's base case for that vehicle class; and adopt the incremental capital costs calculated by EEA for its policy case, converted to 2000 $. The result, if fully applied to EIA's forecasted light-vehicle fuel use in 2025, would be a 27% fuel saving at $0.53/gallon for cars and $0.34/gallon for light trucks.)

Our *State of the Art* calculations are necessarily less direct. Any procedure short of designing from scratch an optimized vehicle of each class is necessarily imperfect, but we believe our methodology, described next and qualified in Box 10, realistically captures the key relationships between vehicle classes as well as the recent progress in hybrid and lightweight vehicle technologies uniquely embodied in the *Revolution* design. The results are summarized in Fig. 20. On a consistent accounting basis, the hybrid *Revolution*'s 3.5× (47-mpg) efficiency gain over *Allroad 2.7T* yields a 72% fuel saving at an incremental capital cost of $3,190. The Cost of Saved Energy is $0.56/gallon at our 5%/y real discount rate and EIA's 2025 vehicle-mi/y.

To obtain this result, we first constructed a base-case model of the light-vehicle fleet from 2000 through 2025 by subclass, matching EIA's forecasted fuel use within a few percent, to support analyses not otherwise possible using EIA's limited model outputs.[342] Then we commissioned Whole Systems Design (WSD, Boulder, CO) to update and expand Hypercar, Inc.'s proprietary 2000 cost analysis.[343] From a 13-vehicle universe of near-peer vehicles (*Technical Annex*, Ch. 5), WSD and Hypercar, Inc. experts chose Audi's 2004 *Allroad 2.7T with Tiptronic* as today's market vehicle closest to *Revolution* in function, performance, features, and price[344]—

(continued on next page)

---

341. Ashuckian et al. 2003.

342. EIA's NEMS outputs, kindly provided to us by EIA's modeling experts, show numbers of vehicles, adjusted EPA fuel economy, estimated on-road fuel economy, and miles traveled. Unfortunately, vehicle-miles traveled and vehicle populations are shown only as aggregated totals, not by vehicle class or subclass. We therefore had to construct a vehicle stock-and-flow model, shown and tested in *Technical Annex*, Ch. 21, to yield this level of detail needed to support our analysis.

343. This consultant appropriately adjusted and resized components, and conservatively applied replacement drivesystem component costs from three proprietary industry sources. These are mass estimates developed for Hypercar, Inc. by Lotus Engineering (Norwich, UK); a Bill of Materials for actual components in Lotus's *Elise* production sports car, which has power and mass broadly comparable to *Revolution*'s; and a confidential teardown of an existing production vehicle with certain features and capacities also similar to *Revolution*'s. The iterative process of adjusting mass and propulsion power requirements went through three recursions for the hybrid and two for the other two variants, adjusting each time such elements as engine, cooling systems, electric motors, traction batteries, transmission, differentials, fuel storage and delivery systems, and exhaust systems. Secondary elements were appropriately adjusted by informal estimate. The fuel-cell variant's stack was downsized (per kW) from the 2000 design, saving cost, reducing peak-load efficiency by five percentage points (note 328, p. 62), and leaving mass unchanged. Details are in the *Technical Annex*, Ch. 5.

Unlike previous studies, which often sought to extrapolate from midmarket cars to all other vehicle classes, our analysis applies to the fleet an integrated heart-of-the-new-market SUV-crossover design specifically tuned to the most demanding requirements, including safety, size, comfort, and performance.

9: Analyzing and extending ultralight vehicle costs (continued)

hence a comparable baseline from which we could estimate incremental costs and efficiencies. Drawing on a variety of studies validated across a wide range of vehicle classes and used to convert manufacturing cost to dealer invoice price and to MSRP, we applied the high-volume Ford *Explorer*'s 79% markup from manufacturing cost to invoice price and the low-volume Audi *Allroad 2.7T*'s 10.4% markup from invoice price to MSRP. We included destination charge (the weight-related factory-to-dealer shipping cost) but not sales tax. Of the hybrid *Revolution*'s calculated incremental pretax retail price of $3,190, we assumed 20% (in line with EIA's assumptions) would reflect the next 21 years of spontaneous business-as-usual improvements, yielding a net incremental cost of $2,544.[345]

Scaling these results to other vehicle classes shows that the *Revolution* hybrid's technology and cost translate into saving 69% of the 2025 light-vehicle fleet's fuel at a Cost of Saved Energy of $0.53/gallon for cars and $0.59/gallon for light trucks. To obtain that result, we assumed that the fuel economy and incremental cost relationships between vehicle classes in the ACEEE full-hybrid case (summarized in Ashuckian et al.) would also apply to our *State of the Art* case. The ACEEE case contains both hybrid powertrains and significant lightweighting, making it a reasonable proxy. We assumed that our hybrid *Revolution* efficiency of 66 mpg and incremental cost of $3,190 was comparable to ACEEE's "compact SUV" category, then scaled mpg and incremental costs to the other vehicle classes proportionately.[346] We applied the resulting savings in each vehicle class to EIA's projected 2025 vehicle-miles, using a 14-year new-vehicle life.[347]

Our cost analysis conservatively omitted three further opportunities:

- It made no allowance for efficiency gains that may come from making the *Revolution* design more similar to mainstream vehicles in acceleration, accessories, and other features. In these and other respects, *Revolution* is truly a luxury design, but we lacked the details and resources to analyze potential efficiency gains from a more "stripped-down" version.

(continued on next page)

344. In 2000 $, the Audi lists at $34,256 MSRP plus $5,102 of options for feature comparability, 6 hp/100 lb, 0–60 mph in 7.6 s, and 18.7 mpg. The comparison is inexact but appears to understate *Revolution's* relative value.

345. To calculate costs and energy savings, we compared the hybrid *Revolution's* 66-mpg fuel economy to the projected fuel economy for EIA's "compact SUV" vehicle class in 2025 (21.9 mpg). We treated the increase in fuel economy between the 2004 Audi *Allroad* and EIA's 2025 compact SUV baseline—equivalent to 20% of the total fuel intensity reduction from the Audi to the *Revolution* hybrid—as a business-as-usual efficiency improvement that should happen in the absence of changes in government policy and business practice, which is EIA's standard and legally mandated assumption. We therefore assumed that 20% of the $3,190 incremental cost for the hybrid *Revolution* relative to the Audi is attributable to efficiency improvements that would have happened anyway, and subtracted that percentage of the cost (totaling $646) to calculate net incremental costs for the compact SUV category of $2,544. This approximation assumes a more or less linear relationship between fuel intensity and cost for the limited improvements considered, which also implicitly include any evolution in feature set over those 21 years.

346. We used that study's "full hybrid" case because it reflects significant weight reduction, though not nearly as much as *Revolution's*, and is most comparable to our *State of the Art* case even though its hybrid powertrains are two generations beyond that of the 2004 *Prius* to which we adjusted the hybrid *Revolution's* efficiency.

347. This is a standard analytic assumption used by NAS/NRC (2001) among others. According to ORNL (2003), the mean car in 2001 was 9 and the mean light truck 8 years old, both growing; for the most recent model year available (MY1990), median survival was 17 years for cars and 15-odd for light trucks, also both growing as reliability and corrosion resistance continue to rise.

Box 9: Analyzing and extending ultralight vehicle costs (continued)

- Any Otto-engine vehicle can gain another ~25–30% in mpg-gasoline-equivalent (~40–45% in mpg of diesel fuel) by switching to a modern diesel engine if, as European automakers believe, such engines can be made to meet emerging U.S. emission rules. Surprisingly clean and quiet diesels are now entering the U.S. market, e.g. in the 2005 Mercedes *E320 CDI*, which meets 45 states' current emission standards, is hoped to meet the rest by 2006,[348] and is 24% more efficient.[349] Diesel-hybrid concept cars are being designed not just for muscle (Figs. 18b, c) but also for fuel economy, like Toyota's ultralight 2001 *ES³* subcompact's 77 mpg gasoline-equivalent.[350] U.S. automakers would find diesel adoption convenient, and it's just passing 50% market share in Europe, but we entirely omitted this major option until air issues are definitively resolved.

- To convert EPA laboratory mpg to actual on-road mpg, this study applied EIA's "degradation factor" (which rises to 0.801 for cars and 0.792 for light trucks in 2025) to reflect EIA's projected congestion, driving patterns, highway speeds, and other real-world shifts. That yields a 2025 estimated on-road mpg about four percentage points below EPA adjusted mpg. This four-point loss may be appropriate for the inefficient vehicles EIA assumes, but significantly understates the on-road efficiency of the far more efficient vehicles we've analyzed.[351]

Together, we believe these conservatisms, plus the considerations in Box 10, more than offset the inevitable uncertainties in our analysis. We are also comfortable with our use of an SUV crossover design—combining the attributes of a rugged off-road vehicle and a luxury sports sedan—as a surrogate for a fleet increasingly dominated by those attributes. In actual use, most SUVs are now car substitutes—perhaps

1–13%[352] go off-road or do heavy towing—and so are ~75% of pickup trucks.[353] Unlike previous studies, which often sought to extrapolate from midmarket cars to all other vehicle classes, our analysis applies to the fleet an integrated heart-of-the-new-market midsize SUV-crossover design specifically tuned to the most demanding requirements, including safety.

348. According to Mercedes executives paraphrased by W. Brown (2004). See also Foss 2004 and Marcus 2004. The tighter emission rules that now prevent this model from being sold in California (and NY, MA, VT, and ME, which use its standards) will apply nationwide from 2007.

349. I.e., 24% excluding or 40% including the 13% greater energy of a gallon of diesel fuel than of modern gasoline.

350. This 733-kg plastic-and-aluminum 4-seat subcompact has low drag (C_d 0.23) and frontal area (1.98 m²). Its ultracapacitor-storage hybrid drive peps up its 1.4-L turbocharged diesel engine and boosts EC-cycle efficiency to 88 mpg of diesel fuel, equivalent to 78 mpg of gasoline: Toyota 2001; *EV World* 2001.

351. This is for three reasons: our *State of the Art* vehicles' lower aerodynamic drag improves their fuel economy at EIA's increased future highway speeds; their hybrid drive recovers braking energy in EIA's increasingly congested urban driving, typically making them *more* efficient in the urban than the highway mode (rather than about one-third less as EIA assumes); and their accessory loads are far lower (e.g., at least fivefold for the *Revolution* design)—a major source of the difference between adjusted-EPA and on-road mpg, since EPA's test procedure leaves air-conditioning and other accessories turned off. The derivation of EIA's *AEO04* degradation factors is described by DACV 2000. Unfortunately EIA's 2025 fleet is not technically characterized—just its driving patterns—so we can't calculate the adjustment needed. Adding a further level of confusion, EIA's "EPA rated" mpg figures in the NEMS database turn out (J. Maples, EPA, personal communication, 10 May 2004) to mean NHTSA CAFE mpg, which are similar but not identical to EPA laboratory mpg; we use the latter to avoid the NHTSA data's varying <1-mpg distortions by model vs. calendar years and by adjustments for alternative-fuel-capable vehicles. EIA's "EPA rated" mpg are not, as one might assume, EPA adjusted mpg. EIA's degradation factor of ~0.8 in 2025 therefore *combines* the conventionally separate steps of converting from EPA laboratory to EPA adjusted mpg (by subtracting 10% from city and 22% from highway laboratory values) and then correcting further to obtain estimated on-road mpg. To fit this unusual and unstated EIA convention, our underlying analysis in *Technical Annex*, Ch. 5 starts with EPA laboratory mpg, then translates the results into the EPA adjusted mpg used there and in this report.

352. Bradsher (2002, pp. 112–114), citing industry interviews and surveys. However, nearly half the intending buyers of SUVs and pickups surveyed in 1998 said they *planned* to drive off-road: Steiner 2003, Table 5.1.7. (Some, perhaps many, may have thought that meant driving on graded dirt or gravel roads.) There appear to be similar, perhaps smaller, discrepancies between intended or actual purchase of towing packages and their use. Such gaps would not be surprising, since SUVs are among the most heavily marketed U.S. products, and that marketing emphasizes rugged off-road fantasies.

353. DeCicco, An, & Ross 2001, p. 16.

10: Comparing light-vehicle prices

It's hard to compare rigorously the costs and prices of light vehicles even in today's market, let alone in 2025's. However, combining accepted, validated, and documented analytic methods can yield a reasonable and probably conservative estimate of the pretax retail price of advanced-composite ultralight hybrid-electric vehicles.

Feature differences prevent exact comparisons between current market vehicles and *Revolution*-like concept designs. *Revolution*'s standard equipment is equivalent to options[354] that add $5,390 (2004 $) to *Allroad*'s MSRP. Some features are simply different: instead of leather seats (a $3,600 extra on *Allroad*), *Revolution* has mesh seats like the market-leading Herman Miller *Aeron* chair's, and genuine (not faux) carbon-fiber trim. *Revolution* isn't designed for towing, which relatively few users need (often the same ~5% who actually drive off-road), while *Allroad* can tow 3,300 pounds. But *Revolution* provides adjustable ride height and exceptional stability control. On balance, *Revolution*'s feature package can fairly be interpreted as adding thousands of dollars to today's SUV base-model MSRPs. It's therefore conservative to assume rough feature parity between the advanced 2000 *Revolution* we costed and a well-loaded 2004 luxury sport-utility crossover vehicle. But several further broad comments help put such comparisons in perspective.

The minor price differences, in either direction, of radically more efficient but uncompromised light vehicles are within the range of normal trimline variations in today's market.[355] For example, the 2000 Ford *Explorer*'s MSRP ranged from $20,495 for a two-door, 2WD base version to $34,900 for a fully loaded four-door, 4WD Limited Edition.[356] This $14,405 spread exceeds any plausible price premium for even the costliest (fuel-cell) *State of the Art* efficiency gain, pessimistically assessed. Yet the inherent feature-richness of advanced vehicles, the customer attributes inherent in hybrid powertrains (smoothness, quiet, low-end torque, abundant onboard power capacity, etc.), and the potential to offer "exciters"[357] should allow automakers to create appealing customer option packages, analogous to but surpassing those of the 2004 *Prius*, that simply fold in superefficiency as an incidental coproduct of market-leading vehicle innovation.

RMI's analysis of the cost of saving fuel, as if that were all that such advanced vehicles offer, invites the narrowest sort of economic comparison between ways of achieving that single goal. In fact, if that were customers' sole criterion for buying cars, only one model would survive in each vehicle class. The global auto industry actually sells a dizzying and dynamic array of models and options because people are complicated and have many kinds of preferences. From a marketing perspective, the public reaction to *Revolution* convinces us that most buyers will want such vehicles for a great many reasons, differing only in where fuel economy comes into their list of priorities, so it's not important how they rank mpg among desired attributes.

(continued on next page)

354. These are the $3,600 Premium package, $750 cold weather package, $1,100 premium audio package, $850 telematics package, $390 tire-pressure monitoring system, $1,350 navigation system, and $950 17" wheels.

355. This insight is due to DeCicco, An, & Ross (2001, p. 20).

356. DeCicco, An, & Ross 2001, p. 20.

357. This is car marketers' term for exciting features buyers didn't expect a car could provide, such as the Japanese *Prius* model's ability to parallel-park itself. A car that perfectly implements everything expected of it, but no more, will generally undersell a model that adequately implements all expected features but also implements an "exciter" even in half-baked fashion.

Heavy trucks

Class 8 trucks—18-wheelers and their kin, with a Gross Vehicle Weight Rating (GVWR) of 33,001 to 80,000 lb—were the fastest-growing user of highway transportation fuel during 1991–2001 (3.6%/y), outpacing even light trucks (3.4%/y).[362] Our analysis shows a surprisingly inexpensive potential to raise Class 8 trucks from EIA's 6.2 to 11.8[363] miles per gallon of diesel fuel (*State of the Art*), and then, with four further truck-specific improvements plus system-benefits, to ~16 diesel-mpg equivalent.

The trucking industry is intensely competitive and worries constantly about fuel (its second-biggest factor cost, whose price correlates closely

> Systematic improvements in weight, drag, engines, tires, and other technical details can double heavy trucks' efficiency at an average cost under 25 cents a gallon, and may save two-thirds with smarter regulatory policies. Omitting these technical improvements costs a trucker four times as much as installing them.

362. ORNL 2003, Table 2.6.

363. Although we adopt EIA's 2000 baseline of 6.19 miles per gallon of diesel fuel, new Class 8 trucks in and after MY2004 may now be getting ~5.9 (implied by Kenworth 2003, p. 18) or even fewer (by some anecdotal accounts) mpg on-road.
(continued on next page)

Box 10: Comparing light-vehicle prices (continued)

New U.S. cars' real prices have risen steadily for 30 years amid business-cycle fluctuations. If the linear-regression trend continued, average real car prices (2000 $) would rise by 11.5% or $2,290 during 2000–2010, and by $5,725 during 2000–2025[358] (three times EIA's assumed $1,765 or 9.6% rise for average light vehicles during 2000–2025). Historic price growth, driven by consumer preferences and incomes and by regulatory requirements, has so far swamped any price growth due to efficiency technologies, and would continue to do so if extrapolated.[359] But the steady growth in expectations, capabilities, and features that customers (and often regulators) expect also tends to be delivered by technologies in or closely related to the efficiency portfolio. Price increases due to saving fuel without also adding other desired attributes are likely to be small.

These cost and price comparisons omit *Revolution*-like vehicles' biggest economic implication: the way they transform automakers' risk/reward ratio by dramatically cutting capital investment, assembly effort and space, and parts count. *Revolution*'s passenger cell's 14 self-fixturing composite parts are easily hand-liftable and snap together for gluing. This and its colorable-in-the-mold body shell make the body shop disappear and the paint shop optional—the two costliest elements of automaking. Product cycle time can also be slashed, especially with further progress toward soft tooling that could ultimately replace the half-billion-dollar football-field-full of up to a thousand progressive steel die-sets that take a thousand engineers two years to design and create. (Molding the *Revolution*'s composite body takes only 14 die-sets—fast and cheap to make—and they run at low pressure to mold polymers, rather than stamp steel.) *Revolution*-like designs could apparently compete on cost and earn market returns, but their strategic agility, capital-leanness, and much smaller minimum production scale may be far more important, offering early adopters a new path to striking competitive advantage.

Finally, we would reemphasize the inexorable progress of technology, which on past form (Fig. 11) seems likely by 2025 to surpass even our hopes, and to surpass by far our 2004 technologies.

358. DeCicco, An, & Ross 2001 p. 21 and Fig. 4.
359. DeCicco, An, & Ross 2001, p. 21.

Michigan's biggest food-grade tanker fleet went from 5 to 12 mpg-equivalent without our proposed technological improvements.

with bankruptcies). While truckers care intensely about their rigs' look and feel, trucking lacks some of the emotional and marketing complications of changing car design, and tractor makers tend to have shorter product development cycles and faster adoption of innovations than do automakers. Yet trucking has specific structural barriers (pp. 150–154 below) that have constrained adoption of many important fuel-saving technologies, creating major opportunities if these barriers are systematically overcome. Our technological analysis (*Technical Annex*, Ch. 6)—firmly grounded in industry experiments and in detailed studies at MIT and two National Labs—finds that full adoption could save ~38% of EIA's forecasted 2025 truck fuel, at a cost below $1 per saved gallon of diesel fuel at the nozzle, or 41% at below $2/gal. These savings rise respectively to 46% and 50% when we add four further truck or driver improvements,[364] whose hard-to-determine cost we conservatively assume to equal the average of the previous gains.

Taken together, the technical potential could save diesel fuel at an average cost of 25¢/gal fuel, vs. EIA's projected 2025 partly-taxed price[365] of $1.34/gal. Average costs per saved barrel of crude oil range from –$1.2 to +$3.7, and the costliest (though tiny) increment of savings costs $26.3–32.9/bbl.[366] The technological savings total ~1.0 Mbbl/d of crude oil in 2025, nearly 4% of EIA's total projected demand. Although only ~20–25% of the technological improvements are retrofittable, a new-truck buyer would pay only about one-fourth as much to install them as not to.

This analysis also doesn't assume seven regulatory changes[367] (whose saving or cost or both we found hard to estimate accurately) that could substantially raise the 2025 saving to perhaps 55–65% of EIA's 2025 heavy-truck fuel use. The most important regulatory change—safely raising GVWR to the 110,000 lb allowed in Europe (Canada allows 138,000 lb)—would raise load per trip by ~53% and cut fuel per ton-mile by ~15–30%, cut emissions and congestion, and enable international shipments to be fully loaded at origin.[368] When Michigan adopted a 164,500-lb limit for its

(note 363 continued from previous page) That's because emission-reducing technologies hastily added by seven makers of heavy-truck diesel engines reduced their fuel efficiency. These technologies avoided even costlier EPA penalties (several thousand dollars per truck) for non-compliance with 2002 non-methane hydrocarbon and NO$_x$ emissions standards set in 1997, under a 1999 consent decree settling government claims that they had installed illegal software to turn off engine emission control systems during highway driving (EPA, undated[a]). Unfortunately, the resulting fuel-cost penalty to truck owners was greater, especially high fuel prices. The same happened to MY2004+ urban buses. By not counting this recent development, and in effect assuming the engine-makers will restore their engines' pre-2004 efficiency while meeting the emissions standards, our analyzed efficiency improvements may be understated.

364. These were (1) allowing a 1-axle increase, (2) navigation technology to reduce wasted miles, (3) real-time fuel-economy display, and (4) better driver's education to optimize acceleration, deceleration, and match of operating conditions to powertrain map (note 376).

365. Including federal and state but not county or local taxes, and assuming 15 ppm sulfur.

366. The cost per saved barrel is negative if the cost of saving the retail diesel fuel is less than the cost of converting crude oil at the refinery entrance into diesel fuel at the retail pump, because then the refinery would have to use cheaper-than-free crude oil in order for the value chain to deliver diesel fuel more cheaply than saving it.

367. These seven omitted regulatory options are: (1) increase maximum GVWR to the European norm of 110,000 lb, (2) further utilize the truck-rail-truck modal shift by stacking-train rail and rail-to-truck transloading, (3) federally increase trailer lengths from 53 to 59 feet, (4) federally increase trailer height to 14 feet from 13.5 feet—already part of some states' standards, (5) allow double and triple trailer combinations, accompanied by disc brakes giving more brakes-per-pound-of-GVWR, (6) reduce speed limits to 60 mph, and (7) reduce empty miles by consolidating loads with large carriers. We estimate that these savings would cumulatively account for at least another 20–40% off any given baseline truck-stock fuel intensity.

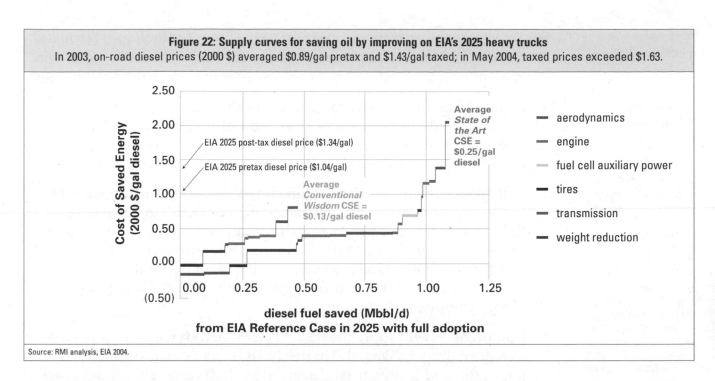

Figure 22: Supply curves for saving oil by improving on EIA's 2025 heavy trucks
In 2003, on-road diesel prices (2000 $) averaged $0.89/gal pretax and $1.43/gal taxed; in May 2004, taxed prices exceeded $1.63.

Source: RMI analysis, EIA 2004.

roads, its biggest food-grade tanker fleet increased load per daily trip by 2.5×, equivalent to raising efficiency from 5 to 12 mpg, *without* any of the technical improvements analyzed here. Safety and roads needn't suffer, because brake effectiveness and the number of axles would increase at least in step with the vehicle's total weight.[369]

Heavier loads needn't harm roads or safety.

Figure 23: The evolution of heavy-truck tractors
L–R: typical ~5-mpg (diesel fuel) Peterbilt 379, ~7.5-mpg[370] Kenworth T2000, PACCAR center-console concept tractor,[371] and engineer/artist's impression (commissioned by RMI) of a *State of the Art* lightweight, highly aerodynamic tractor.[372]

368. Major global shippers, such as a major automaker, have complained that the largest volume of material they ship is air—the empty space in partly-loaded containers.

369. Safety can be sustained and indeed increased, due mainly to better brakes (more stopping power per unit weight) and reduced tire-blowout risk (from better wide-based single tires and automatic pressure control). Road damage depends not on GWVR but on the pressure resulting from distributing that weight through axles to tires and road surfaces, so higher GWVR with even more axles can mean *lower* axle weight and road damage, though in some circumstances it could require bridge upgrades (Luskin & Walton 2001). It may be attractive to offer higher GWVR as part of a package limiting speed to, say, 60 mph (improving safety and saving additional fuel). Exterior airbags might be added too. Some engineers also favor "bullet truck" designs coupling tractor and trailer in ways that could even eliminate the risk of jackknifing. (As illustrated at www.e-z.net/~ts/ts/jack.htm, a rig jackknifes when when the tractor's drive (rear) axle locks its brakes, making the tractor and trailer unsteerable and typically causing a rollover or making the rig sweep across multiple lanes of traffic—the main cause of multi-vehicle pileups involving heavy trucks.)

370. PACCAR 2001; PACCAR 2002.

371. This concept design enhances both fuel efficiency and safety. The wedge shape of the cab reduces drag while providing front underrun protection. The driver's seat is located on the centerline of the vehicle for enhanced visibility. Photo copyright 2004, courtesy PACCAR Inc.

372. Original RMI artwork commissioned from Timothy C. Moore, Whole Systems Technologies, Inc. (Boulder CO); see note 335.

At 65 mph, a heavy truck's tractive load is about 3/5 air drag, 2/5 rolling resistance.

373. What's different is mainly the allocation of vehicle losses. Lavender, Eberle, and Murray (2003) provide Woodrooffe & Associates data showing that a nominal Class 8 base truck driving on a level road at 65 mph and a respectable 6.6 mpg uses 400 kW of fuel, of which 60% goes to engine losses, 3.8% to accessory loads, 2.3% to powertrain losses, and the remaining 34%, or 136 kW, to tractive loads comprising 85 kWh aerodynamic losses and 51 kWh rolling resistance (i.e., 5/8 aero, 3/8 tires). Since this analysis assumes constant speed, braking losses are neglected; for an over-the-road truck these are small but not zero. Hill-climbing energy must also be counted, and isn't recovered except on roller-coaster roads or with hybrid drive. Ignoring these refinements for actual driving cycles, the analysis suggests that saving one kWh of tractive load saves 2.5 kWh of fuel—less than the ~7–8-fold wheels-to-tank multiplier for standard light vehicles (p. 52) because of the big truck diesel engine's nominal 40% efficiency. The authors (two from National Labs) suggest an efficiency goal of 10.3 mpg.

Fig. 22 shows the attractively low cost of the main technologies (*Technical Annex*, Ch. 6). Most are analogous to those for light vehicles[373] and are on the market or under test by top firms. In order of decreasing fuel savings:

- Increase from 5 to 6 axles (as in Canada and Europe), improving trucking (and much container-ship and rail-freight) productivity by perhaps 15–20%—and incidentally easing the security-inspection burden by reducing the number of international container shipments.

- Fully adopt the incremental engine improvements already planned, to achieve a brake thermal efficiency of 55% (DOE's 2012 goal, vs. today's 40–44%), via variable-pitch turbos, turbocompounding, displacement on demand, variable valve timing/lift, common-rail, piezo-injectors, 42-V electrical systems, conversion of hydraulics to electrics, better lubricants, camless diesels, hybrid drive, and homogeneous charge compression ignition.

- Comprehensively apply the past 30 years' aerodynamic improvements to reduce drag. C_d was ~1.0 in the 1970s, reaches ~0.6–0.7 today (Fig. 22b), and in advanced designs (Fig. 23d) can probably approach the ~0.25 of today's best market cars.

- Use lighter, stronger, more durable tractor and trailer materials to save 5% of fuel—both by saving fuel through lower rolling resistance even when hauling light, bulky goods, and by carrying heavier payloads per trip (saving trips) when hauling heavy, dense goods.[374]

- Make air-conditioning and other auxiliary loads efficient, often electrically- rather than shaft-driven, and powered by an efficient APU (auxiliary power unit).

- Fully apply superefficient wide-based single tires and automatic tire-pressure controls.[375]

- Use loadsensing cruise control, reduced out-of-route miles, real-time fuel-economy and gear-optimizing display for driver feedback, and better driver education.[376]

374. Kenworth Trucking Co. (2003) provides data implying that in "some applications such as specialized truckload carriers and tank truck carriers," weight savings can be worth over 30 times as much for their increased payload as for their reduced rolling resistance.

375. Properly designed and operated, this combination needn't increase blowout risk. The automatic inflation system not only saves fuel, but also provides instant low-pressure warning, usually giving the driver time to pull over. Although there's only one tire per axle per side, it should run cooler due to decreased rolling resistance (two rather than four sidewalls are flexing). In any event, the apparent redundancy of a double tire is often illusory because failure of one tire in a pair immediately overloads and blows out the other. Moreover, dual tires can develop unequal pressure and diameter because the inner tire is closer to inboard brakes and can experience less air circulation. Most truckers who use wide-based single tires prefer them for smoother handling, easier maintenance, and better weight distribution as well as significant savings in weight (a half-ton per rig), fuel, and per-wheel taxation (Kelley 2002; Davis 2002; Kilcarr 2002).

376. Uchitelle (2004), for example, describes CR England Inc.'s classes for its 3,800 professional drivers, who had often run their 2,600 heavy trucks' diesels at 1,500 rpm rather than at the more fuel-thrifty 1,200 rpm.

> **Figure 24: The shape of the future? European concept trucks** in tanker and (R) linehaul tractor variants by Prof. Luigi Colani.[377]

Fig. 24 illustrates such aerodynamic and lightweighting gains in a 2001–02 concept tanker truck reportedly 43% more efficient than Europe's 6.4-mpg class average—and, at 11.2 mpg, 90% of the way to *State of the Art*'s 12.5-mpg target without using all its techniques, notably for engines.

Medium trucks

Class 3–7 trucks (GWVR 10,001–33,000 lb) use ~7% of highway-vehicle fuel, and comprise a wide range of non-household trucks and vans. They can generally use the same technologies already analyzed for light and heavy trucks, because nearly all of them closely resemble the trucks in one or the other of these categories.[378] *Technical Annex*, Ch. 7, shows that full use of those technologies in 2025, netted against an assumed 5–6% penalty in fuel economy for emission controls, would save 45% (*Conventional Wisdom*) to 66% (*State of the Art*) of Class 3–7 trucks' gross fuel use at, respectively, $1.23 and $0.85 per gallon of gasoline or diesel fuel. The savings are so large partly because the fleet has so far improved so little in mass, drag, or powertrains, and partly because its typical urban-dominated driving cycle yields especially large savings from hybrid drive. For example, Fedex expects the hybrid drives now being deployed into its 30,000 OptiFleet *E700* light-medium trucks to save 33% of fuel and 90% of emissions—and this fleet is still using conventional platform physics. DOE's Advanced Heavy Hybrid Propulsion System Program targets 50% fuel savings. Our analysis relies mainly on MIT and Argonne National Laboratory studies, and assumes by 2025 the same halving of hybrid powertrains' extra cost that Toyota and Honda expect for their hybrid cars over the next few years.

> Non-household trubs and vans can apply light- and heavy-vehicle technologies to save two-thirds of their fuel at $1 a gallon.

377. Professor Luigi Colani, whose design studio is well known in the German-speaking world, is a Sorbonne-trained aerody-namicist whose biography lists consultancies for many automakers and aerospace firms. The tanker shown at Spitzer Silo-Fahrzeugwerke GmbH, undated and aluNET International, undated, a project of Spitzer Silo-Fahrzeugwerke GmbH, is one of a family of seven developed since 1977. An over-the-road version is said to have been tested at 20.9 L/100 km, and, at FleetWatch 2002, is said to represent a 43% saving from the European fleet average for its class. AkzoNobel 2002 reports the test (at the Bosch track in Boxberg) to have shown a ~30% fuel saving, but it doesn't say compared to what; Professor Colani (personal communication, 12 May 2004) says it was a standard Mercedes truck, but further details are unavailable. Additional tractor and tractor-trailer images are at Colani, undated; www.colani.de, undated; Bekkoame Co. Ltd. 2002; Autotomorrow 1989; www.lkw-infos.de; Luigi Colani Design, undated; and Virtualtourist.com 2003. Schröder (2002) mentions the tractor in one test as 3.96 m high, 2.52 m wide, and 6.16 m long, with a 12.9-L 430-hp diesel engine. An article about the body-work (www.handwerk-ist-hightech.de, undated) says Professor Colani's *AERO 3000* was modified from a DAF *95 XF*. He informed the senior author [ABL] orally of plans to build by autumn 2004, with a Dutch partner, a superefficient heavy truck which he said he expects to achieve C_d ~0.2.

378. Light trucks—Class 1 (≤6,000 lb) and Class 2 (6,001–10,000 lb)—accounted for 71% of total Class 1–8 truck fuel usage in 1997, and Class 8 for 22% (ORNL 2003, Table 5.4). Class 6 (19,501–26,000 lb) used 4% and Class 7 (26,001–33,000 lb), which behave much like Class 8 heavy trucks, used 1.4%. Class 3–5 trucks use only 22% of Class 3–7 truck fuel, which in turn is only 7% of highway-vehicle fuel, so they don't need detailed analysis here.

Fully adopting ◄— **proven innovations in road management could save 1–2% of highway fuel and a great deal of highway-building money and drivers' time.**

Since 2001 congestion cost ~$70 billion per year, and EIA traffic forecasts would make it worse, intelligent highway systems probably save enormously more money than they cost, but we took no account for that wealth creation.

Intelligent highway systems (IHS)

The U.S. National Intelligent Transportation Systems Architecture contains 32 technical and operational options in eight categories. They save congestion, driver time, fuel, money, and often pollution and accidents. We analyzed some of the most obvious opportunities for saving fuel by these means. Full adoption of incident management, signal coordination, ramp meters, and electronic toll plazas on all major roads in 75 U.S. metropolitan areas' would have saved 0.95 billion gallons of the 5.7 billion gallons of fuel wasted by congestion in 2001. Adding a modest amount of advanced routing technologies, and a small part of the potential offered by a diverse additional technical portfolio described in *Technical Annex*, Ch. 8, would have saved another 0.5 billion gal/y in 2001. This 1.45-billion-gallon saving potential in 2001 matches ITS America's[379] 2002–2012 goal, scales to 1.68 billion gal/y (0.9% of total oil consumption) for all highway vehicles in 2025, and is our *Conventional Wisdom* case.

We also considered six other major technologies that could save between 17-plus and 45-plus percent of the fuel otherwise wasted by congestion. These include signal priority modeling for bus rapid transit and trucks, intelligent cruise control, very close vehicle spacing, vehicle classifiers, routing algorithms, and agent-based computing infrastructure, all described and referenced in the final section of *Technical Annex*, Ch. 8. Some of these measures are relatively costly, so we assume only the cheapest one-fourth of the whole portfolio, whose composition will vary with local circumstances. When deployed along with the *Conventional Wisdom* technology suite, those least-cost additional technologies round out our *State of the Art* IHS portfolio. Estimating its fuel savings and costs is particularly difficult, so rather than simply adding up the savings from every option, we conservatively estimate the impact of any subset to be twice the total of the *Conventional Wisdom* portfolio; the actual savings could be far greater.

The costs of both IHS portfolios assumed here are unknown but probably modest, and are at least an order of magnitude smaller than the societal value of driver time saved. (Recall from p. 38 that 2001 congestion cost ~$70 billion per year.) The net cost of our partial IHS portfolio is therefore at worst zero and is probably strongly negative. However, the lack of reliable cost figures doesn't matter because we've already credited IHS with helping to offset rebound (p. 41), so it's not in our oil-efficiency supply curves.[380] If it were, it would probably reduce the average cost per saved barrel.

379. Intelligent Transportation Society of America, www.itsa.org.

380. The deferral value of road investments and avoided accidents would modestly increase the value of saved time. We also chose to count IHS effects outside the supply-curve context so as to avoid the methodological awkwardness of having to put it near the left side of the curve (because of its negative cost), but thereby leaving readers to wonder how far it changes the light-vehicle analysis. We preferred to show the light-vehicle analysis by itself, unperturbed by reduced driving.

Other civilian highway and off-road vehicles

Technical Annex, Ch. 9, discusses the minor oil use by other highway and off-road vehicles, such as agricultural and construction equipment. Urban transit buses are not discussed here but on p. 120, in the context of fuel-switching, because, we'll argue, by 2025 they can and should be 100% converted to using saved natural gas (partly to improve urban air quality), saving an eighth of a million bbl/d with a payback time of about half of a bus's typical operating life. Bus efficiency will thus save natural gas rather than oil.

Trains

Technical Annex, Ch. 10, based on industry and government studies, describes *Conventional Wisdom* technologies to save 13% of trains' 2025 fuel use. Full implementation would save 0.04 Mbbl/d in 2025 at 14¢/gal of diesel or $2.9/bbl crude. *State of the Art* technologies would save 30%, or 0.1 Mbbl/d in 2025, at 26¢/gal diesel or $7.8/bbl crude. These are on top of mostly technological 1%/y improvements—28% during 2000–2025—assumed by EIA. The Swiss railways, which have very active R&D and are already rather efficient, foresee even larger potential savings (up to 60%) from integrating new propulsion concepts (up to 30%), lightweighting (up to 20%), cutting drag and friction (up to 10%), and optimizing operations.[381] A 60% saving in Switzerland is a 66% saving against the 2000 U.S. freight railways' baseline, which is 17% more energy-intensive to start with.[382] The forecast Swiss savings are thus half again as big as our U.S. *State of the Art* savings for 2025, suggesting ours are conservative. The more advanced propulsion concepts, exceeding 310 mph, could also displace the least efficient air travel.

Ships

Marine transportation offers potential to save 31% of its 2025 residual oil use, or 0.2 Mbbl/d, at a cost of $0.12/gal of residual oil using *CW* technologies, or 56% (0.4 Mbbl/d) at a cost of $0.23/gal with *SOA*. The portfolio includes improved hull shape and materials, larger ships, drag reductions, hotel-load savings, and better engines and propulsors, plus a little logistics and routing improvement. Details are in *Technical Annex*, Ch. 11.

Airplanes

Civilian air transport of passengers and freight is projected by EIA to use 86.5% of aviation fuel in 2025; the rest fuels military platforms. We focus here on civilian airplanes, and later (pp. 84–93) apply their lessons to civilian-like parts of the military fleet. We consider here only kerosene-fueled jet airplanes; potential liquid-hydrogen-fueled versions are discussed below at note 916, p. 239.

We count urban transit buses' efficiency gains later under natural gas, because they'll have been converted to use it.

Our *State of the Art* railway energy saving is only two-thirds of what the Swiss National Railway envisages.

381. Jochem 2004, p. 25. In the 1990s, for example, the Danish Railway (SB) developed the Copenhagen S-train, with 46% lower weight per seat than the 1986 model.

382. Swiss freight railways in 2000 used 232 kJ/tonne-km (SSB 2003). The corresponding U.S. figure was 352 BTU/ton-mi or 257 kJ/tonne-km (ORNL 2003, p. 9-10). However, we don't know how much adjustment, if any, is required for the freight dominance of U.S. railways' high-load-factor but one-way coal-hauling.

Proven technologies can cheaply save more than half of the nearly 3% of 2025 oil used by ships.

The industry agrees that airliners in 2025 can cost-effectively save half to two-thirds of forecasted fuel use by the national fleet, or up to 5 percent of U.S. oil use, while improving comfort, safety, and cost.

Taking one pound out of a midsize airplane typically saves ~124 pounds of fuel every year, worth more than $200 over 30 years.

Airplanes' efficiency in flight depends[383] on engine efficiency, weight, aerodynamic lift/drag ratio, layout, load factor, and electric power generation and accessories.[384] Airplanes certified during 1960–2000 showed a 70% decrease in "block fuel use" (gate-to-gate fuel used in defined and idealized "normal" operations), coming about half from better engines and half from better airframes.[385] This impressive progress decelerated somewhat in the 1990s, mainly because the easiest performance gains were already achieved, airlines' financial weakness retarded development of new models, and slow adoption of advanced composites caused weight savings to lag behind engine and aerodynamic improvements. Yet even more than for cars, weight is the most critical factor, because taking one pound out of a midsize airplane typically saves ~124 pounds of fuel every year,[386] worth more than $200 over 30 years. The composite fraction of structural weight—only about 3% in a *767* and 9% in a *777*—will exceed 50% in the next-generation midsize *7E7* and (according to press reports) in the superjumbo *A380*, as noted on p. 56. The historic ~3.3%/y drop in energy intensity may be resumed if such innovations are rapidly taken into the global fleet. Most forecasters doubt this because of the industry's financial weakness, but policy (pp. 154–159) could change that. A leading U.S. team expects a 1.2–2.2%/y drop in energy intensity to 2025 (1.0–2.0%/y without higher load factors);[386a] Airbus expects 2%/y (Fig. 24); DASA[387] opined that even 3.5%/y is theoretically possible.[388]

A fully loaded *7E7*'s expected ~97 passenger-miles per gallon is impressive—like a *State of the Art* car, only going ten times as fast—but is far from the ultimate. Our bottom-up calculation estimates the effects and costs of established techniques for reducing weight and drag, engine losses, and other minor terms. Fortunately, such gains' parametric effects have been extensively analyzed, so we have relied on industry forecasts to 2025. We separately assess small, medium, and large jets (comparable to *737-800*, *777-200ER*, and *747-400*) in EIA's 2025 fleet mix. Regional airplanes today (7% of civilian aviation fuel use, 17% in 2025) are ~40–60% less fuel-efficient than long-haul jets, partly because their short stages,

383. Greene 2004.

384. Such auxiliary loads as air-handling, space-conditioning, lighting, cooking, and electronics have not yet received the systematic and up-to-date attention they deserve. RMI's worldwide observations and discussions with a major aircraft manufacturer suggest that redesigning auxiliary loads could profitably save up to 2% of fuel use in, say, a *7E7* (which will be several times as electricity-intensive as its predecessors because it does electrically many things previously done with fluids). This can save weight and fuel carriage, while improving passengers' comfort, health, and safety. To our knowledge, no manufacturer has yet systematically applied in these uses the efficiency innovations practiced in today's most efficient buildings. Absent a rigorous determination of which of the improvements aren't yet counted in the *7E7* design, this topic is conservatively omitted from our efficiency analysis.

385. Compared with a *DC8–21*: Lee 2000.

386. D. Daggett (Boeing), personal communication, 29 August 2003. A similar analysis for a different, double-aisle airplane yielded a similar result (111 lb/y: D. Daggett, personal communication, 28 May 2004). At EIA's 2025 price of 80.7¢/gal (2000 $) and our 5%/y real discount rate, the 124:1 mass-decompounding ratio yields a 30-year present value of $228 worth of fuel for each pound of avoided weight. Alternatively, nominal industry assumptions imply that saving a pound could be worth more than that in profit (tens of times that much in revenue) if it allowed a pound of extra payload to be carried all the time at market prices (R.L. Garwin, personal communication, 26 May 2004).

386a. Lee et al. 2001.

387. DASA, the Munich-based DaimlerChrysler Aerospace AG, merged in 2000 with Aerospatiale Matra and Casa to form EADS (European Aeronautic Defence and Space Company), the parent of Airbus.

388. Faaß 2001, slide 11. Unfortunately the DASA study graphed there is not publicly available, so we have not graphed its ~0.9 MJ/RP-km (megajoule-per-revenue-passenger-kilometer) potential (20% above RMI's *State of the Art* best case shown in Fig. 25).

Figure 25: Historic and projected airplane energy intensities, 1955–2025

This RMI graph shows the evolution of more efficient kerosene-fueled airplanes. EIA assumes efficiency gains will slow by three-fifths, making the 2025 fleet two to three times less efficient than the most efficient airplanes then expected to be available and cost-effective—a bigger percentage gap than today's. Historical airplane fuel-intensities are from actual quarterly data for 1998–2003, showing the mean and one-standard-deviation error bar.[389] (See Technical Annex, Ch. 12). The discontinuity between historical[390] and projected[391] fleet averages is due to differences in fleet definitions (including cargo, charter planes, and the fraction of international fuels accounted for). EIA projects fleet and new airplane efficiency to increase 0.8%/y and 0.4%/y (1.1%/y and 0.6%/y including the 72%→76% rise in load factor) during 2000–2025. EIA's technology model adopts an assumption of weight-saving materials (99% adoption by 2017, raising seat-mpg 15% vs. 1990) and ultra-high bypass engines (68% adoption by 2025, raising seat-mpg 10% vs. 1990), but EIA considers its other four technologies (propfan, thermodynamics, hybrid laminar flow, and advanced aerodynamics) not cost-effective at $0.81/gal (2000 $) in 2025. In contrast, RMI believes a much more powerful technology portfolio to be competitive. Airplane projections are based on operational data using EIA's projected load factor for the year in which each study is shown. Operational data are analogous to on-road rather than EPA laboratory or adjusted fuel intensity for light vehicles. For example, on an idealized 2000-man mission, *7E7* uses only 0.875 MJ/RP-km, vs. 1.6 MJ/RP-km derived from *767-300–209* and graphed here.[392] The difference, due to operational imperfections and age degradation, can be reduced by better practices and technologies.[393] Boeing's idealized efficiency data are in *Technical Annex,* Ch. 12. These are additional to the airplane-technology-based difference between the fleet-average and airplane projections. The Airbus,[394] EIA,[395] Greene,[396] and NRC[397] projections shown represent fleet averages for the given year, while the Lee et al.,[398] Delft,[399] and RMI projections are airplane-specific.

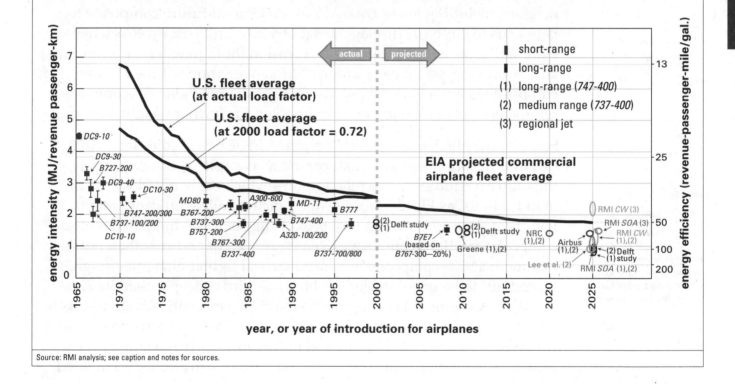

Source: RMI analysis; see caption and notes for sources.

389. BTS 2004.

390. ORNL 2003, Table 9.2.

391. EIA 2004.

392. M. Mirza, Boeing Economic Analysis Department, personal communication, 11 June 2004, based on a standardized 2,000-nautical-mile trip at the 2000 average load factor of 0.72; Boeing, undated (downloaded 13 August 2004).

393. The difference between block and actual fuel use in 1992 averaged ~18%, for complex but well-understood reasons susceptible to considerable improvement (Daggett et al. 1999).

394. Faaß 2001.

395. EIA 2004.

396. Greene 1992.

397. CAT/NRC 1992.

398. Lee et al. 2001. That paper's Fig. 6 inspired Fig. 25 above.

399. Dings et al. 2000.

Gains in airplane efficiency are projected to keep on decelerating to 2025, causing a two- to three-fold "efficiency gap" compared to the best models then available.

A 95%-advanced-composite advanced tactical fighter airframe design turned out to be one-third lighter but two-thirds cheaper than its 72%-metal predecessor.

especially those less than 600 miles, decrease their ratio of cruise flight to less efficient air and ground modes. But big efficiency gains can be had in all sizes, and regional jets may displace some larger airplanes.[400]

Improving different parts of the integrated airplane system tends to be synergistic. Boeing says[401] that as composites make *7E7* lighter but more spacious (Fig. 25a), its one-fifth drop in fuel intensity, vs. a comparably sized *767–300*, will come 40% from better engines,[402] 30% from better airframe materials, aerodynamics, and systems architecture, and the other 30% from "cycling the design": more efficient engines and better lift/drag ratio reduces fuel loading, thus optimizing requirements for the wing and landing gear, thus saving even more weight and fuel, and so on. This "design spiral" is like that of ultralight cars, only more so, because the vehicle is carried by wings rather than wheels. And as with composite cars, composite airplane structures reduce weight while adding other benefits, including lower cost. Airbus's proposed future composite fuselage aims to cut basic fuselage weight by 30% and cost by 40% while eliminating structural fatigue and corrosion (both maintenance concerns) and improving passenger comfort.[403] Moreover, much of the *7E7* and *A380* composite is not advanced polymer composite but "glare"—composite-reinforced metal—leaving even more room for further weight savings.

Some of the efficiency typically projected in design studies tends to get lost in translation into an actual commercial airplane. But conversely, the industry studies we've relied upon—which come out close to our own findings, as Fig. 25 shows—don't include all significant options. For example, a 1994–96 military project suggests that higher advanced-composite fractions could save even more weight and cost than normally assumed: a 95%-composite advanced tactical fighter airframe design turned out to be one-third lighter but two-thirds cheaper than its 72%-metal predecessor.[404] This approach would be especially advantageous in a Blended-Wing-Body passenger aircraft (Fig. 25c)—an advanced design we favor for *State of the Art,* hard to make with *Conventional Wisdom'*s tube-and-wing metal-forming techniques, but ideally suited to molded advanced composites.

In addition, improvements in the air transportation system and logistics, chiefly from information technology, are expected to save an additional 5–10% of system fuel at negative cost, both in the air and on the ground.

400. Lee et al. 2004.

401. Pole 2003.

402. Typically these use lighter, stronger materials at higher temperatures and pressures. Only about a fourth to a third of fuel energy typically moves the aircraft; the rest is discharged as the engine's waste heat (Lee et al. 2004). This isn't for lack of trying—modern engines use single-crystal titanium blades, and peak temperatures are about one-third that of the surface of the sun—but remarkably, further 10–30% improvements are in store.

403. Kupke & Kolax 2004.

404. This DARPA-funded Integrated Technology for Affordability (IATA) design project was conducted in 1994–96 at the Lockheed-Martin Skunk Works® with support from Alliant Techsystems, Dow-UTL, and AECL, and briefed on 20 September 2000 to the Defense Science Board panel "Improving Fuel Efficiency of Weapons Platforms" by D.F. Taggart, then chief engineer of Hypercar, Inc. and previously leader of the IATA effort at the Skunk Works. Although too revolutionary at the time to find a customer, it clearly showed that the same radical simplifications of structure and manufacturing (including fastenerless self-fixturing assembly) that an advanced-composites-dominated design has brought to cars (Lovins & Cramer 2004) should also work for aircraft, both military and civilian. In this instance, compared with the JAST 140 conventional design, the IATA wing/body design was 33% lighter, had a lower recurring production cost (by 77% at T1, 65% at T100, 73% at T250), and had a 48% lower nonrecurring production cost and orders of magnitude fewer parts.

> **Figure 26: Next-generation airplanes.** L–R: Interior vision of Boeing's mostly-composite long-range *7E7 Dreamliner*, to enter service in 2008 with 15–20% fuel saving at no greater cost; Northrop flying-wing *B-2* bomber, showing how the low-signature engines of a Blended-Wing-Body design can be packed inside; artist's conception of a civilian BWB airplane without this potentially efficiency-improving feature;[405] and an artist's conception of a civilian BWB with ultra-efficient engine technology, embedded wing propulsion, and boundary-layer ingestion engine inlets with active flow control.

Many air-traffic-management innovations are also expected to increase safety despite higher traffic volume. All these improvements together could save 45% of EIA's projected 2025 airplane fuel intensity at an average cost of 46¢/gal of saved aviation fuel using *State of the Art* technologies, or 21% at 67¢/gal with *Conventional Wisdom* options. Details are in *Technical Annex*, Ch. 12. Fitting the pattern that emerged in several analyses of road vehicles, the more advanced *State of the Art* technologies tend to save more energy at comparable or lower cost because they use more integrative platform designs that capture more synergies, achieving expanding rather than diminishing returns to investments in saving fuel.

Just as today's car fleet is only half as efficient as a *Prius*, the U.S. passenger jet fleet is only about two-thirds as efficient as a *777*. By 2025, the best new planes could get 2.9× the seat-miles per gallon of today's fleet average, or 2.3× more than EIA's projection, leaving a huge overhang of unbought efficiency. The barriers to efficient aircraft are not necessarily only technological, but partly the understandable conservatism of the manufacturers and regulators, and chiefly, as with light vehicles, arise from business dynamics. Although Boeing appears to be pricing the 20%-more-efficient *7E7* at little or no—even negative (note 663, p. 157)—extra cost, most airlines can't afford rapid fleet replacements, and airframes fly for 20–50 years, usually as hand-me-downs to small airlines, cargo carriers, and developing countries. Airlines are a great industry but a bad business: as Warren Buffett famously calculated,[406] U.S. airlines have collectively earned zero cumulative net profit since the Wright brothers (1903–2003), to which Southwest Airlines' Herb Kelleher added a decade ago, "If the Wright brothers were alive today, Wilbur would have to fire Orville to reduce costs."[407] Bankrupt or capital-strapped operators can't afford to buy the best that technological innovators can make, but adoption can be greatly accelerated, as we'll propose on pp. 154–159.

> Over the next two decades, advanced airplanes can save 45% of projected fuel at 46¢ a gallon. Many of the most sophisticated technologies will cost less than small, incremental savings.

> The U.S. airline industry has run a cumulative net financial loss since the Wright brothers, and remains handicapped by fuel inefficiency.

405. Holmes 2002. The *B-2* achieved a very low radar signature at the expense of fuel economy because of engine airflow distortion. A commercial BWB airplane's buried engines could save fuel, due to smaller exposed surface area, if they used novel active airflow control devices to avoid either a sharp s-bend or a long but heavy and high-drag s-duct.

406. As of 1995, after which the industry made a little money but then lost far more.

407. Jones 1994.

Military vehicles

Huge efficiency gains by the Pentagon—the world's largest oil buyer—could make military force more effective, improve force protection, and cut defense costs by more than $10 billion a year.

Military use of oil is only 1.6% of 2000 and 1.5% of projected 2025 national total use (Fig. 6). However, its implications for security and the macro-economy are disproportionate. In particular, its ability to accelerate a massive technological shift in the civilian economy, as it did with microchips, merits extended discussion here.

DoD buys five billion gallons a year—enough to drive every U.S. car coast-to-coast every four years.

War is among the most energy-intensive human activities, consuming about two-fifths of total U.S. energy in 1941–45.[408] The ~$0.4-trillion/y, 3-million-person Department of Defense (DoD)—reportedly the nation's oldest and largest organization—operates 600,000 structures on 30 million acres in 6,000 locations in 146 countries; 550 public utility systems; hundreds of thousands of land vehicles; hundreds of ocean-going vessels; and more than 20,000 aircraft. Mainly to fuel these platforms, DoD spends upwards of $5 billion a year on energy. It is the largest U.S. buyer of energy, using 1.1% of national and 85% of government energy in 2002. DoD is probably also the world's largest oil buyer—five billion gallons a year, enough to drive every U.S. car coast-to-coast every four years. If the Pentagon were a country, it would rank in the top third of energy users worldwide.

Fighting an intensive Gulf war uses oil at about the same rate at which the U.S. imports oil from Kuwait.

Out of every eight barrels that fueled the Allies' victory over oil-starved Nazi Germany and Japan in World War II, seven came from American wells.[409] That would be impossible today, when warfare is ~15 times as oil-intensive[410] and most U.S. oil is imported. In 2001, U.S. warplanes over Iraq were fueled partly with oil from Iraq, then the nation's sixth largest supplier.[411] In Operations Desert Shield/Desert Storm (1990–91), 75% of oil was sourced in-theater from cooperative Gulf neighbors; Saudi Arabia provided 21 million gallons a day. In the 2002 Afghan campaign, 95% of the Defense Logistics Agency's half-billion gallons of fuel was trucked in from Pakistan, Uzbekhistan, and elsewhere in Central Asia, including Russian jet fuel left over from the 1980s Soviet/Afghan war.[412]

Of the gross tonnage moved when the Army deploys, ~70% is fuel. The Army directly uses only ~$0.2 billion worth of fuel a year, but pays ~$3.2 billion a year to maintain 20,000 active-duty and 40,000 reserve personnel to move it.

The fuel logistics burden

Fighting an intensive Gulf war uses oil, mostly for aircraft,[413] at about the same rate at which the U.S. imports oil from Kuwait.[414] That use is tiny in world oil markets: two wars in Iraq plus one in Afghanistan used a total of only ~103 Mbbl—1.5% as much as the U.S. uses in a year, or 5% of the two billion barrels Saddam Hussein's forces torched in Kuwait.[415]

408. War is both expensive—in 2000 $, an estimated $250 billion for World War I, $2.75 trillion for World War II, and $450 billion for the Vietnam War—and more energy-intensive than the civilian economy's average, by factors estimated at very roughly 1.5, 2, and 3 respectively (Smil 2004).

409. Painter 2002; Klare 2004.

410. Comparing, for example, the 1991 Gulf War with the liberation of Europe at the end of World War II: Copulos 2004.

411. Ebel 2002.   412–415. See next page.

Still, it's an immense logistical strain to deliver that much oil that quickly into theater, often to austere sites, and especially into thirsty platforms that mustn't run dry. Fuel logistics, as much as anything, prevents America's most lethally effective forces from being rapidly deployable and its most rapidly deployable forces from assuredly winning.[416]

Weapons themselves are seldom[417] very energy-consumptive—they merely focus energy into a specific zone of destruction for an extremely short time—but the platforms used to carry weapons systems tend to be extremely energy-intensive and must be fueled by a large, complex, globe-girdling, and (in its own right) energy-intensive logistics chain. Of the gross tonnage moved when the Army deploys, ~70% is fuel, and transporting that fuel to the bases or depots from which it's redistributed costs about 8% as much as the fuel itself.[418] Over 60% of Air Force fuel is used not by fighters or bombers but for airlifting people and materiel, including fuel.[419]

Military efficiency potential

The energy intensity of land, sea, and air platforms reflects four needs: superior tactical performance (speed, maneuverability, endurance); carrying and delivering munitions; carrying armor and other forms of protection; and resisting or offsetting battle damage. All can be systematically improved through better technologies, tactics, and operational concepts. Within these four unique operational constraints, it is feasible, just as in civilian vehicles, to reduce military platforms' fuel use by methodically applying technologies that cut weight, drag, idling, and auxiliary power consumption and that raise the efficiency of converting fuel into motion through engines, powertrains, and propulsors. In military as civilian vehicles, "The most important factor in reducing...demand for fuel... is reduc-

In 2001, U.S. warplanes over Iraq were fueled partly with oil from Iraq, then the nation's sixth largest supplier.

Despite the special requirements of tactical performance, force protection, munitions carriage, and battle damage resistance, military platforms can save oil in the same ways as civilian ones— by cutting weight, drag, idling, auxiliary power, and powertrain losses—only the savings are greater because military platforms are less efficient to start with and their fuel logistics and its vulnerability make savings far more valuable.

412. Erwin 2002a; Cohen 2003. However, for the first two months of Operation Enduring Freedom, "major shortages of fuel plagued the force" despite half of 6,800 Air Force sorties, "flying the wings off airplanes," being for fuel resupply, which Under Secretary of Defense Pete Aldridge described as "a terrible way" to deliver fuel. Granger 2003.

413. In FY2002, 56% of all DoD energy use for both platforms and facilities, and 85% of the oil DoD contracted to procure, was aviation fuel (DESC 2003). In the first seven months of 2002 Afghan operations, only 7% of fuel went to the Army (Cohen 2003).

414. In 1987, the Department of Energy estimated that DoD energy consumption could double or triple in a war (DOE 1987). Applying these factors to the petroleum fraction (79%) of total FY2001 DoD energy consumption (0.774 quadrillion BTU/y—40% less than FY1987, due largely to force reductions) implies that war could raise DoD's oil use by ~0.3–0.6 Mbbl/d, consistent with the Defense Energy Support Center's normal provision of 100 Mbbl/y or 0.27 Mbbl/d. For so long as a wartime optempo (pace and intensity of operations) is sustained, that rise would equate to 12–24% of net imports from the Gulf, or to the 2000 rate of net imports from Kuwait (0.27 Mbbl/d) or Iraq (0.62 Mbbl/d). Actual fuel use in Desert Shield/Desert Storm was 1.9b bbl (0.25 Mbbl/d crude-equivalent); for the first 42 days of Operation Iraqi Freedom, at least 0.24 Mbbl/d (0.12 Mbbl/d over the first 84 days, 0.054 Mbbl/d during 19 Mar 2003 through 9 Feb 2004); and for the less intensive Operation Enduring Freedom (in and around Afghanistan), 0.050 Mbbl/d (1 Oct 2001–11 June 2003). By 9 Feb 2004, these four operations had consumed a total of 4.5 billion gal, energy-equivalent to 103 Mbbl of crude oil—as much oil as the U.S. uses for all purposes every five days. Sources: Cohen 2003; Erwin 2002a; Volk 2004; DESC 2003–04.

415. Laherrere 2004.

416. Logistics failures have defeated generals from Napoleon to Rommel (Van Creveld 1977).

417. The main exception is nuclear weapons because of their exotic materials and the huge energy inputs needed to enrich uranium and produce plutonium. Smil (2004) estimates that at least 5% of all U.S. and Soviet commercial energy used during 1950–90 went into developing and producing these weapons and their delivery systems—not implausible in view of their whole-system cost.

418. In FY2002 for all Services (DESC 2003), dividing delivery cost (p. 32) by value of petroleum products purchased (p. 19). 419. DSB 2001.

Abrams **tanks' inefficient and mostly-idling ~1968 gas turbine halves their fuel efficiency. This delayed the invasion of Iraq by more than a month to stockpile the extra fuel.**

The Air Force spent 84 percent of its fuel-delivery cost on the 6 percent of its gallons that were delivered in midair.

420. NAS/NRC/CETS 1999, p. 148.

421–441. See Box 11.

ing the weight of…vehicles."[420] But there are two key differences: *in military platforms, fuel efficiency is immensely more valuable*—not only in dollars but in lives, and potentially even in the margin between victory and defeat—and *most military structures and engines use decades-old technologies,* offering even more scope for improvement. Box 11 (pp. 86–90) illustrates these valuable opportunities to save oil in DoD's existing inventory.

Beyond the retrofits summarized in Box 11, there's even greater potential scope for more fight with less fuel at lower cost. *Technical Annex*, Ch. 13, presents an initial sketch of how the findings of a seminal 2001 Defense Science Board report could apply to the estimated 2025 fleet of land, sea, and air platforms. The result: 61% *Conventional Wisdom* and 66% *State of the Art* reductions in petroleum-based fuel use by all DoD land, sea, and air platforms, not counting most of the fuel saved by transporting less metal and fuel.

Such radical *State of the Art* savings may surprise those unaware that DoD's official Army After Next goals for 2020 include 75% battlefield fuel (continued on p. 91)

11: Saving oil in existing military platforms

The nearly 70-ton *M1A2 Abrams* main battle tank—the outstanding fighting machine of U.S. (and Saudi, Kuwaiti, and Egyptian) armored forces—is propelled at up to 42 mph on- or 30 mph off-road by a 1,500-hp gas turbine,[421] and averages around 0.3–0.6 mpg.[422] Its ~20–40 ton-

421. Rather than the diesel engine used in all other Army heavy land platforms. Diesels are historically heavier and bulkier, but may not be any more, and use less fuel, which has its own weight and bulk (Erwin 2000).

422. Its nominal fuel consumption (from a 505-gal fuel capacity) ranges from 60 gal/h gross-country to 30+ "while operating at a tactical ideal" to 10 in basic idle mode; nominal consumption averages ~37.5 gal/h; nominal cruising range is 265 mi/505 gal = 0.52 mpg (GlobalSecurity.org 2004). However, worse values, such as cross-country ~0.3 mpg and idling ~16 gal/h, have been reported (Periscope1.com, undated).

423. The late-1960s-technology AGT 1500 gas-turbine engine, out of production since 1992, was supposed to be replaced starting in FY03 or FY04 by the LV100 engine, which was predicted to increase range by up to 26%, halve idling fuel use, and quintuple the AGT 1500's notably poor reliability (Geae.com, undated). The AGT 1500's rated nominal fuel intensity was an unimpressive 0.45 lb/shp-h (pounds-per-shaft-horsepower-hour) (Turbokart.com, undated) or ~31%—much worse at part-load. However, cancellation of *Crusader*, a heavy mobile artillery system that was also to use the LV100, raised (Continued next page.)

mpg is surprisingly close to the ~42 ton-mpg of today's average new light vehicle; the tank simply weighs ~34 times as much, half for armor. But there's more to be done than improving its ~1968 gas turbine:[423] for ~73% of its operating hours, *Abrams* idles that ~1,100-kW gas turbine at less than 1% efficiency to run a ~5-kW "hotel load"—ventilation, lights, cooling, and electronics. This, coupled with its inherent engine inefficiency, cuts *Abrams*'s average fuel efficiency about in half,[424] requiring extra fuel whose stockpiling for the Gulf War delayed the ground forces' readiness to fight by more than a month.[425]

This is one of many striking examples that emerged in a 1991–2001 Defense Science Board (DSB) task force on which one of us (ABL) served under the chairmanship of former astronaut, NASA director, naval aviator, and Vice Admiral (Ret.) Richard Truly. This widely noticed

(continued on next page)

unclassified report[426] covering all Services' land, sea, and air platforms found more than 100 effective fuel-saving technologies that could save much, perhaps most, of their fuel while never impairing and often improving warfighting capability.

The DSB panel examined why a capable meritocracy with more wants than funds hadn't already achieved such large and lucrative savings. The institutional reasons are complex, but one of the biggest is false price signals due to lack of activity-based costing. When weapons platforms are designed and bought, the cost of their fuel has been assumed to equal the average wholesale price charged by the Defense Energy Support Center (DESC), historically around a dollar per gallon. Logistics—moving stuff around—occupies roughly a third of DOD's budget and half its personnel. But when designing and buying platforms, logistics is considered *free,* because the cost-benefit analyses used to justify investments in efficiency are based on the DESC price for fuel, *excluding the cost of delivering it.* This understates delivered fuel cost by a factor of at least three, perhaps several times three (Fig. 27[427])—even by tens or hundreds in some specific cases.

Abrams illustrates why. Since gas turbines, inefficient at best, become extremely so at low loads,[428] a small APU matched to the small, fairly steady 5-kW "hotel load" would save 96% of the fuel wasted in idling the huge gas turbine. *Abrams* was designed with no APU on the assumption that its fuel would cost ~$1/gal with zero delivery cost. But to keep up with a rapid armored advance that outruns resupply trucks, bladders of fuel may have to be slung beneath cargo helicopters and leapfrogged 400+ km into theater in a three-stage relay (eight helicopters at the front end to get one to its destination), consuming most of the fuel in order to carry the rest. Delivery cost can then rise to an eye-popping $600 a gallon, becoming astronomical beyond 400 km.[429] Even delivery by land to the Forward Edge of the Battle Area (FEBA) costs ~$30/gal. If *Abrams*'s designers had considered fuel transport cost, they'd probably have designed the tank very differently. Yet misled by false cost signals, they didn't leave room under armor for an APU. The DSB panel suggested a Russian-style pragmatic improvisation: buy a Honda genset at Home Depot and strap it onto the back of the tank. Most of the time, nobody is shooting at the tank, and the genset will save nearly half *Abrams*'s fuel. If the genset ever gets shot away, *Abrams* is no worse off than it is right now. (The Army has instead begun developing an APU to squeeze into scant under-armor spaces.)

(continued on next page)

(fn 424 continued)
that engine's unit cost, leaving *Abrams* re-engining in limbo (Erwin 2003). There may also be other alternatives, such as the experimental Semi Closed Cycle Compact Turbine Engine, expected to more than double AGT 1500's efficiency yet occupy far less volume (Salyer 1999, slide 33).

424. Using *M1A1* data (79% of the 2000 *M1* fleet), the fleet-average utilization is 205 h/y or 411 mi/y, totaling 55 h/y mobility and 150 h/y idle at 12 gal/h, of which the Army believes 98 h/y or 65% could be displaced by a 0.5 gal/h APU, saving 46% of the tank's total fuel consumption (Moran 2000, slide 14). (The Army calculates average savings of only 32% for the *M1A2* because it assumes the APU uses 4 gal/h. We suspect more advanced APUs could use less fuel and run longer.) Potential APU savings are largely additional to those of making the main engine more efficient, which would easily bring the Army's APU-saving estimate (a fleet-weighted average of 43%) to well above 50%.

425. Salyer 1999, slide 8, assuming a corresponding reduction in the fuel and infrastructure inserted.

426. DSB 2001. Summarized by Truly (2001); in Book 2002; and in Ginsburg 2001.

427. DSB 2001; the previously unassembled data used to compile this chart come respectively from pp. 39, 4 and 20, and 17, adding only the Navy's information about the split of oil delivery modes between oiler (70%) and pierside (30%) at respective costs of $0.64/gal and $0.05/gal (Alan Roberts [OSD], personal communication, 3 April 2001).

428. To produce power without stalling (being aerodynamic devices), gas turbines must keep spinning rapidly regardless of their load; they cannot simply run very slowly like an internal-combustion engine.

Fuel logistics hamstrings the Army

Fuel-wasting design doesn't just cost money; it weakens warfighting. Each tank is trailed by several lumbering 5,000-gallon tankers. An armored division may use 20, perhaps even 40, times as many daily tons of fuel as it does of munitions—around 600,000 gallons a day. Of the Army's top ten battlefield fuel guzzlers, only #5 (*Abrams* tanks) and #10 (*Apache* helicopters) are combat vehicles; three of the top four are trucks,[430] some carrying fuel—not unlike the six-mule Civil War wagons that hauled roughly a ton of materiel, half of it feed.[431] Some 55% of the fuel the Army takes to the battlefield doesn't even get to front-line combat units, but is consumed by echelons above corps and by rear units.[432] This big logistical tail slows deployment, constrains maneuver, and requires a lot of equipment and people. The Army directly uses only ~$0.2 billion worth of fuel a year, but pays ~$3.2 billion a year to maintain 20,000 active-duty personnel (at ~$100,000/y) and 40,000 reserve personnel (at ~$30,000/y) to move that fuel.

(continued on next page)

Figure 27: Uncounted costs of delivering fuel to weapons platforms
Summary of Defense Science Board panel's 2001 findings of a severalfold difference between the undelivered "wholesale" fuel cost assumed when requiring, designing, and procuring weapons platforms (blue) and the "retail" price they actually pay in peacetime (magenta). Combat delivery to the platform can cost far more, and even in peacetime, the magenta bars omit many large infrastructure and staff costs (p. 267).

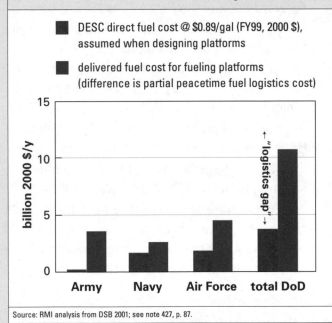

■ DESC direct fuel cost @ $0.89/gal (FY99, 2000 $), assumed when designing platforms

■ delivered fuel cost for fueling platforms (difference is partial peacetime fuel logistics cost)

Fuel used to deploy Army assets via Navy or Air Force lift is ascribed to those Services; the size of these allocations is unknown, but over 60% of Air Force fuel is used for lift. Some Air Force refueling (~16% in Operation Desert Storm) serves Navy and Marine Corps aircraft. Army and Navy data shown are for 1997; Air Force, 1999; Navy includes Marine Corps. Major omissions from the magenta bars include: Army's oil-related equipment and facilities and their ownership cost; Army's fuel delivery into platforms, which can cost hundreds of times the blue bar; Navy's purchase of new oilers; and Air Force's acquisition of ~100 new aerial tankers (now proposed, for tens of billions of dollars). At the FY02 DESC average fuel cost of $1.29/gal (FY02, 2000 $), the delivered fuel price probably rose to ~$12–14b. The direct fuel cost, shown as $3.7b at the FY99 DESC fuel charge, has since risen above $6b in FY2004–05 (2004 $) due mainly to higher volumes delivered (the DESC FY04 fuel cost was $0.91/gal, 2004 $). Delivery not just into theater but into the platform can become enormously costlier in combat: for land forces in Iraq in 2003, the fully burdened logistics cost reportedly averaged around $130/gal (2003 $), or about a hundred times the DESC direct fuel price to which the platforms were designed.

Source: RMI analysis from DSB 2001; see note 427, p. 87.

---

429. Salyer 1999, slide 7.

430. For Army battlefield units broadly: Hunt 2003. Four of the Army's top ten battlefield users are trucks: heavy linehaul, medium tactical, heavy-equipment transporter, and HMMWV ("Humvee"). The Army's quarter-million trucks, driving 823 million miles a year, are sometimes said to be the world's largest fleet: Higgins 2002; Gorsich 2000.

431. Hoeper 1999. This is not a new problem: NRC (1999), at p. 67, quotes Sun Tze's *The Art of War*, ~100 BC, as saying: "Transportation of provisions itself consumes 20 times the amount transported." This appears to be a reference to **2:14**, where Sun Tze notes that foraging off the enemy is always to be preferred, because one cartload of his provisions is equivalent to 20 of your own (since you haven't borne its logistical burden). A summary of military logistics history (Gabriel & Metz 1992, Ch. 3) suggests that Alexander the Great's triumphs were importantly based on a logistics-based early Revolution in Military Affairs.

432. Erwin 2002. The article notes a TACOM finding that if an Army Brigade Combat Team used hybrid vehicles, their range would increase by 180 miles, and each 100 miles would reduce the brigade's fuel needs by 4,000 gallons, nearly a full tanker-truckload.

Abrams tanks idle their main engine ~73% of the time, at less than 1% efficiency, to run a small "hotel load"
(limiting their "silent watch" capability to about a half-hour) because their fuel delivery was assumed to be free.
On the battlefield, rapid fuel delivery can cost $600 a gallon.

This logistics personnel cost thus multiplies the $0.2b direct fuel cost by 16, plus further pyramiding gear and people—and represents a timely opportunity to deploy a whole division of personnel from tail to tooth. In a specifically simulated example, the Army After Next equivalent of today's heavy divisions would save not only ~$0.33 million/d in battlefield fuel, but also would eliminate the need for 9,276 oil, maintenance, and other personnel costing eight times as much—about $2.5 million/d—not counting additional personnel and equipment savings stretching back to the homeland.[433] By 2025, an estimated science and technology investment totaling on the order of $2 billion would be saving ~$1.2 billion *each year*, and rising fast, just on oil-related personnel and infrastructure.[434]

Unarmored fuel carriers are also vulnerable. Attacks on in-theater and rear logistics assets can make a fuel-hungry combat system grind to a halt—as it did, to great upset, in a recent wargame that was stopped because this tactic was considered unfair. (The U.S. is fortunate that the distinctly unsporting Saddam Hussein didn't use it more.) Yet the warfighting benefits of fuel

433. Salyer 2000, slide 19.

434. Salyer 2000, slide 25.

435. The short-run marginal cost components for FY99, in 2000 $, are $17.03 air-to-air cost, $0.22/gal delivery into the tanker on the ground, and $0.89/gal DESC fuel charge delivered to the airbase (DSB 2001).

436. Loitering is important for killing time-sensitive, high-value targets using near-real-time intelligence. Of course, better engines' performance can be exploited by any combination of range, loiter, payload, or other performance metrics. For example, better (IHPTEP) engines, the DSB panel was told, could let Naval combat air patrols carry more payload (due to 36% lower takeoff gross weight) or stay out longer (44% lower fuel burn at constant mission). In antisubmarine helicopters, better engines could increase radius by 430% at constant payload and loiter time, or increase payload by 80% at constant radius and loiter. Such numbers represent very valuable force multipliers, amounting to free new "virtual" ships and aircraft.

economy—in deployability, agility, range, speed, reliability, autonomy, dominant maneuver in an extended battlespace, etc.—are as invisible to platform designers as logistics cost: none of these advantages is yet valued by DoD buyers, so inefficient platforms keep getting bought, wasting oil and money and hobbling warfighters.

Air Force: gas stations in the sky

What about the Air Force? The venerable *B-52H* bombers now being flown by the children of their original pilots (and structurally capable of flying until at least 2037) have inefficient, low-bypass, 1950s-technology engines. By 2010, those could be refitted to today's commercial engines, using 33% less fuel to fly 46% farther. On its usual long-distance and long-loiter-time missions, *B-52H* typically needs midair refueling costing ~$18.1 a gallon (2000 $).[435] (That cost doesn't include at least 55 tankers the Air Force will soon need to replace for more than $10 billion.) Thus the Air Force in FY1999 paid $1.8 billion for two billion gallons of fuel, but delivering that fuel into the aircraft added another $2.6 billion, so the actual *delivered* fuel bill was $4.4 billion: the Air Force spent 84 percent of its fuel-delivery cost on the 6 percent of its gallons that were delivered in midair. Counting that delivery cost, re-engining *B-52H* would repay twice its cost; greatly reduce or even eliminate midair refueling; free up scarce tankers and ramp space for other missions; and enable bombers to loiter for hours over their targets.[436] A Defense Science Board panel in April 2003 unanimously recommended promptly re-engining the *B-52H* fleet. The $3–3.5 billion cost could be privately financed by engine-makers as a shared-savings deal or even a "Power-by-the-Hour™" service

(continued on next page)

lease.[437] A decision is still pending, but on 25 May 2004, DoD's proposed $23.5b 100-tanker acquisition was suspended for further review.

Navy: communities afloat

The Navy has led all Services in institutionalizing energy savings—partly by letting skippers keep for their own ships' needs up to 40% of the fuel dollars they saved.[438] Naval energy savings of 26% during 1985–2002, saving a half-billion dollars, included such innovations as installing fuel-flow gauges and performance curves to optimize cruise speed within mission requirements, and shutting off unneeded engines. The Navy is on track to save 35% by 2010.[439] Just the FY2001 efforts saved 1 Mbbl worth $42 million—enough fuel to support 38,000 steaming hours, and equivalent to getting free fuel for 19 destroyers.[440] But there's far more still to do.

Visiting several surface and submarine vessels during the 1990s, this report's senior author noticed many Naval design details as inefficient as those in civilian buildings and equipment, despite the sixfold higher cost of onboard electricity. Of course, the Navy has unique design imperatives: ships must go far and fast through all the world's climates, project power, protect crews, and fight through gales and missile strikes. Being shot at demands serious redun-

dancy and special operational methods. Cramped space often requires small and twisting pipes and ducts, especially when those that get installed second must snake around those that got installed first. Inefficient modes of running equipment may be required for prudence under certain threat conditions or operational requirements. Nonetheless, the Secretary of the Navy and the Deputy Chief of Naval Operations suspected an opportunity. In 1999–2000 they therefore invited Rocky Mountain Institute (RMI) to examine "hotel loads" on a typical surface combatant—the USS *Princeton*, a billion-dollar *Aegis* cruiser then in the top efficiency quartile of her class, and burning ~$6 million worth of oil a year, a third to a half of it to generate electricity.

RMI's engineers found nearly $1 million/y in retrofittable hotel-load and operational savings in such mundane devices as pumps, fans, chillers, and lights and in the mode of operation of their gas-turbine power generators—uses that consume nearly one-third of the Navy's non-aviation fuel.[441] Such a saving per hull would extrapolate to ~$0.3 billion/y for the whole Navy. The potential savings RMI found were several times the 11% previously estimated by the able engineers at Naval Sea Systems Command (NAVSEA). If fully implemented, RMI's recommendations could save an estimated 20–50% of *Princeton*'s electricity and hence 10–25% of her fuel (perhaps even 50–75% if combined with other potential improvements in power generation and propulsion), while extending range, stretching replenishment intervals, reducing signatures, and moderating machinery wear and crew heat stress. And this doesn't count a further 8% savings potential NAVSEA had already found in the propulsion, power, and combat/command systems that RMI didn't examine. An RMI suggestion for both retrofit and new-ship experiments is under review.

437. Carns 2002.

438. The Incentivized Energy Conservation Program (ENCON) (www.i-encon.com), introduced in the early 1990s and fully adopted in FY2000, is described by Pehlivan 2000. Of measured savings, up to 40% go as cash awards to the ships, 10% for ENCON training and program administration, and 50% to regional commanders to improve ships' readiness. In FY2000, the Atlantic Fleet stopped paying the cash incentives, which ENCON hopes to reinstate soon. The Pacific Fleet currently pays awards totaling $2M/y to ships that "underburn" their baseline fuel-consumption target. Minor cash bonuses also come with awards for which both Fleets compete, and other forms of recognition encourage competition between ships and between Fleets.

439. Navy Information Bureau 613 2002.

440. See Encon 2002.   441. Lovins et al. 2001.

savings, with feasibility shown by 2012, and that by 2000 the Army already considered this "achievable for combat systems."[442] For example, today's armored forces were designed to face Russian *T-72s* across the North German Plain, but nowadays their missions demand mobility. Only one ~70-ton tank fits into the heaviest normal U.S. lift aircraft,[443] so deployment is painfully slow, and when the tank arrives in the Balkans, it breaks bridges and gets stuck in the mud.[444] Army Research, leapfrogging beyond 20- to 40-ton concepts, has proposed a novel 7–10-ton tank[445] that uses ~86% less fuel (~4+ mpg), yet is said to be as lethal as current models and (thanks to active protection systems) no more vulnerable.[446] The Army reckons that such redesign could free up about 20,000 personnel—a whole division plus their equipment and their own logistical pyramid—that are needed to deliver fuel to and in theater. This would save $3-plus billion a year for theater forces, plus more costs upstream.

Yet even this transition may be only a partial interim step. A National Research Council exploration of initial Army After Next (AAN) concepts analyzed deployment of an 8,000-soldier division with ~2,000 vehicles, none exceeding 15 tons. Despite having 30% fewer troops, 48% fewer vehicles, and 30% less weight than a mid-1990s "light" infantry division—or 53% fewer troops, 75% fewer vehicles, and 88% less weight than a "heavy" armored division—the hypothetical AAN division, inserted near-vertically by rotorcraft or tiltrotorcraft, could still need, just to get to the battle area, *fuel weighing three times as much as the entire battle force.*[447] This suggests the potential logistical value of even more radical light-weighting, possibly to a <1-ton ultralight tactical/scout expeditionary vehicle analogous to the *Revolution* composite car (Box 7).[448] A little-known

> **Army Research has proposed a novel 7–10-ton tank that uses ~86% less fuel, yet is said to be as lethal as current models and no more vulnerable. Such redesign could save about 20,000 personnel needed to deliver fuel to and in theater, saving upwards of $3 billion a year.**

442. Salyer 2000, slide 23.

443. That is, *C-130* or *C-17*, which can both use short runways; in principle, a *C-5 Galaxy* can carry two *Abrams* tanks, but it needs long runways and is old and unreliable. *C-130* can lift only a 20-ton vehicle. *C-5* moved 48% of all cargo to Afghanistan and Iraq in Operations Enduring Freedom and Iraqi Freedom, but as all Services strive to get "light, lean, and lethal," such heavy lifting, "some time in the next 10–15 years,…could go away entirely as a requirement," says General Handy, Commander of U.S. Transportation Command Air Mobility Command. This is because the Army is trying to move toward equipment that can all be lifted by a *C-130* or less. However, the Air Force is modernizing its *C-5* fleet because not only lift weight drives its requirement (Tirpak 2004).

444. Newman 2000. *Abrams* is also too big and heavy to cross the Alps overland (due to bridge and tunnel constraints), so it's faster to deploy them to the Mediterranean by sea from the United States than by land from Germany.

445. Using ultralight composite structure and armor, it would be far more capable and protective than the useful family of ~10-ton-class metallic light tanks such as the British *Scorpion,* German *Wiesel,* and the U.S. *M8 AGS* and *M113 Gavin* (neither currently fielded by U.S. forces).

446. That doesn't mean invulnerable. Recently developed anti-armor weapons can reportedly defeat all known and projected forms of armor made of any materials using currently known forms of atomic and molecular bonds, even at prohibitive (meters) thicknesses. In perhaps a decade, such anti-armor technology will probably diffuse to the cheap, portable, and ubiquitous status of today's RPGs, which are themselves a significant threat, with a million tank-busting *RPG-7s* in use in 40 countries, each selling for under $1,000 (Wilson 2004). In the coevolution of arms and armor—despite great effort and much progress with active, reactive, smart, electromagnetic, dynamic, biomimetic, and other techniques—we are getting to the point where the best defense is a good offense, combined with situational awareness, agility, and stealth. This realization is one of the forces driving military transformation's move away from heavy armor; nondeployability and logistics cost and risk simply reinforce that conclusion.

447. NAS/NRC/CETS 1999. However, the panel noted potential mitigation, including, over water or very smooth terrain, the possibility of the Russian wing-in-ground concept, akin to the low-energy flight of large waterfowl just above the surface (NAS/NRC/CETS 1999, p. 68; Granger 2003, pp. 58–59).

448. Such a "*HyperVee*" platform in military use could get >60 mpg with a diesel hybrid or >90 mpg with a fuel cell, yielding ultralow sustainment, signatures, and profile. Being fast, small, and agile, it could hide behind little terrain, and its composite structure could resist small-arms fire and shrapnel with no extra weight, supplementably by light composite appliqué armor. Being thin-skinned, its tactics would presumably include UAV reconnaissance and other tools for situational awareness. It could be made occupant-liftable and field-refuelable; could carry formidable PGM or recoilless weapons; could be made air-droppable and amphibious; and could be highly deployable, with two personnel able to load ~20 weaponized units into one *C-130*. A fuel-cell version could also make ~2.5 gal of pure water per 100 miles, solving the second-biggest sustainment problem—getting drinking water to the warfighters.

When 30 *Abrams* tanks were set against 30 Baja dunebuggies armed with precision-guided munitions, the prompt result was 27 dead tanks (21 completely immobilized) and three dead dunebuggies.

1982 Army experiment suggests possible tactical value too: when 30 *Abrams* tanks were set against 30 Baja dunebuggies armed with precision-guided munitions, the prompt result was 27 dead tanks (21 completely immobilized) and three dead dunebuggies. (In a subsequent experiment, missile-toting dirtbikers apparently outgunned the tanks even worse.[449]) That exercise was done in a desert, not in a forest or city, not under chemical warfare conditions, and reportedly with unimpressive tank tactics, but it's still instructive. With different tactics, light and even ultralight forces, being fast, hard to see, and even harder to hit, may be more effective than familiar heavy forces—especially if they can get to the fight quickly and keep fighting with little sustainment while the tanks and their fuel are still en route.[450]

Such information-enabled breakthroughs are at the core of today's military transformation strategy. A light, agile Army (and a Marine Corps unencumbered by heavy armor) could greatly reduce the burdens on the Navy's and Air Force's lift platforms and their fuel use to insert, sustain, and extract those forces, creating a virtuous circle of oil savings. The Navy is finding similarly important opportunities for speedier deployment and resupply: a 1998 wargame plausibly equipped the 2021 Navy with a 500-ton ship that can carry a million pounds for 4,000 nautical miles, and with ships that can travel at 75 knots.[451] U.S. and Russian designers in 1999 were exploring ships, like Tasmanian wavecutters, that can carry over 10,000 tons for more than 10,000 nautical miles at more than 100 knots.[452] And light forces could greatly facilitate Sea Basing.

A final conceptual example illustrates the scope for major force multipliers that could be more than paid for by their fuel savings and that may even reduce capital costs up front. The Navy designs ships to carry weapons systems. RMI's *Princeton* survey found that onboard electricity, made inefficiently in part-loaded gas turbines, costs ~27¢/kWh, so the present value of saving one watt is nearly $20—not counting the weight or cost of the fuel and electrical equipment, just their direct capital and operating cost. But saving a pound of weight on a surface ship typically saves ~5–10 pounds of total weight because the engines, drives, and fuel storage systems shrink commensurately. In a ship, such "mass decompounding" is less than in an airplane but far more than in a land vehicle. So saving a watt must be worth much more than $20 present value. What is it worth, therefore, to design a watt of power requirement, or a pound, or a cubic foot, out of a Naval weapons system? Nobody knows, because the question hasn't been asked, so weapons systems have clearly not been so optimized. But organizing naval architects' "design spiral" around such whole-system value should yield far lighter, smaller, cheaper, faster, and better "Hyperships." This requires changes in the stovepiped design

449. An interesting compendium on bicycle warfare is at LBI, undated.

450. Modern doctrine for Future Combat Systems is to avoid encounter (through situational awareness and tactics), avoid detection (signature management), avoid acquisition (same plus electronic countermeasures), avoid hit (same plus active protection), avoid penetration (lightweight composite armor), and avoid kill (TACOM 2003). Collectively, these stages of protection are intended to substitute for thick, heavy, but increasingly vulnerable passive armor.

451. Hasenauer 1997.

452. NAS/NRC/CETS 1999, p. 134.

culture—so that whole systems are optimized for multiple benefits (not isolated components for single benefits) purging tradeoffs and diminishing returns, eschewing incrementalism, and rewarding the whole-system results we want. As with automaking, this isn't easy. But it's important to do before others do it to us.

Recent battlefield experience suggests that the Joint Chiefs' transformational doctrine emphasizing light, mobile, agile, flexible, easily sustained forces is vital to modern warfighting. It's very far from most of the forces now fielded; heavy-metal tradition dies hard; porkbarrel politics impedes fundamental reform. But warfighters increasingly see rising risk and cost in vulnerable and slow logistics,[453] compounded by cumbersome procurement that cedes America's technology edge to adversaries who exploit Moore's Law by buying modern gear at Radio Shack. Innovations to turn these weaknesses into strengths could save prodigious amounts of oil, pollution, and money. We estimate that comprehensive military fuel efficiency could probably save upwards of ten billion deficit-financed dollars a year—plausibly several times that (p. 267) if we fully count the scope for redeploying personnel, avoiding vast pyramids of fuel-support personnel and equipment, and achieving the full force multipliers inherent in wringing unneeded oil out of the whole DoD asset base.

Whether such innovations also make the world more secure depends on how well citizens exercise their responsibility to apply military power wisely and create a world where its use becomes less necessary. If we get that right, we can all be safe and feel safe in ways that work better and cost less than present arrangements, and fewer of the men and women in the Armed Forces need be put in harm's way. Military leadership in saving oil is a key, for it will help the civilian sector—by example, training, and technology spinoffs—to make oil less needed worldwide, hence less worth fighting over. We'll return on p. 261 to that vital geopolitical opportunity, which could prove to be DoD's greatest contribution to its national-security mission. If our sons and daughters twice went to the Gulf in ~0.5-mile-per-gallon tanks and 17-feet-per-gallon-equivalent aircraft carriers *because* we didn't put them in 29-mile-per-gallon light vehicles, that's a military *and* a civilian problem—one that both communities must work together to solve.

Feedstocks and other nonfuel uses of oil

One-eighth of U.S. oil is used to make materials, not burned as fuel. More than a fourth of that "feedstock" is used to make asphalt for roads, roofs, and the like. The United States is projected to have 6.34 million lane-miles of paved highways in 2025, 99.6% of them paved mainly with asphalt, a bitumen-rich refined product. Our economic, civil engineering,

> If our sons and daughters twice went to the Gulf in ~0.5-mile-per-gallon tanks and 17-feet-per-gallon-equivalent aircraft carriers because we didn't put them in 29-mile-per-gallon light vehicles, that's a military and a civilian problem—one that both communities can help solve.

453. *Quartermaster Professional Bulletin* 2002.

> Half of 2025 asphalt, and $8 billion a year in paving costs, can be saved by mixing it with rubber crumbs from old tires, making roads' top layer thinner but longer-lived. Uncertain but large savings are also likely in synthetic materials made from oil.

and materials-flow analysis finds that a mixture of asphalt with crumb rubber from old tires[454] can, if fully implemented, replace virtually all of that surfacing asphalt. This asphalt-rubber mixture has long been proven in service from Arizona to Alberta, and has become cost-competitive since its patent expired in 1992. If fully implemented by 2025, it can save 60% of paving asphalt, 51% of total asphalt in all uses, or 0.36 Mbbl/d of crude oil, at an average net cost of *negative* $64/bbl (*Technical Annex*, Ch. 14). That is, asphalt-rubber paving costs less than traditional asphalt paving because it uses a thinner paving layer that also lasts longer, resulting in lower materials- and handling-costs. This decreases total highway agency cost per lane-mile by ~15%, and would save agencies ~$7.7 billion/y in 2025—even more if combined with other paving innovations that make surfaces more pervious, resin-enriched, or light-colored. Moreover, with our *State of the Art* technologies, switching to light-colored pavements can avoid 0.13 percent of U.S. natural-gas use in 2025, because by reflecting the sun's heat they reduce air-conditioning loads that are met on hot afternoons chiefly by inefficient gas-fired combustion turbines (pp. 113–114). The reduced "urban heat island" effect valuably reduces photochemical smog formation. By staying cooler, the pavement also lasts longer and reduces fuel use for vehicular air-conditioners. Asphalt-rubber pavement cracks less and reduces both noise and skids; major accidents fall by two-fifths, or on wet days by half—a valuable benefit to which we assign no economic value.

On the assumption that petrochemical feedstocks will grow in proportion to U.S. industrial output and be trimmed in proportion to industrial direct-fuel intensity, EIA projects that petrochemical feedstocks (excluding asphalt, road oil, and lubricants) will be 9% of 2025 U.S. oil use (including LPG), or 2.5 Mbbl/d. A large portion of all petrochemical feedstocks go to manufacture plastics (apparently ~48% in 1998).[455] And ~63% of the energy consumed by plastics is for feedstocks, the remainder to fuel their processing.[456] Together, plastics-industry feedstocks and their process fuel now use ~4.5% of total U.S. energy.[457] Yet U.S. use of plastics per dollar of GDP shows signs of saturating just as all other major materials have done.[458] Plastics are also an important target for deliberate materials-efficiency

454. In 1998, 270 million tires were scrapped in the U.S., with 70% being recycled or exported according to EERE 2003a. Estimates for tire stockpiles in the U.S. range upwards from 500 million, or 6 MT of rubber. Our analysis finds plenty of available mass of tires even if they become much lighter in *State of the Art* light vehicles.

455. EIA's 1998 *Manufacturing Energy Consumption Survey* (MECS) data (EIA 1998) imply that the inferred use of ~423 trillion BTU of petroleum feedstocks by the plastics sector was ~48% of the 886 trillion BTU of total 1998 petroleum feedstocks other than for asphalt, road oil, and lubricants (EIA 2003c, Table 1.15). We assume this fraction prevails through 2025, implying a 2025 plastics-industry petroleum input of 0.99 Mbbl/d.

456. The MECS data (EIA 1998) show that in 1998, 394 trillion BTU of energy in all forms got used in plastics processing out of the total 1,067 trillion BTU (37%) of first use energy; the remaining 63% was thus feedstocks. We adopt this split as probably conservative for petroleum feedstocks, whose quantities in this sector were withheld by EIA. For the purposes of these calculations, plastics are defined as NAICS Code 325211 only—probably an underestimate, as it doesn't account for the complex value web of polymers and petrochemical feedstocks. However, 1,067 trillion BTU is 4.48% of the total first use energy from EIA 1998 Table 1.2, identical to the unsourced American Plastics Council (APC) estimate and consistent with the 4.0% plastics total primary energy use typical of high-income countries as cited Patel & Mutha 2004.

457. American Plastics Council, undated. APC was unable to provide its source for this information, but EIA 1998 shows 4.48% of U.S. primary energy went as process energy or feedstock (indistinguishably) into NAICS Code 325211, "Plastic Materials and Resins." (However, the 1997 *Census of Manufactures* found that 14% of plastic materials originate as secondary products of other industries (USCB 1997), and the interlinked flows of materials are so complex that quantification is very difficult.) Plastics' large energy use doesn't mean they're not worthwhile: in some cases, such as thermal insulation or vehicle light-weighting, using plastics can save far more energy than their production consumes.

458. Ausubel 1998, at Exh. 8, citing Wernick et al. 1996.

459. The total amount of plastics in municipal solid waste (MSW)—25.4 million tons—represented 11.1 percent of total MSW produced in the U.S. in 2001 (EPA, undated).

gains, if only because of rising costs for disposing of trash, which is 11% plastic.[459] U.S. innovators are already emulating Europe's and Japan's packaging reductions, dematerialization, product longevity, and closed materials loops, like DuPont's billion-dollar-a-year business of remanufacturing used polyester film recovered by reverse logistics. In 2001, the U.S. recycled 5.5% of its discarded plastics;[460] Germany, 57%.[461] We consider Germany's 57% to be a realistic 2025 U.S. target for *State of the Art*, and half that rate (29%) for *Conventional Wisdom*. Net of the 2000 U.S. plastics recycling rate of 5.5%, this implies respective 2025 petroleum feedstock savings of 0.61 Mbbl/d (25%) and 0.27 Mbbl/d (11%). Since German recycling is driven by statutory targets, it can't be rigorously assumed profitable even though the targets are surpassed. But its economics will improve with U.S. experience, so we think it conservative to estimate plastics recycling's 2025 net Cost of Saved Energy at zero.

> Interface, Inc. has developed carpets whose total materials saving, 99.9%, could profitably displace more than 6% of total U.S. petrochemicals.

Many substitutions away from oil are already occurring invisibly: even the adhesive in 3M's Scotch™ Brand tape and in many 3M bandages is now oil-free.[462] This potential to save the petrochemicals industry's products would be revealed as much larger if we included higher-performance and more productively used polymers. For example, Interface, Inc. has developed carpets that are one-third lighter but four times more durable—an 86% materials saving; can be leased as a floor-covering service—another 80% saving because only the worn carpet tiles are replaced; and can then be remanufactured with no loss of quality. If fully applied to the synthetic-carpet industry, the total materials saving, 99.9%, could profitably displace ~6.6% of total U.S. petrochemicals—or ~7.3% counting a wildly popular family of fractal patterns (randomized like leaves on a forest floor) that saves 89% of carpet manufacturing and fitting waste, or 9% of total carpet making, while halving installation and maintenance cost.[463] (Natural or biomass-derived materials offer further major potential for displacing the nylon and other carpet fibers now made from oil.) We conservatively neglect all such further opportunities because their complex analysis exceeds available data and this study's resources.

460. By weight, for the most recent year recorded (EPA 2003a). The 5.5% plastics recovery fraction was, by nearly fourfold, the lowest for any major type of material in trash, although bottle recovery is somewhat better at 21%. The 2000 plastics recovery rate was 5.4% (EPA 2002a). Lacking good massflow data for polymer recycling, our analysis assumes that any molecular inefficiencies and additions in recycling polymers will roughly offset petroleum process energy saved by avoided polymer manufacturing from virgin materials.

461. Includes recycling and energy recovery for 2001. APME 2003; Duales System Deutschland AG 2004. German "extended product responsibility," mandatory deposits, and other policy innovations now spreading to several dozen countries, raised the rate of packaging recycling from 12% in 1992 to 86% in 1997. During 1991–97, such initiatives raised plastic collection by 19-fold and cut home and small-business packaging use by 17% (Gardner & Sampat 1998). German automakers are world leaders in recycling plastics, with unexpected benefits: BMW's Z-1 thermoplastic skin was not only strippable from the metal chassis in 20 minutes on an "unassembly line," but also made repairs much easier (Graedel & Allenby 1996).

462. Uchitelle 2004.

463. Approximately 13 million pounds of carpet go to U.S. landfills daily (Interface Sustainability 2001). This is after accounting for the 4% of carpets that are currently recycled (Interface) and 1% of carpets produced from natural fibers (University of Nebraska, Lincoln 1996). Scaling this value by 2% per year (Global Information, Inc. 2003) equals 19.7 million lb/d in 2025, ~95% made from petrochemicals. In 2003, the U.S. plastics industry produced 282 million lb/d of all polymers.

Full use of advanced-composite light vehicles in 2025, if achieved, would boost polymer demand by ~69%, equivalent to four years' growth. This temporary investment of oil in recyclable polymer would save nearly 100 times that much light-vehicle fuel each year.

The 25% *State of the Art* petrochemicals saving is partly offset (temporarily, until recycling catches up) by our assumption of a light-vehicle shift from metal to polymer autobodies, which would (assuming full implementation) consume 6% of EIA's projected 2025 polymer production rate (equivalent to four years' growth).[464] This ~0.1 Mbbl/d increase in feedstock requirements shrinks the *State of the Art* net feedstock saving to 0.51 Mbbl/d.[465] But on p. 110, we'll show that most of the remaining petrochemical feedstocks can be replaced by biomaterials. Today's forerunners of such carbohydrate-based products include McDonald's potato-starch-and-limestone replacements for polystyrene clamshells and Cargill-Dow's polylactic-acid-based textile fibers.

Lubricants, roughly half in industry and half in vehicles, use 1% of U.S. oil. Most lubricants can be saved by adopting vehicle technologies that need less or no oil (e.g., ultralight hybrids with roughly threefold smaller engines and transmissions, if any, would use correspondingly less oil, and fuel-cell vehicles would use almost none[466]); by re-refining used oils;[467] and by using synthetic oils[468] that last at least twice as long but cost about the same. Systematically combining these methods should save about 34% of 2000 lubricant petroleum use in *Conventional Wisdom* (0.08 Mbbl/d) and 80% in *State of the Art* (0.20 Mbbl/d).[469] Most of the rest should be displaceable with biolubricants (p. 110 below).

464. We estimate 303 million light vehicles in 2025, each with a Body-in-Black™ conservatively containing the same ~116-kg mass of carbon-fiber thermoplastic composites and thermoplastic (assumed all made from oil) as the 2000 *Revolution* design. Adjusting for the nominal 2:1 white-fiber:black-fiber ratio for producing the carbon fiber from polyacrylonitrile (ultimately made from propane), and assuming the nonstructural body panels are pure unfilled thermoplastic, implies ~226 kg of polymer input per vehicle body, or 4.6 MT/y for projected 2025 light-vehicle production. We scale this by 1.08—the ratio of curb weights for the average new *State of the Art* light vehicle in 2025 to the 2000 *Revolution*'s 856.5 kg, noting that EIA's 2025 "Small SUV" is only 1% lighter than the average new vehicle. This 1.08 scaling factor yields 244 kg of polymer input to make the average 2025 light-vehicle body in this fashion. For EIA's 20.4 million new units in 2025, that's 5.0 MT/y, or 10.3% of current U.S. polymer production (48.5 MT in 2003), equivalent to four years' growth in the 80% higher polymer production rate EIA adopts for 2025. Assuming that the nonstructural polymer content of the halved-weight but generally more polymer-intensive *State of the Art* light vehicles remains roughly comparable to the 115 kg (7.6% by mass) in the typical 2001 car (ORNL 2003, p. 4-16), this is a quite modest increase in total polymer production. Over time, such a fleet would become substantially self-sustaining in materials because the extremely durable autobody polymers chosen can be recycled repeatedly, then downcycled. Further refinements, such as adoption of a true monocoque when Class A molding and reparability have matured, should further lighten the Body-in-Black. We make no corresponding adjustment for the advanced composites used by trucks and airplanes because their massflows are relatively small and should be part of forecasted feedstock demand.

465. This forecasted 5 MT/y polymer requirement, or 10.4% of 2000 production of 48.2 MT (APC 2001), would be 6.3% of projected 2025 polymer production, scaled by EIA's index of industrial output. We round this down to 6.0% as a conservative allowance for recycling of early models and of manufacturing scrap. This increases 2025 feedstock consumption by 0.1 Mbbl/d.

466. Lovins et al. (1996) show that an ultralight vehicle using an engine hybrid would eliminate 2, or using a fuel cell would eliminate 5–6 (including 22 L/car-y of motor oil), of the 14 types of fluids now needed to maintain a typical car (whose fluid inventory is ~80 kg), and would require an order of magnitude less fluid input per year. Such vehicles are also likely to use sealed superefficient bearings requiring no grease. For our technology assumption we simply reduce car crankcase-oil usage proportional to mpg, i.e. by 27% for *CW* and 69% for *SOA*. This value implicitly incorporates all the relevant savings, assuming that virtually all the lubricant is crankcase oil.

467. Re-refined used oil is measured against the same standards as virgin oil and can therefore be assumed as a direct replacement. In addition, re-refining uses only 1/3 of the energy required to refine crude oil, saving both process energy and feedstock (Zingale 2002) Currently, only 10% (Buy Recycled Business Alliance 2000) of collected used oil is re-refined in the U.S. vs. up to 60% in other countries such as Germany (Buy Recycled Business Alliance 2000). Therefore, accounting for both re-refining substitution and process energy savings, assuming an increase from 10% to 20% for re-refining in the U.S. for *CW* and an increase to 60% for *SOA*, and a used oil collection rate of 58% as in Germany (International Centre for Science and High Technology 2002), we adopt an overall 10% *CW* saving and 48% *SOA* saving of lubricants remaining after technology efficiency improvements (*CW* = [10%*58%]+[(2/3)*10%*58%] and *SOA*=[50%*58%]+[(2/3)*50%*58%]).

468. Current estimates for synthetic market share range from 6% (Synlubes.com 2004) to 7% (Amsoil, undated). *CW* assumes that 10% of the lubricant market will be synthetics in 2025 with a 50% longer life than conventional lubricants, thereby eliminating the demand for half again as many bbl-equivalents each year (15% total). *SOA* assumes that 20% of the lubricant market will be synthetics in 2025 with double the useful life or 40% total.

469. See next page.

Industrial fuel

For fuel, as distinct from feedstocks, industry uses distillate fuel oil and liquefied petroleum gas, plus small amounts of low-value residual oil and coal-like petroleum coke, to produce process heat and steam. We conservatively estimate that about 11% (*Conventional Wisdom*) or 19% (*State of the Art*) of this 2025 petroleum use can be saved, for $3–4/bbl or less than a three-year simple payback. Our practical experience in heavy process plants suggests a much larger potential—CEF's *Advanced* case resembles the *lowest* savings we've achieved—but data to substantiate this across diverse U.S. industries aren't publicly available.

We therefore rely on the findings of a detailed and peer-reviewed interdisciplinary study by the five National Laboratories with the greatest expertise in energy efficiency.[470] This Clean Energy Futures (CEF) study examined 20-year technoeconomic efficiency potentials. The Labs analyzed industrial fuel and power savings by subsector in a *Moderate* case assuming modest changes in political will and improved use of off-the-shelf technology, and in an *Advanced* case with significant adoption of more sophisticated technologies, partly driven by a carbon-permit-trading system that equilibrates at $50/TC (tonne carbon). We apply the percentage fuel savings from these respective cases to EIA's 2025 industrial fuel use to obtain *Conventional Wisdom* and *State of the Art* savings of industrial fuel and electricity.[471] The resulting actually implementable oil savings in 2025 also assume that saving industrial electricity will back out oil-fired generation first, then gas- and coal-fired generation in proportions determined by a simple load duration curve (LDC) analysis.[472] Details are in *Technical Annex*, Ch. 15.

Buildings

Our analysis of buildings, which use 5.7% of oil in 2025, also relies on the CEF study. Our *State of the Art* instantaneous potential savings in 2025—25% at $3.3/bbl—comes from scaling the percentage savings for the last year of CEF's 20-year *Advanced* scenario (which assumes normal stock turnover) to 100% implementation, and assuming that these percentage savings of natural gas in buildings applied equally to directly used distillate oil and LPG (reasonable because they're priced above natural gas).

One-ninth of 2025 oil is used to fuel industrial processes. Much of this can be profitably saved by furnace and boiler improvements, thermal insulation and re-use, combined production of heat and power, and other well-known and lucrative practices.

The 6% of 2025 fuel-oil use slated for buildings can be mostly displaced by similar efficiency gains; later we'll displace the rest with saved natural gas or with bottled gas.

469. The percentage savings were based on a simplified bottom-up analysis of potentials for these three lubricant saving strategies.

470. Brown et al. 2001; Interlaboratory Working Group on Energy-Efficient and Clean-Energy Technologies 2000; Koomey et al. 2001.

471. Our industrial fuel savings are achievable potentials, not the instantaneous potentials reported here for other sectors. It is not possible to ascertain the full technical potential based on CEF's data and methods. Since CEF's savings already account for stock turnover and policy implementation, we apply 100% of CEF's industrial savings in our *Coherent Engagement* policy scenario.

472. In the electricity efficiency analysis, we backed out all oil used in electricity generation except that in Alaska and Hawai'i. Coal and gas savings are then split 39%:61%, respectively, based on our LDC analysis, using the average U.S. heat rate to calculate coal and natural gas fuel savings per kWh saved.

Our analysis then scales the CEF *Moderate* case's percentage savings proportionately to obtain the *Conventional Wisdom* potential—13% at $1.7/bbl. For both scenarios, we allocate electrical savings' primary fuel displacements as we do for industry. Details are in *Technical Annex*, Ch. 16.

Electricity generation

Less than 3% of oil today makes electricity; ◄──────── **and conversely, less than 3% of electricity is made from oil, nearly all from otherwise useless "residual" oil. But a combination of efficient use and alternative supplies can profitably displace virtually all of that oil.**

Many commentators suppose that energy is energy, so a source of electricity, such as coal-fired or nuclear power stations, can substitute for oil. In general this is not so, and not only because very few vehicles (the users of 70% of oil) run on electricity. In 2000, only 2.9% of U.S. oil was used to produce electricity, and within that 2.9%, only 0.3% of oil used was distillate products; the rest was tarry residual oil (the very bottom of the barrel—a gooey coal-like tar that's hardly good for anything else, though it can be expensively upgraded to lighter products instead). Conversely, only 2.9% of U.S. electricity was made from oil. EIA projects this to drop by 2025 to 1.7%, and the fraction of oil used to make electricity to fall to 1.5% (0.5% in the form of distilled product). The link between oil and electricity is thus tenuous.

The 0.5 Mbbl/d of oil used to produce U.S. electricity in 2000 (mainly in New England, Alaska, and Hawai'i) is projected by EIA to decline to 0.36 Mbbl/d by 2025. In some cases, the most convenient near-term substitute will be natural gas, which can be freed up by using it more efficiently, both in other power plants and in industrial and building applications (see p. 111 below). Our analysis displaces oil used in electricity generation using a combination of more efficient end-use of electricity in buildings and industry and substitution of other generating technologies and fuels. (For example, in Hawai'i, home to 10% of U.S. oil-fired electricity generation in 2002, the cheapest supply-side alternatives are renewables such as windpower, and diverse renewables can meet more than half the need.) Details are in *Technical Annex*, Ch. 17.

New coal and nuclear plants are unsuited to the "peaker" operation needed to displace most oil- and gas-fired power plants, and in any case can't compete with three better ways to do the same things.

Although little oil is used to make electricity, 16% of U.S. electricity in 2000 was made from natural gas, projected to rise to 22% in 2025. As we'll see later (p. 113), saving electricity is a potent way to displace natural gas that can in turn displace oil in buildings and industry. In theory, new coal or nuclear power plants could do the same thing, but for two fatal flaws: they're technically and economically unsuited to the "peaker" operation (few hours per year) that most gas- and oil-fired generation does, and they're manyfold, even tens of times, costlier to build and run than buying electric end-use efficiency. They're also uncompetitive compared to windpower and gas- or waste-fired cogeneration (Box 25, p. 258).

Making electricity at the right scale for the job often makes it cheaper, thanks to 207 hidden advantages revealed by careful examination of financial economics, electrical engineering, and other "distributed benefits" that typically increase decentralized generators' economic value by about tenfold.[473] That's not counted by traditional comparisons of cost per kilowatt-hour. But distributed benefits are real, measurable, and starting to shift market choice. They can greatly expand the scope for profitably displacing oil- and gas-fired generation by relatively small-scale means that can be mass-produced and rapidly deployed.

Combined efficiency potential

So far, we have found a technical potential to cut 2025 oil use by more than half, or almost 15 Mbbl/d (Fig. 28), if *State of the Art* end-use efficiency technologies were fully applied by then. That's enough efficiency to cut 2025 oil imports by two-thirds (Fig. 29). *Conventional Wisdom* saves half as much at half the unit cost or a quarter the total cost, but even the huge *State of the Art* savings cost an average of only $12/bbl, less than half the 2025 oil price of $26/bbl.

Even the most expensive major tranche of *State of the Art* savings—light trucks at 59¢/gal or $19/bbl—is less than EIA's $26 oil price. This comparison omits oil-industry capital expenditures, such as incremental refineries and distribution capacity, that the 5 Mbbl/d of light-truck savings (equivalent to twice today's Gulf imports) could avoid.

More than half the total savings comes from light vehicles, and one-third just from light trucks, which account for over half the growth in oil use to 2025 (Fig. 7). Most of that potential *is on the market in 2004*. If in 2025 every car were a 2004 *Prius* (p. 29) and every light truck were a 2005 *Escape, RX 400h,* or *Highlander* hybrid SUV (Fig. 5)—all of which will doubtless seem charmingly antique in 2025—then the 2025 light-vehicle fleet would save 37% more oil than *Conventional Wisdom* light vehicles do, proving those vehicles' feasibility ~21 years early. Such a hypothetical 2025 fleet replacement with the best MY2005 hybrids would also save 4.5 Mbbl/d. That's only 56% as much oil as *State of the Art* light vehicles would save,[474] emphasizing the importance of lightweighting, but it's still 16% of EIA's forecasted 2025 total oil use, equivalent to twice 2002 net imports from the Persian Gulf. That's not bad for uncompromised vehicles on the 2004–05 market.

It's also worth recalling the major conservatisms behind this assessment (pp. 37–39). In our view, failure of 2004 advanced-composites technologies to reach commercial maturity by 2025—~15 years later than we expect—is less likely than their being supplanted by such laboratory wonders (in 2004) as carbon nanotubes and glassy (amorphous) metals.[475]

More than half of total projected 2025 oil use could be saved by fully deploying the efficiency technologies that all cost less than the projected oil price ($26 per barrel in 2000 $). Saving the average barrel costs only $12. Such big savings could return oil use to pre-1970 levels and cut imports by 70% to pre-1973-embargo levels. Of the light-vehicle savings, 56% would be realized if all light vehicles in 2025 just got the mpg of equivalent 2005 hybrids.

473. Lovins et al. 2002.

474. The calculation is in *Technical Annex*, Ch. 5, and assumes the SUVs get 29 EPA adjusted mpg.

475. Nanotubes, besides their extraordinary and diverse thermal and electrical properties, may cost less than carbon fiber today yet offer roughly 10–100 times its strength per pound (R. Smalley, personal communication, 20 Nov. 2003). Glassy metal, well described in an article of that title by B. Lemley (2004), may likewise cost a few dollars a pound in bulk, yet be six times as strong as steel. Further revolutions, such as synthetic spider-silk, are also starting to emerge from imitating nature's 3.8 billion years of design experience (Benyus 1997). There may even be biomimetic ways to make carbon nanotubes.

If every car on the road in 2025 were a 2004 *Prius* and every light truck were a 2005 *Escape, RX 400h,* or *Highlander* hybrid SUV, then the 2025 light-vehicle fleet would save 16% of EIA's forecasted 2025 total oil use, *equivalent to twice 2002 net imports from the Persian Gulf.*

And it's hard to imagine another 21 years passing without the advantages of smart growth (especially of demandating and desubsidizing sprawl) becoming unbearably obvious, leading to major shifts in land-use policy in much of the United States. (These advantages include improved quality of life, crime reduction, increased real-estate value, and tax relief.) Trying to foresee efficiency potential 21 years ahead is always a shot in the dark, but such is the pace of progress today, and the likely pressure of events to come, that we feel we're more likely to have under- than overstated how much oil-saving by 2025 will look obviously practical and profitable.

Fig. 28 might at first seem to show only that the costliest increments of end-use efficiency approach EIA's 2025 crude-oil price projection of $26/bbl: more precisely, that feeding $26/bbl crude oil into the oil value chain would deliver refined products at a short-run marginal price greater than the cost of displacing those products through end-use efficiency. But efficiency's advantage is actually much greater, because we have not yet counted three further elements of oil's true societal cost, of which the first two are marked on the vertical axis of Fig. 28.

Figure 28: Supply curve summarizing *Conventional Wisdom* and *State of the Art* technologies for efficient use of oil, analyzed on pp. 43–99 above, hypothetically assuming full implementation in 2025. We assume EIA's convention of expressing savings volume in Mbbl/d of product delivered to end users, totaling 28.3 Mbbl/d in 2025. On the y-axis we use a value-chain adjustment for wholesale and retail products to normalize CSE to $/bbl crude. This method (pp. 40–41) accounts for differences in production and delivery costs of different products as well as energy content contained. The total *State of the Art* efficiency potential could save more than half of projected 2025 oil use at an average cost less than half of EIA's projected 2025 crude-oil price. Realistic implementation fractions, rates, and methods for efficient end-use will be discussed starting on p.169 below, and additional oil-saving potential from supply substitutions, starting on p. 103.

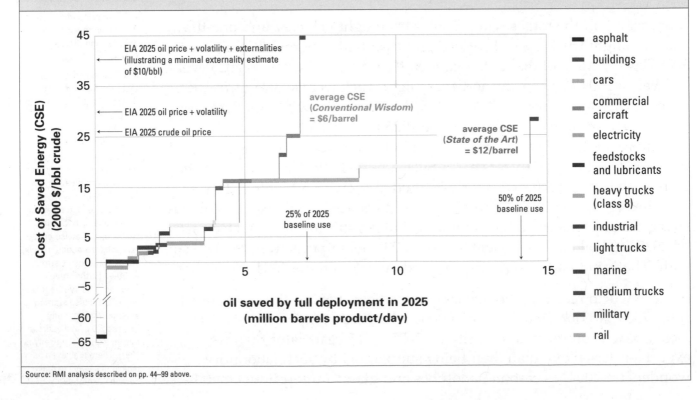

Source: RMI analysis described on pp. 44–99 above.

- *Value of oil's price volatility*: As noted in Box 3, p. 16, properly comparing oil with efficient use—which is financially riskless because its cost is locked in from the moment the equipment is installed—requires adjustment for the financial value of oil's price risk. The market, at this writing, values that risk at $3.5/bbl.

- *Externalized cost*: Externalities—security, avoidable-subsidy, health, environmental, and other costs that are real and quantifiable but not included in oil's market price—add up to some debatable but substantial amount. As noted on pp. 21–22, it's hard to justify an externality value as low as $10/bbl, and rather easy to justify a value of tens of dollars per barrel—comparable to or exceeding oil's market price.

- *Avoidable capital cost*: The long-run avoidable capital cost just to 2025 looks relatively modest (~$0.5/bbl), but in the longer run, replacing reserves and replacing or refurbishing major capital items like refineries and pipelines could cost considerably more.

Thus even the costliest kinds of *State of the Art* end-use efficiency are cheaper than the market price of oil and *much* cheaper than the true social cost of oil. The present value of the societal saving from fully buying efficiency instead of oil in 2025—i.e., the integrated area between the *State of the Art* supply curve in Fig. 28 and a horizontal line extending rightwards at $26/bbl—is thus much larger than the $870 billion implied by valuing 2025 crude oil just at its private internal cost of $26/bbl (20-year net present value in 2025 at ~$70b/y rate of net earnings). The true societal value could be severalfold higher. This surplus can be interpreted in any mixture of at least three ways:

- *Cost conservatism*: Even if efficiency cost far more than we claim, it'd still be a better buy than oil.

- *Quantity conservatism*: We've left so much money on the table that we're not yet contemplating buying nearly as much quantity of oil savings as would be worthwhile.

- *Implementation gap*: By constructing the supply curve at a societal discount rate (a conservatively high 5%/y real), rather than at far higher implicit consumer discount rates (often 50–70-plus %/y)—that is, by taking a long rather than a short view—Fig. 28 shows how savings can be attractive to society even though they may look too costly to consumers. The policy section starting on p. 169 describes how to turn this discount-rate arbitrage opportunity into business profits as well as public goods. The vertical "freeboard" in Fig. 28 represents a large safety margin to accommodate imperfections in that arbitrage.

> Saving half of 2025 oil use is not only half the cost of buying it, but also avoids major societal costs not included in oil's price. This conservatism could accommodate doubled costs of saving oil, or large shortcomings in the policies we'll propose for encouraging private purchasing decisions that better reflect society's long-term best interest.

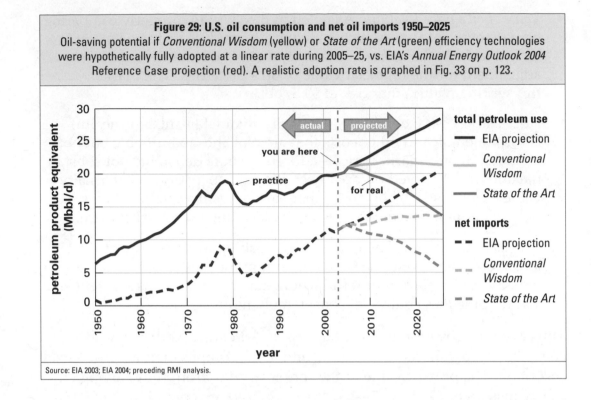

Figure 29: U.S. oil consumption and net oil imports 1950–2025
Oil-saving potential if *Conventional Wisdom* (yellow) or *State of the Art* (green) efficiency technologies were hypothetically fully adopted at a linear rate during 2005–25, vs. EIA's *Annual Energy Outlook 2004* Reference Case projection (red). A realistic adoption rate is graphed in Fig. 33 on p. 123.

Source: EIA 2003; EIA 2004; preceding RMI analysis.

476. In principle there's at least one additional major option—synthetic fuels made from coal. However, we'll suggest that climate-safe ways to use coal to make hydrogen, chiefly by pulling it out of water, are an even higher-value use and are more likely to prove competitive in the more demanding post-efficiency marketplace.

So far, we've only considered how to use oil very efficiently. That's enough, if fully deployed by 2025, to return U.S. oil use and imports to pre-1973 levels (Fig. 29). (Starting on p. 178 we'll consider how quickly this can actually happen.) But our quiver still contains three arrows—the three potential supply-side displacements for the remaining oil use.[476] These all become more effective, rapid, affordable, and attractive when efficient use has shrunk what they must do, as we'll see next. Of course, their contribution can't simply be added to that of efficiency, because whichever is done first (typically efficiency if we choose the best buys first) will leave less oil usage for subsequent measures to displace. But properly integrated, the combined potential is potent indeed.

Fully capturing the profitable end-use opportunities described so far could return 2025 U.S. oil use and oil imports to pre-1973-embargo levels— *before* **the oil-substituting supply options to be described next.**

Substituting for Oil

Nearly half of the remaining oil use can be displaced by substituting cheaper supplies.

Option 2. Substituting biofuels and biomaterials

Liquid fuels made from farming and forestry wastes, or perhaps from energy crops, are normally considered to offer only a small potential at high cost. For example, classic ethanol production from corn, which now provides ethanol oxygenate equivalent to 2% of U.S. gasoline,[477] could expand by only about half by 2025 if not subsidized. Modern production plants of this type, especially if highly integrated,[478] yield net energy, but need favorable resale prices for their byproducts (mainly distiller's dried grains and, in other countries, electricity) to compete with gasoline. And gasoline, as noted on pp. 20–21, is already rather heavily subsidized.

However, that widely held perspective, reflected in our *Conventional Wisdom* biofuels portfolio (Fig. 30a), is outdated. When the National Academies' National Research Council found in a 1999 study that biofuels could profitably provide 1.6 Mbbl/d by 2020,[479] new methods of converting cellulose- and lignin-rich (woody) materials into liquid fuels, e.g. using genetically engineered bacteria and enzymes, were just emerging. Five years later, even newer *State of the Art* technologies now permit biofuels by 2025 to provide 4.3 Mbbl/d of crude-oil equivalent at under $35/bbl ($0.75/gal gasoline-equivalent). Of that amount, 3.7 Mbbl/d is competitive on the short-run margin with EIA's projected $26/bbl oil (Fig. 30b), or more to the extent one counts oil's subsidies and externalities.

Option 2. New technologies can produce a robustly competitive 3.7 Mbbl/d of liquid fuels from biomass, mainly as cellulosic ethanol. Such biofuels can profitably displace a third of the U.S. oil use remaining after efficiency gains. Foreign precedents are encouraging.

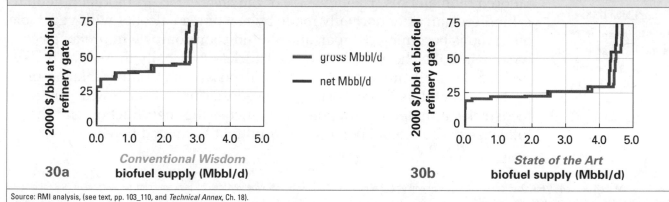

Figures 30a & 30b: Supply curves for the 2025 full-implementation potential of U.S. biofuels, assuming that none ("gross") or all ("net") of the energy required to run the conversion process is derived from biofuels rather than from other energy sources. These graphs account for the energy content and end-use efficiency of the biofuels in today's gasoline- and diesel-fueled engines: when converting them into their equivalent, first as those retail fuels and then as crude oil, we count 1 gallon of diesel fuel as equivalent to 1.1 of biodiesel, and 1 gallon of gasoline as equivalent to 1.23 of ethanol.[480]

30a — *Conventional Wisdom* — biofuel supply (Mbbl/d)

30b — *State of the Art* — biofuel supply (Mbbl/d)

— gross Mbbl/d
— net Mbbl/d

Source: RMI analysis, (see text, pp. 103_110, and *Technical Annex*, Ch. 18).

477. In 2003, 2.8 billion gallons of ethanol were produced, vs. 137.1 billion gallons of gasoline (EIA 2004d, Table 3.4).

478. E.g., Dakota Value Capture Cooperative's single-site closed-loop project in Sully County near Pierre, South Dakota, combining a cattle feed mill, feedlot, anaerobic digester, cogeneration plant, and ethanol plant, and exports ethanol, CO_2, wet distillers byproducts, liquid fertilizer, compost, and cattle. See www.dakotavcc.com.   479. NAS/NRC 1999.

480. The conversion rate of 1.23 gallons of ethanol per gallon of gasoline is calculated as follows: ethanol contains only 67.7% of the heat content of gasoline (84,600 BTU/gal [Higher Heating Value] divided by 125,000 BTU/gal [also HHV]). However, Wyman et al. (1993, p. 875) maintain that, "a 20% gain in engine efficiency can be obtained relative to gasoline in a well-designed engine." Therefore, multiplying 67.7% by 1.2 equals 0.812 gallon of gasoline per gallon of ethanol or inversely, 1.23 gallon of ethanol per gallon of gasoline.

A third or more of road transportation fuels worldwide could be displaced by biofuels in the 2050–2100 time frame.

New technologies roughly double the yields, greatly reduce the energy inputs, and often reduce the capital costs of classical corn-ethanol processes.

The Brazilian ethanol program provided nearly 700,000 jobs in 2003, and cut 1975–2002 oil imports by a cumulative undis-counted total of $50 billion (2000 US$)— more than ten times its total undiscounted 1975–89 real invest-ment, and ~50 times its cumulative 1978–88 subsidy.

The ultimately profitable potential is even larger; NRC found it exceeded 8 Mbbl/d by the end of the century. But just the *State of the Art* 2025 potential, shown in Fig. 30b, is major—13% of EIA's projected 2025 oil demand before (or 18% after) fully applying oil's end-use efficiency potential.[481] Our conclusion, detailed in *Technical Annex*, Ch. 18, is also consistent with the finding by Battelle Memorial Institute's Joint Global Change Research Institute that 9.5 quadrillion BTU/y of biomass energy[482] could be provided without large impacts on the current agricultural system, yielding a few percent more biofuel at *SOA* conversion rates (4.6 Mbbl/d at $36/bbl) than shown in Fig. 30b. Taking a global view, a 2004 IEA biofuels report esti-mates that "…a third or more of road transportation fuels worldwide could be displaced by biofuels in the 2050–2100 time frame."[483] And a study for DoD of how to relieve U.S. oil dependence, like many others lately, recom-mended a large-scale initiative in cellulosic biomass.[484]

Of the *State of the Art* potential, 99% is from ethanol, largely from lignocel-lulosic feedstocks. The new technologies often use very efficient enzymes (many but not all from genetically modified bacteria, and the best about tenfold cheaper than they were two years ago) for both digesting cellu-lose and hemicellulose into sugars and then fermenting them. Other paths include thermal processes demonstrated at pilot-plant scale, such as the Pearson Gasification process, which produces Fischer-Tropsch ethanol from synthesis gas. (The F-T process connects small hydrocarbon mole-cules into long chains, produces a zero-sulfur and zero-aromatics synthet-ic diesel fuel completely compatible with existing infrastructure, and can be applied to syngas made from any hydrocarbon or carbohydrate.) Collectively, such innovations roughly double the yields, greatly reduce the energy inputs, and often reduce the capital costs of classical corn-ethanol processes. They also offer greater scope for coproducing valuable tailored biomaterials. The other 1% of the *State of the Art* biofuel potential is biodiesel, an ester normally made by reacting an alcohol with vegetable oil; it too is becoming cheaper, and should soon compete in pretax price when using the cheaper kinds of feedstocks—especially those which, like used cooking oil, are often currently a disposal cost. Comparable bio-oils usable as diesel fuel can also be produced thermally from a wide range of feedstocks, as noted below, potentially increasing their fraction and the total size of the biofuel potential beyond that examined here.

481. I.e., 3.7 Mbbl/d divided by EIA's projected 2025 oil demand of 28.3 Mbbl/d is 13%, and is 18% when divided by the remaining oil demand of 20.8 Mbbl/d after *State of the Art* efficiency savings.

482. Smith et al. 2004. Assuming our *State of the Art* conversion rate of 180 gal ethanol/dry short ton (dt), this equates to 4.6 Mbbl/d. The intermediate price is $36/bbl crude oil, but unlike ours, is not converted on the short-run margin from the retail product price.

483. This IEA study predicts a post-2010 price for cellulosic ethanol of $0.19/L or $0.72/gal (IEA 2004a, Table 4.5, p. 78)—higher than our predicted *State of the Art* price of $0.61/gal ethanol ($0.75/gal gasoline-equivalent), or slightly lower if Table 4.6 (IEA 2004a, p. 79) is correct in labeling the IEA figures as gasoline-equivalents. The IEA price is based on an NREL estimate (as quoted in IEA 2000), that assumed an ethanol conversion rate of 112 gal/ton vs. our *SOA* conver-sion rate of 180 gal/ton. Substituting the 180 gal/ton rate into the IEA calculation results in a price of $0.57/gal ethanol, which is actually lower than our pre-dicted *SOA* price.

484. Petersen, Erickson, & Khan 2003.

Both ethanol and esterified biodiesel have been proven in widespread use, ethanol typically in 10–85% blends with gasoline and biodiesel in 2–100% blends with diesel oil.[485] Brazil's 29-year-old ethanol program is now the world's low-cost producer. Using cheap sugar cane, mainly bagasse (cane-waste) for process heat and power, and modern equipment, it provides a ~22% ethanol blend used nationwide, plus 100% hydrous ethanol for four million cars.[486] The Brazilian ethanol program provided nearly 700,000 jobs in 2003, and cut 1975–2002 oil imports by a cumulative undiscounted total of $50 billion (2000 US$)—more than ten times its total undiscounted 1975–89 real investment,[487] and ~50 times its cumulative 1978–88 subsidy.[488]

> **Ethanol has replaced about one-fourth of Brazil's gasoline, already eliminating oil imports worth ~50 times its startup subsidy.**

The Brazilian government provided three important initial drivers: guaranteed purchases by the state-owned oil company Petrobras, low-interest loans for agro-industrial ethanol firms, and fixed gasoline and ethanol prices where hydrous ethanol sold for 59% of the government-set gasoline price at the pump.[489] These pump-primers have made ethanol production competitive yet unsubsidized (partly because each tonne of cane processed can also yield ~100 kWh of electricity via bagasse cogeneration—a national total of up to 35 billion kWh/y, ~9% of national consumption).

In recent years, the Brazilian untaxed retail price of hydrous ethanol has been lower than that of gasoline per gallon. It has even been cheaper than gasoline—and has matched our 2025 cellulosic ethanol cost—on an energy-equivalent basis for some periods during 2002–04.[490] Ethanol has thus replaced about one-fourth of Brazil's gasoline, using only 5% of the land in agricultural production. Brazilian "total flex" cars introduced by VW and GM in mid-2003 can use any pure or blended fuel from 100% gasoline to 100% ethanol, and are welcomed because they maximize customers' fuel choice and flexibility.[491] (In contrast, the ~3 million "flex-fuel" vehicles now on U.S. roads, marketed partly to exploit a loophole in CAFE efficiency standards but seldom actually fueled with ethanol, can't go beyond the "E85" blend of 85% ethanol with 15% gasoline.)

> **Brazilian "total flex" cars introduced by VW and GM can use any pure or blended fuel from 100% gasoline to 100% ethanol.**

485. However, not all U.S. biodiesel is blendable with petroleum diesel. Moreover, Congress has at times defined biodiesel (chiefly to promote certain subsidies) as involving only certain feedstocks (such as virgin vegetable oils—excluding, e.g., used cooking oils and animal tallow), or being esterified with only certain alcohols (such as methanol to the exclusion of ethanol and others), or requiring transesterification (thus excluding equivalent fuels that remove long-chain fatty acids' carboxyl group by a thermochemical process instead). Such exclusive definitions may make sense for soybean producers and others seeking favorable treatment for their own option, but make no sense for a country seeking to maximize deployment of and competition between different bio-oils that are equally functional for displacing diesel fuel.

486. Wyman 2004; Goldemberg et al. 2004. The blend is nominally sold as 22% ethanol (range 20–26%), the rest gasoline, while the neat hydrous ethanol is 95.5% pure ethanol and ~4.5% water.

487. Goldemberg et al. 2004.

488. WBCSD 2004, p. 107.

489. Goldemberg et al. 2004.

490. Table 4.4 on p. 77 of IEA 2004a shows that in fact, in mid-2002 and early 2004, Brazilian bioethanol (at ~$0.72/gal gasoline-equivalent) achieved our 2025 bioethanol price of $0.75/gal gasoline-equivalent. See Goldemberg et al. 2004.

491. IPS 2003. McClellan (2004) estimates a ~70% market share for "total flex" vehicles by 2007 in Brazil.

Europe produced 17 times as much biodiesel in 2003 as the United States did.

Germany has seen BP and Shell become the dominant distributors of biofuels, while independent companies like Greenergy have taken the lead in the UK by selling branded biofuel products through supermarkets.

With such a mature sugarcane-ethanol industry, Brazil is gearing up for ethanol exports that could reach 9 million tonnes a year by 2010, over half of it to Japan (the world's largest ethanol importer in 2003) and a sixth to the U.S. The main obstacles are import tariffs designed to protect existing corn-ethanol industries. The U.S. charges 54¢/gal, raising ethanol's landed East Coast price from $1.00 to $1.54/gal, and Europe charges 38¢/gal, but the U.S. tariff wall is leaking. Cargill proposes to dehydrate Brazilian ethanol in El Salvador for tariff-free export to the U.S. under an exception in the Central America Free Trade Agreement, despite heavy opposition from the U.S. corn lobby. Peru is about to open a 25–30,000 bbl-ethanol/d export facility that would be tariff-free under the Andean Trade Preference Act. Meanwhile, China is exploring major investments in Brazil to produce both ethanol and castor oil or biodiesel for shipment to China.[492]

Europe produced 17 times as much biodiesel in 2003 as the United States did, and the EU is demonstrating that a transition to biodiesel is feasible. European countries place high taxes on transportation fuels (as high as 74% of the UK's $5.5/gal price for diesel fuel[493]), but have been able to implement partial (UK, France) and even full (Germany, Austria, Italy, Spain) biodiesel de-taxation.[494] This makes biodiesel competitive with traditional diesel fuel and supports bio-oil feedstock producers as their agricultural subsidies are phased down. In addition, the European Commission Directive of 2003 established biofuel targets of 2% energy content of all transport fuel by 2005 and 5.75% by 2010.[495] Unsubsidized cost-effectiveness will continue to be difficult for biodiesel, however, as competition for feedstocks increases and as prices for the byproduct glycerin fall with increased supply (unless those lower prices elicit major new glycerin markets).

The biofuels transition already underway will have significant impacts on its related industries. Fuel standards will force the development of new relationships among automakers, engine makers, and fuel suppliers in order to evaluate biofuels' impacts on automobile engines and their warranties (such as the Volkswagen/DaimlerChrysler/CHOREN Industries renewable fuels collaboration). European automakers have already approved biodiesel blends of up to 5% and are reportedly evaluating blends up to 30%. Retail fuel distribution will probably remain the same, but the dominant players in the distribution chain may change. Germany has seen BP and Shell become the dominant distributors of biofuels, while independent companies like Greenergy have taken the lead in the UK by selling branded biofuel products through supermarkets and hypermarkets.

492. Bio-era 2004.

493. Calculated from the June 2004 supermarket price of £0.795/L or £3.01/U.S. gallon (Automobile Association 2004), converted at the approximate June 2004 exchange rate of £0.55/$.

494. Automobile Association 2004. The favored feedstocks are rather costly: U.S. biodiesel made from canola (called "rapeseed" in Europe) costs ~$60/bbl on the short-run margin.

495. European Parliament 2003.

In the U.S., the combination of vehicle efficiency and ethanol output analyzed here suggests that by 2025, the average light vehicle's fuel will contain at least two-fifths ethanol, rising thereafter—even more if ethanol is imported. To accommodate regional variations on this average, "flex-fuel" vehicles accepting at least E85 should therefore become the norm for all new light vehicles not long after 2010. "Total flex" vehicles like those now sold in Brazil would further increase the potential to accelerate ethanol adoption and to manage spot shortage of either gasoline or ethanol. In short, many of the fuel-system, commercial, vehicle-technology, and production developments that the U.S. would need for a large-scale biofuel program have already succeeded elsewhere; the main shift would be using modern U.S. cellulosic ethanol conversion technologies.

The input side: biomass feedstocks and rural economies

Our analysis of all feedstocks adopts the authoritative Oak Ridge National Laboratory state-by-state analysis of forest, mill, agriculture, and urban wood wastes and dedicated energy crops.[496] ORNL found an annual potential to produce and deliver 510 million dry short tons (dt) of biomass at below $54/dt without competing with existing food and fiber production or creating soil or water problems. For biodiesel, we rely on the 2002 *Oil Crops Situation and Outlook Yearbook* from the U.S. Department of Agriculture.[497]

The main energy crops we examine for ethanol production are switchgrass and short-rotation woody crops such as hybrid willow and poplar. Switchgrass is a fast-growing perennial Midwest and Southeast grass that curbs soil erosion via extensive ten-foot-deep roots, is drought- and flood-tolerant, can be harvested like hay once or twice a year, but has nearly three times the typical yield of, say, Alabama hay. Such crops could often be profitably grown, preventing the erosion caused by traditional row crops, on the 35 million acres of arable land in the Conservation Reserve Program, which now pays farmers an average of $48/acre-y to grow resource-conserving, soil-holding, non-crop vegetation, preferably in polyculture,[498] rather than traditional crops.[499] Our analysis assumes that

> **Special energy crops can provide ample biofuel feedstocks; diverse waste streams may add more. Sound biofuel production practices wouldn't hamper food and fiber production nor cause water or environmental problems, and can actually enhance soil fertility.**

496. Walsh et al. 2000.

497. Ash 2002. Supplemental sources included Wiltsee 1998 and Duffield 2003.

498. Conservation Reserve Program/Conservation Reserve Enhancement Program (CRP/CREP) lands are often degraded or low-quality, so they especially need to be rebuilt via diverse prairie-emulating polycultures to fix nitrogen

and regenerate a biota-based nutrient- and water-management system. This normally takes a few years to get well established, but haying can start after the first year. The main strategy could be co-cropping or strip-cropping diverse ensembles including such legumes as perennial Illinois bundleflower and biennial sweet clover, and perhaps encouraging warm-season grasses that can associate with nitrogen-fixing bacteria. Ensembles of relatively few plant types can achieve much of the synergy of mature prairies. Some Great Plains prairie remnants have been hayed continuously for 75 years with no fertilizers or supplements, yet no apparent decline in yield. To be sure, such unmanaged prairie meadows have severalfold lower hay yields than highly bred, managed, and fertilized switchgrass fields. The latter, though, are often fertilized with ~120 kg/ha-y of nitrogen, vs. ~150–200 for corn, which takes up the nitrogen only half as efficiently. The basic design questions include whether native prairies' extraordinary biodiversity, which has sustained them with no inputs through millennia of vicissitudes, is "overdesigned" for human biofuel needs, and on a net-energy basis, what compromise between switchgrass monoculture and prairie-like polyculture will optimize the mix of yield, cost, longevity, and resilience: W. Jackson & J. Glover (The Land Institute, Salina KS), personal communications, 25–26 July 2004.

499. Haying is currently allowed on certain CRP and CREP lands, but only once every three years, under considerable restrictions, and incurring a 25% payment reduction (USDA 2004b). New rules would be needed to allow regular haying of deep-rooted perennials and to encourage appropriate perennial polycultures.

Biofuels improve urban air quality, and can reduce CO_2 emissions by 78% for biodiesel or 68% for cellulosic ethanol. Properly grown feedstocks can even *reverse* CO_2 emissions by taking carbon out of the air and sequestering it in enriched topsoil whose improved tilth can boost agronomic yields.

fuel crops would be grown where they're at least as profitable as traditional crops, and that no dedicated energy crops would be available from the Rocky Mountain and Western Plains regions (which probably do have some arid-land native-plant fuel crop potential).

We also consider offal and other animal processing wastes using a recently industrialized thermal depolymerization process that could produce 0.05 Mbbl/d of bio-oil, from $20/t feedstocks, at prices as low as $13.20/bbl. One such process, owned by Changing World Technologies, is analogous to the delayed-coker technology used in oil refining, and has recently been extended to handle many further forms of waste, including feedlot manure, municipal solid waste, sewage sludge, used tires, and automotive shredder fluff. Other such thermochemical technologies are possible.[500] Successful commercial application of this technology to such diverse feedstocks (not included in our analysis) could potentially produce up to an additional million or so barrels per day of biobased oil or two quadrillion BTU/y of other energy forms, effectively closing the loop on a some major waste streams.[501] Some of the feedstock streams, of course, have competing uses, and the competitive-market economics have many uncertainties, so we haven't included these resources in our supply portfolio. On the other hand, some waste streams now incur tipping fees or other disposal costs, making their bio-oil economics potentially favorable. Further European-style restrictions on refeeding animal wastes to animals would increase the U.S. waste streams requiring and paying for disposal.[502]

Since biofuels contain essentially no sulfur, trace metals, or aromatics, they also improve urban air quality, and can reduce CO_2 emissions by 78% for biodiesel[503] or 68% for cellulosic ethanol.[504] Properly grown feedstocks can even *reverse* CO_2 emissions by taking carbon out of the air and sequestering it in enriched topsoil whose improved tilth can boost agronomic yields. Using biofuels as a vehicle for better farm, range, and forest practices can also help to achieve other goals such as reduced soil erosion and improved water quality, and can dramatically improve the economies of rural areas. Our *State of the Art* analysis takes no credit for saving nearly 181 million tonne/y of carbon emissions via biofuels production, which under the emerging trading system, if sold for say $10–50/tonne, could cut the biofuels' net cost by $1–6/bbl.[505] This value alone could increase pretax farm net income[506] by about $26–128 from its 2002 average of just $43/acre-y. The full value could be even larger, and could be supplemented by other revenues from this strategy, as discussed on pp. 162–165.

500. Bridgwater 2003.

501. Assuming 166 Mt/y of municipal solid waste, 15 Mt/y of sewage sludge, and 220 Mt/y of feedlot manure, converted at a 30% mass yield (B. Appel, personal communications, 7 and 10 August 2004).

502. Woolsey 2004.

503. Schumacher, Van Gerpen, & Adams 2004.

504. GM et al. 2001, Fig. 3.6, pp. 3–13. .

505. Assuming a crop yield of 7 tons/acre and an ethanol conversion rate of 180 gal ethanol/ton, 22 barrels of crude-oil-equivalent per acre could be replaced each year. Using a 0.85 kg/L density for crude and an 84% carbon content results in a 2.56 tonne/acre carbon savings. Therefore, assuming a carbon credit price of $10–50/tonne carbon yields $1.16–5.82/bbl-equivalent, or ~$26–128/acre-y.

506. Moreover, Lal et al. (1998), summarized by the same authors in Lal et al. 1999, suggest that the water- and nutrient-holding capacity of increased soil organic content could be worth far more. See also Lal 2003, summarizing scientific literature in which he and his land-grant-university and USDA colleagues find that restorative and recommended practices could sequester in soil enough carbon to offset a fifth of current U.S. carbon emissions (nearly one-third including aboveground forest biomass), and could continue to do so for the next 50 years.

Even without counting carbon and ecological benefits, biofuels' domestic and largely rural production could boost not just the

national economy, but especially rural areas' economy, culture, and communities. An analysis of a proposal for 5-billion-gallon-a-year biofuel production by 2012 (1.8 times 2003 ethanol production) found that cumulatively through 2012, it could save a total of 1.6 billion barrels of oil,[507] cut the trade deficit by $34 billion, generate $5 billion of new investment and 214,000 new jobs, boost farm income by $39 billion, and save $11 billion of farm subsidies.[508] Similar benefits are becoming apparent in Europe, whose 430 million gallons of biodiesel production in 2003 (vs. 25 in the U.S.) won support from both oil and auto companies, as well as from farmers and those wishing to reduce farmers' costly surpluses and subsidies to conform to the 1 August 2004 world trade agreement.

Biofuel development must not exacerbate, but if soundly pursued could help ameliorate, two problems common in farming, ranching, and forestry.[509] The first is unsound practices that deplete topsoil, biodiversity (especially in soil microbiota), groundwater, and rural biotic cultures. The second, due largely to distorting subsidy patterns and to lax antitrust enforcement against giant grain dealers and packing houses, is unhealthy market concentration and near-monopsony: by 2002, 62% of agricultural goods came from just 3% of farms, and most farmers' margins continued to head toward zero.[510] Driven by a combination of customer food-safety concerns, soil erosion, litigation, primary-producer economic desperation, market innovations, and large-scale monoculture's increasing risks, a quiet but pervasive grassroots shift has begun. This shift, away from monocultural cropland, rangeland, and woods is beginning in land-grant universities, extension offices, and farms, ranches, and forest operations around the country. The size of this shift is still small, but its economic logic, and the ecological logic that ultimately drives the economics, is compelling. It is even beginning, though initially on a more limited scale than authorized and intended by law, to be rewarded by the 2002 Farm Bill's popular Conservation Security Program.[511]

507. That saved 1.6 billion barrels of oil is half the nominal mean reserves of the Arctic National Wildlife Refuge, which couldn't produce anything by 2012 even if it were approved and economic today.

508. Urbanchuck & Kapell 2002; Renewable Fuels Association 2004.

509. Hawken, Lovins, & Lovins 1999, Chs. 9–11.

510. USDA 2004a.

511. Like commodity price-support programs but unlike any other soil conservation program, the CSP is open-ended in funding and enrollment, but has so far been artificially constrained by rulemaking that is still in progress and is tracked at www.mnproject.org/csp/index.htm.

In general, treating soil like dirt is proving less profitable and durable than treating it as a biotic community—an extraordinarily valuable form of natural capital to be productively used and reinvested in. Highly integrated "Natural Systems Agriculture" is proving that letting free ecosystem services sponsor fertility and crop protection can match or beat the yields, margins, and risks of practices based on chemical or genomic artifice. Biofuels won't automatically solve any of the basic problems of contemporary agriculture, any more than farming and forestry reforms will spontaneously triumph over deeply entrenched practices and concentration trends that are both reinforced by and reinforcing current public policies. But at a minimum, biofuel efforts can support parallel efforts to achieve these outcomes, if designed around recommended practices. Biofuel productivity, at home and abroad, could also greatly benefit from the new nature-mimicking methods' inherent and increasing advantages. Industry standards of practice and certification procedures, analogous to those now spreading through the world's timber industry, should be designed into international biofuels trade from the start. This is in exporters' interest because it will enable them to be paid for shifting carbon from air to soil, rather than being charged for doing the opposite (mining soil carbon by unsustainable farming practices).

Biomaterials

Besides replacing transportation fuels with biobased fuels, there is an opportunity to replace petroleum-derived materials and feedstocks with bioproducts—industrial and consumer goods derived fully or partly from biomass feedstocks (12.3b lb in 2001).[512] Organic chemicals, including plastics, solvents, and alcohols (175b lb in 2001), represent the largest and most direct market for bioproducts based on the similar basic composition (chiefly carbon and hydrogen).[513] Lubricants and greases (20b lb in 2001) are another sizeable market in which bioproducts are beginning to compete.[514]

After petrochemical feedstock savings of 0.27–0.51 Mbbl/d through plastics recycling (pp. 94–95), biomaterials offer a further 0.6 Mbbl/d[515] crude-oil displacement from petrochemical feedstocks in our *Conventional Wisdom* case and 1.2 Mbbl/d[516] in *State of the Art*. In addition, the considerable variety of biolubricants now emerging makes it reasonable to target 2025 biomaterials lubricant substitution savings of 0.04 Mbbl/d for *Conventional Wisdom* and 0.11 Mbbl/d for *State of the Art*.[517] Details are in *Technical Annex*, Ch. 18.

Industry standards of practice and certification procedures should be designed into international biofuels trade from the start.

In 1999, the National Research Council predicted biomaterials could ultimately displace over 90% of petrochemical feedstocks. Vigorous industrial activity to exploit today's even better techniques ← **suggests the first 1 Mbbl/d is realistic by 2025.**

512–514. Paster, Pellegrino, & Carole 2003.

515. We adopt a linearly extrapolated value of 27% (of 1994 usage) in 2025 from NAS/NRC 1999. Of the 2.159 Mbbl/d petroleum used as feedstocks other than for asphalt and lubricants in 1994 (EIA 2003c, Table 5.11), 27% would be 0.583 Mbbl/d. Subtracting 0.23 Mbbl/d of savings due to plastics recycling (pp. 95–96 above) from the original EIA feedstock demand of 2.075 Mbbl/d in 2025 leaves net feedstock demand in 2025 of 1.845 Mbbl/d, of which 0.583 Mbbl/d is a 32% substitution.

---

516. For the 2025 *SOA* biomaterials substitution potential we adopt a conservative 1.2 Mbbl/d—the unused portion of the available biomass after assuming conversion to biofuels for prices <$26/bbl—for a saving of 55% of the forecasted post-efficiency 2.0 Mbbl/d. The 1.2 Mbbl/d value assumes the same energy-conversion efficiency as the biofuels processes for the biomaterials processes, i.e., the remaining biomass feedstocks would yield enough biomaterials to displace ~1.2 Mbbl/d of crude-oil petrochemicals demand.

517. The *Conventional Wisdom* 19% represents a 25% conversion of the 75% of lubricants that are base oil to biobased oils. The 56% *State of the Art* value represents a 75% conversion of the 75% base oil. These values were then multiplied by 203,700 bbl/d (EIA 2003c, Petroleum Products Supplied by Type, Table 5.11, showing 166,000 Mbbl/d; scaled out to 2025 by the forecasted growth rate of 1.2% from EIA 2004, Table 11).

The price of bioproducts remains generally high compared to those of conventional products, but the cost gap is closing. Biorefineries represent a key price reduction route for bioproducts, operating similarly to petroleum refineries by taking in multiple types of biomass feedstocks and converting them through a complex processing strategy to a variety of coproducts including biofuels, biomaterials, power, chemicals, and heat. Production on a commercial scale will also drive down costs as demonstrated by industry leaders already producing on this scale, including Cargill Dow's Nature-Works, Metabolix's PHA polymer production, and DuPont's 3GT™ polymer platform. The market for bioproducts continues to grow, both by pure market forces and through such policy mechanisms as mandated federal purchases of biobased products (notably by DoD), accelerating the rate at which biomaterials become cost-competitive. DuPont's goal of ~20% biofeedstocks for its giant chemical business by 2010 is a harbinger of the next materials revolution—the shift from hydrocarbons to carbohydrates. The chemical giants are placing bets consistent with the National Research Council's 1999 prediction that biomaterials could ultimately meet over 90% of the nation's needs for carbon-based industrial feedstocks.[518]

> DuPont's goal of ~20% biofeedstocks for its giant chemical business by 2010 is a harbinger of the next materials revolution—the shift from hydrocarbons to carbohydrates.
> The chemical giants are placing bets consistent with the National Research Council's 1999 prediction that biomaterials could ultimately meet over 90% of the nation's needs for carbon-based industrial feedstocks.

Option 3. Substituting saved natural gas

Overview

Today's natural gas shortages can be turned into surpluses by using both electricity and natural gas more efficiently. Our initial estimate is that 12 TCF/y (trillion cubic feet per year) of natural gas, equivalent to 12.7 q/y (quadrillion or 10^{15} BTU/y), can be saved in 2025 at a cost of $0.88/MBTU. Obviously that's far below the mid-2004 futures market price for natural gas ($5/MCF delivered in December 2007[519]). This additional gas efficiency potential has been overlooked by policymakers eager to expand domestic gas drilling and liquefied natural gas (LNG) imports. That omission suggests a risk that costly new LNG terminals, if financed and sited, could be ambushed by demand-side competition.

The quickest and cheapest way to save large amounts of natural gas is to save electricity: improving total U.S. electric efficiency by 5% would lower *total* U.S. gas demand by 9%—enough to return gas prices to $3–4/MBTU for years to come. Improved efficiency should start with the peak loads first, because nearly all onpeak electricity is generated in extremely inefficient gas-fired simple-cycle combustion turbines (see discussion below); well-proven techniques could achieve this in just a few years. Some of the saved gas can be substituted for oil in targeted

> **Option 3.**
> Today's natural-gas shortages can be turned into surpluses by efficiently using both electricity and directly used gas. By 2025, natural-gas equivalent to half of today's usage could be saved at a small fraction of today's gas price. Some of the saved gas can then be substituted for oil in targeted uses, but substitution via hydrogen (an option discussed later) could save even more oil and money.

518. NAS/NRC 1999.
519. *Wall St. J.* 2004a.

Reducing natural gas demand will tame the volatile gas markets, lower gas prices, and potentially cut gas bills by $40 billion per year and electric bills by an additional $15 billion per year.

furnaces, boilers, and high-duty-cycle vehicles like buses, but most can yield the greatest value if used to make hydrogen (p. 227).

Reducing natural gas demand will tame the volatile gas markets, lower gas prices, and potentially cut gas bills by $40 billion per year and electric bills by an additional $15 billion per year.[520] Electricity savings, detailed below, will also reduce the likelihood and severity of blackouts by reversing the trend toward larger, more heavily loaded transmission lines,[521] by providing an instantly usable "fire extinguisher" to correct local power imbalances before they cascade across whole regions,[522] and by penalizing artificial scarcity.[523] In summary, the good news is that by adopting these measures, the U.S. can regain more than adequate North American natural gas supplies.

The degree of future gas substitution will ultimately depend on its price relative to the price of residual and distillate fuel oil, and well as on any equipment-related costs of switching. While we can reasonably surmise that both gas and oil prices would decline as U.S. demand drops (unless overtaken by some combination of unexpectedly high oil demand elsewhere, supply disruption, and depletion), we do not believe accurate predictions are available for how these fuels will be competitively priced against each other. Nevertheless, we are using EIA's forecasted future U.S. fuel prices to be consistent with the overall methodology in this report. We next summarize the findings of our analysis of potential U.S. gas savings and substitutions; details are in *Technical Annex*, Ch. 19.

Saving natural gas

United States natural gas markets are currently deregulated, with wellhead prices set by markets. Customers have open access to the natural gas transportation system, at tariffs defined by regulation—generally federal for interstate transactions and state for intrastate transportation and retail distribution. Gas-fired power plants have dominated new power generation because they offer high efficiency and lower emissions. The resulting growth in demand for natural gas,[524] combined with disappointing recent North American supply and discovery,[525] has eliminated the supply overcapacity "bubble." The tight supply/demand balance, combined with gas seasonality, has led to annualized gas price volatility

520. RMI's $40b/y savings estimate is based on the nominal annual value of bringing gas prices down to $3/MBTU. McKinsey consultants (Colledge et al. 2002) estimated the $15b/y power savings from demand response, but their analysis only looked at energy costs, not avoided distribution capital, so the power-cost savings are probably twice as high, especially if the demand-response investments are even modestly targeted.

521. Lovins, Datta, & Swisher 2003.

Recent calls for LNG imports and other costly expansions of U.S. natural gas supplies overlook larger, ← **cheaper, and faster opportunities to use gas far more efficiently.**

522. Lovins, Datta, & Swisher 2003a, based just on utility-dispatchable load reductions, such as brief interruptions of electric water-heater and air-conditioner loads that are imperceptible to the customer. Such radio-dispatched demand adjustments are successfully used in diverse utility systems worldwide, in locales ranging from Europe to New Zealand.

523. Analysis by one of the authors (EKD) shows that if California had installed additional load management equivalent to 1% of its peak load, then in 2000–01, when some suppliers were withholding power supplies to raise prices, shrewd investors could simply have shorted the power market (bet on lower prices), activated their load management, dropped prices, averted shortages, and taken more than $1 billion from the miscreants. This is far cheaper insurance than building new capacity—let alone asking the same firms to do so, thereby increasing their already excessive market power.

524. EIA 2004, p. 47, reports 1995–2002 growth of 43% in gas-fired generating capacity and 31% in gas use. New combined-cycle plants are far more efficient than older simple-cycle or condensing plants, and most of the recently added ~200 GW of combined-cycle plants outran demand, reducing their capacity utilization (EIA 2004, p. 48).   **525.** EIA 2004, pp. 33–45.

of 60% in recent years, vs. 40% for oil.[526] Gas prices have risen from their previously normal range of $3–4/MBTU to $5–6/MBTU,[527] where they could remain in the absence of either higher supply or lower demand. These high gas prices are a significant motivator for improving end-use efficiency, and helped to make U.S. gas demand 6% lower in 2003 than it was at its peak in 2000.[528] Some of that reduction is permanent "demand destruction" from gas-intensive industries' seeking cheaper fuel by moving overseas.

Gas consumption is projected by EIA to rise precipitously from 23 TCF in 2004 to 31 TCF in 2025.[529] Since domestic gas production is expected to be no more than 24 TCF, gas imports could rise to 7 TCF—hence the recent clamor for LNG facilities, Arctic pipelines, and drilling in lower-48 wilderness areas.[530] Is there a better way? What if we take seriously the repeatedly proven economic reality of competitive market equilibration between supply and demand, and ensure that end-use efficiency can actually be bought if it costs less than supply?

There are significant opportunities to save U.S. natural gas in three primary end-uses:

- Electric power generation

- Residential/commercial buildings gas use

- Industrial gas use

Electric utilities

Eighteen percent of U.S. electricity in 2004 is expected to be gas-fired, consuming 5.7 TCF.[531] By 2025, if electricity is used no more efficiently than EIA projects, natural-gas demand for power generation is forecasted to rise to 8.3 TCF.[532] Since nearly all power at periods of peak demand is gas-fired and inefficiently produced, nearly 25% of the gas used for power generation is used for peak power generation.[533] The leverage at the peak is tremendous. A decrease of just 1% of total 2000 U.S. electricity consumption would have reduced *total* natural-gas use by 2%. This decrease in consumption is readily achievable. California's emergency program to shave peak loads to relieve expected summer 2001 power shortages exceeded its goal of contracting for ~1.3% of total peak demand savings over two years. Its implementation began in the first five weeks, and significant savings were realized in the first nine months.[534] Fig. 31 shows

> **The quickest and cheapest way to save large amounts of natural gas is to save electricity: improving total U.S. electric efficiency by 5% would lower total U.S. gas demand by 9%—enough to return gas prices to $3–4/MBTU for years to come.**

526. NPC 2003, pp. 285, 289.

527. EIA 2004.

528. EIA 2004.

529. EIA 2004's baseline already includes a 34% decrease in gas intensity (gas consumption/GDP).

530. NPC 2003.

> **Nearly all peak-period electricity is made from natural gas—so inefficiently that each percent of peak-load reduction saves two percent of total U.S. gas use. Proven and profitable electric-efficiency and load-management methods can save one-fourth of projected 2025 natural-gas demand at about a tenth of today's gas price.**

531. EIA 2004. In 2003, the gas-fired fraction fell to 16%.

532. EIA 2004 predicts 8.6 TCF in 2020, falling back to 8.3 in 2025 because higher gas prices are projected to make coal more competitive.

533. In 2000, gas used for peak power generation was ~1.26 TCF; we estimate this will rise to 2.39 TCF by 2025.

534. Two decades ago, the ten million people served by Southern California Edison Company were cutting its forecasted 10-years-ahead peak demand by 8½%, equivalent to more than 5% of the peak load at the time, *every year*. This cost the utility about 1–2% as much as new power supplies. Today's technologies and delivery methods are far better.

Since nearly all power at periods of peak demand is gas-fired and inefficiently produced, nearly 25% of the gas used for power generation is used for peak power generation. The gas-saving leverage at the peak is tremendous.

Figure 31: Saving electricity to save natural gas

For moderate reductions in U.S. use of electricity including onpeak periods, each percent of electricity saved also saves nearly two percent of total natural gas consumption. We apply the insights of this 2000 RMI analysis to 2025 below as a reasonable approximation. (EIA projects the gas-fired fraction of U.S. electricity to rise only from 18% in 2000 to 21% in 2025. EIA also projects the combustion-turbine-and-diesel fraction of installed capacity—the kinds mainly displaced by peak shaving—to rise from 12% in 2000 to 15% in 2025.[535]) The graph is based on RMI's plant-by-plant economic-dispatch analysis, unadjusted for the subtleties of regional and subregional power flows and transmission constraints and for some minor uncertainties related to dual-fuel oil/gas units. Electricity savings here include peak periods, either because onpeak savings are specifically encouraged or because efficiency is improved in uses like industrial motors and commercial lighting that operate onpeak as well as at other times. The curve's slope is steeper for electrical savings up to 5% because combustion turbines, rather than more efficient (e.g. combined-cycle) units, are being displaced.

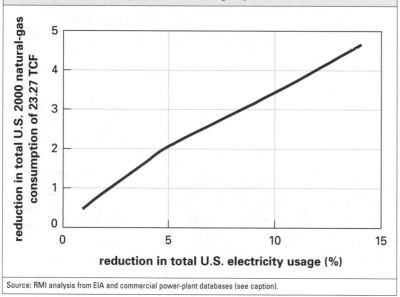

Source: RMI analysis from EIA and commercial power-plant databases (see caption).

this little-known but important relationship between total U.S. electricity savings (that include peak periods) and natural gas savings.

By 2025, EIA projects that the U.S. will have 175 GW of combustion turbines and 202 GW of combined-cycle units, consuming 8.3 TCF of gas.[536] To reduce this consumption, we recommend starting with peak load programs (programs that economically reduce customer electricity demand during a utility's peak generation periods). These are generally cheaper than the capacity cost of a new combustion turbine,[537] but unlike the turbine, consume no gas. Well-managed utilities across the country are actively pursuing these programs, and EPRI (Electric Power Research Institute) has estimated that demand-response programs have the potential to reduce U.S. peak demand by 45 GW—more than 6% of projected demand.[538] RMI conservatively estimates that peak-load management programs[539] can shave enough peak load to save at least ~2% of total electricity consumption, and thus the first ~4% of U.S. gas use could be eliminated for *negative* cost, due to those savings' capacity value and market-hedging value.[539a]

---

535. This capacity allocation would be consistent with a peakier load, but oddly, EIA projects aggregate system load factor to rise from 50.4% to 52.9%. This doesn't affect our analysis.

536. EIA 2004.

537. For example, the peak-load reductions were expected to cost an average of ~$320/kW (2000 $) over all ten state-administered programs (Ceniceros, Sugar, & Tessier 2002). This cost would approximate the national average that utilities reported for their 2000 load-management programs. Subsequent measurement found the California emergency programs' actual costs averaged ~$155/kW: Rudman (2003) summarizing CEC 2003. (This is for the first 509 MW of peak savings evaluated, achieved through 2002, and excludes LED traffic signals, which are meant mainly to save kWh, not peak load.) The programs' cost was decreased by California's two decades of experience and built-up delivery infrastructure, but increased by major savings previously achieved and by the premium paid to procure the new savings very quickly.

538. EPRI 2001.

539. This traditional term includes load-shaving and -shifting both under utility control and by customer choice, the latter often informed by real-time price signals and facilitated by smart meters. Principles and practice are surveyed in NEDRI 2003.

539a. Our economic assessment used the CEF study's costs, which are for efficiency, not load-shifting; we understand the distinction, and didn't double-count the peak-load savings.

Electric end-use efficiency programs assumed in the *Conventional Wisdom* and *State of the Art* scenarios will eliminate 18% and 27% of total 2025 U.S. electricity consumption, respectively.[540] Such programs, reflecting good but not best practice and typically excluding side-benefits (such as reduced maintenance costs that can largely or wholly offset their invest-ment),[541] cost around 2.0¢/kWh and 1.7¢/kWh (2000 $, levelized over the life of the equipment), respectively. If we apply these programs to the projected 2025 power generation dispatch curve, we estimate that 5.1–8.1 TCF of natural gas could be displaced.[542] Subtracting the value of avoided generating capacity and deferred grid capacity, the CSE is 0.8¢/kWh for *Conventional Wisdom* and 0.6¢/kWh for *State of the Art*. When we con-vert this to the cost of saved gas, based on the typical efficiencies of the various types of power plants, we find that *State of the Art* electric end-use efficiency could eliminate 25% of 2025 natural-gas use at an average Cost of Saved Energy of $0.60/MBTU.

> *State of the Art* electric end-use efficiency could eliminate 25% of 2025 gas use at an average Cost of Saved Energy of $0.60/MBTU.

Buildings

As explained on pp. 97–98 and in *Technical Annex*, Ch. 16, we used the five National Laboratories' peer-reviewed Clean Energy Futures (CEF) study[543] to calculate *Conventional Wisdom* and *State of the Art* instanta-neous-potential gas savings in 2025 of 13% (1.28 TCF/y, 1.32 q/y) and 25% (2.57 TCF/y, 2.64 q/y), at CSEs of $1.51 and $1.71/MBTU, respectively. These savings, and those below for industry, are all in gas used directly for heat.

> Conservative National Lab analyses show a profitable potential by 2025 to save non-electric-utility gas use equivalent to another eighth of 2025 natural-gas demand.

Industrial fuel

Industry uses natural gas to produce process heat and steam, as well as for feedstocks, which are treated separately below. Based on the CEF study (p. 97, above), we conservatively estimate that with *Conventional Wisdom* technologies, ~5% of 2025 industrial-fuel natural gas can be saved, equivalent to 0.63 TCF/y (0.65 q/y), at a CSE of $1.50/MBTU. The corresponding ~11% *State of the Art* potential is equivalent to 1.33 TCF/y (1.37 q/y) at a lower CSE—only $1.00/MBTU.[544] Details are in *Technical Annex*, Ch. 15. Our practical experience as efficiency consultants in heavy process plants suggests a much larger potential, but data to substantiate this across diverse U.S. industries aren't publicly available. The CEF study assumes that the stock of industrial equipment, like build-ings, turns over in 40 years and that all the remaining stock gets retrofit-

540. This analysis is based on the CEF study: Interlaboratory Working Group 2000.

541. Lovins 1994, main text and note 36. Moreover, gains in labor productivity or retail sales are often worth an order of magnitude more than the saved energy (Romm & Browning 1994; HMG 2003; HMG 2003a; HMG 2003b).

542. Including the displaced oil-fired electricity generation, and assuming nominal national-average grid-loss estimates of 7% offpeak and 14% onpeak.

543. Interlaboratory Working Group 2000. As for oil savings in buildings (pp. 98–98), we simply applied the CEF *Moderate* and *Advanced* cases' percentage savings to the EIA 2004 Reference Case.

544. Interlaboratory Working Group 2000.

ted over 20 years, but it doesn't show these two effects separately, and hence understates the savings potentially available from more aggressive implementation (as is also true of industrial direct oil savings, p. 97, above).

The following table provides a summary of the straightforward potential gas savings in 2025 from the major sectors we list above.

Table 1: Potential savings of U.S. natural gas via end-use efficiency in electricity, industrial fuel, and buildings, and the corresponding Cost of Saved Energy. The savings shown are realistically implementable by 2025.

Means of savings by sector	Conventional Wisdom		State of the Art	
	gas saved (TCF/y)	CSE ($/MBTU)	gas saved (TCF/y)	CSE ($/MBTU)
electricity generation via demand response	5.1	$0.78	8.1	$0.60
industrial-fuel gas end-use efficiency	0.6	$1.50	1.3	$1.00
residential/commercial buildings' direct gas end-use efficiency	1.3	$1.51	2.6	$1.71
total	7.0	$0.98	12.0	$0.88

Natural gas savings compound. When less natural gas is delivered through the nation's pipeline system, the 3% of gas used as fuel to compress it also decreases more or less proportionally. Conservatively assuming that gas from LNG imports require *no* pipelining (as imports at least to Gulf of Mexico terminals would) and are displaced first, pro-rata compressor savings add a free "bonus" saving of 0.22 TCF/y to the 12 TCF/y of 2025 savings just shown. Moreover, 10–12% of the remaining compressor fuel gas, or a further ~0.09 TCF/y, can be saved by straightforward efficiency retrofits of existing pipeline compressors at a CSE of ~$0.16/MBTU.[545] These two savings increase the total *State of the Art* 2025 gas-saving potential to 12.3 TCF/y at an average CSE of $0.86/MBTU. To the extent the saved gas is in fact re-used, however, either to displace oil directly or to produce hydrogen, rather than being left in the ground, both of these savings would need appropriate adjustment.

Saving 12 TCF/y of gas, or 39% of EIA's total projected 2025 gas use, would reduce gas consumption below U.S. domestic gas production (and indeed below today's consumption), avoid the cost of new imports, and as noted above, cut 2025 gas and electricity bills by probably upwards of $50 billion a year by reducing both quantities used and prices. The question remains, though: would this lower-price saved gas then actually substitute for oil?

545. B. Willson (Director of Engines and Energy Conservation Laboratory and Associate Professor of Mechanical Engineering, Colorado State University, Fort Collins), personal communication, 8 April 2004. In addition, much of the compression energy could be profitably recovered—an untapped gigawatt-scale resource—by reducing gas pressure at the city gate through turboexpanders rather than choke valves. The resulting electricity would probably displace mainly coal. The obstacles to capturing it appear to be structural and regulatory, not technical or economic.

Substituting saved gas for oil

Natural gas has served as a substitute for oil for years; in fact, gas currently used in the end-uses discussed above was at some point substituted for residual fuel oil, distillate fuel oil, or naphtha. Therefore, the question is not whether this substitution is technically feasible, but whether it is economical. The decision to substitute gas is based on four main factors: the difference in fuel prices between gas and the respective oil product, the retrofit capital costs, environmental regulatory emissions requirements, and savings due to the gas equipment's improvement in end-use efficiency vs. the existing oil equipment. Currently, industry's ability to switch from gas to oil is largely limited by environmental regulations on air emissions, whereas the ability to switch from oil to gas has been limited by their relative prices at the point of end-use (the "burner tip").

Natural gas is no longer the cheap and abundant fuel that it once was. During the 1980s and early 1990s, gas was priced to be competitive with residual oil, which in turn is priced roughly 10% below crude oil prices, so gas remained inexpensive. By 2000, gas demand began to outstrip the ability of U.S. infrastructure to supply and deliver it, and prices rose to considerable peaks—up to $10/MBTU.[546] During 2001–03, gas has exhibited higher and more volatile prices than oil. Gas futures, too, are currently trending above oil at $5–6/MBTU,[547] with a higher implied volatility than West Texaco Intermediate crude oil (*Technical Annex*, Ch. 19).

While gas can be saved inexpensively (Table 1), it will then be resold not at its *Cost* of Saved Energy, but at the market *price* that reflects the supply and demand conditions prevailing at the time. Substituting saved gas for oil is not free, but requires capital costs for the conversion. These investments, absent an environmental requirement, would only be made if the

> Regardless of the unknowable future relative prices of oil and natural gas, saved gas can profitably displace at least 1.6 Mbbl/d of 2025 oil, with about 8 TCF/y (equivalent to one-third of 2004 gas demand) of saved gas left over.

546. EIA 2004.
547. *Wall St. J.* 2004a.

Table 2: Estimated non-transportation 2025 oil uses, potentially suitable for gas substitution, remaining after full implementation of *State of the Art* end-use efficiency and substitution of biofuels, biomaterials, and biolubricants. No transportation uses are considered except intra-city buses (p. 120).

Sector	EIA 2025 projected oil use (Mbbl/d)	2025 oil use after full implementation of *State of the Art* efficiency (Mbbl/d)	2025 oil use after full implementation of *State of the Art* efficiency and biosubstitution (Mbbl/d)
industrial fuel	2.82	2.28	2.18
petrochemical feedstocks & lubricants	2.75	2.02	0.79
residential buildings	0.86	0.64	0.64
commercial buildings	0.46	0.34	0.32
intra-city buses	0.05	0.05	0.05
power	0.36	0.04	0.04
total	7.31	5.38	4.03

Cogeneration
was a near-universal
U.S. practice in 1910,
but fell into disuse,
making the U.S.
electricity sector's
fuel productivity
lower in 2004 than
in 1904.

gas commodity price were cheaper or if the gas appliance were significantly more efficient than its oil-fired counterpart. What do these conditions imply about future gas substitution?

To estimate that substitution potential, we assume that the *State of the Art* energy efficiency improvements will be implemented for both oil and gas since they save money for consumers. If their full technical potential is captured by 2025, and biofuels and biomaterials are then fully substituted, then 4 Mbbl/d of non-transportation oil use will remain in 2025 for potential gas substitution, as shown in Table 2, p. 121.

12: Replacing one-third of remaining non-transportation oil use with saved natural gas

Substituting natural gas for industrial fuel oil

Saved natural gas can be substituted for much of the remaining 2.2 Mbbl/d of 2025 industrial fuel oil consumption, which is almost entirely for process heat and (mostly) steam.[548] Even without the lower gas price that might be expected from saving 12 TCF/y, industrial users may find switching to natural gas cheaper, either because industrial-scale gas furnaces are significantly more efficient than their oil counterparts, or because cogeneration (combined heat and power, or CHP) creates an opportunity to displace oil-fired steam boilers with heat that would otherwise be wasted. Our best estimate is that 56% of industrial oil used as fuel, or 1.2 Mbbl/d, raises steam in non-cogenerating boilers.[549]

Cogeneration was a near-universal U.S. practice in 1910, but fell into disuse, making the U.S. electricity sector's fuel productivity lower in 2004 than in 1904.[550] As some U.S. firms and a far larger number abroad demonstrate daily, cogeneration is more energy-efficient than separately producing power and steam, since the waste heat of thermal power generation is used to create the steam, replacing boiler fuel. Thermal efficiencies of cogeneration technologies can be 90% or more—higher than a boiler and far higher than a central power station, but cogeneration displaces *both*. At EIA's projected energy prices, a typical 36-MW$_e$ industrial cogeneration unit would have a Cost of Saved Energy around –$4.52/bbl and an Internal Rate of Return (IRR) of 77%/y (see *Technical Annex*, Ch. 19). Displacing 1.2 Mbbl/d of industrial oil consumption would require 43 GW of cogeneration. Is there enough potential cogeneration available?

548. EIA 2004d.

549. Fifty-six percent of residual and distillate fuel oils used in manufacturing in 1998 were boiler fuel (EIA 1998).

550. Cogeneration could save a projected $5 trillion of global capital costs through 2030, $2.8 trillion in fuel cost, and 50% in the incremental power generation's CO_2 emissions (Casten & Downes 2004; U.S. Combined Heat and Power Association, www.uschpa.org).

551. The CEF analysis was derived for industrial subsectors from Resource Dynamics Corporation's DIStributed Power Economic Rationale Selection (DISPERSE) model. The DISPERSE model assumes that U.S. policies are structured to reduce barriers to financing, siting, utility interconnection, discriminatory tariffs, etc., and therefore support cogeneration. For additional information on barrier-busting policies that would promote the growth of CHP, see Lemar 2001 and Ch. 3 of Lovins et al. 2002.

552. Cogeneration forecast potential based on Lemar 2001.

553. EIA 2001b reports that 72.6% of residences have access to natural gas in their neighborhood, while 57.3% of commercial buildings (67.6% of commercial floorspace) actually use natural gas and 9.7% (9.3% by floorspace) use propane. Presumably more customers may have access to gas than actually use it, but ~44% of buildings that do not currently use gas or propane could switch. Since more oil is saved through efficiency and biofuels substitution in the *State of the Art* scenario, there is less left to be switched to gas (EIA 2001b, EIA 1999).

The CEF study found that 75 GW of new industrial CHP capacity were economically viable in the *Advanced* scenario, assuming that U.S. policies were structured to eliminate barriers to cogeneration,[551] and 40 GW in the *Moderate* scenario.[552] We thus expect that 1.15 Mbbl/d with our *Conventional Wisdom* technologies, and with *State of the Art* technologies, at least 56% of the remaining 2025 industrial oil use, or 1.2 Mbbl/d, could be switched to gas through cogeneration.

Substituting gas in buildings

Since the gas grid does not extend everywhere in the United States, especially in rural areas, we estimate that less than half (0.46 Mbbl/d in *Conventional Wisdom* or 0.39 Mbbl/d in *State of the Art*) of 2025 building oil consumption has the ability to switch to gas.[553] Of this, 0.3 Mbbl/d and 0.26 Mbbl/d, respectively, is projected to be residential building demand that would switch to gas when the existing residential boiler or furnace must be replaced. We assume that this switchover will occur because gas furnaces average one-eighth higher efficiency than their oil-fired counterparts.[554] The Cost of Saved Energy is −$16 to +$3/bbl for *Conventional Wisdom* (average homes) and −$8 to +$18/bbl[555]

554. New gas-fired condensing furnaces for residential use have an Annual Fuel Utilization Efficiency (AFUE) of 94–96%. The equivalent oil-fired furnace has an AFUE of 83–86% (ACEEE, undated).

555. There is less oil to displace in homes that have already implemented efficiency measures so their CSE is higher.

556. Cogeneration for commercial buildings is generally on a smaller scale than for industrial uses. Therefore, the CSE for cogeneration for commercial buildings assumes a 1-MW electric generating capacity, vs. 50 MW capacity for industrial applications.

557. NPC 2003.

558. NPC 2003.

559. NPC 2003, II:54.

560. The National Petroleum Council predicts that gas demand for feedstocks will decrease during 2001–25. However, we do not classify this decrease as saved gas, because the decrease will be made up for either by switching *to* oil or by petrochemical producers' simply leaving the U.S.

for *State of the Art* (high-efficiency homes). See *Technical Annex*, Ch. 19, for details.

The remaining oil consumption is in commercial buildings. Authoritative studies of the relative merits of gas vs. oil commercial building furnaces and boilers were unavailable at the time of this writing. However, cogeneration and tri-generation are likely to substitute for oil-fired heat at almost all locations served by gas, once the onerous backup charges and interconnection barriers are removed. We make the conservative assumption that commercial buildings' natural gas access mirrors the residential building sector's, and estimate that 0.14 Mbbl/d in *Conventional Wisdom* and 0.11 Mbbl/d in *State of the Art* can be saved through cogeneration, at a CSE of $0.22/bbl for both scenarios.[556]

Substituting for petrochemical feedstocks

Natural gas and natural gas liquids (NGLs, which EIA counts as part of petroleum consumption, p. 40) are important to the chemical industry as both fuel and feedstock. Currently, the U.S chemical industry, making more than one-fourth of the world's chemicals, accounts for 12% of total U.S. gas demand, and 24% of this feedstock gas consumption is used directly to make such basic chemicals as ethylene and ammonia.[557] In 1999, when natural gas prices averaged $2.27/MBTU, the average operating margin for the chemical industry was 6.8%, but as gas prices rose to $3.97/MBTU in 2002 (also in nominal dollars), margins fell to 0.6%.[558] The winter 2000–01 gas price spike idled 50% of methanol, 40% of ammonia, and 15% of ethylene capacity.[559] Natural gas prices are generally forecasted by EIA to remain at or above their high 2004 level, so eroding margins will force companies to consider either fuel-switching to oil or moving their operations offshore.[560]

(continued on next page)

Therefore, substituting gas for naphtha feed-stocks is unlikely. However, if our gas-saving recommendations are implemented, natural gas prices will probably decline substantially due to decreased demand. (Indeed, gas-intensive industries can best obtain cheap gas to sustain their U.S. operations by supporting regional and national electricity and gas efficiency.) In that case, companies would probably stay in the country, thereby sustaining U.S. jobs, but might still not switch to gas. Refineries will make less naphtha as they produce fewer refined prod-ucts, but the naphtha is cheaply available, and any left over will be made into gasoline.

Shifting natural gas from peaky power-generat-ing loads to steady industrial and petrochemical loads also has a major hidden advantage: the industry could better time gas-storage injec-tions, further reducing price volatility. This may even reduce average prices by reducing buyers' need to hedge against price volatility and peak-period deliverability problems in a quite imper-fect market. And of course anything that makes natural gas prices lower and steadier improves the competitiveness of U.S. industry and reduces migration offshore, preserving American jobs.

We conservatively omit the following three further ways to save feedstock natural gas:

- substituting biomaterials for gas just as we did above (pp. 93–96; *Technical Annex*, Ch. 18), to save 0.9 Mbbl/d of oil-derived chemical feedstocks (e.g., plant-derived polyhydrox-yalkanoates have properties similar to petro-chemical-based polypropylene's);

- potential savings in petrochemical feedstocks (e.g. from plastics recycling[561]) that would lower natural gas use, just as it does for oil (pp. 93–96); and

- using precision farming and organic methods to reduce the ~0.5 q/y (1998) of natural gas that goes into nitrogen fertilizer, much of which isn't effectively used and simply wash-es away as water pollution.[562]

Other uses

The remaining two uses of oil that could use nat-ural gas as a substitute are small (details are in *Technical* Annex, Ch. 19). We expect intra-city buses to switch from diesel to compressed natu-ral gas (CNG) at relatively low cost.[563] If CNG hybrid buses were deployed, 0.07 q/y of natural gas would displace 0.04 Mbbl/d of diesel fuel at a CSE of $8–16/bbl.[564] Both hybrid and CNG tech-nologies are already commercialized separate-ly—the largest U.S. fleets are respectively in Seattle and Los Angeles—and we expect their combined adoption to occur in both *Convention-al Wisdom* and *State of the Art.* Conversion can occur rather quickly: Beijing recently converted its entire bus fleet to CNG and LPG in just three years. In the electric power sector, the other main remaining oil use that could in principle be substituted by gas, end-use efficiency and dis-placement by renewables eliminates most oil-fired electric power generation (p. 98); any minor potential remaining for gas substitution is neg-lected here. All the rest is located only in Hawai'i and Alaska in areas beyond the gas grid; as a result, no additional gas-for-oil substitution is expected, although there is often major poten-tial from efficiency plus small-scale renewables, both encouraged by high power costs.

561. A Dutch lifecycle assessment found a 31% near-term potential for improving the 1988 energy efficiency of plastic packaging (Worrell, Meuleman, & Blok 1995).

562. A 30–50% potential saving available within a decade was found in the Netherlands (Worrell, Meuleman, & Blok 1995).

563. The reasons for such conversions are often as much to clean up urban air as to cut fuel and maintenance costs.

564. Powertrain hybridization of intra-urban buses, which are relatively inefficient because of their slow, stop-and-go service, should save ~30–37% of their fuel, with an increase of 60% in bus fuel economy; see GM 2004a.

Table 3: Potential 2025 substitutions of saved natural gas (shown in Table 1) **for suitable uses of oil after efficiency and biosubstitution** (shown in Table 2). Considerably larger substitutions would be feasible and could be driven by relative burner-tip prices if known or if influenced by policy (such as carbon trading). The substitutions shown are the minimum expected to be attractive regardless of the relative prices of oil and gas, with no other interventions. The bus term includes both fuel efficiency (via hybridization) and substitution of compressed natural gas for diesel fuel.

Sector	Conventional Wisdom			State of the Art		
	oil saved (Mbbl/d)	gas substitution (TCF/y)	CSE ($/bbl)	oil saved (Mbbl/d)	gas substitution (TCF/y)	CSE ($/bbl)
industrial fuel	1.15	2.89	−$4.52	1.23	3.07[566]	−$4.52
residential buildings	0.30	0.50	−$6.44	0.26	0.43	$4.72
commercial buildings	0.14	0.50	$0.22	0.11	0.43	$0.22
intra-city buses	0.04	0.07	$11.86	0.04	0.07	$11.86
total	1.63	3.96	−$4.08	1.64	4.00	−$2.32

Anything that makes natural gas prices lower and steadier improves the competitiveness of U.S. industry and reduces migration offshore, preserving American jobs.

Without assuming that saved natural gas will be resold for below the burner-tip price of petroleum products, the *State of the Art* methods summarized in Box 12 can still plausibly displace 1.6 Mbbl/d of oil using just 4.0 TCF/y of the 12 TCF/y of saved natural gas. The average cost[565] of this displacement is −$2.3/bbl, dominated by the largest term—industrial cogeneration (Table 3).

The potential 2025 natural gas savings in Table 1 and their substitutions for oil in Table 3 are summarized in Fig. 32 (see next page) as supply curves.

Gas-for-oil substitution could become considerably greater than shown in Fig. 32 if driven by a gas price advantage, environmental constraints (such as ozone restrictions or carbon pricing), or public policy. However, at the modest one-third substitution level shown here, about 8 TCF/y of saved natural gas will still be left over in 2025 for a variety of uses. Two are obvious: combined-cycle power plants (many idled by electric end-use efficiency) or further co- and trigeneration in buildings and industry. Both would displace coal-fired electricity, as would become more likely in a carbon-trading regime. A third use for the leftover gas,

565. CSEs are calculated based on cost of substitution only, except in the case of residential buildings and intra-city buses where substitution and efficiency gains could not be logically separated.

566. Natural gas used for cogeneration would displace not only oil but also coal and other fuels used to generate electricity.

for probably the highest profit margins and the greatest savings in fossil fuel and carbon emissions, would be conversion to hydrogen for use both in vehicles and in co- or trigenerating fuel cells in factories and buildings (pp. 227–242).

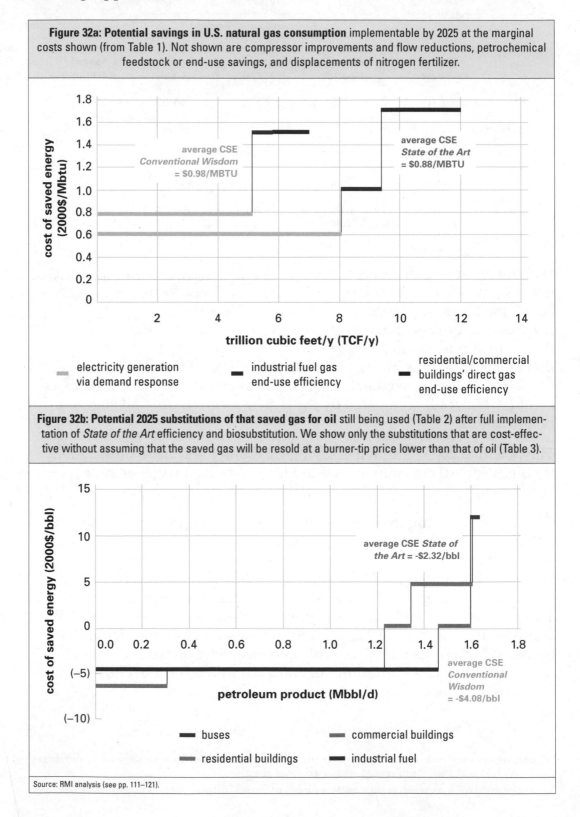

Figure 32a: Potential savings in U.S. natural gas consumption implementable by 2025 at the marginal costs shown (from Table 1). Not shown are compressor improvements and flow reductions, petrochemical feedstock or end-use savings, and displacements of nitrogen fertilizer.

Figure 32b: Potential 2025 substitutions of that saved gas for oil still being used (Table 2) after full implementation of *State of the Art* efficiency and biosubstitution. We show only the substitutions that are cost-effective without assuming that the saved gas will be resold at a burner-tip price lower than that of oil (Table 3).

Source: RMI analysis (see pp. 111–121).

Combined Conventional Potential

To recap: if *all State of the Art* end-use efficiency recommendations were implemented by 2025, 52% of EIA's forecast oil use would be eliminated. And half of this remaining oil use would in turn be displaced by substituting for oil the available and competitive 2025 biofuels/biomaterials/biolubricants (pp. 103–111), and the clearly advantageous portion of substituting saved natural gas (pp. 111–112). In actuality, however, the following section, on Implementation, will show that only 55% of that efficiency potential can be implemented by 2025 by the means described; the other ~45% would remain to be captured soon thereafter.

Given that realistic implementation, one-third of 2025 oil demand would be displaced by the supply substitutions (pp. 43–102). The idealized-efficiency-only Fig. 29 (p. 102) would then turn into the realistic path shown in Fig. 33; the two graphs are similar because the supply substitutions by 2025 nearly offset the not-yet-captured efficiency.

Using oil efficiently and displacing it with cheaper conventional substitutes could meet 80% of forecasted 2025 oil imports. The rest is less than what efficiency will capture soon after 2025. Domestic supply alternatives could even displace that last 20% *plus*, if desired (pp. 227–242), the forecasted domestic oil output. Making America oil-free within a few decades is thus both practical and profitable.

Figure 33: U.S. oil use and oil imports if end-use efficiency, biosubstitution, and saved-natural-gas substitution were realistically implemented during 2005–25, vs. EIA's *Annual Energy Outlook 2004* Reference Case projection. Leftover saved natural gas isn't shown.

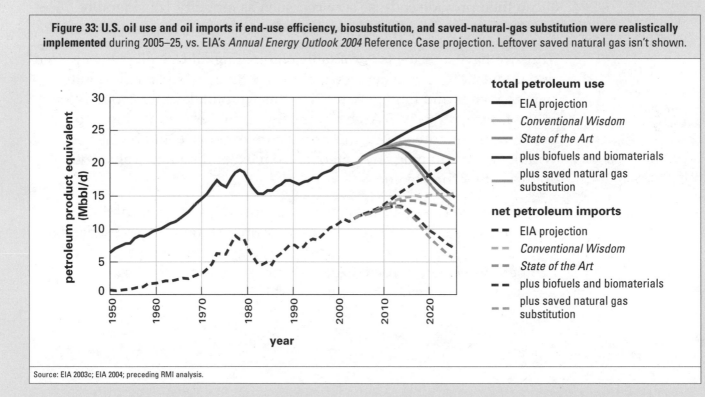

Source: EIA 2003c; EIA 2004; preceding RMI analysis.

We have a recipe for profitably eliminating all U.S. oil use, imported and domestic, over the next few decades, with considerable flexibility in both means and timing. Achieving this would take only about as long in the future as the 1973 Arab oil embargo is in the past. Within two generations, a more prosperous and secure America could be oil-free—possibly without, and certainly with, a modest part of the cost-effective potential from expanding renewable energy sources other than biofuels, notably windpower converted to hydrogen.

But how to capture that combined potential? Next we'll show how innovative business strategies, accelerated by public opinion, can actually capture half of Fig. 29's efficiency potential and the other half soon thereafter. But even with 7 Mbbl/d of savings still to be captured after 2025 as vehicle stocks complete their turnover, the 2025 supply-demand balance could be revolutionized, as charted in Fig. 34. Eighty percent of forecasted 2025 U.S. oil demand—all but 5 Mbbl/d—can be met in that year either by profitable, actually implementable efficiency and alternative supplies or by the 7.8 Mbbl/d of domestic petroleum supply that EIA forecasts for 2025.[567] Adding the 7 Mbbl/d of further efficiency gains to be captured soon after 2025 would thus meet the entire forecasted demand without even needing 2 Mbbl/d of the forecast domestic petroleum output. And as we'll see on pp. 227–242, this doesn't yet count two large further options—substituting leftover saved natural gas in the form of hydrogen, or making still more hydrogen from non-biomass renewables.

The 7.8 Mbbl/d of domestic petroleum output shown isn't actually needed either. That's because the 8 TCF/y of leftover saved U.S. natural gas, plus another 2.5 TCF/y we'll explain on pp. 238–239, can be converted to hydrogen (pp. 227–242), which can be used 2–3 times as efficiently as oil. It can then provide end-use services, such as mobility, considerably greater than the 7.8 Mbbl/d of oil can do.

Thus we have a recipe for profitably eliminating all U.S. oil use, imported and domestic, over the next few decades, with considerable flexibility in both means and timing. Achieving this would take only about as long in the future as the 1973 Arab oil embargo is in the past. Within two generations, a more prosperous and secure America could be oil-free— without even counting any potential from expanding renewable energy sources other than biofuels.

Having charted this journey beyond oil, how do we begin, conduct, and complete it? The business and policy opportunities we present next can take us there, as part of a broader strategy for building a durably competitive economy, revitalized industries, a vibrant rural sector, a cleaner environment, and a safer world.

567. Comprising 4.61 Mbbl/d crude oil and lease condensate, 2.47 Mbbl/d natural-gas plant liquids, 0.48 Mbbl/d other refinery inputs (chiefly from natural gas), and 0.24 Mbbl/d for volumetric gain from domestic crude.

Figure 34: Petroleum product equivalent supply and demand, 2000 and 2005

Supply-demand integration for 2025, using EIA's convention of expressing savings volume in Mbbl/d of petroleum product equivalent. EIA's forecasted demand in 2025 (with 2000 shown for comparison) could be cut in half (third bar from the left) if *State of the Art* end-use efficiency were fully implemented. The following implementation analysis finds that ~55% of that efficiency potential can be captured by 2025 through *Drift* plus *Coherent Engagement* policies, as shown, leaving the other ~45% as the not-yet-captured profitable efficiency potential shown by the vertical arrow. The 20 Mbbl/d of net demand can then be met as shown by a combination of bio-derived oil substitutes, saved and substituted natural gas, and domestic petroleum production, plus 5 Mbbl/d of "remaining supply" to be derived from any combination of: North American oil imports, biofuel imports, saved natural gas (8 TCF/y of saved gas remains for substitution either directly or as hydrogen), buying more efficiency or biosubstitutes than shown (since our analysis, especially for efficiency, stopped short of the forecasted oil price, and far short of the full social value of oil displacement including externalities), or simply waiting a bit longer to finish implementing the remaining 7 Mbbl/d of *State of the Art* efficiency, chiefly by completing the turnover of vehicle stocks.

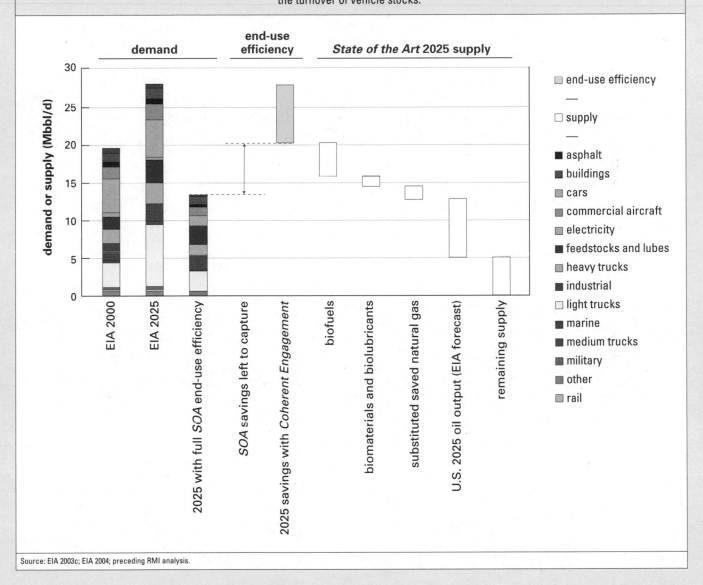

Source: EIA 2003c; EIA 2004; preceding RMI analysis.

Implementation

Strategic vision

The prize

Imagine a revitalized and globally competitive U.S. motor-vehicle industry delivering a new generation of highly efficient, safe, incredibly durable, fun-to-drive vehicles that consumers want. Imagine equally rugged and efficient heavy trucks that boost truckers' gross profits by $7.5 billion per year.[568] Consider the pervasive economic benefits of an advanced-materials industrial cluster that makes strong, lightweight materials cheaply for products from Strykers to bicycles to featherweight washing machines you can carry up the stairs by yourself. Envision a secure national fuels infrastructure based largely or wholly on U.S. energy resources and on vibrant rural communities farming biofuel, plastics, wind, and carbon. Think of over one million new, high-wage jobs, and the broad wealth creation from infusing the economy with $133 *billion* per year of new disposable income from lower crude-oil costs. Recognize with pride that with this new economy, the U.S. is nearly achieving international greenhouse gas targets as a free byproduct. Picture increased energy and national security as oil use heads toward zero, and as the U.S. regains the leverage of using petrodollars to buy what our society really needs rather than handing those dollars to oil suppliers to feed an addiction. Imagine a U.S. military focused on its core mission of defense, free from the distraction of getting and guarding oil for ourselves and the rest of the world. Imagine that the U.S., able once again to practice its admired ideals, has regained the moral high ground in foreign policy. Finally, envision one of the largest and broadest-based tax cuts in U.S. history from eliminating the implicit tax that oil dependence imposes on our country by bleeding purchasing power, inflating military and subsidy costs, and suppressing homegrown energy solutions.

Sound utopian? It is not.

This vision is based on severely practical business solutions to the "creative destruction" dilemma currently faced by the chief executives in the U.S. transportation sector, and on the handful of market-oriented government policies that are needed to help lower the risk of this transition. The business principles are grounded in such classic and prescient works as Joseph Schumpeter's writing on the concept of "creative destruction" (*Capitalism, Socialism and Democracy*, 1943), Michael Porter's *Competitive Strategy* (1980), and Clayton Christensen's and Michael Raynor's *The Innovator's Solution* (2003).

> Since phasing out oil doesn't cost money but saves money, business will lead it for profit. However, supportive rather than hostile public policies would help, and coherent national-security policy can be a vital contributor.

> Applying classic business concepts of competitive strategy to the oil problem can create astonishing gains in national prosperity, security, equity, and environmental quality.

> A $180-billion industrial investment in the next decade can return $130+ billion *per year* in gross oil savings, or $70 billion a year in net savings, by 2025.

> Envision the largest and broadest-based tax cut in U.S. history from eliminating the implicit tax that oil dependence imposes on our country by bleeding purchasing power, inflating military and subsidy costs, and suppressing homegrown energy solutions.

568. Of the ~20b gal/y consumed by trucking, 37% is saved at a net customer gain of ~$1/gal—the difference in cost between the fuel efficiency technologies and the retail price of diesel fuel.

Our business analysis supports an exciting and astounding conclusion: intelligently investing an incremental $90 billion[569] over the next two decades in retooling the domestic automotive, trucking, and airplane industries and another $90 billion in domestic energy infrastructure, could create the capacity to achieve this oil-free future. Yet despite the high rates of return on these investments, they entail too much business risk—perceived or actual—for the private sector to do entirely on its own, quickly enough to meet national needs.

Vaulting the barriers

Risk-aversion has deep roots in the cultures of very large organizations. Their enormous sunk costs, both in physical assets and in psychological habits, create an immune system that stubbornly resists invasion by innovation. This resistance can be shown by rigorous business scrutiny to be destructive: innovation and competition are the evolutionary pressures that make the firm stronger. Nevertheless the "not invented here" mentality stubbornly persists. Wrenching change is always difficult and seldom greeted with enthusiasm. IBM had 77% higher real revenue and 20% higher real earnings in 2000–03 than it did in 1978–81, the pre-PC age when it was the king of mechanical typewriters and mainframe computers, but its transition into the microcomputer age was very hard—a near-death experience. The challenge facing U.S. makers of light vehicles, heavy trucks, and airplanes is equally daunting. But in a competitive global marketplace, the alternative to bold leadership is worse. As General Electric's former CEO Jack Welch put it, if we don't control our own destiny, someone else will.

To complement market forces, and to reduce the risk to the weakened U.S. transportation equipment sector, we need a coherent set of government policies to support the transition. We need economically efficient policies that shift companies' and customers' choices toward higher-fuel-economy vehicles of all kinds while expanding their freedom of choice; help manufacturers to retool their factories and retrain their workers; support the rapid emergence of cost-effective bio-fuels, other renewables, and domestic fuels; upgrade our transportation systems to reduce congestion; align utilities' profit motives with their customers' interests; and eliminate perverse incentives across the domestic-energy value chain. While we can

American business can continue to be threatened by obsolescence and dwindling market share, or can grasp oil displacement's unique opportunity to revitalize key industries.

If America intelligently invested an incremental $90 billion over the next two decades in retooling the domestic automotive, trucking, and airplane industries and another $90 billion in domestic energy infrastructure, we would have the capacity to achieve an oil-free future.

569. $100 billion is needed for new efficient automotive and trucking manufacturing capacity, plus R&D for new platform development. We estimate that ~$30 billion will be spent anyway in the U.S. to meet projected new car demand, for a net increase of $70 billion. An additional $20 billion of incremental investment is needed for airplanes. Therefore, the total incremental investment is $90 billion—essentially the same as the ~$91 billion we estimate would be needed for domestic energy supply infrastructure.

probably never satisfy those pure libertarians who hold that no government intervention can ever be justified, and indeed we think many of today's energy problems spring from ill-advised past interventions, we will make a reasoned case that some limited, targeted, and carefully defined changes in federal, state, and local policy (pp. 169–226) are not just desirable but very important for managing national risks and achieving national goals.

When considering our suggestions to foster this transition and benefit all stakeholders, remember that any long-term vision beyond the comfortably familiar always looks odd at first. In 1900, the U.S. had ~8,000 cars. Fewer than 8% of the two million miles of rural roads were paved. Anyone who'd proposed then that half a century hence, the ubiquitous horse and buggy would be gone, replaced by a wholly unfamiliar infrastructure in which the newfangled oil industry would refine, pipe, and sell a new product called gasoline, would have been dismissed as a dreamer. Anyone who'd predicted that a century hence, 170,000 U.S. retail outlets would be pumping this new fuel into nearly 240 million light vehicles whizzing along 600,000 miles of highway would have been banished as a lunatic. Yet we live in that world today because the genius of private enterprise, building on Henry Ford's 1908 Model T (which got 2.5 million cars on the road during 1908–16), was supported by a series of public policies, from the early decision to have taxpayers finance public roads to President Eisenhower's 1956 Interstate Highway System. The changes proposed here are far less momentous than those. They need virtually no new infrastructure; they use well-established technologies made by existing industries; they meet current user requirements even better than today's technologies do; and they're profitable for both producers and consumers. The issue is how to help them happen smoothly, quickly, and well, so American industry can vault the obstacles to doing what it does best—innovation.

In 1900, the U.S. had ~8,000 cars. Fewer than 8% of the two million miles of rural roads were paved.

Anyone who'd predicted a century hence nearly 240 million light vehicles whizzing along 600,000 miles of highway would have been banished as a lunatic. Yet we live in that world today because of the genius of private enterprise.

We need economically efficient policies that shift companies' and customers' choices toward higher-fuel-economy vehicles of all kinds while expanding their freedom of choice;
help manufacturers to retool their factories and retrain their workers;
support the rapid emergence of cost-effective bio-fuels, other renewables, and domestic fuels;
upgrade our transportation systems to reduce congestion;
align utilities' profit motives with their customers' interests; and
eliminate perverse incentives across the domestic-energy value chain.

At many levels and from many sides, the Big Three ← U.S. automakers face competition so unprecedented and profound that it could either kill them or make them stronger. Their fate hangs in the balance, and time is of the essence.

The endangered automotive sector— why it's important to act now

In 1970, U.S. automobile manufacturers were the envy of the world. The Big Three—Chrysler, Ford, and GM—produced nine out of every ten cars sold in America. Then the 1970s oil price shocks caught them unawares, and Japanese manufacturers swooped in, initially offering smaller and more efficient cars that better met many customers' needs, then leveraging into other segments. Thirty years later, the U.S. automobile sector is on the ropes. The Big Three have been reduced to 59% domestic market share. Their competitive situation is worsening: since 1999, U.S. car manufacturers lost 2% domestic market share *each year* to Japanese and European competition, and now barely sell the majority of the cars within their home market. The last bastion of competitive strength and profits has been the light-truck sector, where the U.S. still maintains 75% market share, but this too is now under frontal assault. The U.S. market position in light trucks is protected by a 25% tariff on imported vehicles, leading the Japanese and German competition to build their factories on U.S. soil. These transplants increasingly make all kinds of light vehicles, from 1990s-style truck-based SUVs to the car-based "crossover" vehicles that outsold them in the first half of 2004 and may portend their decline.[570]

An *Economist* cover story recently questioned whether any of the Big Three would survive the global hypercompetition of the next 10–20 years.

Reliance on lawyers and lobbyists to try to avert competition and regulation has long restrained American automakers from fully exploiting their extraordinary engineering prowess.[571] And so the nation's and the world's largest industry, providing a tenth of all U.S. private-sector jobs (p. 17) and creating the machines that provide core mobility for most Americans, is sufficiently at risk that an *Economist* cover story recently questioned whether any of the Big Three would survive the global hypercompetition of the next 10–20 years.[572] On 16 March 2004, its editorialist opined: "Put bluntly, the short-term outlook for the Big Three is dreadful….If anything, the long-term outlook is worse."[573]

---

570. J. White 2004. Schatz & Lundergaard (2004) report that ~40% of people trading in a traditional truck-based SUV in 2004 are shifting to a different vehicle class or subclass—a quintupling in five years.

571. This incoherence is longstanding: e.g., GM lobbyists killed California's Zero-Emission Vehicle rule, which had given a head start to the world's best battery-electric car (GM's *EV-1*), just as its marketing was gaining momentum. The few hundred early-adopter lessees, forced to return their beloved cars to be scrapped, were embittered. Then a 2001 anti-CAFE-standards lobbying blitz strove to convince Americans that efficient cars are unsafe and unaffordable—unmarketing many of the same OEMs' key innovations, and infuriating the green market segment, which switched its loyalty to Honda and Toyota. GM and DaimlerChrysler may sue, with federal support, to overturn California's proposal to regulate automotive CO_2 emissions. Yet to argue that this is a covert form of efficiency regulation preempted by federal law, i.e. can be complied with solely by raising fuel economy, automakers must deny the feasibility both of biofuels and of their own impressive and heavily advertised hydrogen programs. (This would also reinforce many environmentalists' suspicions that the White House's hydrogen program is a bad-faith stalling tactic, and offend the industry's technical partners in hydrogen.) Stomping on one's own cutting-edge developments can't advance market acceptance, sales, reputation, morale, or recruitment. Such contradictions between strategic goals, marketing messages, and lobbying or litigating positions are unhelpful, polarizing, and futile. Foreign competitors simply market new products without first needing to stop unmarketing them. Yet some major environmental groups bear similar self-inflicted wounds: e.g., if the Sierra Club succeeds in forcing EPA to admit authority to regulate CO_2, it could preempt California's proposed rule.

572. Carson 2003; Maynard 2003.

573. "Buttonwood" 2004.

Much has been written about the causes of the decline of the U.S. automotive sector and the basis of competition. To succeed, car manufacturers need lower costs, higher quality, a breadth of product offerings, a dealer network, and brand loyalty.[574] While U.S. manufacturers have largely closed the cost gap with their Japanese rivals, their continued slide in market share is attributed mainly to persistent gaps in quality and value. This has translated into a loss of brand loyalty. In the 1980s, Lee Iacocca could confidently tell TV viewers, "If you can find a better car, buy it." Later, as competitors pulled ahead, many buyers continued to follow his advice. In short, American car companies must consistently build the cars that consumers want, with better quality and value than anyone else.[575] Yet the industry's ingrained practices—from the old strategy of owning captive rental-car companies to the cultural habit that employees should normally drive the company's products (rather than driving competing ones to understand them better)—have diluted competitive discipline. And Detroit's incrementalist technological style, rooted in corporate culture, has ill served the industry as Japan's bolder strategy gave Toyota and Honda the lead in hybrids.

> ## 13: Guilt-free driving: hybrid cars enter the market
>
> The rapid U.S. growth in hybrid cars illustrates how quickly products that offer all the key attributes (such as family-size, peppy, and guilt-free) can claim market share. Hybrids were introduced in 1999, and, even though they can cost ~$2,500–$4,000 more than a conventional car, are expected to gain a market share of 1.5% by 2005, with a growth rate of a stunning 75% per year. J.D. Power and Associates believes that the reasons for the rapid growth are better hybrid technologies and greater customer product line choice, from small compacts to SUVs. Consumers are seeking to retain their lifestyle with less environmental impact. It was Toyota's hybrid, the *Prius*, that swept the industry's 2004 top awards (p. 29) and whose 22,000-order backlog has forced some dealers, facing year-long waitlists, to stop taking orders. By May 2004, with gasoline prices hovering above $2 a gallon, the 55-mpg *Prius* midsize sedan commanded a $5–8,000 premium in some markets, while U.S. SUVs needed ~$4–5,000 incentives to sell (even Toyota averaged nearly $3,000 incentives across its full product line). Used rental *Prius*es are even reselling for more than the new list price.[573a] Toyota and Honda have taken the lead in the hybrid market, but U.S. automakers are slowly following and will be rolling out competitors starting in late summer 2004 with Ford's *Escape* small SUV (p. 31). (EIA forecasts a 5.5% market share for hybrids in 2025, but assumes that they'll average only 33–38 mpg for cars, 27–32 for light trucks—both worse than any hybrid on the market in 2004.)
>
> 573a. Freeman 2004; Carty 2004.

Success in the dynamic light-vehicle market requires relentless focus on developing attractive product lines that anticipate evolving customer needs. U.S. preferences for more efficient (and often somewhat smaller) cars in the 1970s, aerodynamic cars in the 1980s, and sport-utility vehicles

---

574. Train & Winston (2004) provide an overview of these factors and the relative position of U.S. manufacturers vs. their rivals.

575. Train & Winston (2004) note that while cost was the initial reason for loss of market share to the Japanese, the U.S. car manufacturers consistently missed product-line opportunities, and had declining quality relative to Japanese and European makers, leading to today's battle for brand loyalty based on quality differences.

in the 1990s were all critical trends that defined the basis for growth in market share. Looking forward, customer preferences for safety, comfort, entertainment, fuel economy, performance, and environmental friendliness appear both contradictory and self-evident. Cars are bought as much for emotional as for economic reasons, and most Americans, it would seem, want to drive large, sporty vehicles and feel good about it. Manufacturers of hybrid cars and, imminently, of hybrid light trucks are claiming market share by recognizing and meeting this customer need (Box 13). Similarly, many Americans resent the feeling of having to buy an SUV to protect their families from the heavy, aggressive, incompatible SUVs that increasingly surround them. Makers who first offer family protection without inefficiency and hostility (pp. 58–59) will win those customers.[576]

Many obstacles are blocking or slowing U.S. automakers from the fundamental changes they will need in order to prevail in the global marketplace of the next few decades. Starting on p. 178, we propose a portfolio of market-oriented public policies to break down those obstacles. First we explore more fully what the challenges are, what causes them, why they're serious, and how—like an Aikido master blending with an attacker's energy—the industry can turn serious competitive challenges into transformative opportunities.

Financial weakness, incrementalist culture, and internal contradictions slow U.S. automakers' response to such obvious forms of competition as hybrid-electric vehicles. But ultralight materials, software-dominated vehicle architectures, and even new business models will expand the competitive threat.

Four competitive threats

The first big threat is advanced propulsion technologies. But unlike Toyota,[577] which hopes to expand its global market share from 10% now to 15% in 2010,[578] U.S. automakers' propulsion strategy isn't built around world-class fuel economy: it's the strategy of an Airbus *A380* super-jumbo, not a sleek and economical Boeing *7E7* (Box 14). On the whole, U.S. manufacturers are stubbornly defending their market share in light trucks by making ever larger and heavier gasoline-engine SUVs, backed by ever larger financial incentives such as rebates (around $5,000 in mid-2004) and interest-free loans.

In contrast, Japanese automakers, especially Toyota, have the financial strength to bet on both fuel cells and hybrid powertrains, as well as to invest heavily in both economy and luxury models simultaneously. Indeed, they're bringing hybrids' peppy performance to luxury models, and already their hybrid powertrains are cheap enough that they're about to appear in two of the world's most popular sedans—the Honda *Accord*

576. The sense of protection comes from a combination of size, stiffness, strength, and solid handling (e.g., crosswind stability and excellent suspension). It would doubtless be reinforced by official crash tests and, even more, by videos of astonishing crash performance vs. steel vehicles. We are aware of no evidence that *weight* per se is a customer requirement for light vehicles, and customers who use carbon-fiber sporting goods already know better (pp. 57–60).

577. Toyota's 2004 lineup has the best average car, truck, and overall fuel economy of any full-line manufacturer in the U.S. market, and includes eight of the 20 most efficient models. Unlike some U.S. competitors, Toyota has met CAFE standards throughout its history. Of 2004 Toyota/Lexus vehicles, 100% are California-certified as Low Emission (LEV), 75% as Ultra Low Emission (ULEV). Toyota's 23 models on a leading environmental group's "Best of 2004" list (www.aceee.org) top the industry. Thus Toyota's claim "Cleaner, Leaner and Greener" (Toyota 2004a) is not mere rhetoric.

578. Parker & Shirouzu 2004.

and Toyota *Camry*. Japanese automakers seek to gain first-mover advantage for the next generation of efficient mobility through experience, scale, and brand positioning gained with their hybrid vehicles. Korean firms appear to have similar goals. European automakers, including DaimlerChrysler, are also backing cleaner diesels, based on the EU regulatory environment and European customer preferences, though their acceptability under tightening U.S. fine-particulate regulations is not yet established. While GM is making a major long-term play in fuel cells and is also exploring and partly adopting other technologies, it may lack the financial strength to make significant investments into multiple advanced powertrains, so with only a few mild hybrids during 2004–07, it risks losing market share to Japanese hybrid-makers meanwhile. Only Ford is introducing a "strong hybrid" SUV in 2004, later than hoped, under Toyota technology licenses, and probably using technologies somewhat less advanced than Toyota's latest market offerings. In short, U.S. automakers are trying, but are still playing catch-up.

14: Opening moves: Boeing's bet on fuel efficiency as the future for commercial aircraft

In chess, the opening moves define the strategy each player will use to prevail. In the transportation business, the product lines, manufacturing, and marketing approaches define the competitive strategy. The battle between Boeing and Airbus for dominance in civilian aircraft presents a clear example of the challenge and opportunity in using efficient transportation platforms for competitive advantage, as the combatants have developed opposite strategies.

Airbus entered the commercial aircraft business in the 1990s, and by 2000 had eliminated Boeing's near-monopoly, capturing 40% share. Airbus then announced the behemoth *A380*, a 555-passenger plane designed to move passengers between the major international hubs. Airbus has already received orders for 129 planes. Many major airports can't yet even accommodate a plane that big.

Boeing instead chose a different approach—its *7E7 Dreamliner*—to create business value for the airlines by boosting fuel efficiency 15–20%. As luxurious as *A380*, *7E7* has improved engines, lighter materials, and better aerodynamics (though of course fewer seats). Boeing expects the airlines to fly international travelers more frequently along city pairs, in a similar model to the domestic carrier Southwest. Boeing received its first order for 59 planes (50 from ANA), with more coming in.

As noted in *Fortune*, "The ideal carrier for Boeing's new *7E7* hasn't been invented yet." But the reality of the airline industry is that it suffers from overcapacity and poor financial health. Airlines' difficulty in passing through high fuel costs to their customers and in managing hub congestion favors Boeing. If Boeing is successful in using *7E7* to reverse its competitive fortunes vs. Airbus, it will serve as a parable for the whole transportation sector. The countermoves have already begun: Airbus perceives *7E7* as enough of a threat to its *A330* to be contemplating an *A350* with a more efficient engine (p. 158).

Japanese automakers are entering the carbon-fiber airplane business with the clear intention of cross-pollinating, so ultralight materials and manufacturing methods can start in the airplane business, where they're more valuable, then migrate back into the automotive sector at higher volumes. Over time, the heavy steel cars that now dominate American manufacturing and policy are fated to occupy a shrinking global niche.

A deeper competitive threat comes not from innovative propulsion but from autobody materials. The European Union's policymakers aren't yet committed to a wholesale transition to ultralight materials, but they're quietly backing R&D and a supportive policy framework for light-but-safe cars. European expertise in Formula One racing and some European automakers' moves toward carbon composites, especially in Germany, seem bound to shift EU attention in this direction. Despite similarly limited policy vision in Japan so far, Japanese automakers are entering the carbon-fiber airplane business with the clear intention of cross-pollinating, so ultralight materials and manufacturing methods can start in the airplane business, where they're more valuable, then migrate back into the automotive sector at higher volumes. Over time, the heavy steel cars that now dominate American manufacturing and policy are fated to occupy a shrinking global niche. In materials, propulsion, and overall design, they'll increasingly fit only one country's market (albeit a huge one), threatened from all sides. Increasing monetization or regulation of carbon emissions in key global markets, increasing risk of costly or disrupted oil supplies, and other countries' rising attention to both these issues (p. 167) further heightens U.S. automakers' prospective competitive disadvantage.[579]

An even more subtle competitive threat is in neither propulsion systems nor body materials, but in vehicles' systems architecture. At the 1998 Paris Auto Show, Professor Daniel Roos, who directs MIT's International Motor Vehicle Program and coauthored *The Machine That Changed the World*, warned automotive CEOs that in two decades most of them could well be out of business—put there by firms they don't now consider their competitors:

> In the next 20 years, the world automotive industry will be facing radical change that will completely alter the nature of its companies and products….In two decades today's major automakers may not be the drivers of the vehicle industry; there could be a radical shift in power to parts and system suppliers. Completely new players, such as electronics and software firms, may be the real competitors to automakers.

That future is already emerging. And it could encourage formidable new market entrants. For the software-rich cars of the future, competition will favor not the most efficient steel-stampers but the fastest-learning system integrators and simplifiers—manufacturers like Dell and system companies like Hewlett-Packard or Sony. That sort of competition, too, favors leapfroggers. Most of China's 300 million cellphone owners never had a landline phone; they jumped directly into wireless. Most young Chinese routinely use digital media but have never seen an analog videocassette. To them, a software-rich, all-digital, all-by-wire vehicle will seem natural, while a customary U.S. vehicle, mechanically based with digital displays grafted on, may feel clunky and antique.

579. More than 60% of 2002 light-vehicle sales worldwide were in countries (including China) that have ratified the Kyoto Protocol, and some of the rest, including the U.S., are moving in a similar direction via private market-makers or other forms of national or subnational regulation. The Big Three face greater CO_2 exposure than six of the world's seven other major automakers (all but BMW). Less because of their product mix than because they're behind Toyota in strong hybrids, GM and Ford could need bigger product shifts to deliver a superior efficiency value proposition, and those shifts could become even more awkward if oil disruptions required rapid adjustments (Hakim 2004e; Austin et al. 2004).

Perhaps the greatest peril, though it's only starting to emerge on the fringes of automobility, is transformation of the business model. Traditionally, automakers sell vehicles and oil companies sell gallons. Both want to sell more, while customers prefer on the whole to buy fewer (but more physically and stylistically durable) vehicles that use fewer gallons. These opposite interests don't create a happy relationship. But suppose an automaker or an oil company leased a mobility service (Box 20, p. 196) that provides vehicles or other means of physical or virtual mobility, tailored to customers' ever-shifting needs. Customers would pay for getting where they want to be, not for the means of doing so. Then vehicles and gallons, instead of being the providers' source of profit, turn into a cost: the fewer vehicles and gallons it takes to provide the mobility service that the customer is paying for, the more profit the provider makes and the more money the customer saves. Most major car and oil companies are thinking quietly but seriously about this business model. Most industry strategists fear that the first firm to adopt it on a large scale could outcompete all the rest, both because of a better value proposition and because aligning producers' with customers' interests tends to yield better outcomes for both. There is no guarantee that such transformative business models will start in America. So far, they've tended to emerge in small countries, such as Switzerland and Holland, and in developing countries—that is, in places where congestion and high fuel and land prices force innovation at the most fundamental level, transcending mere technology.

China and India

Preoccupied with obvious competitors in Japan, Korea, and Europe, American automakers risk being blindsided by China's automakers. The Chinese are positioning themselves to enter the world market with a leapfrog play of highly efficient vehicles, backed by the strength of the scale and experience gained in their burgeoning 4.3-million-vehicle/y (2003) domestic market. The Chinese government's National Development and Reform Commission's 2 June 2004 white paper steers the $25.5 billion automaking investment that's expected during 2004–07 to raise output to nearly 15 million vehicles a year, nearly as big as the whole U.S. market. This policy is also raising barriers to market entry (each project must invest at least $241 million including $60 million of R&D), consolidating the fragmented 120-plant automaking sector, and tightening domestic efficiency standards that most heavy U.S. vehicles can't meet (p. 45). Hybrids and lightweighting are specifically to be encouraged.[580]

Moreover, this automotive strategy is intimately linked with a transformative energy strategy. Four weeks after its release, Premier Wen Jiabao's Cabinet approved in principle a draft energy plan to 2020. It makes energy efficiency the top priority, pushes innovation and advanced technology, and emphasizes environmental protection and energy security to "foster an energy conservation-minded economy

It's dangerous to underestimate the dynamism of Chinese manufacturing. Chinese industry is supported by a strong central policy apparatus rooted in five millennia of history, and is enabling the world's most massive construction boom in at least two thousand years.

Integrated advances in China's policies for both cars and energy will probably make its auto industry a major global competitor in the next decade, with India following fast.

In a few decades, a mighty Chinese economy's automakers might have taken over or driven out the Big Three and even bought major Japanese automakers.

580. APECC 2004.

There's also India's younger, smaller, but rapidly maturing auto industry. It's only $5b/y, but is growing by 15% a year. Quality has improved so rapidly, on a Korea-like trajectory, that in 2004, Tata Motors is exporting 20,000 cars to the UK.

and society" in which "the mode of economic growth should be transformed and a new-type industrialization road taken."[581] As other industries have learned the hard way, WTO-governed global competition works both ways, and it's dangerous to underestimate the dynamism of Chinese manufacturing. Chinese industry is supported by a strong central policy apparatus rooted in five millennia of history, and is enabling the world's most massive construction boom in at least two thousand years. Already, too, homegrown Chinese fuel-cell cars are rapidly advancing in several centers, raising the likelihood that Chinese leaders' aversion to the oil trap will be expressed as leapfrog technologies not just in efficient vehicles but also in oil-free hydrogen fueling. In a few decades, a mighty Chinese economy's automakers might have taken over or driven out the Big Three and even bought major Japanese automakers.

In case 1.4 billion Chinese moving rapidly to make something that beats your uncle's Buick isn't enough of a threat, there's also India's younger, smaller, but rapidly maturing auto industry. It's only $5b/y, but is growing by 15% a year. Quality has improved so rapidly, on a Korea-like trajectory, that in 2004, Tata Motors is exporting 20,000 cars to the UK under the MG Rover brand. India "may be better placed than China is to become a global low-cost auto-manufacturing base."[582] A billion Indians, with an educated elite about as populous as France, have already transformed industries from software to prosthetics, using breakthrough design to undercut U.S. manufacturing costs by as much as several hundredfold.[583] India's domestic car market, like China's, is evolving under conditions that favor an emphasis on fuel efficiency.

Unusual U.S. conditions— cheap gasoline, high incomes, ← weak efficiency regulation— don't prevail in most global markets, and blunt the Big Three's competitive edge.

Suppressing the signals

With such competition looming, one might suppose that U.S. automakers would embrace tighter domestic efficiency requirements to help them gird for the challenge. Instead, their visceral and partly understandable revulsion to regulation led them to invest heavily in full-court-press lobbying to freeze or weaken current requirements. That lobbying's success could set the stage for a rerun of Japanese competitors' 1970s market success, but this time against far more competitors than just Japan. Historically low U.S. fuel prices, high personal incomes, and low and stagnant U.S. efficiency standards all encourage U.S automakers to undercompete globally on fuel economy. None of these three peculiarly North American conditions prevails in most of the rest of the world. The disparity could get worse. If the National Highway Transportation Safety Administration adopts its spring 2004 proposal to base CAFE standards on weight class—deliberately rewarding heavier (except the very heaviest) and penalizing lighter vehicles—it will enshrine the already worrisome divergence between U.S. and other, especially European, safety philosophies, making it ever harder for U.S. automakers to market their heavy products abroad (p. 58).

581. APECC 2004, p. 5
582. Farrell & Zainulbhai 2004.
583. Prahalad 2004.

If the U.S. fails to act decisively and coherently during this period, we will not only continue to lose market share: we will ultimately lose the manufacturing base, and those high-wage manufacturing jobs will be lost forever. Clinging to heavy and inefficient product lines will make us the unrivaled leaders in producing products that the world's consumers do not want, in commanding the loyalty of a steadily aging and shrinking customer base, and in depending on perpetually cheap fuel that seems ever less likely to remain reliable. Worse, we will fall behind in the advanced materials technology race, ceding the next generation of high-technology manufacturing jobs to agile and uninhibited competitors overseas. Add the subtler forms of competition in software-dominated vehicles and solutions-economy business models, and the prospects dim further for automakers that perpetuate existing product lines, changing only incrementally, cocooned within a comfortable regulatory and price environment.

> **Clinging to heavy and inefficient product lines will make the U.S. the unrivaled leaders in producing products that the world's consumers do not want, in commanding the loyalty of a steadily aging and shrinking customer base, and in depending on perpetually cheap fuel that seems ever less likely to remain reliable.**

Crafting an effective energy strategy: transformative business innovation

> **U.S. automakers must shift speedily to high efficiency, then beyond oil— or risk suffering the fate of the once-mighty whaling industry.**

Detroit's dilemma is unpalatable: if countries like China and India do leapfrog to ultralight fuel-cell cars, they'll pose a grave competitive threat regardless of oil price, but if they don't, their growth in oil demand, and the cashflow needs of demographically and socially challenged oil exporters, will conspire to keep upward pressure on fuel prices more consistently than in the 1990s, making customers even more dissatisfied with Detroit's slow progress toward oil-frugal cars. For the U.S. economy, either path—importing cheaper superefficient cars or importing costlier oil—creates a drag on growth, drives inflation and interest rates, and destroys good jobs.[584] When thoughtful auto executives say they're uncomfortable having their industry's future depend on unpredictable oil prices, they're right—but in a far deeper sense than they may intend. The imperatives of the end of the Oil Age converge with those of radically shifting automotive technology to compel the linked transformation of these two largest global industries. If their twin transformations dance smoothly together, it'll be sheer delight. But if either industry lags, it'll get stepped on, and more agile partners will cut in.

584. IEA 2004b. From 1970 to 2003, inflation has historically closely tracked the price of oil. U.S. GDP growth has moved inversely with inflation. While the shift in manufacturing and services mix has lowered the direct impact of oil on the U.S. economy, and so has reduced oil intensity, the general vulnerability of the economy to inflationary pressures remains.

The creative destruction dilemma

"Disruptive ← technologies" can make rapid vehicular innovation and industrial transformation the path to success, re-equipping U.S. automakers to compete and prevail in the global marketplace—or can spell their demise if others do it first.

More than 50 years ago, economist Joseph Schumpeter described the process of "creative destruction," where innovations destroy obsolete technologies, only to be overthrown in turn by ever newer, more efficient rivals.[585] Creative responses to economic shifts occur when businesses respond to innovation in ways that are "outside the range of existing practice….Creative responses cannot be predicted by applying the ordinary rules of inference from existing facts, they shape the whole course of subsequent events and their long run outcome."[586] Depending on how radical the change is and how flexible the sector is, the impetus for change can often come from within the industry. In *Capitalism, Socialism, and Democracy*, Schumpeter argued in 1943 that businesses are "incessantly being revolutionized from within by new enterprise, i.e. by the intrusion of new commodities or new methods of production or new commercial opportunities into the industrial structure as it exists at any moment."[587] This process has played out across many industries, most recently those transformed by the Internet. Now, focused partly by the concerns about oil and climate, it has come squarely to the transportation sector.[588] How can this sector's existing players address the creative destruction challenge?

The Big Three are slowly being forced up the value chain by the foreign competition, and may soon find themselves stranded without much of a market.

In *The Innovator's Dilemma*, Harvard Business School professor Clayton Christensen explained how industry leaders get blindsided by "disruptive innovations" because they focus too closely on their most profitable customers and businesses.[589] The U.S. car and truck companies' asset base, supplier networks, and labor contracts are tied to manufacturing highly profitable but inefficient light trucks and SUVs. Their business focus is on how to provide larger, more powerful, and higher-margin vehicles to their most profitable customers in this segment, virtually ignoring the underserved, low-margin small-car segment that has been scooped up by the new Korean entrants Hyundai and Kia. (The Big Three have even come dangerously close to ignoring the entire car sector.) The increasing difficulty of competing in small and medium cars heightens dependence on SUV profits. However, those same SUVs are too large and too fuel-consumptive to gain a market foothold in countries outside the U.S.; the French government has proposed stiff taxes on them, with growing support from other European countries, and the government of Paris is even considering outlawing them as a public nuisance.[590] So while the upsurge in U.S. demand for SUVs was an unusually persistent bonanza for Detroit because competitors at first thought SUVs were a passing fad, the global market share of the Big Three continues to shrink.[591] They're slowly being forced up the value chain by the foreign competition, and may soon find themselves stranded without much of a market. Their dilemma is akin to the Swiss watchmaking industry's plight before Nicholas Hayek's radical simplifiers at Swatch saved their market from Asian competitors—starting with the cheapest commodity watches.

585. Schumpeter 1943/1997.The term probably dates to 1942.

586. Schumpeter 1943/1997.

587. Schumpeter 1943, p. 31.

588. For a discussion of creative destruction applied to the telecommunications sector and the impact of the Internet on industries, see McKnight, Vaaler, & Katz 2001.

589. Christensen 1997.

590. Henley 2004; Power & Wrighton 2004; Naillon 2004.

591. Austin et al. (2004, p. 11) summarizes the strategic trap of U.S. automakers' excessive light-truck dependence.

In *The Innovator's Dilemma*, Christensen observes that the successful incumbents are able to adapt to evolutionary change with what he describes as "sustaining innovations"—those that make a product or service better in ways that customers in the mainstream market already value, like the low direct operating cost of Boeing's new 7E7 (Box 14).[592] The SUV itself was a sustaining innovation for the U.S. car companies, because it was a breakthrough product that could be effectively marketed as offering the automotive industry's best customers more perceived value than before.

Within this framework, the superefficient automobiles discussed on pp. 44–72, together with the new business models they offer (in product line, distribution, sales, aftermarket),[593] are disruptive innovations like the ones Christensen describes. Disruptive innovations create an entirely new market by introducing a new kind of product or service or by enabling new markets to come into being.[594] (The vehicles in our *State of the Art* portfolio are especially disruptive innovations because unlike their *Conventional Wisdom* brethren, they enable and accelerate the shift to hydrogen fuel-cell vehicles and hydrogen as an entirely new energy carrier, as we'll see on pp. 233–234.) The problem is that incumbent companies, no matter how successful, have trouble managing or initiating disruptive changes to their own markets. To see why, we must understand the business challenges faced by the automotive industry.

Business challenges: market, business, and customer realities

Most U.S. light-vehicle buyers scarcely value fuel economy

Businesses and their customers appear to care deeply about energy only when it is not available. Scarcity or disruption of supply creates far more market reaction than an increase in market prices.[595] The response to the 1970s oil shock was a dramatic shift by customers to more efficient vehicles—often this meant smaller vehicles because choices at the time were limited, although, as noted on p. 7, this shift to smaller (mainly imported) cars is actually an urban legend. In fact, only 4% of the 7.6-mpg new-domestic-car efficiency gain during 1977–85 came from making cars smaller.[596] The shift to efficient vehicles, coupled with the political will to

> As then United Auto Workers President Doug Fraser noted in 1980, "If the 1975 [CAFE] legislation had not been enacted, there quite possibly could have been even greater damage inflicted on the industry and its workers by foreign imports."

> Market conditions will continue to retard or block adoption of super-efficient light vehicles, unless new business strategies and public policies shift buyers' behavior.

> U.S. autobuyers count only the first three years' fuel savings— a ~58% underestimate.

---

592. Christensen & Overdorf 2001, p. 114.

593. For example, the wireless services mentioned on p. 63. Smaller-scale manufacturing would permit greater localization and a sales model like that of a Dell customized mail-order computers with onsite General Electric service contracts. (This is a sales model Ford in the UK introduced for servicing conventional cars as a convenience dimension; Ford then found it was also cheaper to deliver than traditional drive-in service shops.) Models will vary widely between cultures—most cars in Japan, for example, are sold door-to-door, often through longstanding relationships, and usually bundled with all the required financial and legal services—but we believe the novel technical characteristics of software-rich ultralight vehicles could transform their market and aftermarket structure as much as their manufacturing.

594. Christensen & Overdorf 2000.

595. Steiner 2003. For example, during the height of the 2000–01 U.S. power crisis, when prices soared, over 60% of business users rated reliability as their most important concern, as compared to prices, which were a distant second (Datta & Gabaldon 2001).

596. See the detailed finding of only a 0.5-mpg gain from 1975–93 shifts in size class (Greene & Fan 1995). Interestingly, although CAFE standards didn't make vehicles significantly smaller, gasoline price spikes have historically done so (Greene 1997, p. 26 & Fig. 10), especially for light trucks.

Buyers underestimate by ~58% the true fuel economy benefits of a typical light vehicle over its 14-year average life, because they count only ~3 of its 14 years of fuel savings—not enough to repay the extra cost of a more advanced and efficient model.

enact CAFE standards and Detroit's impressive response to them, led to a whopping 60% increase in new light vehicles' fuel economy in the decade 1975–84.[597] At the time, most in Detroit were not enthusiastic about this legislative mandate, and many vehemently opposed it, but as then United Auto Workers President Doug Fraser noted in 1980, "If the 1975 [CAFE] legislation had not been enacted, there quite possibly could have been even greater damage inflicted on the industry and its workers by foreign imports."[598] Yet today, most industry observers believe that U.S. customers will continue to buy SUVs until gasoline prices reach $3–4/gal, consistent with experience in Europe where $3–5/gal fuel holds SUVs' market share to one-fifth the U.S. level.[599] What has changed since the oil price shocks of the 1970s?

A big difference is that energy accounts for only 4.5% of the average American's disposable income today, compared with 8% during the 1970s oil shocks. Both disposable income and credit have increased, so higher energy prices don't pinch most households' budgets—until a price spike occurs.[600] Most people can't be bothered to buy energy efficiency as insurance against price spikes. U.S. households typically require paybacks within two years to invest in energy-efficient appliances, an implicit discount rate over 40%/y—an order of magnitude higher than a social discount rate, and several times even a credit-card cost of capital.[601] For the lower-income families on which energy price spikes inflict real hardship,[602] lack of credit and disposable income increases this discount rate substantially, and energy takes a higher fraction of household income but there's less money to invest in efficiency. Thus, the tendency to underinvest in energy efficiency prevails across income levels. Moreover, it applies to vehicles as well as in the home: most vehicle buyers count only the first three years' energy savings.[603] The implication is that buyers underestimate by ~58% the true fuel economy benefits of a typical light vehicle over its 14-year average life.[604]

There is hope. One-fifth of U.S. light-vehicle buyers say they are early adopters, willing to spend $2,500 more for better fuel economy.[605] That's about what a *State of the Art* SUV would cost extra, or as much as a hybrid does today. This early-adopter segment may be large enough to kick-start the market (albeit with a gentle kick), as evidenced by hybrid cars' recent rapid sales growth. In 2004, the problem isn't inventing attractive doubled-efficiency vehicles like today's hybrids (which save nearly twice as much fuel as *Conventional Wisdom* vehicles would), but being unable to make them quickly enough, so Toyota is already planning to build an additional hybrid-car factory.

Based on historic purchasing behavior, though, only a minority of customers will spontaneously adopt a hybrid that saves gasoline at a cost comparable to today's gasoline price, or even a *State of the Art* vehicle that

597. EIA 1994.

598. DeCicco, Griffin, & Ertel 2003, p.6.

599. Hakim 2004d.

600. Hakim 2004d. By 1998, the share of household income paid for energy use was comparable to the share paid in 1973, before the oil prices for most IEA countries soared (IEA 2004).

601. Stern et al. 1986. An energy efficiency project with a two-year simple pay-back and a five-year project life yields a 41%/y IRR.

602. Ball 2004.

603. NAS/NRC 2002a. Honda of America similarly reports that consumers only value fuel savings for the first 50,000 miles of the a car (German 2002) More broadly, the U.S. Department of Energy survey found that average consumers need to be paid back within 2.9 years for an investment in fuel economy (Steiner 2003)

604. Greene et al. 2004.

605. Steiner 2003.

saves gasoline at a cost of 56¢ a gallon. Many more will buy an incremental *Conventional Wisdom* vehicle that saves 61% less fuel than *State of the Art* but at a 71% lower cost per gallon (15¢/gal). Such a vehicle, with an extra cost of only $727, is more attractive to most car buyers because they count only ~3 of its 14 years of fuel savings—not enough to repay the extra cost of a more advanced and efficient model. But once they've bought an incrementally improved vehicle, fewer *State of the Art* vehicles will be bought for the next ~14 years, slowing the fleet's shift to really high efficiency. The market reality is that most customers are slow to adopt very efficient vehicles or appliances, and it takes even longer for those new purchases to become a major fraction of the whole fleet on the road. But the sooner that adoption starts, the sooner it affects the entire fleet. We'll therefore suggest, starting on p. 178, creative ways to jump-start early adoption by customers and correspondingly early retooling by automakers.

Most firms underinvest in energy efficiency too

Even sharp-penciled businesses underinvest in energy efficiency, despite the exceptionally high rates of return on these investments.[606] The discount rate for U.S. business investments in new capital projects is generally estimated at ~15%/y, but investments in energy efficiency projects that are often taken from operational, rather than capital, budgets commonly require a 2-year payback, implying a 41%/y real discount rate if the project has a 5-year life, or 50% over 20 years—around ten times the cost of capital. Many firms nowadays ration capital, despite its record-low cost, so stringently that they require energy efficiency to repay its cost in a single year! There appear to be at least five main reasons for this egregious misallocation of capital:[607]

- The capital budgeting process in most corporations not only allocates capital to the projects with greatest return, but tends to skew capital towards projects with greater growth prospects—those that gain markets rather than cut costs. Hence, new plants will often be built before the old ones are made more efficient.

- Many firms fail to risk-adjust competing investments' returns. They therefore fail to notice that competent investments in energy efficiency are among the lowest-risk opportunities in the whole economy; indeed, they're a bit like insurance, in that their energy savings are worth the most when they're most needed because high energy prices have cut revenues and profits. Investment to gain or keep market share is far riskier than, say, buying an efficient vehicle that is certain to save a rather well-defined amount of fuel and to reduce proportionately the firm's exposure to fuel-price volatility. A firm that takes financial economics seriously will therefore buy efficiency whose returns go right down to, and even a bit below, its marginal cost of capital.

> **Five well-known organizational failures lead most companies to misallocate capital away from very lucrative, low-risk investments to cut energy costs, including those of vehicles.**

606. See review and citations in Lovins & Lovins 1997; DeCanio 1993; DeCanio 1998; Howarth & Andersson 1993; Koomey, Sanstad, & Shown 1996; Lovins 1992.

607. Golove & Eto 1996; Koomey 1990.

**Five main reasons
for misallocation
of capital
(continued):**

- Managers tend to think of energy costs as too small a portion of the overall cost structure, and too diffuse, to merit attention—even though saved energy, like any saved overhead, drops straight to the bottom line, where it can add greatly to pinched net earnings.

- Incentives are often misaligned, so that the party who would save the money from reduced energy use does not own the energy-using equipment, such as a leased commercial office building or a trucking fleet.

- Lack of activity-based costing and cost accountability often obscure energy costs from line managers, who may never even see the bills because they're sent directly to a remote head office.

Once again, the market reality is that nearly all businesses fall far short of buying the economically optimal amount of energy efficiency in their equipment and vehicles. The organizational reasons are complex, but the reality is widely known and is accepted by all knowledgeable analysts. If we want to change that behavior, we must change the underlying conditions that cause it. Otherwise it should come as no surprise that given such customer indifference, manufacturers are reluctant to invest in retooling their product lines to produce more efficient cars, trucks, and airplanes. It simply looks too risky to make big investments to make new products that customers may not buy.

**Nearly all businesses
fall far short of buying
the economically
optimal amount of
energy efficiency
in their equipment
and vehicles.
So it should come as
no surprise that
manufacturers are
reluctant to invest in
retooling their prod-
uct lines to produce
more efficient cars,
trucks, and airplanes.**

The investment required to launch a new automotive product line can be around $1–2 billion.[608] Boeing and Airbus are spending $10 and $12 billion, respectively, to develop their newest civilian airplane platform.[609] Truck product line development costs ~$0.7–1 billion.[610] For the transportation sector, therefore, developing a major new product line is a daunting risk, even a bet-your-company decision. That's why Ford, for example, chose to add hybrid powertrains to existing product lines (reportedly making the hybrid *Escape* potentially profitable[611]) rather than design a new hybrid platform from the ground up.

Having already placed some bets on hybrids (mainly Ford so far) and fuel cells (chiefly GM and DaimlerChrysler, each to the tune of $1 billion), U.S. automakers no longer have the financial strength to shift to ultralight autobodies at the same time. And they may worry that if they did place that bet, they'd miss the opportunity to edge out their rivals by incremental improvements in conventional markets that they thoroughly understand. Given today's market conditions and torpid policy environment, this reaction is superficially plausible. And it's reinforced by the volatile way capital markets respond to energy prices.

---

608. For example, the Saturn cost $2 billion to launch. DaimlerChrysler spent over $2 billion developing its lineup of mini-vans (Greenberg 2001). Ford even spent $6 billion on the *Mondeo*, the first "World Car" (Law 2004).

609. Bloomberg.com 2004a; Nelson.com, undated.

610. Thomas 2002.

611. Parker 2004.

Capital markets are notoriously fickle, with some reason, and most of all in the feast-and-famine world of energy overshoots. Many leading investors today still bear thick scar tissue from the mid-1980s, when public policy pushed hard to expand energy supplies at the same time that earlier policies and price signals from 1979's second oil shock invisibly but dramatically increased end-use efficiency. These two trends met head-on in 1985–86 as efficiency captured the market sooner, shrank the revenues that were supposed to repay the supply investments, glutted energy markets, crashed prices, and bankrupted many suppliers. (Those with short memories periodically try to persuade investors to rerun this bad movie, generally reaching the same sad ending.) Herd-instinct investors, who lack a long view and steady nerves, tend to make energy technology stocks soar after disruptive events. These stocks then tend to crash as energy markets stabilize.[612] Less seasoned investors who haven't experienced the painful reality of market equilibration amplify these extremes by behaving as if only increased supply, not increased efficiency, is real, reliable, and bankable. Ignoring efficiency can be terminal.

The risk of being risk-averse

No wonder many analysts openly doubt if consumers will adopt hybrid cars in enough volume to justify even the modest investments made by Ford, Toyota, and Honda. Although rapid market adoption so far seems to defy cynicism,[613] a policymaker for a U.S. automaker even remarked in mid-2004 that *Prius* "has not been accepted by the American public." Ironically, Toyota was simultaneously announcing a near-doubling of *Prius* production and considering building a U.S. plant to make more, *Prius* was flying off dealers' lots faster than any other car in America for the tenth straight month (nearly twice as fast as the runner-up), and some *Prius* dealers were extracting price premia greater than the rebates his company was paying everywhere to sell its flagship products. Doubting the staying power of a successful rival is easy but imprudent, especially when it's as formidable a firm as Toyota.

Large incumbent firms like to stay within their management comfort zone and to choose either incremental or sustaining innovations. Yet business history teaches us that no matter how big or old the company, this strategy will ultimately succumb to the onslaught of innovative competitors. Disruptive innovations, and the companies that undergo transformative change to adopt them, ultimately defeat creatures of habit; in the long run, standing pat is a losing strategy. However accustomed its customers and compliant its regulators may be, any big, muscular firm will turn stiff and sluggish without frequent stretching. The market says so. Competing against aggressive innovators, Ford and GM rank number 3 and 4 in revenues among the *Fortune* 500 companies, but 80th and 87th in market capitalization.[614] As we noted on p. 30, their combined market capitalization plus DaimlerChrysler's is less than Toyota's. Moreover, 95% of GM's

It's easy but dangerous to be complacent about competitors' progress. Winning depends on strategy as well as tactics.

Business history teaches us that no matter how big or old the company, the strategy of incremental innovations will ultimately succumb to the onslaught of innovative competitors. Disruptive innovations, and the companies that undergo transformative change to adopt them, ultimately defeat creatures of habit; standing pat is a losing strategy.

612. Datta & Gabaldon 2003.
613. Golfen 2004.
614. Hakim 2004b.

market capitalization is based on value from existing assets, rather than new growth opportunities: apparently the market doesn't believe GM has the capability to break out of incremental innovation.[615] U.S. automakers rank near the bottom in return on equity, and often make more money from financing than from manufacturing vehicles.[616] All who know first-hand these firms' extraordinary technical capabilities and their pivotal role in the U.S. economy hope for a magic turnaround, but Disney's First Law notwithstanding, wishing won't make it so.

Financial weakness is rooted in, and reinforces, underlying organizational flaws. Christensen observes that incumbent organizations have tremendous inertia due to their capabilities, processes, and values (defined not as ethics, but as "the standards by which an employee sets priorities to judge what [business opportunities] are attractive or unattractive").[617] McKinsey's Foster and Kaplan note a similar phenomenon they call "cultural lock-in," wherein companies maintain their old mental models and are unable to move beyond incremental innovation.[618] We recognize, and sympathize with, the formidable leadership and management challenge that the Big Three and their associated business network face in trying to inspire and reward breakthroughs in a culture of caution—one where it's definitely easier to get permission than forgiveness, and (as the Japanese proverb puts it) the nail that sticks up gets hammered down. But we believe that a combination of leadership from within, integration of new technologies, and public policy reinforcement from without holds a timely answer to this challenge.

Milton Friedman, viewing the enormous capacity of the business system to block change, once remarked that the problem with capitalism is capitalists. (He added that the problem with socialism is socialism.) Yet through the harsh and necessary discipline of creative destruction, market capitalism, the most powerful engine of wealth creation the world has ever known, bears the seeds of its own renewal.

> Market capitalism, the most powerful engine of wealth creation the world has ever known, bears the seeds of its own renewal.

> Ford and GM rank number 3 and 4 in revenues among the *Fortune* 500 companies, but 80th and 87th in market capitalization— their combined market capitalization plus DaimlerChrysler's is less than Toyota's.

615. Christensen & Raynor 2003.

616. The joke around Detroit is that the Big Three make cars so they can loan people money to buy them. Maybe it's not a joke. In 2003, Ford Motor Company's Financial Services organization posted income (before taxes) of $3.3 billion while the Automotive business had $0.1 billion in income before tax and excluding special loss items (Ford Motor Company 10-K, 12 March 2004). GMAC, the financing organization of General Motors, posted $2.8 billion of net income vs. GM's automotive net income of $0.6 billion (General Motors Corporation 10-K, 11 March 2004).

617. Christensen & Overdorf 2000.

Business opportunities: competitive strategy for profitable transformation in the transportation sector

In *The Innovator's Solution*, Clayton Christensen and Michael Raynor discuss how incumbent companies can create disruptive innovations rather than be destroyed by them. They argue for a managerial approach that demands a focus on disruptive innovation, and for the fundamental changes in the internal business processes and values that are needed to reshape an organization. McKinsey's Foster and Kaplan argue for the same focus on disruptive technologies, but choose a different managerial solution that focuses on adaptive processes and the decisiveness of private equity managers. Both concur on the fundamental principle that the innovation focus should be on disruptive, not sustaining or incremental, innovations—and that management must start this effort when the current business is in its prime, which is far earlier than most managers expect. By the time a business is mired in low-margin, commoditized incrementalism, it no longer has the strength and agility to break out of the swamp, and falls easy prey to determined predators.

The business cases detailed in *Technical Annex*, Ch. 20, and summarized next, show that the transition to *State of the Art* cars, trucks, and airplanes will be profitable for manufacturers, particularly as the normal and expected technological progress continues to pare their manufacturing investment risks. Since the superefficient technologies offer new and better value propositions for end-users (pp. 61–73), producers must develop better production techniques and business models to manufacture and deliver them, as we discuss next, and should welcome and seek supportive public policies to ease their manufacturing conversion (pp. 178–207).

America's transition to radically more efficient light vehicles, in particular, is of historic dimensions. It will deliver a 64–78-plus-mpg SUV (for example) to customers, at an attractive price, *without compromising any customer attribute*. This will occur fast enough and soon enough only if business and investment risks are lowered so that the perceived benefits of shifting corporate cultures and strategies will exceed the perceived hazards. The *business* risk can be lowered if companies stimulate customer demand without shifting preferences between vehicle types or sizes; we'll describe on pp. 178–203 how to do this. The *investment* risk can be lowered if companies take a new approach to developing and manufacturing high-efficiency vehicles. This requires two breakthroughs: *new manufacturing processes that lower the capital investment,* and *significantly improved carbon-composite (or lightweight-steel) manufacturing processes to cut variable production costs (materials, fabrication, and finishing).* These co-evolving breakthroughs can already be seen in the laboratory and are starting to enter the market (pp. 56–57).[619] Their refinement and scaleup will doubtless require some trial-and-error, but both these breakthroughs already appear to have

---

Superefficient vehicles offer superior value propositions not just for customers but also for automakers.

Delivering a 64–78-plus-mpg SUV (for example) to customers, at an attractive price, *without compromising any customer attribute* **requires two breakthroughs—** *new manufacturing processes that lower the capital investment* **and** *significantly improved carbon-composite (or lightweight-steel) manufacturing processes to cut variable production costs.* **These can already be seen in the laboratory and are starting to enter the market.**

618. Foster & Kaplan 2001.

619. Whitfield (2004) partially updates the status of two developments described above on pp. 56–57.

progressed beyond the realm of potential showstoppers, because they combine in new ways proven techniques that are already successfully practiced in other contexts, and they draw on a risk-managed portfolio of diverse methods. So how can these manufacturing breakthroughs cut the investments, variable costs, and risks of making *State of the Art* light vehicles? And how can analogous transformations be accelerated in the heavy-truck and airplane businesses?

Ultralight composite vehicles can create breakthrough manufacturing advantages.

Lowering light vehicles' manufacturing risk

New automotive platform development is and will remain an extraordinarily costly, demanding, and exacting business. However, its investment requirement has recently been reduced from an average of $2 billion to ~$1.5 billion. The development cycle has also become much faster, falling from ~60 to ~18 months, as design and even crash-pretesting shifts from physical prototypes to the sophisticated on-screen virtual-design and simulation software proven in such aircraft as *777* and *B-2*.[620] Product-development costs and times for *State of the Art* light vehicles should be no greater, and may well be smaller, due to unprecedented parts de-proliferation (which lowers the integration complexity), modular but integrated vehicle operating software, and the greater technical (though not cultural) simplicity of designing and producing vehicles from advanced composite materials.[621]

Assembly plants can need two-fifths less capital investment and incur lower variable costs. Development cycles may also become faster and cheaper. The business logic is compelling for automakers— and the vehicles save fuel at far lower cost than today's best-selling hybrids.

Manufacturing investment and variable cost

Advanced-composite autobodies can considerably reduce the required capital investment for building new car manufacturing/assembly plants. (The steel industry claims competitive production cost for its ULSAB-ATV concept design, though for different reasons.) As Box 15 explains, with ultralight composite autobodies, the cost of a 50,000-vehicle/y greenfield assembly plant could drop to ~$185 million, or $3,700/vehicle-y—about 40% less than the $6,150/vehicle-y at GM's most modern C-flex plant,[622] which in turn is nearly one-fifth cheaper than typical Japanese transplant facilities.[623] The cost reduction is due primarily to the elimination of the paint shop, and secondarily to far fewer and lower-pressure presses, cheaper tooling (adjusted to the same lifetime), no welders, and simplified assembly. *State of the Art* vehicles' redesign also lowers the minimum

620. Mateja & Popely 2004; Weber 2002; Gould 2004.

621. Proprietary estimates of current product development costs for carbon-composite vehicles obtained from D.R. Cramer (Hypercar, Inc.), personal communication, 22 July 2004, based on diverse 1998–2004 internal analyses.

622. Proprietary estimates of current production costs for a *State of the Art* vehicle (from Hypercar, Inc., updated in 2004 by Whole Systems Design [Box 9]) are consistent with the $3,700/vehicle-y investment estimate, and the advanced-composite autobody costs are far below those stated by Cramer & Taggart 2002. GM's 130,000 vehicle/y Lansing Grand River facility (Ward's Auto World 2002, *Automotive Intelligence News* 2004), its most modern assembly plant, cost $800 million but is half the size and cost of its predecessors, and "embodies everything we've learned about lean manufacturing," says Gary Cowger, president of GM North America (Weber 2002). Production ramp-up reached a total of 59,128 units in 2003 (Garsten 2004).

623. JAMA 2003.

15: Radically simpler automaking with advanced composites

A large part of the expense of creating a light vehicle comes from the dizzying complexity of its manufacturing process. A typical car can easily contain some 10,000–15,000 separate parts or even more.[624] Automakers, on average, have devolved about a third of their total engineering effort to their parts suppliers, and that fraction is rising, in many cases to two-thirds. In the manufacturing plant, these thousands of parts must be coordinated so that there are just enough parts available, not too many, all defect-free, in exactly the right place at the right time. Up to about a hundred (sometimes more) different steel body parts are stamped from flat sheetmetal into final shape in gigantic presses, using progressive tool-steel die-sets to form each part gradually through several successive hits. Those tools cost about a half-billion dollars, not counting the high-pressure presses they fit into (p. 73).

Once stamped, the body parts are brought together and precisely positioned by giant jigs while hundreds of robots join them together with ~2,000+ spot-welds into the "body-in-white"— the car's basic frame, body, and "closures" before finishing. Then the body is cleaned and coated by a rust-inhibitor. Painting, the hardest step, accounts for about half an assembly plant's total capital cost (a new paint shop typically costs ~$100–200 million) and for at least a quarter of the total cost of creating a painted steel part. After drying and inspection, the painted body moves slowly down an assembly line where workers, with some robotic help, add the other major components such as engine, drivetrain, suspension, brakes, wheels, wiring, and interiors.

Advanced-composites autobodies can eliminate or greatly simplify body manufacturing and final assembly, slashing both capital and operating costs. A composite autobody could be made from 10–20 parts rather than the 60–100 typical of a modern steel unibody.[625] Incoming inventory, welding, trim, body assembly, and worktime in final assembly could be reduced. Also, by making autobody parts from advanced composites molded at modest pressures rather than from stamped sheet steel, and laying color in the mold (integral to the polymer matrix or as a dry film coating), steel stamping operations and painting could be completely eliminated and replaced by composite forming equipment, either with no paint line or with a simpler one for clearcoating in-mold-pigmented composite parts. As in-mold color matures further, current designs, which add shiny cosmetic polymer exterior panels over the structural carbon-composite passenger cell, might even evolve to a true "monocoque": like an egg, the shell is the structure. But even using current techniques, the combination of structural and exterior-panel elements would be simpler to form, assemble, and finish than today's steel unibody. And integrated design that emphasizes lightweighting and parts-reduction not only halves vehicle weight, making the propulsion system far smaller and cheaper; it can also eliminate or combine many other current vehicle systems.[626]

624. A source estimating 20,000 parts in a 1996 car (*Life* 1996, p. 20) reports that Ransom E. Olds's ~1901 first model, perhaps the first to subcontract mass-produced parts for later assembly, had only 443 parts. Of course, it also looked like an open horse-carriage, with a 5-kW 4-stroke engine, 2-speed transmission, and none of a modern car's most basic passenger amenities.

625. Parts count depends on definitions: a Lotus has two main body parts, but they're augmented by others. We normally count the elements of, say, an underbody, door, or hood (such as foamcore, hardpoint mounting bracket, fiber, and resin) as constituting a single part. This isn't strictly comparable to steel parts-count conventions, but broadly speaking, the approach described in Cramer & Taggart 2002 and in Lovins & Cramer 2004 reduces body parts count by fourfold.

626. Lovins & Cramer 2004.

The cost of a 50,000-vehicle/y greenfield assembly plant could drop to ~$185 million, or $3,700/vehicle-y— about 40% less than GM's most modern plant, which in turn is nearly one-fifth cheaper than typical Japanese transplant facilities.

State of the Art **vehicles' redesign also lowers the minimum efficient scale of manufacturing from nearly 150,000 vehicles per year to around 50,000.**

Investment in such manufacturing plants would be financially justified, as long as there is a market for the vehicles.

627. The production cost analysis, described on pp. 62–73 and in *Technical Annex*, Ch. 5, assumed manufacturing-cost-to-invoice markups of 79% and invoice-to-MSRP markups of 10.4%, both consistent with industry margins for acceptable returns on capital; above-average U.S. auto-assem-

efficient scale of manufacturing from nearly 150,000 vehicles per year to around 50,000. The less lumpy cashflow (plus quicker ramp-up due to simpler manufacturing) requires and risks less investment, and the more agile plant allows a closer and more dynamic match to customer needs.

If advanced-composite autobodies cut manufacturing capital costs to this extent, as considerable proprietary analysis suggests they can, then the total manufactured costs of the new generation of high-efficiency vehicles could be competitive with today's comparable cars.[627] The composite manufacturing technologies discussed on p. 57 are already becoming available to make carbon-composite autobody parts for less than 20% of the cost of aerospace composites, with at least 80% of their performance.[628] Fig. 20 (p. 65), for example, shows that a gasoline-engine, nonhybrid, but ultralight advanced-composite midsize SUV could sell for just 1.6% more than the most nearly comparable steel SUV on the 2004 market, yet use 58% less fuel. Its Cost of Saved Energy, 15¢/gal, is one-fifth that of a conservative estimate for the popular 2004 *Prius* hybrid, and yields a one-year simple payback time at $1.50/gal.[629] Fig. 20 also shows that an ultralight advanced-composite hybrid SUV would save fuel at a cost of 56¢/gal— still one-third below *Prius*'s—for a three-year simple payback. Yet these figures are not for a midsize sedan like *Prius*, but for an uncompromised midsize SUV crossover vehicle with a slightly roomier interior than a 2000 *Explorer* and with superior simulated crashworthiness (Box 7, p. 62). These comparisons suggest that such an ultralight vehicle, even with hybrid drive, could command a far broader market than *Prius* enjoys today. With just hybrid drive and no ultralighting, that market is big enough for Toyota to have slated 4% of its total 2005 production, or 300,000 vehicles, for hybrid powertrains.[630] Ultralighting saves far more fuel but costs about the same (Fig. 21, p. 66).

Since a *State of the Art* ultralight-hybrid light vehicle made from either advanced composites or lightweight steels could thus be profitably sold at a competitive cost, we conclude that investment in such manufacturing plants would be financially justified, as long as there is a market for the vehicles. Today's hybrids, as we just discussed, provide an encouraging hint at that market, but hybrids are still a tiny part of total vehicle sales. There are more fundamental reasons to expect robust demand for *State of the Art* vehicles.

bler wages; and a greenfield plant working two shifts at 90% uptime, 64% working hours, hence 58% availability. Porsche Engineering's analysis for the steel industry's ultralight-steel backstop technology (p. 67, above) is methodologically similar and, for the nonhybrid gasoline-engine *ULSAB-ATV* charted in Fig. 21 (p. 66), shows an extra production cost of about zero.

628. E.g., Whitfield 2004.

629. For this comparison, since there is no exact nonhybrid comparable, we assume the efficiency of a Toyota *Echo* and a 2004-$ marginal price of ~$1,900. Toyota has certified $3,150 for purposes of Colorado's hybrid tax credit (Colorado Department of Revenue, Taxpayer Service Division 2003), which is based on marginal manufacturing cost adjusted to equivalent retail price. However, since Toyota is widely believed to have shaved its actual margin, we use the much lower $1,900 estimate (2004 $)—close to expected MY2007 full pricing (note 178, p. 30)—to ensure conservatism. At the declared $3,150 marginal price, *Prius*'s Cost of Saved Energy would be $1.35/gal (2000 $).

630. President Fujio Cho confirmed this figure, subject to production constraints, at the Traverse City CEOs' conference, with two-fifths being non-*Prius* models: Porretto 2004.

Market adoption

Both theoretical demand (estimated from decades of purchasing behavior and recent customer surveys) and revealed behavior from the rapid initial market entry by hybrid vehicles clearly indicate that there is a market for higher-efficiency vehicles across the broad spectrum of light-vehicle product lines. The size of the early-adopter segment is commonly estimated to range from a low of 3–5%—revealed by hybrid automakers' short-term production plans—to a high of nearly 20% from market surveys. The market itself will demonstrate the degree of adoption over the next five years as the hybrid car class expands, and this will, in turn, inform automakers about potential initial market size for broader categories of next-generation vehicles.

To the extent that the next-generation light vehicle is a truly disruptive technology that provides superior mobility services at lower cost, hence greater value, customers can broadly adopt it with astonishing speed. A comprehensive 1999 review of disruptive technologies' historical adoption found that technologies using the existing infrastructure can move from 10% to 90% capture of the capital stock within 12–15 years (p. 6, above),[631] implying an even faster increase in their share of new-vehicle sales. The new generation of automobiles and light trucks will need new manufacturing infrastructure if they're made of composites (lightweight steels use conventional fabrication), but will need little concurrent investment in additional infrastructure—just routine upgrading of repair shops and skills to handle composite bodies (more like boatbuilding than sheetmetal work) and hybrids (a little extra test equipment and training for the electrical components). Indeed, given hybrid vehicle manufacturers' emphasis on making hybridization transparent to the user,[632] hybrid powertrains could in principle be adopted with a speed comparable to, say, airbags (0–100% of the new-vehicle market in seven years) or anti-lock braking (0 to nearly 60% in eight years).[633]

Since 2000, hybrids' U.S. sales have indeed grown at an average annual rate of 89% from a nearly zero base.[634] If that kept up for seven years, it would amount to millions of vehicles a year, but that's not a sound analytic method. Rather, we must look to the basic principles that govern all new technologies' market adoption.

Innovation diffusion theory suggests that speed of diffusion and permeability of markets both rise if the new technology is perceived as superior, easy to use, matched to customers' needs, testable without obligation (as one can do with rental and loaner vehicles), understandable (or unnecessary to understand—e.g. one can use a cellphone without understanding what goes on inside it), socially compatible, low-hassle, low-risk, and reversible (as by reselling a car). Today's hybrid vehicles pass all these tests nicely. We believe *State of the Art* cars will too. They can and should sell because they're *better*, not because they're efficient (p. 46): not because they're green, but because they're a superior product that redefines market expectations.[635]

The same attributes that have made other innovations diffuse rapidly can also apply to superefficient light vehicles.

State of the Art **cars can and should sell because they're better, not because they're efficient: not because they're green, but because they're a superior product that redefines market expectations.**

631. Grübler, Nakićenović, & Victor 1999.

632. Ford's *Escape* hybrid designers even included red-light creep, which a hybrid wouldn't normally have.

633. Federal Reserve Bank of Dallas 1997.

634. R.L. Polk & Co. data cited in Porretto 2004.

635. Most drivers don't know or care what their autobody is made of, so long as it's safe, solid, free of squeaks and rattles, durable, and attractive. Advanced composites do all of these things better. They also don't rust or fatigue, can bounce undamaged off a 6-mph collision that could cause thousands of dollars' worth of damage to a steel car, and can even be radar-stealthy. We can easily envisage advanced-composite bodies attracting not customer resistance but bragging rights.

Diffusion studies also find, however, that it can take a decade or more to achieve the first 10% market capture. The importance of the size of the early-adopter segment thus becomes plain: if not enough people adopt the new technology, it can languish for too many years for the automobile manufacturers to make a profitable return on their product development investment. This then delays even more the successive generations of follow-on innovations.

Government policies can unblock this product evolution and greatly reduce the risk to automakers by stimulating the market to cross the chasm of early adoption with high speed and confidence. Starting on p. 186, we'll discuss and simulate the most important way to do this: policies known as "feebates,"[636] which reward a shift to more fuel-efficient vehicles without distorting choices between vehicle classes or burdening public revenues. If enacted regionally or nationally, feebates alone would create the incentive for manufacturers to accelerate and increase their investments in developing and making very efficient vehicles. Our policy portfolio also includes complementary policies to increase early demand and accelerate supply of advanced technology vehicles.

We believe this combination of underlying market demand, slimmed investment and production costs, manufacturing breakthroughs, and policy-accelerated market uptake (pp. 178–203, summarized on pp. 180–181) suffices to create a profitable and highly competitive business model for advanced vehicles. We therefore turn to the other two transportation sectors clearly at competitive risk, and able to contribute notably to oil savings: heavy trucks and aviation.

Restoring profitability in the trucking sector

Investments in fuel efficiency can help bring back financial health to the trucking sector. Its structure and business conditions are quite favorable for a comparatively rapid transition to more efficient fleets, because buyers and sellers of new trucks are relatively concentrated, and both have strong economic incentives to improve fuel efficiency in order to restore or increase profits (*Technical Annex*, Ch. 20).

There are two major categories of trucks: heavy trucks (Class 8, pp. 73–77) and medium trucks (Classes 3–7, p. 77). U.S. Class 8 trucks consume ~1.5 million barrels of diesel fuel per day—10.4% of the nation's *total* oil use, and over three times the total usage of energy of Classes 3–7 (78% of whose fuel use is in the heaviest categories, Classes 6 and 7).[637] Among medium and heavy trucks, the big ones matter most.

The U.S. trucking industry at first appears highly fragmented, with more than 56,000 for-hire and private *fleets*.[638] Barriers to entry are low; for example, the minimum efficient scale for LTL (less-than-truckload) operations is 2 million ton-miles hauled annually, equivalent to just five trucks.[639]

The U.S. trucking industry at first appears highly fragmented. However, the upper end of the market is concentrated: the hundred largest for-hire fleets own 18% of the total Class 8 stock. Moreover, their turnover represents a whopping 55–60% of the total demand for new Class 8 trucks.

High-volume, profit-hungry new-truck-fleet buyers can induce truckmakers to shift rapidly to doubled-efficiency models—once the buyers ← realize it's possible.

636. This term, a combination of "fee" and "rebate," was probably coined by Professor A.H. Rosenfeld at the University of California, Berkeley, now a California Energy Commissioner. The concept was suggested independently in the 1970s both by him and by the senior author of this report, but may have been devised even earlier by IBM scientist Dr. R.L. Garwin. In Europe, feebates are often called a "bonus/malus" system—a term probably due to Professor E.U. von Weizsäcker.

637. EIA 2004; DOT 1977; ORNL 2003.

638. ATA 2004.

Seventy percent of these long-haul trucks are "for-hire trucks" driven by carriers that supply services using tractors and trailers they own.[640] However, the upper end of the market is concentrated: the hundred largest for-hire fleets own ~395,000 tractors, 18% of the total Class 8 stock.[641] Moreover, these owners are the critical early adopters, since they renew their fleets about every five years. This turnover represents a whopping 55–60% of the total demand for new Class 8 trucks, so new sales are highly concentrated in a small group of companies.

The trucking industry has strong incentives to save fuel, because its operations are barely profitable. The top hundred companies' profit margins in 1999–2000 averaged ~3.0–3.1%, and the very top performers achieved 4.9–5.0%.[642] Fuel accounts for 13–22% of the costs of the typical trucking company. The biggest are best able to buy in bulk and to equip drivers with such sophisticated technologies as wireless systems that let them shop for the lowest real-time price, optimizing their route for the best fuel prices along the way as well as to minimize miles and hours traveled. This is a business imperative, because a mere 15–20% rise in fuel costs could wipe out the entire profit margin of the *best* companies. Yet not all truckers can pass on the fuel costs to their customers, and small operators with less purchasing power often become unable to make their debt payments. This explains the numerous trucking protests, in the U.S. and around the world, when oil prices rise.

The converse is also true. If efficient trucks can cost-effectively reduce fuel cost and exposure to uncontrollable fuel price volatility, then profits will rise in proportion to the net benefit. Truck efficiency improvements across the entire U.S. Class 8 truck stock could save 38% of its year-2000 fuel use at an average at-the-nozzle cost of $0.25 per saved gallon of diesel fuel, discounting the saved fuel at 5%/y real over the average life of the truck (pp. 73–77).

Since nearly two-thirds of all new Class 8 trucks are bought by the 100 biggest companies, these companies could lower their own fuel bill by 45%[643] within their average five-year fleet turnover period by purchasing highly efficient trucks—if those were for sale.[644] All adoptable measures with marginal internal rates of return (IRR) of at least 15% would yield an average IRR of 60%/y.[645] Using the EIA forecast of diesel fuel price in 2025—$1.33/gal (2000 $)—and the same amount of driving would raise the average IRR to over 80%/y.

As a specific illustrative case, we estimate that if a firm like Swift Transportation Co., Inc. switched its entire fleet to *State of the Art* trucks, its net profit margin would increase by ~103%. In 2003, Swift had revenue of $2.4 billion, owned 14,344 tractors, and had a net after-tax margin of 3.3%. By implementing all *State of the Art* fuel efficiency measures that each achieve an IRR of at least 15%, Swift would save 45% of its current truck fuel. This would bring Swift's average new-truck mpg from 6.7 to 11.3,

The trucking industry has strong incentives to save fuel, because its operations are barely profitable.

639. Assuming a 25% load factor and 67,000 mi/y of driving. See Giordano 1997.

640. ATA 2001.

641. The hundred largest fleets have an average trailer-to-tractor ratio of 2.2, and 83% have a ratio of 1.5 or greater (Transport Topics 2003).

642. BTS 2000.

643. For the specific measures discussed in the prior section on heavy truck technical potential and with marginal internal rates of return greater than 15%. Who operates the truck at different phases of its life doesn't matter if the market that determines resale value is reasonably efficient.

644. This figure is based on RMI's business case evaluation from actual 2001 data on a sample of 100 companies, and is relative to their fuel use in 2003. On average, these firms achieved 6.2 mpg, paid only $1.08/gal (2000 $) net of any bulk-purchase discounts, and drove each truck 115,000 mi/y.

645. We used data from 14 of the top 100 trucking companies to calculate the average price for diesel and the average VMT (Vehicle Miles Traveled). The 2003 average diesel price was derived from 2001 reported fuel costs and VMT, using the industry average fuel economy of 6.2 mpg and EIA's ratio of 2003 to 2001 diesel prices. See *Technical Annex*, Ch. 20.

The 100 biggest companies could lower their own fuel bill by 45% within their average five-year fleet turnover period by purchasing highly efficient trucks with an average IRR of 60%/y.

646. We are also mindful that bringing a large new class of buyers into the heavy-truck market, as we propose for light vehicles, would require major capacity expansions that could raise short-term prices and whose sales may not be sustainable over the long term as the fleet becomes saturated with advanced tractors.

647. Smith & Eberle 2003; USCB 1999; KPMG LLP 2004; Navistar 2003; PACCAR 2003.

648. Please see the Trucking Business Case spreadsheet (*Technical Annex*, Ch. 20) for details.

with an average IRR of 70%/y. After the fifth year, Swift's after-tax profit margin would rise from 3.3% to 6.7%.

Similarly, private carrier fleets serving companies such as Wal-Mart®, Coca-Cola®, or SYSCO® *each* account for 0.3–0.5% of the national Class 8 truck stock, and, unless the carriers pass their fuel costs on to their clients (Wal-Mart, etc.), the private carriers also have clear incentives to upgrade their fleets.

Most of the existing fleet, however, is owned by many smaller fleets and independent truckers, who tend to buy their trucks used from the large private carriers and run them for the rest of their useful life. Owning the trucks far longer than private carriers, these smaller operators drive twice as many cumulative total miles per truck; yet they're also unlikely to have the cash or credit to upgrade their vehicles early. These truckers, responsible for ~60–65% of total Class 8 fuel use, will have to wait for *State of the Art* vehicles to trickle down to the used-truck market. Nevertheless, the five-year resale cycle is much quicker than for light vehicles or airplanes, so although policies could readily be devised to accelerate adoption by bringing used-truck buyers into the new-truck market, we have chosen not to do so.[646] Instead, we focus on the ~23% of the Class 8 operators that buy ~60% to ~75% (averaging nearly two-thirds) of all new trucks and are eager customers for efficiency improvements. Given the very positive customer economics, we expect that the first manufacturer to make this shift will gain substantial market share.

The Class 8 truck manufacturing market is highly concentrated: four major players (DaimlerChrysler, Volvo, Navistar, and PACCAR) sell 99.5% of U.S. heavy trucks. Unlike cars, the efficiency improvements described on pp. 73–77 do not require a major change of platform design nor new product lines. Instead, the improvements are about equally divided between lightweighting, making the body more aerodynamic, and modernizing the engine.

While we don't have firm capital estimates of the investment cost, clearly it is comparatively modest. For the four big truckmakers, we estimate that a cumulative total investment of ~$18 billion would be required during 2005–25 to retool 15–24 plants, or ~$750 million per plant[647]—about a half-year's worth of revenue per plant. This proposed investment is well within the range of what these manufacturers already plan to invest. When annualized, it is equivalent to 50–70% of current (2003 actual) and forecast (2004–06) investment rates that those four OEMs already *specifically target at high-performance vehicles and next-generation diesel engine technologies*, often using a more incremental approach. In addition to these costs, truckmakers would incur a ~$3–5 billion total charge for product-line development costs.[648]

RMI expects that an informed market will make these changes on its own. The major customers for new trucks receive high returns from more efficient vehicles, as do the truck manufacturers from increased profits due to selling more expensive trucks. The technology improvements necessary to make the vehicles more aerodynamic and lightweight are substantially easier technically than for cars (*Technical Annex*, Ch. 6), and most are well proven. These innovations account for two-thirds of trucks' potential fuel savings. The other third comes from engine improvements, which will require more R&D, but that's the core product-development business of such capable firms as Cummins, Caterpillar, and Detroit Diesel.

Our judgment is that the main missing ingredient for radically increased efficiency in the trucking sector is better customer information on what's possible. RMI's recent conversations with the heads of two very large Class 8 fleet operators substantiate this hypothesis. These savvy business leaders were astonished that more than a few percent of truck energy could be profitably saved. On learning of the *State of the Art* potential, their basic reaction was, "Let's build one, and if it works, we'll simply tell the truckmakers that we want them to make such trucks for us." When our consulting practice previously advised one of these same firms on an experimental building, its design required a certain technology that could readily be made but hadn't been brought to market. When we asked the leading vendor's sales department for one, they said, "Sorry, sir, it's not in the catalogue." When we replied, "Our client is X Corporation, and if they like this product, they'll buy a truckload a day indefinitely," the answer instantly changed to "Yes, sir! When do you want it?" That energy-saving, profit-enhancing product was duly delivered, successfully tested, and widely propagated.

The opportunity to do the same with Class 8 trucks is starting to be validated. In 2004, one of the most innovative, engineering-intensive, and successful bulk carriers in the U.S.[648a] redesigned a Class 8 tractor-trailer combination from scratch in collaboration with a major truckmaker. The goals—25% higher payload, doubled fuel economy, enhanced safety and driver ergonomics, and reduced emissions—did turn out to appear feasible, and a prototype is planned to be built in late 2004. Interestingly, the technology suite didn't include the C_d reductions and superefficient engines emphasized on pp. 73–77 above, but is expected to achieve comparable results by emphasizing careful integration of off-the-shelf improvements. This implies that our *State of the Art* portfolio conservatively omitted some collectively significant technological opportunities.

The business opportunity for the truck manufacturers is not selling more trucks in the U.S. per se, but selling trucks that provide higher value to their customers, yielding decisive advantage in margin or market share. The same product improvements will also make the trucks more competitive in other countries where the diesel prices are higher, notably in Europe, where the reduced CO_2 and other emissions would also provide a strong marketing advantage. For medium trucks, major development efforts are already underway in Europe and Japan to reduce radically the

RMI expects that an informed market will make these changes on its own.

The main missing ingredient for radically increased efficiency in the trucking sector is better customer information on what's possible.

648a. Logistics Management, Inc. (Bridgeview, IL). Tom Wieranga, President (contactable via RMI), personal communication, 16 August 2004.

noise and emissions of urban delivery trucks; this is accelerating global demand for the most advanced technologies, such as fuel cells. And of course the same spectrum of demands occurs in the Pentagon's truck fleet, perhaps the world's largest (p. 88, note 430), with the added incentive of the huge logistics costs for delivering fuel. When one also considers DoD's need for superefficient diesel engines for medium and heavy tactical vehicles, using military procurement to insert advanced technologies rapidly into the heavy-truck market faster becomes a key enabler for military transformation.

Revitalizing the airline and airplane industries

Fuel costs are the airline industry's biggest variable cost except labor. Because of their high volatility, fuel costs are the industry's financial Achilles' heel. Per passenger-mile, you pay airlines about the same as you pay to own and run your car, but like low-income households, airlines gush red ink whenever fuel prices spike up. Meanwhile, overcapacity is depressing the near-term growth prospects of airplane manufacturers. How do we address both problems, so as to revitalize the airline industry and reduce oil dependence at the same time?

The key to this puzzle is that fuel savings from new airplanes are very cheap per gallon, but new planes are expensive. The legacy airlines are too broke to buy many new planes, so when the profitable discount carriers buy very efficient new planes, they displace their high-cost competitors[649] even faster, accelerating the market exit of the legacy carriers and the cost savings to customers.

If policymakers decide that they wish to save the legacy airlines, a good way to give them a better chance of survival—better for society than, say, simply throwing federal dollars at their operating deficits or assuming their $31 billion in pension obligations[650]—would be an innovative loan guarantee program for the airline industry to purchase or lease new fuel-efficient aircraft (Box 16). Current-dollar jet fuel prices rose 54% to $1.18/gallon between May 2003 and May 2004, increasing fuel costs to 2.13¢/seat-mile.[651] As we noted on p. 17, each time the jet fuel price increases 1 cent, it costs U.S. airlines $180 million a year.[652] Higher fuel prices cost the three largest U.S. carriers—United, American, and Continental—an additional $700 million in 2004.[653] But if new efficient aircraft used *Conventional Wisdom* technologies, U.S. airlines' fuel cost would drop 29% to 1.51¢/seat-mile, saving $6.2 billion per year. Those savings would rise to $8.4b/y with *State of the Art* planes, which would cut fuel costs to 1.14¢/seat-mile, even at mid-2004 fuel prices.

The economics of fuel efficiency are compelling. Over its 30-year life, one *7E7* will save over $7 million in present-valued fuel costs compared with the *767* it replaces (or $5.3 million vs. the *A330* with which it competes), yet its capital cost is comparable or lower.[654] If United had reconfigured

Next-generation airplanes save fuel cheaply (or even better than free), but legacy airlines can't afford them. Federal loan guarantees can make such acquisitions financeable, and should be coupled with scrappage of the inefficient old planes now parked.

Fuel savings from new airplanes are very cheap per gallon, but new planes are expensive. The legacy airlines are too broke to buy many new planes, so when the profitable discount carriers buy very efficient new planes, they displace their high-cost competitors even faster.

649. U.S. legacy airlines' total cost is 9.5–11.5¢/seat-mile; low–cost carriers', 6–8¢/seat-mile.

650. M.W. Walsh 2004.

651. New York Harbor jet fuel prices were used (EIA, 2004e, p. 26, Table 15).

652. Tully 2004, p. 101.

653. *Financial Times* 2004.

just 9% of its 2003 fleet with similarly efficient planes, its net income would have increased by $34 million.[655] (*State of the Art* planes could roughly double those savings.) Even incremental retrofits can be attractive. For example, Southwest is executing a plan to attach blended winglets to all of its *737-700*s at a cost around $710,000 per plane.[656] The project will improve each plane's fuel efficiency by 3–4%, saving ~$113,000 more than the winglets cost (present-valued at 5%/y real over 30 years). If Southwest applied this technology to its entire 2003 fleet of 388 aircraft, it would invest nearly $300 million to cut operating costs by 0.6%, paying back in 8 years and earning a real IRR of ~12%/y.[657] So if fuel savings are profitable, why aren't all airlines updating their fleets like Southwest, especially with new planes?

The answer lies in the structural changes in the U.S. airline industry and the financial state of the U.S. airlines. The major U.S. carriers are facing devastating competition from discount carriers whose lower-cost business model is based on a more efficient point-to-point service, lower embedded labor costs, and lower non-labor operating costs. Low-cost carriers' market share has risen from 5% in 1987 to 25% in 2004. The market capitalization of the six biggest discounters is now $18 billion, far higher than the $4 billion market capitalization of the six largest traditional airlines.[658] Southwest Airlines alone has a tenth the market share and a twelfth the revenue of the Big Six combined—but nearly three times their *combined* market capitalization.

The major airlines, having borrowed ~$100 billion to stay alive,[659] are now carrying so much debt that either they're in bankruptcy or their credit ratings have slipped to junk-bond status. This makes it hard for them to finance the new fuel-efficient (and often more lightly crewed) jets they need. And if they were to do so, the present-valued lifetime fuel savings are only ~6% of the capital cost of a new plane—critical to operating margins, but hardly enough by itself to justify turning over the fleet when cash is scarce.[660]

> **If new efficient aircraft used *Conventional Wisdom* technologies, U.S. airlines' fuel cost would drop 29%, saving $6.2 billion per year. Those savings would rise to $8.4b/y with *State of the Art* planes.**

> **Southwest Airlines has a tenth the market share and a twelfth the revenue of the Big Six combined—but nearly three times their market capitalization.**

654. The *7E7* replaces the current *767*. Even at the EIA estimate for 2025 jet fuel prices of 81¢/gal (2000 $, based on $26/bbl crude), its lifetime fuel savings at the U.S. airlines' current weighted-average cost of capital (13%/y) are $7.4 million, based on flying 900 flights/y, each of 3,500 nautical miles. From airlines' perspective, the fuel savings are only 6% of the ~$120 million price of a new *7E7*. We assumed a nominal 30-y aircraft life (Ferguson 2004).

655. This illustrative example assumes that United Airlines replaced its 37 *767-300*s and 10 *767-200*s with 47 *7E7*s. At a fuel saving of 23.8% vs. a *767-200* and 17.3% vs. a *767-300* (M. Mirza, Boeing Economic Analysis Dept., personal communication, 11 June 2004, based on a standardized 2,000-nautical-mile trip at the 2000 average load factor of 0.72), *7E7* would have saved 18.7% of the fuel used by those 47 aircraft (8.8% of United's fleet). Assuming an even distribution of miles flown across United's 532-aircraft fleet, this replacement would have saved 18.7% of $183 million/y (8.8% × $2,027 million/y fuel expense), or $34.2 million/y. (Fuel expense and fleet data from UAL Corporation 10-K, filed 2 March 2004.)

656. Martin, Rogers, & Simkins 2004. Our IRR calculation assumes Southwest's weighted-average real cost of capital is 10%/y, close to its actual WACC of 10.5% at mid-2004, and assumes a constant real fuel price of 81¢/gal (2000 $), equaling EIA's 2025 forecast.

657. Calculations based on the expected saving of 110,000 gal/plane-y at the EIA 2025 price forecast of 81¢/gal.

658. Tully 2004.   659. Jenkins 2004.

660. Of course, it's not worth buying a new car just for its fuel savings either, but when one needs a new car anyway, its potential fuel savings are a much larger fraction of total capital cost than for a new airplane. Airplanes are usually more fuel-efficient than cars, counting actual load factors for both (see the right-hand seat-mpg axis of Fig. 25 on p. 81; actually planes have about three times the load factor of cars). However, their capital cost per seat is two orders of magnitude higher, because they travel ten times faster, for 2–3 times the lifetime and ~20–30 times the operating hours, and are made at five orders of magnitude lower volume.

While major airlines are cutting back on plane orders, the low-cost carriers have orders for 500 new jets over the next 5 years—more than the 357 jets Continental Airlines currently flies.[661] The low-cost carriers would be well advised to consider very fuel-efficient planes too. As discount carriers move from regional point-to-point service (whose short stages increase fuel use per seat-mile) to transcontinental flights, their flights surpass the trip lengths at which the value of fuel-efficient new planes starts to increase more and more rapidly. Efficiency saves more on longer trip lengths because the base benefit of more efficient planes is compounded by the reduced amount of fuel they must carry for the longer trips vs. their heavier and less efficient counterparts. On a standard 2000-mile flight, a typical existing widebody would have to carry at least 11,594 gallons of total fuel, of which 818 gallons are needed just to carry fuel. This is only a 7% overhead, but for longer missions, the fuel needed to carry fuel rises

Efficient new planes like the *7E7* and its successors could easily be stalled by the least efficient one-fifth of the fleet that's now parked. If traffic picks up and those parked planes resume service, they'll not only waste fuel and continue to bleed operating budgets they'll also slow the adoption of far more efficient new models, and hence the development of next-generation *State of the Art* airplanes too. That's why we propose to link the scrappage of inefficient parked planes to loan guarantees for financing efficient new planes.

16: Flying high: fuel savings arbitrage

The airlines are starting to draw on $10 billion in federal loan guarantees to help them out of bankruptcy. While the airlines have used bankruptcy to address labor costs, they have not fixed the structural problem of fuel cost. The economics of fuel efficiency are compelling, but the major airlines lack the balance-sheet strength to retrofit their fleet. Rather than simply bail out the airlines, and hope they recover, why not double down on the bet, and finance the restructuring of their fleet to achieve far greater national benefits?

Our proposed program calls on commercial banks and the federal government to arbitrage discount rates and liquidity by providing financing for the airlines to restructure their fleet toward increased fuel efficiency. Airlines could receive federal loan guarantees to buy or lease any new aircraft that meets a high target for fuel efficiency, from any manu-

facturer (competition is good), provided that for each plane so financed, an inefficient parked plane is scrapped. (A trading system would allow buyers who don't own parked planes to satisfy the scrappage obligation.) Fuel savings would help repay the commercial financing, just as energy efficiency financing does in buildings and factories. This program addresses the overcapacity problem that is stifling the sale of new aircraft, and would stimulate orders for new planes.

Airlines would be allowed either to purchase or to lease the new fuel-efficient aircraft, but would be encouraged to enter into operating leases, thereby reducing their on-balance-sheet debt and improving their ability to borrow. A program of this nature need not be limited to the legacy airlines; a similar program could be crafted for the new planes bought by the low-cost carriers.

661. McCartney 2004.

until at the limit of a 747's globe-girdling range, nearly two gallons must be loaded to have one gallon left at the destination. By contrast, a *State of Art* widebody plane would need to carry only 6,716 total gallons of fuel while transporting 173 more passengers.[662]

If the next generation of planes can deliver fuel efficiency at below the EIA projected 2025 jet fuel price of 81¢/gallon, as is clearly the case (pp. 79–83), then the discounters should spend the extra money to acquire these planes. If they want to stay competitive, the future is already here: a *7E7* can save one-fifth of the fuel used by the *767* it replaces, but at the same or lower real capital cost.[663]

Yet rapid adoption of efficient new planes like the *7E7* and its successors could easily be stalled by the least efficient one-fifth of the fleet that's now parked. If traffic picks up and those parked planes resume service, they'll not only waste fuel and continue to bleed operating budgets (making airlines even less able to escape from the fuel-cost trap); they'll also slow the adoption of far more efficient new models, and hence the development of next-generation *State of the Art* airplanes too. That's why, in Box 16, we propose to link the scrappage of inefficient parked planes to loan guarantees for financing efficient new planes. The parked fleet is worth more to society dead than alive—counting not just their fuel waste, but the opportunity cost of their delaying the adoption and development of ever more efficient successors—and this linkage seems a simple way to activate bounty-hunters.

> The parked airplane fleet is worth more to society dead than alive.

Getting generation-after-next planes off the ground

The underlying economics of *State of the Art* Blended-Wing-Body aircraft are compelling even when compared to excellent *Conventional Wisdom* planes like the *7E7* they'll ultimately replace. *State of the Art* planes will save 30% more fuel than *Conventional Wisdom* planes, delivering fuel savings at only 43¢ per gallon of saved jet fuel, far below the EIA price of 81¢ per gallon in 2025. We therefore expect that these planes could be adopted by the airlines. The question is when, and how that schedule can be accelerated.[664]

> Even more efficient successor planes should be readied promptly to start saving even more fuel after 2015. Military requirements can accelerate their development.

By 2025, EIA projects a 60% increase in passenger miles and a 130% increase in cargo miles. To meet this increased travel demand, EIA projects about 15,000 new airplanes to be sold between 2005 and 2025, a third

662. Calculated by using average-widebody and *SOA* aircraft gal/seat-mile data from *Technical Annex*, Ch. 12. Seating (295 passengers) and incremental fuel burn (0.005 gal per flight-hour per pound of weight added) are determined based on a widebody aircraft fleet made up of 31% *747-400*s, 51% *767*s, and 18% *777*s. Fuel reserves are based on Federal Aviation Requirement 91.151, which mandates 30 minutes of cruising speed fuel for daytime flights.

663. The weighted-average price of all *767-200ER*, *-300ER*, and *-400ER* airplanes placed in world service in the past five years was $119 million (2000 $), while the *7E7* is estimated to sell for $112±4.7 million (2000 $), implying a negative Cost of Saved Energy.

664. Packaging issues may also arise in small sizes, such as for regional aircraft, but the sort of advanced-composite construction method used in the Lockheed-Martin Skunk Works' advanced tactical fighter in the mid-1990s (p. 62, note 326) should help to fit more passengers and cargo into a smaller, lighter, and cheaper Blended-Wing-Body airplane.

The overarching national aviation goal should be to ensure that new planes bought in the short term are as efficient as they can be (like *7E7*); that *State of the Art* successor models are developed and brought to market with due deliberate speed; and that both airframe manufacturers and their customers find it advantageous and feasible to adopt the most efficient airplanes available at any given time.

of which will be regional jets.[665] Airlines are willing to pay more for reductions in operating costs: the investment per seat for long-range aircraft increased 130% during 1959–95.[666] But some airlines need financing, and all need superefficient planes to choose from.

Worldwide commercial airline production is largely a duopoly comprising Boeing and Airbus. These companies are in a continuous high-stakes engineering design competition to beat the rival's performance. Currently they each have a new plane in development for release in the next four years (Box 14). Airbus is set to release the 555-seat *A380*, a plane designed to compete with Boeing's *747*, around 2006. Boeing in turn is designing the *7E7 Dreamliner* to replace its own *767* and *757* models and compete against Airbus's *A330*. Airbus is worried enough to begin to design a more-fuel-efficient engine upgrade for its *A330*, though that platform's higher weight and drag will limit its ability to compete with *7E7*.[667] Both manufacturers chose to target the competition's signature aircraft, and each claims to have surpassed the other's current operating efficiency by at least 15%.

Development costs are around $10–12 billion for a new model aircraft.[668] Airbus projects that the *A380* project will not reach breakeven until the 251st plane is sold (even longer if list prices are discounted). Based on the adoption pattern of the *747-400* released in 1989, this volume may take longer than four years to achieve.

Technology innovation is not just about improved efficiency, however. Technological innovation enables, and sometimes creates, new business models. Airbus is betting on the continuation of the existing hub-and-spokes business model by even larger fleets, justifying gigantic airplanes. Boeing is betting that the discounters' point-to-point regional business model will spread to transcontinental and intra-regional flying. Boeing may also be contemplating design variants larger or smaller than the *7E7* base model to hedge its market-structure bet, whereas the *A380* will offer less size flexibility. At any size, Boeing's more efficient technology should be attractive to airlines facing volatile and possibly high fuel prices.

RMI expects that this battle will play itself out over the next five to ten years. If Boeing begins to gain the advantage, then its business strategy will have been proven by the market. We expect this to spur investment by all airline manufacturers in a more efficient generation of aircraft. A complete cycle of new airplane development takes up to about a decade, followed by another couple of decades to replace older models.[669] Therefore, *State of the Art* planes would not come on line until 2015 or beyond, regardless of technological and manufacturing improvements, and much of their benefit comes after 2025. Our scenario analysis below assumes that after 2015, new *State of the Art* planes would be phased into the fleet. Of course, feebate-like incentives could accelerate this adoption, but may not be necessary. The overarching national aviation goal should be to ensure that new planes bought in the short term are as efficient

665. EIA 2004.

666. Babikian et al. 2000.

667. Lunsford & Michaels 2004.

668. Wallace 2003; BBC News 2000; note 609.

669. Flug-Revue Online 2000.

as they can be (like *7E7*); that *State of the Art* successor models are developed and brought to market with due deliberate speed; and that both airframe manufacturers and their customers find it advantageous and feasible to adopt the most efficient airplanes available at any given time.

An obvious way to accelerate *State of the Art* civilian airplane development is smart military procurement, since Blended-Wing-Body or "flying wing" designs—under development by Boeing, NASA, and others since the early 1990s—and their associated technologies, such as next-generation engines, also have broad military applications, initially for tankers, weapons systems, and command/control, and later for heavy lift and cargo applications. The Blended-Wing-Body concept is under continuing study by Boeing's Phantom Works and Integrated Defense Systems branches for military use. A 17-ft-wingspan scale model was flight-tested in 1997 in collaboration with Stanford University, and an improved 21-ft-wingspan model is under development with Cranfield Aerospace (UK). DARPA and other agencies are helping with concept development for military applications, and Boeing and its competitors would happily build on that expertise to bring medium-to-large Blended-Wing-Body airplanes to the commercial market as market conditions warrant. Thus with airplanes as with heavy trucks, the key enabling technologies are of such strong military as well as civilian interest for both cutting costs and transforming capabilities (pp. 84–93) that military science and technology development should be one of the leading elements of any coherent national effort to displace oil. Across the range of land, sea, and air platforms, this is most true for advanced lightweight materials, as we see next.

> With airplanes as with heavy trucks, the key enabling technologies are of such strong military as well as civilian interest for both cutting costs and transforming capabilities that military science and technology development should be one of the leading elements of any coherent national effort to displace oil.

Creating a new high-technology industrial cluster

> Advanced ultralight materials, engines, and other efficiency technologies are the foundation of oil savings and a stronger industrial and employment base. Their accelerated military and civilian development should be vigorous, coordinated, and immediate.

Technological advances are generally and rightly considered the main engine of economic growth.[670] *State of the Art* ultralight-hybrid vehicles and their associated advanced technologies are in the same tradition as the technological changes that were so vital to the U.S. economy in the twentieth century. Throughout their lifecycle, these vehicles will consistently favor high-productivity production processes and supply high-skill, high-wage, high-value-added jobs with large and widely distributed economic multipliers.

Automaking has undergone several major transformations before, often triggered by new materials.[671] Our proposal for the transformation of the transportation sector is underpinned by technological improvements in

670. For example, see Anton, Silbergilt, & Schneider 2001; see also Christensen & Raynor 2003, which argues that corporations accrue higher market value from their ability to adopt innovations.

671. Amendola 1990: "The choice of materials has always been one of the major technical problems in planning, designing and manufacturing a car.... [T]he very history of the automobile industry is rich in innovations strictly related to decisive choices about materials used. For instance, the introduction of the Model T Ford in 1908, which is often referred to as the beginning of the modern automobile industry, was associated with a very important innovation in the area of materials: use of a high-strength vanadium steel alloy in critical chassis components. This innovation is considered by historians as 'the fundamental chassis design choice.'"

The military and aerospace sectors are the most likely candidates to build the initial primary market demand that would enable the advanced materials sector to gain the requisite scale economies.

advanced materials and their manufacturing techniques, powertrains (especially using electric traction), power electronics, microelectronics, software, aerodynamics, tires (another materials-dominated field), and systems integration. Collectively, these form a new high-technology industrial cluster that will expand U.S. competitiveness beyond the transportation sector alone—much as the development of the microchip, cross-fertilized with other technologies, has created the largest and most dynamic sector of the modern economy, and the information revolution in turn has transformed the entire economy.[672] How can another such co-evolution (in the automotive sector and beyond) be encouraged in order to synchronize the industrial development strategy? And rather than stifling this evolution with planning, how can creative policy maximize opportunities for the broadest and most durable kind of wealth creation?

RMI's analysis strongly suggests that the military and aerospace sectors are the most likely candidates to build the initial primary market demand that would enable the advanced materials sector to gain the requisite scale economies. The diffusion of military innovations into wide civilian use has encouraging precedents. The best-known example is the microchip:[673]

> In 1976, U.S. military purchases accounted for 17% of IC [integrated-circuit] sales worldwide ($700 million out of total sales of $4.2 billion)—a significant market share that gave DoD leverage in defining product specifications and directions. In the next 20 years, the U.S. military market increased only marginally, to $1.1 billion, while the commercial market exploded to $160 billion. The military market now [in 1999] accounts for less than 1% of sales, and the commercial market has become the dominant force in setting IC product directions. Although lower prices have resulted, the DoD is now compelled to use commercial IC products and adapt them to meet military requirements, as necessary.

Such investments often have surprising and serendipitous spin-offs. Military R&D in advanced aero-engine turbines is obviously the basis of today's modern commercial aircraft, which could hardly get off the ground without those lightweight, fuel-efficient, high-bypass engines. Less obviously, those commercial engine technologies in turn are the basis for the combined-cycle gas-fired power plants that have rapidly transformed the global electric power industry.

The advanced materials we envisage for efficient cars and trucks, especially the carbon-fiber composites, are historically based on aerospace technology. The business challenge arises because aerospace applications typically have about a thousand times smaller volume and a thousand times higher cost than automotive ones. Direct technology transfer is therefore insufficient; R&D is needed for mass production of advanced-composite structures that meet the automotive industry's requirements of high volume and low cost. As noted in our earlier discussion of the lightweighting revolution (p. 57), such efforts in the private sector already show promise, and military attention could greatly accelerate their application.[674]

672. This topic is discussed by Davis, Hirschl, & Stack 1997. In a July 2001 interview, Davis states that "…the way that we make things—the tools and the technology and the science and the technique—all those things are such a fundamental part of the economy that when they change everything else changes with it. The main player today is the microchip, which was commercially introduced around 1971, because it makes so many other breakthroughs in human activity possible—from manufacturing to agriculture, to medicine, transportation, how we produce all forms of culture."

673. NAS/NRC/CETS 1999, p. 137. In FY1977, DoD R&D represented 40% of federal spending for basic research and over 70% of all federal investment in microelectronics and electrical engineering (NAS/NRC/CETS 1999, p. 138).

674. Whitfield 2004.

Non-aerospace military needs, especially for lightweight land and sea platforms, are an important pathway to this commercialization because they often need higher production volumes and lower costs than military aircraft. As previously discussed (pp. 84–93), military mission requirements focus strongly on lighter, stronger, cheaper, and more energy-efficient vehicles to fit today's rapid-response and agility-based doctrine and to lower logistics cost and vulnerability. The military has the R&D budget to support the development of advanced materials (composites and lightweight steel), and already does so to a degree. The military clearly has the scale. If DoD were to adopt the changes proposed to its Humvee (HMMWV) production alone, a 10,000-unit yearly production run of the multipurpose vehicle would require 5 million pounds of carbon fiber. This represents over 6% of the current worldwide production capacity of carbon fiber for all applications (80 million pounds). By 2025, the U.S. automobile industry alone could demand ~1.7 billion pounds of carbon fiber, 21 times current worldwide production, corresponding to compound growth of 15%/y.[675] And this rapid expansion is feasible: composite industry sources estimate that within five years the industry could be ready for cost-effective mass production of carbon-fiber-based civilian and military vehicles.[676]

The synchronized timing of the co-evolution is important. For example, Ford's first round of *Escape* hybrid SUVs is limited not by the market or its manufacturing capacity, but by Sanyo's nickel-metal-hydride buffer-battery manufacturing capacity, because soaring demand for Japanese hybrids keeps the supply chain rather fully occupied.[677] Therefore, military technology support should be launched *now* in order to have the capacity ready in time for the automakers' shift. To minimize exposure to the cumbersome DoD budget process, early commitments should focus on DARPA and the more agile R&D and early-application Service organizations.

The new industrial cluster would bring national benefits far beyond military prowess and budget savings. It would create a significant number of high-technology manufacturing jobs, which we estimate to be roughly analogous to the labor intensity of the chemicals sector (2.3 jobs per million dollars of annual revenue using the narrowest definition and excluding all multipliers). The 2025 carbon-fiber demand mentioned above would fetch ~$8 billion per year, creating ~20,000 new direct jobs.[678] For our projected *State of the Art* vehicle production volume, these jobs may either go to the steel sector for new lightweight steel or to the polymer composite sectors, or to some mixture; market competition will sort that out, but either way,

> By 2025, the U.S. automobile industry alone could demand ~1.7 billion pounds of carbon fiber, 21 times current worldwide production, corresponding to compound growth of 15%/y. The industry could be ready for cost-effective mass production of carbon-fiber-based civilian and military.

675. Based on 8 million *SOA* cars with an average of 212 lb of carbon fiber per car—196 lb/car (Hypercar, Inc. proprietary mass-budget analysis, D.R. Cramer, personal communication, 11 May 2004) times 1.08 scaling factor (p. 96, note 164, above).

676. Levin 2002. However, big speculative price swings that now deter investment in carbon-fiber production capacity would need to be smoothed by making futures and options markets in structural carbon.

677. MSNBC News 2004.

678. Calculated on the basis of 8 million *State of the Art* cars built in 2025, each with 212 lb of carbon fiber, and one manufacturing job created for every 43.4 tons of carbon fiber produced. Job creation numbers derived from Alliance of Automobile Manufacturers economic contribution study on plastics and rubber producers (McAlinden, Hill, & Swiecki 2003, p.25).

it means good jobs.[679] There are probably many times more jobs, too, in converting raw carbon fiber into cars than in making the fiber. Looking forward to the hydrogen economy, which ultralight vehicles can help accelerate (pp. 233–234), several studies on fuel-cell manufacturing predict on the order of hundreds of thousands of new jobs.[680] Clearly, this cluster of new automotive-and-energy-related technologies could be an important engine of economic growth. It is indeed plausible that jobs lost in, say, petroleum refining and petrochemicals would be more than offset by new jobs that apply broadly similar skills to polymer manufacturing and application—especially as mass-produced fuel cells, too, switch their materials to molded and roll-to-roll polymers.

The national benefits that will grow out of the new advanced-materials industrial cluster go far beyond the direct jobs it creates. These new technologies have the potential to be as pervasive and transformative as plastics were in the 1960s. Advanced polymer composites have already entered boatmaking, military and civilian airplanes, bicycles, and sporting goods, and are now poised to enter the automotive sector and beyond. Lightweight steel also has the potential to extend steel usage well beyond the realm of traditional applications. Whichever advanced light material comes to dominate future automobile construction (most likely a diverse mix, each used to do what it does best), the materials applications throughout society will extend far beyond their originally intended mobility applications.

Restoring farming, ranching, and forest economies

Farming has never been an easy business, and the decline in U.S. agricultural communities' population, income, and cultural vitality has been relentless. An average of 450,000 agricultural jobs (farm proprietors and employees) have been lost each decade since 1970.[681] The U.S. and many other OECD countries have responded to this decline with ever-increasing subsidies for the agricultural sector. These subsidies not only distort markets and farming practices,[682] but also hobble the global development process, depressing poor countries' food exports and domestic-market food production to a degree that recently triggered a revolt and blocked further trade liberalization.[683] Traditional thinking on U.S. biofuels is that

> **Rural and small-town America can gain enormously in income, jobs, and stability through biofuel production and related revenues— while the country gains half a ← Saudi Arabia's worth of stable, uninterruptible, all-domestic fuel supplies.**

679. For a discussion of job impacts from carbon composites, see Lovins et al. 1996, Ch. 6.

680. "PricewaterhouseCoopers predicts that by 2013 the North American fuel cell industry will represent 108,000 direct and indirect jobs associated with manufacturing stationary fuel cell units...." (*Fuel Cell News* 2003). The Breakthrough Technologies Institute predicts 189,000 direct and indirect jobs produced by the fuel cell industry (BTI 2004).

681. Calculated from Bureau of Economic Analysis, Regional Economic Accounts, Local Area Personal Income (BEA, undated).

682. The U.S. currently provides a $0.53/gallon ethanol subsidy, and proposed a $1/gallon biodiesel subsidy in the 2002 Senate Energy Bill (Peckham 2002). Europe has used a combination of oilseed-production subsidies and biodiesel tax exemptions (p.106) to ensure competitive pricing and therefore, market adoption of biodiesel (CRFA, undated). However, "...tying government subsidies to commodity prices has distorted the agriculture market and made farmers dependant on government handouts" (Hylden 2003).

683. The 1 August 2004 framework agreement to remove agricultural export subsidies (which the U.S. denies it has) and substantially reduce direct crop subsidies (which have powerful political defenders) will be slow and hard to convert into actual desubsidization in the U.S. and EU. However, the agreement increases the need for a different and trade-equitable way to strengthen rural economies.

they are yet another in the long line of subsidized crops, representing an agricultural bailout by urban and suburban dwellers.[684] But this view, based on corn-ethanol conversion, is now badly outdated (p. 103).

Once cellulosic biofuel technology lowers the cost of ethanol below the equivalent crude oil price benchmark of $26/bbl, as has already occurred for sugarcane ethanol in Brazil (p. 105), the game changes fundamentally. It's no longer about who can lobby best for crop subsidies, but about strategic investment in a new and more secure rural-based domestic fuels infrastructure that competes, without subsidy, even with today's subsidized gasoline (i.e., producible for $0.75/gal gasoline-equivalent at the plant gate, p. 103). The benefits of such substitution are well established: greater energy security, increased agricultural employment, and reduced carbon intensity among others.[685] The business question is whether or not next-generation biofuels and biomaterials make financial sense to farmers and agricultural processors.

From the farmer's perspective, the fundamental business decision is based on the value per acre vs. alternative agricultural crops. Promising crops proposed for biofuels (p. 107) include switchgrass and such short-rotation woody crops as hybrid poplar and willow. Based on our *State of the Art* analysis, a cellulosic ethanol cost of $0.61/gallon ($0.75/gallon of gasoline equivalent) implies that biofuel refiners can pay $54 per dry ton for these crops and still make an adequate return on capital from their operations. A representative switchgrass yield of 7–10 ton/acre-y yields revenue of $431–637/acre-y.

That revenue from the biofuel crop, much or even most of it from land otherwise unsuitable for or reserved from conventional cropping, is just the beginning. Much of the same land can be simultaneously used for windpower in the nation's extensive windy areas, notably on the High Plains. Farmers can also capture three kinds of carbon credits: from the fossil fuel displaced by both the biofuels and the windpower, and from the net increase in soil carbon storage. Soil carbon accumulates because biofuel-feedstock farming using USDA-recommended soil conservation practices can be better than carbon-neutral: such farming methods can fix airborne carbon (CO_2) into soil to improve fertility, water retention, and biodiversity (which in turn can substitute for fertilizers, pesticides, and other costly inputs). USDA's new Conservation Security Program begins to recognize and reward farmers' investments in these vital assets, both prospectively and retroactively. Despite official U.S. nonparticipation in global carbon-trading regimes, the farm-sector benefits of reduced CO_2 emissions are efficiently available from private trading regimes now emerging around the world.

> An average of 450,000 agricultural jobs (farm proprietors and employees) have been lost each decade since 1970. But once cellulosic biofuel technology lowers the cost of ethanol, the game changes fundamentally. It's no longer about who can lobby best for crop subsidies, but about strategic investment in a new and more secure rural-based domestic fuels infrastructure that competes, without subsidy, even with today's subsidized gasoline.

684. Indeed, the recent Energy Bill foundered partly on a bipartisan gridlock between the rural states and the urban areas on the degree of ethanol subsidies that the urban areas would be forced to pay (Coon 2004; Taylor & Van Doren 2003).

685. According to AUS Consultants, Inc., increasing ethanol output to 5b gal/y by 2012 would reduce crude oil imports by 1.6b bbl cumulatively, cut the U.S. trade deficit by $34 billion, and eliminate $10.6 billion of direct government payments to farmers. Environmentally, net CO_2 emissions are cut by 78% for biodiesel (Schumacher, Van Gerpen, & Adams 2004) and 68% for ethanol (assuming a E85 fuel blend—GM et al. 2001, Fig. 3.6).

The renewable fuels farming system can provide farmers with total revenues of ~$500–900/acre-y not counting any of the $100–500/acre-y carbon offset revenue from windpower production. This income level compares favorably with gross revenues generated from such traditional crops as corn ($325/acre-y), wheat ($118), and soybeans ($281). Together these pure-net income streams could quadruple pretax net farm income.

The carbon offsets from biofuel production could potentially be worth $26–128/acre-y, assuming carbon prices of $10–50/tonne carbon.[686] Lease payments for windpower production (worth ~$1,000–1,600/acre-y to the turbine owner) can provide an additional $50–80/acre-y for areas with Class 4 winds or better, which are widespread on the Great Plains.[687] The carbon offsets from the wind turbines' output would be worth an additional $100–500/acre-y,[688] some of which could probably be captured by the landowner in a competitive market. Finally, soil carbon storage can add a further $3–15/acre-y.[689]

Collectively, the renewable fuels farming system can provide farmers with total revenues of ~$500–900/acre-y (Table 4), not counting any of the $100–500/acre-y carbon offset revenue from windpower production (in case the windpower developer captures all of that benefit). This income level compares favorably with gross revenues generated from such traditional crops as corn ($325/acre-y), wheat ($118), and soybeans ($281),[690] all of which require far costlier inputs and operations than harvesting perennial switchgrass. Better yet, about $80–220/acre-y of carbon revenues and wind royalties (again ignoring carbon offsets from windpower) incur *no* out-of-pocket costs to the farmer or rancher—they're third-party payments for byproducts of the main farming activity—and together these pure-net income streams could quadruple pretax net farm income, which averaged only $43/acre-y in 2002 (p. 108). Obviously not every farmer can capture all these kinds of income, and exact values will differ widely, but equally obviously this approach holds promise of major improvements in farm economics, and analogously for ranch and forest operations.

Table 4: Potential farm revenue and net income from clean energy and carbon offsets (assuming carbon trading at ~$10–50/tonne carbon). Windpower net income counts only royalties from wind-turbine siting, on the assumption that the carbon offset value from the wind electricity's displacing fossil fuels would be captured by the windfarm developer, not the landowner.

Product	Product value, 2000 $/acre-year	Carbon offset value, 2000 $/acre-year	Value to farmer, 2000 $/acre-year
biofuels	431–637 (switchgrass)	26–128	457–765 including >26–128 net
windpower	1,000–1,600	100–500	50–80 net
soil carbon	–	3–15	3–15 net
total	1,431–2,237	129–643	510–860

686. Assuming a crop yield of 7 ton/acre-y and an ethanol conversion rate of 180 gal ethanol/ton, 22 barrels of crude equivalent per acre could be replaced each year. Using a 0.85 kg/L density for crude and an 84% carbon content results in 2.56 tonne/acre-y carbon savings.

687. The American Wind Energy Association estimates that income to farmers from wind rights amount to $50–80/acre. Annual income from a single 1.5-MW wind turbine will be perhaps $3–4,000 per year (depending upon how much electricity is generated), and only ~0.5 acre will be used to site the turbine within the ~50–75 acres dictated by spacing requirements (AWEA 2004a).

688. Assuming a wind energy output of 40 MWh/acre-y, displacing coal-fired generation that releases 0.25 tonne carbon/MWh, yields a savings of 10 tonne carbon/acre-y or $100–500/acre-y (at $10–50/tonne carbon).

689. Assuming sequestration of 0.3 tonne carbon/acre-y (Swisher 1997; Swisher et al. 1997) worth $10–50/TC yields $3–15/acre-y of pretax net revenue to the farmer.

690. Revenue per acre was calculated by multiplying partly irrigated crop yield in bushels/acre (USDA/NASS 2002, Table 33—Specified Crops Harvested Yield per Acre Irrigated and Non-Irrigated) by the estimated 2003/04 price per bushel (USDA 2004).

The new demand for bioenergy crops, plus the other new agricultural revenues, should provide a major boost to rural employment. Estimates vary, but could be as high as 780,000 new agricultural sector jobs from biofuels production based on national production of 24.9 billion gal/y of ethanol.[691] Our 2025 *State of the Art* ethanol volume, 57.7 bgal/y, is 2.3 times that big, corresponding at our 23% lower job intensity to 1.45 million added jobs—clearly a rough approximation, but equivalent to nearly half of *total* U.S. agricultural employment today.

Table 4 summarizes how five potential new revenue streams to the agricultural economy—biofuels, windpower, and carbon offsets from both of these energy sources, as well as from soil carbon storage—could exceed those from conventional farming, while reducing input costs and local impacts on land and water resources. Thus reducing oil dependence, fossil-fuel consumption, and greenhouse gas emissions can help American agriculture to become *more profitable* as well as more sustainable.

There are broader whole-system benefits as well. From a government perspective, a cost-effective biofuels program would allow the government to restructure the billions of dollars in farm subsidies that are paid each year—$11.7 billion in 2002 (2000 $) including $1.9 billion to corn, $1.7 billion to the Conservation Reserve Program, and $0.7 billion to soybeans.[692] Potentially, some 5% of the annual expenditure, or $540 million per year, could be eliminated or substantially reduced.[693] (Of course, if greater net farm income were simply offset by reduced subsidies, farmers would be no better off in aggregate, but there could be significant distributional effects, since current subsidies are widely considered to favor big over small operations.) Finally, of course, having a greater mix of energy supplies from domestic sources increases national energy security: the ~4 Mbbl/d of cost-effective biofuels (p. 103) would be the all-American equivalent of about half a Saudi Arabia, but undisruptable and inexhaustible. As the Apollo Project's advocates put it, would we rather depend on the Mideast or the Midwest?

> **Rural employment could be as high as 780,000 new agricultural sector jobs from biofuels production.**

> **The ~4 Mbbl/d of cost-effective biofuels would be the all-American equivalent of about half a Saudi Arabia, but undisruptable and inexhaustible— would we rather depend on the Mideast or the Midwest?**

691. Urbanchuk 2003. Assuming 57 bgal/y of ethanol production from our *SOA* scenario at its feedstock cost of $11.3 b/y, and the agricultural "Job Creation Multiple" of 28 jobs created per million dollars of revenue (Laitner, Goodman, & Krier 1994) implies the creation of 743,000 jobs—lower than the Urbanchuk estimate, but significant. Alternatively and probably more accurately, an average 40 Mgal/y ethanol plant adds 694 jobs throughout the economy (RFA 2004); our proposed output would need 1,300 such plants, creating 957,000 jobs.

692. Environmental Working Group 2002.

693. Urbanchuk 2001. That study assumes that loan deficiency payments will be eliminated and government payments will be reduced, therefore lowering direct payments to farmers by $7.8 billion during 2002–16, or $540M/y.

Sooner or later, the market will provide super-efficient cars, trucks, and airplanes. The opening moves have already been made to determine who will sell them. The game will move swiftly. Foreign rivals now enjoy a lead from their national policies. The United States must catch up— not by copycat efficiency mandates, but by policy innovations tailored to the U.S. business conditions we've just described.

Neither competitive forces nor oil-market concerns will wait for business-as-usual.

If we don't act soon, the invisible hand will become the invisible fist

The market will ultimately deliver more efficient cars, trucks, and airplanes. Indeed, it already has begun to do so with the introduction of doubled-efficiency hybrid vehicles in the past few years and Boeing's *7E7* in 2007–08. But will it be U.S. or foreign manufacturers who reap the benefit of this market transition? If U.S. business and political leaders are not decisive now, we could end up replacing imported oil with imported cars and airplanes. And while competitive global markets will ultimately bring efficient fleets to U.S. buyers, this could take so long that the U.S. automotive sector exits just as its successors enter. Let's therefore recap the business and policy challenge before we move on to the policies that can help business leaders to address it timely.

The fundamental business problem in U.S. automaking is the disparate financial strength of the Big Three and their competitors. The Big Three simply do not have the ability to invest quickly in an entirely new and properly broad product line, even at the lower product development and production costs we've described, without giving up one of the strategic R&D programs they're already conducting. Of course the Big Three can, should, and do incorporate lighter and stronger parts into their existing product lines and new platforms, but that's incremental change, while the coming global shift in automotive technology and markets requires radical and rapid change. Neither competitive forces nor the oil-market concerns discussed on pp. 8–25 will wait for business-as-usual.

By contrast, Toyota, and to a lesser degree Honda, Nissan, and others, have the financial strength and the business strategy to adopt holistic bundles of new technology rapidly in new product lines. They continue to have the benefits of their domestic markets, access to lower-cost capital, and the *keiretsu* supply-chain system, plus the lower-cost, high-quality lean manufacturing system made famous by Toyota and the support of their domestic and regional markets.

Korean automakers should not be overlooked. They've gained more points of global market share in the 1990s than any other country and are considered a disruptive force in the automobile market.[694] They have succeeded in the way Toyota pioneered, by entry into the lowest-profit-margin segment of the business, the small car market. Like Toyota, their strategy is to leverage that position into the higher-margin segments. What better way than with breakthrough technology? The same opportunity is doubtless occurring to India's burgeoning automakers.

694. Christensen & Raynor 2003, p.61.

The Chinese have the potential to build a new automobile industry from scratch, and they show every sign of preparing to leapfrog the West. To appreciate the power of a massive domestic market with patriotic buying behavior, overseen by a farsighted central policy, consider China's growth in the technology sector. Over the past five years, China has sustained a 40% annual growth rate in high-tech exports, and now manufactures 35% of the world's cellphones. China has passed the U.S. to become the world's largest mobile phone market (as noted on p. 6, note 46, it has more cellphone users than the U.S. has people), and China Mobile and China Unicom are the numbers one and three largest mobile carriers globally.[695]

The explosive growth of Chinese automotive manufacturing capability is already positioning it as a tremendous threat to U.S. automakers (p. 135).[696] In 2003 alone, sales of Chinese-made vehicles in China grew by more than one-third (p. 2). Not only are Chinese companies investing in automaking, but General Motors plans to invest $3 billion in its Chinese operations over the next three years,[697] and GM's competitors are similarly ambitious. Yet China's intention to serve more than its home and regional market could hardly be plainer: the State Development and Reform Commission's 2 June 2004 white paper (p. 135) says, "Before 2010, our country will become an important vehicle making nation, locally made products will basically satisfy domestic demand, and we will enter the international market in a big way."[698] Shanghai Automotive Industry Group already hopes to partner with MG Rover Group Ltd., buy Ssangyong (Korea's fourth-biggest automaker), and become one of the world's top ten automakers.[698a]

China, Europe, and Japan all have the advantage of technology-forcing regulations that stimulate demand for new, more efficient cars. These rules appear to reflect some rivalry, and the gap between these regulations and U.S. rules is widening. China's 2004 white paper requires that the "average fuel consumption for newly assembled passenger vehicles by the year 2010 will be reduced by at least 15 percent compared to the level of 2003"; this applies better-than-U.S. minimum standards to *every* new vehicle (not just their average) and bars used-car imports.[699] European automakers, as an alternative to legislated standards, have voluntarily committed to the equivalent of 39 mpg by 2008 (25% lower fuel intensity) and are considering 46 mpg (another 15% intensity drop) by 2012.[700] New legislation in Japan requires 23% fuel-economy gains during 1995–2010, to levels up to 44 mpg depending on vehicle class, via the "Top Runner" program (p. 45, note 225) committing all new vehicles to approach the most fuel-frugal vehicle in their class.[701] Canada's Climate Action Plan, with 2004 bipartisan endorsement, promises 25% mpg gains by 2010 despite the close integration of its auto industry with that of the U.S.

China, Europe,
and Japan all have
the advantage of
technology-forcing
regulations that
stimulate demand
for new,
more efficient cars.

695. Cai 2003; Fu 2004.

696. China Economic Net 2004.

697. Zhengzheng 2004; Agencies 2004a.

698. Blanchard 2004.

698a. Wonacott 2004.

699. Bradsher 2003.

700. European automakers are implementing a voluntary standard of 140 grams of CO_2 per km by 2008 and negotiating a standard likely to be 120 gCO_2/km for 2012. European emissions averaged 166 gCO_2/km in 2002, down 11% from 186 in 1995. That progress reflects mainly dieselization, but Chancellor Schröder, at the request of German automakers, recently asked the EU to accelerate dramatically the Euro-5 standards that will reduce fine-particle emissions.

701. Fulton 2004.

China's intention to serve more than its home and regional market could hardly be plainer: "Before 2010, our country will become an important vehicle making nation, locally made products will basically satisfy domestic demand, and we will enter the international market in a big way."

In striking contrast, no increase is contemplated in the U.S. 27.5-mpg average car standard—passed in 1975 and first effective in MY1984—and the 2003 1.5-mpg increase in U.S. light-truck standards to just 22.2 mpg for MY2007 will yield little or no actual gain.[702] This growing gap hardly bodes well for U.S. exports to an increasingly integrated global market. As we'll show next, efficiency standards aren't the only or even the best way to improve fleet efficiency, but if, for whatever cause, new American cars' efficiency continues to stagnate, then most foreign buyers, and an increasing share of U.S. buyers, simply won't want them.

However, a key competitive opportunity remains as unexploited by foreign as by U.S. policymakers. While the U.S., Japan, and Europe are all providing generous R&D funding for the fuel cell as the next-generation engine, all of their official programs give far more limited attention to the near-term practical potential for a lighter, stronger platform and body to get to fuel cells sooner and solve the hydrogen storage problem (p. 233), while saving far more gasoline and diesel fuel meanwhile. The United States has at least as great technological breadth and depth in advanced materials as Japan and Europe, and a more entrepreneurial flexible market system for rapidly exploiting that capability.

Capital quickly migrates to those companies that demonstrate the ability to earn superior returns. The invisible hand of the market, as described by Adam Smith, was an early attempt to describe the movement of capital in society. The speed of capital migration has accelerated of late, so the invisible hand will feel more like the invisible fist when it hits those automakers that fall behind in the competitive race for the next-generation vehicle.

The entire extra business investment needed to reach ~77% market capture in 2025 by super-efficient cars and light trucks and ~70% by efficient heavy trucks—some $70 billion spread over a decade or two—is what the United States now spends directly every seven months to buy foreign oil that's largely wasted.

Do U.S. business leaders and policymakers really want to wait for the market to deliver the next generation of efficient mobility via leisurely meandering, or should we enact the few critical strategy and policy shifts that would transform the market more quickly and potentially save and revitalize the U.S. transportation manufacturing sector? As we debate this, consider that the entire extra business investment needed to reach ~77% market capture in 2025 by superefficient cars and light trucks and ~70% by efficient heavy trucks—some $70 billion spread over a decade or two—is what the United States now spends directly every seven months to buy foreign oil that's largely wasted.

702. That's because the higher standard would be roughly offset by a proposed extension of the current law's "flex-fuel" loophole, which credits ethanol-blend-capable vehicles with fuel savings (up to 1.2 mpg for MY1993–2004) even if they never use alternative fuel blends (other than normal oxygenates); very few actually do. Sales in the CAFE-exempt >8,500-lb GWVR category, such as *Hummer*, have also increased since Oak Ridge National Laboratory found 5.8 million such exempt "heavy light trucks" on the road at the end of 1999, accounting for 9% of light trucks' total fuel use (NHTSA, undated).

Crafting coherent supportive policies

Government's role in implementation

Since the journey beyond oil is not costly but profitable, free enterprise will lead it in pursuit of greater profit, stronger competitive advantage, and lower business risk. But as the previous 41 pages have shown, the existing policy framework is indifferent, inconsistent,[703] rife with distortions, and scarcely focused on accelerating fundamental innovation. Current policy encourages only routine rates of spontaneous market progress that are too little and too late for national needs, maintaining a business environment that is far too risky for key American industries in a world full of resourceful and determined rivals.

We said on p. 1 that governments should steer, not row. They should set the rules of a fair and free marketplace, not choose its outcomes nor supplant the private firms that do the work. But the preceding business cases compel us to conclude that some judicious, coherent, and supportive steering in the direction of accelerating technological leapfrogs can turn serious business risks and societal challenges into major national benefits.

To make the transition faster, cheaper, and surer, policy must accelerate oil efficiency by:

- shifting customer choice strongly toward advanced-technology vehicles while expanding freedom of choice, so enterprise can deliver uncompromised, indeed enhanced, service and value in ways that also produce public goods;

- reducing the risk of retooling, retraining, new capacity, and widely beneficial R&D;

- supporting private investment in innovative domestic energy supply infrastructure;

- purging perverse incentives (i.e., stop doing dumb things); and

- expanding alternatives for fair access, at honest prices, to all competing modes of access and mobility, including smart development that requires less travel.

As we describe innovative ways to achieve these goals, please bear in mind a bedrock need for firms and governments at all levels: systematic and comprehensive "barrier-busting" is vital to let people and companies respond efficiently to the price signals they already see. That alchemy of obstacles into opportunities—or as Interface, Inc.'s Chairman Ray C. Anderson says, "stumbling-blocks into stepping-stones"—is described more fully elsewhere,[704] in a broader context than just oil and transportation. It underlies all the specifics that follow.

Since phasing out oil is not costly but profitable, business will lead it for profit. Coherent public policy can steer in the right direction by expanding choice and adoption, and speeding development and production, of advanced-technology vehicles. It can also foster alternative energy supplies, reward what we want rather than the opposite, and enhance competition between different modes of transport and ways to need them less.

703. Most strikingly in the huge tax deductions offered for "business" use of the heaviest and least efficient SUVs—a heavily marketed tax break that can cover most of the cost of, say, a dentist's buying a *Hummer*.

704. Lovins & Lovins 1997, especially pp. 11–20.

Cynicism about governments is millennia old and often deserved (Box 17). But to the widespread assumption that not much about oil use can or will change, and perhaps even less if government gets involved, we suggest five replies:

- Throughout history, in such crises as World War II, democracies have risen magnificently to meet and defeat great dangers. Such mobilizations, including U.S. automakers' six-month crash-conversion to military production (p. 1), spring from extraordinary leadership. But creeping crises short of this cataclysmic character can also be mastered by less conspicuous and more routine ways of just paying attention.

- For example, with astonishing benefit and virtually no disruption, the United States has already demonstrated extremely rapid oil and energy savings during 1977–85, led by government but implemented largely by the private sector (pp. 7–8). The savings called for here are considerably slower than those that were already achieved with so little fuss that, less than two decades later, they're already nearly forgotten.

Did anyone notice that national water productivity in 2000 was only 2.36 times its 1975 value, and per-capita withdrawals were down 26% (while per-capita energy use rose 5%)? Did we have a terrible problem of needing to muster national will to suffer the pain of achieving this miracle?

17: *Gridlock as Usual* according to Thucycides, ca. 431–404 BCE

In his 24 June 1963 speech in Frankfurt's Paulskirche cathedral, President Kennedy paraphrased and quoted a noted Athenian soldier and historian:[705]

Thucydides reported that the Peloponnesians and their allies were mighty in battle but handicapped by their policy-making body—in which, he related, "each [faction or state] presses its own end...which generally results in no action at all....They devote more time to the prosecution of their own purposes than to consideration of the general welfare—each supposes that no harm will come of his own neglect, that it is the business of another to do this and that—and so, as each separately entertains the same illusion, the common cause imperceptibly decays."

705. Kennedy 1963. Cebrowski (1999) used a similar quotation when President of the Naval War College. The quoted portion is apparently adapted from Thucydides 431 BCE (the 1910 Crawley translation). The original (including the paraphrased part) in *The Peloponnesian War* 1.141.6–7 is characteristically terse:

[6] μάχῃ μὲν γὰρ μιᾷ πρὸς ἅπαντας Ἕλληνας δυνατοὶ Πελοποννήσιοι καὶ οἱ ξύμμαχοι ἀντισχεῖν, πολεμεῖν δὲ μὴ πρὸς ὁμοίαν ἀντιπαρασκευὴν ἀδύνατοι, ὅταν μήτε βουλευτηρίῳ ἑνὶ χρώμενοι παραχρῆμά τι ὀξέως ἐπιτελῶσι πάντες τε ἰσόψηφοι ὄντες καὶ οὐχ ὁμόφυλοι τὸ ἐφ' ἑαυτὸν ἕκαστος σπεύδῃ· ἐξ ὧν φιλεῖ μηδὲν ἐπιτελὲς γίγνεσθαι. [7] καὶ γὰρ οἱ μὲν ὡς μάλιστα τιμωρήσασθαί τινα βούλονται, οἱ δὲ ὡς ἥκιστα τὰ οἰκεῖα φθεῖραι. χρόνιοί τε ξυνιόντες ἐν βραχεῖ μὲν μορίῳ σκοποῦσί τι τῶν κοινῶν, τῷ δὲ πλέονι τὰ οἰκεῖα πράσσουσι, καὶ ἕκαστος οὐ παρὰ τὴν ἑαυτοῦ ἀμέλειαν οἴεται βλά-ψειν, μέλειν δὲ τινι καὶ ἄλλῳ ὑπὲρ ἑαυτοῦ τι προϊδεῖν, ὥστε τῷ αὐτῷ ὑπὸ ἁπάντων ἰδίᾳ δοξάσματι λανθάνειν τὸ κοινὸν ἁθρόον φθειρόμενον.

- Energy isn't the only example of such rapid change (Fig. 35). During 1975–2000, U.S. withdrawals of water per dollar of GDP fell at an average compounded rate of 3.4%/y—faster than the ~2.7%/y which we propose for 2000–25 oil efficiency. To be sure, though energy and water use both depend on composition of GDP, the two resources are quite different, and they're saved by different actors and means.[706] But among their similarities is that usage of both appeared to rise in lock-step with GDP until the mid-1970s, when that correlation was deliberately broken, causing steady declines in usage not only per dollar of GDP but also per capita. Did anyone notice that national water productivity in 2000 was only 2.36 times its 1975 value, and per-capita withdrawals were down 26% (while per-capita energy use rose 5%)? Did we have a terrible problem of needing to muster national will to suffer the pain of achieving this miracle? Does anyone doubt it was a good idea? Can you imagine our water situation today if we hadn't done it? This water-efficiency revolution came mainly from millions of sensible corporate and personal choices within a slowly improving policy framework, such as starting to price water on the margin, reduce subsidies to its use, educate users, and make markets in saved water. These policy shifts drove many business shifts, such as paying attention to water, improving technical designs, and bringing water-thrifty products to the marketplace (encouraged by national standards for plumbing fixtures).[707] The result is astounding, and this invisible chapter in U.S. resource-productivity history is far from over.

Five replies
to the assumption that
oil use can't or won't
change that much
(continued)

Figure 35: Water productivity, 1950–2000. During 1950–2000, U.S. GDP more than quintupled and population nearly doubled, yet total water withdrawals[708] were lower in 2000 than in 1980. Per dollar of GDP, water withdrawals were 59% lower in 2000 than in 1950, and 62% lower than their peak in 1955. To most Americans, this stunning progress in water productivity was completely invisible, quietly driven by private decisions supported by mainly decentralized public policy. Yet without it, we'd now be withdrawing 2.5 times as much water as we actually do, and most of the country would be in a severe and continual water crisis. Making today's oil problems fade away over the next few decades can have similar dynamics, advantages, and ultimately invisibility if we gently steer the system in the right direction.

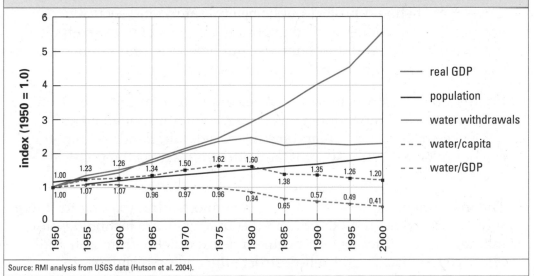

Source: RMI analysis from USGS data (Hutson et al. 2004).

706. The biggest water savings were in agricultural irrigation and thermal power plants (due mainly to fewer new nuclear plants, which need more cooling water per kWh, and more combined-cycle plants). However, important gains were also made in industry, buildings, and landscaping irrigation.

707. Rocky Mountain Institute helped to speed this process 16 years ago by simply publishing a thorough catalog of little-known market offerings. The industry soon took over that informational function.

708. Hutson et al. 2004.

Five replies
to the assumption that
oil use can't or won't
change that much
(continued):

- The same success of unobtrusive but pervasive policy shifts is evident in increased electric efficiency at the state level. For example, aligning utility with customer interests and adopting building and appliance efficiency standards early held per-capita use of electricity virtually flat since the mid-1970s in California, while it rose by more than half in the rest of the country. The savings helped California achieve faster economic growth.[709] Similar results were achieved in New England households after 1989. Vermont households held electricity use steady during 1974–90, then lowered it by an eighth. Nobody felt hampered; they simply wrung better services at lower cost from less electricity and more brains.

- As we'll show, the shifts we're proposing in automaking are slower than those the industry actually achieved in the 1970s and 1980s, less capital-intensive, and probably a good deal more profitable. And they require less invention than such previous requirements as the Clean Air Act, which was passed—with justified faith in American ingenuity—before the industry had even developed the catalytic converter.

709. Contrary to a widespread myth, California's 2000–01 power shortages were not due to unexpectedly soaring demand, nor to a shortage of generating capacity, which continued to expand through the 1990s but in more cost-effective nonutility and decentralized forms (Lovins 2001a). Mostly, the shortages were due to a perfect storm of poorly designed restructuring and rational (if sometimes illegal) market response to its unintended perverse incentives.

710. Or at least very close to it if other considerations make a theoretically second-best solution preferable.

711. Democracy, as law professor Harold Green remarked, is based not on the expectation of truth but on the certainty of error. Cyberneticists express the same idea when they say that systems without feedback are stupid by definition. Policies gang oft agley; as FDR remarked in the Depression, we can't know that this or that will work, but we must try. With the humble awareness that unintended consequences accompany most policy interventions, we nonetheless think the ideas suggested next merit consideration, testing, and refinement in the forge of experience.

For implementation methods, policymakers can draw on decades of experience—chiefly in Europe, Japan, and North America, but increasingly also in developing countries whose abundant needs and talents often incubate clusters of innovation. However, the U.S. policy toolkit, despite some past successes, has been mired in twenty years of trench warfare, and is ripe for renewal. In general, U.S. car companies favor fuel taxes while U.S. oil companies favor car-efficiency standards, and these two titanic lobbies have fought each other to a draw since 1975. It's time to seek fresh solutions.

After briefly reviewing the lessons of those two dominant post-1973 policy tools, we'll propose modern alternatives that meet clear criteria. To make our own biases explicit, we believe that:

- Government should protect public health, safety, and security; enhance equity, choice, and competition; align incentives so efficient markets produce, and don't destroy, public goods; and remove unnecessary obstacles to more perfect markets.

- Energy policy instruments should be company-, entrant-, and technology-neutral, innovation-accelerating, economically efficient,[710] evidence-shaped, market- and results-based, fair, nondiscriminatory, easily understood, transparent, and attractive across the political spectrum.

- The instruments to be preferred are revenue-neutral (paying for themselves with no net flow to or from the Treasury), are technology-forcing, reward continuous improvement, learn quickly from rich and effective feedback,[711] and self-destruct after their job is done.

Since all five of this study's coauthors have studied or taught economics, yet we're all field practitioners—not armchair theorists who lie awake at night wondering whether what works in practice can possibly work in theory—we feel compelled to add another comment, hinted at on pp. 25–28. The market is a powerful and efficient tool for the short-term allocation of scarce resources. But markets also have limits.[712] They're not good at long-term, and especially at intergenerational, allocation; generally aren't concerned with distributional equity (markets are meant to be efficient, not fair); may not tell us how much is enough; reveal cost and perhaps value but not values; and can't substitute for politics, ethics, or faith. Markets are wonderful tools, and we apply and refine them extensively, but they can't do everything, and their purpose is far from the whole purpose of a human being.

With this understanding, let's first explore why and how the goals of traditional tax- and mandate-based U.S. policy instruments can be better achieved without them.

Fuel taxes

The United States taxes gasoline and diesel fuel at some of the lowest rates in the world, manyfold lower than Europe and Japan do. Much higher taxes are the most obvious, economically doctrinaire,[713] and politically difficult way to signal the true social costs of buying and burning oil and the public goods of using less of it. Such conservatives as University of Chicago Nobel economist Professor Gary Becker,[714] Hudson Institute director of economic policy studies Dr. Irwin Stelzer,[715] and columnist Charles Krauthammer,[716] as well as commentators ranging from environmental writer Gregg Easterbrook to Ford Motor Company Chairman Bill Ford, Jr., all favor this solution.[717] (Taxing aviation fuel *at all*—it's tax-free nearly worldwide, thanks to an intricate network of hundreds of treaties that were meant to promote air travel and succeeded with a vengeance—would shrink this giant distortion between transportation modes.[718] But let's focus here on road vehicles' fuel.)

> The U.S. policy toolkit, despite some past successes, has been mired in twenty years of trench warfare, and is ripe for renewal.

> America underprices mobility fuels, but their economically correct pricing, though useful, isn't effective, sufficient, or necessary for encouraging the purchase of efficient vehicles. It's more useful for a different purpose—signaling the social cost of traveling.

712. The austere preconditions for a perfect market—e.g., perfect information about the future, perfectly accurate price signals, perfect competition, no monopoly or monopsony, no unemployment or underemployment of any resource, no transaction cost, no subsidy, no taxes—clearly don't describe the world any of us inhabit. The differences between that theoretical world and the real world are what makes business innovation possible and profitable.

713. Since Arthur Cecil Pigou proposed them in 1918. He is generally credited with the now-common distinction between private and social marginal products and costs, and with the idea that the resulting market failures can be corrected by "internalizing the externalities" through taxes and subsidies. (Ronald Coase in 1960 showed that absent transaction costs, private transactions on broadened property rights could do the same thing without governments.)

714. Becker 2004. Dr. Becker estimates that a 50¢/gal "terrorist protection tax" on gasoline would cut gasoline use by ~10%, and suggests it be used to increase stockpiles.

715. Stelzer 2004. Dr. Stelzer particularly likes taxes on oil imports (for which, as we noted at p. 13, note 97, there is legal authority). Of course, the U.S. already taxes its oil imports—via DoD's part of our tax bills (p. 20)—and so does OPEC.

716. Krauthammer 2004.

717. Gross 2004.

718. The Chicago Treaty regime's prohibition of aviation fuel taxes doesn't bar CO_2 emissions fees. A new EU-U.S. "open skies" aviation agreement wasn't signed in mid-2004 partly because many EU countries propose such fees, but the U.S. wants them charged only on EU airlines, not on U.S. airlines operating within Europe (a view echoed by the UK). A 188-nation Montréal conference will try again in September 2004 to soften U.S. intransigence.

We consider the high gasoline taxes favored by most major U.S. allies and trading partners to be theoretically sound and generally helpful, but the weakest possible signal to buy an efficient vehicle, insufficient, and nonessential.

719. Former Federal Reserve Chairman Paul Volcker and former Council of Economic Advisors chairman Martin Feldstein have proposed that carbon taxes (equivalent to efficient trading) be used to cut federal budget deficits, and Ford Motor Company has reportedly supported using a carbon tax to replace part of California's sales tax (Morris 1994, note 1). Europe is shifting toward taxing less the things we want more of (like income and jobs) while taxing more the things we want less of (like depletion and pollution). See Repetto et al. 1992; PETRAS 2002; and the green tax shifting papers at www.redefiningprogress.org/publications/

720. An enduringly bizarre aspect of American political life is that Americans seem to prefer OPEC ministers rather than members of the U.S. Congress to be the ones raising their prices at the pump, and OPEC countries (and unintentionally, in small part, terrorists) rather than the U.S. Treasury to receive the revenues.

With a big caveat, we consider the high gasoline taxes favored by most major U.S. allies and trading partners to be theoretically sound and generally helpful in improving economic efficiency, because fuel prices omit important costs to society, and prices that tell the truth are always better than prices that lie about what things really cost. High gasoline taxes needn't be regressive if immediately recycled into corresponding cuts in other taxes, especially the most regressive ones such as payroll taxes. Fuel taxes could take various forms, including carbon charges from cap-and-trade CO_2 markets,[719] though these wouldn't send a big price signal: $25 per tonne of carbon is equivalent to only 6¢/gal, well within normal short-term price fluctuations. So what's the caveat? High gasoline taxes also have serious defects beyond their obvious political challenges.[720] They are:

- the weakest possible signal to buy an efficient vehicle.[721] Since U.S. taxed gasoline is only about an eighth of the total cost of owning and running a car, this price signal is first diluted ~7:1 and then shrunk to insignificance by consumer discount rates—which are so high that the difference between a 30- and a 40-mpg car, though consequential for society, will seem to the short-sighted buyer to be worth only about the price of a set of floor mats, hardly worth the hassle of laborious learning and negotiations;[722]

- insufficient (if it were sufficient, the many foreign countries with $4–5/gallon gasoline prices would be driving *State of the Art* vehicles by now, but they aren't[723]—in fact transportation is the fastest-growing CO_2 source in Europe);

- nonessential and hence not worth arguing about, because there are even better ways to encourage people to choose efficient vehicles.

The main virtue of higher gasoline taxes would be in reducing miles driven *after* the car is bought.[724] This effect, though weak, is clearly observable; but we'll propose alternative ways to achieve that goal too, without increasing net cashflow to the Treasury. So without denying the sound economic principle of proper pricing, we think there are more creative, politically palatable, and effective ways to signal the value of efficient vehicles—especially at the point of purchase where that decision is focused. We'll return to the most important such option—feebates—as soon as we've argued that efficiency standards, too, are no longer the best policy choice for America.

721. IEA 2001. The graph on p. 22, for example, shows that around 1997, new cars were about an eighth more efficient in Britain and Germany than in the U.S. (where they were larger, p. 27), but were less efficient in Japan (where they were generally smaller) despite its severalfold higher fuel taxes.

722. Greene 1997, pp. 4–7. This near-indifference to efficiency by customers, in turn, causes producers to see in such incentives a low incentive but a high investment risk (Greene 1997, p. 8).

723–724. See next page.

Standards, mandates, and quotas

Before we similarly note the limitations of efficiency standards, let's also note their historical context. In the decade after Congress enacted Corporate Average Fuel Economy (CAFE) standards in 1975 as one of the *least* controversial elements of the Energy Conservation and Policy Act,[725] U.S. oil use dropped 7% and oil imports dropped 23% while GDP grew 37%. Informed by detailed analyses and hearings, the standards were carefully set at levels that could be met cost-effectively (or very nearly so) with straightforwardly available technologies. They therefore did not—as many feared and some still claim—prove costly, inefficient, or unsafe.[726] In hindsight, CAFE standards and their milder light-truck equivalent were largely responsible for nearly doubling car efficiency and increasing light-truck efficiency by more than half in their first decade. (A gas-guzzler tax on cars—though not on light trucks—and a few years of high oil prices after the 1979 spike helped too.) CAFE was the cornerstone of America's OPEC-busting oil savings in 1977–85 (pp. 7–8), and helped to avert even graver erosion of U.S. automakers' market share by more efficient Japanese imports (p. 140).

The 1975 law required CAFE standards to enforce "maximum feasible fuel economy," considering technological feasibility, economic practicality, fuel-economy effect of other standards, and the nation's need to conserve energy. (Lawmakers have lately tried to add other criteria.) The standards were thus meant to evolve as automotive technology became more energy-efficient—as indeed it did by one-third during 1981–2003 (p. 8), at prices the public paid. Yet during 1975–2003, the standards weren't raised at all, contrary to the strong wishes of three-fourths of Americans in 1995.[727] Instead, the standards have become such anathema to most U.S. automakers that they've been broadly changed only twice[728]—weakened 5.5% for cars in MY1986–88 (after world oil prices fell by half, due substantially to CAFE-induced efficiency gains), then strengthened 7% for light trucks during MY2005–2007. Thus the 21.0-mpg light-truck standard that Congress voted in 1975 to take effect in MY1985 got delayed 20 years.[729] During 1995–2000, Congress expressly forbade even *considering* any CAFE increases. Now the responsible agency, the National Highway

> Foreign countries and even states are pulling dangerously far ahead of U.S. efficiency standards, but there are even more economically efficient, effective, flexible, and speedy ways to shift to fuel-frugal, high-performance, market-leading vehicles.

> Roughly 85–90% of the world's energy twenty years from now will be used by products not yet manufactured, and many of these will be made in China.

---

723. In general, they're simply driving less, partly because they often have more sensible land-use and better public-transportation alternatives. The EU is having to introduce new non-price policy instruments and voluntary agreements (backed up by a tacit threat of mandates) to bring next-generation vehicle efficiency to market, because gasoline taxes near the limits of political tolerance aren't enough to achieve this. As the IEA (2001, p. 57) puts it, "Even big changes to fuel prices may not have much additional effect on vehicle choices." To mention a simple empirical observation, the state of Hawai'i has gasoline prices 50¢/gal higher than the mainland U.S., yet its' fleet mix is not appreciably more efficient than the U.S. national average.

724. In the short run, partly due to rigidities in land-use patterns and alternative transportation options, vehicle travel is remarkably unresponsive to cost. The International Energy Agency concludes that "a 10% increase in fuel prices results in only a 1–3% decrease in travel" (IEA 2001, p. 12).

725. Bamberger 1999. The key votes approving CAFE's authorizing statute (EPCA) were 300–103 in the House and 58–40 in the Senate (U.S. Congress 1975).

726. Greene 1997.　　　　　　　　727. Greene 1997, Table 3.

728. Plus three single-year weakenings—by 7% in 1979 for the 2WD light-truck standard in MY1981, by 7% in 1984 for the average light truck in MY1985, and by 4% in 1988 for the car standard in MY1989 (Bamberger 2003).

729. Bamberger 2003, Table 1.

Traffic Safety Administration (NHTSA)—while making some commendable safety improvements and perhaps reducing some of the "gaming" that has seriously undercut CAFE's goals—is proposing a weight-based rewrite that may weaken this foundation of America's oil-saving success while undermining future auto exports (pp. 58, 206–208). In response to this federal inaction and erosion, many states are starting to act on their own.[730]

Undeterred, many other nations also continue to tighten national technical standards for fuel efficiency (p. 167), as WTO rules permit so long as the standard is rationally based and nondiscriminatory. Standards have a long record of effectiveness not only in vehicle efficiency and emissions (such as the Clean Air Act) but also in raising the energy efficiency of buildings and appliances. U.S. appliance standards, for example, have already saved 40 billion watts (GW) of peak electricity demand in refrigerator/freezers and 135 GW in air conditioners, compared with, say, the 61 GW of load lost in the 14 August 2003 Northeast blackout. So far, the federal government has spent ~$2 per household devising and implementing nine residential appliance efficiency standards to combat two market failures—customers' taking a far shorter view of future energy savings than society does, and split incentives (most appliances are bought by landlords, homebuilders, and housing authorities who won't pay the utility bills). By 2020, that $2-per-household investment in minimum standards will have stimulated each household to spend an additional $950 on efficiency, thereby saving $2,400—a $150 billion net saving to the national economy.[731] The rise of efficiency standards for everything from lights to motors and buildings to cars in rapidly growing economies like China's is fortunate, since roughly 85–90% of the world's energy twenty years from now will be used by products not yet manufactured, and many of these will be made in China.

Standards also have their limits. Imposing mandates can be less efficient than market mechanisms.[732] Standards aren't as fine-grained or transparent to customers as methods that translate vehicles' efficiency directly into their sticker price. Standards are readily gamed, as CAFE has been to near-perfection. Moreover, absent political consensus to take seriously the CAFE law's provision for updating, the standards, once set, are static. And once standards are met, they can halt backsliding but foster no further innovation, because they include no reward for beating the standard. Standards also don't take account of different firms' differing markets, circumstances, and ability to comply at different costs; in contrast, tradable permits for sulfur, nitrogen-oxide, and lead pollution have achieved very large pollution reductions and dollar savings simultaneously, surpassing their promoters' fondest hopes.[733]

730. The leader, California, is making rules in 2004 to implement "maximum feasible cost-effective reduction" in light vehicles' CO_2 emissions starting with MY2009; the 2002 authorizing law excludes mandatory trip reduction, any additional fees or taxes, or banning any vehicle category. The growing move for coastal Eastern states, challenged by ozone nonattainment, to adopt California's standards could give its CO_2 rule strong market influence if it survives threatened legal challenges. Of course, as noted earlier (note 685), a CO_2 standard can be met by switching to low- or no-fossil-carbon fuels, or partly by such other means as CFC refrigerant abatement, rather than solely by better mpg.

731. LBNL, undated. Nonetheless, many still oppose and block cost-effective standards on apparently ideological grounds. For example, a recent rollback of federal air-conditioner standards threatened to waste 1.34 TCF of gas over the next 25 years, but was reversed in court. DOE is still delaying standards for major categories of gas-fired furnaces, boilers, and water heaters that could save 5.5 TCF/y over the next 20 years.

732. A typical exposition of this thesis is Kleit 2002. However, Greene (1997) argues that a combination of standards and fuel taxes works better than either alone, due to consumers' "satisficing" behavior, producers' risk aversion, and the sluggishness and partial oligopoly of vehicle-efficiency markets.

733. Stavins 2001. The most famous market-based program, EPA's SO_x allowance trading system, has cut SO_x by 6.5 million tons since 1980 at an estimated cost saving of $1b/y. One of the first U.S. tradable permit programs, for lead in the 1980s, met its environmental goals, saved ~$250M/y, and provided measurable incentives for technology development and diffusion. See also EPA 2002.

Automakers also complain that CAFE standards can push customers toward smaller cars that meet their needs less well, might be less safe, and are far less profitable to make. This hardly seems a serious problem, since during 1975–2003 the market share of small cars fell by 15% while that of SUVs rose 22%, nearly surpassing them in total sales.[734] Further-more, under CAFE automakers can sell and customers can buy whatever vehicles they wish, subject to a small ($55/car-mpg) penalty paid, at least in theory, by noncompliant manufacturers.[735] Some, including the UAW, assert that CAFE has tilted competition to favor imported cars, although this is hard to square with historical evidence.[736] Nonetheless, the critique persists that CAFE distorts customer choice.

Regardless of the merits, which are complex and controversial, the parties to the CAFE dispute, chiefly auto and environmental lobbies, are so firm-ly dug into polarized positions, and the subject has become so politically toxic, that any end-run around it is likely to be preferable. Our policy approach not only achieves the oil-saving and competitive-strategy goals better; *it may not even require federal legislation* (which is only one way to implement policy), and far from raising tax burdens, it *should markedly reduce the federal budget deficit.*

These attributes are desirable not only to evade gridlock, but also because the legislative sausage-factory is prone to opaque back-room negotiations that too often turn temporary, narrow, pump-priming interventions—especially tax expenditures—into such eternal entitlements that some U.S. energy sectors have been milking subsidies for more than a half-century.[737] (Depletion allowances were introduced in 1918 to spur energy output for World War I.[738]) Moreover, while carefully targeted tax expenditures can be effective,[739] their design often rewards spending, not results, and may discriminate against anyone who doesn't pay taxes.

For all these reasons, we prefer the innovative, market-oriented policies described next. They are flexible enough to offer choices between federal and regional or state implementation, so that the federal government can lead, follow, or get out of the way. They offer similarly wide choice for administrative vs. legislative implementation. And they offer, we believe, a trans-ideological appeal conspicuously absent from the proposals that have deadlocked federal energy policy for the past few years. We'll start with the five major steps that the federal government (other than DoD) should take—and that state governments could take absent federal leadership—to reduce oil use in light vehicles. We'll next list an assortment of other fed-eral opportunities, and then move to those distinctively available to states, the military, and civil society. Finally, we'll assess budgetary impacts, which turn out to be gratifyingly positive. We won't formally analyze "free riders" (people who'd have done as hoped even without incentives) because we don't think this is an important problem, especially when offset by "free drivers" (early adopters who follow incentivized adopters' good example).

The parties to the CAFE dispute, chiefly auto and environmental lobbies, are so firmly dug into polarized positions, and the subject has become so politically toxic, that any end-run around it is likely to be preferable. Our policy approach not only achieves the oil-saving and competitive-strategy goals better; *it may not even require federal legislation* **(which is only one way to implement policy), and far from raising tax burdens,** *it should markedly reduce the federal budget deficit.*

734. EPA 2003, p. 32.

735. These civil penalties since 1983 total >$0.5 billion. European automakers regularly pay ~$1–20+M/y as a cost of doing business in the U.S. Asian makers and DaimlerChrysler have never incurred the penalty. Ford and GM have on occasion, but have never had to pay it thanks to retroactive loopholes.

736. Greene 1997, pp. 30–32; NAS/NRC 2001, p. 6-2. The Academy recommended eliminating both the dual-fleet rule and the dual-fuel allow-ance now in CAFE rules.

737. EIA 1999a.

738. Lovins & Heede 1981, p. 28.

739. Datta & Grasso 1998.

Better policies ← to guide market evolution toward both business success and national security goals can cut government expenditure and avoid new federal legislation. Synergistic reforms can change federal policy from a brake to an accelerator, and profitably lift advanced vehicles' market share from zero to more than three-fourths.

Federal policy recommendations for light vehicles

Our policy and technology recommendations for light vehicles closely match those published in 2003 by a task force of the Energy Future Coalition. The Transportation Working Group was chaired by Dennis R. Minano (GM's Vice President for Environment and Energy 1993–2003) and comprised the Big Three automakers, a Tier One supplier, the United Auto Workers, Shell, and three leading technology- and business-oriented environmental groups.[740] After "an intensive review of the best ways" to bring advanced automotive technologies "more quickly and in greater volumes into the marketplace," the group agreed on four central recommendations:

Initiative 1: Establish incentives for manufacturing and purchasing advanced technology vehicles.

Already, U.S. manufacturers are preparing to produce and market a range of more efficient advanced technology vehicles. But without external incentives, the transition to the broad manufacture and consumer acceptance of vehicles with advanced fuel-saving technologies will be slow, too slow to help significantly on the issues of [oil] dependence and climate in the necessary timeframe. To accelerate the deployment of these vehicles into the marketplace, the Working Group recommends a mix of manufacturing and consumer incentives that will partially offset the higher purchase price of these vehicles and reduce manufacturers' capital needs as they retool to produce these vehicles. These incentives should, though, be sharply targeted. The Group recommends that, to qualify for either incentive, a vehicle must, at a minimum, meet performance criteria relating to fuel use.

Initiative 2: Ensure the availability of clean fuels for advanced vehicles [i.e., cleaner gasoline and diesel fuel, biofuels such as ethanol and biodiesel, and hydrogen].

Initiative 3: Invest in the aggressive development of fuel cells.

Initiative 4: Reduce vehicle miles traveled.

Since Initiatives 2–3 are treated elsewhere in this report, and Initiative 4 is beyond its scope (p. 38), we focus here on the Work Group's Initiative 1. It aims at "getting millions, not thousands, of advanced technology vehicles on the road quickly" via "significant [consumer and manufacturer] incentives that primarily focus on lowering consumer costs for advanced fuel-saving technology vehicles, as well as incentives for U.S. manufacture of these vehicles" via facility conversion credits and complementary support via government fleet purchasing. The purpose and effect of our proposals exactly mirrors those of this consensus, but we suggest some improvements in detailed structure to improve efficiency and avoid tax burdens. For example, we favor mechanisms that reward producers for making and selling efficient vehicles (and their components) rather than for spending money; similarly for customers, we suggest revenue-neutral feebates scaled to efficiency rather than tax credits scaled to expenditures. Despite such differences in detail, we're encouraged by the striking parallels between the task force's consensus based on its diverse stakeholder interests and our independent recommendations based on the preceding business-model analysis and public-policy goals.

740. EFC 2003, Summary of Recommendations: Transportation Working Group, pp. 1–3 and App. A: Working Group Reports, pp. 1–14.

Let's start with our conclusions about how a suite of policies can greatly accelerate the introduction and adoption of advanced vehicle technologies, as summarized in the following graphical double-spread (Fig. 36). Our strategy uses eight policies to shift demand toward efficient vehicles and to mitigate manufacturers' risk-aversion and illiquidity when they retool to meet that demand. These policies were simulated and refined via a model of light-vehicle sales and stocks that we constructed for this report, based on the conceptual structure and price elasticities from a 1995 U.S. Department of Energy study.[741] Our treatment of feebates is consistent with an important peer-reviewed 2004 paper by noted researchers at DOE and its Oak Ridge National Laboratory;[742] although their model is more complex and is structured differently, it responds similarly to feebates. Box 18 explains the model structure and key assumptions that yield the results in Fig. 36. Starting on p. 186, we'll explore each of the policies simulated in Fig. 36.

As a reminder: *Conventional Wisdom* vehicles are like today's steel, gasoline-engine vehicles, but with consistent use of the straightforward and moderate improvements—nearly all in the propulsion system—that some market vehicles already include (such as variable valve timing). *Conventional Wisdom* vehicles embody the kinds of incremental improvements analyzed in the National Research Council's 2001 study, summarized above on pp. 49–51. As we said on p. 69, *CW* vehicles save 27% of the fuel used by the light vehicles assumed in EIA's forecast of U.S. oil use to 2025. In contrast, *State of the Art* vehicles are ultralight hybrids, which cost more and save much more. The two are compared in cost and savings in Fig. 21, p. 66. The efficiency of today's relatively heavy hybrids falls in between these two categories and is not specifically modeled in our study, so those vehicles can be considered either a proof of the conservatism of *CW* vehicles or a stepping-stone to *SOA* vehicles, which add ultralight construction and other refinements to today's best hybrid powertrains.

"[W]ithout external incentives, the transition to the broad manufacture and consumer acceptance of vehicles with advanced fuel-saving technologies will be slow, too slow to help significantly on the issues of [oil] dependence and climate in the necessary timeframe. To accelerate the deployment of these vehicles into the marketplace, the Working Group recommends a mix of manufacturing and consumer incentives that will partially offset the higher purchase price of these vehicles and reduce manufacturers' capital needs as they retool to produce these vehicles."

— Energy Future Coalition Transportation Working Group, comprising DaimlerChrysler, Ford, GM, Visteon, UAW, Shell, Natural Resources Defense Council, Union of Concerned Scientists, and World Resources Institute

741. Davis et al. 1995.
742. Greene et al. 2004.
743–745. See box 17 on p.182.

CAUTION: ENTERING CALCULATIONAL THICKET.

The next two pages simply and graphically summarize our main light-vehicle policies and their simulated effects.

Figure 36 shows each policy's incremental effects on the sales of new vehicles and the on-the-road vehicle stock.

Box 18 explains more technically how we simulated these effects.

If you don't need to know how our model works, we suggest you read just pages 180–181, then skip to p. 185. And if you don't need an in-depth understanding of our proposed federal policies, you can skip all the way to p. 204 or even to p. 207.

Figure 36: How RMI's eight proposed policies, described next, **can stimulate demand for and accelerate production of *State of the Art* light vehicles** (green)—and, as a side-effect, of *Conventional Wisdom* (yellow) ones too—compared with EIA's forecast (made in January 2004 and extending to 2025) of relatively inefficient vehicles (red). For each successive policy step, market share of new vehicles is graphed on the left, and the light-vehicle fleet on the road (the vehicle stock) on the right. On the left, the *Conventional Wisdom* and *State of the Art* market shares in 2025 are shown in yellow and green, respectively. On the right, the boldface roman-type number is the light-vehicle petroleum product saving compared with EIA's forecast for 2025; the boldface italic number is the 2004 net present value (NPV) for vehicles purchased between 2005–25 (over the 14-y vehicle life) of customers' net savings, i.e. the fuel saving at EIA's forecast retail gasoline price minus the vehicles' extra pretax retail price; and the lightface italic numbers are the 2025/2050 average mpg of the fleet.

NEW SALES (*CW*, *SOA*)
percentage of EIA forecast sales; last two graphs on p. 181 exceed 100% due to scrappage

STOCK (million vehicles)
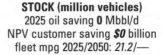
2025 oil saving **0** Mbbl/d
NPV customer saving *$0* billion
fleet mpg 2025/2050: *21.2/—*

2025 share: 0%, *0%*

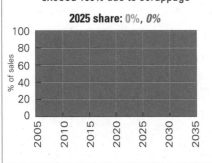

a. EIA forecast without *Conventional Wisdom* or *State of the Art* technology
EIA projects that all new light vehicles are "EIAmobiles." They include 5% (1.1 million) new hybrids in 2025, but those get only 34 mpg for cars and 27 for light trucks (worse than today's hybrids). EIA's average new light vehicle in 2025 is thus only 0.5 mpg more efficient than it was in 1987.

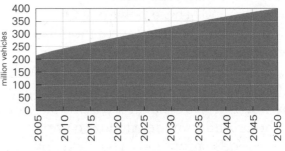

53%, *0%*

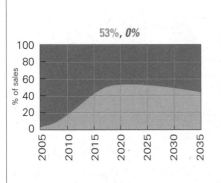

Drift scenario
b. Allowing incremental 27% efficiency gains beyond EIA's technology assumptions leads those *Conventional Wisdom* vehicles to capture half the market (declining slightly later as EIAmobiles improve) because *CW* (assumed to be static) pays back in a few years. To distinguish the effects of *State of the Art* vehicles, we don't show them until case **e.**

1.6, *$179*, 23.7/24.8

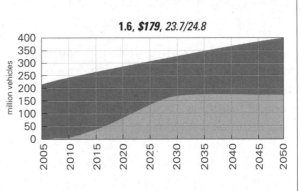

94%, *0%*

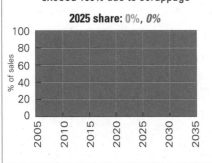

***Let's Get Started* scenario**
c. The first and most important *Coherent Engagement* policy is feebates, starting here at the basic $1,000/0.01-gpm (gallons per mile) level that effectively lets buyers see 14, not 3, years' fuel savings. This nearly drives EIAmobiles out of the market.

2.7, *$295*, 26.4/28.3

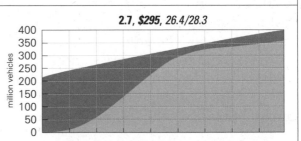

99%, *0%*

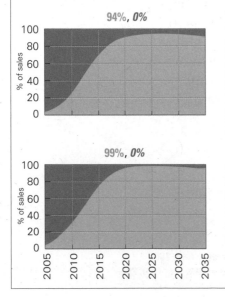

d. This scenario also includes the low-income scrap-and-replace program. It's not a big oil-saver, but it's vital for equitable social development, and creates a profitable new million-vehicle-a-year market.

2.8, *$323*, 26.7/28.4

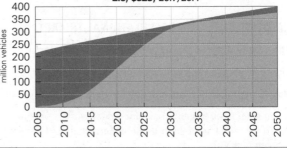

Figure 36 (continued)

Implementation

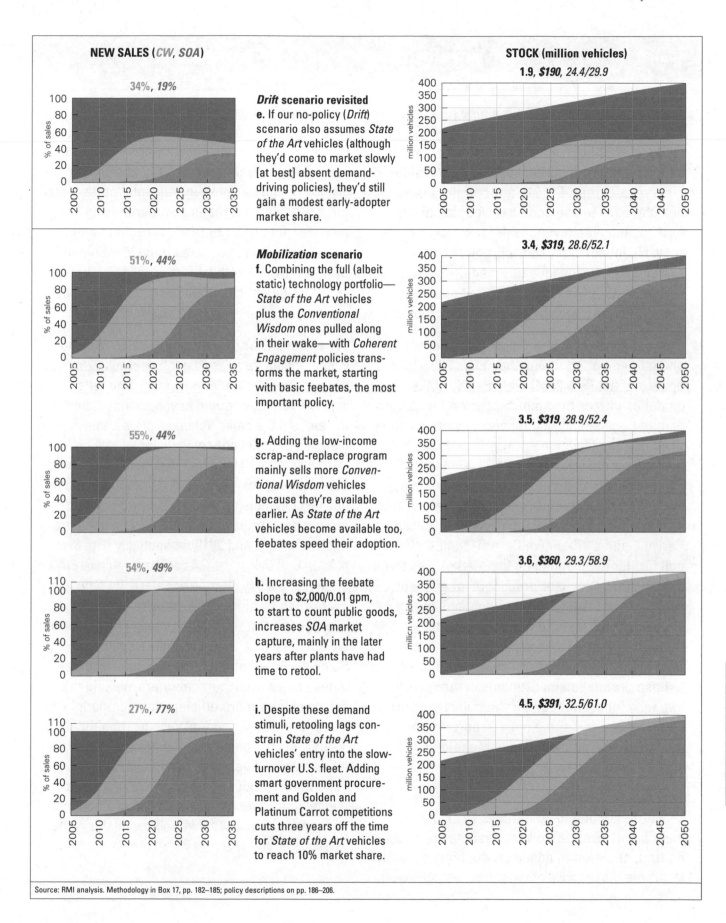

NEW SALES (*CW*, *SOA*)

STOCK (million vehicles)

Drift scenario revisited
e. If our no-policy (*Drift*) scenario also assumes *State of the Art* vehicles (although they'd come to market slowly [at best] absent demand-driving policies), they'd still gain a modest early-adopter market share.

Mobilization scenario
f. Combining the full (albeit static) technology portfolio— *State of the Art* vehicles plus the *Conventional Wisdom* ones pulled along in their wake—with *Coherent Engagement* policies transforms the market, starting with basic feebates, the most important policy.

g. Adding the low-income scrap-and-replace program mainly sells more *Conventional Wisdom* vehicles because they're available earlier. As *State of the Art* vehicles become available too, feebates speed their adoption.

h. Increasing the feebate slope to $2,000/0.01 gpm, to start to count public goods, increases *SOA* market capture, mainly in the later years after plants have had time to retool.

i. Despite these demand stimuli, retooling lags constrain *State of the Art* vehicles' entry into the slow-turnover U.S. fleet. Adding smart government procurement and Golden and Platinum Carrot competitions cuts three years off the time for *State of the Art* vehicles to reach 10% market share.

Source: RMI analysis. Methodology in Box 17, pp. 182–185; policy descriptions on pp. 186–206.

18: Modeling the effects of policy on light vehicle sales and stocks

To explore the effects of our suggested policies, RMI constructed a peer-reviewed dynamic model of U.S. light vehicle fleet sales and stocks. It's fully described and downloadable (*Technical Annex*, Ch. 21), structurally simple, flexible, easy to use and alter, yet able to capture essential behaviors with reasonable accuracy. No model can exactly predict complex systems, but we believe this model—unique, to our knowledge—provides a sound and transparent basis for assessing our policy proposals.

Our model tracks car and light truck fleets by annual age cohort. It matches EIA's 2001–25 fleet forecast (EIA 2004) within ~3%. RMI's model estimates how public policy affects both demand and supply. Eight policies were summarized graphically on the previous two pages, and will be described in the following text. The five policies that stimulate *sales* are feebates, low-income scrap-and-replace, federal fleet procurement, its coordination with a "Golden Carrot," and a "Platinum Carrot" competition to pull further innovation into the market. The three policies that stimulate *production* of efficient vehicles are manufacturer conversion incentives (modeled as federal loan guarantees, though they could take other forms), military R&D investment, and early military procurement (whose production investments in turn create capacity for production for the public market). Feebates are by far the most important, and could achieve all the benefits of the demand-side policies but ~5–10 years later.

Each year, our model uses the previous year's sales of cars and of light trucks to adjust the "pivot point" (Box 18) to keep feebates revenue-neutral, and then to adjust production so manufacturers make more of what has just sold well.

The feebate affects customers' benefit/cost ratio, calculated as the rebate for an efficient car (Box 18) plus the present value of its 3-year fuel saving—discounted at 5%/y (p. 39)—all divided by the vehicle's incremental pretax retail price. Benefit/cost ratios shift purchasing behavior according to DOE's historic price elasticities, which are assumed to be identical for *SOA* and *CW* vehicles. From purchasing behavior, RMI's model calculates vehicle stocks, fuel savings, and their retail-customer net value.

We assume EIA's projections of sales mix and vehicle-miles traveled in each year to 2025. Thus our assumptions about how many and what kinds of vehicles people buy, how much they're driven, and the sales volumes, prices, and efficiencies of conventional vehicles are all EIA's. Our *CW* and *SOA* vehicles' cost and mpg come from Boxes 7–10 (pp. 62–73). Our model endogenously computes only how quickly those two vehicle categories get adopted, assuming introduction in 2005 and 2010 respectively (Fig. 37a, p. 183). Our *CW* and *SOA* vehicles achieve EIA's projected 2025 0–60-mph acceleration time in every year, so before 2025, they're peppier than average (by a gradually decreasing amount), but we don't assume they'll therefore sell better. Some 90–95%[743] of the efficiency gain from feebates comes from manufacturers' making the same vehicles more efficient, but our model conservatively counts *no* fuel savings from the other 5–10%, which comes from customers' buying a different mix of vehicles. We model technological progress under all policies as the gradual adoption of *State of the Art* vehicles, all bought instead of *Conventional Wisdom* vehicles rather

(continued on next page)

743. Davis et al. 1995; Greene et al. 2004 (for the ~95% figure).

than EIAmobiles (thus conservatively minimizing oil savings). We assume that scrapped vehicles have the same mpg as other vehicles contemporaneously retired. We assume that all light vehicles last 14 years,[744] although carbon-composite *SOA* vehicles should last far longer (and could be designed for fuel-cell retrofits). We assume that a given policy yields only one unique outcome, different policies yield different outcomes, and an economically indifferent manufacturer will split choices 50/50. Our model's output agrees well with two DOE model results.[745]

Adoption in each year equals demand times retooling fraction (Fig. 37a); *CW* and *SOA* vehicles can't be adopted faster than manufacturers retool to produce them. Thus if everyone wanted *State of the Art* vehicles but only 50% of automakers' capacity had been retooled to produce them, then only half the demand would be met; the rest would default to *Conventional Wisdom* vehicles (or, to the extent they too weren't yet available or demanded, to EIA's inefficient base-case vehicles). Conversely, if manufacturers had retooled to make every vehicle *State of the Art*, their sales would nonetheless be limited by demand. Thus our model matches annual demand with supply insofar as this supply is available within the practical constraints of retooling.

744. Survival rates for RMI's cohort model are based on Table 3.9 and 3.10 of ORNL 2003. VMT is based in Table 3.6 and 3.7, scaled up to EIA's projections through 2025, then extrapolated linearly.

745. RMI's model is annually dynamic, whereas Greene et al. (2004) model a static pivot point and assess a one-year snapshot ~10–15 years in the future. Nonetheless, when we tested our model by introducing NRC vehicles, it predicted mpgs 5% above to 10% below those predicted by Greene et al. (*Technical Annex*, Ch. 21). As for oil savings, Patterson, Steiner, & Singh (2002) show that a weighted-average vehicle stock average of ~53 mpg corresponds to refined-product use of 7.3 Mbbl/d, which scales to ~5.4 Mbbl/d using RMI's vehicles. RMI's model finds 5.1 Mbbl/d—reasonable agreement given the differences in assumed technology costs and policies. Of course, these models have different purposes: RMI's calculates from consumer preferences, while Patterson, Steiner, & Singh's only asks what mpg would be needed to achieve a given oil saving.

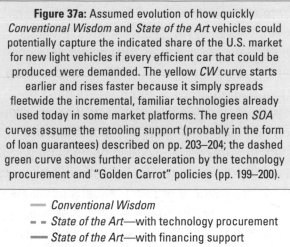

Figure 37a: Assumed evolution of how quickly *Conventional Wisdom* and *State of the Art* vehicles could potentially capture the indicated share of the U.S. market for new light vehicles if every efficient car that could be produced were demanded. The yellow *CW* curve starts earlier and rises faster because it simply spreads fleetwide the incremental, familiar technologies already used today in some market platforms. The green *SOA* curves assume the retooling support (probably in the form of loan guarantees) described on pp. 203–204; the dashed green curve shows further acceleration by the technology procurement and "Golden Carrot" policies (pp. 199–200).

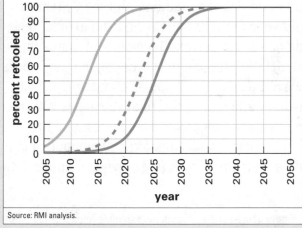

Source: RMI analysis.

Our best judgment of the practical constraints on retooling and retraining is shown in Fig. 37a, based on standard logistic s-curves and reflecting a moderate mix of policies that include federal action to relieve automakers' and suppliers' financial constraints as described later on pp. 203–204. By "priming the pump," our other proposed policies should affect not just demand (their main aim) but also retooling rates, and this is shown schematically in Fig. 37a's dashed green line as a three-year acceleration of the initial "takeoff" phase of making *State of the Art* vehicles.

(continued on next page)

How soon could manufacturers start producing *State of the Art* vehicles? For advanced-composite versions, Fig. 37b illustrates how this could plausibly occur in 2010 based on a concerted effort launched in 2005 by one or more major market players. Automakers don't traditionally start designing platforms whose production methods aren't long perfected and practiced, but they've lately been doing such parallel development with certain light-metal production innovations where prudent fallback positions were available. In this case, ultralight steel (pp. 55, 67) offers such a "backstop" using conventional fabrication methods. But the dynamics shown in Fig. 37b appear realistic in light of six main factors: current development status (pp. 56–57), U.S. technological depth, market imperatives, the speed and power of modern virtual design techniques, the relative simplicity of tooling to make composite autobodies, and the technological shortcuts already embedded in our assumed designs (e.g., using cosmetic exte-

rior panels so composite structures don't need Class A finish). To make Fig. 37b feasible basically requires at least one decisive automaker or Tier One supplier, and there are many candidates. The 2010 date might even be surpassed by the most aggressive competitors.

Different policies match different technological worldviews, so we considered presenting different policy packages matched to the *Conventional Wisdom* and *State of the Art* vehicle technologies. We chose instead to describe a single policy package focused on accelerating *State of the Art* vehicles to achieve radical and profitable oil savings. In that world, *Conventional Wisdom* vehicles' incremental oil savings are also available in the marketplace, but are pulled along as a byproduct of accelerating *State of the Art* vehicle adoption. To be sure, the production of *Conventional Wisdom* vehicles starts sooner in

(continued on next page)

Figure 37b: Assumed schematic schedule for launching 50,000/y production of *State of the Art* vehicles in 2010 (0.25% of that year's light-vehicle sales), based on advanced-composite production technology demonstrated in mid-2004 at 1×1-m scale (or on BMW technology, pp. 56–57), then perfected for large-scale use through a larger industry/federal R&D effort (pp. 204–206). Delays would either correspondingly delay *SOA* vehicles' introduction and fuel savings or require a switch to light-steel substitutes (pp. 55, 67), but we consider this schedule feasible.

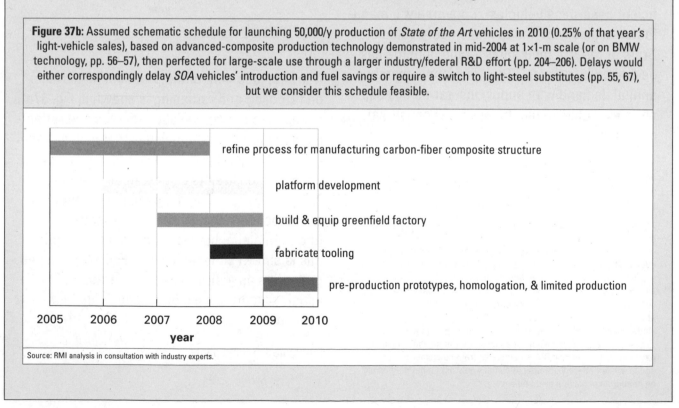

Source: RMI analysis in consultation with industry experts.

A major lesson of Fig. 36 is that despite a strong portfolio of both technologies and policies, the stock of light vehicles on the road in 2025 gets only 32.5 mpg, compared with 21.2 mpg in EIA's projection. By 2050, the 32.5 has risen to 61.0 mpg, reflecting the maturation of stock turnover. These very long lead times are inherent in the dynamics of the enormous, long-lived, slow-moving vehicle stock, the lead times of retooling, and the supertanker-like momentum of the whole automotive system. The policy lesson is clear: start quickly and work aggressively to get very efficient vehicles on the road as soon as possible in large numbers. It's like the king who, in the legends of several cultures, told his gardener he wanted to plant a tree. "Sire, it will take a hundred years to grow," replied the gardener. "Then," said the king, "we must plant it this afternoon!"

So what are the policy instruments that would accelerate adoption and production of *State of the Art* vehicles as dramatically as Fig. 36 shows? What are the key insights from that policy modeling? As mentioned in Box 18, the first and most important instrument is feebates, because they stimulate consumer demand for, and industry supply of, ever more efficient vehicles. Feebates aim to ensure that the most efficient vehicles at any given time are the highest-margin vehicles, so manufacturers are eager to develop and sell them. Policy must also help to accelerate supply; this requires the conversion of existing factories to build *State of the Art* vehicles to meet that burgeoning demand, and may also require new factories. An integrated suite of policies is needed here: early military science and technology investment to coalesce, strengthen, and expand the advanced materials sector; guaranteed civilian and military government procurement of advanced vehicles in the early years (a "Golden Carrot")

Box 18: Modeling the effects of policy on light vehicle sales and stocks (continued)

this scenario, and since they are much cheaper, they're adopted more quickly (Fig. 37b). Although they save only 39% as much fuel as *State of the Art, Conventional Wisdom* vehicles therefore yield most of the total oil savings from all light vehicles by 2025. However, *State of the Art* vehicles, after the delay caused by their later start and slower retooling, complete their takeover not long after 2025, ultimately saving far more oil. And in any event, the red (inefficient) vehicles that underpin EIA's forecast are completely squeezed out of the market by 2020 under our full *Coherent Engagement* policy scenario (Fig. 36i).

Even the impressive oil saving shown in Fig. 36i is conservative, mainly because we assume no technological progress beyond 2004 (p. 37) and no adoption of fuel cells. In practice, since *State of the Art* vehicles greatly accelerate the market entry of affordable fuel cells (pp. 233–234), those should achieve production scale at competitive cost late in the period. They would save about two-fifths more energy than shown for the appropriate fraction of *State of the Art* gasoline-hybrid vehicles and would entirely displace hybrids' remaining *oil* use, since the hydrogen for the fuel cells (pp. 227–242) would come from saved natural gas or renewables or both.

Rebates for buying efficient vehicles, paid for by fees on inefficient ones, can expand customer choice, create both consumer and producer surpluses, cut fuel costs by hundreds of billions of dollars in net present value, and save millions of barrels ◄─ of oil every day. Incentives would favor efficient vehicles, not smaller ones, and the automakers who make the best vehicles, whatever their market segment.

so as to build industry manufacturing experience and volume more rapidly; a "Platinum Carrot" prize competition to reward early mass-market adoption of even more advanced vehicles; and throughout, especially at first, the financial support to prime the pump by providing the U.S. automaking industry with the financial liquidity needed to restructure its manufacturing capacity. In addition, we suggest a low-income lease-and-scrap program designed to help reduce the burdens on the welfare system and further expand the market for efficient new vehicles. The rest of this section details how these policies would work, as well as some additional options that should be thoughtfully considered.

Feebates

The centerpiece of our policy recommendation is the "feebate," which provides a rebate for or levies a fee on each new vehicle depending on its efficiency.[746] Buyers of new light vehicles that exceed a certain annually defined fuel economy benchmark, called the "pivot point," would receive a rebate to be subtracted from the purchase price. The amount of the rebate would depend on how much the vehicle's fuel economy exceeds the pivot point for vehicles of that size. Conversely, buyers of new vehicles with fuel economies lower than the pivot point for vehicles of that size would pay a corresponding surcharge on their purchase price. The feebates we propose are revenue-neutral, with no net flow of dollars into or out of the Treasury. Instead, the fees paid by buyers of less efficient vehicles (which impose social costs) would be used to pay the rebates to buyers of more efficient vehicles (which save social costs), with a tiny bit left over to pay the feebates' administrative costs. Feebates are typically described as a dollar value for every *gallon per mile* difference from the pivot point (see Box 19)—not mile per gallon, since the goal is to save gallons in a linearly proportional manner (i.e., all gallons saved are equally valuable).[748] As the fleet

---

19: How feebates work

Feebates lower the prices of efficient vehicles, so people buy more of them, and raise the prices of inefficient vehicles, so people buy fewer of them. Each year, the fees pay for the rebates (plus the minor administrative costs[747]). Consider, for example, a feebate of $1,000 per 0.01 gpm, with a pivot point of 23 miles per gallon (0.043 gpm) for the midsized SUV class. A Nissan *Pathfinder* getting 18 miles per gallon (1/18 mpg = 0.056 gpm), is 0.013 gpm worse than this benchmark value or "pivot point," so *Pathfinder* incurs a $1,300 fee. Ford's new *Escape* hybrid SUV gets (let's suppose) 36 miles per gallon, or 0.028 gpm—0.015 gpm better than the pivot point—so it would earn a $1,500 rebate. These changes in the vehicles' retail prices are typically smaller than the sales incentives that most automakers now offer out of their own profit margins, and are economically about equivalent to the hybrid tax credits offered by some states such as Colorado. In this example, the feebate would be revenue-neutral if slightly more *Pathfinder*s than *Escape* hybrids were sold.

---

747. We haven't explicitly accounted for administrative costs because in well-run programs, based on extensive utility experience, they should be very small—well within analytic uncertainties. But they must be budgeted and paid for.

746. Greene et al. 2004; Koomey & Rosenfeld 1990. See also note 636.

748. See next page.

becomes more efficient, the pivot point would gradually shift[749] toward lower fuel intensity (higher mpg), eventually surpassing *Conventional Wisdom* vehicles. If we ever ran out of worthwhile technologies, we could declare victory and stop.

U.S. feebates should be structured to be revenue-neutral, technology-neutral, and neutral as to vehicle size so as to enhance and not distort customer choice. We therefore suggest having the feebate system apply the same slope ($/gpm) to each and every new light vehicle without exception, but with a separate pivot point for each size class (measured by interior volume or areal footprint as the best metric of customer utility—not by weight).[750] Size-class-based feebates will preserve the competitive position of each automaker regardless of where in the market it concentrates its offerings, and thus put no U.S. automaker at any disadvantage.[751] Feebates apply to each vehicle, not to the average of all sales by each manufacturer. However, treating feebates by size class also nearly eliminates the potential for shifting customer choice between classes, and avoids complaints about interference with freedom of choice. Whatever size of vehicle you prefer, you have a choice whether to get one that's more or less efficient, with the corresponding rebate or fee attached. So a business buying a powerful, high-capacity Class 2b truck would pay no more (and may pay less) for a fuel-efficient version of that vehicle with feebates than for an inefficient version in a system like today's, without feebates—and that business will also pay far less for fuel. All gain, no pain.

Unlike standards, feebates reward and propel continuous improvement.[752] Feebates are provided to the customer, but they actually incentivize the manufacturer to incorporate energy efficiency improvements that cost less than the feebate "reward," thus maintaining an attractive retail pricepoint. Unlike fuel taxation, feebates directly signal the value of efficiency to the buyer at the time and place of choosing the vehicle. Feebates are a continuous mathematical function, and are completely transparent and predictable to manufacturers and customers, making feebates more efficient than standards. They're also less prone to "gaming," although any system will be gamed somehow. And feebates make money for everyone: under a $1,000/0.01-gpm feebate, automakers' net sales would increase by nearly

The centerpiece of our policy recommendation is the "feebate," which provides a rebate for or levies a fee on each new vehicle depending on its efficiency, with no net flow of dollars into or out of the Treasury.

Feebates should be structured to be revenue-neutral, technology-neutral, and neutral as to vehicle size so as to enhance and not distort customer choice.

Unlike standards, feebates reward and propel continuous improvement.

748. Basing linear feebate slopes (rates) on mpg instead of gpm would introduce serious distortions, since a 1-mpg increase in a 15-mpg vehicle saves 10 times more gallons per mile than a 1-mpg increase in a 48-mpg vehicle. However, it is conventional and appropriate to express the pivot point in mpg for easy comparison with federal efficiency labels.

749. If each year's setting of the pivot point were purely retrospective, the continuous improvement of market offerings would prevent revenue-neutrality. The calculation should therefore be based on estimated sales mix for the year about to occur, much as EPA now does when estimating each model year's sales-weighted efficiency, or as state utility regulators do when calculating electricity and gas tariffs for a future "test year." Although sales projections even a year ahead are always uncertain, the industry's production lead times would allow each model's mpg to be closely estimated far enough in advance that the balancing account needed to true-up annually for cumulative revenue-neutrality should run a small net balance, averaging sufficiently close to zero, and probably reducing estimation errors by learning over time.

750. We rejected two alternatives sometimes discussed. Size class could be considered in size-specific feebate calculations under a single uniform pivot point for all vehicles, but that would be more complex and less transparent. Or feebates could be customized for each automaker: that would of course be manufacturer-neutral but at the expense of distorting customer choice between subclasses, removing a spur to competition between automakers, and creating a potential barrier to market entry.

751. Japan's "Top Runner" system of improving light-vehicle efficiency (note 225, p. 45) also permits trading between classes.

752. This is one of feebates' main advantages over the NAS/NRC 2001 proposal of merely grafting tradeable permits onto the system of CAFE standards (unless the trading cap decreased over time).

Unlike fuel taxation, feebates directly signal the value of efficiency to the buyer at the time and place of choosing the vehicle.

Treating feebates by size class also nearly eliminates the potential for shifting customer choice between classes, and avoids complaints about interference with freedom of choice.

A business buying a powerful, high-capacity Class 2b truck would pay no more (and may pay less) for a fuel-efficient version of that vehicle with feebates than for an inefficient version in a system like today's, without feebates—and that business will also pay far less for fuel.

$10b/y,[753] while customers would save ~$15b/y through 2020.[754] Astute manufacturers will also multiply their higher volumes times the higher margins earned by superior value proposition and first-mover advantage.

Feebates would apply to *all* new light vehicles, rather than distorting the market by discriminating between different types (e.g., CAFE exempts the heaviest light vehicles, like *Hummer,* and the gas-guzzler tax applies only to cars, leading makers to ensure that their least efficient vehicles are legally classified as light trucks so they avoid the tax; otherwise a 15-mpg *Expedition* would cost $3,000 extra). We see no reason to perpetuate in fee-bate structure the highly gamed historic distinction that CAFE regulations now draw between cars and light trucks,[755] nor between imported and American-made vehicles; these simply distort the market.[756] We haven't modeled size-class disaggregation, but, as Greene et al. (2004) found by modeling up to 11 subclasses, it wouldn't make much difference to our findings.

Endorsed by the National Research Council's 2001 study, feebates would best be adopted federally for uniformity to both manufacturers and customers, and for ease of administration. In time they would supplant CAFE standards by making them (and the gas-guzzler tax) irrelevant, though for the time being those should remain to deter recidivism. But if the federal government failed to act, many states are poised to step in, having already considered such initiatives for more than a decade.

In 1990, for example, the California Legislature approved an early CO_2-based feebate, DRIVE+, by a 7:1 margin, though it was then pocket-vetoed by Governor Deukmejian because one of the Big Three opposed it (another was neutral; the third's position is unknown). The concept enjoys 3:1 support in recent California private polling and is likely to return there soon. A state feebate can easily piggyback onto existing new-vehicle sales, excise, or use taxes. Massachusetts and Vermont have long considered varying a 5% state tax rate within a range of 0–10%, based on efficiency compared to other vehicles in each vehicle's size class. Similar discussions are underway in at least five other states.[757] The vehicle's sales sticker could and should show how its sales tax is derived from its federally rated mpg—though the Department of Transportation criticized that display of

---

753. Greene et al. (2004) found that under a $1,000 per 0.01 gpm feebate, manufacturers' sales revenues would increase by $9.7 billion—the excess of revenue gains (from selling more expensive vehicles) over revenue losses (from selling fewer vehicles).

754. The per capita savings are based on a calculation by the California Air Resources Board on the savings of California consumers under a nationwide, carbon-based feebate system (Ashuckian et al. 2003, pp. 3–16).

755. This distinction would remain in CAFE rules unless, as we hope, NHTSA abolishes it as an arbitrary anachronism (all the more so with the rapid rise of crossover vehicles). However, it would become irrelevant in step with CAFE itself as fleet efficiencies rapidly improved under the influence of feebates. We also see no current reason to exempt any class of customers (e.g., farmers) from feebates, which would affect only new vehicle purchases, not existing vehicle operations, and are meant to offer all kinds of customers more efficient choices of all kinds of road vehicles, but wouldn't apply to vehicles meant and licensed for almost exclusively off-road use, such as tractors.

756. The UAW asserts that this CAFE rule discourages automakers from moving production offshore. Our policy recommendations should considerably increase the net benefit to automakers of sustaining and expanding U.S. production.

757. Totten & Settina 1993.

vital customer information in an unadjudicated advisory opinion that effectively discouraged Maryland from enforcing its 1992 feebate law (and deterred many other states from adopting feebates), on grounds that now appear clearly unsound[758] and readily avoidable.[759]

The Province of Ontario's feebate system, operating since 1991, has had predictably inconclusive results because it's invisible to customers and offers only a flat C$100 rebate, although the sliding-scale fee on gas-guzzlers can rise to C$4,400. However, it's interesting because it was adopted by a consensus of automakers, the Canadian Auto Workers, car dealers, and environmentalists.[760] Similar incentives are also gaining popularity in Europe, and are gradually evolving from one-sided inefficiency taxes (all stick, no carrot) to full feebates. Austria in 1992 raised its 32% new-vehicle purchase tax to 37% for the least efficient models, but scaled the increase down to zero for the most efficient. Efficiency-based fees are also in force in Denmark, Sweden, and Germany. Diverse jurisdictions from Europe to some Australian states base fees on vehicle weight.[761] A full feebate likely to take effect on 1 January 2005 in France is graduated in seven steps: it would charge €3,500 for the least efficient one-third of new light vehicles (such as large SUVs) while rebating up to €700 to the cleanest and most efficient one-sixth. French automakers make mainly midsize family cars (the half of sales that would have no net fee or rebate) or more efficient ones, which would get rebates, so they quietly favor the proposal, which would mainly crimp sales by their German and Japanese competitors.[762]

Because they work at both ends of the purchase decision—carrot and stick combined—and affect what most buyers focus on intently (the net purchase price of the vehicle), feebates are strikingly effective. A $1,000/0.01-gpm U.S. feebate "slope," illustrated in Box 18 and compellingly analyzed by Greene et al. (2004), would let new-car buyers behave as if they were considering fuel use or savings over the entire 14-year nominal life of the vehicle (no matter who owns it), rather than only for its first three years as they do now. That is, this $1,000/0.01-gpm slope is societally efficient

Under a $1,000/0.01-gpm feebate, automakers' net sales would increase by nearly $10b/y, while customers would save ~$15b/y through 2020.

A full feebate likely to take effect on 1 January 2005 in France would charge €3,500 for the least efficient one-third of new light vehicles (such as large SUVs) while rebating up to €700 to the cleanest and most efficient one-sixth. French automakers quietly favor the proposal.

---

758. Chanin 2003, especially pp. 747–753; Clinton 1999 reflects the constitutional principles of states' rights and establishes a strong administrative presumption in favor of promptly issuing federal preemption waivers requested by states, except where preemption is clearly vital to the national interest. It cannot, however, bind judicial determinations of the zone of federal preemption. Chanin (2003) compellingly argues that states need not even invoke CO_2 regulation (as California did with the 2002 Pavley Act, AB1493, which many other states may effectively adopt) to implement non-preempted feebates, provided their fee is not so exorbitant as to leave buyers only a Hobson's choice. (Her logic appears unaffected by the Supreme Court's preemption decision of 28 April 2004 in an air-quality case (AQMD 2004; U.S. Supreme Court 2004).

759. Absent federal leadership via uniform feebates, states could apparently adopt policies that reasonably influence (not mandate) vehicle choice without restricting what makers may produce or customers buy, and by separating the required federal mpg label from any state feebate label calculating a feebate from the federal mpg rating. Caselaw (Chanin 2003, pp. 752–754) doesn't appear to hold that the "related to" clause in CAFE preemption stops states from doing anything that might mention or influence customers' efficiency or emission choices in any way (e.g., by the existing fourfold differences in state gasoline taxes). A different issue might arise in California under AB1493—that law prohibits the California Air Resources Board's automotive CO_2 regulations from imposing vehicle taxes—but nothing stops the state legislature from doing so (it already does) or from basing taxes or feebates rationally on CO_2 emissions, weight, or even simply on federally rated mpg (Chanin 2003).

760. Morris 1994, "Ontario's Automobile Feebates." However, the consensus was under governmental duress.   761. Michaelis 1997.

762. Henley 2004. In presenting this key element of his National Health and Environment Plan, Prime Minister Raffarin noted that air pollution kills more than 30,000 French citizens a year, and 7–20% of cancers in France are believed to have an environmental cause. A senior UK advisor has suggested a 3–4× increase in SUVs' ~$300/y road tax (Power & Wrighton 2004).

because it arbitrages the difference in the discount rates used by new-car buyers and by society. Our model indicates (Fig. 36) that a feebate with this slope would raise the 2025 new-sales share of *Conventional Wisdom* vehicles from 19% to 44% for cars and from 45% to 56% for light trucks. Because of their later arrival into their market and their slower retooling (Fig. 37a), *State of the Art* vehicles' new-sales share would rise from 20% to only 45% for cars, and from 18% to only 43% for light trucks. Because *SOA* vehicles are more efficient, they'd be 11% of the 2025 stock but provide 34% of oil savings from non-EIA vehicles.

Many, including ourselves, would consider it economically efficient to double the feebate slope to $2,000/0.01 gpm to begin reflecting the public value of reduced oil use and a revitalized light-vehicle sector. (This is economically equivalent, at our 5%/y real discount rate over 14 years, to valuing saved gasoline at an extra 26¢/gal and saved short-run marginal crude oil at an extra $3.6/bbl—far below the externality estimates on pp. 21–22.) The resulting fees and rebates would then approach the ~$4,000–5,000 rebates now commonly paid by manufacturers to customers to promote the sale of large SUVs—but, in complete contrast to those incentives, feebates wouldn't reduce the automakers' profit margins. A $2,000/0.01 gpm feebate would increase *State of the Art* vehicles' market share by another five percentage points, although *SOA* share in the on-the-road fleet rises by only half that much because of the early years' production bottleneck. Despite the persistent production constraint, the higher feebate saves an extra ~0.2 Mbbl/d in 2025 (almost all from increased *State of the Art* sales). The accelerated *State of the Art* introduction would save even more oil thereafter—by 2035, an extra 1.23 Mbbl/d. We have not evaluated even higher feebate slopes, though our downloadable model can easily be used to do this.

Feebates should be considered not just for light vehicles but also for medium and heavy trucks, perhaps for other vehicles such as buses and trains, and conceivably for airplanes (for which we made a different suggestion on p. 156, tailored to that industry's unusual business conditions). Broadly speaking, anything that moves and uses oil would be a potential candidate for this powerful, flexible, simple, market-oriented, and versatile policy instrument and its variants.[763] Indeed, feebates are so powerful that in time, they could achieve all the benefits of our entire policy package (except retooling incentives). But to increase the speed and confidence of the shift to advanced technology vehicles, to capture further benefits, and to ensure a balanced and diversified group of mutually reinforcing instruments, we also suggest a wider portfolio, including the other policies described next.

763. For example, we haven't analyzed the potential to pay feebates not to autobuyers but to automakers, thus leveraging the roughly twofold markup from bare manufacturing cost to MSRP—though making the price signal opaque to the customer and relying entirely on competitive forces to pass it through to the retail level. (Some manufacturers fear the public may not trust them to do this, creating ill feeling.) Manufacturer rebates have been done advantageously with smaller energy-saving items, notably compact fluorescent lamps (von Weizsäcker, Lovins, & Lovins 1997, p. 166). Moreover, about a fourth of the successful U.S. utility incentive programs to promote electric efficiency in the 1980s and 1990s rewarded not just retail buyers but also "trade allies": e.g., PG&E got a bigger saving at a third the cost by paying rebates not to buyers of efficient refrigerators but to the appliance-store associate who *sold* them. The chance to earn this $50 bonus rather than nothing (for selling an inefficient unit) led the stores to stock only efficient units; the rest were sold elsewhere or, one hopes, not made. Another option: pay dealers' carrying charge for very efficient cars—enough incentive to swing a market (as B.C. Hydro did to flip the market for big electric motors in just three years [von Weizsäcker, Lovins, & Lovins 1997]). States that wanted to save oil faster could experiment with such high-leverage dealer or salesperson incentives even under a uniform federal feebate.

Low-income scrap-and-replace program

Welfare reform has been the subject of great interest over the past decade. The root causes of poverty in America have been identified as a combination of lack of capital, lack of skills, failure to form families,[764] lack of reliable transportation,[765] and low-wage earners' need for certain welfare benefits not typically provided by low-wage jobs, such as health care.[766] Much effort has been put into strategies that address these issues, specifically programs that help welfare recipients transition to the working world.[767] A major question is how to keep them working and help keep them from reverting to poverty. Our focus here is on the impact of improving timely, reliable transportation for low-income Americans, going beyond the laudable existing public transport initiatives to address issues such as transport for those who work outside peak travel times of public transit, and for those living in rural areas not served by public transit. There is a growing consensus that limited mobility is an important "missing link" in a comprehensive strategy for reducing and ultimately eliminating poverty.

Our second policy initiative therefore links and thus helps to solve three distinct but related problems: lower-income Americans' limited personal mobility and disproportionately burdensome fuel purchases (both part of the "poverty trap"), their inability both to gain from and to contribute to the prompt benefits of transforming automaking, and the slow (~14-year) spontaneous turnover of the nation's light-vehicle stock, which retards the adoption and hence the development of more efficient models.

We outline two alternative ways to address these three problems. Both proposed mechanisms involve best-practice[768] and preferably nationwide[769] scrappage of qualified inefficient cars. They also create a profitable new million-vehicle-a-year market to replace the scrapped ones; increase oil savings and pollution prevention; and improve equity and social welfare. The two mechanisms differ only in which low-income used-car buyer segment they help—the most marginal used car buyers, who can barely afford a used car, or the least marginal buyers, who already buy first-generation used cars. We recommend that a neutral expert body like the U.S. Government Accountability Office (GAO) determine which mechanism and design details would produce greater social welfare benefits, and recommend a policy, which may well include both mechanisms, for pilot tests to support nationwide rollout.

Low-income Americans pay as much for driving as for food. But about $0–3 per day extra can provide a very efficient and reliable new car *plus* its fuel, while a clunker gets scrapped. Affordable personal mobility may be the missing link in reducing welfare dependence while opening a new million-vehicle-a-year market.

We aim to create the same revolution in affordable personal mobility as was achieved in affordable home-ownership after World War II. If that mobility is superefficient, a low-income household can afford not only to get but also to drive a reliable vehicle, gaining the mobility that is the key to America's opportunity.

764. ISP/ASPE/HHS 1983; NCSL, undated.

765. "According to the Community Transportation Association of America, JOBS program studies have concluded that the lack of affordable transportation presents a barrier even more serious than the lack of child care to prospective JOBS clients." Kaplan 1997; Cotterill & Franklin 1995.

766. Fraker et al. 2004, p. 16.

767. Sawhill 1999.

768. Kallen et al. 1994.

769. Horowitz (2001, p. 121) shows that "... it is far more cost-effective to attempt to transform a national market through long-term coordinated coast-to-coast efforts that permit market preferences to evolve and mature, than it is to temporarily manipulate local markets through piecemeal programs that are highly variable from place to place and from year to year. In short, persistent efforts to educate producers and consumers and inform them of energy efficiency benefits appear to be more capable of building sustainable sales volumes and market shares than the alternative of financial subsidies." (Note 29 in IEA 2003b). We recommend staging from regional pilot programs to national rollout.

770. IEA 2003b.

771. Raphael & Stoll 2001. This is basically because in most U.S. metropolitan areas, "one can commute greater distances in shorter time periods and, holding distance constant, reach a fuller set of potential work locations using a privately-owned car rather than public transit" (which also may not match the irregular hours of many low-income workers' jobs). Other benefits include greater ease of getting and holding a job (because one can get to it reliably), more family time and stable homes (less time on often slow public transportation), access to a wider choice of food and other goods at more competitive retail prices than the urban core offers, and less or no exposure to volatile gasoline prices. Of course, the quoted statement doesn't mean that only black and Latino/a families make up the lowest income quintile; most low-income rural Americans are white. However, black families accounted for 16% of the lowest-income quintile in 2002 ("White and Other" accounted for the remaining 84%), and for decreasing percentages of the higher income quintiles—14%, 11%, 9%, and 6% (BLS, undated).

Either way, the goal is clear and compelling: to create the same revolution in affordable personal mobility as was achieved in affordable home-ownership after World War II—applying to all U.S. working families an expanded version of Henry Ford's vision that his cars should be affordable to the workers who built them. But our goal goes further: to make that mobility superefficient, so that a low-income household can afford not only to get but also to *drive* a reliable vehicle, gaining the mobility that is the key to America's opportunity.

Affordable and superefficient personal mobility, especially if offered in many states or nationwide,[770] would bring life-changing benefits to low-income Americans, especially in areas poorly served by public transit: for example, "raising minority car-ownership rates to the car ownership rate of whites would narrow the black-white employment rate differential by 45 percent and the Latino[/a]-white employment differential by 17 percent."[771] The vehicles driven by low-income citizens are not only slightly less efficient,[772] but also tend to be the least reliable and often the most polluting and least safe in the fleet. Correcting these conditions and making personal mobility affordable is more valuable than the gasoline savings, which for a nominal million-vehicle-a-year program would accumulate over a car's lifetime to ~0.2 Mbbl/d with *Conventional Wisdom* or 0.4 Mbbl/d with *State of the Art* compact cars.[773]

An instructive analogy comes from America's historic national commitment to make home ownership more affordable.[774] Many can now afford a home[775]—but not driving between home, job, and retail stores. That's costly at best, and when gasoline prices soar, it can become prohibitive,[776] making some families choose between feeding the children and fueling the car, without which there's no paycheck. For the average low-income household, mobility is normally as costly as food.[777] In cities with long commutes, mobility now costs more than housing.[778] Yet without credit, a marginally better car is a stretch and a new car is an impossible dream.[779]

772. Khazzoom (2000a, p.26) notes that 1993 U.S. households with average incomes ≤$15k vs >$50k had average vehicle efficiency of 19.8 vs 20.1 mpg. No newer data are available, although qualitatively, the 2001 partial Department of Transportation data appear comparable. Driving was 49% lower in the 1993 lower-income households (14,109 vs. 27,740 miles).

773. Assuming savings from annual replacement of 1 million 23-mpg MY1985 cars with 37.5- and 90-mpg cars over 2010–24 (14-year average lifetime), saves 0.2–0.4 Mbbl/d.

774. Andrew 2004. Home ownership rose from 64% in 1994 to nearly 69% in 2003; among African-Americans, from 42% to 48%; among Latino/as, from 41% to 46%.

775. At least to finance the home if not to pay the utilities—efficient building and appliance design typically gets too little attention.

776. Ball 2004. The squeeze has reportedly reduced mid-2004 revenues at Wal-Mart and Target.

777. Tan 2000, pp. 29–35. In 2002, before the run-up in gasoline prices, the average low-income (bottom-quintile) U.S. household devoted 35% of its $19,061 annual income to housing, 17% to mobility (chiefly by car), 17% to nutrition, 9% to utilities, fuel, and public services, and 7% to health care. In contrast, the average household's $57,835 income was split 32%, 20%, 13%, 6%, and 5%, respectively.

778. Ball 2004. In sprawling Tampa, where 75% of jobs are over ten miles from the city center, transportation costs more than housing.

779. Three-fourths of U.S. families earning less than $15,000 a year own cars; otherwise, lacking effective public transportation, they'd be largely immobilized. But investment in automotive efficiency or reliability is beyond reach. In that paycheck-to-paycheck world, cars tend to be fourth- to sixth-hand clunkers bought for cash, tinkered with and coaxed into running for just another month.

Fortunately, substituting clean, efficient cars for dirty and often inefficient ones benefits everyone. Prematurely retiring "super-emitters"[780] would disproportionately save oil, save money for those most in need, and improve urban air and public health.[781] Specifically targeting such cars is a cost-effective way to reduce pollution, and even the broader scrappage we propose is still worthwhile for society[782] So what are the two ways we suggest to scrap qualified inefficient cars, save oil, and provide efficient, reliable mobility to non-creditworthy lower-income citizens?

Our first proposed mechanism combines scrappage of qualified cars and financing of new cars with high-volume procurement. A federal agency such as the General Services Administration (GSA), which now buys most federal government vehicles, would competitively procure, at a fair unit margin to the winning automaker, additional but highly efficient new vehicles. It would then lease these at federal rates to qualified non-creditworthy low-income citizens, possibly via competing for-profit firms. The bulk-bought vehicles must correctly express aggregated customer preferences for reliable, efficient mobility and for other desired vehicle attributes.[783] For every efficient new car bought and leased, slightly less than one older, less efficient, more polluting vehicle would be scrapped. For maximum flexibility, these two transactions need not necessarily involve the same driver or household, although such linkage would be simple and worth considering. The lease would be very inexpensive because of the large-scale procurement, especially since the GSA would be buying one very efficient model. The program can create five other benefits, accruing to various parties but all monetizable: future saved fuel, two emissions credits, cheaper insurance bought in bulk, and the lessees' avoided purchases of replacement clunkers. Low-income lessees, who suffer grievously when gasoline prices spike, would benefit further from the program's bulk-buying price-hedged (constant-price) gasoline,[784] in much the way that many large private fleets now buy their fuel.

> **Raising minority car-ownership rates to the car ownership rate of whites would narrow the black-white employment rate differential by 45 percent and the Latino[/a]-white employment differential by 17 percent.**

780. I.e., vehicles emitting many times the average pollutant levels per mile. A recent study by major car and oil companies found from roadside real-time emission measurements in Denver that even as newer, cleaner vehicles emitted less of the smog-forming pollutants, the fraction emitted by the dirtiest tenth of the vehicles held steady or rose: by 2003 it accounted for 69% of the fleet's CO, 75% of HC, and 54% of NO_x. (WBCSD 2004, p. 100). Similar issues are far more acute in most giant cities in developing countries, where similar remedies would be worth considering—not just for cars but also for, e.g., the dramatically pollution-reducing two-stroke scooter retrofits developed at Colorado State University: a $200 retrofit can cut CO emissions by ~1 ton/y and cut fuel use 32% (M. Defoort [Engines and Energy Conversion Laboratory, CSU, Ft. Collins CO], personal communication, 2 August 2004).

781. Now that U.S. new-vehicle efficiency has been nearly flat for two decades, the opportunity to save a great deal of *fuel* by scrapping the *oldest* vehicles is largely gone; but the least efficient vehicles are also often the heaviest, most aggressive, and least compatible with their lighter roadmates. Where this is true, scrapping them would improve public safety (and slightly increase recovery of currently scarce scrap steel).

782. Not *all* scrappage is worthwhile. We tested *Kelley Blue Book* prices and EPA efficiency data to check the "scrappage resource" supply curves for some popular models, relating their age to the $/bbl cost of saving oil by scrapping them. Most of the inherently inefficient heavy models are relatively new and valuable, making their CSE relatively high. Scrapping older cars is often a more cost-effective oil-saver, but the amount saved is smaller.

783. See notes 812–813 below for lessons from other kinds of aggregation-and-procurement programs. Microcredit experience suggests that the default rate may be surprisingly low, and the collateral is excellent.

784. Low-income customers would especially benefit from constant-price gasoline. The posted price at the pump would appear to vary, but the lessee's special credit card would be charged the constant price. (Car-sharing firms like FlexCar, whose hourly fees include fuel, use special credit cards that work only with a specific vehicle and are electronically cancelled in the event of fraud or default.) The hedging could, for example, piggyback off the Defense Energy Support Center (p. 87) hedge purchases for all DoD gasoline supply, which like other military fuels is provided at constant prices known far in advance. Indeed, the new car's high efficiency could motivate still another innovation: leasing not just a car but a mobility service solution where lessor and lessee share the benefit of the fuel savings. This alignment of provider with customer interests illustrates the powerful "solutions economy" business model (pp. 135, 196) described by Hawken, Lovins, & Lovins 1999, Ch. 7, and in the forthcoming book *The Solutions Economy* by J.P. Womack & D.T. Jones.

Many can now afford a home—but not driving between home, job, and retail stores. For the average low-income household, mobility is normally as costly as food. In cities with long commutes, mobility now costs more than housing.

The analysis in *Technical Annex*, Ch. 22, finds that low-income customers could lease an efficient new compact or midsize *Conventional Wisdom* car—safe, clean, comfortable, insured, reliable, warranted, with a five-year extended service plan—for an incremental cost of ~$3/day without feebates, or ~$2.3/day with feebates. Starting around 2010, *State of the Art* vehicles with feebates could reduce that incremental cost to about 15¢ a day. For early adopters, the "Golden Carrot" aggregated-procurement incentives described on pp. 199–200 could even cut that to zero—or perhaps even less, earning a return to help finance participation for the neediest.

785. Moral hazard would be minimized via ensuring certain disclosure requirements relating to an individual lender's historical lower threshold for making credit available, and via the ability to compare confidentially the thresholds across multiple lenders.

786. The Federal Family Education Loan Program Program (FFELP), and to some extent Sallie Mae (SLMA, the Student Loan Marketing Association). Sallie Mae was established by Act of Congress in 1972 as a Government-Sponsored Enterprise, floated on the NYSE in 1984, privatized in 1997, and renamed in 2002 (Sallie Mae, undated). When the Education Act was passed in 1965, FFELP was set up to cover any defaults on student loans that were issued by banks, but by the early 1970s, this repayment provision for delinquent loans proved too slow and inadequate, and the banks underserved the demand

Our second proposed mechanism includes the same scrappage program, but doesn't use government procurement, and has a different financing mechanism. It would provide affordable mobility in the form of efficient new cars, but this time to customers who buy, not lease, and whose credit record marginally disqualifies them from buying a new car. This program would similarly retain the demand-supply balance in the used car market, and would therefore raise quality for all used-car buyers rather than disproportionately for the lowest-income buyers. The financing mechanism would simply guarantee reimbursement to current auto lenders for incremental defaults on loans made to the marginal next-in-line new-car borrower category, and would therefore almost exclusively engage existing market mechanisms and financial institutions. The cost would largely consist of reimbursing the incremental defaults.[785] This is analogous to the student loan program developed to ensure financing for this roughly equally risky customer segment.[786] It could involve a separate office with sole responsibility for reimbursing the incremental defaults, but there would be no need for a "designated agent" such as car dealers or car rental companies.[787] Regardless of who originates the retail loans and whose cars they finance, a "Carrie Mae" institution could provide a reimbursement guarantee for financing efficient new cars into a new low-income market while relying on today's financial services infrastructure for screening and execution. Existing financial services companies (FSCs) would compete for a piece of the action,[788] given an

because the lag between declaration of default and government repayment crimped the lenders' liquidity. Sallie Mae fixed this problem by buying the student loans very shortly after issuance. This increased both liquidity and loan volume: relieved of default risk, each bank could fully satisfy loan demand from the next student cohort.

787. Instead, dealers, who have traditionally originated loans on-the-spot mainly for their parent automakers' financing arm or third parties, would compete with newer entrants, such as the financial service companies (FSCs) that lend to many segments of the consumer market. FSCs also finance cars, and have recently become very efficient at doing so by mailing directly to qualifying buyers a voucher or check spendable at any dealership. FSCs do this today for relatively safe customers, mailing vouchers just like preapproved credit-card offers to those with FICo scores above ~660 (Fair Isaac's Company, Inc. scores—a standard consumer-finance rating system analogous to Moody's or S&P, with a maximum possible score of 800). Under our proposal, the new-car voucher simply has far better collateral (note 792).

788. FSCs already know the sub-prime auto market very well, and would likely be eager to expand their servicing via deepening, if a reimbursement guarantee were to be offered. Carrie Mae would define qualifying levels of new-car efficiency, as well as mechanisms for the FSC and Carrie Mae itself to certify scrappage.

attractive business model.[789] It would be essential to clearly define under what circumstances the default reimbursement guarantee kicks in, so that the risk profiles of these loans are completely defined by a qualification mechanism that specifies who qualifies and for how much credit.[790]

The scrappage arrangement is identical for both mechanisms. Carrie Mae would define qualifying levels of inefficiency and mechanisms for the buyer or lessor to certify scrappage. "Cash for Clunkers" programs that pay customers or bounty-hunters to scrap old-but-still-driven cars have been implemented or considered in at least five states (AZ, CA, DE, IL, ME),[791] revealing important program-design lessons.[792] Vehicle scrappage must target only vehicles that would otherwise actually drive enough miles to make it worthwhile.[793] And to avoid driving up prices for parts for collectors' vintage vehicles, either the public should be allowed to scavenge them before scrappage (with notice to collectors' groups when a noteworthy vehicle is received), or collectable vehicles should be excluded from the program. In any event, new-car procurement could be linked with the "Golden Carrot" incentive described on pp. 199–200.)

789. The expected loan risk in this used-car segment is about the same as that of the student loans Sallie Mae buys today, so with risk and cost guaranteed via the reimbursement policy, and the lender's net loan-to-value ratio well below one, interest should be high among FSCs. Sallie Mae loan clients (students) have ~20–40% default rates; sub-prime auto borrowers, an estimated ~20–35%. Although default rates are proprietary, one deep sub-prime auto lender—Texas-based Drivetime, www.drivetime.com—reportedly charges well over 20%/y for its lowest-rated used-car buyers, who probably FICo-score well below 550. This implies expected default rates around 25–40%, so for the riskiest new-car buyers, ~20–35% seems reasonable. However, unlike an uncollateralized student loan, the FSC's loan is secured by the new car, which is easily traced, can be repossessed (wireless transponders are cheap), and is more valuable because of its high efficiency and modernity. The guarantor's cost is thus essentially the transaction cost of depreciation, repossession and resale, with significant principal remaining. Default rates should be further reduced because nearly 100% financing (no down payment, just normal finance costs) improves the borrower's strained cashflow; most repairs are free under warranty; and the increased ability to get to work reliably reduces the risk of losing one's job if the car breaks down. The lower-income borrower's new ability to build a sound credit history and equity in the new car—a far more valuable asset than the previous clunker—is an added incentive. Some sub-prime lenders even install radio-controlled devices that disable a car on its next start if the loan is in default after several days' warning, but this might prove inappropriate or unnecessary.

790. For example, if an FSC's historical baseline cut-off FICo score were 660 and if, after seeing the terms offered by the reimbursement guarantee, the FSC were induced to deepen its lending cutoff point to 640, the reimbursement would pay for any defaults within this FICo range that were incremental to the FSCs documented historical default rate at the 660 level. So if defaults went from 20% at the 660 level to 23% for the 640-to-660 borrowers, the guarantee would reimburse 3 percentage points of those guarantees, or 13% of all defaults for this segment. With this guarantee, the FSC could treat the 640-to-660 borrower segment on an equal footing with the 660-level borrowers to whom the FSC already lends.

791. And about a dozen other countries, mostly paying ~$500–1,500 and meant to reduce local air pollution (IEA 2001, pp. 87–89). The most ambitious effort, in Italy in 1997, scrapped 1.15 million light vehicles or ~4% of the national fleet in a year. Payment was scaled to engine displacement, and was conditional on buying a new car—conveniently for firms like Fiat—but sales then dropped, predictably, by about the same amount.

792. A decade-old but still useful guide is Kallen et al. 1994.

793. E.g., by strictly enforced requirements such as valid registration for at least one year prior to scrapping and demonstrating roadworthiness by driving vehicles to the dealership, then ensuring that vehicles turned in are scrapped so that they do not re-appear. Empirical evidence (Dill 2004) suggests that scrappage incentives tend to attract lower-income households that drive their clunkers more, rather than higher-income households seeking to dispose of a surplus vehicle. However, low-income households with the highest driving levels are unlikely to be attracted by a $500 scrappage bonus because that's not enough to buy a replacement clunker. About three-fourths of vehicles scrapped in Bay Area programs would otherwise have been driven, as program designers assumed, for about three more years (Dill 2004). Some programs specifically target the most polluting cars (World Bank 2002), or those that have just failed smog tests. Some, like British Columbia's Scrap-It, offer a variety of compensation options including a free transit pass (which most participants choose [Clean Air Initiative Asia, undated]).

Automakers would sell a million additional vehicles a year into this new market and would make a profit on every one of them. That offtake would also lower the risk of developing new fuel-efficient platforms.

So far, most scrappage programs have been on a sufficiently modest scale not to dry up the clunker supply and make older used cars unaffordable to those who most need their mobility. However, a successful large-scale scrappage effort could in principle have a slightly regressive effect,[799] chiefly affecting minorities and low-income rural residents.[800] This would be offset in part by the decline in used-car prices when the leased cars are resold into the used car market, since pre-leased cars typically resell for less than pre-owned private cars. Further, the estimated ~1:1.2 ratio of inefficient old cars scrapped to efficient new cars financed (to be adjusted in the light of experience) avoids regressivity at the low end of the used-car market by not scrapping one additional used car for every eleventh

20: More antidotes to regressivity

The combination of the suggested low-income lease-and-scrap program plus feebates (for which all new-car buyers are eligible) should eliminate the potential for burdening low-income drivers, and on the contrary should much improve their access to affordable personal mobility. However, if needed, further options are available.

Our analysis hasn't fully counted all ways in which careful financial engineering can cut risks and hence costs. (By such methods, one firm has systematically cut public-sector and university housing finance costs by more than half.)[794]

Car-sharing programs[795] in the U.S. and Europe typically cut annual driving by ~30–70% without loss of convenience or mobility. Some services, like FlexCar,[796] claim to take six cars off the road for every car they field; the hourly lease fee includes premium insurance, fuel, reserved parking, and maintenance. ZIPcar claims 7–10× reductions, implying that some infrequent drivers give up their cars in favor of cheaper occasional rentals. A more fully integrated offering like the 58,000-member, 1,750-vehicle, 1,000-site Mobility Car Sharing Switzerland[797] delivers superior mobility at lower cost with no self-owned car. Such concepts may hold special promise for low-income communities to cut costs.[798]

794. UniDev LLC (www.unidevllc.com), for a good-sized California project, recently cut the annual income required to qualify for a $338,000 house from $106,000 to $43,000 and for a 1,000-ft² two-bedroom apartment from $81,000 to $39,000.

795. WBCSD 2004, pp. 139–141. The European and U.S. car-sharing news sites are respectively www.carsharing.org and www.carsharing.net; the World CarShare Consortium is at http://ecoplan.org/carshare/cs_index.htm. U.S. car-sharing typically saves money if you drive less than ~7,500 mi/y, and is available in more than three dozen cities. We aren't aware of a car-sharing service designed specifically for low-income U.S. communities, but suspect it could offer some attractions.

796. See www.flexcar.com/vision/impact.asp.

797. This service, www.mobility.ch, is now available to ~60% of the population of Switzerland. It combines in a single fee a free or discounted pass for public transportation and a short-term service to drive the vehicle of your choice (in some cities, dropped off to and picked up from your location by a bicycle courier). It could be extended to include more services, such as a cashless backup taxi service, a travel agency, and a broadband Internet service provider (for videoconferencing and, soon, virtual presence). Such business models work because not everyone needs a car at once; the average U.S. private car has an asset utilization of only 4%, so it stands idle 96% of the time.

798. A possibly apocryphal, but financially plausible, story relates that several hundred residents of a distressed Massachusetts town sold their cars, pooled the proceeds into a nonprofit group, and bulk-bought a fleet of identical, efficient Honda cars—enough to get the dealer price, and thanks to the nonprofit ownership, tax-free. Every two years, they sold the fleet and bought a new one, thus staying in warranty and remaining a qualified dealer. They also bulk-bought insurance, fuel, and a two-person maintenance staff (formerly employed seasonally to keep up the town's snowplows). Car-sharing—cars were booked and checked out like a library book—increased asset utilization, providing more mobility from fewer cars with lower total cost. The alleged net annual savings totaled about $5,000 per household—a huge boost, equivalent to one-fourth of total income for the bottom quintile of American households.

new car bought.[801] This ratio also aids market entry by households that have not previously owned a car—a fraction that's been declining but that, in 1999, still included 27% of households below the poverty line.[802] (Box 20 mentions other remedies for regressivity.) Since cars would qualify for scrappage based on the "Reasonably Reliable Test,"[803] we conclude there is little reason to sunset the scrappage policy (hence also the financing mechanism) before 2025. If saturation of the target segment(s) ever became problematic, that would be a nice problem to have and is best dealt with at the time. As more efficient new cars make old ones relatively less efficient, the societal value of accelerating their scrappage rises.

Under either mechanism, all Americans, especially those with lower incomes, would enjoy the same or greater personal mobility, and average real used-car prices wouldn't rise (because the scrap/replace ratio is less than one). Low-wage earners would see lower operating costs and higher-quality, more reliable personal mobility at a cost, compared with their current arrangements, ranging from a few dollars a day to zero or even slightly negative. Since the new cars meet far stricter emission standards than the scrapped clunkers, air pollution should decrease. High fuel efficiency would reduce CO_2 emissions too. Congestion probably wouldn't increase appreciably, because most of the new trips by previous non-car-owners would be in the opposite direction to inbound suburbanites' commutes, and many would also occur at different times. And if the program works as intended, automakers would sell a million additional vehicles a year into this new market and would make a profit on every one of them. That offtake would also lower the risk of developing new fuel-efficient platforms.[804]

Smart government fleet procurement

The 2002 federal vehicle fleet, both civilian and nontactical military, contained more than 470,000 light vehicles and 21,000 heavy trucks. When state and municipal fleets are included, a total of nearly four million vehicles, over half of them light vehicles, are a part of one government

> Governments buy billions of dollars' worth of light vehicles every year. They can help mold the market by shopping as intelligently as a demanding private purchaser.

> The federal government alone spent $1 billion in 2002 to buy and lease light vehicles; all governments, billions of dollars.

799. A $1,000/0.01 gpm feebate rate (Greene et al. 2004) would probably reduce demand for cars by ~0.5%, reducing light-vehicle replacement rates by ~100,000 cars/y in 2025. But over the medium-to-long term, this reduces the supply of cars to the secondary market, increasing used-car prices by a couple of percent: e.g., a price elasticity of demand of −1.0 implies that scrapping 1 million cars would raise the average used-vehicle price by $198 (2000 $) in 2005, based on the July 2003 average used-vehicle price of $9,092. See also note 801 and Box 20.

800. Raphael & Stoll 2001; Schachter, Jensen, & Cornwell 1998; Stommes & Brown 2002.

801. The twelfth car offsets the regressivity that might be introduced by feebates. For economic efficiency and Pareto optimality (making someone better off but nobody worse off), we propose decoupling the purchase and scrappage transactions. This would indeed permit focusing scrappage on the least-efficient vehicles, further increasing oil (and perhaps pollution) savings, but our model doesn't assume this.

802. BTS 2001, Fig. 1. Fig. 2 shows 18% of 1999 households were without cars in the central city but only 4% in rural areas.

803. Kallen et al. 1994.

804. Initially, the lease-and-scrap program adopts *Conventional Wisdom* vehicles because of their much lower cost and early availability; later, the program could shift to *State of the Art* cars as they became available. This will increase the rate of saving oil and may reduce the incremental cost to lessees, especially with feebates.

The federal fleet alone in 2002 (light, medium, and heavy vehicles) drove five billion miles and used a third of a billion gallons of fuel.

fleet or another.[805] The federal government alone spent $1 billion in 2002 to buy and lease light vehicles;[806] all governments, billions of dollars. Taxpayers would be better served if the several hundred thousand annual vehicle purchases had efficiency and operational strings attached.

We recommend that federal and state agencies be promptly required to purchase American-made vehicles from the 10% most efficient in their class, subject to operational requirements. This extends the policy of Massachusetts, whose Republican Governor, Mitt Romney, requires purchase of only the most efficient and best-lifecycle-value vehicles, all with ultra-low emissions and no less than 20 mpg city rating (EPA adjusted). His policy also allows purchase of four-wheel-drive vehicles only when "absolutely necessary for emergency or off-road response" (not just helping non-emergency state personnel get to work in inclement weather), and light trucks only where justified by need (such as pickups for highway cleanup); otherwise more efficient platforms must be substituted.[807] Comparable smart procurement is appropriate for light, medium, and heavy vehicles. Since the federal fleet alone in 2002 (light, medium, and heavy vehicles) drove five billion miles and used a third of a billion gallons of fuel,[808] the fuel savings can be considerable. Citizens will have the educational value of seeing more of the most efficient models on the road and the satisfaction of seeing their tax dollars better spent. The shift of market share to makers of the most efficient platforms will encourage the other automakers to develop such platforms. Lifecycle-cost acquisition policies should become universal, and would be strongly reinforced by feebates.

Currently, the top 10% of models within each size class (or subclass if so restricted by operational needs) would include all hybrids and a smattering of other efficient models. To the manufacturer, hybrids today cost more per saved gallon (2004 *Prius* ~$1.75/gal, *Civic Hybrid* ~$2.13/gal)[809] than they will in ~2007 as powertrains' marginal cost falls by half. For example, *Accord Hybrid* and *Camry Hybrid* should then both have a CSE around 80¢/gal. But that's still well above our *State of the Art* ~2010 projection of 56¢/gal, which will itself be a moving target. And even *State of the Art* vehicles, though very worthwhile, have a higher Cost of Saved Energy than the far less efficient but 12¢/gal *Conventional Wisdom* vehicles. The public sector should lead the market shift by backing the highest-saving cost-effective (*SOA*) vehicles, and until those are available, modern hybrids. Many but not all private purchasers (Fig. 36) will choose to do the same, especially when even minimal ($1,000/0.01 gpm) feebates shift their fuel-saving time horizon from 3 to 14 years.

805. FHWA 2002; GSA 2003.

806. GSA 2003.

807. Executive Office for Administration and Finance (Commonwealth of Massachusetts) 2003.

808. GSA 2003.

809. These very rough estimates compare a 2004 *Prius* with a $4,000 (2003 $) incremental retail *cost*—the actual incremental retail price is considerably lower—with a 36-mpg 2004 Toyota *Echo* (there's no exactly comparable model because *Prius* is a "ground-up" new platform). We compare the 2004 *Civic Hybrid* (5-speed manual, 48 mpg) with a 5-speed 2004 *Civic* nonhybrid (34 mpg) and use the actual $2,560 incremental price (2003 $).

"Golden Carrots" and technology procurement

Beyond routine government procurement, there's a wider toolkit of "technology procurement" for pulling new technologies into the market faster. Many variants are in use in many countries. We have evaluated which variants could fit U.S. light-vehicle markets. Box 21 lists some of them, and suggests ample and flexible scope for technology procurement with or without a government role. The focus here is not on the individual technologies that go into a vehicle, but the whole vehicle as a system.[810]

Business risk-takers are best incentivized by real carrots, not just by "sticks painted orange."[810a] A particularly juicy flavor could use existing government procurement programs, often, but not necessarily, civilian, to pull better technologies into production by guaranteeing to buy a certain number of them, for a certain number of years, at a certain minimum price, if they meet certain specifications substantially more advanced than anything now available. The aim is thus not just to buy a widget, but to make much better, even sooner, the widgets that one is buying anyway.

Such governmental "Golden Carrot" programs were pioneered by Hans Nilsson and his colleagues in Sweden, whose Agency for Public Management (Department for energy efficiency [Kansliet] at NUTEK), among other roles, aggregates all public-sector procurement, giving it strong market clout. During 1990–2000, "Golden Carrots" were offered for 32 new energy-saving products in six major categories serving Swedish government buyers and residential, commercial, and industrial customers. Some of those products created new export markets. Various targeted procurement designs were tested.[811] Naturally, each sector turned out to have different success factors, and success varied between projects. But overall, the key to success was the vigor and strict neutrality of the procurement process, with no preference for any firms, countries, or designs. We suggest procurement led by the federal General Services Administration and large states, to offer substantial, high-confidence markets to early providers of advanced technology vehicles. (If aggregation is difficult because of state- or regional-level dealer-relationship arrangements, it may be possible to do "virtual aggregation" unbundled from actual procurement, with appropriate manufacturer netbacks to dealers.) In addition, we suggest dangling an even more valuable kind of carrot for which automakers would stretch even higher.

Governments and large fleet owners buy hundreds of thousands of vehicles every year. That purchasing power can pull very efficient vehicles into the market much earlier.

Business risk-takers are best incentivized by real carrots, not just by "sticks painted orange."

During 1990–2000, "Golden Carrots" were offered for 32 new energy-saving products in six major categories serving Swedish government buyers and residential, commercial, and industrial customers. Some of those products created new export markets.

810. Technology procurement policies with government involvement often don't involve the government as the primary buyer. In cases when the government is the buyer, only in rare circumstances (e.g., military) does it guarantee sales numbers, price, and/or a time period for sales. The buyer could as well be a cooperative of private entities. Independent of who's buying and any level of guarantees, there is normally a coordinator of the whole exercise, and that coordinator is often but not necessarily a government employee. In the absence of guarantees, the coordinator's primary role is to aid market development via a carefully planned set of steps detailed elsewhere; see Olerup 2001.

810a. This phrase is Steve Wiel's when he was a Nevada Public Service Commissioner.

811. Olerup 2001.

812–817. See Box 21 on p. 200.

21: Golden Carrots: theme and variations

Golden Carrots (defined on p. 199) have elicited efficient products from windows (Sweden) to photocopiers (EPA, DOE, and International Energy Agency—a multinational procurement project), from lighting can fixtures and miniature compact fluorescent lamps (Pacific Northwest National Laboratory) to rooftop air conditioners (DOE, PNNL, and Defense Logistics Agency).[812] Golden Carrots have also been used by many European governments, and the resulting lessons are well described.[813] Sweden even undertook an exploratory battery-electric car procurement in 1994–96, including the normal steps: an active buyers' group, media coverage, targeted informational materials, exhibitions, and rewards for providers of the first product batch. All these phases merit in-kind and financial support. Initial production support in a U.S. context could be done by loan guarantee, purchase, or prize. Many combinations are possible: e.g., failing to win a first-past-the-post competition shouldn't exclude other manufacturers from loan guarantees for capacity to make products meeting the criteria.

Golden Carrots are a special case of a broader "Technology Procurement" approach that needn't rely on government procurement, but aims additionally or instead at the general market. The emerging international pattern is for a neutral public body to:

1. organize and aggregate selected high-volume buyers and market influencers (such as utilities),

2. closely understand the business and technology needs of diverse and often fragmented buyers,

3. aggregate those users' specifications into highly desirable product attributes,

4. develop technical specifications with buyers and makers,

5. solicit competitive bids for compliant new products,

6. select one or (preferably) more winning bidders,

7. help them with marketing and customer education to maximize purchase and ensure that diffusion takes root, and

8. keep driving further technological improvements.

Private fleet operators, such as car-rental and taxi companies, would be suitable participants for such aggregations.

Another popular format is to offer a prize paid out as the first x units are sold by cutoff time y. In 1993, the U.S. EPA and 24 utilities, combined into the Consortium for Energy Efficiency (CEE), created the Super-Efficient Refrigerator Program to improve the appliance that uses

(continued on next page)

---

812. PNNL 2003; Hollomon et al. 2002, p. 6.125; Wene & Nilsson 2003.

813. Olerup 2001; Wene & Nilsson 2003; Suvilehto & Öfverholm 1998 (whose Appendix 2 tabulates which activities have been applied to which products); IEA 2003b.

814. Frantz 1993.

815. Whirlpool apparently quietly continued making a comparable model for some time under Sears's Kenmore label. Later, the industry agreed on tighter federal standards from 1998, but after Whirlpool launched an effort to boost efficiency further, its domestic competitors sought and got a three-year delay in the new standards, causing Whirlpool to quit the Association of Home Appliance Manufacturers in protest. Some would draw the sobering lesson that while the competitors were busy using their lobbying muscle to soften the competitive edge that Whirlpool's SERP-driven innovation had gained, foreign competitors were quietly gaining ground on all of them—unsettlingly like the auto business.

"Platinum Carrot" advanced-technology contest

In 1714, the British Parliament offered a huge cash prize—£10,000 to £20,000, depending on precision—for inventing a way to measure ships' longitude. The result prevented countless shipwrecks and revolutionized world trade.[818] In the 1780s, the French Academy offered a 100,000-franc prize for a process to extract sodium hydroxide from sea salt, and so created the modern chemical industry. The 1927 Orteig Prize for which Charles Lindbergh flew the Atlantic was one of about three dozen aviation prizes offered during ~1908–15. Indeed, the lure of privately funded prizes is credited with jumpstarting the U.S. aviation industry, and the 1895 Great Chicago Car Race (based mainly on innovation, not speed) with "giving birth to the American auto industry"[819] by engaging Charles Duryea and his contemporaries in both cooperative and competitive efforts at a time when American car tinkers were scattered and coherent development was centered in Europe. This tradition continues. Round-

> The first firm to make and sell a serious number of highly advanced vehicles should get a ten-figure prize, substituting competitive juice for bureaucratic soup.

> The lure of privately funded prizes is credited with jump-starting the U.S. aviation industry and giving birth to the American auto industry.

818. Sobel 1995. However, John Harrison's precision-clockmaking effort, launched in 1730 and culminating in a half-degree-precise clock in 1761, met with skepticism: the Longitude Board refused to believe longitude could be determined without astronomical measures. It awarded only half the prize, then kept demanding more evidence and more clocks, until ultimately King George III bypassed the Board and awarded the balance.

819. Macauley 2004; NAS/NAE 1999.

Box 21: Golden Carrots:

theme and variations (continued)

about one-sixth of the electricity in American homes. SERP offered a $30-million prize to the manufacturer that could produce, market, and distribute the most efficient refrigerator at the lowest price, using no ozone-depleting chemicals and beating the 1993 federal efficiency standard by at least 25%.[814] Whirlpool beat the 13 other entrants with 30–41%, and the runner-up, Frigidaire, announced that it too would bring its entry to market. The contest accelerated by about six years the U.S. introduction of market-

816. Ledbetter et al. 1999.

817. Later, the New York Power Authority teamed with CEE and the federal Department of Housing and Urban Development to elicit and market an efficient apartment-sized refrigerator via all housing authorities, utilities, and weatherization providers; since 1997, more than 200,000 units with better than doubled efficiency have been installed, kicked off by a 20,000-unit procurement by the New York City Housing Authority (CEE 2004; DOE 2003). Such efforts need to aim high because technology changes quickly. For example, these refrigerators were a useful advance, but they use ~5 times as much electricity as a larger, privately built unit in use at RMI since 1984, which in turn uses ~2–3 times as much as the 2004 state of the art.

leading superefficient refrigerators, even though Whirlpool didn't collect the whole prize (payable as the first quarter-million units were sold) because its sales fell ~30–35% short. The firm dropped the new model before the July 1997 sales deadline, blaming the unit's higher price;[815] federal evaluators cited "insufficient and problematic marketing."[816] But units twofold more efficient still, recently introduced by Danish and Japanese competitors, should soon hit the U.S. market, so Whirlpool was merely ahead of its time and its detractors were short-sighted.[817] Indeed, a general lesson of technology procurement programs is that they often help the losing entrants too: they further refine their products and often come back with seriously competitive products, but meanwhile the process has put the first mover into gear. At worst, such contests help to prepare manufacturers to compete effectively as better products, from makers at home or abroad, begin to attack their core markets.

the-world nonstop flight, human-powered cross-English-Channel flight, and other extraordinary aviation achievements were induced by monetary rewards. At this writing, aerospace composites wizard Burt Rutan and his competitors are vying for the $10-million Ansari X-Prize for the first private space flight.[820]

In 1999, the National Academy of Engineering recommended that Congress encourage more extensive experiments in speeding innovation by prizes and contests.[821] As we demonstrated in the first 32 pages of this book, the goal of bringing drastically more efficient light vehicles into the market is a high national priority: it is important enough to warrant a large incentive. We therefore recommend a federal "Platinum Carrot" prize for the first U.S. automaker that can produce and sell into the market 200,000 uncompromised 60-mpg gasoline-fueled midsize SUVs (or their attribute equivalents in other subclasses), meeting the most advanced emission and safety standards and capable of total gasoline/ethanol fuel flexibility. Qualifying sales could be to any U.S. customers, civil or military, private or governmental, and may permit double-dipping with Golden Carrot incentives, at any prices the parties agree upon.[822]

The prize will have to be large enough to induce several automakers to participate, and provide for recovery of most of the full-program development costs of a next-generation vehicle, say around $1 billion. The goal is to bring new efficiency technologies to market in uncompromised vehicles at a competitive price—hence the sales requirement. Alternatively, the prize could be paid out per vehicle sold; effectively this would be a $5,000/vehicle subsidy to early adopters (worth ~$10k when leveraged to retail), but could help such vehicles work down the cost curve to become fully cost-competitive at production scale. The prize could be winner-take-all, or could be split among the top few contestants (e.g., in a 5:3:1 ratio) according to competitive standing in sales by a certain date.

For comparison, the precompetitive 1993–2001 Partnership for a New Generation of Vehicles spent ~$1.5 billion[823] of federal funds,[824] roughly matched by the Big Three, and its FreedomCAR/FreedomFuel successor was announced as a $1.7-billion program ($0.72 billion new, the rest reprogrammed) spread over five years. As Mary Tolan of Accenture noted, "$1.7 billion over five years does not drive the private sector into

We may have already proposed enough policies on the demand side support to support automakers' financing leapfrogs, not just wanting to. However, the Big Three have such weak balance sheets and guarded competitive prospects that they may simply lack the creditworthiness and liquidity to place the needed big bets—especially to retool in the short term before most of the new market growth has occurred.

820. Additional information available at www.xprize.org.

821. NAS/NAE 1999, p. 1.

822. Entrants might choose to sell at $5,000 below cost if they were confident of making it up by winning the prize—or to discount even deeper if they felt this would win them greater value from first-mover advantage in selling enough vehicles to catch up with their loss-leader discounts. That'd be up to them.

823. In mixed current dollars, as is the following $1.7 billion figure for 2001–06.

824. Often to much better effect than was widely reported. It developed not only useful concept cars (Fig. 10) but also significant manufacturing improvements and, most importantly, major rivalry in advanced technology vehicles, both within the U.S. and worldwide. Reports of deepening rifts between the Big Three over reluctance to do their best work in view of their competitors indicated PNGV's success in this key regard.

Crafting coherent supportive policies: *Federal policy recommendations for light vehicles:* "Platinum Carrot" contest

Implementation

action"[825]—but then again, a billion-dollar prize may get more respect. Both federal automotive programs have had value. But they would be usefully complemented, at the least, by a developer-driven, wholly competitive approach motivated by real money—a competition where all entrants are free to take their best shot in their own way. If successful, the prize could then be repeated with the bar set, say, ~70% higher, corresponding to a fuel-cell version. By then, still further potential, chiefly from more advanced materials, should be evident and worth incentivizing—much as aviation prizes, in less than a century, have progressed in distance from a 25-meter flight to a round-the-world nonstop, and in height from a thousand feet to outer space.

Supporting automotive retooling and retraining

The five preceding initiatives aim to shift demand strongly toward advanced technology vehicles, secure early markets for them, and reduce or remove the market risk of their aggressive development. These initiatives may collectively be big enough to pay for automakers' development and conversion costs for the first one or two million vehicles within a normal business model. We may therefore have already proposed enough prices on the demand side to support automakers' actually financing leap-frogs, not just wanting to.[826] However, we have also argued that the Big Three have such weak balance sheets and guarded competitive prospects that they may simply lack the creditworthiness and liquidity to place the needed big bets—especially to retool in the short term before most of the new market growth has occurred. Such financial constraints on retooling would not be a risk to incur lightly. For the competitive reasons described on pp. 130–137, the outcomes could be worse than Chrysler's need for a $2.6 billion (2000 $) bailout by 1979 federal loan guarantees[827] in the wake of the 1970s oil shocks, than Ford's close approach to a similar fate, and than GM's near-miss in 1992, when it was reportedly within an hour of a fatal credit downgrade.

In the spirit of the task-force report we quoted on p. 178, we therefore assume for present purposes that a convincing case can be made for further support. It would apply to converting production capacity, and probably also to building new capacity, to produce *State of the Art* vehicles and their distinctive key systems and components. U.S. facilities of both automakers and their Tier One and Two suppliers would be eligible. If and as needed, measured and temporary federal conversion support could be structured in several ways, aimed at reducing risk and improving liquidity. We prefer a federal loan guarantee for new or retrofitted plant and equipment installed in the U.S. (but open to all automakers), refundable to the government if utilized and if the plant fails to operate for an agreed period, and specifically targeted to advanced (*SOA*-level) technology vehicle production, tightly defined. Associated retraining would also qualify, again carefully defined. The budgetary cost to the

> Before advanced vehicle markets become large and vibrant, hard-pressed American automakers may need loan guarantees for the liquidity to convert their factories quickly enough to meet demand ahead of foreign competitors.

825. Tolan 2003.

826. Carson 2003 and pp. 130–137 summarize the basic issues: overcapacity, high fixed costs (notably health-care), pension obligations (GM's, with more than two pensioners per employee, exceeds its market cap), rigidities in labor and dealer relationships, and a deteriorating competitive posture.

827. The loans were later repaid, so the federal guarantee was not called, and the government, haven taken the usual equity stake, was able to sell its shares in 1983 for a $311-million profit. The 1990 Federal Credit Reform Act requires the estimated cost of federal credit extensions to be estimated and budgeted; the outstanding total of federal loan guarantees is now well into eleven figures, though presumably most will never be used. Risk can be shared by partial (rather than 100%) guarantees and, at a higher cost, by subordinating the guaranteed debt.

If and as needed, measured and temporary federal conversion support could be structured in several ways aimed at reducing risk and improving liquidity.
We prefer a federal loan guarantee— the support should reward success, not effort.

Treasury would be offset by warrants on the firm's equity, as in the Chrysler bailout, and risk should be shared.[828] We suggest the loan-guarantee format because the borrowers, though enjoying the increased credit and liquidity of the federal debt rating, would be on the hook for the loan and have an incentive to invest it wisely. Direct federal financing should be unnecessary given this alternative, but might be considered for reasons we haven't thought of. Tax credits may be the least attractive option, but if granted, should be paid per vehicle produced to stringent and market-leading (not incremental) efficiency and emissions targets: the support should reward success, not effort.[829]

Using a federal loan guarantee to buy down an automaker's interest rate by about two-fifths is equivalent to cutting ~$153 off the manufacturing cost, hence ~$300 off the retail price, of a typical *State of the Art* vehicle. This is helpful, and should support the early, pre-demand-stimulus retooling rate shown in the solid green line in Fig. 37a (p. 183). But over the long run, it's much less important than the demand stimuli we've proposed. Nor is money the only constraint on how rapidly the industry can change course. Retooling rate is a function of not just investment risk perception and liquidity, but also physical, labor, and institutional constraints and (less easily analyzed but perhaps more important) cultural constraints—how quickly people, especially in groups, can change their attitudes and mindsets. Abundant, cheap financing cannot push these other rate-limiting steps beyond a certain point, so it's highly effective up to a point, but then less so.

The Pentagon can be the biggest money-saver from advanced transportation technologies. Its R&D should lead the rapid development of the advanced materials industrial cluster and other key enabling technologies— investing more money in American ingenuity to save oil, so we can all spend much less trying to get and guard it. Federal energy R&D also needs serious funding, restructuring, and a focus on best buys.

R&D and early military procurement

The "Military vehicles" section, on pages 84–93 above, described the compelling doctrinal, operational, and budgetary reasons for the Pentagon to bring superefficient land, sea, and air tactical platforms rapidly to market. The special logistical burdens of nontactical vehicles, such as the global hauling of materials by heavy trucks and lift aircraft, make these as big a priority as tactical platforms. Science and technology targets for rapid insertion span across the whole gamut of military equipment. They range from cheap but ultralight structural materials (especially advanced composites)—which can also have immediate benefits for theater force protection—to fuel-cell APUs for tanks, other armor, and heavy trucks. Current government and private R&D, both military and civilian, generally emphasizes propulsion systems but badly underinvests in lightweight materials and advanced manufacturing (Fig. 19, p. 64). Most official assessments reinforce this error by virtually ignoring platform physics,

828. Chrysler's equity holders gained more value than the guarantee-protected debt holders (Chen, Chen, & Sears. 1986).

829. This lesson was repeatedly learned the hard way with renewable energy tax credits. Structured to reward expenditure, they attracted rent-seekers to compete with sound firms, spoiled market acceptance with fly-by-night operators and shoddy products, and may even have retarded achievement. Restructured for results, as for the wind production tax credit, they have proven highly successful in driving rapid technological and business learning— except where, as for that particular credit, Congress keeps turning off the tap more or less annually, which is another effective way to kill the U.S. industry and cede its opportunities to foreign competitors.

though encouragingly, lightweight-ing is gaining adherents even faster in DoD than in Detroit. Advanced materials (pp. 159–162) are the nexus where military and civilian needs most clearly converge and where collaboration can advance the oil and national security needs of both communities. This makes it impera-tive to focus DoD's science and technology resources far more intensively on such key enabling technologies for saving fuel. Design competitions to smash the comfortable boundaries of design integration and produce breakthrough efficiency at lower cost should also prove valuable.

> A recent rough estimate suggested that one-sixth of all energy in the United States is consumed by aerodynamic drag in transportation systems, with potential savings around \$20b/y from applying known drag-reduction techniques. The main obstacle is severe fragmentation between institutions and across disciplines.

Basic and applied research focused across intellectual boundaries can pay unexpectedly large dividends. For example, a recent rough estimate suggested that one-sixth of *all* energy in the United States is consumed by aerodynamic drag in transportation systems, with potential savings around \$20b/y from applying known drag-reduction techniques.[830] These estimates may be too high—we estimate that about half, not three-fifths, of U.S. transportation energy overcomes fluid drag—but that's still a huge number meriting a concerted attack. The main obstacle is severe fragmen-tation of effort between institutions and, more seriously, across disci-plines.[831] That opportunity cries out for a focused national civil/military development effort, perhaps organized by DARPA (with Defense Science Board guidance) in concert with diverse civilian experts. Further expan-sion of the sometimes lively collaboration and cross-pollination between military developers (such as DARPA and the Services' research centers) and other centers of excellence (National Laboratories, private firms, and nonprofits) can also speed such technologies' development and transfer to wide civilian use, but will require simpler contracting mechanisms so innovative small groups can play. Risk- and benefit-sharing can accelerate through R&D consortia where, for example, parties keep the intellectual property they brought, but cross-license any results of their collaboration.

Broader reforms in civilian energy R&D are also long overdue.[832] Its real out-lays have fallen by nearly three-fifths since 1980, bringing the U.S. into dead last among top industrial nations in the fraction of R&D devoted to energy.[833] The private sector, far from picking up the slack, is generally slashing even more muscle from its R&D budgets; few Wall Street analysts seem to realize that most industries are eating their seed corn and are gravely underinvest-ing in R&D. Sound civilian energy R&D priorities are also unlikely to emerge from the Department of Energy so long as it remains driven by tra-ditional constituencies and distracted by its mainly nuclear-weapons and waste-cleanup responsibilities; it should be restructured as purely civilian agency with a purely energy-focused mission.[834] Its R&D on manifestly uncompetitive energy technologies (such as fission and fusion) should be halted, greatly increasing the funds available for options that actually show and have proven their promise. DOE's priorities should be realigned to

830. Wood 2004. Further scrutiny may refine the strik-ing initial estimate that 60% of U.S. transportation energy is dissipated by fluid drag. The cost estimates appear dubious in detail but in the right general direction.

831. Including (Wood 2004) "aerodynamics, transportation, hydrodynamics, wind engi-neering, environmental sciences, chemistry, medical engineering, combustion, manufacturing, etc."—and we'd add, materials and, most importantly, biomimetics.

832. PCAST 1997.

833. Margolis & Kammen 1999.

834. Nuclear weapons pro-grams, for example, could go to DoD and nuclear waste management and cleanup to EPA.

emphasize energy efficiency more than supply, to match the nation's energy needs (chiefly for decentralized heat and mobility fuels, not centralized electric power generation), and to strengthen integrative whole-systems insights and design processes.

Automotive efficiency and safety regulation: first, do no harm

Federal regulators are fixing some old auto-safety problems but threatening to make new ones that are as dangerous for automakers as for their customers. New materials and designs can save both lives and oil— if allowed to.

Our feebate-centered policy recommendations, with their targeted supplements (pp. 191–209), should gradually render moot the details of CAFE rules, because virtually all vehicles will beat CAFE handily. However, we meanwhile endorse the Academy's call to abolish those rules' archaic car/light-truck distinction and dual-fuel loophole. And to the extent feebates don't meet and beat CAFE standards, and further CAFE reforms are required, here's our menu of CAFE reforms. We would treat all light vehicles identically in safety regulations (not relax or except the rules for light trucks); abolish the 8,500-lb limit that now lets "heavy light" passenger vehicles like the *Hummer* evade many existing rules; expose all light and "heavy light" vehicles to the gas-guzzler tax (which could, however, be repealed as feebates took effect);[835] extend both efficiency and safety regulation to all Class 3–4 ("light medium") vehicles; repeal the scandalously quadrupled business tax break for vehicles over 6,000 lb;[836] and purge any other incentives for automakers to make vehicles heavier and less efficient. These reforms could be gracefully phased in about as quickly as feebates will eliminate their bite by profitably shifting customer demand toward efficiency.

Our feebate-centered policy recommendations should gradually render moot the details of CAFE rules, because virtually all vehicles will beat CAFE handily.

These reforms could be gracefully phased in about as quickly as feebates will eliminate their bite by profitably shifting customer demand toward efficiency.

More broadly, NHTSA's 2004 CAFE rulemaking must not inhibit or penalize progress toward light-but-safe vehicles (pp. 57–60) by shifting, as now proposed, from fleet-average to weight-based class average efficiency standards that would reward heavier vehicles with looser efficiency requirements and penalize downweighting (except for the heaviest vehicles) with stricter standards. Incentivizing weight would damage national energy security, public safety, and automakers' export prospects, and would so clearly fly in the face of the scientific and engineering evidence before NHTSA[837] that it would invite challenge as arbitrary and capricious. Box 22 suggests ways to reinforce what NHTSA is doing well and correct what it's doing badly.

835. Substituting feebates would incidentally eliminate the gas-guzzler tax's discrimination against cars and in favor of light trucks—much as Germany's 16 states, for example, have recently equalized vehicle taxes between these two classes.

836. This figure is further distorted by the practice of counting SUVs' weight including their rated payload, which is excluded for normal purposes of regulating cars. Under the Jobs and Growth Act 2003, "the entire cost of all but one large SUV—the *Hummer H1*—can be deducted" in the first year by any business buying one for ≥50% business use, up to $100,000; for the *H1*, the total deduction is $106,000 out of the $110,000 price (Taxpayers for Common Sense 2003). Many tax advisors now steer light-vehicle buyers to a list (e.g., Bankrate.com 2003) to ensure that their proposed purchase is *heavy* enough to qualify for the maximum "business" tax break. If any business tax break for light vehicles is desired, it should be at least neutral as to weight, and ideally calibrated to efficiency per unit of interior volume or footprint area (not weight). Meanwhile, things have come to such a pass that on many residential streets in California and elsewhere, thanks to old 6,000-lb weight limits, most of today's larger SUVs are already technically illegal (Bowers 2004).

837. Including Lovins 2004a.   838–839. See Box 21.

NHTSA should mine its data for the engineering reasons why, at any given weight, some vehicles are several times as crashworthy as others: these design differences hold the key to huge, low- or no-cost safety gains without changing cars' manufacturing or materials at all.

22: Realigning auto-safety policy with modern engineering

NHTSA assumes a weight/size relationship as an inflexible fact, when actually it's a major technical policy *variable* that policy should be designed to *influence* strongly; yet neither NHTSA nor the NRC report on which it relied has considered the new materials that can radically decouple size and strength from mass. The agency's weight-based approach rests on logically and technically invalid extrapolation from a dubious *historic correlation* (note 317, p. 60) to the *future causality* of risk in fleets with different designs and, probably very different materials. This led NHTSA to adopt the false assumption that heavier means safer. If the aggressivity and compatibility issues of recent years are any indication, that way lies an even more absurd mass arms race in which you drive a *Hummer*, she drives an 18-wheeler, and he drives a locomotive. Such a future would ensure, not only a greater toll on the roads, but also the isolation and ultimately the failure of American automakers' offerings within more discriminating global markets whose safety rules are based on a rigorous systems engineering approach to crash safety. As we noted on p. 60, the dean of industry safety research, retired GM safety-analysis leader Dr. Leonard Evans, though long a vociferous critic of CAFE standards, agrees that lighter but stronger materials can save fuel, emissions, and lives simultaneously.

838. NHTSA should also intensify its historically weak efforts to distinguish mass from size in its historic crash-safety data; conduct a convincing public analysis to check if its historic weight/risk correlations are artifactual (note 317, p. 60); and most importantly, launch an open public process, in collaboration with European and Japanese lightweight-vehicle safety experts, on how the light-but-safe safety philosophy emerging abroad (note 301, p. 58) can best be refined, allowed, and encouraged in a U.S. context.

839. M. White 2004.

NHTSA should stimulate innovation in making *all* (and particularly large) vehicles lightweight *and* crashworthy *and* compatible with all other vehicles. NHTSA should mine its data for the engineering reasons why, *at any given weight*, some vehicles are several times as crashworthy as others: these design differences hold the key to huge, low- or no-cost safety gains without changing cars' manufacturing or materials at all.[838] Sound science, the rapid emergence of ultralight-vehicle structural and manufacturing options, and common sense all point to the need for a federal safety policy that respects markets, encourages innovation, promotes public health, and advances national competitiveness. Such a policy should:

- be performance-based, not prescriptive; technology-neutral; as far as possible technology-forcing; and supportive, not destructive, of national efficiency goals;

- decouple fuel-economy choices from vehicle-size-class choices (if desired) by encouraging size/mass decoupling, via normalizing fuel intensity to size (e.g., gal/mi per interior ft^3)—*not* to mass;

- be at least neutral as to vehicle mass, carefully avoiding any incentives for a further spiral of the "mass arms race";[839] and

- favor the *downward* rather than upward harmonization of mass within the fleet (if one *does* wish to influence mass).

(continued on next page)

Modest federal ← **policy tweaks can similarly accelerate other kinds of oil-saving technologies and practices throughout the economy.**

New technologies, bioenergy sources, trade rules, and policies can systematically revitalize rural and small-town America while ← **protecting soil, community, and climate.**

Other federal policy recommendations

Supporting investment in domestic energy supply infrastructure

There is a rapidly emerging consensus that accelerating cellulosic biomass conversion and other biofuel production, if done right, is an important part of any oil-displacement strategy. The Energy Future Coalition's Bioenergy and Agriculture Working Group, representing diverse stakeholders, recommends four sensible initiatives:[840]

- Direct DoD to conduct a "fly-off" competition as it does for military hardware, aimed at building 5–10 commercial-scale demonstration plants within five years and testing them to determine which processes work best. This would be funded with $1 billion to be flexibly spent at DoD's discretion. Such a competition should greatly accelerate the early plant phase of development that the private sector would otherwise undertake more timidly, and would be a cheap way to gain the needed technological learning on a timescale that better fits national urgency.

- Increase federal bioenergy R&D funding from $0.15 to $0.5b/y;[841] allocate it more on technical and less on political considerations (Congressional "earmarks" have recently overallocated increased hydrogen funding, but with scant regard to technical merit); and emphasize applied fundamentals.

- Redirect agricultural export subsidies—to be purged under the 1 August 2004 World Trade Organization agreement—to developing biofuel markets in ways that conserve soil and that encourage, measure, and reward carbon fixation in soil. The National Research Council should assess the impacts of shifting crop subsidies to soil conservation, energy crops, and the bioenergy industry. (Some private assessments have lately suggested that the phaseout of subsidies would suffice to put the bioenergy industry on a sound footing as a durable source of income to revitalize farm, ranch, and forest economies and cultures.)

840. EFC 2003, "App. A: Working Group Reports: Report of the Bioenergy and Agriculture Working Group."

841. For comparison, the 2002 Clean Coal Technology Initiative allocated $2 billion over 10 years to R&D for coal—a massive, profitable, and centuries-old industry. The 2002 Farm Bill allocated $75 million for biofuel R&D over 6 years.

22: Realigning auto-safety policy with modern engineering (continued)

Meanwhile, NHTSA's commendable efforts of the past few years to reduce the aggressivity and incompatibility of high, heavy vehicles (such as large SUVs and pickups), and to improve their stability, should be strongly encouraged and accelerated. Innovations like Honda's Advanced Compatibility Engineering Body Structure—already on the market in Japan and about to enter the U.S. market—prove the effectiveness and economy of such redesign. During the transitional period, while very heavy "light" vehicles continue to be offered, and while light (though not necessarily smaller) vehicles increase their market share, such design reforms will be especially important to public safety. Of course, driver behavior, such as intoxication and seat-belt usage, is enormously more important to safety than vehicle design, and should continue to be seriously addressed by NHTSA and law-enforcement agencies.

- Use government policy to increase the use of bioproducts and assess their benefits, for example:

    ○ Adopt a national renewable-fuels standard[842] and an electricity renewable portfolio standard.

    ○ Expand existing tax incentives for renewable energy production (e.g., windpower's Production Tax Credit) to include environmentally acceptable but wasted biomass.

    ○ Give other fuels with equal or better lifecycle environmental performance the same tax treatment afforded to [corn-derived] ethanol under current law (i.e., create a level playing field between all biofuels).[843]

    ○ Develop USDA labeling for biobased content, and encourage government procurement of such products.

    ○ Increase EPA's efforts to promote alternative transportation fuels in ozone nonattainment areas.

The only Working Group recommendation we disagree with is that automakers should continue to receive CAFE credits for "flex-fuel" vehicles. Although our feebate proposal should rapidly render CAFE irrelevant, we think any requirements for the capability to use alternative fuels should be separate from those for fuel economy. In addition:

- As we noted earlier (p. 107), within about a decade, the fuel flexibility of at least E85 and preferably Brazilian-style "total flex" vehicles should be the norm for new U.S. light vehicles; otherwise cellulosic ethanol supply, blended or neat, could outrun the fleet's ability to use it.

- The official definition of "biodiesel" should be broadened to include all neat or blendable diesel fuels made from wastes; the current congressional definition, written to advance certain crop producers' interests, uses a narrow chemical definition and feedstock requirement (favoring virgin and edible feedstocks over used and inedible ones), and even excludes bio-oils blendable with petroleum diesel fuel. The best waste streams to begin with are those already being collected, especially if they now incur a disposal cost.

In Sweden, whose farming and forestry sectors provide a strong platform for biofuels, the government is suggesting a requirement for half of the biggest filling stations to offer at least one renewable fuel by 2008, and will soon require public procurement to buy efficient fuel-flexible cars and fill them with renewable fuels. Many of the larger Swedish cities already offer free parking for hybrids and flexible-fuel vehicles, exempt them from the forthcoming (2005) Stockholm congestion charge, and reduce by 20% the usage tax on company cars if they're environmentally preferred. Sweden and other European countries also have well-advanced plans and propos-

In Sweden, the government is suggesting a requirement for half of the biggest filling stations to offer at least one renewable fuel by 2008, and will soon require public procurement to buy efficient fuel-flexible cars and fill them with renewable fuels.

842. The Senate has passed a 5-billion-gal/y-by-2012 ethanol standard, meant mainly to boost corn ethanol production from its current 3 billion gal/y. We think 5 billion gal/y is likely to be exceeded anyhow, but would like to encourage the rapid development of cellulosic ethanol. Three good methods would be to set the bar much higher, e.g., 25 billion gal/y by 2015 (10% of U.S. motor fuel), perhaps twice that by around 2020; to establish a credit trading system to elicit least-cost solutions; and to count multiple credit, phased down from an initial value of say 3:1, for each gallon of cellulosic ethanol in order to reward early adopters, then taper off that incentive as the technology matures. More broadly, since innovation by definition will produce surprises, we urge its broad encouragement by encouraging all kinds of conversion of waste streams into mobility fuels, emphasizing those compatible with existing infrastructure. Otherwise, biofuels policy will continue to be balkanized by the rent-seeking behavior of specific technology advocates, channel owners, and feedstock producers.

843. We expect these subsidies would trend downwards, and would not need to exceed subsidies to gasoline if gasoline's price properly reflected its social cost.

als for filling stations that provide, as some already do, a diverse and flexible mixture of fuels: a normal gasohol (E5–E10) or similar gasoline-ethanol blend that any unconverted car can use (such as Brazilian-style E22), E85, hydrous ethanol (with due care in cold climates), various biodiesel blends, and hydrogen. The menu would gradually evolve away from oil, toward renewables, and toward a higher hydrogen/carbon ratio. Rural filling stations where ethanol is available, but natural gas is not, could advantageously choose deliveries of just ethanol and gasoline (ultimately just ethanol) and, as demand justifies, could reform some of the ethanol onsite to hydrogen for fuel-cell vehicles.[844] Perhaps direct-ethanol fuel cells will make the reforming altogether unnecessary.[845]

Our other previous biofuel recommendations (pp. 107–110) include: changing the Conservation Reserve Program rules to allow perennial no-till cropping of soil-holding energy crops, especially in polyculture; promoting low- and no-input production of such feedstocks; and establishing recommended-practices standards for domestic-biofuel production, and labeling and tracking for imported-biofuel production, so that bioenergy helps to protect and enhance tilth, not degrade it. We also urge great care in developing, licensing, and applying genetically modified organisms for biofuel production: some being created, especially those that can digest both C5 and C6 sugars, could do immense mischief if they escaped, propagated, and perhaps swapped their genes into other organisms. Current U.S. regulatory structures are not up to this task: national regulation of GMO crops was indeed structured so that *nobody* is responsible for ensuring public health and safety—especially the manufacturers that wrote the rules.[846]

Encouragingly, biofuels can nicely reconcile legally acceptable ways to strengthen rural economies with the 1 August 2004 World Trade Organization's agreement to phase out export and crop subsidies in developed countries (notably the U.S. and EU). (These subsidies were deemed to be an impermissible bias against developing-country farmers.) Support for rural economies can now be done not for its own sake but as fair compensation for providing valuable public and private nonagricultural services: from renewable energy supply to soil protection to carbon sequestration. A recent legal analysis found that America's soil conservation programs and biofuel and renewable energy development programs do comply with WTO rules, because these programs: have clear environmental and conservation objectives, don't distort global trade through direct price supports, and meet certain program-specific criteria such as minimum periods of land set-asides. However, to insulate these programs from WTO attack, the analysis recommends that Congress legislatively confirm the programs' clear environmental and conservation purposes and document their environmental benefits.[847]

America's soil conservation programs and biofuel and renewable energy development programs do comply with WTO rules.

844. Reforming ethanol requires a higher temperature than natural gas but lower than gasoline, and not only allows but welcomes water content, which can even be much higher than would be permissible as a direct vehicular fuel.

845. An autothermal ethanol reformer has been demonstrated (Deluga et al. 2004).

846. Lovins 1999.

847. Dana 2004.

Heavy-vehicle policy

We already proposed proven regulatory changes that could greatly increase the purely technological oil savings available from heavy trucks (p. 74, note 367; p. 75, note 369), including:

- Raise federal Gross Vehicle Weight Rating (GWVR) to the European norm of 110,000 lb, trailer length from 53 to 59 ft, and trailer height from 13.5 to 14 ft (some states have already done these or more).

- Allow double- and triple-trailer combinations if accompanied by disc brakes that increase braking power per pound of GWVR so as to improve safety.

- Remove obstacles to expanded stacking-train rail and rail-to-truck transloading, so railways are better used for long hauls via expanded truck-rail-truck intermodality.

- Reduce heavy-truck speed limits to 60 mph.

- Remove any regulatory obstacles to consolidating loads with large carriers.

Properly done, these should sustain or improve safety and not increase (possibly decrease) road wear. There might be a modest need to accelerate repair of the most deficient bridges, but this should be done anyway for public safety.

Objective national research should also seek to resolve over the next few years whether advanced filtration, computer controls, and other methods can make light-vehicle diesel engines acceptable in California and other areas with strict air quality standards (especially for ultrafine particulates). German automakers seem to think so; as mentioned earlier, they've persuaded Chancellor Schröder to ask the EU to accelerate by three years the new Euro-5 standards, which from 2010 could cut fine particulates by up to 99%. EPA, which has been tightening its standards as medical research reveals more unpleasant surprises, is skeptical and may require considerably lower emissions; so may California regulators, who are allowed to set their own stricter standard. In any event, resolving this issue is a vital prerequisite to rethinking emissions from future diesel-powered heavy vehicles, and hence for the U.S. role for biodiesel (though not for ethanol). If diesel technology turned out to be unacceptable for long-run public health, such alternatives as fuel cells would need to be accelerated. Meanwhile, welcome recent initiatives are starting to clean up off-road, railway, and marine diesels through better technology, lower-sulfur fuel, and reduced idling (substituting APUs or dockside hookups)—Canadian locomotives turn out to idle 54–83% of the time.[848]

Simple reforms, many already adopted by states or foreign countries, can greatly improve Class 8 trucks' efficiency and profitability while safeguarding public health and safety.

Welcome recent initiatives are starting to clean up off-road, railway, and marine diesels through better technology, lower-sulfur fuel, and reduced idling.

848. WBCSD 2004, p. 92.

Regulatory reform
in fuel, gate, and slot
pricing can give
airlines a fair shot at
success and improve
the quality of travel.

Aircraft policy

Aviation fuel's treaty-bound freedom from taxation may be coming to an end, none too soon. We suggest that this distortion (competing mobility fuels are taxed, often heavily) be corrected by environmental user fees, on the emerging European model. Zürich and some other European airports have also pioneered variable but revenue-neutral landing fees calibrated to the noise, emissions, or other nuisances of the various types of aircraft, so as to signal correctly their relative public value. Nearly half of landings at Zürich now pay less than before, while the most polluting planes pay 35% more in a steep graduated fee structure meant to accelerate cleanup.

Besides the loan-guarantee/scrappage program suggested on p. 191, we suggest policy encouraging a level playing field for hub-and-spokes vs. point-to-point business models. In practice, this would mean allocating gates and slots through the market rather than letting them continue to be hoarded by "fortress hub" monopolists.[849] If that means the monopolists can't compete with point-to-point carriers, that should be their problem, not their customers'.

Charging drivers
what driving really
costs, making
markets in avoided
travel, and designing
communities around
people, not cars,
can make access
and mobility cheaper,
fairer, and more
pleasant.

The best way not to
need to travel is to be
already where you
want to be, so you
needn't go some-
where else.

Other transportation policy

A fully rounded transportation policy to foster affordable mobility with less or no oil is not all about vehicles and fuels. It must also deal with dwindling gasoline tax revenue (as vehicles become more efficient, and perhaps switch to other fuels that may not be taxed the same as gasoline), improved intermodal transportation, and smart growth.

The core of any sensible transportation policy is to allow and promote fair competition, at honest prices, between all ways of getting around or of not needing to. The best way "not to need to travel," i.e. to generate "negatrips," is to be already where you want to be, so you needn't go somewhere else. That could mean more sensible land-use, plus virtual mobility that moves only the electrons while leaving the heavy nuclei behind.[850] Another key element of transportation policy is to ensure equitable access for all Americans, in ways that improve customer choice, the quality of our communities, and the air we all breathe.

Real-time,
congestion-based
road pricing
is a good replace-
ment for lost gasoline
tax revenues.

Shifting taxation from fuel to roads and driving

More efficient vehicles will reduce fuel purchases and hence motor-fuel tax revenues, even if all forms of fuel, including biofuels and hydrogen, are taxed comparably to gasoline (which would be counterproductive and hard to justify from economic principles, since gasoline taxes are supposed to reflect externalities, not a mere desire for government revenue).

---

849. The airport nearest RMI's headquarters is dominated by such a firm, with the result that—in between the sporadic periods it had competitors over the past two decades—the airline has sometimes charged more to fly 25 minutes to its fortress hub in Denver than to fly from there to Europe.

850. Many transportation policy achievements and proposals are surveyed in Hawken, Lovins, & Lovins 1999, pp. 40–47.

Offsetting this tax loss will require other ways to fund building and repairing roads, bridges, and other highway infrastructure.[851] To be sensible, forward-looking, and economically efficient, user fees charged on roads or driving should be real-time and congestion-based: if government is charging such fees, it might as well do it in a way that reflects the true social cost of taking a trip right now. Signaling that cost will reduce the need to build and maintain infrastructure in the first place, as well as save time, accidents, and pollution. Signaling that cost also allows fair competition by other modes of physical mobility and, indeed, by other means of access, such as substituting virtual for physical mobility, or co-location to design out the need for travel.

There is extensive and encouraging experience, particularly in Europe, with real-time and congestion-based tolling on highways for both passenger and freight vehicles.[852] Another handy tool is cordon pricing in cities, similar to the policy recently introduced in London, which cut traffic by 16% within months, and to those used in several Norwegian cities and in Singapore.[853] U.S. experiments with electronic tolling and other forms of automatic road charges[854] are encouraging, and the interoperable telemetric devices emerging throughout the Northeast could be adapted to real-time congestion-based pricing. The same is true of parking fees[855] and bridge and ferry tolls: if they're charged electronically, the cost of adding time and congestion information is usually small. Some privately built highways even charge a toll based on real-time congestion, but guarantee its refund if a "service quality guarantee" (so many minutes to a given destination) isn't met; then drivers can decide if reduced time-of-travel-uncertainty is worth the price.

A realistic, cost-based approach to driving would for the first time send efficient market signals to drivers, reducing sprawl, travel, congestion, pollution, and oil use. It would ensure that drivers not only get what they pay for, but also pay for what they get. And it would improve equity between drivers and the one-third of Americans—a growing class as our demographic grays—who are too old, young, poor, or infirm to drive. Sooner or later, this "immobilized class" will start insisting that drivers pay their own way without burdening the taxes of those who can't drive and thus end up paying twice for mobility—once for the socialized costs of others' car-based mobility, and again for their own alternatives.

> User fees charged on roads or driving should be real-time and congestion-based.

> A realistic, cost-based approach to driving would ensure that drivers not only get what they pay for, but also pay for what they get. And it would improve equity between drivers and the one-third of Americans who are too old, young, poor, or infirm to drive.

851. To offset gasoline-tax revenues lost to greater fuel economy (p. 41), we had to assume some unspecified mix of user fees totaling ~24¢/gal-equivalent to sustain 2004 revenues and 62¢/gal to achieve revenues scaled to EIA's 2025 forecast. Some ways of doing this are more efficient, effective, and palatable than others, but the choice should be local and isn't ours to make.

852. Perkins 2002; Viegas 2002; Perett 2003.

853. IEA (2001) estimates that cordon pricing in all major metropolitan areas could cut 2010 light-vehicle consumption by ~3–6% (IEA 2001, p. 15). Acceptance by the public is typically raised by linking toll-ring revenue to improvements in public transportation and transport infrastructure.

854. IEA (2001, p. 110) and California's SR-91 experience suggest that allowing toll-paying drivers with low occupancy to use HOV lanes, so they become "HOT" (High Occupancy/Toll) lanes, increases those lanes' utilization and acceptance, and that their usage is increased mainly by a diverse set of drivers suffering occasional urgency rather than by wealthy drivers using them routinely.

855. Overprovision of seemingly free parking is the biggest single cause of U.S. urban congestion. Parking cash-out—so driving competes more fairly with other modes of mobility and access—is a useful solution (IEA 2001). If combined with a U.S. national parking tax of $1/h (up to $3/d), parking cash-out is estimated to be able to cut light-vehicle travel, fuel use, and CO_2 by 4–7% by 2010 (IEA 2001, p. 16).

A whole-systems ◄───
approach to trans-
portation should
focus on intermodal
competition, integra-
tion, and innovation-
risk management.

The Houston-sized
city of Curitiba has
the second-highest
car ownership in
Brazil but the lowest
car drivership, the
cleanest urban air,
and the highest
quality of life.

Avoiding unwanted
mobility is the most
powerful long-run ◄───
focus for transporta-
tion policy.

856. CyberTran
(www.cybertran.com),
for example, being an ultralight rail system manyfold
cheaper, more compact,
and more flexible than conventional light rail, holds
promise for retrofit within
as well as between cities.
Unfortunately it falls
through the cracks between
conventional categories, so
it has long been unable to
attract the program-defined
government R&D funding it
merits. The technology was
originally developed at the
Idaho National Engineering
Laboratory as an alternative
to the hour-long bus com-
mute to the remote site for
experimental nuclear reactors, but that didn't create a
niche for it within DOT.

Integrating transportation systems

A fair transportation policy would also include improved intermodal
and mass transit options such as Bus Rapid Transit and improved light
rail. (Western Europeans use their well-integrated and convenient public
transport for a tenth of their urban trips; Canadians, 7%; Americans,
2%. The Houston-sized city of Curitiba has the second-highest car ownership in Brazil but the lowest car drivership, the cleanest urban air, and
the highest quality of life.) It's unrealistic to expect most American cities
to approach downtown Tokyo's 92%-rail commuting, but uncivilized to
have a rail system that many cities in the developing world would scorn.
With new technologies ranging from CyberTran® to hybrid-electric bicycles, American industry could indeed zoom ahead of foreign competitors—if the U.S. government had the flexibility to recognize and support
such innovations' emergence,[856] e.g., by insuring against first-adopter
technical risk, much as EPA used to do for innovative wastewater systems. (If the novel wastewater system didn't work, despite the expectations of EPA's technical experts, EPA would pay for replacing it with a
conventional one, so the early adopter could seek the benefits without the
risk.) Similar risk management could break the logjam on commercializ-
ing technologies like CyberTran.

Is this trip necessary (and desired)?

Sound policy would also include encouraging smart growth designed to
reduce sprawl and the need for driving. Most importantly, it would stop
subsidizing and mandating sprawl, so we would have much less of it.
Personal mobility in America is often as undesired as it's excessive.
It comes increasingly from the deliberate segregation and dispersion of
where we live, work, shop, and play, and its effect is to fragment our
time, erode our communities, weaken our families, and raise our taxes to
pay costs incurred by developers but socialized to everyone. Americans
travel more miles than all other industrial nations combined, and U.S.
light vehicles emit as much greenhouse gases as all of Japan. This is neither necessary nor economic, and it may not be making us happier.
Indeed, designing cities around cars, not people, makes them unlivable.
And it is hardly a worthy model for the rest of the world, which as a
whole is only half as good at birth control for cars as for people.

Finally, a good transportation policy would tackle problems in freight
transportation, creating a more efficient intermodal system that would
shift freight transport from trucks to rail and/or ships as much as possible and worthwhile. A comprehensive, economically efficient transportation policy for both goods and people is vital, but its design is outside the
scope of this study, and our savings calculations assume none of it.

Non-transportation federal policy

The main oil-saving national policies we suggest outside the sphere of transportation are few and simple. For example, the same discount-rate arbitrage that we suggest for vehicle buyers would also make sense in buildings and industry, so anyone considering buying energy efficiency will take as long a view of its benefits as society does. The many ways to do this include: proposed laws (such as S.2311 and H.R. 4206 in 2004) offering comprehensive tax incentives for substantial long-lived efficiency improvements in equipment and buildings;[857] broader and faster building and equipment efficiency standards; further improvements in and enforcement of procurement policies; fundamental improvements in how buildings and equipment are *designed*;[858] feebates for buildings (as a few jurisdictions now do for water and sewer hookups); educating real-estate-market actors about the valuable labor-productivity, retail-sales, and financial-return benefits of efficient buildings;[859] and applying widely an innovation now used to make the capital market for energy savings efficient by providing a standard way to measure, aggregate, and securitize them just like home mortgages.[860]

Federal energy policy should take a coherent approach to mobility and access, land-use, and safety. A more difficult but equally important shift would be to ensure that our energy prices tell the truth—shorn of subsidies and reflecting external (larcenous) costs now imposed on people at other times and places than the energy point of sale. We hope we live to see such honest prices. Another critical policy objective would be to encourage and permit all ways to produce and save energy to compete fairly, no matter which kind they are, what technology they use, how big they are, or who owns them. That fundamental reform would be revolutionary in a system long attuned to constituents' needs rather than the broad public interest.

With or without these basic reforms, a more subtle, seldom noticed, and perhaps even more important federal opportunity offers arguably the greatest single leverage point in national energy policy: correcting a glaringly perverse incentive in the retail price formation of regulated gas and electric distribution utilities in 48 states, as noted in the next section. This principle could be federally articulated and encouraged,[861] even though its implementation is largely a matter for the states, (including Territories and Tribes), to whose responsibilities and opportunities we turn next.

> Proven methods of pricing, finance, and design can help use energy in ways that save money. An even more revolutionary notion: let all ways to produce or save energy compete fully and fairly.

> The same discount-rate arbitrage that we suggest for vehicle buyers would also make sense in buildings and industry, e.g., via feebates for buildings and by applying widely an innovation now used to make the capital market for energy savings efficient: by providing a standard way to measure, aggregate, and securitize them just like home mortgages.

857. This is not just for saving electricity: PG&E estimates that by 2001, standards and utility incentives had cut California's direct use of natural gas (not for power generation) by more than one-fifth.

858. RMI's *10XE* ("Factor Ten Engineering") project aims to change fundamentally how engineering is done and taught, so as to achieve radical—order-of-magnitude—energy and resource savings, usually at lower capital cost and with improved performance. Hawken, Lovins, & Lovins 1999 give examples.

859. Note 541 and Innovest 2002, which found one-third better stock-market and financial performance by leaders in energy management within the commercial property sector. Similar studies for the retail merchandising and retail food sectors are found at Energy Star, undated.

860. Such as the International Performance Measurement and Verification Protocol, www.ipmvp.org, now used nearly worldwide to finance energy and water savings, both new and retrofit, in the private, public, and nonprofit sectors.

861. Before the current expansionist tendencies of the Federal Energy Regulatory Commission's jurisdiction—defined by the 1932 Federal Power Act as relating solely to interstate power transactions—there was ample and often encouraging precedent for federal laws that required each state at least to consider certain utility regulatory reforms. Unfortunately, in recent years some state and federal courts have flatly ignored key provisions of such landmark federal laws as the National Utility Regulatory Policies Act (1978), on the strange principle that since some states have restructured their electricity markets, PURPA must be a dead letter nationwide, even though Congress forgot to repeal it.

States: incubators and accelerators

If the federal government doesn't lead, it should follow by letting the states try experiments, then perhaps standardizing what would work best nationwide. And if the federal government won't follow, it should get out of the way: not preempt state experiments that create public goods (from Maryland feebates to California CO_2 reductions), not favor the worst buys first, and not reward the opposite of what we want (e.g., paying oil companies to find oil, the Pentagon to protect it, and a business owner to buy a *Hummer* to waste it).

It is constitutionally axiomatic, but often forgotten, that under federalism, powers not specifically reserved to the national government are reserved to the states. The states have their own challenges, but on the whole, their vast diversity and greater grassroots vitality tend to make their governments more creative, dynamic, and accountable than the often-gridlocked federal government. Moreover, states can interact more directly with communities—an even more accountable and often effective level of action than state government. Thus a galaxy of extraordinarily effective energy-saving actions were conceived and executed at a city, county, town, village, and neighborhood level all across America in the 1970s and early 1980s, often encouraged by state energy offices funded by the U.S. Department of Energy.[862] Those successes, now forgotten by all but old-timers,[863] offer an encouraging template for reforging the links between government, civil society, and the ultimate engines of action—the social atoms of the firm, household, and individual.[864]

Transportation

The Northeast Advanced Vehicle Consortium in New England,[865] and the network of sophisticated California agencies with their Northeastern counterparts who prefer California's to federal air standards, illustrate strong state leadership in transportation. They provide a framework for implementing feebates at a regional or state level if federal action falters. As we noted earlier (p. 189), federal preemption could be avoided by careful legislative drafting, even if the federal government refused to waive the CAFE authority whose legally mandated bar-raising it's been refusing to implement. States are also free to implement scrappage programs, as some already have.[866]

In such areas as utility and insurance regulation, car- and fuel-tax collection, and land-use, states and localities are emerging as leading innovators.

If the federal government won't follow, it should get out of the way and not reward the opposite of what we want (paying oil companies to find oil, the Pentagon to protect it, and a business owner to buy a *Hummer* to waste it).

States have a large and effective menu of ways to lead in transportation reforms.

862. At that time, DOE had a lively local-programs office led by Tina Hobson (now Senior Fellow at Renew America). Federal funds were later slashed by more than 80%, but Congress still provides ~$0.3b/y. The National Association of State Energy Officials (www.naseo.org), with a vast reservoir of field experience, illustrates the extent of this underinvestment by noting that Alabama's commercial/industrial efficiency program generated more than $750 for each dollar spent. Only a few states, such as California and North Carolina, have durably institutionalized their energy efforts, and many are at annual risk of disappearing into budget-deficit crevasses.

863. Outstanding examples are reviewed by Alec Jenkins in Lovins & Lovins 1982, Ch. 17, pp. 293–334.

864. Political theory has a lot to say about the relationship between the individual and the nation-state, but is relatively weak on the structure and function of communities. RMI's Economic Renewal Program has long found communities a peerless arena for social innovation.

865. Additional information available at www.navc.org.

States are the almost exclusive arbiters of the ground-rules that govern zoning, land-use, road pricing, and other basic underpinnings of travel demand. Those policies can either incur or avoid the "enormous costs of sprawl," which a Bank of America study found "has shifted from an engine of California's growth to a force that now threatens to *inhibit* growth and degrade the quality of our life."[867] States can also encourage local use of sprawl-reducing mortgages, such as Fannie Mae's *Location Efficient Mortgage* and *Smart Commute* products,[868] to achieve major increases in disposable income and reductions in traffic.[869] In addition, states can:

- Adopt Pay-at-the-Pump collision liability insurance (Box 23, p. 218)— an excellent candidate for national standardization once state and regional models have been refined. It should save ~$11 billion a year.

- Supplement national or state feebates with direct auto-dealer incentives. The sales associate who pockets a $100 special state bonus for selling a superefficient car, on top of normal commission, will push such sales more enthusiastically.

- Pay carrying charges for dealers to stock superefficient but not ordinary cars. This would incentivize automakers to fill the inventory pipeline with diverse advanced-technology models, especially in areas served by smaller dealers. Otherwise, initially thin sales might reduce advanced vehicles' public exposure by making them a special-order item that sells poorly because there are none on the lot.

- Realign light vehicles' registration fees not so much with market value as with lifecycle value—market value plus present-valued lifetime fuel consumption—so the public-goods value of efficient vehicles is re-signaled annually.[870] (Even better would be to include clear externalities.) The current *ad valorem* system encourages drivers to hang onto old, inefficient cars rather than buy new, efficient ones.

> A galaxy of extra-ordinarily effective energy-saving actions at a city, county, town, village, and neighborhood level all across America in the 1970s and early 1980s offer an encouraging template for reforging the links between government, civil society, and the ultimate engines of action—the social atoms of the firm, household, and individual.

> The sales associate who pockets a $100 special state bonus for selling a superefficient car, on top of normal commission, will push such sales more enthusiastically.

> Realign light vehicles' registration fees not so much with market value as with *lifecycle* value—market value plus present-valued lifetime fuel consumption—so the public-goods value of efficient vehicles is re-signaled annually.

866. Howevor, some further **state actions** remain ensnarled. Many states have long wanted to offer hybrid cars free access to HOV lanes, but most have concluded this is illegal until EPA corrects a regulatory mistake that makes such discretionary access—meant to save oil—depend not on the vehicles' fuel economy but solely on whether they burn an approved alternative *fuel.*

867. Bank of America et al. 1996

868. Modeled on Fannie Mae's *Energy Efficient* and *Home Performance Power* products, which finance energy-saving home improvements (new or retrofit) and apply the proceeds to mortgage qualification ratios, these products increase borrowing power for homebuyers whose location near workplaces or transit can reduce their commuting costs. These innovations are all part of Fannie Mae's ten-year, $2-trillion *American Dream Commitment*® to bring homeownership to an additional 18 million Americans in targeted groups.

869. Studies in three cities found that, compared with sprawl, higher urban density cuts driving by up to two-fifths, proximity to transit by one-fifth (Holtzclaw et al. 2002).

870. Implementing the OECD "Polluter Pays Principle" (which the U.S. officially accepts in principle), most European car ownership taxes depend on some combination of engine type and displacement, fuel type, vehicle age, and gross vehicle weight (in Sweden, Norway, and the Netherlands). British and French ownership taxes depend on CO_2 emissions. Denmark's move from a weight- to an inefficiency-based tax in 1997 has cut fuel intensity by 0.5 km/L (1.2 mpg) for gasoline vehicles and by 2.3 km/L (5.4 mpg) for diesel vehicles. Emissions may also be considered, as in Tokyo and some other Japanese prefectures, to correct the current perverse incentives that clean new vehicles are taxed at far higher rates than dirty old ones (Hirota & Minato 2002).

23: Pay-at-the-Pump car insurance

Since both insurance and state fuel taxation are state issues, a key opportunity for state leadership to save light-vehicle fuel and reduce the cost of driving, especially for low-income citizens, is Pay-at-the-Pump (PATP) automotive liability insurance.[871] Current third-party auto collision insurance costs the same no matter how few or many miles are driven.[872] Many drivers buy no insurance, usually because they can't afford it, and hope they won't get caught (most don't, though there may be consequences).[873] Those who drive less or play by the rules thus subsidize both high-mileage and uninsured drivers. Moreover, since low-income people drive only about half as many miles as the well-to-do, they pay about twice as much per mile, thus cross-subsidizing the rich—and paying not in affordable slices but in unaffordably large chunks.[874] PATP was suggested as far back as 1925, and Senator Moynihan tried to include it in his 1967 reforms.[875] With the socialized costs of uninsured motorists (and resulting litigation) rising, this idea's time has finally come, in a hybrid form that melds the best of the PATP and traditional insurance payment systems, and should overcome the objections sometimes raised to previous versions.

Specifically, we propose that basic third-party property-damage and bodily-injury insurance be bought at the fuel pump via the existing state fuel-tax system and repaid to each state's insurance issuers in proportion to their current-year market share. Other insurance and extra coverage would be paid to one's chosen company just as now, trued up for any risk premia or for competitive differences between insurers. This is simply a smarter way to pay about one-third of your insurance bill, and reduces everyone's bills because there are no longer any uninsured motorists (you can drive without insurance, but not without fuel). Uninsured motors would be automatically assigned to a carrier *pro rata* on their market share. Insurance companies would gain more customers with no marketing effort; PATP should sustain or improve their profitability.

PATP also reminds drivers every time they refill the tank that part of the variable cost of driving is exposure to collision risk, and that, like fuel use, this cost can be reduced by driving less. To this extent, the variabilized price signal would be more efficient than the present flat-rate lump-sum.[876] It might seem at first that drivers of efficient cars get cross-subsidized by drivers of

(continued on next page)

871. Khazzoom 2000. A well-known popular treatment (Tobias 1993) entangled the concept with no-fault and partly public insurance—among the main reasons the insurance industry successfully opposed it in every state where a campaign was run at the time.

872. Although accident rates don't vary linearly with miles driven, they do depend more on congestion, which is related to collective driving: by definition, traffic density equals vehicle-miles divided by lane-miles of capacity. Obviously, too, driving more miles exposes you to more potential accidents.

873. Collision liability insurance or its equivalent is mandatory throughout the United States. The Insurance Information Institute (www.iii.org/individuals/auto/a/canidrive) states that NH, TN, and WI require only financial responsibility, FL requires only property-damage liability coverage, and the other 46 states and District of Columbia require both bodily-injury and property-damage liability coverage.

874. The last survey data (1993), from EIA 1997's *Household Vehicles Energy Consumption 1994* (this survey was discontinued in 1994 but may perhaps be revived), showed 49% fewer miles/vehicle-y at household incomes <$15,000 than for those ≥$50,000 (Khazzoom 2000a, p. 26). Interestingly, the respective average vehicle efficiencies were 19.8 and 20.1 mpg. Not surprisingly, a 1993 survey of 799 low- and moderate-income Californians found 89% in favor of PATP—96% among the majority without insurance (Khazzoom 2000a, p. 25)—and the concept was strongly supported by low-income advocacy groups (Khazzoom 2000a, p. 24, note 38).

875. Khazzoom 2000a.

876. Unlike "Pay as you Drive" insurance—another way to variabilize the cost—there's no need to check how many miles each car travels (via periodic odometer checks or real-time GPS or other telemetry), and all drivers are covered to the extent they drive, rather than leaving some with the option of driving uninsured. The PATP portion of insurance premia would be automatically adjusted up or down with fleet fuel economy. It also marginally incentivizes fuel economy.

- Encourage localities to grant parking preferences to efficient cars, as some American and European cities already do.

- Help their highway departments buy rubberized asphalt early and often to capture the states' dominant share of the $8b/y of agency savings on paving costs. Some of these savings may then be recycled into accelerated bridge upgrades and repairs (p. 211).

Electricity and natural-gas pricing

Saving natural gas, largely by saving electricity, is a key element of displacing oil, so we must pay attention to all three forms of energy, not just the direct use of oil. States have original and unique jurisdiction relating to all three, such as intrastate transportation and the retail pricing of electricity and natural gas. Almost every state has a utility commission that regulates jurisdictional private (and sometimes, in part, public) utilities; many still regulate distribution utilities' formation of retail prices. Due to historical accidents, all states except Oregon and California currently do this in a way that rewards utilities for selling more energy and penalizes them for cutting customers' bills. The National Association of Regulatory Utility Commissioners, with rare unanimity, resolved in 1989 that this perverse incentive should be fixed, and nine or so states did so. By 2000, all nine except Oregon reversed this reform (often inadvertently), as they became distracted by restructuring or succumbed to short-term political pressures to freeze electric *rates* (prices)—a conceptual blunder, because customers pay not rates but *bills* (price multiplied by consumption).

> **States hold the most potent U.S. energy-policy lever: aligning retail utilities' financial interests with their customers'.**

> **All states except Oregon and California currently reward utilities for selling more energy and penalizes them for cutting customers' bills.**

Box 23: Pay-at-the-Pump car insurance (continued)

inefficient cars, but in fact, charging per gallon, not per mile, also has a rational basis: the vehicular efficiency being rewarded will increasingly come from lightweighting, which reduces aggressivity toward other vehicles and toward pedestrians. The combination of PATP with our earlier proposals for low-income access to efficient vehicles is particularly attractive for both equity and economic efficiency.

Implementing PATP today would add a typical insurance charge of ~$0.45/gal at the pump, but reduce insurance bills by more than that: the average annual fixed cost per car would fall by ~$250 (2003 $), and the total cost of driving

would fall.[877] The California Energy Commission estimates a net effect of reducing light-vehicle fuel consumption by 4% by 2020, saving California drivers $1.3 billion in direct non-environmental costs (which would scale to ~$11 billion nationwide) in present value.[878] We already counted the appropriate net effects of PATP in calculating net driving rebound (p. 41, above). PATP would best be implemented nationally, but even if it were done in just a state or region, past experience with different taxes suggests only modest and declining "retail leakage" from some drivers' tanking up out-of-state to avoid the premium.

877. Khazzoom 2000a; Ashuckian et al. 2003, pp. 3-4 – 3-9.
878. Ashuckian et al. 2003.

The solution is arrestingly simple: use a balancing account to decouple utilities' profits from their sales volumes, then let utilities keep as extra profit a small part of what they save their customers. This is the most important single way to make natural gas and electricity cheap and abundant again.

States can diversify their energy supplies to include renewables in a way that decreases their citizens' costs and risks.

Then California, chastened by the costly consequences of nearly destroying its world-leading efficiency programs, restored its successful old solution, and other states are now starting to follow suit.

The solution is arrestingly simple:[879] use a balancing account to decouple utilities' profits from their sales volumes, so they're no longer rewarded for selling more energy nor penalized for selling less, and then let utilities keep as extra profit a small part of what they save their customers, thus aligning both parties' interests. This is the most important single way to make natural gas and electricity cheap and abundant again. It can be supplemented by state financing, typically by revolving funds to invest in efficiency and renewables: the largest of these, San Francisco's $100-million bond issue, is expected to pay for itself with a profit to the taxpayers. Honolulu's $7.85-million revolving fund for City buildings' energy improvements is expected to earn $2 million net.

Renewable energy

Recent federal gridlock has hatched more state energy leadership and spread it into regional compacts with greater scale and leverage. In mid-2004, even as the federal government pushed fossil-fuel development across the Western states, the nine states of the Western Governors' Association, led by Governors Schwarzenegger (R-CA) and Richardson (D-NM), unanimously agreed to develop 30 GW of clean (generally renewable) electric capacity by 2015, raise energy efficiency 15% by 2020, and seek to become "the Saudi Arabia of wind and solar energy."[880] Thirteen states have officially adopted mandatory "renewable portfolio standards" for their electricity or energy supply portfolios; Governor Pataki (R-NY) has set a 25% goal for the next decade. This is not just prudent diversification but also sound financial economics, because renewables like solar and wind energy, especially when diversified and aggregated over a substantial area, can be bought on fixed-price contracts with no material price risk to the developer (nobody hikes the price of sun and wind, so once installed, it's a constant-cost resource within the modest statistical fluctuations of weather and microclimate). An optimized portfolio should therefore include renewables in the energy supply portfolio even if they appear to cost more per kilowatt-hour, for the same reason that an optimized investment portfolio should include riskless Treasury debt even if it yields less.[881] And in fact, some renewables, such as well-sited windpower, are now clearly competitive on price alone, thanks partly to state and federal public-goods R&D that's helped to launch new industries.

879. Some of the best retired state utility regulators, via the nonprofit Regulatory Assistance Project, advise their peers how to do it both in the U.S. and abroad: www.raponline.org.

880. Cart 2004. Additional information available at www.westgov.org.

881. This argument, elaborated chiefly by Dr. Shimon Awerbuch, is summarized and documented in Lovins et al. 2002, pp. 163–167.

Military policy:
fuel efficiency for mission effectiveness

As the rest of the federal government leads, follows, or gets out of the way, there's one part of the government that is trained, prepared, and obliged to lead: the Department of Defense. We showed on pp. 84–93 why DoD absolutely requires superefficient land, sea, and air platforms to fulfill its national-security mission. To be sure, as a byproduct of platform efficiency, DoD will also greatly enhance its warfighting capability and trim probably tens of billions of dollars per year off its overstressed budgets; but the most important result will be the Pentagon's ability to deploy and sustain agile, effective forces. The more the military can be relieved of the duty to protect oil, the safer will be our troops, our nation, and the world. And the military's spearheading of lightweighting and other efficiency technologies will greatly hasten the day it will be relieved of this unnecessary mission.

Right now, the Pentagon's requirements-writing, design, and procurement of military platforms place a modest rhetorical priority but a low actual priority on fuel efficiency. The Defense Science Board (DSB) task force's report of 31 January 2001 set out the needed reforms.[882] It was briefed to the full DSB in May 2001, released mid-August 2001, and concurred with by the Joint Chiefs of Staff 24 August 2001.[883] Eighteen days after that came 9/11, which diverted attention from any further action. Decisive adoption is now overdue. Fortunately, there are growing signs, chiefly within the Services, of interest in shifting in-house and contractor design professionals toward integrative, whole-system thinking that can "tunnel through the cost barrier" to radical energy efficiency at lower capital cost.[884] The main missing ingredient is turning efficiency aspirations into actual requirements and acquisitions. Leadership to do so must come from the Secretary of Defense.

This need is driven partly by a growing realization among the senior uniformed and civilian leadership that cost is a strategy—that organizations and processes must deliver requisite capabilities dramatically quicker and cheaper, not just in first cost but in the total long-term cost of using what we buy. A strategic approach to cost must therefore emphasize strategies not just for sharply reducing acquisition and operating costs (often by changing metrics, e.g. properly counting logistics), but also by suppressing the monetary cost of war, countering adversaries' strategies for imposing cost, and reducing the likelihood and intensity of war itself (p. 261). As the fuel-efficiency strand of that strategy emerges, DoD could also take practical steps with shared-savings pilot tests under the proposed National Defense Energy Savings Bill.[885]

> **Light, agile forces can't do their job if they drag a heavy logistical tail. But innovative techniques promise to transform this vulnerability into major warfighting gains, tail-to-tooth realignments, fiscal savings, and civilian spinoffs.**

> **The more the military can be relieved of the duty to protect oil, the safer will be our troops, our nation, and the world. And the military's spearheading of lightweighting and other efficiency technologies will greatly hasten the day it will be relieved of this unnecessary mission.**

882. DSB 2001, p. 87, note 426.

883. Fry 2001. The only non-concurrence was over whether "fuel efficiency" should be a mandatory Key Performance Parameter expressed in operational requirements documents and whose nonattainment is cause for program termination; the Joint Staff believed "fuel efficiency should not adversely impact meeting an operational requirement." We don't interpret this subordination of fuel efficiency to operational requirements as a denigration of fuel efficiency's great importance, and believe it can be required in other effective ways than as a KPP.

884. Lovins 2003a; Hawken, Lovins, & Lovins 1999, especially Ch. 6.

885. S.2318 cosponsored by Senators Collins (R-ME), Bayh (D-IN), Roberts (R-KS), and Reed (D-RI); see the Alliance to Save Energy 2004.
The bill died when CBO "scored" its obligations without its contractually offsetting savings. CBO and OMB should fix this unwarranted practice.

Civil preparedness: evolving toward resilience

Meanwhile, homeland security is at risk as intelligent adversaries threaten to exploit the profound and longstanding vulnerabilities of America's overcentralized, brittle energy systems (p. 12).[886] Our centralized systems—the regional power grids, oil and gas pipeline networks, and the like—could be brought down by single acts of sabotage; indeed, large pieces of the power grid keep failing all by themselves. Building more giant power lines and power stations will make this problem worse, because at its root, the problem is one of system architecture, not of inadequate capacity: the bigger they come, the harder they fall. However, the demand-response strategy we proposed on pp. 111–122, initially as a quick way to save trillions of cubic feet of natural gas per year at negative net cost, also happens to make the electricity system more resilient in much the same way that many distributed, instantly usable fire extinguishers help to protect a flammable building. Dispatching even a small amount of load management into a transmission system that's about to tip into cascading blackout can instantly correct the supply/demand imbalance before it can propagate. Whether one is designing precautions against terrorists or tree-limbs, saboteurs or squirrels, instant local response from the demand side (and from intelligently self-dispatching distributed generators), in an omnidirectional grid, is a key missing element of energy security.

> **In evolving away from today's overcentralized and highly vulnerable domestic energy system, efficient use buys the most bounce per buck, and more diverse, dispersed, renewable supplies can make major supply failures impossible by design.**

Another basic finding of our 1981 Pentagon analysis of domestic energy vulnerability and resilience (p. 12) is that the most "bounce per buck" comes from using energy more efficiently. For example, tripled-efficiency light vehicles with the same number of gallons in their fuel tanks can run three times as far before refueling. If their fuel supply is disrupted, that leaves three times as long to mend it or to improvise new supplies. Alternative supplies can also support three times as much mobility, greatly increasing flexibility.

In the tightly coupled oil supply chain, where crude-oil stockpiles like the Strategic Petroleum Reserve are many steps and miles from users' needs for refined products, and where major stocks of products are equally vulnerable to attack, the most important way to buy resilience is end-use efficiency. Thus efficient vehicles (and other oil uses) act as a fine-grained, highly distributed Strategic Petroleum Reserve—already delivered to customers, presenting no high-value targets, invulnerable to cascading system failures (such as vulnerable pipeline networks), and profitable to boot. That's an element of energy security and national resilience that no people in a dangerous world can afford to be without.

> **The most important way to buy resilience is end-use efficiency.**

886. Lovins & Lovins 1982; Lovins et al. 2002; Lovins, Datta, & Swisher 2003.

Civil society: the sum of all choices

For the past 95 pages we've analyzed American business opportunities and policy needs. But the bedrock supporting those major actors is the awesome power of more than 280 million diverse citizens who, given good information, have shown for two and a quarter centuries an uncanny knack for ultimately making farsighted choices. For all the ills and errors of our society, the power of its democratic roots and its rich networks of interlocking communities is immense, and growing ever more so in the Internet age. Despite initial concerns that the information revolution would only empower tyrants and spread darkness with the speed of light, the record so far suggests that more people have already been liberated by the microchip than ever were by the sword. And as communities of home and work, interest and faith, begin to coalesce and interlock, linked electronically in new networks that erase the isolation of distance and status, citizens' power becomes a rising tide that can drive great social movements. The more diverse the elements of that power, the greater the power of the whole. ·

Just as informed citizens drive politics, so informed customers drive business. For all the concern about manipulation by concentrated media and skillful advertising in both the civil and commercial spheres, any business executive knows that customers are ultimately in control. The franchise, the license to do business, depends critically on public approbation. One of the biggest challenges of leading a large organization is that anyone in it, in a thoughtless moment, can do something stupid that makes the public unwilling to buy that company's products. Such a reputational loss can in the end prove fatal. The converse opportunity is to be the kind of company people are eager to deal with. And any "green CEO" knows that the biggest win from earning a sterling reputation, and from removing any contradiction employees might have felt between what they do at work and what they want for their kids, is an unassailable lead in recruitment, retention, and motivation of their people.

In such a world, where reputation is such a precious but fragile asset, civil society has an unprecedented power to reward the leaders and punish the laggards in making business serve not just narrow economic ends but also broad societal ones. Nongovernmental organizations, already a sizeable chunk of the economy and perhaps the leading source of social innovation, amplify this bottom-up power of engaged citizens to help steer business in creative new directions.

By mindful market choices, collaboration with innovative firms, and disapprobation of laggards, civil society can drive business and government innovation as powerfully as it did in the California electricity crisis, when informed and mobilized customers undid 5–10 years' previous demand growth in just six months.

Because we lead better than we follow—more a bunch of lone wolves than a flock of sheep—we are greater together than we could ever be apart, able to lead and innovate from the bottom up as well as any people on earth.

Some citizens organize to work with companies; others, to combat them. But whether civil society and corporations coevolve in a predator-prey relationship, warily circling each other, or overtly cooperate in innovation, they are the two most important partners in today's tripolar world of business, civil society, and government. Increasingly, civil society and private enterprise are teaming up to do together what government should do but can't or won't. In new patterns, we find new ways to join together and learn together.

In this kaleidoscope of ad-hoc collaborations and shifting alliances, leadership from both sides and all levels is vital, and goes far beyond mere management. (As Admiral Grace Hopper said, "Manage things; lead people.") But the most important leadership still comes from the people, from the urban neighborhood and the village square, the schoolroom and the factory, the church and the Little League field. It comes from the convenience-store counter and the truck stop, from the seat of a tractor and the back of a horse. We Americans are an adventurous, independent, and ornery lot. Because we lead better than we follow—more a bunch of lone wolves than a flock of sheep—we are greater together than we could ever be apart, able to lead and innovate from the bottom up as well as any people on earth. Even top-down leadership can elicit that bottom-up power if done with proper respect. As Lao Tze said,[887]

> Leaders are best when people scarcely know they exist,
> not so good when people obey and acclaim them,
> worst when people despise them.
> Fail to honor people, they fail to honor you.
> But of good leaders who talk little,
> when their work is done, their task fulfilled,
> the people will all say: "We did this ourselves!"

887. In the classic *Tao Tê Ching*, #17.

Beyond gridlock: changing politics

In our society, citizens are not mere passive consumers but the wellspring of emerging values and opinions that drive business and political evolution. The silent but inexorable motion of belief systems and alliances, like the shifting of tectonic plates, can cause sudden realignments. In crafting an approach with broad appeal across the political spectrum, we are mindful of the potential for new and unexpected coalitions to form:

- Advocates for elders, the handicapped, the sick, and the impoverished can join environmentalists in favoring equitable access to mobility for all, especially non-drivers.

- Quality-of-life and community advocates can join anti-tax conservatives in insisting that developers pay their own way, rather than burdening the rest of the community with higher taxes for the road, school, public-safety, and other costs their projects impose.

- Conversely, canny real-estate developers who know the unique profitability of neotraditional and "new urbanist" design can join with both environmentalists and family-focused conservatives to create great places to raise families. These are designs that focus on pedestrian neighborhoods, not traffic engineering, so that as Alan Durning puts it, cars can become a useful accessory of life rather than its central organizing principle.

- The progressive environmental/labor axis can join with both hard-nosed industrialists and faith communities committed to stewardship in new ways of doing business that, as Ray C. Anderson says, "do well—very well—by doing good."[888]

- Rural and farm advocates can find their most deeply felt needs— cultural as much as economic—converging with those of four possibly unfamiliar allies: industrialists building new bioenergy enterprises, environmentalists protecting land, water, and climate, military leaders seeking new ways to strengthen the roots of national security, and advocates for the world's impoverished farmers, seeking fair trade undistorted by old-style American crop subsidies.

Such lists can be almost indefinitely expanded. We offer these examples of seemingly unlikely bedfellows not as amusing artifacts but as a stimulus to thought about the new, trans-ideological politics of a path beyond oil based on common sense, shared interests, and good business.

Realigning policy with public needs can forge broad and powerful new coalitions around clear, common-sense objectives and the values shared across a land of diverse patriots.

888. Hawken, Lovins, & Lovins 1999.

Too long has our nation been riven by energy-driven conflicts between regions and cultures—Midwestern coal-miners and -burners vs. friends of Northeastern lakes and trees, oil- and gas-exporting vs. -consuming states, automaking powerhouses vs. oil-dependent and climate-sensitive states, the urban core vs. the suburbs, old-timers vs. immigrants. Our divisions spread deeper, too, when diverse cultural roots have been nurtured in different soils: for example, between those not versed in country things and those who can say, in farmer-poet Wendell Berry's words, that "What I stand for is what I stand on." There are many causes of these divisions. But in innumerable ways, both obvious and subtle, our oil habit has been an important part of what has divided us.

Our immense national diversity—an undying source of strength and delight—will never wholly transcend such differences of interest, emphasis, and agenda. But as many of the underlying causes of those tensions are revealed as artifacts of an obsolete and uneconomic energy strategy, those causes can increasingly be sublimated into a healthy source of cohesion. We can then begin to collaborate on the great national project of the 21st Century: building together in America a secure, convivial, and prosperous life after oil.

Option 4. Substituting hydrogen

Beyond mobilization to a basic shift in primary energy supply

On pp. 123–125 we summarized the technical means to cut 2025 oil demand by more than half. In the Implementation section (pp. 127–226) we explained in business and policy terms how to achieve these goals, thereby breaking OPEC's pricing power and indeed making oil relevant only to countries that choose not to adopt similarly profitable approaches themselves For the U.S., this takes three integrated steps: saving oil at less than half its price, biosubstitution at up to the oil price, and substituting saved natural gas at levels that make sense regardless of the oil (and gas) price. The remaining oil demand, 13.5 Mbbl/d, could then be provided by the 7.8 Mbbl/d of forecast domestic oil output plus 5 Mbbl/d of "balance." That "balance" could come from any combination of six other resources: waiting for the additional 7 Mbbl/d of cheap efficiency already underway to be fully implemented, importing North American biofuels or oil, eliciting more efficiency or biosubstitutes by starting to count oil's unmonetized costs, or substituting more of the 8 TCF/y of leftover saved natural gas via hydrogen or compressed-natural-gas vehicles. Three other points bear emphasis:

- Of the 2025 oil demand, 4.4 Mbbl/d will fuel cars and light trucks. After 2025, *State of the Art* vehicles will continue to be adopted until they start to saturate the market. They'll be two-thirds of the light-vehicle stock by 2035, when all transportation will use only 12.9 Mbbl/d (extrapolating EIA's demand forecast beyond its end in 2025). The supply/demand balance will thus be even better in 2035 than in 2025—total demand down to 10.6 Mbbl/d, the remainder, after domestic supply substitutions, down to 3.3 Mbbl/d. And it will still keep improving, with a rich menu of options to choose from.

- If we hadn't saved half the oil by end-use efficiency, then trying to do the same thing with supply-side substitution alone, notably biofuels, would ultimately have run into supply constraints and very high prices (Fig. 30, p. 103) as well as competition with food crops and constraints in water availability and land-use. These issues, often cited by critics of biofuels, are artifacts of very high demand for mobility fuels. This is unnecessary if we use a least-cost combination of efficient use *and* alternative supply.

- Examining the structure of our tools for modeling the effects of policies, we estimate that a modest fraction of the *Mobilization* scenario's oil savings (~35% of light-vehicle savings and an unknown fraction for other end-uses) might occur anyway through spontaneous market uptake of incremental technologies. However, we definitely don't rec-

---

Option 4.
Superefficient light vehicles create a robust business case for hydrogen-fuel-cell propulsion. Deployed in concert with fuel cells in buildings, this permits a rapid, practical, profitable, and self-financing hydrogen transition, a durable all-domestic energy supply strategy, and many other important benefits. Oil-related carbon emissions would fall, then cease. The need for natural gas and financial capital would be modest and may shrink.

Efficient oil use, biosubstitutes, and the obviously profitable substitutions of saved natural gas for oil can halve oil use by 2035 despite rapid economic growth, but the trajectory of oil use can be aimed irreversibly toward zero by an advantageous (though not essential) further option— making the leftover saved gas, or other abundant energy such as windpower, into hydrogen.

Three other points (continued):

ommend such inaction, because it would forego most of the benefits. The total of benefits available from fully implemented *Mobilization* (*State of the Art* technologies accelerated by *Coherent Engagement* policies), for the projected 2025 level of services, includes $133 billion a year in avoided oil purchases, or a net benefit of $70 billion a year. It also provides all the resulting side-benefits, such as reduced exposure to oil-price volatility, lower global oil tensions, reduced emissions, deferred depletion, etc., plus the benefits of industrial and rural revitalization. Even under the same policies, incremental *Mobilization* technologies (in the *Let's Get Started* scenario) would achieve less than half of these benefits at more than half of their cost. Such a failure of nerve would leave far too much money on the table.

We know that optimal results depend both on advanced oil-displacing technologies *and* on policies to support their rapid adoption. But a question remains: is this as good as we can do, or is another step beyond today's *State of the Art* technologies already coming into view as technical progress, accelerated by the policies we've suggested, continues its virtuous spiral?

The leftover saved gas could be used even more effectively than simply burning it as a direct fuel. If it were instead converted to hydrogen, it could make U.S. mobility completely oil-free.

A further important potential step—the hydrogen transition—would be optional but advantageous. We noted on p. 124 that the 8.2 TCF/y of leftover saved gas could be used even more effectively than simply burning it as a direct fuel. If it were instead converted to hydrogen, which can be used 2–3 times as efficiently,[889] then it could meet the transportation needs within both the 5 Mbbl/d "balance" requirement and the 7.8 Mbbl/d of domestic oil output if desired, making U.S. mobility completely oil-free.[890] Since hydrogen can be produced from any other form of energy, including renewables, hydrogen also holds the key to the long-term elimination of oil use for transportation (even including airplanes) and all other uses. We thus stand poised for the final checkmate move in the Oil Endgame, the move that can deliver total energy independence—the hydrogen economy.

889. Lovins 2003b. DOE states the factor is 2.5 (Garman 2003). (Burning H_2 in an internal-combustion engine, instead of using it to run a fuel cell, reduces its efficiency advantage over hydrocarbons to ~1.3–1.5 and compromises its economic case.) In stationary applications, onsite H_2 cogeneration or trigeneration typically offers at least twice the efficiency of a central fossil-fueled power station plus an onsite combustion heater.

To illustrate its power, we show an altered version of Fig. 33 from p. 123. This time, in Fig. 38, we convert the 8 TCF/y of leftover saved gas into hydrogen. This graph demonstrates that even if hydrogen realizes only 10% stock capture by 2030, it already would make a significant difference in oil consumption because it *eliminates oil use entirely*. There are so many attractive ways to make hydrogen that this illustrative 10% can be increased as much as desired.

890. This also provides an "insurance policy" in case the oil savings from efficiency and biofuels so depress world oil prices that the costlier parts of the 7.8 Mbbl/d of U.S. oil output become uncompetitive and get shut in or left undeveloped.

Once hydrogen is introduced, the complete elimination of oil use is inevitable; the only question is how fast this would happen.

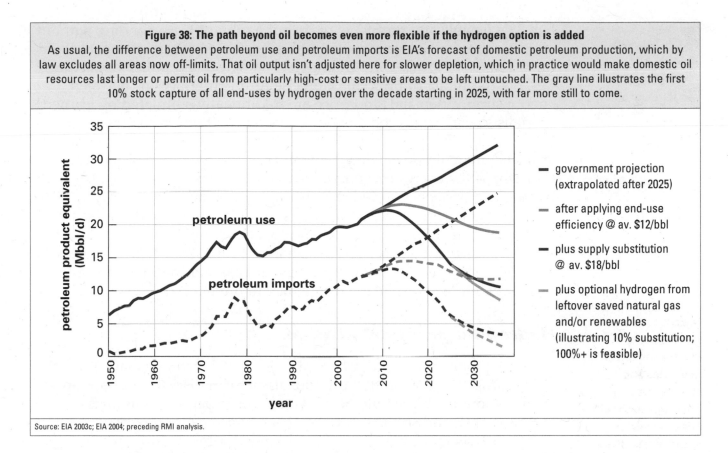

Figure 38: The path beyond oil becomes even more flexible if the hydrogen option is added
As usual, the difference between petroleum use and petroleum imports is EIA's forecast of domestic petroleum production, which by law excludes all areas now off-limits. That oil output isn't adjusted here for slower depletion, which in practice would make domestic oil resources last longer or permit oil from particularly high-cost or sensitive areas to be left untouched. The gray line illustrates the first 10% stock capture of all end-uses by hydrogen over the decade starting in 2025, with far more still to come.

Legend:
- government projection (extrapolated after 2025)
- after applying end-use efficiency @ av. $12/bbl
- plus supply substitution @ av. $18/bbl
- plus optional hydrogen from leftover saved natural gas and/or renewables (illustrating 10% substitution; 100%+ is feasible)

Source: EIA 2003c; EIA 2004; preceding RMI analysis.

Thus, once hydrogen is introduced, the complete elimination of oil use is inevitable; the only question is how fast this would happen. For primary fuel substitutions, substituting one primary fuel for another, such as the successive shifts from wood to coal to oil to gas, has historically required approximately 50 years for each shift, although they overlapped. Other complex technology substitutions such as railways or electrification that required technical interdependence, significant infrastructure, and large scale have also required 40–50 years. There are some compelling reasons to believe that hydrogen could displace other fuels more quickly. The integration of fuel cells[891] into vehicles and buildings will be made far simpler by the technological and efficiency improvements already in place if the *State of the Art* technology portfolio is implemented in a timely fashion. *Coherent Engagement* policies will already have removed barriers, and aligned incentives for introducing distributed hydrogen technologies and for accelerating the development and adoption of successive generations of hydrogen fuel cells. As we'll discuss below, there will be an abundance of diverse primary energy sources for the hydrogen transition. These factors suggest to the authors that hydrogen could largely or wholly displace oil 25–30 years after it is introduced. Embarking on the hydrogen transition, whatever its exact timing, sets the trajectory of oil use unmistakably and permanently downward.

891. The fuel cell, invented in 1839, is a modular electrochemical device. Many high-school chemistry students do an experiment in "electrolysis," using an electric current to split water into hydrogen and oxygen. A fuel cell does the same thing backwards: it chemically recombines hydrogen with oxygen (typically from the air) on a catalytic membrane, with no combustion, to produce an electric current, pure hot water, and nothing else. There are several kinds of fuel cells. Those expected to be first applied in vehicles typically use direct hydrogen produced separately by "reforming" a hydrocarbon or carbohydrate with steam. Some higher-temperature types of fuel cells can use hydrocarbon fuels directly.

Hydrogen could largely or wholly displace oil 25–30 years after it is introduced.

Fig. 38's flexible and profitable recipe for a vibrant U.S. economy without oil is illustrative. Such a mapping of how complementary elements could unfold helps to provide insight into technological and policy opportunities, not to predict or prescribe a precise future. Interactions between energy supply, demand, and price are traditionally simulated by learned specialists using large econometric or general-equilibrium computer models. While the feedbacks reflected in dynamic models are often real, not mere artifacts or circular logic, they generally capture too much or too little (or both) of the energy/economic system's immense complexity. For this reason, and because we pledged a transparent system-level analysis using downloadable spreadsheets so readers could scrutinize and change our assumptions (p. 33), we unapologetically offer simpler but not simplistic scenarios. They are neither forecasts nor fantasies. They fall, as Professor Paul Steinhart used to say, "between the unavoidable and the miraculous." They seek more to enable the future than to predict it (pp. *xxiv*, 34).

Despite recent skepticism by the underinformed, industries and governments are pressing ahead with billions of dollars' worth of R&D that is making the hydrogen transition practical and profitable.

Hydrogen: practical after all

In that exploratory and indicative spirit, we sketch here the main elements of a hydrogen transition that is optional—we can displace oil profitably even without it—but would be advantageous in profits, emissions, fuel flexibility, and security. It would also reduce calls on natural-gas resources, whether by stretching them longer or by avoiding those of highest private and public cost. Ultimately, hydrogen would make possible a completely renewable solution to mobility fuels, so they could not be cut off, would never run out, and wouldn't harm the earth's climate. Done well, these fuels could also cost less per mile and have steady, predictable prices.

Along the way, we briefly address some of the salient misunderstandings that have led many otherwise well-informed commentators to criticize the hydrogen economy as infeasible, uneconomic, dangerous, or polluting. These misconceptions are dealt with in a documented white paper by this report's senior author.[892] Capable technologists worldwide would not already have created 172 prototype hydrogen cars and 87 hydrogen filling stations[893] if they were simply sloppy thinkers or deluded dreamers. Rather, they have developed practical solutions to the problems that many recent studies (often propagating each other's errors) carelessly assume to be formidable or insoluble. As energy venture capitalist Robert Shaw says of the hydrogen transition, "Those who think it can't be done shouldn't interrupt those doing it."

892. Lovins 2003b.

893. Cars from www.hydrogen.org/ index-e.html, filling stations from M.P. Walsh 2004a.

Some of the business leaders now doing it were quoted in the frontispiece of this book. A few additional quotations reinforce the impression that they are doing it not for amusement but with the intention of making money:

> "Our vision is that, from the year 2020, more than a third of all BMW vehicles sold in Europe will be hydrogen-powered," says company chairman Joachim Milberg….Ferdinand Panik, director of DaimlerChrysler's fuel-cell project in Germany, reckons hydrogen fuel cells will power a quarter of new cars world-wide by 2020.
>
> — *ATLAS OF POPULATION & ENVIRONMENT,*
> AMERICAN ASSOCIATION FOR THE ADVANCEMENT OF SCIENCE[894]

> "General Motors is on record saying that we expect to begin selling hydrogen fuel cell vehicles by 2010, and we hope to be the first manufacturer to sell one million fuel cell vehicles….[A]s the price of hydrogen and electricity per kilowatt decrease, we see the convergence of the power and transportation infrastructures. The new model will cause hydrogen and electricity—made from various sources—to become the two principal energy carriers. Hydrogen and electricity are interchangeable via fuel cells and electrolyzers—leading to a distributed energy network wherever one or the other is present—and also leading to unprecedented new business opportunities."
>
> — LARRY BURNS, VP R&D AND PLANNING,
> GENERAL MOTORS CORPORATION, 10–11 FEB. 2003[895]

> "We are basically moving to a hydrogen economy.***[W]e believe the hydrogen fuel cell is the big answer."
>
> — RICK WAGONER, CHAIRMAN AND CEO,
> GENERAL MOTORS CORPORATION, 2003[896]

> "The fuel cell is the most promising option for the future. We are determined to be the first to bring it to market."
>
> — JÜRGEN HUBBERT, DAIMLERCHRYSLER[897]

> "Work on the fuel cell is no longer motivated exclusively by technological and environmental considerations, but has become a genuine competitive factor. We view the fuel cell as an economic opportunity that will help safeguard high-tech jobs and business success in the future."
>
> — DR. FERDINAND PANIK, FUEL CELL PROJECT DIRECTOR,
> DAIMLERCHRYSLER, 12 NOV. 1999[898]

> "Fuel cell vehicles will probably overtake gasoline-powered cars in the next 20 to 30 years."
>
> — TAKEO FUKUI, MANAGING DIRECTOR, R&D,
> HONDA MOTOR CO.[899]

> "We want to meet our customers' needs for energy, even if that means leaving hydrocarbons behind."
>
> — SIR MARK MOODY-STUART,
> CHAIRMAN, ROYAL DUTCH/SHELL GROUP[900]

Billions of dollars have already been invested in hydrogen fuel cells by most of the world's major automotive and oil companies (GM, Daimler-Chrysler, and Shell have each placed billion-dollar bets, with major efforts also at Toyota, Honda, and BP), scores of leading manufacturing and

Capable technologists worldwide have developed practical solutions to the problems that many recent studies carelessly assume to be formidable or insoluble.
"Those who think it can't be done shouldn't interrupt those doing it."

894. Pearce & Boesch, undated.

895. Burns 2003.

896. First portion from Sehgal 2003, second from Wagoner 2003.

897. Hubbert, undated.

898. DaimlerChrysler Communications 1999.

899. Fukui 1999.

900. *Economist* 2001.

materials companies (such as United Technologies and DuPont), and the large existing hydrogen industry (Air Products & Chemicals, LindeAG, Air Liquide, and more). Some of the most formidable potential competitors haven't yet even announced their presence. Automakers alone are continuing to invest more than a half-billion dollars a year to bring fuel cells to market; they're interested not just in fuel cells' doubled efficiency and zero emissions but also in their ruggedness, light weight, and simplicity. A fuel-cell powertrain has about a tenth the parts count of an engine-based powertrain, and with some 700 million cars and trucks in the world, increasing about 8% a year, that's a lot of avoidable parts. Then there is substantial R&D by the military, which has long used fuel cells in submarines and spacecraft and is eager to apply them in land, sea, and air platforms. Many of these investments have been to good effect, as will become clear from announcements over the next year or so. Steady progress with the details of materials and manufacturing engineering is now making fuel cells sufficiently durable (already over 10,000 hours in some realistic field tests) to support commitments to the manufacturing scale-up needed to make them cheap.

901. Solomon & Banerjee 2004.

The United States' $1.2-billion hydrogen R&D commitment is following in the footsteps of substantial hydrogen R&D efforts[901] in Canada, Japan, Europe (with special efforts in Germany, Norway, and Iceland), South Korea, China, and elsewhere; California and Michigan even have significant state-level hydrogen programs. The efforts in China and Japan merit special notice because of these countries' competitive threat in automaking (pp. 132–136, 166–168). China is believed by some analysts to be already the world's number two hydrogen producer. Japan's R&D investment, proportionate to the United States', started earlier and is well integrated across fueling infrastructure, vehicles, and stationary uses. Its aggressive and specific goals include 50,000 fuel-cell vehicles by 2010 and 5 million by 2020, plus 2.1 and 10 GW of stationary power generation by those years (respectively including ~1.2 and ~5.7 million household-size fuel cells). Model hydrogen-related building and safety regulations are to have been redesigned by 2004, and Japan's industrial standards for hydrogen equipment are intended to shape global ones. These are among the hallmarks of a serious strategic effort, and they are intensifying.

Fuel cells, in short, have already passed the stage of potential show-stoppers and are well along the path of serious commercialization. So, as we'll suggest, are the other parts of the hydrogen system needed to sustain a practical route from here to there. So in broad outline, what would a hydrogen transition look like? How could it enable the United States to rely completely on domestic energy sources to fuel its economy not just while natural gas resources last, but indefinitely? And from the perspective of broad national benefit, how could its radical improvements in three sectors—vehicles, energy distribution, and overall energy infrastructure—make the hydrogen transition rapid and profitable?

Eight basic questions

→ Hydrogen's rationale, market, safety, storage, cost, infrastructure, ultimate energy sources, and transitional path are all solved or soluble problems. The logical sequence is from today's hybrid cars to ultralight gasoline hybrids to ultralight hydrogen hybrids—preferably using fuel cells, but potentially with internal-combustion engines as an optional backup.

Why is hydrogen important, and is it safe?

Hydrogen is important because it is a new, extremely versatile, and abundant energy carrier that is cleaner, safer, and potentially more economic to use for mobility and distributed applications than either natural gas or oil. As a carrier, hydrogen is made from other energy sources such as gas, oil, coal, or electricity (including renewably produced electricity), and can deliver any kind of energy services. The hydrogen industry is already large—it makes about 50 million tonnes of hydrogen a year, or one-fifth as many cubic feet as the world's entire natural-gas production—yet has an enviable safety record spanning more than a half-century. Any fuel is hazardous and needs due care, but hydrogen's hazards are different and generally more tractable than those of hydrocarbon fuels.[902]

How would a light vehicle safely and affordably store enough hydrogen to drive 300+ miles?

Inexplicably, recent studies from such normally informed sources as the Office of Technology Policy, National Academy of Sciences, and American Physical Society (not actually independent studies, but largely copied from each other) have claimed that hydrogen storage is an unsolved problem, a "potential showstopper," and requires basic materials breakthroughs.[903] They're wrong; the storage problem has been solved for at least four years. The solution, though, is not to find a new way to store hydrogen, but to adopt vehicles whose better platform physics let them drive as far using three times less hydrogen. For example, in 2000 the *Revolution* concept-car design showed that properly integrating ultralighting, reduced aerodynamic drag and rolling resistance, and other improvements can triple vehicle efficiency without changing the fuel and prime mover. This reduction in the energy needed to move the vehicle largely overcomes the roughly fourfold[904] higher bulk of compressed hydrogen gas (at the 5,000 psi that's now standard in off-the-shelf and extremely safe carbon-fiber tanks) vs. gasoline for the same driving range. The skeptics simply forgot to count the potential to make the *vehicle* more efficient, as distinguished from its powertrain. But using an ultralight (optimally an advanced-composite) autobody not only makes the hydrogen tanks small enough to fit or "package" well, leaving plenty of room for people and cargo, as shown in Fig. 39; it also makes the fuel cell three times smaller. That makes it competitive many years earlier, because needing three times fewer kilowatts,

The storage problem has been solved for at least four years. The solution, though, is not to find a new way to store hydrogen, but to adopt vehicles whose better platform physics let them drive as far using three times less hydrogen.

902. See NHA, undated; EERE, undated. It follows that the risks of wide public deployment are comparable to or less than those of the existing wide public deployment of other fuels, including gasoline. However, historic doctrines governing tort liability may not adequately recognize this (Moy 2003). The United States also has some 44,000 code jurisdictions, each with a fire marshal with probably a different and often an underinformed conception of hydrogen safety, so considerable effort will be needed, and is starting in the U.S. and abroad, to modernize codes and standards.

903. E.g., Service 2004. See Lovins & Williams 1999; Lovins & Cramer 2004; Lovins 2004b.

904. The compressed hydrogen actually has an eighth the energy per unit of volume of gasoline, but is used at least twice as efficiently in a fuel cell as gasoline is in an engine.

Figure 39: Ultralight vehicles solve the hydrogen storage problem

Packaging for the fuel-cell *Revolution* concept-SUV virtual design described on pp. 62–68 shows that such efficiency-tripling platform physics can shrink the hydrogen tanks by threefold (the three tanks shown provide a 330-mile average driving range on 3.4 kg or 138 L of hydrogen at 5,000 psi or 345 bar), yet still offer a spacious interior (five adults in comfort, and up to 69 ft³ of cargo space with the rear seats folded flat). The fuel cell (in rear) also becomes three times smaller and more affordable. This design used three hydrogen tanks only for an analytically convenient match to standard sizes; one or two tanks in custom sizes would be lighter and cheaper, and conformal shapes are also possible. Ford and others have demonstrated that such tanks are extremely crashworthy, partly because they're supported by interior pressure. These government-approved tanks are standard in the industry; some makers are starting to use 10,000 psi, but ultralight vehicles make this higher pressure and cost unnecessary. The transverse tanks in this design have room to move axially in a side-impact collision. The exterior of the *Revolution* show car is Fig. 18d on p. 61. See also Box 7, pp. 62–63 above.

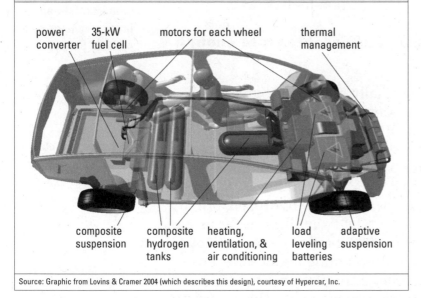

power converter | 35-kW fuel cell | motors for each wheel | thermal management

composite suspension | composite hydrogen tanks | heating, ventilation, & air conditioning | load leveling batteries | adaptive suspension

Source: Graphic from Lovins & Cramer 2004 (which describes this design), courtesy of Hypercar, Inc.

the automaker can afford to pay three times as much per kilowatt—a price realized at probably tens of times lower cumulative production volumes.[905]

Under what conditions is hydrogen a cheaper light-vehicle fuel than oil?

What matters is the total cost per mile driven, not the cost of the fuel per unit of energy contained. Since hydrogen must be made from other forms of energy, it is economic to deploy only if it is more efficiently used than the fuel it was made from, thus justifying the investment, energy input, and other operating costs needed to convert it. Like gasoline made from crude oil, or electricity made from coal, hydrogen is a more "refined," efficiently usable, valuable, and costly form of energy than the natural gas, electricity, or other resource it's made from. But if the price of hydrogen per BTU is, say, twice that of gasoline, but each BTU of hydrogen also propels the car twice as many miles as a BTU of gaso-

> **What matters is the total cost per mile driven, not the cost of the fuel per unit of energy contained.**

line, *and* if the car is priced the same, then the driver is indifferent. Or if the car is priced higher but the hydrogen has a sufficiently greater efficiency edge, then the driver is again indifferent. Of course, car buyers are not so simple-minded as to care *only* about cost per mile: the enormous diversity of vehicles on the market demonstrates how many other factors matter too (and often matter more). But just to focus for the moment on cost per mile, Fig. 40 illustrates the relationship between fuel price, fuel-cell

905. At an 80% experience curve, meaning that each doubling of cumulative production volume reduces real unit cost by 20%, a two-thirds cost reduction is achieved by five doublings of cumulative production volume. Five doublings are a factor of 32.

906. A good fuel cell is inherently far more efficient than a good gasoline engine and modestly more efficient than a good diesel engine. The fuel cell's most efficient operating point is also at the relatively low power at which most driving occurs, rather than at high power as for Otto engines (Williams, Moore, & Lovins 1997, Fig. 8). Both engines and fuel cells can be advantageously hybridized to match their "map" (efficiency vs. load) with varying tractive loads and to recover braking energy for re-use. Hybridization usually brings greater percentage savings to engines than to fuel cells, but this is sensitive to many assumptions about hardware, driving cycles, and control algorithms. The fuel-cell vehicle analyzed here combined a 35-kW fuel cell with a 35-kW high-power buffer battery, mainly because for the time being, batteries cost less per kW than fuel cells. When that ceases to be true, the battery will become smaller. Ultimately it may disappear if developers can perfect a reversible fuel cell, whose electrolytic (backwards) operation to store braking energy would be buffered with an ultracapacitor for charge-acceptance rate. The byproduct oxygen could optionally be stored and used to supercharge the fuel cell, making it smaller.

efficiency, and capital cost for the two most efficient versions of the *Revolution* ultralight midsize SUV concept-car designs (Fig. 20 on p. 65)—propelled by a gasoline-hybrid-electric powertrain or a hydrogen-fuel-cell hybrid[906]— vs. their conventional 2004 Audi *Allroad 2.7T* comparable competitor.

This comparison assumes that the fuel-cell vehicle will sell for 23% more than the gasoline-hybrid version. Fig. 20 on p. 65 shows that this premium is entirely due to the fuel-cell powertrain's costing ~$6,000 more to manufacture than the gasoline-hybrid powertrain. So long as that remains true, and the retail price premium for the fuel-cell vehicle remains $10,300, Fig. 40 shows that the fuel-cell version can't save enough fuel to repay its higher capital cost. However, this could, and probably will, change in any or all of three ways by the time the fuel-cell vehicles get to market sometime during the following decade:

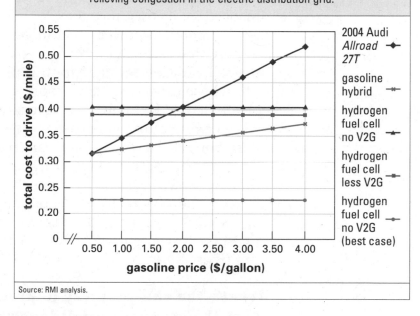

Figure 40: How can fuel-cell vehicles compete with gasoline hybrids?
The toughest competitor will be not inefficient, heavy, gasoline-engine cars but ultralight hybrids, assuming the prices and efficiencies of the gasoline-hybrid and fuel-cell-hybrid midsize crossover-style SUV variants shown in Fig. 20, p. 65. Hydrogen delivered into such a fuel-cell ultralight SUV for $4/kg can compete against a gasoline-hybrid SUV with equal platform physics (mass, drag, and rolling resistance) only if fuel cells become cheaper than we assumed, or if, as shown in the lowest curve, they have durable membranes and the vehicles are plugged in as power stations when parked and earn appreciable revenue from Vehicle-to-Grid (V2G) operation. The range of V2G credits shown is from Lipman et al.,[907] and reflects a range of 10,000 to 40,000-h fuel-cell life and less or more favorable spreads between natural-gas and electricity prices. The high V2G revenues that yield the lowest cost curve in this graph could instead be considered a surrogate for capturing some of the distributed benefits of relieving congestion in the electric distribution grid.

Source: RMI analysis.

- Fuel cells and other hydrogen equipment may become cheaper than we assumed. One-third of the fuel-cell SUV's extra retail price, nearly enough to make the fuel-cell car compete with the hybrid, is due to what now look like conservatisms in our assumed cost of the fuel-cell system and hydrogen tanks.[908] Most of the rest of the premium should disappear at higher production volumes. At very high volumes when fuel cells are fully mature, a fuel-cell car might ultimately even cost less to build than a gasoline-engine car; that's certainly the intention of the world's main automakers.

907. Lipman, Edwards, & Kammen 2004.

908. The most detailed public-domain mass-production cost analysis (originally from Directed Technologies, Inc., which did much of Ford Motor Company's fuel analysis) states that this vehicle's 35-kW fuel-cell system should cost about $1,723 at an early production volume of 300,000/y, and its tanks, to hold its 3.4 kg of hydrogen, should cost about $704 more than a normal gasoline tank: Ogden, Williams, & Larson 2004, p. 15, converted from 1998 to 2000 $. RMI's consultants' cost analysis assumed a ~60% costlier fuel-cell system (excluding its output power electronics) and 150% costlier tanks than this, adding nearly $4,000 to the assumed retail price shown in Fig. 20. (The fuel-cell system in this context means the stack plus auxiliaries—air compressors, heat exchangers, humidification systems, safety devices, and control systems—but excludes the hydrogen tanks and associated plumbing.) Fig. 20 also shows a ~$600 lower manufacturing cost for the fuel-cell than for the hybrid SUV in the category of chassis components, partly because the fuel-cell variant is 24 kg lighter than the hybrid. We haven't attempted to update the advanced-composites costs, which in light of recent manufacturing-process progress will probably be lower than we assumed for all the variants.

Three ways this could
change (continued):

Hydrogen fuel cells
today, **installed in
the right places and
used in the right way,
can economically
displace less
efficient central
resources for deliver-
ing electricity, paving
the way for hydrogen
use to spread rapidly,
financed by its own
revenues.**

- Fuel cells may become more efficient. Our analysis assumed a peak fuel-cell efficiency five percentage points lower than a 2003 norm (p. 62, note 328); this was a good economic choice, but further technological progress may make it unnecessary.[909]

- The vehicle may earn revenue from selling back power to the grid when parked—so-called Vehicle-to-Grid or V2G operation, which RMI proposed in the early 1990s.

Our insights into the full economic value of distributed power suggest that hydrogen fuel cells *today*, installed in the right places and used in the right way, can economically displace less efficient central resources for delivering electricity, paving the way for hydrogen use to spread rapidly, financed by its own revenues.[910] This logic normally refers to stationary uses—combined power generation, heating, and perhaps cooling in buildings and industry. But it could also apply to power generation in parked fuel-cell vehicles designed for this purpose. Using a more durable fuel cell (whose extra cost we've counted), such plug-in "power stations on wheels" could sell power to the grid when and where it's most valuable—during afternoon peaks in downtown load centers. The first couple of million adopters may even earn back as much as they paid to buy their cars. The fuel cells in a full hydrogen-fuel-cell light-vehicle fleet would ultimately have very many times the grid's total generating capacity, so it doesn't take very many V2G-operated vehicles adopters to put most coal and nuclear power plants out of business. Even at relatively high volumes, the power's resale value to congested urban grids can be significant (Figs. 40–41).

What's the cheapest way to produce and deliver hydrogen to meet the economic conditions required for adoption?

We envisage a distributed model for hydrogen production and delivery that integrates the infrastructures of natural gas, electricity, buildings, and mobility. Instead of building a costly new distribution infrastructure for hydrogen, or repeating the mistake of burdening supposedly cheaper central production with prohibitively costly distribution, we'd use the spare offpeak capacity inherent in existing gas and electricity distribution infrastructures, then produce the hydrogen locally—chiefly at the filling station, called "forecourt" production—so it requires little or no further distribution. Hydrogen could thus be made, compressed, stored on-site, and

---

909. Many firms are developing materials that can run more efficiently by boosting operating temperature without unduly degrading membrane life. One major developer states that a 5°C-higher temperature can make a typical fuel-cell car 100–200 kg lighter—a big win if the membrane lasts.

910. Swisher 2003; Lovins et al. 2002. There are obvious applications in commercial buildings that need ultrareliable power for computers and other digital loads, such as the well-known Omaha credit-card processing center, or buildings isolated from the grid, such as the Central Park police station (both successfully using ~$3,000/kW phosphoric-acid fuel cells). But there are also important early niche markets in industry. Microchip fabrication plants need ultrareliable power, cooling, ultrapure hot water, and hydrogen—all valuable outputs of a fuel cell and its on-site natural-gas reformer, making even retrofits an attractive proposition that several chipmakers are now considering. GM and Dow are also implementing a large pilot project that uses fuel cells to turn byproduct hydrogen from electrochemical processes back into electricity and useful heat to run the process. Such opportunities abound throughout industry.

delivered into vehicles for ~$4/kg (less with cheap natural gas or at Costco scale) with small-scale, on-site natural gas reformers. This assumes that delivered gas prices remain below $8/MBTU—a very safe assumption in our view, whether based on North American gas or on LNG, which would nominally deliver gas to a filling station for ~$6/MBTU. We assume conventional miniature thermal steam reformers, which several firms are now bringing to market. Their natural-gas-to-hydrogen conversion efficiency is 72–75%. If a new type of one-step reformer with lower capital cost and higher efficiency (83–85%) scales down to this size, its production costs would be significantly lower than Fig. 42 shows.

GM estimates that 11,700 forecourt reformers could provide a station within two miles of 70% of U.S. population, and permit refueling every 25 miles along the 130,000-mile National Highway System (NHS)—all for a total investment of just $12 billion, assuming rather costly facilities.[911] This would eliminate the "chicken-and-egg problem" (which comes first, the fueling stations or the cars they fuel?) at less than a tenth the real cost of the NHS itself. The 6,500 non-NHS stations in 100 metro areas could fuel 1 million vehicles, equivalent to several million at the more fuel-frugal *State of the Art* platform efficiency. More stations would then be added as needed to serve growing demand. (The U.S. now has ~170,000 gasoline filling stations, and their number is shrinking.) The roll-out needn't take long: Deutsche Shell said a few years ago that if desired, it could put hydrogen pumps into all its German filling stations in about two years.

Roughly 70% of gasoline filling stations, serving ~90% of U.S. gasoline demand, already have natural gas service. The rest could reform their hydrogen from either LPG or ethanol, which has the advantage that it can be wet (hydrous)—avoiding the costly step of removing virtually all the water—because the reformer needs steam as well as ethanol.[912] As for climate impact, standard miniature reformers would emit ~2–3 times less CO_2 per mile that gasoline cars emit today. Several oil companies even think they'll find ways to collect that CO_2 from filling-station-scale reformers and turn it into value. And of course biofuel reformers wouldn't affect the climate at all.

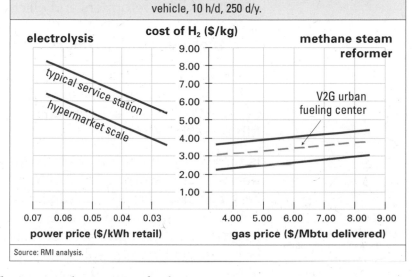

Figure 41: Cost of distributed hydrogen production
Based on ~2003 technology for miniature reformers and electrolyzers, both sited at the filling station, RMI analysis shows that the electricity or gas prices shown can support delivery of 5,000-psi hydrogen into light vehicles at the approximate $/kg costs shown for two different filling-station sizes, one standard (serving about as many cars as a normal million-gallon-a-year gasoline filling station) and one hypermarket-scale (ten times as big). The dashed line shows that a 500-vehicle urban parking facility, equipped with a 1-MW stationary fuel and a gas reformer for refueling, could deliver hydrogen at an intermediate cost (undercutting a standard filling station by ~$0.5/kg) if it captured the revenues from an average of 10 kW of net power resold from each parked vehicle, 10 h/d, 250 d/y.

Source: RMI analysis.

Instead of building a costly new distribution infrastructure for hydrogen, or repeating the mistake of burdening supposedly cheaper central production with prohibitively costly distribution, we'd produce the hydrogen locally—chiefly at the filling station— so it requires little or no further distribution.

911. McCormick 2003.

912. Deluga et al. 2004; Morrison 2004. Intelligent Energy Inc., chaired by former Shell chair Sir John Jennings, has even demonstrated a shoebox-size direct ethanol fuel cell (www. intelligent-energy.com).

Implementation

Option 4. Substituting hydrogen: *Eight basic questions:* Cheapest way to produce and deliver hydrogen?

Alternatively, sites that can buy electricity for under 3¢/kWh—mostly during off-peak periods or in areas with excess hydroelectricity or wind power—may find on-site electrolysis competitive.[913] These two ubiquitous and competitive retail commodities, natural gas and electricity, will compete in both spot and forward markets, and the market will determine the winner. We fully expect the hydrogen transition to be initially fueled by natural gas. Ultimately, as renewables (chiefly windpower) become cheaper and natural gas costlier, renewably produced electricity may gain the advantage.[914] Fig. 41 shows a reasonable estimate for the cost competition between distributed gas reformers and electrolyzers using near-term technology.

Are there enough primary energy sources for this transition?

After *State of the Art* efficiency improvements are deployed to the degree practical by 2025, plus biosubstitutions, the U.S. will consume 20.4 Mbbl/d of oil in 2025. Of this, light vehicles and trucks will consume 63% or 12.9 Mbbl/d (25.4 qBTU/y).

Is there enough natural gas in North America to fuel the hydrogen transition without resorting to LNG imports? Our previous analysis says yes, both because so much gas can be profitably saved and because fuel-cell vehicles are so efficient that they need relatively little gas to make their hydrogen. *If* hydrogen fuel-cell road vehicles, both light and heavy, were twice as efficient as gasoline- and diesel-fueled *State of the Art* technologies,[915] they'd need in 2025 only 8 qBTU/y (or 70 million tonnes a year) of hydrogen delivered to the tank. To reform this much hydrogen from natural gas at state-of-the-art 85% efficiency would require 9.4 qBTU/y (9.2 TCF/y) of natural gas. These numbers decline rapidly as more efficient vehicles are phased in. We showed in Fig. 21 on p. 66 that an average *State of the Art* light vehicle at EIA's 2025 sales mix would get 73 mpg. If hydrogen fuel cells improve this gasoline-hybrid fuel economy proportionately to the *Revolution* SUV variants shown in Fig. 20, p. 65, then that 73 mpg would become 119 mpg-equivalent. However, since the fuel would switch from gasoline to hydrogen, the fuel-cell vehicle would not just reduce but *eliminate* the hybrids' remaining oil use, which is 4.4 Mbbl/d for all light vehicles in 2025 and 2.2 in 2035 (extrapolating EIA's forecast of vehicles and vehicle-miles from its end in 2025). Of course, as fuel-cell vehicles phase in over time, the vehicle stock will also be getting more efficient—as it must do for the hydrogen to be attractive. Thus if we could substitute a fuel-cell vehicle for all light vehicles on the road in 2035 (which will virtually all be *State of the Art* ultralight hybrids as shown in Fig. 36i, p. 181), then the entire road-vehicle stock would need only 5.8 qBTU/y (51 million tonne/y) of hydrogen, which could be made from 6.6 TCF/y of natural gas.

As our discussion of natural gas showed on pp. 112–116 above, improved electric and direct-gas end-use efficiency and electric load management could cost-effectively save 12.0 TCF/y of gas by 2025—a value we consider conservatively low. Further, since we are no longer making gasoline in

913. Electrolyzers are somewhat like fuel cells run backwards, so they too should become much cheaper with mass-production. They may have a cost advantage at small scale, e.g., for home use or very small filling stations.

914. For niche markets and perhaps more, one would then need to consider whether advanced lithium batteries, which become ever better and cheaper for cellphones and laptop computers, might get cheap and light enough so that an advanced battery-electric powertrain might beat a fuel-cell one. See *Technical Annex*, Ch. 24.

915. Heavy vehicles start with good diesel engines, which are more efficient than gasoline engines, but would probably be replaced not with proton-exchange-membrane (PEM) fuel cells but with more efficient high-temperature (e.g., solid-oxide) fuel cells, perhaps with topping and bottoming cycles added. Doubled efficiency is therefore still an approximately realistic starting-point for this estimate.

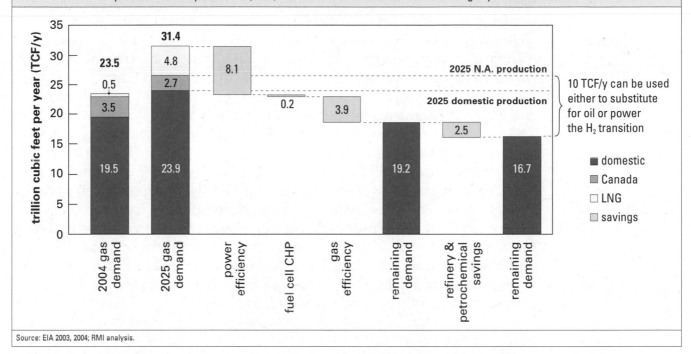

Figure 42: Reducing EIA's 2025 natural-gas demand forecast by 41% via electric and gas efficiency, substitution of fuel-cell combined-heat-and-power ("FC CHP") to back out the remaining combined-cycle gas power stations, gas savings in refineries (displaced by substituting hydrogen for hydrocarbon fuels), and displacement of gas in petrochemicals by biomaterials (or offshore migration). Naturally, unless directed elsewhere by government intervention, saved gas will flow to the uses with the highest netback margins. Competition between the cost of extracting or saving gas and the value of saving it (then reusing it for cogeneration, hydrogen production, process heat displacements, etc.) will determine whether all the forecast gas production occurs.

Source: EIA 2003, 2004; RMI analysis.

a hydrogen world, natural gas that is currently used to make hydrogen in oil refineries could be redeployed, saving 0.5 TCF/y of gas. In addition, we would expect at least two-thirds of U.S. refineries to close (since there is no longer much market for petroleum-based transportation fuel, and the remaining refineries would supply the remaining petroleum-fueled vehicles, airplanes, and machinery), saving an additional 1.0 TCF/y of natural gas from process heat and power. This would increase further if aircraft shifted to liquid hydrogen—a surprisingly practical and attractive option.[916] One additional TCF/y would be saved by the eventual offshore migration of U.S. petrochemicals manufacturing, or—as we would prefer—through substitution by biomaterials. This brings 2025 gas demand down from 31.4 TCF to only 18.5 TCF. That's 8.2 TCF below the forecast 2025 North American gas deliverability of 26.6 TCF (Fig. 42). Thus we

A sensible hydrogen transition may even require less financial capital than business-as-usual.

916. Liquid hydrogen is the lightest known fuel, four times bulkier but 2.8 times lighter than jet fuel per unit energy, or about as dense as high-density Styrofoam—hence its use in space rockets. Using it to fuel jetliners requires superinsulated tanks, which are bulky but light, permitting ~20–25% higher payloads. Design studies for such "cryoplanes" by Boeing, NASA, Airbus (for the EU), and others confirm cleaner burning and better safety than jet fuel (kerosene). Although Airbus thought efficiency would drop, Boeing (for a nominal *767* platform) found a ~10–15% gain—enough to offset the liquefaction energy—because of hydrogen's net effects on mass, drag, climb, cruise, and engine efficiency: Daggett 2003, and personal communication, 16 June 2003. The Air Force tested liquid hydrogen in a *B-57* in 1956; Tupolev, in a *Tu-154* in 1988. Airbus's 35-partner consortium (dieBrennstoffzelle.de, undated), under EU funding, has already established the concept's basic feasibility and safety. Boeing has announced work on fuel-cell applications for both propulsion and auxiliary power, and expected in 2003 to flight-test an experimental one-seat aircraft with propellers driven by a 25-kW fuel cell after battery-boosted takeoff (Knight 2003). Dutch researcher Ing. P. Peeters believes the ultimate solution, especially for regional and other smaller airplanes, would be a fuel-cell, superconducting-electric-motor, unducted-fan-driven design (personal communication, 3 May 2004). At Mach 0.65, he predicts energy savings of 55% vs. *747-400* (7,000-km mission, 75% load factor, 415 seats) and 68% vs. *737-400* (1,000 km, 70% load factor, 145 seats). This implies substantial savings, vs. even a very efficient future kerosene-turbofan design.

have enough gas supply to fuel the hydrogen transition in 2035, even before all the *State of the Art* light vehicles are phased in. The gas savings are summarized in Fig. 42.

This analysis assumes that all of the needed hydrogen would be reformed from natural gas. In fact, some hydrogen would be made from electrolysis, particularly using off-peak power, low-cost hydropower (such as spring spillpower), and renewables. In fact, the wind potential of the Dakotas alone could make 50 million tonnes of hydrogen per year[917]—enough, at *State of the Art* efficiency, to fuel every highway vehicle in the United States.[918] Dakotas windpower is only a fraction of the national potential: adding Texas, Kansas, and Montana augments the Dakotas' output by 1.5-fold. Windpower is now a $7-billion-a-year global industry. It adds 2% a year to Germany's total supply of electricity (now 10% renewable), provides a fifth of Denmark's, could provide upwards of half Europe's residential electricity by 2020, and now includes such giants as General Electric. Obviously windpower can make enough all-American hydrogen, plausibly at competitive long-run cost,[919] to do everything we're proposing here to do with natural gas. This makes frontier gas projects (Rockies wildlands, North Slope, etc.) optional. Nearly unlimited amounts of hydrogen could also be produced from coal, which is very good at pulling hydrogen out of steam, if emerging ways to keep the carbon permanently out of the air fulfill their promise. And finally, although it's too early to tell for sure, there are tantalizing indications that a sensible hydrogen transition may even require less financial capital than business-as-usual, partly because it needs less fuel and partly because upstream investments tend to be lower for gas than for oil.

The Dakotas alone could make 50 million tonnes of hydrogen per year—enough, at State of the Art efficiency, to fuel every highway vehicle in the United States.

917. Elliott et al. (1991) estimated the Dakotas' Class 3+ wind potential, net of environmental and land-use exclusions (50% of forest area, 30% of agricultural and 10% of range lands, 20% of mixed agricultural/range lands, 10% of barren lands, and 100% of urban, wetlands, and parks and wilderness areas), at 2,240 TWh/y (equivalent to 58% of total U.S. 2002 net generation) at 50-m hub height for 750-kW turbines. Today's ~2-MW turbines have 100-m hub heights, where the wind is much stronger (its extractable power rises as the cube of windspeed), and would normally do much better than the assumed 25% efficiency and 25% losses. Moreover, recently discovered larger-than-expected high-level wind would probably further increase the potential (Archer & Jacobson 2003). At a nominal 75% electrolyzer efficiency, the total wind electricity from these two states could produce 50 million tonnes of hydrogen per year (Lower Heating Value = 120 MJ/kg) on-site, less irrecoverable losses (perhaps on the order of 10%) in transmitting electricity or hydrogen to market. The electrolyzers might also be able to sell byproduct oxygen for gasifying coal or biomass. At a nominal ~40% capacity factor, characteristic of good but not outstanding wind sites with modern turbines, the wind capacity required would be ~640 GW, approaching the total U.S. generating capacity of ~750 GW. This would be a considerable undertaking, but plausibly economic (Leighty 2003). When considering the expense, recall that the U.S. Senate has little trouble voting as much as tens of billions of dollars in subsidies for a clearly uneconomic pipeline to transport 35 TCF/y of stranded gas from Alaska's North Slope. (Such a pipeline, especially via the Canadian route, might make more economic sense if it carried hydrogen instead, reformed at the wellhead with CO_2 reinjection.) For general background on large-scale windpower, see www.awea.org; www.ewea.org; Reeves 2003; Chapman & Wiese 1998; and L. Brown 2004.

918. In 2000, all U.S. highway vehicles used 20.7 qBTU of gasoline (77%) and diesel fuel (23%), 74% of it gasoline in light vehicles (ORNL 2002, p. 2-6). With the more than quintupled-efficiency *SOA*-class fuel-cell light vehicles (119 mpg with fuel cells vs. EIA's 22.6) and roughly tripled-efficiency *SOA*-class fuel-cell heavy vehicles, that 22 EJ (exajoules = 1018 J) of highway-vehicle petroleum fuel could be displaced by ~4.6 qBTU/y of H2, or 40 MT/y, leaving room for traffic growth.

919. Wind machines dedicated to powering electrolyzers could eliminate the cost, maintenance, and uptower weight of the gearbox and power electronics.

What technologies are required to enable the hydrogen transition?

The hydrogen transition depends on superefficient vehicles and distributed generation taking hold in the U.S., more than either of these breakthroughs depend on the hydrogen economy. There has been much misplaced angst about whether the U.S. should invest now in efficient vehicles or in hydrogen technologies. This debate makes as much sense as arguing about whether star athletes should play football or baseball, which occur during different seasons. The answer is, of course, "both": first today's gasoline hybrids, then ultralight hybrids, then ultimately fuel-cell ultralight hybrids. (Some experts believe an intermediate step—efficient hybrids with small hydrogen-fueled internal-combustion engines, like hybrid successors to Ford's *Model U* concept car—may also make sense;[920] these could be considered a partial backstop technology in case cheap, durable fuel cells take longer to commercialize than expected.) In the case of hydrogen, efficiency and distributed generation should clearly come first because these set the stage for the hydrogen economy, which will have trouble competing without them. That is, *hydrogen needs* State of the Art-*class vehicles far more than they need hydrogen.* However, once we have such vehicles and once fuel cells become cheaper, there will be a robust business case for producing the hydrogen that those vehicles would then use.

Hydrogen needs State of the Art-class vehicles far more than they need hydrogen. However, once we have such vehicles and once fuel cells become cheaper, there will be a robust business case for producing the hydrogen that those vehicles would then use.

How can the U.S. profitably make the transition from oil to hydrogen?

The transition will certainly be profitable for automotive and fuel cell manufacturers. We have suggested elsewhere an orderly and integrated sequence of deployment steps that can make it self-financing.[921] However, the hydrogen economy presents a paradox for oil companies. They will already have lower total net income from efficiency adoption (if they sell less oil but don't invest in the efficiency improvements), although the rest of society will have greater income and earnings. If they redefined themselves as *energy* companies, however, they could make more profit by embracing hydrogen than by clinging to petroleum's steadily declining energy market share. Fundamentally, the margins on hydrogen could be greater than the remaining margins on gasoline, for three reasons. First, hydrogen will monetize gas reserves earlier, increasing their present value. On a global basis, oil is becoming increasingly expensive to find and exploit, while gas is comparatively plentiful but is often stranded and remote from market. Second, fuel margins from hydrogen depend on the efficiency of converting the fuel into torque at the wheels. The more efficient the fuel cell is, the more suppliers can charge for the hydrogen, because it competes at the wheels of the car, not per BTU but per mile. Third, refinery assets will be underutilized due to decreased gasoline production. Some of them are strategically located near urban centers and therefore have the potential to become hydrogen production centers.

The margins on hydrogen could be greater than the remaining margins on gasoline.

Oil companies will be able to make more profit from their oil by taking hydrogen out of it in a reformer than having to add more hydrogen to it in a refinery.

920. Thomas 2004.

921. Lovins & Williams 1999; Lovins 2003b.

(Some refineries make more profit today as merchant electricity generators than from selling refined products. Merchant hydrogen is an analogous play and should be especially attractive for near-urban refineries because they've already bought their methane steam reformers and other infrastructure; they would need only to deliver the hydrogen to nearby buyers.)

The oil companies that position themselves to become future hydrogen suppliers will survive the transition and prosper. Depending on the cost of oil reforming technology and the relative cost of carbon credits vs. carbon sequestration, it may make more economic sense to *reform* rather than *refine* oil: H minus C will be worth more than H plus C, or symbolically, (H–C)>(H+C). Oil companies will be able to make more profit from their oil by taking hydrogen out of it (and using it to split off more hydrogen from steam) in a reformer than having to add more hydrogen to it in a refinery.[922] They're already good at both these processes, but their emphasis would shift.

922. U.S. refineries use ~7 MT/y of hydrogen to make high-octane gasoline and to desulfurize diesel fuel. These applications worldwide are responsible for most of the 11%/y growth in hydrogen production.

When could this transition occur?

The oft-described technical obstacles to a hydrogen economy—storage, safety, cost of the hydrogen, and its distribution infrastructure—have already been sufficiently resolved to support rapid deployment starting now in distributed power production, and could be launched in vehicles upon widespread adoption of superefficient vehicles. (The stationary fuel-cell markets will meanwhile have cranked up production to achieve serious cost reductions, even if they capture only a small market share: two-thirds of all U.S. electricity is used in buildings, and many of them present favorable conditions for early adoption.) Automotive use of fuel cells can flourish many years sooner if automakers adopt recent advances in crashworthy, cost-competitive, ultralight autobodies. We certainly believe that the transition could be well underway by 2025, and if aggressively pursued, it could happen substantially sooner. Two keys will unlock hydrogen's potential: early deployment of superefficient vehicles, which shrink the fuel cells so they're affordable and the fuel tanks so they package, and integration of deployment in vehicular and in stationary uses, so each accelerates the other by building volume and cutting cost.[923]

Two keys will unlock hydrogen's potential: early deployment of superefficient vehicles, which shrink the fuel cells so they're affordable and the fuel tanks so they package, and integration of deployment in vehicular and in stationary uses, so each accelerates the other by building volume and cutting cost.

The hydrogen option is not essential to displacing most or all of the oil that the United States uses. But it's the most obvious and probably the most profitable way to do this while simultaneously achieving other strategic advantages.

In sum, the hydrogen option is not essential to displacing most or all of the oil that the United States uses. But it's the most obvious and probably the most profitable way to do this while simultaneously achieving other strategic advantages—complete primary energy flexibility, climate protection, electricity decentralization, vehicles-as-power-plants versatility, faster adoption of renewables, and of course deeper transformation of automaking and related industries so they can compete in a global marketplace that's headed rapidly in this direction.

923. This thesis (Lovins & Williams 1999) is now integral to many major players' business strategies, and is briefly summarized in Lovins 2003b.

Implications and Conclusions

Endgames in chess have just two players. Their dance of their moves and countermoves shapes the outcome with an intricacy that only the world's finest grandmasters and fastest computers can hope to anticipate, and that only in broad strokes. The Oil Endgame has innumerable players, and its complexity is far too great to grasp or foresee. But its implications merit discussion relating to employment, allies and trading partners, developing countries, oil-exporting countries, oil companies, other energy industries, military affairs, the federal budget, and environment and public health. We then conclude with some broad lessons and next steps.

> The opportunities just described have profound and encouraging implications for virtually all stakeholders, turning many old problems into new win-win opportunities.

Implications

Employment

A welcome effect of displacing oil with cheaper alternatives is significant creation of good jobs, both to produce the biofuels and the oil-saving hardware, and through respending the saved oil expenditures, turning a cash outflow into a domestic multiplier of jobs and income. Such increased employment on a broad geographic and skill base is a vital sociopolitical need in most industrialized countries. Renewable energy is already making new jobs in Europe, which expects 0.9 million net by 2020 (over half from biofuels)[924] and may get even more as the pace of switching to renewables accelerates (the current EU target for electricity is 20%-renewable by 2010). Denmark reportedly has about three times as many jobs from manufacturing wind turbines, in which it's the world market leader, as from its electric utility industry.

> Investing in efficiency and renewables tends to make far more new jobs directly than it displaces old ones; lower-cost energy services will induce respending, hence further job creation throughout the economy.

In the United States, our rough estimates suggest that by 2025, the higher-value vehicles being made by the revitalized automotive industry could generate ~240,000 new automaking and supplier jobs;[925] making their lightweight materials could generate possibly some more, due to higher value-added (pp. 161–162); and producing biofuels, nearly 780,000 jobs just from 10% displacement of gasoline by ethanol by 2020, or nearly 1.5 million jobs at our projected 2025 ethanol volume (p. 165). Inevitably, some jobs will also be displaced. By 2020, ~86,000 jobs, mainly within the petroleum industry, will be lost, with some positions such as petroleum engineers, refinery technicians, and pump operators eliminated.[926] However, many of those skilled

> We estimate a net increase in U.S. jobs, due to efficiency improvements, of more than a million jobs by the year 2025 just from producing oil-saving hardware and biofuels. Respending the net saving in oil dollars—$133 billion a year by 2025, equivalent to a very large tax cut—should also stimulate employment considerably.

924. ECOTEC 1999.

925. Estimated from EIA's 21.6-million-light vehicle sales projection for 2025, 77% new-sales share of *SOA* vehicles in 2025 (Fig. 36i), 75% domestic manufacturing share (as in 2003 per *Automotive News* 2003, pp. 16, 20, 25), additional manufacturing cost of $2,544 per unit (p. 70 above, note 345), the 1998 coefficient of 7.57 direct and supplier jobs (excluding respending multiplier) per million 2000 $ of automaking revenue (McAlinden, Hill, & Swiecki 2003, pp. 8, 16), and a ~0.5% sales loss from gross price elasticity. These inputs yield 239,000 marginal automaking and supplier jobs due to the higher value-added to make *State of the Art* vehicles. We didn't try to calculate potential shifts, in either direction, in job intensity; this is just a first-order approximation.

926. Bezdek & Wendling 2003.

and versatile people are likely to be rehired by successor industries, such as biorefineries, in the revitalized rural economy (pp. 162–165). Over all end-uses (those just counted explicitly plus a conservative estimate for trucks, airplanes, buildings, and industry), we estimate a net increase in U.S. jobs, due to efficiency improvements, of more than a million jobs by the year 2025 just from producing oil-saving hardware and biofuels. Respending the net saving in oil dollars—$133 billion a year by 2025, equivalent to a very large tax cut—should also stimulate employment considerably.

Allies and trading partners

"Under current circumstances," former CIA Director R. James Woolsey recently testified, "an oil crisis will affect all our economies, regardless of the source of our own imports. We must think in terms of the world's dependence, not only our own."[927] Moral, cultural, and historical ties aside, there are compelling commercial reasons for encouraging allies and trading partners to engage in their own versions of the *Mobilization* strategy. The U.S. invests heavily in the military security of Western Europe, Japan, South Korea, Taiwan, and Israel, none of which has oil; indeed, they depend on oil and oil imports even more than we do. Those relationships are important for other reasons. Many countries are more worried about oil than the United States seems to be, and may well choose to embark on a new path of aggressive oil displacement once they realize it's possible. The more oil such friends join in saving, the more the common oil problem diminishes. America should therefore invest the persuasive power of its own example, the creativity of its scientists and technologists, the competitive skills of its businesspeople, and the energy of its citizens in making the transition beyond oil a compelling global trend. The alternative is spending blood and treasure to get and keep access to oil that others, for their own deeply held reasons, will increasingly seek to deny to developed countries in general and to the United States in particular.

In our professional careers, the coauthors of this report have worked on energy issues in the private and public sectors in more than fifty countries worldwide. Each society has a unique economic structure, culture, and climate, and they differ widely in styles of governance (e.g., laissez-faire vs. dirigiste). Yet so far we have not found one to which a variant of the technological and policy approach described here could not be effectively adapted if skillfully tailored to local conditions.

The main obstacle to hatching home-grown versions in some countries has been their erroneous conviction, born of their striking progress in saving energy two or three decades ago, that they are already as energy-efficient as they can be. Of no country on earth is that true. There are, of course,

---

Any country, including America's even more oil-dependent partners abroad, can advantageously apply similar oil-displacing opportunities, differing only in detail. A strong U.S. example will be critical; expecting others to do what we say, not what we do, would be hypocritical.

A helping hand, technical and policy collaboration free of "not-invented-here" constraints, a friendly rivalry in who can save oil fastest, and the spillover of U.S.-led technology acceleration into global markets would do wonders for rapidly reaching a "tipping point" that turns global oil consumption irrevocably downward.

---

927. Woolsey 2004.

many differences; savings in places like Western Europe and Japan may be modestly smaller and costlier than in the U.S. But savings will still be large and lucrative, because the differences are less important than the similarities. A strong U.S. example, a helping hand, technical and policy collaboration free of "not-invented-here" constraints, a friendly rivalry in who can save oil fastest, and the spillover of U.S.-led technology acceleration into global markets would do wonders for rapidly reaching a "tipping point"[928] that turns global oil consumption irrevocably downward.

Developing countries

The World Bank estimates that 2.3 billion people today have no access to electricity and 1.6 billion have no access to modern fuels. For many of those people, life is nearly as nasty, brutish, and short as it was a thousand years ago. Such deprivation, hunger, preventable disease, and illiteracy are blots on the world's conscience. Turning these conditions into opportunities for shared wealth creation is an unimaginably large opportunity for which the pioneers of "Bottom of the Pyramid" thinking and action make a powerful business case.[929]

Leapfrog development

Among the several billion people who are starting to get ahead, most notably in the burgeoning commercial centers of China and India, the oil-displacing potential for leapfrogging over obsolete development patterns is stupendous. Societies that are building housing, offices, factories, and infrastructure and are producing appliances, vehicles, and industrial equipment have the chance to do it right the first time and to adopt world-class resource efficiency. In fact, failure to do so is one of the heaviest drags on development, because inefficient resource use diverts most of the investment into costly supply-side projects, leaving too little to buy the things that were supposed to use the resources. For example, the financial capital needed to build a factory making quintupled-efficiency compact-fluorescent lamps or heat-blocking superwindows is about a thousandfold less, and pays back about ten times faster, than the capital otherwise needed to expand the supply of electricity to provide the same increase in light or comfort. The product of intensity times velocity of capital implies about a ten-thousandfold saving from buying "negawatts" wherever they're cheaper than megawatts. This strategy—based on rewarding electricity providers for reducing bills rather than selling energy—could turn the power sector, which now gobbles about one-fourth of the world's development capital, into a net exporter of capital for other development needs.[930]

This shift is even more vital and timely for developing countries, which are over twice as oil-intensive as rich countries but can afford oil even less. Making advanced energy efficiency the cornerstone of the development process can also free up enormous amounts of scarce capital to fund other development needs. This strategy may especially commend itself to China and other Asian nations eager to escape or avoid the oil trap.

928. This characteristic of nonlinear systems means that a process of change reaches the point where a small, seemingly unimportant, incremental change tips the system into a wholly different mode of behavior. Malcolm Gladwell (2000) illustrates with a rhyme: "Tomato ketchup / in a bottle, first none'll come, / and then the lot'll."

929. Prahalad 2004.

930. Lovins & Gadgil 1991

What does this have to do with oil? A lot. Building an oil-frugal or even an oil-free economy from scratch is easier than converting an oil economy to kick the habit. Superefficient energy use, built in the first time, actually *reduces* the capital cost of many buildings and industrial processes; non-oil supplies suffer less hard-currency outflow and price volatility; and the high capital intensity of oil-related supply investments is avoided. It's gratifying that many developing countries are eager to progress past the oil trap without falling in, and disappointing that bilateral and multilateral aid and advice efforts are doing so little to help them execute this emerging strategy. The opportunity is unprecedented; the prize is vast; the time is short. China's mid-2004 energy strategy, making efficient use the top national priority (pp. 135–136, above) is an act of farsighted leadership that we hope others, in both the developing and developed worlds, will emulate.

Climate change and development

There's a striking convergence between the goals of accelerating equitable global development, averting oil dependence by those not already suffering from it, and helping developing countries avoid becoming as much of the climate problem as developed countries now are. As Lord Browne, Group Chief Executive of BP plc, recently wrote:[931]

> It would be morally wrong and politically futile to expect countries struggling to achieve basic levels of development to abandon their aspirations to grow and to improve their people's living standards. But it would be equally wrong to ignore the fact that by 2025, energy-related carbon dioxide emissions from development countries are likely to exceed those from the member states of the Organization [for] Economic Cooperation and Development. Instead of being daunted by the scale of this challenge, policymakers must recognize the scale of the opportunity: developing countries have the potential to leapfrog the developed world's process of industrialization, thereby providing an enormous opportunity to improve energy efficiency and reduce emissions.

He elaborated this theme in the same spirit as our case for displacing oil:

> Seven years after the Kyoto meeting, it is becoming clear that the reduction of greenhouse gas emissions is a soluble problem, and that the mechanisms for delivering the solutions are within reach. In that spirit of cautious optimism, it is time to move beyond the current Kyoto debate…. [T]he costs of deep-water oil and gas development have fallen by a factor of three over the last 15 years, dramatically extending the frontier of commercial activity. There is no reason to think that research and development in the area of benign energy systems would be less successful….Counterintuitively, BP found that it was able to reach its initial target of reducing emissions by 10 percent below its 1990 levels without cost. Indeed, the company added around $650 million of shareholder value, because the bulk of the reductions came from the elimination of leaks and waste. Other firms—such as electricity generator Entergy, car manufacturer Toyota, and mining giant Rio Tinto—are having similar experience. The overwhelming message from these experiments is that efficiency can both pay dividends and

"Developing countries have the potential to leapfrog the developed world's process of industrialization, thereby providing an enormous opportunity to improve energy efficiency and reduce emissions."

— *Lord John Browne,
Chairman, BP plc*

931. Browne 2004.

reduce emissions.[932]...Neither prescriptive regulations nor fiscal interventions designed to collect revenue rather than to alter behavior provide the answer. Rather, governments must identify meaningful objectives and encourage the business sector to attain them by using its knowledge of technology, markets, and consumer preferences.

The global economy, oil savings, and development

We've already noted the salutary effects of biosubstitution on rural economies and hence on the prospects for replacing agricultural subsidies, especially in the U.S. and EU, with real revenues for new rural outputs. This could be a big step toward letting developing-country farmers compete fairly to serve both home and export markets (p. 210). The future we envisage may or may not entail large-scale international trading of biofuels, such as Brazilian ethanol. It would certainly involve dwindling trade in oil—a roughly $400-billion business in 2002. But the decline of oil as an important trade commodity should be more than offset by the rise in trade for oil-displacing technologies and materials. Correcting highly suboptimal investments in using oil and spending its proceeds should also markedly improve global economic efficiency, vitality, and equity.

What would happen if not just other OECD nations but also the emerging economies of Brazil, Russia, India, and China (the BRIC nations) followed the U.S. lead and secured their own energy-efficient futures? According to Goldman Sachs,[933] the BRICs' economies will be half the size of the G6 by 2025, and will overtake their GDP by 2045. Therefore, these countries' energy development path matters a great deal to the overall energy markets and the health of the global economy. Our initial view is if these nations achieved the levels of energy efficiency we've described for *State of the Art* technologies, then total global demand for oil in 2025 would stabilize at close to 2000 levels, while accommodating tremendous economic growth that doubles the BRIC nations' GDP.

This suggests that advanced technology, which all the BRIC nations and many more can perfectly well produce and improve further, can provide a vehicle for increased and broader prosperity without the associated problems of environmental degradation and climate change. Oil would have a decreasing impact on the global economy, further limiting OPEC's pricing power (as well as that of the LNG cartel), thereby reducing the risk of periodic global recessions triggered by oil-price volatility. Moreover, this implies that the global gap between the haves and the have-nots can be reduced, since, for example, consumer products would be increasingly affordable if they did not come with a big energy bill attached to operate them. Finally, for oil-producing nations, it means that the inevitable reforms in their economies and political systems must be accelerated.

If Brazil, Russia, India, and China achieved the levels of energy efficiency we've described for *State of the Art* technologies, then total global demand for oil in 2025 would stabilize at close to 2000 levels.

932. RMI estimates that operational energy and carbon savings are broadly similar among Shell, BP, and ExxonMobil, which modestly reports that over 25 years, its refineries and chemical plants "have improved their energy efficiency by more than 35 percent and opportunities have been identified to achieve an additional 15 percent improvement" (ExxonMobil 2004).

933. Wilson & Purushothaman 2003.

Oil-exporting countries

At first blush, oil-exporting countries seem to enjoy a favorable position. Their national oil companies or similar entities own some 94% of global oil reserves (international oil companies own only ~6%). Their oil assets seem to be appreciating. They are becoming, on the whole, better able to fend off unwanted advances (or worse) from more powerful states that want their oil. At today's high oil prices, they are raking in cash. An important side-effect of the Iraq war and the subsequent oil-price "risk premium" is that Iran, which was in dire straits, Saudi Arabia, which had run down its financial reserves, and many other cash-strapped oil exporters have rapidly replenished their Treasuries. This equips them to weather downturns, bargain harder, defer or buy off internal reforms longer, and even pursue regional ambitions with greater effectiveness and resolve. For oil buyers, these were largely unanticipated and unwelcome outcomes.

An extremely rapid shift away from oil could outpace exporters' adaptive capacity, but in a global market, with strong calls on oil for development in China, India, and elsewhere, the practical pace may well be more measured. However, even full loss of oil markets wouldn't eliminate crude oil's value: the hydrogen it contains is probably worth more without the carbon than with the carbon, even if nobody pays for carbon not released. Exporters can use this prospect to hedge their bets as they diversify their economies.

Nonetheless, there is a shadow side for the oil-exporters as well. Though oil discoveries need not be a curse and can be a blessing, still too few oil-rich states have followed a successful development path and steered safely past the ill effects that often flow from oil wealth (pp. 18–19). In many of the key exporting nations, huge development deficits have persisted and often are worsening under severe demographic pressures (p. 22). For all exporters, even those with sound development priorities and prudent fiscal management, oil prices fluctuate unpredictably, and massive shocks to oil markets could occur at any moment (and in due course probably will, no matter what the United States does). Oil price volatility makes these nations vulnerable to a host of ills—even more vulnerable than their customers are, because oil is a small part of the buyers' economy but far more, even most, of the sellers' economy. However it may occur, less oil revenue means higher unemployment, more disaffected young men, lower investments, higher debt, deeper stagnation, more tendency to turn inwards and to disengage from the global economy,[934] stronger calls for change, more opportunities for demagogues, and rising instability and extremism. Oil wealth is not always to be envied: both its gain and loss can hurt.

Indeed, it is now becoming clear that one of the main drivers of oil price is the cashflow expectations of major exporters, particularly Saudi Arabia as the key setter of production and price. Industry estimates suggest the Kingdom needs an oil price significantly above $30—well beyond the previous OPEC target price band (if not corrected, as it probably should be, for the reduced purchasing power of the U.S. dollar). For some major exporters, notably Venezuela, the perceived need is probably well above $40.

934. Woolsey (2004) remarks: "It is sometimes said that whoever is in power in Saudi Arabia, the Saudi Government will have to sell substantial oil to the world. This is not the case, however, if those who take power wish to live in the 7th century. We can hope for movement in the Kingdom toward reform and subsequent stability under the sort of policies advocated, in however limited a fashion, by the Crown Prince. But we certainly cannot prudently count on such a course of events."

Just as oil is regaining premium market value and key exporters need such value more than ever to sustain their stability and aspirations, here comes the threat that their oil may not ultimately find a market—an outcome that in the context of climate protection has already led OPEC to advance the remarkable proposition that oil exporters deserve "compensation" for any oil not bought[935] (an implied global take-or-pay contract unique in the history of commerce). The outcome of a U. S. transition beyond oil, however, is not so clear-cut. Depending largely on who else adopts a similar course, how much, and how soon, exporters may end up selling their oil later, or to others instead, or in other forms such as hydrogen that may even be more valuable than crude oil or refined products. Only the broad contours of these diverging futures are clear; many details, especially of timing, remain hazy. What is absolutely obvious is that exporters were going to face a stark need for diversification anyway, and may face it sooner rather than later. That may not be such a bad thing for them. Better to face it sooner with thoughtful planning than later as differential depletion and cut-throat competition over scarcer and more concentrated supplies force unwelcome choices in haste and even chaos.

From economic history, one might suspect that major oil exporters' high desired prices reflect significant inefficiencies and rent-seeking behaviors characteristic of statist commodity monopolists. Like many commodity producers before them, these nations will ultimately need to relinquish government control of the economy, privatize their state-run enterprises, cut loose freeloaders, and reform their regulatory institutions. Otherwise they cannot discipline their markets and attract the foreign direct investment needed to broaden their economies. The sooner they start, the longer they might remain in power and the greater their chance of a graceful post-oil transition.

Comparative advantage between competing exporters may shift to those who first diversify their offerings and their economies, not around the margins but fundamentally. It may even make sense for any major holder of oil assets who doesn't believe in the value-enhancing hydrogen prospect to liquidate those holdings early, while market values are high, and invest in hedges. One obvious hedge is investing in the business of making the things that save oil, such as *State of the Art* vehicles and their key enabling technologies. Such a "negabarrel straddle" is bound to make money on either oil or vehicles, and if the hydrogen play succeeds, it'll win both sides of the bet at once. Meanwhile, similar or greater opportunities beckon another key player that's under even more unforgiving economic pressure—major international oil companies.

Oil-exporting countries own some 94% of global oil reserves.

Industry estimates suggest the Kingdom needs an oil price significantly above $30.

935. Barnett, Dessai, & Webber 2004.

The creative destruction challenge
for oil companies

Oil is a great industry but over the long run not a great business: capital-intensive, long-lead-time, a price-taker in a volatile market, a target of political interference and public opprobrium, and based on a dwindling asset. Shifting the business from oil supply to energy services, and redeploying assets accordingly, offers higher returns, lower risks, and higher-value uses of oil companies' skills and hydrocarbons. Biofuels are an excellent product-line extension, and extracting hydrogen from oil in a reformer will generally be more profitable than adding more hydrogen to crude oil in a refinery. Gracefully managing the inevitable transition will be hard but feasible and highly rewarding, especially for early adopters. It will be easier if deliberately planned than if chaotically forced by external events or by depletion seen only in hindsight.

Just as the end of a game of chess is often the most difficult part strategically, so the endgame of oil will be the most strategically difficult for the oil companies. It will require them to think about their assets in a completely different light, to evaluate new business models and processes, and to set up new organizational structures that have the priorities and capabilities necessary to seize the emerging business opportunities. In short, the endgame will require recognition of the disruptive challenge, the vision to understand its dimensions, and the will to meet it.

If the U.S. automotive, truck, and aircraft sectors are successful in revitalizing themselves through efficiency, then the world's oil companies will indeed face the challenge of transforming their businesses to meet new market realities—a process Joseph Schumpeter aptly described as "creative destruction" (p. 128). Major oil companies derive nearly 70% of their enterprise value from the expected future value of their oil and gas reserves.[936] For each barrel of oil sold, more than two-thirds of the margin is in upstream exploration and production (E&P), with downstream refining and marketing often yielding little profit. Yet as the largest consumer of oil, the United States, becomes more efficient, it could potentially use 40–50% less oil by 2025 than conventionally predicted. Displacing product demand shrinks the potential for those fat E&P margins to drive total corporate profits.

We envision two potential scenarios: (1) the rest of the world follows the U.S. lead and global oil demand drops, leading (if nothing else is done) to concomitant drops in oil prices and reserve valuation, and (2) only OECD countries follow the U.S. lead, but demand in the developing world grows rapidly to offset those savings eventually, thereby maintaining the price of oil within the OPEC price band then prevailing. Given the tendency for advanced technologies to diffuse widely where they convey a cost or efficiency advantage, the special incentive for developing countries to adopt a leapfrog development strategy, and the evident eagerness of China (among others) to do so, we believe that oil companies should focus on the former scenario, and we will therefore address it here.

Clayton Christensen observes that most big companies can see disruptive changes coming, and have the managerial, technological, product portfolio, asset base, and deep cash pockets to address them. Nevertheless, few large companies have been successful in launching disruptive products or businesses. Christensen comments, "What managers lack is the habit of think-

936. The valuation of oil companies falls into three classes: the investor-owned supermajors (ExxonMobil, BP, Shell, TotalFina, Chevron/Texaco, ConocoPhillips), the pure plays (e.g., Anadarko), and the national oil companies (e.g., CNOOC). We estimate that in 2003, 70% of the total valuation of the supermajors is based on the valuation of their reserves using data from J.S. Herrold and analyst reports. The impact of changes in reserves and their valuation can be empirically seen during the recent drop in Shell's share price after the announcement of overstated reserves.

937. Christensen & Overdorf 2001   938. Perez 2002.

ing about the organization's capabilities as carefully as they think about individual people's capabilities." Further, he notes, "In the largest companies, [cultural and individual] values—particularly those that determine what are its acceptable gross margins and how big an opportunity has to be before it becomes interesting—define what the company can and cannot do."[937] This defines the core challenge of leadership in major oil companies.

Specifically, if the oil companies take seriously the possibility of the fundamental market changes we have described, then they will begin to explore investments in new technology clusters that would act as a bridge for their businesses through the transition ahead. Carlota Perez at Sussex University has studied the relationship between technology revolutions and the behavior of financial capital, focusing on the tendency for new technologies to arrive in waves, as Schumpeter described, rather than in continuous, incremental steps. "Technological change occurs by clusters of radical innovations forming successive and distinct revolutions that modernize the whole productive structure," according to Perez.[938] The group of technologies employed in ultralight hybrid vehicle production is just such a cluster, with revolutionary implications. This tendency toward clustering, and the accompanying boom-and-bust industry cycles implied, are scale-free properties of technology evolution in the economy at large. Such clustering happens at all levels, across all industries, with the same self-organizing organic logic as punctuated equilibrium in evolutionary biology. And such a clustering is triggering the endgame for the "golden age" for petroleum. But the major oil companies are large enough to manage the transition by diversifying their portfolios of technology investments in a variety of new directions.

In fact, these companies can see the efficiency- and even the hydrogen-based future coming, and one of them, Shell, published in 2001 a credible scenario for how and when the transition could occur (Box 24)—one that includes a China-led leapfrog to superefficient cars and hydrogen fuel cells, and shows global oil use stagnant until 2020 and declining thereafter.[939] Today, efficiency, hydrogen and renewables appear to be small and insignificant business opportunities with lower margins than the existing oil business, and they are often downplayed in the strategic planning and business development process. The oil industry, however, is no longer monolithic in its strategic response to this business challenge. Already, three large oil companies—Shell, BP, and Norsk Hydro—have created, and placed significant capital and organizational resources behind, their hydrogen, renewables, or energy services groups.[940] As a demonstration

> Major oil companies derive nearly 70% of their enterprise value from the expected future value of their oil and gas reserves. For each barrel of oil sold, more than two-thirds of the margin is in upstream exploration and production.

> Shell published in 2001 a credible scenario that includes a China-led leapfrog to super-efficient cars and hydrogen fuel cells, and shows global oil use stagnant until 2020 and declining thereafter.
> Three large oil companies—Shell, BP, and Norsk Hydro—have created, and placed significant capital and organizational resources behind, their hydrogen, renewables, or energy services groups.

939. Remarkably, the October 2001 Shell Group Planning scenarios *Exploring the Future: Energy Needs, Choices and Possibilities: Scenarios to 2050* laid out a discontinuity-driven future somewhat similar to that presented in this report: Shell International 2001. See Box 24.

940. ChevronTexaco has a hydrogen business unit and ExxonMobil has stakes in fuel-cell companies. However, these groups are not positioned as the organizational equivalents of the traditional upstream, downstream, and supply and trading groups, but are treated more as business experiments within the existing organization. To our knowledge, none of the national oil companies or Japanese *motouri*s have made significant business investments in renewables, energy service companies, or hydrogen.

24: Shell's visionary energy futures

Royal Dutch/Shell Group is widely considered the best company for scenario forecasting. Shell uses long-term energy scenarios—looking out over 50 years to understand how energy systems could change, thereby informing its business decisions. The work is based on its worldwide experience in diverse energy businesses, serving energy consumers, and developing and applying technology. The two scenarios developed by Shell International in its 2001 report, *"Exploring the Future: Energy Needs, Choices and Possibilities: Scenarios to 2050,"* explore different paths to a sustainable energy system, and contrast an evolutionary progression from coal, to gas, to renewables (or possibly nuclear) against the potential for a hydrogen economy that's supported by developments in fuel cells, advanced hydrocarbon technologies, and carbon dioxide sequestration. Here's a rough paraphrase:

Scenario 1: Dynamics as Usual

The energy transition described by the *Dynamics as Usual* scenario continues past dynamics. Societal demands for cleaner, more convenient energy drive a gradual shift from high- to low-carbon fuels; and towards electricity as the energy carrier. The path towards a range of new renewables is relatively direct—supported by strong gas growth in the medium term—but only after advances in energy storage and the development of a next generation of renewables around 2025. By 2050, renewables could account for a third of world primary energy and could supply all incremental energy. But underlying this transition is a process of intense competition, maturing new technologies, and shifting social priorities, which make the transition anything but smooth: that is to say, dynamics as usual.

Key stages:

2005	Hybrid vehicles proliferate
2010	"Dash for Gas"; renewable pump priming
2015	Oil price shock triggers resource expansion
2020	OECD renewables stall at 20% of electricity supply; gas security concerns emerge
2030	New nuclear stalls; next generation of renewables emerge
2040	Oil scarcity drives biofuels expansion

Scenario 2: The Spirit of the Coming Age

The Spirit of the Coming Age is based on the impact of a major discontinuity in energy technology. The driver is a superior end-use technology pulled by consumers, which remakes the energy system around it. The key point is the potential for new technologies to emerge from unexpected parts of the energy system. An indirect path toward renewable energy is followed, with advanced hydrocarbon technologies (coal gasification) providing a bridge to a hydrogen economy in countries like China and India, and eventually creating a large demand for renewables and nuclear. On the surface this world appears chaotic because of the disruptive new technology. The early period is one of wide experimentation, with the eventual winners hard to see. But underneath, a new infrastructure logic is emerging, although this becomes clear only after several decades.

(continued on next page)

of its commitment, Shell and Norsk Hydro have created new business divisions for renewables, equal to the existing traditional business divisions.[941]

These firms view themselves not as oil companies but as energy companies: BP's rebranding as "Beyond Petroleum" was more than just creative advertising. As energy companies, they recognize that during this century, oil production is likely to peak, and that we are already entering the age of gas as a transition to the future hydrogen age.[942] Shell, BP, and Exxon-Mobil hydrocarbon reserves are heavily weighted towards gas compared to their counterparts at ChevronTexaco, Total, and ConocoPhillips.[943]

941. Behind the scenes, some other oil majors that might outwardly appear inimical to such new ventures are in fact engaged in often useful and sometimes exciting R&D that is seeking to gain internal political traction.

942. See for example, the several speeches on Shell's website regarding the future of energy and the coming age of gas: Brinded 2004; van der Veer 2004; de Segundo 2003.

943. As of 1Q03, the gas fraction of the oil and gas reserves, using a nominal ratio of 6b CF gas = 1 Mbbl crude oil, was: Shell 47% (before reserve restatement), BP 43%, ExxonMobil 44%, ElfTotalFina 33%, ConocoPhillips 29%, ChevronTexaco 27%.

Box 24: Shell's visionary energy futures (continued)

Key stages:

2005	First stationary and vehicular fuel cells—high consumer interest
2010	Gas resource outlook expands; Fuel-cell fuel distribution innovations; renewables limited to niches
2015	Convergence around fuel cells for transport and stationary uses—gas network backbone
2020	Unconventional oil and gas expand in China and India; fuel cells reach 25% of light-vehicle sales in OECD
2030	Solid H_2 storage transition; renewables pulled by strong H_2 demand
2040	H_2 infrastructure expansion

The two scenarios have five features in common:

1. The important role of natural gas as a bridge fuel over at least the first two decades and the importance of reducing supply security fears,

2. The disruptions that oil markets will face as new vehicle technologies diffuse,

3. The shift towards distributed or decentralized heat and power supply for economic and social reasons,

4. The potential for renewables to be the eventual primary source of energy and the importance of robust energy storage solutions, and

5. The difficulty of identifying winning services or technologies in a period of a high innovation and experimentation.

The key differences between the two scenarios, and their dominant energy products, reflect different energy resource potentials, the timing and nature of technology possibilities, and social and personal priorities—in such areas as health, security, the environment, convenience, aesthetics, and the openness to change.

The increased use of natural gas for power generation and, in the longer term, as a source of hydrogen could increase gas demand and improve the value of gas reserves relative to oil. And as we suggested on p. 242 and will discuss just below, it could even uphold and enhance the ultimate value of oil reserves.

In the near term, investments in clean, renewable biofuels could present attractive options for oil companies, especially insofar as the use of these fuels is compatible with existing petroleum distribution and handling infrastructures. By blending biofuels into gasoline and diesel pools, oil companies can improve the environmental performance attributes of their products, especially climate impact, while paving the way for even more fundamental shifts in technology in the years ahead. The oil majors are already experimenting with biofuels in regional markets around the world, developing new purchasing, investment, and branding strategies to take advantage of opportunities for blending renewable fuels with conventional petroleum-based hydrocarbon products.

As biofuels, especially ethanol, begin to account for a greater proportion of U.S. gasoline supplies (pp. 103–111), some oil companies may begin to integrate backwards along this supply chain. Several recent developments indicate that some oil companies—and even automobile companies—could already be headed in this direction:

Biofuels offer an attractive transitional product. In February 2004, Shell and BP/Aral began blending up to 5% biodiesel into their diesel supplies in Germany.

- Royal Dutch/Shell Group has invested $46 million to acquire a 22.5% equity stake in Iogen Energy Corp., a Canadian company developing a new enzyme-based technology to produce ethanol from biomass crop wastes. Shell is also engaged in research and development of other biomass-to-liquids processes based on Fischer-Tropsch technologies that convert synthesis gas from biomass feedstocks into high-quality, custom-tailored, zero-sulfur diesel fuel components.

- Volkswagen and DaimlerChrysler are investors in an innovative biomass-to-liquids technology being developed in Germany by Choren, a company whose name was chosen based on the symbols for carbon, hydrogen, and oxygen plus the word "renewable."

- Both Shell and BP are experimenting with blending biodiesel into their diesel pools on a significant scale in Europe. In February 2004, Shell and BP/Aral began blending up to 5% biodiesel into their diesel supplies in Germany, which produces and consumes more biodiesel than any other country in Europe. Biodiesel blends are already widely used in France and Italy.

At the same time that oil companies are increasing their investments in natural gas, biofuels, and energy services, and adapting their infrastructures to lower-than-projected oil demand levels, they may be well advised to step back from very-high-cost oil development projects in deep waters and remote areas of the world. Making accurate judgments about which new oil investments will be economic is the most fundamental strategic and cultural challenge facing the industry, and it is one that may well lead to significant divergences in performance among the major oil companies in the decade ahead.

The question arises as to what the future valuation on the oil reserves would be if the transition to hydrogen-based technologies comes sooner than conventionally expected. The traditional view is that the oil reserves are valued based on the discounted value of their expected future production and the anticipated net margin (future price minus cost to develop). This view assumes that the future price for the oil reserves is the price of crude oil, i.e., what the market will pay for the potential to produce hydrocarbon refined products. What if it is not? What if the future price for the oil reserves is based simply on the price of hydrogen? After all, what oil companies own is *reserves of hydrocarbons,* which can be used in refineries, reformers, or other sort of chemical processors. Asked another way: under what conditions will the hydrogen in the oil be worth more without the carbon than with it (mathematically, when is H–C > H+C)? To what extent could that relationship remain true even if nobody pays for keeping carbon out of the atmosphere? The long-run valuation of oil reserves may ultimately depend on the cost of the technology for converting these hydrocarbons into hydrogen and the cost of carbon sequestration. (The same is true for coal.) As these technologies bring the delivered cost of hydrogen closer to the delivered cost of reformed natural gas (or hydrogen from windpower electrolysis), the long-run valuation on these crude-oil reserves will rise accordingly.

> **What if the future price for oil reserves is based on the price of hydrogen?**
> If oil is a competitive way to make hydrogen, it could become more valuable than it is now as a hydrocarbon.

Our premise is that the future hydrogen value chain will be profitable. As discussed in the prior section on hydrogen (pp. 227–242), this is based on the ability of the fuel-cell vehicle to have a lower total lifecycle cost than the ultralight gasoline-hybrid vehicle. If we use distributed rather than centralized infrastructure, delivering hydrogen fuel into the vehicle for less than $4/kg does not appear to be the limiting factor; rather, this future scenario will depend mainly on the performance, cost, and durability of the fuel cell. It would be unwise to bet that those requirements cannot be met by at least one, probably many, of the able competitors now in this race. If this happens, it can be the biggest gamechanger in hydrocarbons since Drake, Spindletop, and the other epochal events that gave birth to the oil industry, because it will fundamentally change how the value of mobility, power, and heat is ultimately delivered to the customer.

Certain oil company assets may be quite valuable in this future value chain. Gas fields, pipelines, storage facilities, and other midstream infrastructure will be highly valuable, some more so than today. Some refineries may be well positioned within urban areas to serve as hydrogen manufacturing facilities. Higher-quality retail assets (if they have the cost structure to compete with new retail formats like hypermarkets), especially the brand itself, will be important in selling all transportation fuels at retail, not just oil. Just as oil companies are only now understanding their refineries as energy centers that convert energy and molecules across the oil, gas, power, and chemical value chains, so too must they incorporate the value of their assets within the future hydrogen value chain.

Until the hydrogen future occurs, what will happen to the oil companies' profits? The danger is straightforward. By 2025, which is not very long in the farsighted oil business, if *State of the Art* efficiency technologies are adopted, oil companies could be selling 40% less oil (50% less if biofuels are adopted), and at least 17% less gas than the EIA forecast demand.[944] The price of both fuels would also undoubtedly be lower than today's expectations (barring other demand- or supply-side surprises). Accordingly, gross revenues could decline by significantly more than 40%. We doubt that oil companies have the cost structure that will enable them to cut costs fast enough to address such a revenue shortfall. Moreover, most of their capital is tied to assets that directly support the oil value chain. The refining sector will be particularly hard hit, since the return on these assets is directly tied to capacity utilization.[945] Capacity to upgrade heavier fractions to gasoline in particular will be stranded by plummeting demand for gasoline. In the absence of new profit streams, absolute profit will fall sharply. Domestic E&P could be especially hard-hit because of its inherently higher cost vs. less mature provinces.

Major oil companies have tremendous assets that transcend the narrow oil niche: technical know-how, energy infrastructure assets, energy market knowledge, globally recognized brands, customer relationships, cash flow, strong balance sheets, and, most importantly, their extremely talented people. As energy companies entering the era of efficiency, they should recognize that solutions-economy business models (p. 193, above) with less volatile margins may grow rapidly. Indeed, services based on efficiency and non-crop renewables (such as windpower) are financially riskless, increasing their value on a risk-adjusted basis vis-à-vis hydrocarbon margins. In addition, expanded customer relationships could open the door to additional "service uplift"—higher margin from selling efficiency retrofits or even wider service bundles, perhaps ultimately including access and mobility services (p. 196). The more forward-looking energy companies have already begun such experiments, with BP's Energy Services and

A post-oil world will still need energy—just less of it and in different forms than previously supposed. Collectively, hydrogen, biofuels, other renewables, and energy services will earn substantial profits. Standing pat is not a sound strategy.

944. In addition to the absolute drop in volume, refineries' product slate will shift away from the light side of the barrel (*Technical Annex*, Ch. 23). For example, EIA predicts 46% of 2025 petroleum products will be gasoline, but by the time all *State of the Art* efficiency is phased in, the mix would be only 29% gasoline, and biofuel substitution would reduce that to zero. In general, the slate shifts toward middle distillates, which in turn could be displaced by greater emphasis on biodiesel or on heavy-vehicle fuel cells.

945. Refining margins in all refinery market zones are highly correlated to the underlying capacity factors or asset utilization, which in turn are directly the result of the demand for petroleum products within that market zone vs. the refining capacity. Thus, in 2003–04, Singapore refining margins are at historic highs due to unprecedented Chinese demand for oil products. Conversely, these refining margins reached a low ebb during the Asian Economic crisis of 1997–98 when overall Asian demand for oil products fell sharply and refining utilization dropped.

Shell's PULSE Energy.[946] Similarly, the renewables business has a considerable first-mover advantage, since the location of the renewables projects and the ability to acquire or develop transmission is critical to the overall value of the project, and both these kinds of assets are often first-come-first-served. Such new kinds of businesses would not fit today's priorities at most major oil companies; hence the management challenge.

A post-oil world will still need energy—just less of it and in different forms than previously supposed. Collectively, hydrogen, biofuels, other renewables, and energy services will earn substantial profits. Energy services and renewable businesses have the potential to earn attractive returns on capital in the near term;[947] perhaps more importantly, they could offer higher returns than those available from reinvestment in conventional upstream and midstream petroleum development. The ability to convert hydrocarbons to hydrogen will dictate upstream profits for oil, gas, and coal, which will all be competing in the hydrogen market—against each other and against biomass, wind, and the new sources of renewably produced hydrogen likely to emerge. Biofuel margins will meanwhile help support the downstream business assets.

While it may be true that the total margins in the new energy value chain may be lower than the existing ones, companies that move swiftly and cohesively will capture a large share of these, while those that fall behind will suffer and decline. As with automaking, standing pat is not a sound strategy. Building new whaling ships was a bad investment decision in 1850 after the arrival of kerosene fuel, well before kerosene achieved even a 5% market share: the fleet-size vs. product-sales history in Fig. 1 on p. 4 implies that the 1850s and beyond brought much grief for shortsighted shipowners. In our view, building new downstream oil facilities could be a bad investment during the onset of the new efficiency era (of which today's hybrid vehicles are a harbinger) and of competitive biofuels. The key to success, Christensen notes, will be to recognize what new capabilities will be needed to compete, and then to acquire them timely.

Other energy industries

The post-oil future is clearly attractive for natural gas, renewables, and virtually all forms of energy efficiency, whether in conversion, distribution, or end-use. Surprisingly, it may even prove attractive for coal—not as a direct combustion fuel (the main use, fueling central stations, will be increasingly challenged to compete with efficiency and distributed gener-

> Building new downstream oil facilities could be a bad investment during the onset of the new efficiency era (of which today's hybrid vehicles are a harbinger) and of competitive biofuels.

> A post-oil future is bullish for natural gas, renewables, and efficiency. It may even prove advantageous for coal, which may, with successful carbon sequestration, be a low-cost long-run way to pull hydrogen out of water. Nuclear power's inherently high costs will deny it a competitive role, with or without an oil or hydrogen transition.

946. In 1999 (finalized 10-K filing on 30 June 2000), Shell Development Australia formed a joint venture with Woodside Energy Limited and United Energy and Energy Partnership (Ikon Energy Pty Ltd) to create PULSE ENERGY, an energy retail company operating in Eastern Australia's deregulated electricity and gas markets (Shell Australia Limited 1999, p. 5).

947. For example, the leading US ESCO, Quanta, had 1999–2002 gross margins of 15–20%, with net of 4–7%. There are no publicly traded non-manufacturing renewable pure plays. However, we observe that private renewable developers tend to earn about 14–16% return on equity from their projects.

**No matter what happens to oil, climate, or hydrogen,
the future for nuclear power is bleak.**

25: What about nuclear power?

We noted on p. 98 that U.S. electricity is nearly unrelated to oil, although on pp. 113–115 we showed an indirect linkage (saving or displacing gas-fired electric generation can free up natural gas to displace oil in other end-uses). Regardless, nuclear power[948] has no prospects in market-driven energy systems, for a simple reason: new nuclear plants[949] cost too much to build. In round numbers, electricity from *new* light-water reactors will cost twice as much as from new windfarms, five to ten times as much as distributed gas-fired cogeneration or trigeneration in buildings and factories (net of the credit for their recovered heat), and three to thirty times as much as end-use efficiency that can save most of the electricity now used.[950] Any one of these three abundant and widely available competitors alone could knock nuclear power out of the market, and there are three, with more on the way (ultimately including cheap fuel cells). None of these competitors was included, however, in the widely quoted 2003 MIT study of nuclear power.[951] It found that if new nuclear plants become far cheaper, are heavily subsidized (at least initially), and benefit from heavy carbon taxation or its trading equivalent, then they may become able to compete with new coal-fired or gas-fired combined-cycle power stations. However, those, too, are uncompetitive with the three cheaper options that weren't examined—and these comparisons ignore 207 "distributed benefits," which typically favor decentralized options by about an extra tenfold.[952]

In these circumstances, new nuclear plants are simply unfinanceable in the private capital market, and the technology will continue to die of an incurable attack of market forces—all the faster in competitive markets. This is true not just in the U.S., where the last order was in 1978 and all orders since 1973 were cancelled, but globally. Rather than selling a thousand units a year as they'd predicted, nuclear salesmen scour the world for a single order, generally heavily subsidized, while vendors of competing technologies often struggle with too many orders. Only in a handful of countries with centrally planned energy systems that lack market accountability might the odd order still occasionally be placed. During 1990–99, nuclear power worldwide added 3.2 billion watts per year (it grew at a 1% annual rate, vs. 17% for solar cells and 24% for windpower). In recent years, windpower worldwide

(continued on next page)

948. We refer here to nuclear fission, not fusion. Fusion seems much further off. The best its advocates have been able to claim is that fusion power might, decades and billions of dollars' R&D hence, become about as cheap as fission, which itself can't compete in the modern market. Fusion's copious fast-neutron fluxes would also be ideal for turning natural uranium or thorium into bomb materials. Best to cut our losses. An existing, free, well-engineered, highly reliable fusion reactor is appropriately sited 93 million miles away.

949. Advocates of nuclear power often slide past this point—that the argument is about whether to build *more* nuclear plants—by referring to the low *operating* costs of *existing* nuclear plants whose high capital costs are already sunk.

950. Lovins 2001b. During 1989–96, the senior author of this report led perhaps the world's most detailed assessment of electricity-saving technologies, now published as the *Technology Atlas* series, and a couple of meters of supplements, from RMI's spinoff E SOURCE (Boulder CO, www.esource.com).

951. Deutch & Moniz 2003. Our comparison relies on this study's correctly calculated 2000 $ busbar cost of 6.7¢/kWh, implying a delivered cost upwards of 9.3¢/kWh (2002 $) if we conservatively assume the average embedded (not marginal) cost of U.S. transmission and distribution (Lovins et al. 2002).

952. Lovins et al. 2002.

has added ~6–7 billion watts per year. No vendor has made money selling power reactors. This is the greatest failure of any enterprise in the industrial history of the world. We don't mean that as a criticism of nuclear power's practitioners, on whose skill and devotion we all continue to depend; the impressive operational improvements in U.S. power reactors in recent years deserve great credit. It is simply how technologies and markets evolved, despite the best intentions and immense effort. In nuclear power's heydey, its proponents saw no competitors but central coal-fired power stations. Then, in quick succession, came end-use efficiency, combined-cycle plants, distributed generation (including versions that recovered valuable heat previously wasted), and competitive windpower. The range of competitors will only continue to expand more and their costs to fall faster than any nuclear technology can match.

Even if something much worse than the worrisome recent events at Davis-Besse and Mihama never occurs and the technology's other outstanding issues are resolved, nuclear power has no future for purely economic reasons. Monetizing carbon emissions won't help, because it would equally advantage at least two of the three strongest competitors (efficiency and windpower) and partly advantage the other (gas-fired co-/trigeneration). There is thus no analytic basis for the MIT authors' personal opinion that *all* energy options will be needed, so nuclear power merits increased subsidies—thereby, though they didn't say so, retarding its competitors by tilting the playing field against them and diverting investment away from them.

The widespread economic fallacy of counting the wrong competitors is commonly accompanied by another blunder: ignoring opportunity cost (the impossibility of spending the same dollar on two different things at the same time). Let's use an illustration slanted to favor nuclear power. If saving a kWh cost as much as 3¢ (well above average), while delivering a new nuclear kWh cost as little as 6¢ (extremely optimistic), then each 6¢ spent on a nuclear kWh could have bought *two* efficiency kWh instead. Buying the costlier nuclear kWh thus perpetuated one kWh's worth of fossil-fueled generation that's otherwise avoided by choosing the best buys first. (The same logic applies to any other costly option, such as a solar cell, that's bought instead of cheaper options like electric efficiency.) The MIT study found that only a major expansion of nuclear power would justify the high costs of addressing its many challenges: a tripling of world nuclear capacity, for example, would be needed to cut by 25% the conventionally projected *increase* in world CO_2 emissions to 2050. But because it's so much costlier than other ways to reduce CO_2, and because it diverts funds from efficiency, such nuclear expansion would actually make climate change worse than if cheaper options were bought instead.

Nuclear advocates have long hoped that a hydrogen transition would finally give them an economic rationale. But whether the hydrogen is made by splitting water with nuclear electricity or with a chemical reaction driven by nuclear heat, the economics are so far out of any competitive range[953] that spending a billion dollars to prove this experimentally is a clear waste of money. The advocates' other last hope was new (or recycled old) nuclear technologies, such as the South African pebble-bed reactor—a Holy Grail of reactor developers for decades, with no

(continued on next page)

953. Lovins 2003b.

Coal may prove a very cheap way to produce bulk hydrogen without climate shifts.

ation), but as a feedstock. Coal contains less hydrogen than oil, let alone natural gas, but is an exceptionally cheap and effective feedstock for syngas processes, especially those that drive steam reformers producing hydrogen. Ultimately this may prove a very cheap way to produce bulk hydrogen. The precondition will almost certainly be success in sequestering the resulting carbon dioxide, because the world's coal resources are limited not by geology but by the capacity of the atmosphere to accept carbon without climate shifts. The insights being assembled at places like Princeton University's BP-funded Carbon Mitigation Initiative will reveal whether this hope is realistic. Meanwhile, a tour d'horizon of breakthroughs in renewable hydrogen production, much of it direct (not via electrolysis) and based on biological or biomimetic photochemistry, reveals many dark horses pulling up fast. And no matter what happens to oil, climate, or hydrogen, the future for nuclear power is bleak (Box 25).

25: What about nuclear power? (continued)

success yet, no solution to the basic economic problem, and a much higher risk of proliferating nuclear weapons.[954] Even a little proliferation, especially to non-state actors, obviously destroys U.S. national security, since anonymous nuclear attacks with no return address, e.g., via shipping container, and with no physical base to retaliate against, can be neither deterred nor punished, and are very difficult to prevent.[955] The only semi-effective defense is prevention, by removing the technical ingredients and innocent "cover" for proliferation, and by eliminating the social and political conditions that feed and motivate the pathology of hatred.

954. The proposed design has some innovative and evolutionary features. Its key economic uncertainty is whether its passive safety design is convincing enough to avoid building a containment structure, which its lower power density would render large and costly. (A no-containment design is unlikely to be licensable in most countries, partly because of terrorist risk and partly because, as the late Dr. Edward Teller pointed out decades ago, any leak in the helium/steam heat exchanger can send steam into the reactor core where it can cause a coal-gas reaction, form methane and hydrogen, and perhaps explode. Every high-temperature gas-cooled reactor built so far has suffered substantial leaks in its helium coolant circuit.) The ESKOM developers claim a capital cost, without containment, of about \$1,000/kW, about 2–3 times less than for a [contained] light-water reactor; independent analysts estimate more like \$2,000/kW, generally with containment. The claimed busbar cost of ~2.6¢/kWh at a 6%/y discount rate would still be uncompetitive against the three options named above, whether for producing electricity or hydrogen. Proliferation could be a show-stopper: the 8% ^{235}U fuel is 84% of the way, in separative work, to 90% enrichment, and each 2.4 GW of pebble-bed electric capacity would require an enrichment plant with a capacity of 500 tonnes of separative work per year (TSWU/y), implying hundreds or thousands of such enrichment plants for large-scale deployment. Professor Hal Feiveson of Princeton summarizes the result: "Lots of enriched uranium close to bomb quality, lots of [enrichment] plants, lots of incentive for innovation to make [enrichment] cheaper and quicker. To me this is an unsettling prospect"—especially since uranium-based bombs are relatively easy to design and make. No technical or political solution to this problem exists. Indeed, *any* nuclear power technology is proliferative because it provides the materials, equipment, skills, and innocent-looking civilian cover for making bombs, as the world is now rediscovering to its potentially immense cost. Conversely, acknowledging the right parenthesis in the nuclear enterprise, and helping all countries substitute cheaper and inherently nonviolent energy options, would make proliferation far more difficult by making the ingredients of do-it-yourself bomb kits harder to get, more conspicuous to try to get, and politically costlier to be caught trying to get, because the reason for wanting them would be unambiguously military (Lovins, Lovins, & Ross 1980; Lovins & Lovins 1979).

955. Bunn & Wier 2004.

U.S. military force structure, posture, and doctrine

On 9/11, a few dollars' worth of weapons and an operating budget on the order of a half-million dollars blew a trillion-dollar hole in the economy and killed three thousand Americans. Although the survival rate approached an extraordinary 90% in the World Trade Center and 99.5% at the Pentagon, the psychological and political impact changed our lives and shook the world. This story is far from over. America's inherent technical vulnerabilities and open society make it possible for a few people to do great harm.

The world's best armed forces, costing more than $13,000 a second,[956] are not keeping us safe from ferocious, capable, and globalized adversaries. As we reflect on why this is so and why the dangers seem to be getting worse, it doesn't take long to realize that oil is a key part of the larger context. Tensions over oil are large and rising, but some of the gravest threats to U.S. security also have indirect roots in oil. Nuclear proliferation, for example, has been greatly facilitated and disguised by a worldwide civilian nuclear power enterprise whose great impetus came from the 1970s oil shocks. The United States' major commitment to and promotion of nuclear power and "research reactors" sowed dragons' teeth around the world. It also set an unassailably bad example: if a nation with some of the world's richest and most diverse energy resources felt it needed nuclear power, then surely any nation less endowed had a strong case for pursuing it too, or at least pretending to. American and foreign vendors armed with big export subsidies were eager to help. The logical conclusion was privatization into the entrepreneurial Khan network's one-stop shopping for home-made nuclear bombs. And the links continue to mutate: the U.S. has lately gone to war over nuclear and other weapons of mass destruction in oil-funded Iraq, tried to buy off a bomb program with oil in North Korea, and is in an unsettling standoff over the mullahs' bomb program in oil-funded Iran, which is discouraging such meddling with an implicit threat to choke world oil flow (p. 11).

American forces are stretched thin today by their engagement not only in Iraq but also in Afghanistan, where a major pipeline project is among the potential stakes (as also in the unsettled Georgian Republic), and across oil-rich Central Asia. But these local conflicts may pale in comparison to the emerging geopolitical fault lines summarized by one leading military thinker who remarked, "It would be irresponsible to ignore the potential military malignancies that come as a result of increased competition for energy." Maintaining ever larger, costlier, and more stressed forces to try to wrest energy from others (and somehow avoid colliding with a giant

Not needing oil implies nega-missions in the Persian Gulf—Mission Unnecessary. This could save Service members' lives, regional tensions, and up to $50+ billion in annual peacetime readiness costs. It would also permit an undistorted view of other security interests in the region. Reducing competition over oil, dangerous uses of petrodollars, oil's drag on global development, current military postures' reinforcement of Islamic grievances, oil vulnerabilities, and perceptions that U.S. actions are motivated by oil should fundamentally improve security conditions, diminish conflict, and help uproot terrorism.

Perhaps the recent confirmation of what many of us feared—that Iraq would be less like Singapore on the Euphrates than like Yugoslavia with oil—will heighten incentives to escape from oil pressures once and for all.

956. The FY05 U.S. military budget (Function 050, adding back the $19 billion of omitted DOE nuclear weapons funding, Function 053) is $420.7 billion (2004 $)—nearly as much as the rest of the world combined, 8.2 times the latest available (2002) budget for the number two spender (China), more than 29 times the combined ~2003 military spending of seven "rogue states" (Cuba, Iran, Iraq, Libya, North Korea, Sudan, Syria), and ~3.6 times the 2002–03 spending of those seven states plus Russia and China (Hellman 2004).

like China) seems a less astute choice than solving the technical and policy problem with homegrown innovation—civilian and military—and investing the money instead into peaceful and productive enterprise… then helping everyone else do the same. Rivalries over resources like oil are a problem we needn't have, and it's cheaper not to.

To be sure, the technological equivalent of a demand-side "nega-OPEC" wouldn't free U.S. forces from commitments and involvement in the Middle East; but not being so deeply embroiled in the region as a customer for oil would certainly increase flexibility. Perhaps the recent confirmation of what many of us feared—that Iraq would be less like Singapore on the Euphrates than like Yugoslavia with oil—will heighten incentives to escape from oil pressures once and for all (pp. 22–23). Over decades, America might even come to have the sort of normal relationship with its former oil suppliers that it now enjoys with its former suppliers of naval masts in the 1820s (Norway), coal for refueling the U.S. Navy a century ago (various Pacific Island nations), and natural rubber in the 1920s to 1940s (various Southeast Asian nations). It would truly shock and awe certain nations in the Middle East if America could treat them as if they didn't have oil. This would, furthermore, give the world no reason to continue thinking that U.S. actions abroad are motivated by oil.

Toward a new strategic doctrine

The journey beyond oil is but a part of a larger evolution in building security in its fullest sense: freedom from fear of privation or attack. Moreover, the means we propose for doing this from the bottom up are the province of every citizen, not the monopoly of national governments; do not rely on the threat or use of violence; make other nations more secure, not less; and save enough money to pay for other key national needs. By making oil not worth fighting over, this transition is part of the evolution of strategic doctrine toward a "new strategic triad": conflict prevention and avoidance ("presponse"), conflict resolution, and nonprovocative defense.[957]

A gratifying number of military leaders have been reflecting on their recent experience of what works—one might call it "preemption of failed states" or "preventative humanitarian relief."[958] Now they're seeking creative ways to counter disenfranchisement, ignorance, poverty, and injustice, all of

> It would truly shock and awe certain nations in the Middle East if America could treat them as if they didn't have oil. This would, furthermore, give the world no reason to continue thinking that U.S. actions abroad are motivated by oil.

> General Marshall foresaw in 1947 that freedom from fear of privation or attack would be the best bulwark against violence. That same vision would make a strong foundation for evolving military doctrine, and would encourage DoD leadership in moving the nation beyond oil.

957. Shuman & Harvey 1993; Lovins 2002a. Nonprovocative defense reliably defeats aggression without threatening others. Its layered deployment in nonprovocative postures creates a stable mutual defensive superiority (each side's defense is stronger than the other side's offense) and gives each side, by design, at most a limited capacity to export offense. This entails force structures and deployments that minimize capability for preemptive deep strikes or strategic mobility; maximize homeland defense; and exhibit four objectively observable attributes: low vulnerability, low concentration of value, short range, and dependence on local support. Unfortunately, current *Quadrennial Defense Review 2001* doctrine, by promoting the very opposite in the form of the global SWAT teams required by short-term exigencies, creates a long-term contradiction with these requirements. This may cause the U.S. to behave in ways that cause such "global cop" forces to be used, and worse, will elicit the kinds of asymmetric attacks to which it is most vulnerable. That is, doctrine based on global power projection can in the long run not bolster but undercut U.S. security. The nearest we can imagine to a solution to this paradox is to strive mightily to prevent conflict, merit trust, and try to make the global-cop role temporary and brief by making the world safer. Getting off oil is a good place to start.

which rank among terrorists' best recruiting tools. These are not the only root causes of terrorism, of course, and many terrorists are neither ignorant nor poor, but these root causes certainly nurture terrorism. Like many uncomfortable truths, this is a very old idea. Martin Luther King, Jr., said, "violence is the voice of the unheard" and "peace is not the absence of war, it is the presence of justice." General George Marshall stated in 1947, "There can be no political stability and no assured peace without economic security," so U.S. policy must "be directed not against any country or doctrine, but against hunger, poverty, desperation, and chaos." That was right then and it's right now. As the then Deputy Chief of Naval Operations, Vice Admiral Dennis McGinn, remarked after 9/11, "It doesn't matter if we kill the mosquitoes if we haven't drained the swamp."[959] Prime Minister Tony Blair, on 2 October 2001, eloquently called for "above all justice and prosperity for the poor and dispossessed, so that people everywhere can see the chance of a better future through the hard work and creative power of the free citizen, not the violence and savagery of the fanatic."

In a world that manufactures some 15 billion transistors every second,[960] huge gaps in the relative quality of life are instantly broadcast around the globe, increasing resentment, empowering demogogues, and fostering "Jihad vs. McWorld" polarization. Yet abundance by design, turning scarcity into plenitude through advanced energy and resource productivity, may be the most important single element in restoring hope that one's children will have a better life. That hope is not just for citizens of the earth's richest nation; it should be available to all. Winning the respect and affection of others requires the extension to all of an equal moral entitlement to the fundamental values of American civics: the shared and lived belief that security rests on economic justice, political freedom, cultural pluralism, respect for law, and a common defense. Defeating the enemies of these values will require comprehensive engagement not only in the military and diplomatic, the economic and humanitarian, the informational and political spheres, but also at the level of ideology. Lieutenant Colonel Tony Kern (USAF Ret.), a teacher of military history, put it thus: "This war [on terrorism] will be won or lost by the American citizens, not diplomats, politicians or soldiers"—that is, it will be won by patience, will, and moral choice. To prevail, the stars we steer by must include such pursuits as democratization, transparency, anticorruption, ecologically informed development, resource efficiency, fair trade, demand-side drug policies, diversity, tolerance, and humility.

As world history shifts into fast-forward, one security concept is dying, another struggling to be born. During the Cold War, security was consid-

General George Marshall stated in 1947, "There can be no political stability and no assured peace without economic security," so U.S. policy must "be directed not against any country or doctrine, but against hunger, poverty, desperation, and chaos."

Abundance by design, turning scarcity into plenitude through advanced energy and resource productivity, may be the most important single element in restoring hope that one's children will have a better life.

958. Recently enunciated preemption doctrine is on the right track in seeking to prevent attacks by others, but mistakes the means. From the perspective of effects-based operations, the effect of preventing attacks on the United States should be achieved by the most economical means, which rarely if ever include early projection of military force.

959. To which Senator Joseph Lieberman added, "While we drain the swamp, we must also seed the garden [of Islamic Reformation]."

960. G. Dyson, personal communication, 10 August 2004.

ered a predominantly military matter. Appended and subordinated to military security were economic security and energy-and-resources security (such as Naval forces in and around the Gulf). Environmental security wasn't even on the agenda; in fact, it was officially viewed as inimical to security and prosperity. But in the post-Cold-War view, we need to add back the missing links between all four kinds of security, and to turn the wasted resources into prosperity and harmony. Imagine these four elements of security as vertices of a tetrahedron—an immensely strong structure, especially if it is filled up with justice, whose presence, as Dr. King said, means peace.

These overarching goals and doctrinal elements can, indeed must, start with practical particulars. Earlier in this report (pp. 85–93, 204–206, 221), we emphasized how the Pentagon can achieve multiple huge wins in national security from single expenditures. The same technology development and insertion needed for mission effectiveness, doctrinal execution, and strategic cost reduction (pp. 85–93) also supports the civilian spinoffs that the civilian economy needs (pp. 204–206). Military trainees who later re-enter the civilian workforce, military leaders who later retire to run civilian enterprises, and the power of the military example to inform and inspire civilian energy advances are also not to be underestimated. In every way, helping to move the country and the world away from future wars over oil could be the American military's greatest contribution yet to lasting security. Military innovation in decentralized facility power is already starting to provide such leadership in resilient electricity systems for civil preparedness (p. 222); the scope for similar leadership in moving beyond oil is enormously greater. Collaboration will also help bridge the growing and worrisome gulf between the civilian and military cultures within our society.

Helping to move the country and the world away from future wars over oil could be the American military's greatest contribution yet to lasting security.

We don't pretend this will be easy. Military hierarchies can resist change as adeptly as civilian bureaucracies. Congressional micromanagement for parochial ends (shades of Thucydides' lament on p. 170) is appallingly pervasive. The extraordinarily slow and cumbersome procurement process that makes it impossible to do anything for years ahead, if then (a process one official recently called "the tunnel at the end of the light") is like swimming in molasses. But from bottom to top, the military meritocracy is also full of talented, dedicated, courageous people who can move out smartly to implement changes, even radical changes, if they make sense and save money. If not only the civilian leadership (p. 221) and the Congress, but also the uniformed leadership, emphasizing the Joint Chiefs and mid-level officers, put radical oil efficiency and displacement at the core of the military mission, doctrine, and culture, they will unleash from within an ultimately unstoppable force. The key is to change perceptions not just in the Pentagon, but in combat units, because changes in operations and procurement *requests* must precede effective changes in force structures and tactics. Practice may often precede theory, too: the operators and logistical supporters of superefficient platforms will be astonished by how much more they can do with how much less fuel, and will start applying that lesson throughout their areas of responsibility and communities of interest. Since technical changes in platforms may be easier (and seem less threatening) than operational changes in cultures, fixing the strikingly inefficient hardware is probably the best and most concrete place to start—right now. Not doing so is costing lives, wasting tens of millions of dollars each day, degrading combat capability, and squandering time.

U.S. federal budget

From a budgetary perspective, the most striking feature of the policies that we propose are that they are remarkably revenue-neutral, particularly when compared to the seemingly endless litany of tax credits usually proffered to reduce U.S. oil dependence. While we do not claim to have performed a rigorous analysis of future federal budget implications, we can offer several insights into how these policies are likely to affect the Treasury. The most striking conclusion is that *our policies will make money for the government, with no new taxes, thereby reducing the deficit.*

Many of our policies are revenue-neutral by design. For example, feebates (pp. 186–190) are explicitly revenue-neutral, since the fees paid by buyers of less efficient light vehicles are used to fund rebates to buyers of more efficient models, keeping them in balance year by year. Further, if the federal government replaced its own half-million-vehicle fleet over the course of a decade using our proposed government procurement policies (pp. 197–203), by 2025 it would save nearly $2 billion (present valued) from the $350 million in annual fuel savings. How? The answer is simple. The net present value of the fuel savings over the vehicles' 14-year lifetimes, at the government's energy-savings discount rate of 3%/y, is ~$8,200. This far exceeds the incremental retail price of *State of the Art* vehicles ($2,544 from p. 70, note 345, excluding any government bulk-purchasing discount), so the government saves nearly $5,700 in present value for every vehicle it buys.

Our preferred form of financial support for automakers' and suppliers' conversion (p. 203–204) is qualified loan guarantees, not tax credits, because that's revenue-neutral to the government, and borrowers are given the correct incentive to invest wisely. Defaults on loans wouldn't be an expense to the Treasury because of offset equity warrants. Thanks to feebates, the loan beneficiaries would be producing the most profitable cars in the industry. Feebates therefore present good asset risk mitigation, both from a project finance perspective and from the lender's perspective.

Similarly, financial support for low-income leasing (pp. 191–197) would be made within the constraints of financing criteria acceptable to the

The revenue-neutrality of almost our proposed policies should yield tens of billions of dollars' present-valued net reduction in the federal deficit, excluding military savings that could approach that value each year. Even if reduced gasoline-tax revenues aren't offset by road-user fees, they'd about be offset by increased income-tax revenues from the oil savings' general economic stimulus.

industry in light of collateral value and default rates. Based on experience in micro-credit programs in other countries and in revolving low-income energy-efficiency loans in the U.S., it is plausible that default rates could be dramatically lower due to peer pressure exerted by the community and the incentive to build a personal credit rating. Since the ultimate interest rate will be defined by the empirical default rate, we believe the government itself will be no worse off by extending its credit as we have proposed. In fact, it may be much better off if welfare rolls are reduced as a result of the program: if scrap-and-replace reduces welfare rolls by just 1%, as is plausible once low-income wage-earners gain the affordable personal mobility they need to reach more job opportunities, the federal government will save $166 million each year—dwarfing any projected losses from default.

Just on the civilian side, our suite of policy recommendations will make the government money— plausibly billions of dollars in present value. The gross annual military savings could be an order of magnitude larger.

One concern about improved vehicle efficiency is the corresponding reduction in fuel-tax receipts at both federal and state level. It's economically efficient to increase user fees to offset that lost tax revenue (pp. 212–213); however, policymakers who don't like this option should recall that *the increase in income tax revenues from the income freed up and the economic stimulus created by not purchasing unnecessary oil almost entirely offsets the decline in gasoline tax receipts.* How is this possible? Fuel expenditures act like a regressive tax on society, insidious and pervasive. It follows that a reduction in fuel expenditures acts like a tax cut, and a progressive one at that. Therefore, we relied on the most recent evaluation of large-scale tax cuts from the Congressional Budget Office, which states that every dollar of tax cut increases GDP by $1.50.[961] To determine the future federal income-tax revenues from a reduction in oil expenditures, we used this relationship, and deducting consumer savings and lost oil company profits from GDP, then applied standard estimates for personal and business taxes.[962] We found that by 2025, in our *Mobilization* scenario, annual GDP would increase by $77 billion, income-tax receipts would increase by $8.4 billion, while gasoline taxes would decrease by $9 billion, yielding an annual shortfall of only $0.6 billion, half of which would be made up from fuel savings in the civilian fleet alone.

The revenue-neutralitiy of our proposed policies will be mirrored at the state level, especially if states and municipalities, which collectively own more than 3.3 million vehicles today, invest in efficient vehicles.

The only remaining unfunded costs in our policies are the $1-billion "Platinum Carrot" prize and additional civilian R&D funding for efficiency and renewables vital to oil displacement. Most of that R&D increase would be

961. The Congressional Budget Office (CBO) found that the GDP multiplier for tax cuts is 1.5. Reducing oil expenditures is a far more progressive form of tax relief than the proposed tax cuts, therefore, one might expect an even higher GDP multiplier, we conservatively use the same one as CBO (Sturrock & Woodward 2002).

962. The crude oil price and taxes account for 76.6% of the retail price of fuel (Bonsor, undated). Thus we applied this value to the retail fuel savings, deducted the consumer savings rate of 8%, to arrive at the total change in disposable income. This was then multiplied by 1.5 to arrive at the GDP effects. The average tax rates are 9.6% and 1.75% per dollar of GDP for households and businesses, respectively.

reprogrammed from unpromising current budget priorities, but if we generously assume additional R&D spending totaling $10 billion spread over 5–10 years, that brings the total net federal civilian investment to just $11 billion. What are the direct benefits from this investment? Just the asphalt savings (pp. 93–94) for all roads are worth $7.7 billion per year,[963] which would pay for the government investment and the remaining annual gasoline tax shortfall (if any) within 2–3 years—not bad.

Note that we haven't counted military R&D expenditures (pp. 204–206), because these must pass existing tests of cost-effectiveness based on DoD's internal budgetary savings, which will probably reach several billion dollars a year in direct fuel costs plus some unknown but probably large multiple of that in avoided logistics costs (pp. 84–93). On p. 93, we estimated that the ultimate DoD savings could well be ten or tens of billion dollars *per year* once forces are realigned to move saved logistics resources from tail to tooth and large support pyramids related to logistics are wrung out. The Defense Science Board panel was able to estimate such systemic savings only for one platform—an efficient tank—and only in theater, but that saving was still over $3 billion a year (p. 91). Department-wide, the details are very complex, but the fundamentals are simple: the Pentagon spends roughly a third of its total budget on logistics (p. 87), or ~$140 billion in FY05; ~60–70% of the tons moved are fuel (p. 85); and full deployment of *State of the Art* platforms would directly save ~64% of the fuel, *not* counting the multipliers for avoided transportation of platforms and fuel (other than midair refueling). Multiplying these terms easily yields tens of billions of dollars a year, reinforcing the caution in the caption of Fig. 27 (p. 88) that the DSB panel's logistics estimates of delivered fuel cost "omit many large infrastructure and staff costs."

The bottom line is that just on the civilian side, our suite of policy recommendations will make the government money—plausibly billions of dollars in present value. The gross *annual* military savings could be an order of magnitude larger. Both civilian and military investments should pay back within a few years or less.

It's not for us to determine what to do with the savings. But national security ultimately depends on a world where aspirations to a decent life are realistic and attainable, for all, for ever. There's plenty of room to argue about the cost of meeting basic human needs worldwide and to suggest innovation in how services are delivered honestly and effectively. But for what it's worth, the UN Development Programme says every deprived person now alive could have clean water, sanitation, basic health, nutrition, education, and reproductive health care for ~$40 billion a year, or ~4% of global military spending (of which the U.S. spends nearly half).

963. See *Technical Annex*, Ch. 14, for calculations of rubberized-asphalt costs and savings. We didn't analyze the split between federal and state highway-budget savings, on the assumption that most or all marginal savings to the states ultimately relieve calls on federal transfer payments for building and maintaining roads.

Where is the determination to build a muscular coalition to create a safer world in these fundamental ways? There's been commendable recent progress, but it's nowhere near the level of vision that General Marshall brought to this challenge half a century ago. This may be a fit area for American leadership, informed by the skilled humanitarian-relief experts in the Services. These fundamental elements of conflict prevention and avoidance may be higher priorities than expanding the costly means to defeat conflicts that could have been stopped before they got started.

Environment, public health, and quality of life

Our *Mobilization* scenario for the Oil Endgame was meant to save oil and money, and it does. But among many free side-benefits, it would also avoid burning enough fossil fuel by 2025 to meet 61% of U.S. obligations under the unratified Kyoto Protocol that's meant to start stabilizing the earth's climate. Specifically, full adoption of the efficiency and cellulosic-ethanol potential in our *Mobilization* scenario for 2025 would reduce total U.S. emissions of fossil-fuel carbon dioxide from EIA's Reference Case by 2.13 billion tonnes per year[964]—equivalent to 42% of U.S. emissions in 1990 (5.00b tonne/y) or to 36% of 2001 emissions (5.79b tonne/y). This would reduce 2025 emissions from 8.14b tonne/y to just 3% above their 2000 level (5.86b tonne/y)—61% of the way to the Kyoto target (4.65b tonne/y, or 7% below the 1990 level, by 2008–12). That performance despite EIA's projected 101% GDP growth would probably be better than any nation on earth expects to achieve. At the current U.S. and European market value of such reductions, ~$5 per tonne of CO_2 equivalent,[965] or the threefold higher value that credible projections suggest for 2020, the potential market value of our *Mobilization* scenario's CO_2 reductions would be ~$10–30 billion per year by 2025.[966] This reduction is only a byproduct of the oil displacements we've described; it excludes the major potential for profitably reducing emissions from burning coal, chiefly by profitably saving more electricity than we assumed: we adopted only the parts of the CEF (Five Labs)[967] study relevant to saving oil, not the additional profitable potential to save coal as well.

The profitable oil savings, without yet saving any coal, would meet two-thirds of the United States' unratified Kyoto Protocol obligation by cutting 2025 CO_2 emissions 2.1 billion tonnes a year. Reduced smog, water pollution, noise, and auto-accident frequency, deaths, and injuries would also be free byproducts of the better technologies.

964. Of this reduction, 1.8 billion tonne/y comes from oil savings, 0.22 billion tonne/y from gas savings, and another 0.1 billion tonne/y from coal displaced by the cogeneration we assumed in displacing industrial oil use. Obviously, much more coal could be displaced by electric end-use efficiency alone.

965. In the U.S., more than 22 major companies have begun trading carbon through the Chicago Climate Exchange. For more information, see www.chicagoclimateexchange.com.

966. Once CO_2 emissions are limited (a safe bet by 2025), then all reductions assume the market value, either as savings to those who emit too much and would have to buy on the market, or as surplus reductions that those below their allocation could sell. Of course, if the total amount of reductions is large, they will have an impact on the market price (more supply and less demand leads to a lower price). While we do not directly address this scenario, our assumption of $15 per tonne of CO_2 is on the low side of what is generally expected in 2025.

967. Brown et al. 2001; Interlaboratory Working Group on Energy-Efficient and Clean-Energy Technologies 2000; Koomey et al. 2001.

The U.S. annually reports more than 30,000 deaths, 330,000 hospital admissions, and 6.6 million asthma attacks due to particulate and ozone pollution.[968] EPA's mandatory national ambient air quality standards are designed to protect the most at-risk people with a reasonable margin of safety. Yet more than 474 U.S. counties, home to 160 million people, don't yet meet the ozone standard and ~130 counties, with 60 million people, don't yet meet the standard for fine particulates.[969] Estimates of compliance costs to bring areas into attainment vary tremendously, but the number is large: EPA analysis concludes that the *annual* cost of partially meeting the ozone standard will be $2.6 billion and the cost of partially meeting the fine-particulates standard, $6 billion.[970]

Ozone is produced in a chemical reaction of nitrogen oxides (NO_x) and volatile organic compounds (VOCs, such as unburned hydrocarbons) in the atmosphere. On-road mobile sources (cars, SUVs, buses, trucks, etc.) produce 34% of national NO_x emissions and 29% of VOC emissions. While fuel efficiency conventionally does much less to reduce tailpipe NO_x emissions than VOCs,[971] the 2004 *Prius* powertrain we assumed is currently the world's cleanest, reducing NO_x by an order of magnitude, even before ultralighting downsizes the engine and its massflow.[972] In addition, our policies would prematurely scrap old, inefficient cars. Old cars generally don't have modern emissions controls, so they emit disproportionally more ozone-causing pollutants than newer cars.[973]

Significant reductions in ozone precursor emissions are also easily possible in the electricity generation sector. As shown in Fig. 31 on p. 114, a 5% reduction in total U.S. electricity consumption saves 9% of total U.S. natural-gas consumption. That results in a ~400,000 tonne/y reduction in NO_x and a ~450,000 tonne/y reduction in non-methane organic gases, which are related to VOCs. There are no national markets for ozone precursors, but some NO_x markets exist in severe non-attainment areas such as Southern California, the Northeast, and Houston. In these markets, the NO_x allowance price has ranged from $500 to $7,500, recently hovering at ~$1,500/ton.[974] If such prices prevailed in a national market, the reductions

Our *Mobilization* scenario would avoid burning enough fossil fuel by 2025 to meet 61% of U.S. obligations under the unratified Kyoto Protocol despite doubled GDP. This reduction excludes the major potential for profitably reducing emissions from burning coal.

968. Abt Associates 1999; Abt Associates 2000. This is a conservative estimate and based solely on effects of ozone and particulate matter.

969. EPA 2003b.

970. The EPA 1996 estimate of compliance cost is on the low end of the spectrum.

971. NO_x is formed when nitrogen and oxygen from the ambient air are present at high temperatures, as is the case in a car combustion chamber. Since these elements are not derived from the fuel, conventional efficiency has little impact. Rather, NO_x is controlled in standard cars by controlling the fuel/air mix, installing catalytic converters, and recirculating exhaust gases.

972. Exhaust VOCs come from incomplete combustion of gasoline, and evaporative VOCs come from fuel evaporation, primarily during refueling. Fuel efficiency would reduce evaporative VOCs simply by requiring fewer fill-ups. Ultralight hybrids would also reduce NO_x by more than is conventionally calculated because of the downsized engine, more optimal engine operation, sophisticated controls, and idle-off with electric (not ignition-driven) restart. Current literature on how modestly efficiency reduces tailpipe NO_x is thus very conservative for our *State of the Art* ultralight-hybrid designs.

973. Super-high emitters make up ~9% of the U.S. fleet, but account for ~17% of hydrocarbon emissions (EPA 1993).

974. EPA 2001.

would be worth more than a half-billion dollars per year. Whether the cleaner urban air is monetized or not, it should significantly improve public health. And, if the national fleet of vehicles does switch to hydrogen fuel cells, all tailpipe emissions will be eliminated, since fuel cells emit nothing but hot drinkable water.

Other environmental, and related financial, benefits from displacing oil include reduced spills onto land and water, and reduced leakage of petroleum products into groundwater. Cleanup of the leaked MTBE gasoline additive, for example, is estimated to cost more than $140 billion.[975] Quality-of-life improvements include reduced congestion (pp. 212–219), which cost ~$70 billion in 2001; the 10–15% lower general noise levels from asphalt-rubber paving (more with low-rolling-resistance tires); and those surfaces' reduced rutting and cracking. In addition, public health would be improved by the estimated~43% reduction in major accidents after that repaving[976] (p. 94, above), and by the substantial reduction likely in crash-related deaths and injuries due to less aggressive, more stable, and more energy-absorbing advanced-composite vehicles (pp. 57–60).

975. Kitman 2004.
976. Carlson 2004.

Conclusions

When we win the Oil Endgame, what is the prize? Using the same Yankee ingenuity that secured our independence two and a quarter centuries ago, we can once more secure our independence from a different form of remote tyranny. Like the first Declaration of Independence, forming the intention to win the Oil Endgame is a statement of political will. But this second Declaration of Independence is much more: it is also a competitive strategy for business and an operational strategy for the military, because achieving national competitiveness through advanced energy efficiency will fortify both profits and security. Business leaders are realizing that energy efficiency is a key to low-cost production, profitable operations, and beating the competition. But winning this game together as a nation means more than that: it is the key to creating a world where one would want to live and do business, where more customers can afford to buy one's products, and where life and commerce can thrive undisturbed by violence.

American business leaders are starting to find their voice as leaders of something greater and more visionary than raising next quarter's earnings per share. From making decisions every day under the discipline of the market and the challenge of uncertainty, they've learned that for companies, as for countries, the world is shaped by surprises. They know that the long-run winners are those whose foresight leads them to create adaptive mechanisms to handle discontinuity gracefully. Business leaders understand that the world energy system is especially subject to big surprises, ranging from oil-supply interruptions, price swings, and political upheavals to climate change and oil depletion. Economist Edgar R. Fiedler remarked, "He who lives by the crystal ball soon learns to eat ground glass." But as seasoned executives know after picking ground glass out of their teeth for years, surprises are the evolutionary pressure that invigorates and empowers agile businesses. Surprises are like the meteorite-induced climate shock that distinguishes the smart, scurrying mammals from the previously dominant reptiles. Planning for a surprise-free energy future is dangerous; indeed the biggest possible surprise would be if there were no surprises. Based on that expectation, the earlier and greater our reduction in oil dependence, whether for reasons of precaution or profit, the less massive and disruptive oil's future shocks will be. As Paul Roberts says in *The End of Oil*, "the real question…is not *whether* change is going to come, but whether the shift will be peaceful and orderly or chaotic and violent because we waited too long to begin planning for it."[977] When the "insurance premium" of mitigating the likelihood and effects of future shocks is negative, because the substitutes cost less than the oil, the case for buying the substitutes promptly becomes a compelling theme in any business case.

We should fear ignorance, inattention, and inaction, but embrace insight, foresight, and mobilization. American business can lead the nation and the world into the post-petroleum era, a distinctively vibrant economy, and real security, in its deepest sense of freedom from fear of privation or attack. We just need to realize that we are the people we have been waiting for.

977. Roberts 2004, p. 14.

Business leaders know that the most precious thing you can buy is time. A story from the oil industry conveys the concept. In the early 1980s, Royal Dutch/Shell Group's engineers were designing the equipment to bring oil ashore from the new Kittiwake field in the North Sea. They were sweating out the last few percent of cost when the strategic planners told them, "You're assuming that you'll be able to sell this oil for $18 a barrel. But by the time it gets here, we think the market will have crashed and you'll only be able to sell it for $12. If you can't beat that, then you can all go home and we'll leave the oil where it is, because we can't lose money on every barrel and make it up on volume." Once the engineers recovered from the shock, they realized they'd previously been asked the wrong question—how to land the oil as quickly as possible, whatever it cost, rather than how to land it as cheaply as possible even if it took a bit longer. By asking that new question, they got very different engineering answers. And not only did they cut the landed cost so much that the oil made money even at $12 (the price in fact hit slightly below $12 right on cue), but the new cost-conscious technologies they invented also made, for example, $30 oil into $18 oil. Most importantly, this new approach postponed the economic depletion of oil, buying precious *time* in which to develop still better technology that could postpone economic depletion still further. Today, the inexpensive new ways to save and substitute for oil have a similarly critical function: they don't simply save money, but also buy time for fuller adaptation and further innovation.

Buying time, however, is of no use if the time isn't well spent. Buying time is no excuse for inaction. The stunning oil savings of 1977–85 were squandered by two decades of cheerful inattention: one commentator called that stagnant period "the years that the locusts have eaten." Today's oil anxieties and costs are the direct result of mid-1980s choices to abandon oil efficiency as no longer necessary, rather than to consolidate and make permanent the advantage we'd temporarily won. Since then, the cultural memory of energy efficiency has decayed: most Americans, including most journalists, know less about its nature and potential than they did twenty years ago, and most of its institutional structure has been systematically dismantled. So today, we contemplate once more the same play that won in 1977–85, but we're no longer a knight and a rook ahead and threatening our opponent's queen. We go into this endgame with advantages of will, wit, and positional flexibility, but careless mistakes can still cost us victory, because in the endgame, events move swiftly, whether in the realm of geopolitics and terrorism or of the creative destruction of business.

As Paul Roberts says in *The End of Oil*, "[T]he real question… is not whether change is going to come, but *whether* the shift will be peaceful and orderly or chaotic and violent because we waited too long to begin planning for it."

To outmaneuver leapfrogging competitors, we estimated that revitalizing the critical industrial sectors will need some ninety billion dollars of private-sector investment. That may appear daunting, but from a national perspective it is modest: indeed, it's less than the direct and indirect cost of a single run-up in oil price like that of 2004. We also suggest straightforward ways to marshal the needed resources. Our suggested policies enlist the power of the capital markets to come to the aid of businesses that can't make the transformative investments unaided. For key supporting R&D, chiefly in materials, we call upon the military to develop rapidly the innovations that can meet its own needs for unfettered mobility, then to share these technologies with the civilian sector, just as it did with microchips and jet engines. And even more than accelerating supply of oil-saving techniques, our proposals accelerate demand for them while expanding market choices.

The coming surprises will be the sieve that sorts the quick from the dead. Firms that are quick to adopt innovative technologies will be the winners of the 21st century; those that deny and resist change will join the dead from the past millennium. We know that for our automakers, truckmakers, airplane makers, and energy companies, the leadership challenge of overcoming organizational inertia and cultural habit is vast, yet we believe that the leaders of American industry can meet that challenge.

This report promotes the kind of innovation that discards wrong old thinking as much as it searches for good new ideas.[978] As inventor Edwin Land said, "People who seem to have had a new idea have often just stopped having an old idea." Stopping having an old idea is difficult, but practitioners and teachers of creativity have good ways to make it easier. Working in an organization noted for uninhibited vision across boundaries, we find it easier than many to ask "Why not? The United States has chosen before to replace some materials completely, whether in the marketplace (whale oil) or by government fiat (chlorofluorocarbons, asbestos); why not oil? What would it take? What would it cost? Might it even *save* money?"

As we've synthesized the answers to these questions, we've become more and more astonished that nobody seems to have added it all up before. This suggests that the responsible institutions, both public and private, have suffered not so much from a dearth of knowledge—perhaps a surplus was more their problem—as from the problem the 9/11 Commission identified, namely a lack of imagination. Clearly our nation needs to invest more in the culture, pedagogy, institutions, and habits of recognizing and spreading innovations rapidly when they occur—rather than denying their existence—and then applying them promptly, so we don't accumulate another quarter-century's worth of unused advances before anyone notices. Henry Ford said, "I cannot imagine where the delusion

> The responsible institutions, both public and private, have suffered not so much from a dearth of knowledge—perhaps a surplus was more their problem— as from the problem the 9/11 Commission identified, namely a lack of imagination.

978. In the same spirit, science searches not for truth but for error; it seeks to falsify what we wrongly thought was true.

Oil dependency is compromising national goals, betraying expectations, limiting choices, and raising costs.
This strikes at the heart of the basic definition, within the study of statecraft, that a powerful nation is one with the broadest array of options. Our need for oil, once vital to building our strength, now weakens it and diminishes us as a nation. America's opportunities to displace oil with cheaper alternatives can help remake us into whom we aspire to be.

that weight means strength came from."[979] Before World War II, Albert Einstein considered "huge cars with great horsepower" to be "disgusting" and opined that efficient transport could move people using only the power of "a small lawnmower engine."[980] Yet it took roughly one century and half a century, respectively, to learn these lessons. We all need to learn faster, and not just to learn in theory, but to adapt in thinking and adopt in practice. As the adage says, "I hear and I forget; I do and I remember; I teach and I understand."

This report implies, too, the urgent political necessity to change fundamentally how national energy policy is made. A bunch of hogs at the trough, jostling to gobble their fill, is not a good model. This approach has deadlocked federal energy policy for decades, acutely so for the past two years, not so much because of bitter partisanship and intra-party wrangling, but because the whole process is mistaken at root. Elected representatives today seek to fulfill the wish-lists of enough constituencies to count the votes, to hold worthy and popular, even crucial, provisions hostage to parochial and inferior ones, and to attract enough lobbying muscle (and, one might indelicately add, campaign contributions that bear the odor of corruption) to pass the bill before anyone has read it too carefully. This approach is not only a disgrace to democracy and an affront to good governance; it simply doesn't solve the energy problem, which, like health care, will keep coming back and back until it's properly dealt with. In 2002, sensing the looming energy-policy trainwreck, Rocky Mountain Institute and another independent nonprofit group, the Consensus Building Institute, tried a quick, low-budget policy experiment. We simply convened a powerful, diverse, and bipartisan group of private- and public-sector energy leaders and asked them to try to come together around their hidden points of consensus. It worked. An integrative, visionary, practical, and comprehensive framework quickly emerged from what people already agreed on but had never been asked about. Since that National Energy Policy Initiative,[981] two larger efforts, the Energy Future Coalition and the ongoing work of the National Energy Policy Commission, have been greatly expanding on this general approach. Sooner or later, when legislators feel they have reached rock bottom, they'll try building energy policy on consensus, and they'll be astonished at how well it works. Focusing on the things we agree about can make the things we don't agree about superfluous.

979. Lacey 1986, p. 44.

980. Letter of C. Scribner, Jr., (Chairman, Charles Scribner's Sons Publishers, New York) to Robert A. Hefner III, 8 July 1987; kindly provided by Mr. Hefner (personal communication, 2 August 2004).

981. NEP Initiative 2002; McFarlane & Lovins 2003.

One more reflection seems necessary, from our perspective as citizens concerned for the future of the United States, its standing in the world, and the value of the principles on which it was founded. As we have consulted hundreds of experts in national security, in foreign policy, and in the energy industries, one theme has emerged with surprising breadth and consistency, and it is this: America's actions, principles, and national ideals are constrained and distorted by the deepening addiction to oil. In all that the United States does in the world, oil dependency is compromising national goals, betraying expectations, limiting choices, and raising costs. This strikes at the heart of the basic definition, within the study of statecraft, that a powerful nation is one with the broadest array of options. Our need for oil, once vital to building our strength, now weakens it and diminishes us as a nation. America's opportunities to displace oil with cheaper alternatives can help remake us into whom we aspire to be.

This report is not an end but a beginning. It is meant to start a new conversation that explores in depth the potential to create a profitable transition beyond oil. No doubt this analysis contains errors and omissions; public scrutiny of this full report[982] will find these flaws and determine whether they're material. What's wrong or missing should be fixed. What's right should be implemented decisively. Barrels and years are a-wasting. Competitors are gaining. There's security to be bolstered, profit to be earned. It's time to move. *We*, we the people, are the people we have been waiting for.

982. See the 24 chapters and numerous spreadsheets of the *Technical Annex* posted at www.oilendgame.com.

Figure 4:   2004 Toyota *Prius*, photo courtesy of Toyota Motor Sales, USA, Inc.

5a: 2005 Ford *Escape*, photo courtesy of Ford Motor Company

5b: 2005 Lexus *RX 400h*, photo courtesy of Toyota Motor Sales, USA, Inc.

5c: 2005 Toyota *Highlander*, photo courtesy of Toyota Motor Sales, USA, Inc.

5d: 2005 *Mercedes Vision Grand Sports Tourer*, photo copyright DaimlerChrysler Corporation

9a: Honda *Insight*, photo courtesy of American Honda Motor Corporation, Inc.

9b: Honda *Civic Hybrid*, photo courtesy of American Honda Motor Corporation, Inc.

10a: 2000 GM *Precept*, photo courtesy of General Motors

10b: 2000 Ford *Prodigy*, photo courtesy of Ford Motor Company

10c: 2000 Dodge *ESX3*, photo courtesy of DaimlerChrysler Corporation

13a: 2003 Daihatsu *UFE-II* hybrid, photo copyright Daihatsu Motor Corporation

13b: 1996 Pantila 4-seat *Coupé*, photo courtesy of Horlacher AG

13c: 1999 BMW *Z22*, photo courtesy of BMW of North America, LLC

13d: 2001 VW "Ein-Liter-Auto," photo copyright Volkswagen AG

16:   *SLR McLaren* crush cones, photo copyright DaimlerChrysler Corporation

17a–b: Kenny Brack Texas Motor Speedway crash, photo copyright Fort Worth Star-Telegram

18a: 1991 GM 4-seat *Ultralite*, photo courtesy of General Motors Media Archive

18b: 2002 Opel 2-seat *Eco-Speedster*, photo courtesy of General Motors Media Archive

18c: 2004 Toyota *Alessandro Volta*, photo courtesy of Toyota Motor Sales, USA, Inc.

18d: 2000 Hypercar *Revolution*, photo courtesy of Hypercar, Inc.

23a: Peterbilt 379, photo copyright Peterbilt

23b: Kenworth T2000, photo courtesy of Kenworth

23c: PACCAR center-console concept truck, photo courtesy of PACCAR, Inc.

23d: Lightweight, highly aerodynamic tractor, photo copyright Rocky Mountain Institute

24a–b: Professor Luigi Colani's European concept tanker truck, photo copyright Colani DAF

24c: Professor Luigi Colani's European concept linehaul tractor, photo copyright Colani DAF

26a: Interior vision of *7E7 Dreamliner*, photo copyright Boeing Image Licensing

26b: Flying wing *B-2* bomber, photo copyright Northrop Grumman Corporation

26c: Artist's conception of a BWB airplane, photo copyright Boeing Image Licensing

Figures

1: Rise and fall of the U.S. whaling fleet, 1821–84 (p. 4)

2: U.S. net oil imports and sources in 2000 and (approximately) in EIA's 2025 projection (p. 9)

3: World oil consumption and real price, 1970–1Q2004 (p. 15)

4: Toyota's 2004 *Prius* (p. 29)

5: Four hybrid SUVs (p. 31)

6: The end-uses of U.S. oil in 2000 and projected for 2025 (p. 36)

7: Transportation Petroleum Use by Mode, 1970–2025 (p. 37)

8: U.S. oil intensity, 1975–2025 (p. 43)

9: Two mild hybrids (p. 48)

10: Three 2000 PNGV diesel-hybrid midsize concept sedans (p. 50)

11: 1990–2004 comparison of absolute mpg vs. incremental costs for new U.S. automobiles (p. 51)

12: Weight vs. energy intensity (p. 54)

13: Four composite concept cars (p. 55)

14: The strength of ultralight carbon-fiber autobodies (p. 58)

15: Advanced composites' remarkable crash energy absorption (p. 59)

16: *SLR McLaren* crush cones (p. 59)

17: Formula One racecar crash (p. 60)

18: Four carbon-fiber concept cars (p. 61)

19: Two-thirds of a *State of the Art* light vehicle's fuel saving comes from its light weight (p. 64)

20: An ultralight hybrid SUV saves 72% of today's comparable model's fuel at 56¢/gal (p. 65)

21: 1990–2004 comparison of absolute mpg vs. incremental costs for new U.S. light vehicles: ultralighting doubles the savings (p. 66)

22: Supply curves for saving oil by improving on EIA's 2025 heavy trucks (p. 75)

23: The evolution of heavy-truck tractors (p. 75)

24: The shape of the future? European concept trucks (p. 77)

25: Historic and projected airplane energy intensities, 1955–2025 (p. 81)

26: Next-generation airplanes (p. 83)

27: Uncounted costs of delivering fuel to weapons platforms (p. 88)

28: Supply curve summarizing *Conventional Wisdom* and *State of the Art* technologies for efficient use of oil (p. 100)

29: U.S. oil consumption and net oil imports 1950–2025 (p. 102)

30: Supply curves for the 2025 full-implementation potential of U.S. biofuels (p. 103)

31: Saving electricity to save natural gas (p. 114)

32: a. Potential savings in U.S. natural gas consumption (p. 122)
b. Potential 2025 substitutions of that saved gas for oil (p. 122)

33: U.S. oil use and oil imports if end-use efficiency, biosubstitution, and saved-natural-gas substitution were realistically implemented (p. 123)

34: Petroleum product equivalent supply and demand, 2000 and 2005 (p. 125)

35: Water productivity, 1950–2000 (p. 171)

36: How RMI's eight proposed policies can stimulate demand for and accelerate production of *State of the Art* light vehicles (p. 180)

37: a. Assumed evolution of how quickly *Conventional Wisdom* and *State of the Art* vehicles could potentially capture the indicated share of the U.S. market for new light vehicles if every efficient car that could be produce were demanded (p. 183)

b. Assumed schematic schedule for launching 50,000/y production of State of the Art vehicles in 2010 (p. 184)

38: The path beyond oil becomes even more flexible if the hydrogen option is added (p. 229)

39: Ultralight vehicles solve the hydrogen storage problem (p. 234)

40: How can fuel-cell vehicles compete with gasoline hybrids? (p. 235)

41: Cost of distributed hydrogen production (p. 237)

42: Reducing EIA's 2025 natural-gas demand forecast by 41% (p. 239)

— Figure 38 reprise (back cover)

Tables

1: Potential savings of U.S. natural gas (p. 116)

2: Estimated non-transportation 2025 oil uses, potentially suitable for gas substitution (p. 117)

3: Potential 2025 substitutions of saved natural gas for suitable uses of oil after efficiency and biosubstitution (p. 121)

4: Potential farm revenue and net income from clean energy and carbon offsets (p. 164)

Acknowledgments

This work was made possible by numerous organizations and individuals during a period of nearly two years, and built on several decades of research before that. We thank here those whose special efforts and generosity most contributed to this report, as well as those whose names have been omitted through their preference or our inadvertence. As noted on p. *ii*, only the authors, not those acknowledged below, are responsible for the content of this report.

We are deeply grateful to Mr. George P. Shultz, his assistant Susan Schendel, and Sir Mark Moody-Stuart for their respective Forewords, which so clearly and graciously introduce this work to its policy, security, and business audiences.

In the Office of the Secretary of Defense, we greatly appreciate the financial support provided for this research by Dr. Andrew Marshall (director of the Office of Net Assessment), Assistant Secretary of Defense Dr. Linton Wells II, Jaymie Durnan, and Rebecca Bash, and in the Office of Naval Research, by Rear Admiral Jay Cohen, Captain John C. Kamp, and Anthony Nickens. Complementary private funders included the William and Flora Hewlett Foundation, an anonymous private foundation, the Rose Family Foundation, Grant Abert, The Winslow Foundation, The Harold Grinspoon Charitable Foundation, the Katz Family Foundation, and individual donors. In addition, the dissemination of this report has been generously supported by the William and Flora Hewlett Foundation, the Compton Foundation, Deborah Reich, Jeff Tannenbaum, TAUPO, Brian and Allie Quinn, and an anonymous donor.

In accordance with Rocky Mountain Institute's normal practice, this report was made available as a confidential draft, in whole or in part, to 139 topical and general peer reviewers, chiefly in industry. Those who kindly provided helpful and attributable critiques included Dr. David B. Brooks (Friends of the Earth Canada), Dr. Irvin C. Bupp (formerly Cambridge Energy Research Associates), Ralph Cavanagh (Natural Resources Defense Council), Vice Admiral Arthur K. Cebrowski (USN, Ret., Office of the Secretary of Defense), David R. Cramer (Fiberforge), David L. Daggett (Boeing), Dr. Richard Danzig (formerly Secretary of the Navy), Dr. Lois-ellin Datta (Datta Analysis), Reid Detchon (Energy Future Coalition), David Dwight PE (Fiberforge), Dr. Peter Fox-Penner PE (Brattle Group), Dr. Jonathan Fox-Rubin (Fiberforge), Prof. Chip Franck (USA, Ret., Naval Postgraduate School), Dr. Richard L. Garwin (IBM), Dr. Victor Gilinsky (formerly RAND Corp.), Jim Harding (Seattle City Light), Col. Bill Holmberg (USMC, Ret., New Uses Council), Bill Joy (formerly Sun Microsystems), Richard G. Kidd III (U.S. Department of State), Dr. Tim Lipman (University of California, Berkeley), Stephen F. Millard (National Defense University), James T. Mills, Sr., C. Michael Ming (K. Stewart Energy Group LLC), Timothy C. Moore (Whole Systems Design), Tom Morehouse (Institute for Defense Analyses), Philip Patterson (U.S. Department of Energy), Ing. Paul Peeters (Peeters Advies), John L. Petersen (The Arlington Institute), Brian Peterson (Explorer Fund Advisors), Christopher Platt (Boardroom), Commander Eric Rasmussen MD, MDM, FACP (U.S. Navy), Dr. Roger Saillant (PlugPower), Gary D. Simon (Sigma Energy Group), Prof. Paul Sullivan (National Defense University), Dr. C.E. (Sandy) Thomas (H2Gen Innovations, Inc.), Richard B. Ward (Shell International), Tom Wieringa (Logistics Management, Inc.), R. James Woolsey (Booz Allen Hamilton), Dr. Sue Woolsey (Paladin Capital), and John Wing (Wing Group).

Acknowledgments (continued)

Among the hundreds of experts who helped us find, refine, and understand key information, we are especially grateful to: Robert Adler (U.S. Energy Information Administration), Arnold Almaguer (Mercedes-Benz), Jeff Alson (U.S. Environmental Protection Agency), Dr. Feng An (Argonne National Laboratory), Ray C. Anderson (Interface, Inc.), Brian S. Appel (Changing World Technologies, Inc.), Dr. Shimon Awerbuch (SPRU, University of Sussex), J. Baldwin, Dr. Susan Bales (Office of Naval Research), Dr. Thomas R.M. Barnett (Naval War College), Dr. Heinz Baumann (Roswell Park Cancer Institute), Rudolf Beger (formerly European Automobile Manufacturers' Association), Gerry Bemis (California Energy Commission), Prof. R. Stephen Berry (University of Chicago), Dr. Mike Bertolucci (Interface Research Corporation), Rodger H. Bezdek (Management Information Services, Inc.), Mark A. Bolinger (Lawrence Berkeley National Laboratory), Lieutenant Commander Paul C. Brown (U.S. Navy), Kevin Brubaker (Environmental Law and Policy Center), Prof. Clark Bullard (University of Illinois at Urbana-Champaign), Tom Burke (Rio Tinto), Larry Burns (General Motors), Chris Calwell, Dr. Chuck Calvano (Naval Postgraduate School), General Mike Carns (USAF, Ret.), Prof. Christopher J. Castaneda (California State University, Sacramento), Prof. Luigi Colani (Studio Colani), Anthony Corridore (Deloitte), Dr. Goli Davidson (Metron Aviation), Stacy Cagle Davis (Oak Ridge National Laboratory), Dr. John DeCicco (Environmental Defense), Dr. Etienne Deffarges (formerly Accenture), Morgan Defoort (Engines and Energy Conversion Laboratory, Colorado State University), Prof. Mark A. Delucchi (University of California, Davis), Dr. Phil DePoy (Naval Postgraduate School), Bill Doak (U.S. Navy), John Doerr (Kleiner Perkins Caufield & Byers), Mike Dolan, David Doniger (Natural Resources Defense Council), Dr. K.G. Duleep (Energy and

Environmental Analysis, Inc.), Dr. Gwynne Dyer, Dr. Ron Earley (U.S. Energy Information Administration), Michael T. Eckhart (American Council for Renewable Energy), Dr. Leonard Evans (Science Serving Society and International Traffic Medicine Association), Christopher Flavin (Worldwatch Institute), William L. Francoeur (Jet Information Services, Inc.), Dr. Herman T. Franssen (Center for Strategic and International Studies, former Chief Economist, International Energy Agency), Dr. John Gage (Sun Microsystems), David Garman (Acting Under-Secretary, U.S. Department of Energy), Steve Gatto (Biofuels International), Billy Glover (Boeing), Dr. David L. Greene (Oak Ridge National Laboratory), Ing. Thomas Guéret (International Energy Agency), Etan Gumerman (Lawrence Berkeley National Laboratory), Mark Gunter, Priscilla Halverson (Capital One), Sonia Hamel (Commonwealth of Massachusetts), Prof. James Hamilton (University of California, San Diego), Hal Harvey (William and Flora Hewlett Foundation), Dr. Allen W. Hatheway (Hatheway.net), Eric Haymes (Mojave Jet–USA), John Heffinger (Kelley Blue Book, www.kbb.com, whose database he generously shared), Robert K. Hefner III (GHK Co.), Dr. Richard Heinberg (New College of California, Santa Rosa), David Hermance (Toyota Technical Center), Admiral James Hogg (USN, Ret., Naval War College), Dr. Roland Hwang (Natural Resources Defense Council), Kelly Ibsen (National Renewable Energy Laboratory), Ing. Diego Jaggi (ESORO AG), Claire Jahns (Chicago Climate Exchange), Jorg-Olaf Jansen (DKR), Prof. Michael C. Jensen (Harvard Business School), Dr. Eberhard Jochem (Swiss Federal Institute of Technology, Zürich), Steve Johnson (Honda), Russell Jones, Prof. Daniel M. Kammen (University of California, Berkeley), Murali Kanakasabai (Chicago Climate Exchange), Dr. Kamal Kapadia (University of California, Berkeley), Chris Kavalec (California Energy Commission),

Acknowledgments (continued)

Maryanne Keller (formerly Furman Sellz), Dr. Hisham Khatib (World Energy Council), Dr. Nasir Khilji (U.S. Energy Information Administration), Ben Knight (Honda), Doug Koplow (Earth Track, Inc.), Prof. William Kovarik (Radford College), Herman P.C.E. Kuipers (Shell Global Solutions), Dr. John D. Kuzan (Exxon-Mobil), Dr. Joosung J. Lee (Massachusetts Institute of Technology), Dr. Mark D. Levine (Lawrence Berkeley National Laboratory), Perry Lindstrom (Energy Information Administration), Alan Lloyd (California Air Resources Board), Chris Lotspeich (Second Hill Group), Elizabeth A. Lowery (General Motors), John Lumbard (Lumbard Investment Counseling), Eddie Mahe (Foley & Lardner LLP), John Maples (U.S. Energy Information Administration), Jan Mares (U.S. Department of Homeland Security), Lourdes Maurice (Federal Aviation Administration), Robert C. McFarlane (Energy and Communications Solutions, LLC), Vice Admiral Dennis McGinn (USN, Ret., Battelle Science and Technology International), Bruce McHenry (Discussion Systems), Dr. Paul E. Mertz (INTEGeR Consult), Clayton L. Meyers (NASA), Alexander Milton, Mansoor Mirza (Economic Analysis, Marketing, Boeing), Dr. Fareed Mohamedi (PFC Energy), Mike Naylor (formerly General Motors), Charles Nicholson (BP), Dr. Peter Niederer (Swiss Federal Institute of Technology, Zürich), Hans Nilsson (FourFact), Dr. Joan Ogden (University of California, Davis), Richard O'Neill (The Highlands Group), Prof. David S. Painter (Georgetown University), Prof. David W. Pearce (University College, London), John Pike (GlobalSecurity.org), Prof. Robert S. Pindyck (Massachusetts Institute of Technology), Jacek Popiel (Sturman Industries), Ed Porter, Alan Quasha (Quadrant Management), Prof. Eva Regnier USA (Naval Postgraduate School), Eugene Reiser (U.S. Energy Information Administration), Ronald J. Reisman (NASA Ames Research Center), Paul Roberts, Prof. Marc H. Ross (University of Michigan), Joel M. Rubin (U.S. Department of State), Joseph Ryan (William and Flora Hewlett Foundation), Academician Roald Z. Sagdeev (University of Maryland), Dr. Richard Sandor (Chicago Climate Exchange), Dr. Andreas Schafer (Massachusetts Institute of Technology), Dr. Lee Schipper (World Resources Institute), Robert Schnapp (U.S. Energy Information Administration), Robert Schorlemmer (ZERI), Prof. Betty J. Simkins (Oklahoma State University), Prof. Kenneth A. Small (University of California, Irvine), Francis Stabler (Naval Postgraduate School), Dr. Walter Stahel, Leigh Stamets (California Energy Commission), E.W. (Bill) Stetson (Foundation for Our Future), JB Straubel, Prof. Joel A. Tarr (Carnegie Mellon University), Alan Taub (General Motors), Wim Thomas (Shell), Andy Tobias, Michael Totten (The Center for Environmental Leadership in Business), Richard H. Travers (R.H. Travers Company), Vice Admiral Richard Truly (USN, Ret., National Renewable Energy Laboratory), Jean-Pierre Uchello (GlobalSecurity.org), Dr. Roger Vardan (General Motors), Mark W. Verbrugge (General Motors), Dr. Philip K. Verleger Jr. (PK-Verleger LLC), Dr. Anant Vyas (Argonne National Laboratory), Prof. Dr. med. Felix Walz (Swiss Federal Institute of Technology, Zürich), Walter Wardrop (National Research Council of Canada – IRAP), Lloyd Weaver PE, Rick Weber (Freightliner), Adam Werbach (Common Assets), Chowen C. Wey (NASA), Prof. Bryan Willson (Engines and Energy Conversion Laboratory, Colorado State University), Major General Frances Wilson (Naval Defense University), Sherry Winkler (U.S. Navy), Tamara Woolgar (Canadian Centre For Energy Information), Dr. Ernst Worrell (Lawrence Berkeley National Laboratory), and Deborah Zemke (formerly Ford Motor Company). We are especially indebted to our many additional informants in the automotive, truck, and oil industries.

Among the researchers not already listed as coauthors on the title page, we especially appreciate the contributions of contractor Andrew H. Baumann and Rocky Mountain Institute's Catherine Greener, Christina Page, Will Clift, and Jeff Possick. Funds for this project were raised by RMI's Development staff, including Ginni Galicinao, Peggy Hill, and director Dale Levy. Communications about the project, and many improvements in its clarity, were contributed by RMI *Newsletter* editor Cameron Burns, communications specialist Jenny Constable, and communications director Karen Nozik. The senior author is particularly grateful to Missy Morgan for invaluable and unfailing support of his difficult logistical needs. Robert K. and MeiLi Hefner, and Lydia Andrada and Bonifacio Sanchez, provided generous hospitality in London during the page-proof stage. Essential strategic counsel came from many members of RMI's Board of Directors, especially Chairman John C. Fox and Executive Director Marty Pickett, and from RMI Senior Fellows Dennis McGinn (Vice Admiral, USN, Ret.) and Dr. Eric Rasmussen (Commander, USN).

For production, we thank Ian Naylor, whose steadfast professionalism persisted through endless revisions to his beautifully rendered cover artwork, and the exceptional skill of editor Beatrice Aranow, who patiently untangled our prose, honed our thinking, and crossed all the "t"s without crossing the eyes. Rocky Mountain Institute's production effort was led by the gifted and devoted graphic art director Ben Emerson, whose information design has made this unusually complex work navigable by its diverse audiences. We are grateful also to the rest of the RMI production team for their painstaking work: Anne Jakle, Tyler Lindsay, Ann Mason, Morley McBride, and Bill Simon. This project would not have been possible without high-speed Internet connections linking the authors' Macintosh computers in Snowmass, Kona, Washington, DC, and Boulder.

Above all, we owe a deep debt to our partners and spouses—Judy, Ann, Priscilla, Elizabeth, Elizabeth, and Liv—and to daughters Ariana Datta and Mary Emerson and son Conrad Emerson for their love, patience, and understanding during this book's gestation and birth.

— ABL

Snowmass, Colorado
3 September 2004

About the publisher and authors

ROCKY MOUNTAIN INSTITUTE (www.rmi.org) is an independent, nonprofit, nonpartisan, entrepreneurial applied research center founded in 1982 by resource analysts Amory and Hunter Lovins in Snowmass, Colorado. Its ~50 staff foster the efficient and restorative use of natural and human capital to make the world secure, just, prosperous, and life-sustaining. Most of the Institute's $6-million annual budget is funded by programmatic enterprise, chiefly consultancy for the private sector. The Institute has also spun off four for-profit firms. About one-third of revenues come from foundation grants and individual donations; government support is rare and seldom sought. RMI does not lobby or litigate. Its extensive business experience includes strategic and technical consultancy, often at Chair and CEO level, for scores of major energy companies worldwide, and its services have recently been provided for or requested by more than 70 *Fortune* 500 companies.

AMORY B. LOVINS is cofounder and CEO of Rocky Mountain Institute. A consultant experimental physicist educated at Harvard and Oxford (where he received an MA by virtue of being a don), he has advised the energy and other industries for over 30 years, as well as the U.S. Departments of Energy and Defense. Published in 28 previous books and hundreds of papers, his work in ~50 countries has been recognized by the "Alternative Nobel," Onassis, Nissan, Shingo, and Mitchell Prizes, a MacArthur Fellowship, the Happold Medal, nine honorary doctorates, and the Heinz, Lindbergh, Hero for the Planet, and World Technology Awards. He advises industries and governments worldwide, including major oil companies, and has briefed 18 heads of state. Since 1990, he has led the development of quintupled-efficiency, uncompromised, competitive automobiles and a profitable hydrogen transition strategy. Much of his work is synthesized in *Natural Capitalism* (www.natcap.org) and *Small Is Profitable: The Hidden Economic Benefits of Making Electrical Resources the Right Size* (www.smallisprofitable.org), one of the *Economist*'s top three business and economics books of 2002. He is a member of the Society of Automotive Engineers, American Physical Society, and International Association for Energy Economics, and is a Fellow of the American Association for the Advancement of Science, World Academy of Arts and Sciences, and World Business Academy. *Automobile* magazine has called him the 22nd most powerful person in the global car industry; the *Wall Street Journal*, one of 39 people in the world most likely to change the course of business in the 1990s; *Newsweek*, "one of the Western world's most influential energy thinkers."

Mr. Lovins's security background includes devising the first logically consistent approach to nuclear nonproliferation (technical papers[983] and two books); performing for DoD the definitive unclassified study of domestic energy vulnerability and resilience;[984] co-developing a "new security triad" of conflict prevention, conflict resolution, and nonprovocative defense;[985] lecturing at the National Defense University, Naval War College, and Naval Postgraduate School on least-cost security and on how new technologies will transform missions and force structures; keynoting the Chief of Naval Operations' 2003 Naval-Industry R&D Partnership Conference; leading for Admiral Lopez the overhaul of the Naval Facilities Engineering Command's design process (later extended to other Services); leading a 2000–01 Office of Naval Research analysis for the Secretary of the Navy of how to save ~$1 million/y of hotel-load electricity aboard a typical surface combatant (*USS Princeton* CG-59);[986] and serving on a 1999–2001 Defense Science Board panel, chaired by Vice Admiral (Ret.) Richard Truly, whose report *More Capable Warfighting Through Reduced Fuel Burden* identified multi-billion-dollar-a-year DoD fuel-saving potential.[987]

E. KYLE DATTA, Managing Director of RMI's consulting practice, is also CEO of New Energy Partners, an energy consulting and renewable development firm in Hawai'i. He is a former Vice President of Booz|Allen|Hamilton (BAH), where he was Managing Partner of the Asia Energy Practice, later led the U.S. Utilities practice, and received the firm's Professional Excellence Award in 1995 and 1997. In his 12 years with BAH, he developed deep expertise in and across the energy value chain, including upstream, refining, retail, power, chemicals, and renewables. He is also coauthor of *Small Is Profitable: The Hidden Economic Benefits of Making Electrical Resources the Right Size*. He holds BS, MES, and MPPM degrees from Yale University. He is a member of the Distributed Energy Research Advisory Council, the Natural Energy Laboratory of Hawai'i Authority, and the board of directors of Foresight Energy. In this report he shared overall strategic direction and content responsibility, led the business and policy analyses, and performed the hydrocarbon substitution analyses.

> Rocky Mountain Institute is an independent, entrepreneurial, nonprofit applied research center working chiefly with the private sector to foster advanced resource productivity. The authors have extensive experience in and with all sectors of the energy industries.

983. Summary in Lovins, Lovins & Ross 1980; typical unclassified support in Lovins 1980.

984. Lovins & Lovins 1982: Foreword by ex-JCS Chair ADM (Ret.) Tom Moorer and ex-USECNAV, later DCI, Jim Woolsey.

985. Shuman & Harvey 1993.

986. RMI report under ONR Grant #N00014-01-1-0252 (Lovins et al. 2001), summarized at Lovins 2001.

987. DSB 2001.

ODD-EVEN BUSTNES, a member of RMI's Energy/Resources and Commercial/Industrial consulting practices (and Special Aide to the CEO 2002–04), holds a Dartmouth BA (High Honors) in Engineering and Government, an Oxford MSc in Chemical Engineering, and a Princeton MPA in Economics. He has been an associate consultant in energy and telecoms with McKinsey & Company, a financial analyst of the shipping sector for Union Bank of Norway Securities, a UNICEF water program analyst in Perú, a Norwegian Special Forces paratrooper, a high-altitude mountaineer on four continents, and an Olympic rower. His primary responsibilities in this report included the heavy- and medium-truck, aircraft, train, ship, Intelligent Highway Systems, and asphalt analyses, and co-leadership of the business-case and implementation modeling.

JONATHAN G. KOOMEY, Senior Fellow at RMI, is on a leave of absence from Lawrence Berkeley National Laboratory (LBNL), where as a Staff Scientist he led the End-Use Forecasting Group. He holds a Harvard AB *cum laude* in History of Science and MS and PhD degrees from the Energy and Resources Group at the University of California at Berkeley. He is the author or coauthor of seven previous books and more than 130 articles and reports on energy efficiency and environmental policy. He serves on the Editorial Board of the journal *Contemporary Economic Policy*. He has received the Fred Burgraff Award from the National Research Council's Transportation Research Board and two outstanding performance awards from LBNL—one for leading the economic integration and buildings analyses for the first "Five Labs Study" in 1997. His LBNL group analyzes markets for efficient products, improves their energy and environmental characteristics, and develops recommendations for DOE/EPA policymakers to save energy and money and prevent pollution. He was the 2003–04 MAP/Ming Visiting Professor of Energy and Environment at Stanford University, is now a consulting professor at Stanford, is the recipient of an Aldo Leopold Leadership Fellowship for 2004, and is a holder of a second degree black belt in Aikido. His main responsibilities in this report included light-vehicle economic modeling and fleet analyses and the integrated calculations of oil efficiency potentials, as well as other important conceptual and technical contributions throughout the entire project.

NATHAN J. GLASGOW, a member of RMI Research & Consulting Practice and (from September 2004) Special Aide to the CEO, holds a BA in Human Biology from Stanford and an MA in Economics from the University of California at Santa Barbara. His experience includes project and office management for the nation's leading rammed-earth building firm, founding and leading a software firm, programming, biomedical research, and service as a volunteer firefighter and EMT. He performed extensive modeling for the implementation and business-case portions of this report, including construction of the light-vehicle cohort model, as well as providing diverse graphics and research support throughout.

JEFF BANNON, RMI Research Intern, holds a BA in Political Science from the University of California at San Diego and an MS in Environmental Science and Management from the Donald Bren School of Environmental Science and Management at the University of California at Santa Barbara. A certified ZERI practitioner, he lived for over five years in Japan, where he worked for the CEO of E-Square, Inc. in Tokyo, worked for the Japanese Ministry of Education (Monbusho), learned Japanese, and earned a black belt in Aikido. He has traveled widely, doubled a clothing store's sales to over $1 million in a year, and has been the senior buyer for San Diego's largest independent foreign trading company. For this report, he researched the whaling history module, helped develop the supply curves for auto efficiency, and supported the senior author in preparation of many other portions of this report. In July 2004 he became Environment Manager for the new town of Haymount, Virginia.

LENA M. HANSEN, RMI Research Intern, received a BA with distinction in Physics with Astronomy and in Dramatic Art at University of North Carolina Chapel Hill and a Master's degree in Environmental Management from Duke, where she was a founding Executive Committee member of the campus's Greening Initiative. She has interned with the Alaska Center for the Environment (public lands) and Western North Carolina Alliance (transit planning and environmental education) and been an assistant stage manager for Chapel Hill's Playmakers Repertory Company. She contributed to the business-case and policy sections of this report.

JOSHUA HAACKER, an analyst with RMI's consulting practice, holds a Rensselaer Polytechnic Institute BS in Chemical Engineering *summa cum laude* and a Harvard MBA. He has been Vice President of Project Management at Vulcan Power Company, a strategy consultant to the Alaska Conservation Foundation, Operations Business Leader and Customer/Supplier Leader at Procter & Gamble, and an engineering intern with Norton Company and General Electric. He synthesized this report's biofuels research and contributed to the feedstocks/lubricants, natural-gas, and business-case analyses.

JAMIE FERGUSSON, 2003 RMI Research Intern, graduated from Cambridge University with a BA and MA in Zoology, then spent two years producing and directing wildlife films throughout Africa on behalf of *National Geographic* and the BBC. He then worked as a management consultant for and co-founded a new strategy consulting practice, Credo, which now employs 40 professionals in London and Munich. Jamie is currently studying for both an MBA and an MES in Environmental Management at Yale. He has rowed at Cambridge and sailed the Atlantic. In this report he wrote the oil-price volatility analysis and early drafts of the biomass section in the *Technical Annex* before moving on to summer positions at the World Bank and BP.

JOEL N. SWISHER, PE, team leader of RMI's Energy & Resources Services, has more than 20 years' wide experience in clean energy technology and distributed, resilient energy systems design. He earned a Stanford BS in Civil Engineering, MS in Mechanical Engineering, and PhD in Energy and Environmental Engineering, and was Stanford's 2002–03 MAP/Ming Visiting Professor of Energy and Environment. He has authored more than 100 professional publications, including coauthoring *Tools and Methods for Integrated Resource Planning*. Those written at RMI include *Cleaner Energy, Greener Profits: Fuel Cells as Cost-Effective Distributed Energy Resources* and *The New Business Climate: A Guide to Lower Carbon Emissions and Better Business Performance*, and (as coauthor) *Small Is Profitable: The Hidden Economic Benefits of Making Electrical Resources the Right Size*. He recently led the design of an economically efficient, security-enhancing electricity strategy that now guides the City of San Francisco's $100-million efficiency/renewables investments. He was previously founder/president of E4, an energy consultancy for industries, utilities, European governments, the Electric Power Research Institute, and such financial institutions as the World Bank. A registered civil and mechanical engineer, he speaks five languages and has twice been U.S. national champion in his age group in orienteering, in which he still competes. In this report he helped to guide the general analytic strategy and refine the electricity and gas analyses.

JOANIE HENDERSON, a member of RMI's Commercial & Industrial Services team, holds a BA *cum laude* in Economics, emphasizing energy management and design, from Sonoma State University. She has participated in many RMI client and research projects and created supply-chain greenhouse gas emissions inventories and reduction recommendations. Her research informed many parts of this report. She is an EMT and volunteer firefighter.

JASON DENNER, mechanical engineer (BSME, University of Vermont), is a consultant and researcher on RMI's Commercial & Industrial Services team, with expertise in industrial processes, product manufacture, and design. While at RMI he has developed collaborative innovation techniques for market-leading clients in the hydrocarbon, chemicals, mining, food- and plastics-processing, packaging, and semiconductor industries. He has applied these techniques with client teams at industrial facilities on four continents to develop breakthrough process improvements and define profitable energy- and water-efficiency opportunities. He has diverse experience in product design methodology, tools, and end-to-end execution, and has part-owned and managed all aspects of a small manufacturing firm through its transition to a lean, team-based organization. For this report he performed the military platform analysis in the *Technical Annex* and contributed to the automotive business case.

JAMES NEWCOMB is Managing Director for Research at Bio Economic Research Associates (bio era). He leads the firm's strategic consulting practice, including research on biofuels and other emerging opportunities and issues in the bioeconomy. He was formerly President and CEO of E SOURCE, a leading provider of information on energy-efficient technologies and services to utilities and corporations worldwide (spun off from RMI in 1992). Previously, he was managing director of Cambridge Energy Research Associates, where he led CERA's natural-gas practice. He was educated at Harvard University (BA, Economics) and the University of California at Berkeley (MA, Energy and Resources). He contributed mainly to the biofuels, natural-gas, and oil-industry sections of this report.

GINNY YANG, a Development Associate at RMI, received a BSE in Environmental Engineering *magna cum laude* from Duke University and was an Accenture consultant for such clients as Nortel Networks, Cadence Design Systems, and Oracle. She has been a volunteer hospital-design biophilia researcher and a Peking University natural-capitalism teaching assistant. She supported this report's business-case research.

BRETT FARMERY, RMI Research Intern, holds a Carnegie-Mellon honors BS in Chemical Engineering and is a 2005 Harvard MBA candidate. He has four years' experience as an Accenture analyst and consultant with oil distribution and paper products clients and as execution architect on a global enterprise-software project. He supported much of this report's business-case research and implementation modeling.

References

Abdul Baqi, M.M. & N.G. Saleri. 2004. "Fifty-Year Crude Oil Supply Scenarios: Saudi Aramco's Perspective." Center for Strategic and International Studies (CSIS), 24 February.

Abernathy, W. J. 1978. *The Productivity Dilemma.* Baltimore, MD: Johns Hopkins University Press.

Abt Associates. 1999. *Out of Breath: Adverse Health Effects Associated with Ozone In the Eastern United States.* Cambridge, MA: Abt Associates (October). www.abtassociates.com/reports/ozone.pdf

Abt Associates. 2000. *The Particulate Related Health Benefits of Reducing Power Plant Emissions.* Cambridge, MA: Abt Associates (October). www.abtassociates.com/reports/particulate-related.pdf

ACEEE (American Council for an Energy-Efficient Economy). Undated. "Top-Rated Energy-Efficient Appliances, Gas and Oil Furnaces." www.aceee.org/consumerguide/topfurn.htm#77gas

Aerospace Technology. Undated. "Freighters." www.aerospace-technology.com/projects/freighters_gallery.html

AFP (Agence France Presse). 2004. "Toyota to Sell Hybrid Camry in U.S.: Report." *Channel NewsAsia,* 12 March. www.channelnewsasia.com/stories/afp_world_business/view/75071/1/.html

Agencies. 2004. "Kuwait Tightens Port Security after Terror Threat." *Arab Times,* 10 May.

Agencies. 2004a. "GM to Invest $3b in China in Three Years." *China Daily,* 7 June. www2.chinadaily.com.cn/english/doc/2004-06/07/content_337263.htm

AkzoNobel. 2002. "Spitzer-Colani-Truck im Sikkens Kleid." Press release, 16 October. www.akzonobel.de/press/20021016-1139.php

Alliance to Save Energy. 2004. "National Defense Energy Savings Act." Fact sheet. Washington, DC: ASE (May). www.ase.org/uploaded_files/policy/NDESA%20Fact%20Sheet.pdf

aluNET International. Undated. "Extraordinary Aluminium Bulk Tanker Truck Designed by Colani. Spitzer's Pioneering Work." www.alunet.net/shownews.asp?ID=1166&type=3

Alvarez, L. 2004. "Britain Says U.S. Planned to Seize Oil in '73 Crisis." *N.Y. Times,* 2 January.

Amendola, G. 1990. "The Diffusion of Synthetic Materials in the Automobile Industry: Towards a Major Breakthrough?" *Research Policy* 19(6): 485–500 (December).

American Iron and Steel Institute. 2002. "New Steels Can Help Vehicles Achieve Five-Star Crash Rating, Double Fuel Economy at No Additional Cost." Press release, 30 January. www.autosteel.org/press_room/2002_avc_short.htm

American Physical Society. 1975. "Efficient Use of Energy." *AIP Conference Proceedings 25.* New York: American Institute of Physics.

American Plastics Council. 2001. "APC Year-End Statistics for 2001." http://environmentalrisk.cornell.edu/C&ER/PlasticsDisposal/AgPlasticsRecycling/References/APC01.pdf

American Plastics Council. Undated. "Energy Efficiency FAQ." www.americanplasticscouncil.org/s_apc/sec.asp?TRACKID=&SID=6&VID=86&CID=349&DID=1149 (downloaded 21 May 2004).

Amsoil. Undated. "Synthetic Motor Oil Claiming Larger Share of Market." www.1st-in-synthetics.com/articles83.htm

An, F. & A. Rousseau. 2001. "Integration of a Modal Energy and Emissions Model into a PNGV Vehicle Simulation Model PSAT." SAE 2001-01-0965. Warrendale, PA: Society of Automotive Engineers.

An, F. & D.J. Santini. 2004. "Mass Impacts on Fuel Economies of Conventional vs. Hybrid Electric Vehicles." SAE 2004-01-0572. Warrendale, PA: Society of Automotive Engineers. www.sae.org

An, F., A. Vyas, J. Anderson, & D. Santini. 2001. "Evaluating Commercial and Prototype HEVs." SAE 2001-01-0951. Warrendale, PA: Society of Automotive Engineers.

An, F., W. Wu, Y. Jin, & D. He. 2003. "Development of China Light-Duty Vehicle Fuel Consumption Standards." Transforming Transportation Conference, World Resources Institute, Washington, DC, 13 January. www.embarq.wri.org/documents/newvisionschina/an.pdf

Andrew, E.L. 2004. "The Ever More Graspable, and Risky, American Dream." *N.Y. Times,* 24 June, C-1.

Ansari X Prize. Undated. www.xprize.org

Anton, P., R. Silbergilt, & J. Schneider. 2001. *The Global Technology Revolution: Bio/Nano/Materials Trends and Their Synergies with Information Technology by 2015.* Arlington, VA: National Defense Research Institute, RAND. www.rand.org/publications/MR/MR1307

APECC (Auto Project on Energy and Climate Change), China Program. 2004. "APECC News Briefing Auto/Energy/Pollution." 1(1): 3–4 and 1(2): 3–6 (the bilingual text of the new policy), July. fengan@ameritech.net

API (American Petroleum Institute). Undated. "Used Oil Management System." www.recycleoil.org/Usedoilflow.htm

APME (Association of Plastics Manufacturers in Europe). 2003. "Plastics 2001 & 2002: An Analysis of Plastics Consumption and Recovery in Europe." Brussels, Belgium: Association of Plastics Manufacturers in Europe. www.apme.org/dashboard/business_layer/template.asp?url=http://www.apme.org/media/public_documents/20011017_201404/literatuur_general_00.htm&title=Literature+-+General+papers

AQMD (South Coast Air Quality Management District). 2004. "AQMD Will Seek to Continue Implementing Fleet Rules." Press release, 28 April. www.aqmd.gov/news1/2004/scotus_opinionpr.html

Arabialink.com. 2002. "Terrorist Attack on Saudi Oil Terminal Thwarted." *GulfWire Digest* 167 (21–27 October). Citing Dow Jones, AP, 14 October. www.arabialink.com/Archive/GWDigests/GWD2002/GWD_2002_10_21.htm#NS2, and http://abcnews.go.com/sections/wnt/DailyNews/Saudi021014_terror.html

Archer, C.L. & M.Z. Jacobson. 2003. "Spatial and Temporal Distribution of U.S. Winds and Wind Power at 80 m Derived from Measurements." *J. Geophysical Research* 108(D9): 4289–4309.

Ash, M. 2002. *Oil Crops Situation and Outlook Yearbook.* Washington, DC: Market and Trade Economics Division, Economic Research Service, U.S. Department of Agriculture (October). www.ers.usda.gov/publications/so/view.asp?f=field/ocs-bby

Ashuckian, D., G. Bemis, D. Fong, C. Kavalec, L. Stamets, & S. Stoner. 2003. *Final Staff Draft Report. Appendix C: Petroleum Reduction Options (Task 3).* Sacramento, CA: California Air Resources Board and California Energy Commission (August). www.energy.ca.gov/fuels/petroleum_dependence/documents

ATA (American Trucking Associations), Economics and Statistics Group. 2001. *Twenty from The Top: A Benchmarking Guide to the Operations of For-Hire Truck-Load Carriers: 2001 ed.* www.ttnews.com/20top/2004/20Top04.asp

ATA. 2004. *ATA Truck Fleet Directory 2004.* Available for purchase at www.truckline.com/store/index.asp

Auffhammer, M. 2004. "China, Cars, and Carbon." *Giannini Foundation of Agricultural Economics Agricultural and Resource Economics Update* 7(3): 9–11. www.agecon.ucdavis.edu/outreach/areupdatepdfs/UpdateV7N3/V7N3_4.pdf

Austin, D., N. Rosinki, A. Sauer, & C. le Duc. 2004. *Changing Drivers: The Impact of Climate Change on Competitiveness and Value Creation in the Automotive Industry.* Zürich: Sustainable Asset Management and Washington, DC: World Resources Institute (July). http://pubs.wri.org/pubs_description.cfm?PubID=3873

Ausubel, J.H. 1998. "The Environment for Future Business: Efficiency Will Win." *Pollution Prevention Review* 8(1): 39–52 (Winter). http://phe.rockefeller.edu/future_business

Automobile Association. 2004. "UK Fuel Prices June 2004." www.theaa.com/allaboutcars/fuel/fuel_report_june04.html (downloaded 7 July 2004).

Automorrow. 1989. "AUTOMORROW '89 World's First Alternative Car Festival Bonneville Salt Flats, Utah October 25–November 1." Press release. www.automorrow.com/articles/auto89press.html

Automotive Intelligence News. 2002. "The Opel Eco-Speedster: Sports Car Prototype as a Bold Stroke to Launch Opel's Diesel Campaign." autointell-news.com, 2 October. www.autointell-news.com/News-2002/October-2002/October-2002-1/October-02-02-p5.htm

Automotive Intelligence News. 2004. "GM Celebrates Start of Construction On New $800 Million Lansing Area Assembly Plant." autointell-news.com, 9 March. www.autointell-news.com/News-2004/March-2004/March-2004-3/Mar-17-04-p3.htm

Automotive Intelligence. Undated. "Daimler-Chrysler: The Dodge ESX3, Low Fuel Consumption." autointell.net. www.autointell.net/nao_companies/daimlerchrysler/dodge/dodge-esx3-01.htm

Automotive News. 2003. *Market Data Book* (May).

Automotive.com. 2004. "Nearly 40% of Car Buyers Say Gas Prices Have Affected Vehicle Purchase Decision," 4 May. www.automotive.com/news/25/1440/

Auto-Motor-Sport Journal. 1999. **19:** 42ff.

Autoweb.com.au. 2000. "Fit for Practical Use: DaimlerChrysler Presents Two Fuel Cell Cars," 9 November. www.autoweb.com.au/A_53197/cms/newsarticle.html

AWEA (American Wind Energy Association). 2004. "Wind Energy Potential—Top 20 U.S. States." Fact sheet. Washington, DC: AWEA. www.awea.org/pubs/factsheets.html

AWEA. 2004a. "Wind Energy for Your Farm or Rural Land." Fact sheet. Washington, DC: AWEA (8 June). www.awea.org/pubs/factsheets/WindyLandownersFS.pdf

Awerbuch, S. & R. Sauter. 2002. "Oil Price Volatility and Economic Activity: A Survey and Literature Review." Draft research paper. Paris: International Energy Agency (September).

Babikian, R., J. Lee, S. Lukachko, & I. Waitz. 2000. "Low-Emission Aircraft Study." Poster. Center for Technology, Policy, and Industrial Development and Aero-Environmental Research Laboratory. Cambridge, MA: MIT. http://web.mit.edu/aeroastro/www/people/iaw/LEAS_Poster.pdf

Bacon, R. 2004. "Taxation of Energy." *Encyc. of Energy* **6:** 13–25. San Diego: Elsevier.

Baer, R. 2003. *Sleeping with the Devil.* New York: Crown.

Baer, R. 2003a. "Addicted to Oil." Interview with Robert Baer by Elizabeth Shelburne. *Atlantic Unbound,* 29 May. www.theatlantic.com/unbound/interviews/int2003-05-29.htm

Baer, R. 2003b. "The Fall of the House of Saud." *The Atlantic Monthly,* 19 May. www.frontpagemag.com/articles/ReadArticle.asp?ID=7892

Bahree, B. 2004. "As Fresh Prospects Dry Up, Petroleum Industry Strikes Deals." *Wall St. J.,* 18 May, p. A1. http://online.wsj.com/article/0,,SB108483037979413835,00.html?mod=todays_us_page_one

Bahree, B. & P.A. McKay. 2004. "Oil Prices Near $40 a Barrel, Casting Long Shadow." *Wall St. J.,* 5 May, p. A1.

Bakhtiari, A.M.S. "World Oil Production Capacity Model Suggests Output Peak by 2006–07." *Oil & Gas J.* (26 April): 19–21.

Ball, J. 2004. "For Many Low-Income Workers, High Gasoline Prices Take a Toll." *Wall St. J. Online,* 12 July. http://online.wsj.com/search#SB108958257586260720

Bamberger, R. 1999. "Automobile and Light Truck Fuel Economy: Is CAFE Up to Standards?" Congressional Research Service Issue Brief 90122 (9 August). www.ncseonline.org/NLE/CRSreports/Air/air-13.cfm?&CFID=14312713&CFTOKE59772486

Bamberger, R. 2003. "Automobile and Light Truck Fuel Economy: The CAFE Standards." Updated Congressional Research Issue Brief IB90122 (19 June). www.ncseonline.org/NLE/CRSreports/03Jul/IB90122.pdf

Banerjee, N. 2004. "Attacks Drive Price of Oil to $40 a Barrel." *N.Y. Times,* 12 May. www.nytimes.com/2004/05/12/business/worldbusiness/12oil.html?th

Banerjee, N. 2004a. "Tight Oil Supply Won't Ease Soon." *N.Y. Times,* 16 May. www.nytimes.com/2004/05/16/business/16OIL.html?th

Bank of America, Greenbelt Alliance, Low Income Housing Fund, & California Resources Agency. 1996. "Beyond Sprawl: New Patterns of Growth to Fit California." Summary at www.bankofamerica.com/environment/index.cfm?template=env_reports_speeches&context=sprawl

Bankrate.com. 2003. "Vehicles That Qualify for Generous Tax Break." Bankrate.com, 5 November. www.bankrate.com/brm/itax/biz_tips/20030403b1.asp

Barnett, J., S. Dessai, & M. Webber. 2004. "Will OPEC Lose from the Kyoto Protocol?" *En. Pol.* **32**(18): 2077–2088.

Barone, M. 2002. "Our Enemies the Saudis." *U.S. News & World Report,* 3 June. www.usnews.com/usnews/issue/archive/020603/20020603021062_print.php

BBC News. 2000. "The Super Jumbo Fact File." BBC News, 23 June. http://news.bbc.co.uk/2/hi/business/675654.stm

BBC News World Edition. 2003. "U.S. Troops Engage Further in Colombia." BBC News, 18 January. http://news.bbc.co.uk/2/hi/americas/2670913.stm

BEA (Bureau of Economic Analysis, U.S. Department of Commerce). 2004. "Gross Domestic Product (GDP)," 30 April. www.bea.gov/bea/dn/home/gdp.htm (downloaded 30 April 2004 using the 29 April 2004 revision).

BEA. Undated. "Regional Economic Accounts, Local Area Personal Income." www.bea.doc.gov/bea/regional/reis/default.cfm#a

Becker, G. 2004. "Let's Make Gasoline Prices Even Higher." *Bus. Wk.,* 31 May. www.businessweek.com/magazine/content/04_22/b3885046_mz007.htm

Bekkoame Co. Ltd. 2002. www.bekkoame.ne.jp/~kotoandq/data/fr54.jpg

Benyus, J. 1997. *Biomimicry.* New York: William Morrow.

Berenson, A. 2004. "An Oil Enigma: Production Falls Even as Reserves Rise." *N.Y. Times,* 12 June.

Bezdek, R. & R. Wendling. 2003. *Potential Long-Term Impacts of Changes in U.S. Vehicle Fuel Efficiency Standards.* Washington, DC: Management Information Services, Inc. (January). www.misi-net.com/publications/CAFE_Article.pdf

Bijur, P. Undated. Quotation at www.worldwide.fuelcells.org/sp_base.cgim?template=sp_quotes, confirmed and dated to late 1990s by P.I. Bijur, personal communication, 11 May 2004.

Bio-era (Bio-Economic Research Associates). 2004. "Biofuels Trade Policies Stir Controversy." Boulder, CO: Bio-era (10 June). www.bio-era.net/modules/wfsection/article.php?page=-2&articleid=21

Birch, S. 2000. "BMW's Secrets Revealed." *Automotive Engineering Intl. Online/Global Viewpoints* (October). www.sae.org/automag/globalview_10-00/05.htm

Blanchard, B. 2004. "China Wants Strong Home-grown Car Industry." *Planet Ark,* 2 June. www.planetark.org/dailynewsstory.cfm/newsid/25348/newsDate/2-Jun-2004/story.htm

Bleviss, D. 1988. *The New Oil Crisis and Fuel Economy Technologies: Preparing the Light Transportation Industry for the 1990s.* New York: Quorum Books.

Bloomberg. 2004. "New Mobile Phone Subscriptions Booming in China." *Taipei Times,* 25 May, p. 10. www.taipeitimes.com/News/biz/archives/2004/05/25/2003156911

Bloomberg. 2004a. "All Nippon to Sign Boeing 7E7 Contract by September (Updated)," 4 June. http://quote.bloomberg.com/apps/news?pid=10000101&refer=japan&sid=akhqzXX4kCYg

BLS (Bureau of Labor Statistics). Undated. "Consumer Expenditure Survey." http://data.bls.gov/labjava/outside.jsp?survey=cx

BMW Group. 2001/2002. *Sustainable Value Report 2001/2002. Reducing Weight to Benefit the Environment.* www.bmwgroup.com/e/nav/index.html?http://www.bmwgroup.com/e/0_0_www_bmwgroup_com/5_verantwortung/5_4_publikationen/5_4_1_umweltbericht/5_4_1_1_umbeltbericht/5_4_1_1_2_focus/5_4_1_1_2_2_leicht.shtml

Boeing. Undated. "747 Fun Facts." Boeing.com. www.boeing.com/commercial/747family/pf/pf_facts.html

Boeing. Undated (downloaded 13 August 2004). "Boeing 7E7 Dreamliner Will Provide New Solutions for Airlines, Passengers." Boeing.com. www.boeing.com/commercial/7e7/background.html

Bohi, D.R. & M.A. Toman. 1996. *The Economics of Energy Security.* Norwell, MA: Kluwer Academic Publishers.

Bonsor, K. Undated. "How Gas Prices Work." Howsuffworks.com. http://money.howstuffworks.com/gas-price2.htm

Book, E. 2002. "Pentagon Needs Accurate Accounting of Fuel." *National Defense* (March). www.nationaldefensemagazine.org/article.cfm?Id=750

Bowers, A. 2004. "California's SUV Ban." Slate.com, 4 August. http://slate.msn.com/id/2104755#ContinueArticle

Bowlin, M. 1999. "Clean Energy: Preparing Today for Tomorrow's Challenges." Speech delivered at Cambridge Energy Research Associates 18th Annual Executive Conference: *Globality and Energy: Strategies for the New Millennium,* Houston, TX, 9 February. www.bp.com/genericarticle.do?categoryId=98&contentId=2000318

BP (British Petroleum). 2003. *BP Statistical Review of World Energy 2003.* www.bp.com/subsection.do?categoryId=95&contentId=2006480

Bradley, J. 2004. "At the Crossroads." *Al-Ahram Weekly On-Line* 689 (6–12 May). http://weekly.ahram.org.eg/2004/689/re4.htm

Bradsher, K. 2002. *High and Mighty: SUVs— The World's Most Dangerous Vehicles and How They Got That Way.* New York: Public Affairs.

Bradsher, K. 2003. "China Set to Act on Fuel Economy." *N.Y. Times,* 18 November.

Breckenridge, T. 2002. "A Bright Light; David Goldstein is Saving the Earth One Kilowatt-hour at a Time." *The Cleveland Plain Dealer,* 1 December.

Bridgwater, A.V. 2003. "Renewable Fuels and Chemicals by Thermal Processing of Biomass." *Chem. Engineering J.* **91**(2): 87–102 (15 March).

Brinded, M. (Group Managing Director, Royal/Dutch Shell Group; CEO, Shell Gas & Power). 2004. "The Vital Role of Gas in a Sustainable Energy Future." Speech delivered at CERA conference, Houston, TX, 11 February. www.shell.com/static/media-en/downloads/speeches/mb_ceraweek_11022004.pdf

Broadman, H.G. & W.W. Hogan. 1988. "Is an Oil Tariff Justified?" *En. J.* **9**(3): 7–29.

Brosius, D. 2003. "Carbon Fiber Gains Traction with Automakers." *Composites Technology* (August). www.compositesworld.com/ct/issues/2003/August/159

Brosius, D. 2003a. "Thermoplastic Composites Making an Impact." *Composites Technology* (February). www.compositesworld.com/ct/issues/2003/February/4

Brosius, D. 2003b. *Reinforced Plastics Automotive Supplement* (February), pp. 21–58.

Brown, L.R. 2004. "Europe Leading World Into Age of Wind Energy." Washington, DC: Earth Policy Institute (8 April). www.earth-policy.org/Updates/Update37.htm

Brown, W. 2004. "Hailing the Diesel's Return." *Wash. Post,* 21 March, p. G01. www.washingtonpost.com/wp-dyn/articles/A8394-2004Mar19.html

Brown, M.A., M.D. Levine, W. Short, & J.G. Koomey. 2001. "Scenarios for a Clean Energy Future." *En. Pol.* **29**(14): 1179–1196 and LBNL-48031. Berkeley, CA: Lawrence Berkeley National Laboratory.

Browne, J. 2004. "Beyond Kyoto." *Foreign Affairs* (July/August).

Brylawski, M.M. & A.B. Lovins. 1995. "Ultralight-Hybrid Vehicle Design: Overcoming the Barriers to Using Advanced Composites in the Automotive Industry." SAMPE (Society For Advanced Materials & Process Engineering). RMI T95-39. Snowmass, CO: Rocky Mountain Institute. www.rmi.org/sitepages/pid175.php

BTI (Breakthrough Technologies Institute). 2004. *Fuel Cells at the Crossroads: Attitudes Regarding the Investment Climate for the U.S. Fuel Cell Industry and a Projection of Industry Job Creation Potential.* Washington, DC: Breakthrough Technologies Institute (27 May). www.ipd.anl.gov/anlpubs/2004/05/50246.pdf

BTS (Bureau of Transportation Statistics). 1999. "Official Airline Information 1999. Form 41, Schedule P-5.2 and Schedule T-2 for 1968–98." Washington, DC: BTS. www.bts.gov/oai/sources

BTS. 2000. "2000 Selected Earning Data Top 100 Class 1 Motor Carriers of Property." Washington, DC: BTS. Available as Excel file at www.bts.gov/mcs/data/html/prop00.html

BTS. 2001. *Transportation Statistics Annual Report 2001.* Washington, DC: BTS. www.bts.gov/publications/transportation_statistics_annual_report/2001/html/chapter_04_figure_01_083.html

BTS. 2004. "Aviation Data Library: Data Tables Schedule P-51 and Schedule T-2 of database Form 41." www.transtats.bts.gov/Databases.asp?Mode_ID=1&Mode_Desc=Aviation&Subject_ID2=0 (downloaded 7–12 July, 2004).

Buchanan, P.J. 2003. "Whose War?" *American Conservative,* 24 March. www.amconmag.com/03_24_03/cover.html

Bunn, M. & A. Wier. 2004. *Securing the Bomb: An Agenda for Action.* Washington, DC: Nuclear Threat Initiative and the Project on Managing the Atom, Harvard University (May).

Burns, L. 2003. "Fuel Cell Vehicles Driving the Hydrogen Economy." Remarks to the Fuel Cells Tech Tour, Sacramento, CA, 10–11 February. www.gm.com/company/gmability/environment/news_issues/speeches/burns_techtour_032003.html

"Buttonwood." 2004. "Ford Focus." *The Economist Global Agenda,* 16 March. www.economist.com/agenda/displayStory.cfm?story_id=2515212

Buy Recycled Business Alliance. 2000. "Re-refined Oil." www.nrc-recycle.org/brba/fs/rerefinedoil.htm

Cai, M. 2003. "The Chinese Telecom Market Still Promises Tremendous Opportunities." *HomeToys.* Dallas, TX: Park Associates (April). www.parksassociates.com/press/articles/2003/hometoys_china.htm

Car.Kak.net. 2003. "Opel ECO-Speedster: Diesel Prototype Pursues World Records." www.car.kak.net. http://car.kak.net/modules.php?op=modload&name=news&file=article&sid=1105

Carlson, D. 2004. "The Asphalt-Rubber Industry Perspective." *Proceedings of the Rubber Modified Asphalt Conference,* Grand Rapids, MI, 19–20 May.

Carns, Gen M.P.C., DSB Chairman. 2002. "Defense Science Board Task Force on B-52H Re-Engining." Washington, DC: Office of the Under Secretary of Defense For Acquisition, Technology and Logistics, DoD. www.globalsecurity.org/wmd/library/report/2002/b52.pdf

Carrico, T.M. 2000. "Ultra*Log." Defense Advanced Research Projects Agency's Advanced Logistics Project. www.darpa.mil/DARPATech2000/presentation.html

Carson, I. 2003. "Extinction of the Car Giants." *Economist,* 14 June.

Cart, J. 2004. "Western Governors Back Greater Role for Clean Energy in Region." *L.A. Times,* 23 June, p. B6.

Carty, S.S. 2004. "UPDATE: Hefty Incentives Boost May U.S. Auto Sales." *Wall St. J. Online,* 3 June.

Casten, T. & B. Downes. 2004. "Economic Growth and the Central Generation Paradigm." Presentation to International Association for Energy Economics, Oak Brook, IL, 14 July.

CAT/NRC (Committee on Aeronautical Technologies/National Research Council). 1992. *Aeronautical Technologies for the Twenty-First Century.* Washington, DC: National Academy Press.

Cavanaugh, K. 2004. "Big Trouble from Tiny Particles?" *L.A. Daily News,* 7 March.

Cavin, C. 2004. "Brack Continues Recovery with his Return to Stage." *IndyStar, 1* April.

Sturrock, J. & Woodward, G.T. 2002. "Economic Stimulus: Evaluating Proposed Changes in Tax Policy." Washington, DC: Congressional Budget Office (January).
http://www.cbo.gov/showdoc.cfm?index=3251&sequence=0

Cebrowski, A.K. 1999. "The Road Ahead: 21st Century War College, 21st Century Warfare, 21st Century Navy." Presentation at All Flag Officers Conference, Newport, RI, 10 February. www.nwc.navy.mil/press/Review/1999/summer/note-su9.htm

CEC (California Energy Commission). 2003. "Final 2002 Report, Evaluation of the California Energy Commission's AB29X and SB5X Peak Load Reduction Program Elements." Consultant Report, P400-02-0029CR. San Francisco, CA: Nexant (5 May). www.nexant.com/docs/CEC/ExecSum2002.pdf

CEE (Consortium for Energy Efficiency). 2004. "Super-Efficient, Apartment-Sized Refrigerator Initiative." Boston, MA: CEE. www.cee1.org/resrc/facts/sear-fx.php3

Ceniceros, B., J. Sugar, & M. Tessier. 2002. "Zero to 60 Megawatts in 8.4 Seconds: How to Rapidly Deploy a Peak Load Reduction Program." Paper presented at American Council for an Energy-Efficient Economy (ACEEE) 2002 Summer Study Session, Pacific Grove, CA, 18–23 August. www.energy.ca.gov/papers/2002-08-18 aceee_presentations/PANEL-04_CENICEROS.PDF

CETS (Commission on Engineering and Technical Systems). 1999. *Review of the Research Program of the Partnership for a New Generation of Vehicles: Fifth Report.* Washington, DC: National Academies Press. http://books.nap.edu/books/0309064430/html/67.html#pagetop

Chanin, R.L. 2003. "California's Authority to Regulate Mobile Source Greenhouse Gas Emissions." *NYU Annual Survey of American Law* 58: 699–754.

Chapman, J. & S. Wiese. 1998. "Expanding Wind Power: Can Americans Afford It?" Washington, DC: Renewable Energy Policy Project (November). http://solstice.crest.org/repp_pubs/articles/chapman/chapman.html

Chen, A., K.C. Chen, & R.S. Sears. 1986. "The Value of Loan Guarantees: The Case of Chrysler Corporation." *Research in Finance* 6: 101–117.

China Economic Net. 2004. "New Auto Rules State Joint Venture Guidelines." *China Daily,* 2 June. http://en.ce.cn/Industries/Auto/t20040602_980324.shtml

Christensen, C. 1997. *The Innovators Dilemma.* Cambridge, MA: Harvard University Press.

Christensen, C. & M. Overdorf. 2000. "Meeting the Challenge of Disruptive Change." *Harvard Business Review on Innovation* **78**(2): 67–77 (1 May).

Christensen, C. & M. Raynor. 2003. *The Innovators Solution: Creating and Sustaining Innovative Growth.* Cambridge, MA: Harvard Business School Press.

Clean Air Initiative Asia. Undated. "British Columbia, Scrap-It, Mandatory Scrappage Program." cleanairnet.org. www.cleanairnet.org/caiasia/1412/article-37169.html

Clini, C. & M. Moody-Stuart. (Co-Chairmen, Renewable Energy Task Force). 2001. *Final Report to the G8 Summit* (July). www.renewabletaskforce.org/report.asp

Clinton, W.J. 1999. Executive Order no. 13132, 64 FR 43255, 10 August. www.dwd.org/pdf/exeorder.pdf

CNN International. 2004. "China Looks for Shared Solutions." CNN.com, 25 May.

Coelho, S.T. & J. Goldemberg. 2004. "Alternative Transportation Fuels: Contemporary Case Studies." *Encyc. of Energy* **1**: 67–80. San Diego: Elsevier.

Cohen, J.M. (RADM). 2003. "Shipbuilding Technologies." *SHIPTECH 2003*. Department of the Navy Science and Technology. www.nsrp.org/st2003/presentations/cohen.pdf

Colani, L. Undated. "Colani: Visions in Design." www.colani.ch/frame.htm

Colledge, J., J. Hicks, J.B. Robb, & D. Wagle. 2002. "Power by the Minute." *The McKinsey Quarterly,* no.1. www.mckinseyquarterly.com/article_abstract.aspx?ar=1142&L2=3&L3=48

Colorado Department of Revenue, Taxpayer Service Division. 2003. "FYI Income 9: Alternative Fuel Income Tax Credits" (December). www.revenue.state.co.us/fyi/html/income09.html

COMPOSIT. Undated. "The Future Use of Composites in Transport: Research Cluster: Lightweighting of Composite Structures for Transportation Systems: State-of-the-Art." www.compositn.net/Clusters/Cluster%20-%20Lightweighting%20-%20State-of-the-Art%20-%20Comparison.htm

Composites World. 2004. "Chrysler Reveals Carbon Fiber-bodied Concept at Detroit Auto Show." Compositesworld.com, March. www.compositesworld.com/hpc/issues/2004/March/381

Composites World. 2004a. "Industry Overview: Sports and Aerospace Applications." *High-Performance Composites: Sourcebook 2004.* www.compositesworld.com/sb/ov-hightech

Coon, C.E. 2004. "Energy Bill Too Weighted Down to Power the Country." *The Heritage Foundation Backgrounder* (#1736), 17 March. www.heritage.org/Research/EnergyandEnvironment/bg1736.cfm

Copulos, M.R. 2003. "The Real Cost of Imported Oil." *Wash. Times,* 23 July. http://washingtontimes.com/commentary/20030722-093718-6082r.htm

Copulos, M.R. 2004. "The Economic Impacts Of Import Dependence on Mineral and Energy Commodities." Testimony before the House Resources Subcommittee on Energy and Mineral Resources, 2 March. www.nma.org/pdf/cong_test/copulos_030404.pdf

Cordesman, A.H. 1993. *After the Storm.* Boulder, CO: Westview Press.

Cordesman, A.H. 2002–04. *Saudi Arabia Enters the 21st Century.* Washington, DC: Center for Strategic and International Studies (CSIS). www.csis.org/burke/saudi21/

Cordesman, A.H. 2004. *Energy Developments in the Middle East.* Washington, DC: Center for Strategic and International Studies (CSIS), 15 March draft. www.csis.org/burke/meep

Cotterill, R.W. & A.W. Franklin. 1995. "The Urban Grocery Store Gap." *Food Marketing Pol. Iss.* **8** (April). Storrs, CT: University of Connecticut Food Marketing Policy Center. www.fmpc.uconn.edu/ip/ip8.pdf

Crain, K.C. 2004. "Ford Expands Hybrid Lineup with Mercury Mariner." *Automotive News,* 12 April. www.autonews.com/article.cms?articleId=47879

Cramer, D.R. & M.M Brylawski (Hypercar). 1996. "The Ultralight-Vehicle Hybrid Design: Implications for the Recycling Industry." Society of Plastics Engineers Recycling Division's 3rd Annual Recycling Conference, Chicago, 7–8 November.

Cramer, D.R. & D.F. Taggart. 2002. "Design and Manufacture of an Affordable Advanced-Composite Automotive Body Structure." *Proceedings of the 19th International Battery, Hybrid and Fuel Cell Electric Vehicle Symposium & Exhibition (EVS-19),* Seoul, Korea. www.hypercar.com/pdf/Hypercar_EVS19.pdf

CRFA (Canadian Renewable Fuels Association). Undated. "Biodiesel Around the World." www.greenfuels.org/bioworld.html

CRS (Congressional Research Service). 1975. "Oil Fields as Military Objectives: A Feasibility Study." Report to USHR Committee on International Relations. Washington, DC: CRS (21 August). www.mtholyoke.edu/acad/intrel/Petroleum/fields.htm

CRS. 1992. *The External Costs of Oil Used in Transportation.* CRS Rpt. 92-574 ENR. Washington, DC: CRS (17 June).

Cummins, C. 2004. "Oil Prices Face Slippery Triggers in Futures Market." *Wall St. J.,* 18 May, p. C1. http://online.wsj.com/article/ 0,,SB108480321622013367,00.html?mod= todays_us_money_and_investing

Cummins, C. 2004a. "As Threats to Oil Facilities Rise, U.S. Military Becomes Protector." *Wall St. J.,* 30 June, p. A1.

Daalder, I.H. & J.M. Lindsay. 2003. *America Unbound: The Bush Revolution in Foreign Policy.* Washington, DC: Brookings Institution Press.

DACV (Decision Analysis Corp. of Virginia). 2000. *Updates to Degradation Factor Analysis: Final Report, Subtask 4.* Report to EIA, Task 90230, Contract DE-AT01-99E1. McLean, VA: DACV (6 July).

Daggett, D.L. 2003. "Commercial Airplanes: Hydrogen Fueled Airplanes." Hydrogen Production & NW Transportation Conference, Seattle, 16 June. www.pnl.gov/energy/ hydrogen/presentations/daggett.pdf

Daggett, D.L., D.J. Sutkus, Jr., D.P. DuBois, & S.L. Baughcum. 1999. "An Evaluation of Aircraft Emissions Inventory Methodology by Comparisons with Reported Airline Data." NASA Contractor Rept. 1999-209480, Boeing Commercial Airplane Group report to NASA Langley Res. Ctr. (June).

Daihatsu Motor Company. 2003. "Daihatsu Exhibits Open-Top Sports 4WD and Ultra Fuel Economy Car at the 37th Tokyo Motor Show." Daihatsu.com, 14 October. www.daihatsu.com/news/n2003/03101401

DaimlerChrysler AG. 2004. "Mercedes-Benz Vision Grand Sports Tourer." www.babez.de/mercedes/vision.php

DaimlerChrysler Communications. 1999. "Innovation Symposium 1999: The Fuel Cell as an Economic Opportunity." Press release, 12 November. www.electrifyingtimes.com/ daimlerchryslerfuelcell.html

Dana, D. 2004. "WTO Legal Impacts on Commodity Subsidies: Green Box Opportunities in the Farm Bill for Farm Income Through the Conservation and Clean Energy Development Programs." Chicago: Environmental Law & Policy Center (20 July). www.elpc.org/energy/ WTO.Farm%20Bill%20Paper.July%2020.2004.pdf

Darley, J. 2004. "A Tale of Two Planets." *Petroleum Review* (April): 16–17. http://postcarbon.org/DOCS/2004/03/ JulianDarley.Saudi-Simmons.2004-03-15.htm

Das, S. 2004. "Material Use in Automobiles." *Encyc. of Energy* **3**: 859–869. San Diego: Elsevier.

Datta, K. & D. Gabaldon. 2001. "Risky Business: The Business Customer's Perspective on U.S. Electricity Deregulation." San Francisco, CA: Booz, Allen & Hamilton.

Datta, K. & D. Gabaldon. 2003. "Winner Take All." *Public Utility Fortnightly,* 15 October.

Datta, L.-e. & P.G. Grasso. 1998. *Evaluating Tax Expenditures: Tools and Techniques for Assessing Outcomes: New Directions for Evaluation, No. 79* (September). San Francisco, CA: Jossey-Bass. www.josseybass.com/ WileyCDA/Section/id-5510.html

Davis, M. 2002. "Tire Manufacturers Offering New Designs for Today's Commercial Truck Marketplace." *Modern Bulk Tranpsorter,* 1 November. http://bulktransporter.com/mag/ transportation_tire_manufacturers_offering

Davis, L.E., R.E. Gallman, & K. Gleiter. 1997. *In Pursuit of Leviathan.* Chicago, IL: University of Chicago Press.

Davis, L.E., R.E. Gallman, & T.D. Hutchins. 1988. "The Decline of U.S. Whaling: Was the Stock of Whales Running Out?" *Bus. History Rev.* **62**: 569–595.

Davis, J., T.A. Hirschl, & M. Stack. 1997. *Cutting Edge: Technology, Information Capitalism and Social Revolution.* New York: Verso.

Davis, W.B., M.D. Levine, K. Train, & K.G. Duleep. 1995. "Effects of Feebates on Vehicle Fuel Economy, Carbon Dioxide Emissions, and Consumer Surplus." DOE/PO-0031. Washington, DC: Office of Policy, U.S. DOE (February). http://eetd.lbl.gov/ea/teepa/pdf/DOE-PO-0031.html

DeCanio, S.J. 1993. "Barriers within Firms to Energy-Efficient Investments." *En. Pol.* **21**(9): 906–915.

DeCanio, S.J. 1998. "The Efficiency Paradox: Bureaucratic and Organizational Barriers to Profitable Energy-Saving Investments." *En. Pol.* **26**(5): 441–454.

DeCanio, S.J. 2003. *Economic Models of Climate Change: A Critique.* Basingstoke, UK: Palgrave Macmillan.

DeCicco, J., F. An, & M. Ross. 2001. "Technical Options for Improving the Fuel Economy of U.S. Cars and Light Trucks by 2010–2015." Washington, DC: American Council for an Energy-Efficient Economy (April). www.aceee.org/store/ proddetail.cfm?CFID=204867&CFTOKEN= 65569880&ItemID=264&CategoryID=7

DeCicco, J., R. Griffin, & S. Ertel. 2003. "Putting the Brakes on U.S. Oil Demand." Washington, DC: Environmental Defense.

Delucchi, M.A. 1998. "The Annualized Social Cost of Motor-Vehicle Use in the U.S., 1990–1991: Summary of Theory, Data, Methods, and Results." UCD-ITS-RR-96-3 (1). Davis, CA: Institute of Transportation Studies, UC Davis (June). www.its.ucdavis.edu/publications/ 1996/RR-96-03%20(01).pdf

Delucchi, M.A. & J. Murphy. 1996. "U.S. Military Expenditures to Protect the Use of Persian-Gulf Oil for Motor Vehicles." UCD-ITS-RR-96-03(15). Davis, CA: Institute of Transportation Studies, UC Davis (April). www.its.ucdavis.edu/publica- tions/1996/rr-96-03-15.pdf

Deluga, G.A., J.R. Salge, L.D. Schmidt, & X.E. Verykios. 2004. "Renewable Hydrogen from Ethanol by Autothermal Reforming." *Science* **303** (13 February): 993–997.

de Saint-Exupéry, A. 1948. *Citadelle/The Wisdom of the Sands.* Paris: Gallimard.

DESC (Defense Energy Support Center). 2003. *Fact Book 2002: 25th Edition.* www.desc.dla.mil/ DCM/Files/fact02.pdf

DESC. 2003–04. "Fuel Usage" boxes, *Fuel Line* (Spring 2003 through Winter 2004 issues). www.desc.dla.mil/DCM/DCMPage.asp?pageid=206

de Segundo, K. 2003. (Chief Executive Officer, Shell Renewables). "A Renewable Energy Future? Challenges and Opportunities." Speech delivered at Macaulay Institute, Aberdeen, 10 October. www.shell.com/speeches

Deutch, J. & E. Moniz. *The Future of Nuclear Power.* Cambridge, MA: MIT (29 July). http://web.mit.edu/nuclearpower

dieBrennstoffzelle.de. Undated. "Wasserstoff- flugzeug Cryoplane." www.diebrennstoffzelle.de/ h2projekte/mobil/cryoplane.shtml

Diem, W., B. Corbett, R. Schreffler, & E. Mayne. 2002. "BMW Races into Carbon Fiber." *Ward's Auto World,* 1 September. www.wardsauto.com/ ar/auto_bmw_races_carbon_2

Dill, J. 2004. "Scrapping Old Cars." *Access* **24** (Spring): 22–27. www.uctc.net/access/access.asp

Dings, J., P.M. Peeters, J.R. van der Heijden, & R.A.A. Wijnen. 2000. "ESCAPE: Economic Screening of Aircraft Preventing Emissions." Delft, the Netherlands: CE, Peeters Advies, Aerospace Engineering/Delft University of Technology. www.cedelft.nl/eng/publicaties/ 00_4404_16e.html

Djerejian, E.P. 2004. Statement to House Appropriations Committee, 4 February. http://appropriations.house.gov/_files/ edward_djerejian_testimony.pdf

DOC/BEA (U.S. Department of Commerce/ Bureau of Export Administration). 1999. *The Effect on the National Security of Imports of Crude Oil and Refined Petroleum Products.* Washington, DC: DOC/BEA (November). http://efoia.bis.doc.gov/sec232/crudeoil/ Sec232Oil1199.pdf

DOC/BEA. 2001. "Section 232 Investigations: The Effect of Imports on the National Security." Washington, DC: U.S. Dept. of Commerce (January). http://efoia.bis.doc.gov/sec232/ imports/imports.pdf

DoD (U.S. Department of Defense). 2001. *National Defense Budget Estimates for FY2002.* Washington, DC: USDoD (August).

DOE (U.S. Department of Energy). 1987. *Energy Security: A Report to the President of the United States.* Washington, DC: DOE (March).

DOE. 1991. *National Energy Strategy: Powerful Ideas for America,* First Edition. Washington, DC: DOE (February).

DOE. 2003. "Building Technologies Program: Super-Efficient Apt.-Sized Refrigerator." Washington, DC: DOE (9 January). www.eere.energy.gov/buildings/emergingtech/page1a.html

Donnelly T., D. Kagan, & G. Schmitt. 2000. *Rebuilding America's Defenses.* Washington, DC: The Project for the New American Century (September). www.newamericancentury.org/RebuildingAmericasDefenses.pdf

DOT (U.S. Department of Transportation). 1997. *Vehicle Inventory and Use Survey.* http://library.queensu.ca/webdoc/ssdc/b2020/vius97.htm

Dougher, R. 1999. "Fueling Confusion: Deceptive Greenpeace Study Premised on Flawed Estimates of Subsidy." Washington, DC: American Petroleum Institute (3 November).

Dreyfuss, R. 2003. "The Thirty-Year Itch." *Mother Jones,* March/April. www.motherjones.com/news/feature/2003/03/ma_273_01.html

DSB (Defense Science Board). 2001. *More Capable Warfighting Through Reduced Fuel Burden.* Washington, DC: Office of the Under Secretary of Defense for Acquisition and Technology (January). www.acq.osd.mil/dsb/reports/fuel.pdf Summarized at www.rmi.org/sitepages/pid939.php

Duales System Deutschland AG (The Green Dot). 2004. "2003 Environmental Performance Balance." www.gruener-punkt.de/Recycling_rates_remain_at_a_high_level.1061+B6Jkw9MQ__.0.html (updated May 2004).

Duffield, J. 2003. "2003 Updated Data for U.S. Biodiesel Development: New Markets for Conventional and Genetically Modified Agricultural Products." Washington, DC: Office of Energy, Economic Research Service, US Department of Agriculture.

Dukes, J. 2003. "Burning Buried Sunshine: Human Consumption of Ancient Solar Energy." *Climatic Change* 61: 31–44.

Dunne, J. 2001. "GM's Five-Passenger Precept Hybrid Gets an Honest-to-Goodness 80 MPG." *Pop. Mech.,* January. http://popularmechanics.com/automotive/concept_cars/2001/1/GM_hybrid_gets_80_mpg

Dyer, G. 2004. "If Saudi Arabia Falls." GBN Global Perspectives. Emeryville, CA: Global Business Network (2 June).

Ebel, R.E. (Director, Energy Program, Center for Strategic and International Studies). 2002. "Geopolitics of Energy Into the 21st Century." Remarks to the Open Forum, U.S. Department of State, Washington, DC, 30 April. www.state.gov/s/p/of/proc/tr/10187.htm

ECCJ (Energy Conservation Center Japan). Undated. "Effects of the Top Runner Program." www.eccj.or.jp/top_runner/chapter4-0.html

Economist. 2001. "The Slumbering Giants Awake." Economist.com, 8 February. http://economist.com/surveys/displayStory.cfm?Story_id=497418

Economist. 2002. "Self-Doomed to Failure." Economist.com, 4 July. www.economist.com/displaystory.cfm?story_id=1213392

Economist. 2003. "The End of the Oil Age." Editorial in *The Economist,* 23 October. www.economist.com/opinion/displayStory.cfm?story_id=2155717

ECOTEC. 1999. "The Impact of Renewables on Employment and Economic Growth." ECOTEC Research and Consulting Ltd. (Birmingham, UK). Brussels, Belgium: European Commission, Directorate General for Energy. www.eva.ac.at/(en)/publ/pdf/alt99.pdf

Edmunds.com. 1999. "Concept Cars: Ford Prodigy," 1 January. www.edmunds.com/news/autoshows/articles/42918/page015.html

EERE (U.S. Department of Energy, Energy Efficiency and Renewable Energy). 2003. "FreedomCar." www.eere.energy.gov/vehiclesandfuels/program_areas/freedomcar/index.shtml

EERE. 2003a. "Consumer Energy Information: EREC Reference Briefs Scrap Tire Recycling," June.

EERE. Undated. "Hydrogen, Fuel Cells & Infrastructures Technologies Program." www.eere.energy.gov/hydrogenandfuelcells/codes

EFC (Energy Future Coalition). 2003. *Challenge and Opportunity: Charting a New Energy Future.* Washington, DC: EFC. "Summary of Recommendations: Transportation Working Group": www.energyfuturecoalition.org/full_report/summ_recomendations.pdf. "Appendix A: Working Group Reports": www.energyfuture-coalition.org/full_report/app_transportation.pdf

EIA (Energy Information Administration). 1994. "U.S. Vehicle Fuel Efficiency by Model Year." Washington, DC: EIA. http://ftp.eia.doe.gov/pub/consumption/transportation/tab5_94.pdf

EIA. 1997. *Household Vehicles Energy Consumption 1994.* Washington, DC: EIA (August). http://tonto.eia.doe.gov/FTPROOT/consumption/046494.pdf

EIA. 1998. *Manufacturing Energy Consumption Survey (MECS).* Washington, DC: EIA. www.eia.doe.gov/emeu/mecs/contents.html

EIA. 1999. "1999 Commercial Buildings Energy Consumption Survey (CBECS) Detailed Tables." Washington, DC: EIA. www.eia.doe.gov/emeu/cbecs/detailed_tables_1999.html

EIA. 1999a. "Federal Financial Interventions and Subsidies in Energy Markets 1999: Primary Energy." SR/OIAF/1999-03. Washington, DC: EIA. www.eia.doe.gov/oiaf/servicerpt/subsidy

EIA. 2001. "Energy Price Impacts on the U.S. Economy." Washington, DC: EIA (10 April). www.eia.doe.gov/oiaf/economy/energy_price.html

EIA. 2001a. *Petroleum Supply Annual 2000, Vol. I.* Washington, DC: EIA (June). http://tonto.eia.doe.gov/FTPROOT/petroleum/0340001.pdf

EIA. 2001b. "Home Energy Use and Costs: 2001 Residential Energy Consumption Survey." Washington, DC: EIA. www.eia.doe.gov/recs/contents.html

EIA. 2001c. *Annual Energy Review 2000.* Washington, DC: EIA (August). www.eia.doe.gov/emeu/plugs/plaer00.html

EIA. 2002. "Estimated Consumption of Vehicle Fuels in the United States 1993–2002." Washington, DC: EIA (September). www.eia.doe.gov/cneaf/alternate/page/datatables/table10.html

EIA. 2002a. *Emissions of Greenhouse Gases in the United States 2001.* Washington, DC: EIA (December). ftp://ftp.eia.doe.gov/pub/oiaf/1605/cdrom/pdf/ggrpt/057301.pdf

EIA. 2003. *Annual Energy Outlook 2003.* DOE/EIA-0383. Washington, DC: EIA (January). http://tonto.eia.doe.gov/FTPROOT/forecasting/0383(2003).pdf

EIA. 2003a. "Persian Gulf Oil and Gas Exports Fact Sheet." Washington, DC: EIA (April). www.eia.doe.gov/emeu/cabs/pgulf.html

EIA. 2003b. "EIA's Natural Gas Outlook through 2025." Presentation Given by Guy Caruso at Colorado Oil and Gas Association, Denver, CO, 5 August. www.eia.doe.gov/oiaf/presentation/ng/ngoutlook.html

EIA. 2003c. *Annual Energy Review 2002.* Washington, DC: EIA (24 October). www.eia.doe.gov/aer/contents.html

EIA. 2004. *Annual Energy Outlook 2004.* DOE/EIA-0383. Washington, DC: EIA (January). www.eia.doe.gov/oiaf/archive/aeo04/index.html

EIA. 2004a. *International Petroleum Monthly* (March). www.eia.doe.gov/ipm/contents.html

EIA. 2004b. *International Energy Outlook 2004.* DOE/EIA-0484. Washington, DC: EIA (April). www.eia.doe.gov/oiaf/ieo/index.html

EIA. 2004c. *Short Term Energy Outlook.* Washington, DC: EIA (April). www.eia.doe.gov/emeu/steo/pub/3atab.html (downloaded 5 May 2004).

EIA. 2004d. "Monthly Energy Review" (May). http://tonto.eia.doe.gov/FTPROOT/ monthlyhistory.htm

EIA. 2004e. "Weekly Petroleum Status Report." www.eia.doe.gov/pub/oil_gas/petroleum/ data_publications/weekly_petroleum_status_ report/historical/2004/2004_06_09/pdf/table15.pdf (downloaded 9 June).

EIA. Undated. "U.S. Petroleum Prices." www.eia.doe.gov/oil_gas/petroleum/info_glance/ prices.html

Electrifyingtimes.com. 2000. "Ford Prodigy," 10 January. www.electrifyingtimes.com/ fordprodigy.html

Elliott, D.L., L.L. Wendell, & G.L. Gower. 1991. *An Assessment of the Available Windy Land Area and Wind Energy Potential in the Contiguous United States.* PNL-7789. Richland, WA: Pacific Northwest Laboratory (August).

Encon. 2002. "ENCON Wins Presidential Award!" www.i-encon.com/2002yir.htm

Endreß, V.A. 2001. "Volkswagen: Ein-Liter-Auto billiger als der Lupo." *Financial Times Deutschland,* 30 April. www.ftd.de/ub/in/ 1070491.html?q=null

Energy Star. Undated. "Good Management Is Good Business." www.energystar.gov/ index.cfm?c=business.bus_good_business

Environmental Working Group. 2002. "Farm Subsidy Database." www.ewg.org/farm/ region.php?fips=00000&progcode=total&yr=2002

EPA (Environmental Protection Agency). 1993. "Automobiles and Ozone." EPA 400-F-92-006. Washington, DC: EPA (January). www.epa.gov/ otaq/consumer/04-ozone.pdf

EPA. 1996. *Regulatory Impact Analyses (RIA) for Ozone and PM.* Washington, DC: EPA.

EPA. 1998. "MTBE Fact Sheet #3: Use and Distribution of MTBE and Ethanol." Washington, DC: EPA (January). www.epa.gov/OUST/mtbe/ mtbefs3.pdf

EPA. 2001. "NO$_x$ Allowance Market Analysis." Washington, DC: EPA (April). www.epa.gov/ airmarkets/trading/noxmarket/pricetransfer.html

EPA. 2002. *Clearing the Air: The Facts About Capping and Trading Emissions.* Washington, DC: EPA (May). www.epa.gov/airmarkets/ articles/clearingtheair.pdf

EPA. 2002a. *Municipal Solid Waste in the United States: 2000 Facts and Figures* (June). www.epa.gov/epaoswer/non-hw/muncpl/pubs/ report-00.pdf

EPA. 2003. *Light-Duty Automotive Technology and Fuel Economy Trends: 1975 through 2003.* EPA420-R-03-006. Washington, DC: EPA (April). www.epa.gov/otaq/fetrends.htm

EPA. 2003a. *Municipal Solid Waste in the United States: 2001 Facts and Figures.* EPA530-R-03-011 (October). www.epa.gov/epaoswer/non-hw/ muncpl/msw99.htm

EPA. 2003b. "Overview: Ozone and PM2.5 Current Air Quality." Washington, DC: EPA (May). www.epa.gov/oar/oaqps/pm25/ pm03training.pdf

EPA. Undated. "Municipal Solid Waste. Commodities: Plastics." www.epa.gov/ garbage/plastic.htm

EPA. Undated (a). "Heavy Trucks, Buses, and Engines." www.epa.gov/otaq/ hd-hwy.htm#regs,www.ganet.org/dnr/environ/ techguide_files/apb/HDDE_Requirements.ppt

EPRI (Electric Power Research Institute). 2001. "The Western States Power Crisis: Imperative and Opportunities." Palo Alto, CA: EPRI (25 June). www.epri.com/corporate/ discover_epri/ news/HotTopics/ WesternPwrCrisis.pdf

Erwin, S.I. 2000. "Engine Competition Fuels Diesel-vs.-Turbine Debate." *National Defense* (April). www.nationaldefensemagazine.org/ article.cfm?Id=57

Erwin, S.I. 2002. "Army's Next Battle: Fuel, Transportation Costs." *National Defense* (April). www.nationaldefensemagazine.org/ article.cfm?Id=769

Erwin, S.I. 2002a. "War on Terrorism Tests Logisticians' Skills." *National Defense* (July). www.nationaldefensemagazine.org/ article.cfm?Id=839

Erwin, S.I. 2003. "Army Seeks Short-Term Payoff from Future Combat Systems." *National Defense* (December). www.national defensemagazine.org/article.cfm?Id=1283

European Commission. 2002. "Meeting the Challenges in Aircraft Emissions: Commission Looks into Clean Alternative to Fossil Fuel." Press release, 29 May. http://europa.eu.int/ rapid/pressReleasesAction.do?reference=IP/02/ 769&format=HTML&aged=1&language= EN&guiLanguage=en

European Parliament. 2003. "Directive 2003/30/EC of the European Parliament and of the Council of 8 May 2003 on the Promotion of the Use of Biofuels or Other Renewable Fuels for Transport." *Official J. of the European Union.* L 123/42 (17 May). www.dft.gov.uk/stellent/ groups/ dft_roads/documents/page/ dft_roads_028406.pdf

EV World. 2001. "Toyota ES3 Claims 88 MPG," 24 November. http://evworld.com/ view.cfm?section=article&storyid=267

Evans, L. 2004. "How to Make a Car Lighter and Safer." SAE 2004-01-1172. SAE (Society of Automotive Engineers) World Congress, Detroit, MI, 10 March.

Evans, L. & M.C. Frick. 1993. "Mass Ratio and Relative Driver Fatality Risk in Two-Vehicle Crashes." *Accident Analysis & Prevention* **25**(2): 213–224.

Executive Office for Administration and Finance (Commonwealth of Massachusetts). 2003. "A&F Bulletin 10—Use of State Vehicles by Executive Agencies." Boston, MA: A&F (1 December). www.mass.gov/eoaf/docs/ administrativebulletin10.pdf

ExxonMobil. 2004. "The Why and How of Energy Efficiency." Advertisement, *N.Y. Times,* 8 July, p. A23.

Faaß, R. 2001. *CRYOPLANE: Flugzeuge mit Wasserstoffantrieb.* Presented to Airbus Deutschland GmbH, Hamburg, 6 December. www.haw-hamburg.de/pers/Scholz/ dglr/hh/text_2001_12_06_Cryoplane.pdf

Fagan, M. 2000. "Sheikh Yamani Predicts Price Crash as Age of Oil Ends." *Daily Telegraph,* 25 June. www.telegraph.co.uk/news/ main.jhtml?xml= %2Fnews%2F2000%2F06%2F25%2Fnoil25.xml

Fairfield County Business Journal. 2004. "Connecticut's Fuel Cell Industry Maintains Dominance," 3 May. www.fairfieldcountybusinessjournal.com/ current_issue/050304fss01.html

Fairley, P. 2004. "Hybrids' Rising Sun." *Technology Review* (April): 34–42. www.technologyreview.com/articles/ fairley0404.asp

Farrell, D. & A.S. Zainulbhai. 2004. "A Richer Future for India." *McKinsey Quarterly,* Special Edition, pp. 50–59.

Fazzio, J. 2000. "Re-refined Oil Programs." Defense Supply Center: Richmond.

Federal Reserve Bank of Dallas. 1997. *Time Well Spent: The Declining Real Cost of Living in America: 1997 Annual Report.* Dallas, TX: Federal Reserve Bank of Dallas. www.dallasfed.org/fed/annual/1999p/ar97.pdf

Ferguson, R.B. 2004. "Rightsizing Design." *eWEEK: Enterprise News & Reviews,* 23 February. www.eweek.com/ print_article/0,1761,a=119526,00.asp

FHWA (Federal Highway Administration). 2002. *Highway Statistics 2002.* www.fhwa.dot.gov/ policy/ohim/hs02/index.htm

Financial Times. 2002. "Toyota Says Hybrid Car Making Money," 29 September. www.evworld.com/ view.cfm?section=communique&newsid=2752

Financial Times. 2004. "A Long Day's Journey into Night: The Low Cost Threat Means Some U.S. Airlines Are Struggling to Survive," 15 June. Downloaded at www.pressindex.com/uk/home

FleetWatch. 2002. "2002 IAA Hanover Truck Expo," October. www.fleetwatch.co.za/ magazines/Oct02/54-HanoverArticle-2.htm

Flug-Revue Online. 2000. "Airbus A3XX." www.flug-revue.rotor.com/FRTypen/FRA3XX.htm

Ford, Jr., W. C. 2000. Untitled speech delivered at 5th Annual Greenpeace Business Conference, London, 5 October. http://media.ford.com/article_display.cfm?article_id=6217

Ford, H.J. & S. Crowther. 1923. *My Life and Work.* Garden City, NY: Doubleday. www.gutenberg.net/etext05/hnfrd10.txt

Ford Vehicles. Undated (downloaded 10 April 2004). "Escape Hybrid." Fordvehicles.com. www.fordvehicles.com/escapehybrid/index.asp?bhcp=1

Ford Vehicles. Undated (a) (downloaded 10 April 2004). "Escape Hybrid FAQs." Fordvehicles.com. www.fordvehicles.com/escapehybrid/faqs/index.asp?bhcp=1#faq3

Foss, K. 2004. "Preview Mercedes-Benz E-320 CDI." Car-data.com. www.car-data.com/xpage.preview/pre.template.asp?mfg=mercedes&model=e320cdi

Foster, R. & S. Kaplan. 2001. *Creative Destruction: Why Companies that are Built to Last Underperform the Market and How to Successfully Transform Them.* New York: Doubleday.

Fraker, T.M, D.M. Levy, R.B. Olsen, & R.A. Stapulonis. 2004. "The Welfare-to-Work Grants Program: Enrollee Outcomes One Year After Program Entry." Report to Congress by Mathematica Policy Research, Inc. (February). http://aspe.os.dhhs.gov/hsp/wtw-grants-eval98/outcomes1yr04/

Frankel, G. 2004. "U.S. Mulled Seizing Oil Fields in '73." *Wash. Post,* 1 January.

Franssen, H. 2004. "Creating Regional Stability: The Middle East." NATO Advanced Research Workshop on Emerging Threats to Energy Security and Stability, The Windsor Group, St. George's House, Windsor Castle, UK, 23–25 January.

Frantz, S. 1993. "The Race to Make the Fridge to the Future." *Home Energy Online Magazine,* January/February.

Freedom House. 2003. "FH Country Ratings." www.freedomhouse.org/ratings/index.htm

Freeman, S. 2003. "Toyota's Prius Hybrid Named Motor Trend's 'Car of the Year.'" *Wall St. J.,* 26 November, p. D3.

Freeman, S. 2004. "Forget Rebates: The Hybrid-Car Markup." *Wall St. J.,* 10 June, p. D1.

Freeman, S., G. Zuckerman, & J.B. White. 2004. "Glut of SUVs Prompts Round of Discounts." *Wall St. J.,* 19 May, p. D1. http://online.wsj.com/article/0,,SB108491530310414905,00.html?mod=todays_us_personal_journal

Frei, P., R. Käser, R. Hafner, M. Schmid, A. Dragan, L. Wingeier, M.H. Muser, P.F. Niederer, & F.H. Walz. 1997. "Crashworthiness and Compatibility of Low Mass Vehicles in Collisions," SAE 970122. Warrendale PA: Society of Automotive Engineers.

Frei, P., R. Käser, M.H. Muser, P.F. Niederer, & F.H. Walz. 1999. "Vehicle Structural Crashworthiness with Respect to Compatibility in Collisions." Working Group on Accident Mechanics at the Universities of Zürich (October). www.biomed.ee.ethz.ch/~agu/pdf/Compatibility.pdf

Frum, D. & R. Perle. 2003. *An End to Evil.* New York: Random House.

Fry, S.A. (VADM USN, Director, Joint Staff). 2001. "Memorandum for the Under Secretary of Defense for Acquisition, Technology, and Logistics." Washington, DC: Office of the Chairman, The Joint Chiefs of Staff (24 August).

Fu, J. 2004. "Nation Tops TV, Cell Phone, Monitor Production." *China Daily,* 5 February.

Fuel Cell News. 2003. "Fuel Cell Investment Yields Jobs, BTI Study Concludes," 27 October–2 November. www.fuelcellsworks.com/InsidetheindustryOct26-03.html#02

Fukui, T. (Honda Motor Co.). 1999. Quoted in *Bloomberg News,* 5 June. Quote found at www.nextechmaterials.com/Ohio_Fuel_Cell_Initiative.htm

Fulton, L. 2004. "Transportation and Energy Policy." *Encyc. of Energy* 6: 196. San Diego: Elsevier.

Gabriel, R.A. & K.S. Metz 1992. *A Short History of War.* Pennsylvania: Strategic Studies Institute, U.S. Army War College. www.au.af.mil/au/awc/awcgate/gabrmetz/gabr0000.htm

Ganesh, K. 2000. "Vorsprung durch Technik BMW?" *BS Motoring Weekly,* 9 September. www.bsmotoring.com/2000/00sep09_2.htm

Gardner, G. & P. Sampat. 1998. "Worldwatch Paper #144: Mind Over Matter: Recasting the Role of Materials in Our Lives." Washington, DC: Worldwatch Institute. www.worldwatch.org/pubs/paper/144.html

Garman, D. 2003. "Freedom Car: 'Free Ride' or Fuel Economy Savior? An e-FFICIENCY NEWS Point-Counterpoint." *Alliance to Save Energy Newsletter,* 21 May.

Garsten, E. 2004. "Flexible and Profitable, GM Lansing Shoots to Top." *Detroit News,* 22 February. www.detnews.com/2004/specialreport/0402/22/a14-70492.htm

Gary, I. & T.L. Karl. 2003. *Bottom of the Barrel: Africa's Oil Boom and the Poor.* Baltimore, MD: Catholic Relief Services (June). www.catholicrelief.org/get_involved/advocacy/policy_and_strategic_issues/oil_report.cfm

Geae.com. Undated. "GE Transportation—Aircraft Engines: LV100." www.geae.com/engines/military/lv100/spotlight_advantages.html

German, J. (American Honda Motor Co., Inc). 2002. Statement before the Committee on Commerce, Science and Transportation, U.S. Senate, 24 January. http://commerce.senate.gov/hearings/012402german2.pdf

Germancarfans.com. 2004. "Mercedes-Benz Vision Grand Sports Tourer Details," 8 January. www.germancarfans.com/news.cfm/newsid/2040108.001/page/1/mercedes-benz/1.html

Gerth, J. & S. Labaton. 2004. "Oman's Oil Yield Long in Decline, Shell Data Show." *N.Y. Times,* 8 April. www.nytimes.com/2004/04/08/business/08OIL.html?ex=1082398756&ei=1&en=ee512a458338e2d1

Gibson-Smith, C. 1998. "Future Growth and Sustainability—BP and Sustainable Development." Cambridge University Engineers Association Annual Conference, Cambridge, UK, 25 September. www.bp.com/genericarticle.do?categoryId=98&contentId=2000431

Ginsburg, J. 2001. "The Most Fuel-Efficient That the Military Can Be." *Bus. Wk.,* 3 September. www.businessweek.com/magazine/content/01_36/b3747102.htm

Giordano, J. 1997. "Returns to Scale and Market Concentration Among the Largest Survivors of Deregulation in the US Trucking Industry." *Applied Economics* 29(1): 101–110. http://ideas.repec.org/a/taf/applec/v29y1997i1p101-10.html

Gladwell, M. 2000. *The Tipping Point: How Little Things Can Make a Big Difference.* Boston: Little Brown and Co.

Gladwell, M. 2004. "Big and Bad." *The New Yorker,* 12 January, pp. 28–33.

Glanz, J. 2004. "15 Miles Offshore, Safeguarding Iraq's Oil Lifeline." *N.Y. Times,* 6 July, p. A1.

Global Information, Inc. 2003. "U.S. Demand to Reach 20 billion square feet in 2007." *Carpets and Rugs Report,* June. www.the-infoshop.com/study/fd14561_carpets_rugs.html

GlobalSecurity.org. 2004. "M1 Abrams Main Battle Tank." www.globalsecurity.org/military/systems/ground/m1-specs.htm

GM (General Motors). 2003. "Hydrogen, Hybrids Highlight Los Angeles Tech Tour." Press release, 13 August. www.gm.com/company/gmability/adv_tech/600_tt/650_future/techtour_081303.html

GM. 2004. "Hybrid Bus Fact Sheet." GMability Advanced Technology. www.gm.com/company/gmability/adv_tech/images/fact_sheets/allison_bus.html

GM. 2004a. "GM Tech Tour Showcases GM/Allison Transmission-powered Hybrid Transit Bus." Gmability Education 9–12. www.gm.com/company/gmability/edu_k-12/9-12/fc_energy/hybrid_allison.html

GM, ANL (Argonne National Laboratory), BP (British Petroleum), ExxonMobil, & Shell. 2001. *Well-to-Wheel Energy Use and Greenhouse Gas Emissions of Advanced Fuel/Vehicle Systems— North American Analysis* (June). www.transportation.anl.gov:80/pdfs/TA/164.pdf

Goldemberg, J., S.T. Coelho, P.M. Nastari, & O. Lucon. 2004. "Ethanol Learning Curve—the Brazilian Experience." *Biomass & Bioenergy* **26**: 301–304.

Golfen, B. 1996. "Car Scrappage Plan Will Roll into Phoenix; Program Designed to Cut Air Pollution." *The Arizona Republic,* 14 December.

Golfen, B. 2004. "The Drive to Save; Hybrid, Diesel Technology Catching On." *Arizona Republic,* 22 May, p. 1A.

Golove, W.H. & J.H. Eto. 1996. *Market Barriers to Energy Efficiency: A Critical Reappraisal of the Rationale for Public Policies to Promote Energy Efficiency.* Berkeley CA: Lawrence Berkeley Laboratory. LBL-38059 (March). http://eetd.lbl.gov/ea/ems/reports/38059.pdf

Gong, Z. 2004. "10 Years Later, China Issues New Auto Lines." *China Daily,* 1 June. www2.chinadaily.com.cn/english/doc/2004-06/01/content_335625.htm

Goode, G. B. 1887. *The Fisheries and Fishery Industries of the United States, Sec. V, Vol. II.* Washington, DC: USGPO. www.nefsc.noaa.gov/history/stories.html

Gorsich, D. 2000. "The Role of Vehicle Intelligence in Army's 21st Century Truck Program." ivsource.net. http://ivsource.net/archivep/2000/jun/a000625_army21ctruck.pdf

Gould, L. 2004. "GM Speeds Times to Market Through Blistering Fast Processors." *Automotive Design & Production* (July). http://autofieldguide.com/articles/070407.html

Graedel, T.E. & B.R. Allenby. 1996. *Design for Environment.* Englewood Cliffs, NJ: AT&T & Prentice-Hall.

Granger, M.G. (Maj.). 2003. *Moving an Expeditionary Force: Three Case Studies in Afghanistan.* Ft. Leavenworth, KS: School of Advanced Military Studies, U.S. Army Command & General Staff College (22 May). http://handle.dtic.mil/100.2/ADA415877

Greenberg, K. 2001. "Motown Slowdown Reaches SUVs—Detroit Automakers Slump Affects Sport Utility Vehicle Market." *Brandweek,* 4 June. http://articles.findarticles.com/p/articles/mi_m0BDW/is_23_42/ai_75452063

Greene, D.L. 1990. "CAFE or Price? An Analysis of the Effects of Federal Fuel Economy Regulations and Gasoline Price on New Car MPG, 1978–89." *Energy J.* **11**(3): 37–57.

Greene, D.L. 1992. "Energy-Efficiency Improvement Potential of Commercial Aircraft." *Annual Review of Energy and the Environment* **17**: 537–573

Greene, D.L. 1997. "Why CAFE Worked." Oak Ridge, TN: ORNL (6 November). http://ntl.bts.gov/data/cafeornl.pdf

Greene, D.L. 2004. "Transportation and Energy, Overview." *Encyc. of Energy* **6**: 179–188. San Diego: Elsevier.

Greene, D.L. & J. DeCicco. 2000. "Engineering-Economic Analysis of Automotive Fuel Economy Potential in the United States." *Annual Review of Energy and the Environment* **25**: 477–536.

Greene, D.L. & Y.H. Fan. 1995. "Transportation Energy Intensity Trends, 1972–1992." *Transportation Research Record* **1475** (25–28 January): 10–19. Washington, DC: Transportation Research Board.

Greene, D.L., J.L. Hopson, & J. Li. 2003. "Running Out of and Into Oil: Analyzing Global Oil Depletion and Transition Through 2050." ORNL/TM-2003/259. Oak Ridge, TN: ORNL (October).

Greene, D.L., J.L. Hopson, & J. Li. 2004. "Have We Run Out of Oil Yet?" DOE presentation, 14 April. www-cta.ornl.gov/cta/Publications/Publications_2003.html

Greene, D.L. & M. Keller. 2002. "Dissent on Safety Issues: Fuel Economy and Highway Safety." Appendix A in *Effectiveness and Impact of Corporate Average Fuel Economy (CAFE) Standards.* Washington, DC: National Academies Press. http://books.nap.edu/html/cafe/appA.pdf

Greene D.L., P.D. Patterson, M. Singh, & J. Li. 2004. "Feebates, Rebates and Gas-Guzzler Taxes: A Study of Incentives for Increased Fuel Economy." *En. Pol.* In press. Oak Ridge, TN: ORNL. doi:10.1016/j.enpol.2003.10.003, online from 16 December, 2003 at www.sciencedirect.com

Greene, D.L. & N.I. Tishchishyna. 2000. "Costs of Oil Dependence: A 2000 Update." ORNL/TM-2000/152. Oak Ridge, TN: ORNL (May). www.esd.ornl.gov/benefits_conference/oilcost_tq.pdf

Greenspan, A. 2002. "Monetary Policy and the Economic Outlook." Testimony before the Joint Economic Committee, U.S. Congress, Washington, DC, 17 April. www.federalreserve.gov/boarddocs/testimony/2002/20020417/default.htm

Gross, D. 2004. "The Prius and the Olive Tree: Why Are Conservatives Supporting Higher Gas Taxes?" *Slate,* 27 May. http://slate.msn.com/id/2101349/

Grübler, A., N. Nakićenović & D.G. Victor. 1999. "Dynamics of Energy Technologies and Global Change." *En. Pol.* **27**: 247–280.

GSA (U.S. General Services Administration). 2003. *FY2002 Federal Fleet Report.* Washington, DC: GSA (February). www.gsa.gov/gsa/cm_attachments/GSA_DOCUMENT/FFR2002_R2K-g6_0Z5RDZ-i34K-pR.pdf

Hakim, D. 2003. "GM Puts Off Its Hybrids, Letting Ford Go First." *N.Y. Times,* 6 November.

Hakim, D. 2004. "Automakers Unveil Plans for More Hybrid Models." *N.Y. Times,* 6 January.

Hakim, D. 2004a. "Average U.S. Car is Tipping Scales at 4,000 Pounds." *N.Y. Times,* 5 May.

Hakim, D. 2004b. "The Big Three Fear That Toyota Is Becoming the Big One." *N.Y. Times,* 20 May, p. C8.

Hakim, D. 2004c. "Toyota Gives the Big 3 a Run for Their Money." *International Herald Tribune,* 21 May. http://iht.com/articles/520957.html

Hakim, D. 2004d. "Moving to Fuel Efficiency: Smaller SUVs Draw More Attention as Gas Prices Rise." *N.Y. Times,* 22 May.

Hakim, D. 2004e. "Catching Up to the Cost of Global Warming." *N.Y. Times,* 25 July.

Hall, D.C. 2004. "External Costs of Energy." *Encyc. of Energy* **2**: 651–667. San Diego: Elsevier.

Hasenauer, H. 1997. "Wargaming the Army After Next." *Soldiers Online,* December. www.army.mil/soldiers/dec97/text/t-aan.html

Hawken, P.G., A.B. Lovins, & L.H. Lovins. 1999. *Natural Capitalism.* Boston: Little Brown & Co. www.natcap.org

Heck, P. 2004. "A First Glimpse at Climate Change to Come?" Swiss Re. www.swissre.com/INTERNET/pwswpspr.nsf/alldocbyidkeylu/ABOD-5WSGHA

Hellman, C. 2004. "Last of the Big Time Spenders." Washington, DC: Center for Arms Control and Non-Proliferation. http://64.177.207.201/static/budget/annual/fy05/world.htm

Henderson, S. 2002. "The Coming Saudi Showdown." *Weekly Standard,* 15 July. www.washingtoninstitute.org/media/henderson/henderson071502.htm

Henley, J. 2004. "France Launches Radical Green Tax on Bigger Cars." *Guardian,* 23 June. www.guardian.co.uk/print/0,3858,4954154-110970,00.html

Herrmann, H.-G. 2003. "Lightweighting in Automotive Industry." RBP/S, 26.02.2003 1. European Aeronautic Defence and Space Company/Corporate Research Centre (14 March). www.compositn.net/Downloads/Presentation%20-%20Lightweighting%20-%20DaimlerChrysler%20-%201pp.pdf

Herrmann, H.-G., C. Mohrdieck, & R. Bjekovic. 2002. "Materials for the Automotive Lightweight Design." DaimlerChrysler Research & Technology (Research Center Ulm) presentation to FKA/IKA conferences New Advances in Body Engineering, Aachen, 28 November.

Hersh, S.M. 2001. "King's Ransom." *New Yorker,* 22 October. www.newyorker.com/printable/?fact/011022fa_FACT1

Higgins, A. 2004. "In Quest for Energy Security, U.S. Makes New Bet: On Democracy." *Wall St. J.,* 4 February, p. A1.

Higgins, R. 2002. "Army, Government, Industry Team to Develop Better, Cleaner Trucks: Gore Kicks off 21st Century Truck Initiative." *NAC News.* www.tacom.army.mil/tardec/nac/newsletter/21cen.htm

Hirota, K. & K. Minato. 2002. "Comparison of Vehicle Related Taxes by Cross-Section." Better Air Quality in Asian and Pacific Rim Cities 2002 (BAQ2002), Hong Kong, 16–18 December. www.cse.polyu.edu.hk/~activi/BAQ2002/BAQ2002_files/Proceedings/PosterSession/48.pdf

HMG (Heschong Mahone Group). 2003. "Daylight and Retail Sales." California Energy Commission (CEC) Tech. Rpt. P500-03-082-A-5. www.h-m-g.com

HMG. 2003a. "Windows and Offices: A Study of Office Worker Performance and the Indoor Environment." CEC Tech. Rpt. P500-03-082-A-9. www.h-m-g.com

HMG. 2003b. "Windows and Classrooms: A Study of Student Performance and the Indoor Environment." CEC Tech. Rpt. P500-03-081-A-7. www.h-m-g.com

Hodgman, C. D., R. C Weast, & S. M. Selby, eds. 1961. *Handbook of Chemistry and Physics, 43rd Edition.* Cleveland, OH: CRC (The Chemical Rubber Publishing Co.).

Hoeper, P.J. (Asst. Sec. of the Army for Research Development & Acquisition). 1999. "How Healthy Is Our Fleet?" Keynote address given at Tactical Wheeled Vehicles Conference, Monterey, CA, 1 February. www.dtic.mil/ndia/tactical/hoeper.pdf

Hollomon, B., M. Ledbetter, L. Sandahl, & T. Shoemaker. 2002. "Seven Years Since SERP: Successes and Setbacks in Technology Procurement." Washington, DC: Federal Energy Management Program. http://eere.pnl.gov/femp/publications/SevenYearsSinceSERP.pdf

Holmes, B. 2002. "The Vision for Wings on America." Presented at the NASA Langley Research Center and Daily Press Colloquium and Sigma Series Seminar, Holmes Colloquium, 10 September. http://sats.larc.nasa.gov/documents.html

Holtzclaw, J., R. Clear, H. Dittmar, D. Goldstein, & P. Haas. 2002. "Location Efficiency: Neighborhood and Socio-Economic Characteristics Determine Auto Ownership and Use—Studies in Chicago, Los Angeles and San Francisco." *Transp. Planning & Technology* 25(1): 1–27. www.nrdc.org/media/pressreleases/020610.asp

Hooker, M.A. 1996. "What Happened to the Oil Price-Macroeconomy Relationship?" *J. of Monetary Economics* 38: 192–213.

Horowitz, M.J. 2001. "Economic Indicators of Market Transformation: Energy Efficient Lighting and EPA's Green Lights." *En. J.* 22(4): 95-122.

Hosken, G. 2004. "African Coastline a Major Target for Pirates." *The Star* (South Africa), 17 February. http://dehai.org/archives/dehai_news_archive/feb-mar04/0286.html

Howarth, R.B. & B. Andersson. 1993. "Market Barriers to Energy Efficiency." *En. Economics.* 15(4): 262–272 (October). www.sciencedirect.com/science?_ob=ArticleURL&_udi=B6V7G-458XJRG-5Y&_coverDate=10%2F31%2F1993&_alid=190215123&_rdoc=1&_fmt=&_orig=search&_qd=1&_cdi=5842&_sort=d&view=c&_acct=C000050221&_version=1&_urlVersion=0&_userid=10&md5=cc1c6e6596cb5a10f54e707fae58b219

Hubbert, J. (DaimlerChrysler). Undated. Quoted at www.nextechmaterials.com/Ohio_Fuel_Cell_Initiative.htm

Hunt, E. 2003. "An Army of Hybrids?" *TidePool,* 21 March. www.tidepool.org/original_content.cfm?articleid=70243

Hutson, S.S., N.L. Barber, J.F. Kenny, K.S. Linsey, D.S. Lumia, & M.A. Maupin. 2004. *Estimated Use of Water in the United States in 2000; U.S. Geological Survey Circular 1268.* Washington, DC: USGS (March/May). http://water.usgs.gov/pubs/circ/2004/circ1268/pdf/circular1268.pdf

Hylden, J. 2003. "Growing Pains: America Needs a New Approach to Support Farmers." *Harvard Political Rev.,* 25 January. www.hpronline.org/news/2003/01/25/Cover/Growing.Pains-356763.shtml

HyWeb. 2004. "HyWeb Overview-Hydrogen Cars." L-B-Systemtechnik GmbH. www.h2cars.de

iafrica.com. 2003. "McLaren Supercar Hit by VW Golf,"19 November. http://iafrica.com/news/sa/286419.htm. See photo at www.automotiveforums.com/vbulletin/showthread.php?t=155172

IAGS (Institute for the Analysis of Global Security). Undated. "Iraq Pipeline Watch." www.iags.org/iraqpipelinewatch.htm

ICC (International Chamber of Commerce) Commercial Crime Services. 2004. "Piracy Takes Higher Toll of Seamen's Lives," 28 January. www.iccwbo.org/ccs/news_archives/2004/Piracy_report_2003.asp

ICC Commercial Crime Services. 2004a. "Weekly Piracy Report." www.iccwbo.org/ccs/imb_piracy/weekly_piracy_report.asp (downloaded Spring 2004).

ICTA (International Center for Technology Assessment). 1998. "The Real Price of Gas." Washington, DC: International Center for Technology Assessment. www.icta.org/projects/trans/realpricegas.pdf

IEA (International Energy Agency). 2000. *IEA Bioenergy Task 27.* Appendix 1, "Liquid Fuels from Biomass: North America; Impact of Non-Technical Barriers on Implementation." Paris: OECD/IEA (15 September). www.liquid-biofuels.com/FinalReport1.html

IEA. 2001. *Saving Oil and Reducing CO$_2$ Emissions from Transport: Options and Strategies.* Paris, France: OECD/IEA. www.iea.org/dbtw-wpd/textbase/nppdf/free/2001/savingoil.pdf

IEA. 2003. *Findings of Recent IEA Work 2003.* Paris: OECD/IEA (April). http://library.iea.org/dbtw-wpd/textbase/nppdf/free/2003/findings.pdf

IEA. 2003a. *Oil Market Report.* Paris: OECD/IEA (10 December). www.oilmarketreport.org

IEA. 2003b. *Creating Markets for Energy Technologies.* Paris: OECD/IEA. www.iea.org/dbtw-wpd/bookshop/add.aspx?id=57

IEA. 2004. *Oil Crises and Climate Challenges, 30 Years Of Energy Use in IEA Countries.* Paris: OECD/IEA (16 April).

IEA. 2004a. *Biofuels for Transport: An International Perspective.* Paris: OECD/IEA (April). http://library.iea.org/dbtw-wpd/bookshop/add.aspx?id=176

IEA. 2004b. *Analysis of the Impact of High Oil Prices on the Global Economy.* Paris: OECD/IEA (May). www.iea.org/Textbase/Papers/2004/High_Oil_Prices.pdf

IMF (International Monetary Fund). 2002. "Money Matters: An IMF Exhibit— The Importance of Global Cooperation: Reinventing the System (1972–1981)." Part 4 of 7. www.imf.org/external/np/exr/center/mm/eng/rs_sub_3.htm

Ingriselli, F. 2001. Testimony to U.S. House Committee on Science, 23 April; also to Electric Transportation Industry Conference, Sacramento, 13 December. www.gvest.com/gvest_sp121301.html

Innovest. 2002. "Energy Management & Investor Returns: The Real Estate Sector." New York: Innovest Strategic Value Advisors (October). www.energystar.gov/ia/business/guidelines/assess_value/reit.pdf

Insurance Information Institute. Undated. "What Are the Driving Laws in My State? Automobile Financial Responsibility Laws." iii.org. www.iii.org/individuals/auto/a/stateautolaws

Interface Sustainability. 2001. "Interface Joins Carpet Industry in Signing Recycling Agreement." www.interfacesustainability.com/mostory.html

Interlaboratory Working Group on Energy-Efficient and Clean-Energy Technologies. 2000. *Scenarios for a Clean Energy Future.* ORNL/CON-476 and LBNL-44029. Oak Ridge National Laboratory and Lawrence Berkeley National Laboratory (November).

International Centre for Science and High Technology. 2002. "Used Oil Technology: Perspectives and Problems." Expert Group Meeting: Perspectives on Cleaner Technologies for Sustainable Chemistry, Trieste, Italy, 29–30 April. www.ics.trieste.it/ActivityDetailsArchive.aspx?pcode=1.1&idx=165&activity_id=21

IPS (InterPress Service). 2003. "New Alcohol Fuel Technology Introduced in Brazil." *Ethanol Latest News,* 26 August. http://running_on_alcohol.tripod.com/id35.html

Isidore, C. 2004. "GM: Hybrid Cars Make No Sense." CNN.com, 6 January. http://money.cnn.com/2004/01/06/pf/autos/detroit_gm_hybrids/index.htm

ISP/ASPE/HHS (Office of Income Security Policy/Office of the Assistant Secretary for Planning/Evaluation and U.S. Department of Health and Human Services). 1983. *Overview of the Final Report of the Seattle-Denver Income Maintenance Experiment.* Washington, DC: HSP/ASPE/HHS (May). http://aspe.hhs.gov/hsp/SIME-DIME83/report.htm

JAMA (Japanese Auto Manufacturers Association). 2003. "Japan's Automobile Manufacturers: A New American Dynamic." Washington, DC: JAMA (November). www.japanauto.com/library/brochure_Nov2003.htm

JEC Composites Magazine. 2003. "Weighing Up the Advantages," 12 August. www.globalcomposites.com/news/news_fiche.asp?id=991&

Jehl, D. 2003. "Al Qaeda Links Seen in Attacks on Top Saudi Security Officials." *N.Y. Times,* 30 December.

Jenkins, H.W., Jr. 2004. "Let Failure Be an Option." *Wall St. J.* op-ed., 23 June, p. A17.

Jochem, E., ed. 2004. *Steps Towards a Sustainable Development: A White Book for R&D of Energy-Efficient Technologies.* Zürich: Novatlantis–Sustainability at the ETH Domain (March). www.novatlantis.ch/pdf/weissbuch_def.pdf

Jochem, E. 2004a. "Material Efficiency and Energy Use." *Encyc. of Energy* 3: 835–844. San Diego: Elsevier.

John's Stuff. 2004. "Toyota Prius—2004 Tech Presentation." http://john1701a.com/prius/presentations/2004-prius_tech-presentation_01.htm

Johnson, C. 2000. *Blowback: The Costs and Consequences of American Empire.* New York: Henry Holt & Co., LLC.

Johnson, C. 2004. *The Sorrows of Empire: Militarism, Secrecy, and the End of the Republic.* New York: Metropolitan Books.

Jones, D. 1994. "Kelleher Mixes Wit, Wisdom: Southwest CEO Explores Industry." *USA Today,* 9 June.

Jordan Times (Amman). 2004. "Kuwait Beefs Up Port Security After Warnings," 10 May. http://tides.carebridge.org/GTU/DT-GTU012.htm#_Kuwait_beefs_up_port_security_after

Kahane, C.J. 2003. *Vehicle Weight, Fatality Risk and Crash Compatibility of Model Year 1991–99 Passengers Cars and Light Trucks.* DOE HS 809 662. Washington, DC: NHTSA (National Highway Traffic Safety Administration), October. www.nhtsa.dot.gov/cars/rules/regrev/evaluate/pdf/809662.pdf

Kallen, R.S., H.A. Learner, R. Michaels, & M. Truppa. 1994. *Components of a Model Accelerated Vehicle Retirement Program.* Chicago: Environmental Law and Policy Center (1 June).

Kaplan, A. 1997. "Transportation and Welfare Reform." *Welfare Information Network.* 1(4): May. www.financeprojectinfo.org/Publications/transita.htm

Karl, T.L. 1997. *Paradox of Plenty: Oil Booms and Petro-States.* Berkeley: University of California Press.

Karl, T.L. 2004. "Oil-Led Development: Social, Political, and Economic Consequences." *Encycl. of Energy* 4: 661. San Diego: Elsevier.

Käser, R., M. Muser, O. Spieß, P. Frei, J.M. Guenat, & L. Wingeler. 1995. "Passive Safety Potential of Low Mass Vehicles." *Proceedings of the International Conference on the Biomechanics of Impact,* Brunner, Switzerland.

Kelley, S. 2002. "Single-Minded." *Etrucker,* 1 August. www.etrucker.com/apps/news/article.asp?id=24659

Kennedy, J.F. 1963. "A New Social Order." Speech delivered at the Paulskirche, Frankfurt, Germany, 24 June. www.geocities.com/~newgeneration/paulsk.htm

Kenworth Truck Company. 2003. *White Paper on Life Cycle Cost.* Kirkland, WA: Kenworth Truck Company (February). www.kenworth.com/Kenworth_White_Paper.pdf

Kerr, S. 2004. "Gun Attack Kills Expatriates in Saudi Port City." *Wall St. J.,* 3 May, p. A18.

Khazzoom, J.D. 2000. *Pay-at-the-Pump (PATP) Auto Insurance.* RFF Discussion Paper 98-13-REV: February 1998 report, revised February 2000. Washington, DC: Resources for the Future. www.rff.org/Documents/RFF-DP-98-13-REV.pdf

Khazzoom, J.D. 2000a. *Pay at the Pump (PATP) Auto Insurance: Criticisms and Proposed Modifications.* RFF Discussion Paper 99-14-REV: January 1999 report, revised May 2000. Washington, DC: Resources for the Future. www.rff.org/Documents/RFF-DP-99-14-REV.pdf

Kilcarr, S. 2002. "Tire Update." *Fleet Owner,* 1 September. http://driversmag.com/ar/fleet_tire_update

Kim, C-R. 2003. "Hybrids Can Be Cheap to Make, Toyota Says." Forbes.com, 2 October. www.forbes.com/business/newswire/2003/10/02/rtr1097450.html

Kitman, J. 2004. "Refining Graft: The Oil Industry May Yet Dodge the Cleanup of MTBE." *Harper's Magazine* (August).

Klare, M. 2001. *Resource Wars: The New Landscape of Global Conflict.* New York: Metropolitan.

Klare, M. 2004. *Blood and Oil: The Dangers and Consequences of America's Growing Oil Dependency.* New York: Metropolitan.

Kleit, A.N. 2002. *Impacts of Long-Range Increases in the Corporate Average Fuel Economy (CAFE) Standard: Working Paper 02-10.* Washington, DC: American Enterprise Institute/Brookings Institution (October). www.aei.brookings.org/admin/authorpdfs/page.php?id=206

Knight, W. 2003. "Fuel Cell-Propelled Aircraft Preparing to Fly." *New Scientist,* 12 May. www.newscientist.com/news/print.jsp?id=ns99993717

Kochan, A. 2003. "BMW Slashes Cost of Carbon-Fiber Panels." *Automobilwoche,* 8 September.

Kohl, W.L. 2004. "National Security and Energy." *Encyc. of Energy* 4: 193–206. San Diego: Elsevier.

Koomey, J.G. 1990. *Energy Efficiency Choices in New Office Buildings: An Investigation of Market Failures and Corrective Policies.* PhD Thesis, Energy & Resources Group, University of California, Berkeley, April. http://enduse.lbl.gov/Info/JGKdissert.pdf

Koomey, J.G. & A.H. Rosenfeld. 1990. "Revenue-Neutral Incentives to Promote Efficiency and Environmental Quality." *Contemporary Policy Issues* 8(3): 142–156 (July).

Koomey, J.G., A.H. Sanstad, & L.J. Shown. 1996. "Energy-Efficient Lighting: Market Data, Market Imperfections, and Policy Success." *Contemporary Economic Policy* 14(3): 98–111 (July).

Koomey, J.G., D.E. Schechter, & D. Gordon. 1993. "Cost-Effectiveness of Fuel Economy Improvements in 1992 Honda Civic Hatchbacks." LBL-32683. Berkeley, CA: Energy and Resources Group (May). http://enduse.lbl.gov/Info/Honda.pdf

Koomey, J.G., C.A. Webber, C.S. Atkinson, & A. Nicholls. 2001. "Addressing Energy-Related Challenges for the U.S. Buildings Sector: Results from the Clean Energy Futures Study." *En. Pol.* 29(14): 1209–1222 and LBNL-47356.

Koplow, D. 2004. "Subsidies to Energy Industries" *Encyc. of Energy* 5: 749–764. San Diego: Elsevier.

Koplow, D. & A. Martin. 1998. "Fueling Global Warming: Federal Subsidies to Oil in the United States." Washington, DC: Greenpeace (June). www.greenpeace.org/~climate/oil/fdsuboil.pdf

Kovarik, B. 1998. "Henry Ford, Charles Kettering and the 'Fuel of the Future." *Automotive History Rev.* **32** (Spring): 7–27. www.radford.edu/~wkovarik/papers/fuel.html

KPMG LLP. 2004. "Competitive Alternatives, The CEO's Guide to International Business Costs" (February). www.competitivealternatives.com/report/sections/careport_ch5.pdf

Krauthammer, C. 2004. "Tax and Drill." *Wash. Post,* 21 May, p. A25.

Kuipers, H. 2000. Remarks at Brennstoffzellen-Antrieb Conference (IIR Deutschland GmbH), Frankfurt, 20–21 November.

Kupke, M. & M. Kolax (Airbus). 2004. "CFRP-Fuselage—Ensuring Future Competitiveness." In *Material & Process Technology–The Driver for Tomorrow's Improved Performance,* Proceedings of the Society For Advanced Materials & Process Engineering (SAMPE), 25th Jubilee International Conference, Paris, 30 March–1 April. Ed. K. Drechsler. Aalsmeer NL: SAMPE Europe, pp. 432–437.

Kyodo News. 2004. "Nissan to Cut Weight of All Models Up to 10%." *Japan Today,* 1 June. http://news.japantoday.com/e/?content=news&cat=3&id=300537&page=4

Lacey, R. 1986. *Ford: The Men and the Machine.* Boston: Little Brown & Co.

Laherrere, J. 2004. "Oil and Natural Gas Resource Assessment: Production Growth Cycle Models." *Encyc. of Energy* **4**: 617–631. San Diego: Elsevier.

Laitner, S., I. Goodman, & B. Krier. 1994. "DSM as an Economic Development Strategy." *The Electricity J.* **7**(4): 62–69 (May).

Lal, R. 2003. Testimony to U.S. Senate Committee on Environment and Public Works Concerning the Potential of Agricultural Sequestration to Address Climate Change, Washington, DC, 8 July. http://epw.senate.gov/108th/Lal_070803.htm

Lal, R., J.L. Kimble, R.F. Follet, & C.V. Cole. 1998. *The Potential of U.S. Cropland to Sequester Carbon and Mitigate the Greenhouse Effect.* Boca Raton, FL: CRC/Lewis Publishers.

Lal, R., J.L. Kimble, R.F. Follet, & C.V. Cole. 1999. "Managing U.S. Cropland to Sequester Carbon in Soil." *J. Soil Water Conservation* **54**: 374–381.

Lavender, C., C. Eberle, & A. Murray. 2003. "Heavy Vehicle Mass Reduction and Manufacturing Challenges." DOE Workshop: Tooling Technology for Low Volume Vehicle Production, Detroit, 18 November.

Law, A. 2004. "Ford Future." Edmunds.com, Special Reports. www.edmunds.com/advice/specialreports/articles/102021/article.html

LBI (Light Bicycles Infantry). Undated. "Militarized Folding All/Extreme Terrain 'Mountain' Bikes." www.geocities.com/pentagon/5265/atb.htm

LBNL (Lawrence Berkeley National Laboratory). Undated. "The Collaborative Labeling and Appliance Standards Program (CLASP)." http://eetd.lbl.gov/clasp/; swiel@lbl.gov

Ledbetter, M.R., J.M. Norling, S.D. Edgemon, G.B. Parker, & J.W. Curtis. 1999. "U.S. Energy-Efficient Technology Procurement Projects: Evaluation and Lessons Learned." PNNL-12118. Richland, WA: Pacific Northwest National Laboratory (February). www.eere.energy.gov/buildings/emergingtech/pdfs/lessons_learned_ab.pdf

Lee, J.J. 2000. *Historical and Future Trends in Aircraft Performance, Cost, and Emission.* MSc thesis, MIT. www.mit.edu/people/jjlee/docs/lee_thesis.pdf

Lee, J.J., S. Lukachko, & I.A. Waitz. 2004. "Aircraft and Energy Use." *Encyc. of Energy* **1**: 29–38. San Diego: Elsevier.

Lee, J.J., S. Lukachko, I. Waitz, & A. Schafer. 2001. "Historical and Future Trends in Aircraft Performance, Cost, and Emission." *Annual Rev. Energy and the Environment* **26**: 167–200.

Leighty, B. 2003. "Transmission of Large-Scale Stranded Renewables." Renewable Hydrogen Forum, Washington, DC, 10–11 April. www.ases.org/hydrogen_forum03/Leighty.pdf

Lemar, P. 2001. "The Potential Impact of Policies to Promote Combined Heat and Power in U.S. Industry" *En. Pol.* **29**(14): 1243-1254 (November).

Lemley, B. 2004. "Glassy Metals." *Discover*, April, pp. 46–51.

Leone, R.C. & B. Wasow. 2004. "George Bush's Fiscal Finger of Fate Inflates Gas Prices." *L.A. Times,* 1 April. http://healthandenergy.com/tax_cuts_increase_oil_prices.htm

Levin, D. 2002. "Carbon Components Coming to European Automobiles." *Detroit News,* 11 December. www.detnews.com/2002/insiders/0212/31/inside-33249.htm

Lexus. Undated. "Lexus Hybrid." www.lexus.com/models/hybrid/index.html (downloaded 1 January & 6 January 2004).

Life. 1996. "Hot for the Road: 100 Years of the Automobile in America." *Life* Collector's Edition, Winter, p.20.

Lipman, T.E., J.L. Edwards, & D.M. Kammen. 2004. "Fuel Cell System Economics: Comparing the Costs of Generating Power With Stationary and Motor Vehicle PEM Fuel Cell Systems." *En. Pol.* **32**: 101–125.

Lovaas, D. 2004. "Suburbanization and Energy." *Encyc. of Energy* **5**: 765–776. San Diego: Elsevier.

Lovins, A.B. 1977. *Soft Energy Paths: Toward a Durable Peace.* San Francisco: Friends of the Earth International.

Lovins, A.B. 1980. "Nuclear Weapons and Power-Reactor Plutonium." *Nature* **283**: 817–823 (28 February), **284**:190 (1980).

Lovins, A.B. 1992. *Energy-Efficient Buildings: Institutional Barriers and Opportunities, Strategic Issues Paper II.* Boulder, CO: E SOURCE.

Lovins, A.B. 1994. "Apples, Oranges, and Horned Toads: Is the Joskow & Marron Critique of Electric Efficiency Valid?" *Electricity J.* **7**(4): 29–49.

Lovins, A.B. 1999. "Redesigning Evolution." *Science* **285**: 1489 (3 September). www.sciencemag.org/cgi/content/full/285/5433/1489c

Lovins, A.B. 2001. "All Energy Experts on Deck!" *RMI Solutions Newsletter.* Snowmass, CO: Rocky Mountain Institute (Fall/Winter). www.rmi.org/sitepages/pid955.php

Lovins, A.B. 2001a. "California Electricity: Facts, Myths, and National Lessons." RMI U01-02. Worldwatch Institute, State of the World Conference Aspen, CO, 22 July. www.rmi.org/images/other/Energy/U01-02_CalifElectricity.pdf

Lovins, A.B. 2001b. "Why Nuclear Power's Failure in the Marketplace Is Irreversible (Fortunately for Nonproliferation and Climate Protection)." Nuclear Control Institute's 20th Annual Conference, Nuclear Power and Nuclear Weapons: Can We Have One Without the Other? Washington, DC, 9 April. www.nci.org/conf/lovins/lovins-transcript.htm

Lovins, A.B. 2002. "FreedomCAR, Hypercar®, and Hydrogen." Invited testimony to Energy Subcommittee, House Science Committee, Washington, DC, 26 June. www.rmi.org/images/other/Trans/T02-06_FreedomCAR.pdf

Lovins, A.B. 2002a. "How To Get Real Security." Adapted from remarks at National Defense University. *Whole Earth Review* **109** (Fall). www.rmi.org/images/other/Security/S02-13_HowRealSecurity.pdf

Lovins, A.B. 2003. "Energy Security Facts." Snowmass, CO: Rocky Mountain Institute. www.rmi.org/images/other/S-USESFbooklet.pdf

Lovins, A.B. 2003a. "More Fight, Less Energy, at Lower Cost!" Keynote to CNO's Naval-Industry R&D Partnership Conference, Washington, DC, 5 August.

Lovins, A.B. 2003b. *Twenty Hydrogen Myths.* Snowmass, CO: Rocky Mountain Institute (20 June). www.rmi.org/images/other/Energy/E03-05_20HydrogenMyths.pdf

Lovins, A.B. 2004. "Energy Efficiency, A Taxonomic Overview." *Encyc. of Energy* **2**: 383–401. San Diego: Elsevier.

Lovins, A.B. 2004a. "Comments on NHTSA Docket No. 2003-16128, RIN 2127-AJ17, Reforming the Automobile Fuel Economy Standards Program." Washington, DC: DOT (27 April). http://dms.dot.gov/search/document.cfm?documentid=279026&docketid=16128

Lovins, A.B. 2004b. "Comment on APS Hydrogen Report." *Physics and Society* (July). www.aps.org/units/fps/newsletters/2004/july/commentary.cfm#lovins

Lovins, A.B., M.M. Brylawski, D.R. Cramer, & T.C. Moore. 1996. *Hypercars: Materials, Manufacturing, and Policy Implications.* Snowmass, CO: Rocky Mountain Institute.

Lovins, A.B. & D.R. Cramer. 2004. "Hypercars, Hydrogen, and the Automotive Transition." *Intl. J. Vehicle Design* **35**(1/2): 50–85. www.rmi.org/sitepages/pid175.php#T0401

Lovins, A.B., E.K. Datta, T. Feiler, K.R. Rábago, J.N. Swisher, A. Lehmann, & K. Wicker. 2002. *Small Is Profitable: The Hidden Economic Benefits of Making Electrical Resources the Right Size.* Snowmass, CO: Rocky Mountain Institute. www.smallisprofitable.org

Lovins, A.B., E.K. Datta, & J. Swisher. 2003. "Towering Design Flaws." *The Globe and Mail,* 23 August, p. A15.

Lovins, A.B., E.K. Datta, & J. Swisher. 2003a. "Enlightening Blackouts." *RMI Solutions Newsletter.* Snowmass, CO: Rocky Mountain Institute (Fall/Winter). www.rmi.org/sitepages/pid1058.php

Lovins, A.B. & A. Gadgil. 1991. "The Negawatt Revolution: Electric Efficiency and Asian Development." Snowmass, CO: Rocky Mountain Institute. www.rmi.org/images/other/Energy/E91-23_NegawattRevolution.pdf

Lovins, A.B. & R.H. Heede. 1981. "Hiding the True Costs of Energy Sources." *Wall St. J.,* 17 September, p. 28.

Lovins, A.B., C. Lotspeich, R. Perkins, J. Rogers, & E. Orrett. 2001. *Energy Efficiency Survey Aboard USS Princeton CG-59.* Report to the Office of Naval Research. N000014-01-1-0252. Snowmass CO: Rocky Mountain Institute (June).

Lovins, A.B. & L.H. Lovins. 1981. *Energy/War: Breaking the Nuclear Link.* Washington, DC: Friends of the Earth.

Lovins, A.B. & L.H. Lovins. 1982. *Brittle Power: Energy Strategy for National Security.* Foreword by ex-JCS Chair ADM (Ret.) Tom Moorer and ex-USECNAV, later DCI, Jim Woolsey. Andover, MA: Brick House. Out of print but reposted at www.rmi.org/sitepages/pid533.php

Lovins, A.B. & L.H. Lovins. 1997. *Climate: Making Sense* and *Making Money.* Snowmass, CO: Rocky Mountain Institute. www.rmi.org/images/other/Climate/C97-13_ClimateMSMM.pdf

Lovins, A.B. & L.H. Lovins. 2001. "The Alaskan Threat to Energy Security" (retitled by editor "Fool's Gold in Alaska"). *Foreign Affairs* **80**(4): 72–85 (July/August). Hypertexted and heavily annotated at www.rmi.org/images/other/E-FoolsGoldAnnotated.pdf. See also updates at www.rmi.org/sitepages/pid785.php and www.rmi.org/images/other/E-FuzzyMath.pdf

Lovins, A.B., L.H Lovins, & L. Ross. 1980. "Nuclear Power and Nuclear Bombs." *Foreign Affairs* **58**: 1137–1177.

Lovins, A.B. & B.D. Williams. 1999. "A Strategy for the Hydrogen Transition." National Hydrogen Association Annual Meeting, Vienna, VA, 7–9 April. www.rmi.org/images/other/Trans/T99-07_StrategyH2Trans.pdf

Luft, G. 2004. "U.S.A., China on Collision Course Over Oil." *L.A. Times,* 4 February. www.iags.org/la020204.htm

Luft, G. 2004a. "A Crude Threat." *Baltimore Sun,* 6 April. www.iags.org/n050904b.htm

Luft, G. & A. Korin. 2003. "Terror's Next Target." *J. of Int. Security Affairs* (December). www.iags.org/n0111041.htm

Luigi Colani Design. Undated. "Luigi Colani Rolley." www.jsdi.or.jp/~jun/LuigiColani-rolley.html

Lumpkin, J.J. 2002. "Mid-East Oil a Potential al-Qaida Target, U.S. Nervous." *AP,* 17 October.

Lunsford, J. & D. Michaels. 2004. "Airbus May Modify Its A330 Plane." *Wall St. J.,* 23 July.

Luskin, D. & C.M. Walton. 2001. *Effects of Truck Size and Weights on Highway Infrastructure and Operations: A Synthesis Report.* Report 0-2122-1. Austin, TX: Center for Transportation Research, University of Texas (March). www.utexas.edu/research/ctr/pdf_reports/2122_1.pdf

Lyke, M.L. 2004. "Sales of Gas-Guzzling SUVs Sputter as Fuel Costs Climb." *Seattle Post-Intelligencer,* 19 May. http://seattlepi.nwsource.com/local/173947_gasguzzlers19.html

Macauley, M.K. 2004. "Advantages and Disadvantages of Prizes in a Portfolio of Financial Incentives for Space Activities." Testimony to USHR Science Committee. Washington, DC: Resources for the Future (15 July). www.rff.org/rff/Publications/Testimony.cfm

MacFarquhar, N. 2004. "Saudi Attack Spurs More U.S. Workers to Pull Up Stakes." *N.Y. Times,* 3 June.

Maher, B. 2002. *When You Ride ALONE, You Ride With Bin Laden: What the Government SHOULD Be Telling Us to Help Fight the War on Terrorism.* Beverley Hills, CA: New Millennium Press.

Mallet, V. 2004. "China Is Biggest Oil Consumer After U.S." *Financial Times* (London), 21 January, p. 1.

Margolis, E. 2002. "America's New Middle East Empire." Truthseeker.com, 9 December. www.thetruthseeker.co.uk/article.asp?ID=395

Margolis, R. & D. Kammen. 1999. "The Energy Technology and R&D Challenge." *Science* **285** (30 July): 690.

Markus, F. 2004. "First Drive: 2004 Mercedes-Benz E-320." Motortrend.com, April. www.motortrend.com/roadtests/sedan/112_0404_first_e320/index.html

Marshall, J.M. 2002. "Bomb Saddam?" *Wash. Monthly,* June. www.washingtonmonthly.com/features/2001/0206.marshall.html

Martin, A., D.A. Rogers, & B. Simkins. 2004. "Southwest Airlines: The Blended Winglet Project." Oklahoma State University Working Paper. Stillwater, OK: Oklahoma State University.

Mateja, J., & R. Popely. 2004. "A Fresh Approach—Model Introductions Usher in a New Way of Doing Business for Domestics." *Chicago Tribune,* 5 February.

Maynard, M. 2003. *The End of Detroit: How the Big Three Lost Their Grip on the American Car Market.* New York: Doubleday.

McAlinden, S.P., K. Hill, & B. Swiecki. 2003. "Economic Contribution of the Automotive Industry to the U.S. Economy—An Update." Study for Alliance of Automobile Manufacturers. Ann Arbor, MI: Center for Automotive Research (Fall). www.autoeverywhere.com/fullstudy.pdf

McCartney, S. 2004. "United Hubs Under Attack by Discounters." *Wall St. J.,* 15 June.

McClellan, B. 2004. "Old Idea Made New: Ethanol Fuel Gains Respect." wardsauto.com, 30 June. http://wardsauto.com/ar/auto_old_idea_made

McCloskey, D.N. 1996. *The Vices of Economists—The Virtues of the Bourgeoisie.* Amsterdam: Amsterdam University Press.

McCormick, B. (Executive Director of Fuel Cells, GM). 2003. "Hydrogen: 'The First Step," Hart World Fuels Conference, Washington, DC, 22 September.

McCraw, J. 2000. "Dodge ESX3." *Pop. Mech.* March. http://popularmechanics.com/automotive/motor_sports/2000/3/dodge_hybrid/print.phtml

McCusker, J.J. 1991. "How Much Is That in Real Money? A Historical Price Index for Use as a Deflator of Money Values in the Economy of the United States." *Proceedings of the American Antiquarian Society* **101**(2): 297–383 (October).

McFarlane, R.C. & A.B. Lovins. 2003. "We Can Take Politics Out of Energy Policy." *Dallas Morning News,* 18 May. www.rmi.org/images/other/Energy/S03-03_PoliticsOutOfPolicy.pdf

McKnight, L., P. Vaaler, & R. Katz. 2001. *Creative Destruction: Business Survival Strategies in the Global Internet Economy.* Cambridge, MA: MIT Press.

McMillan, J. 2001. "U.S.-Saudi Relations: Rebuilding the Strategic Consensus." Strategy Forum, Institute for National Strategy Studies, National Defense University. www.ndu.edu/inss/strforum/SF186/sf186.pdf

Meacher, M. 2004. "Plan Now for a World Without Oil." *Financial Times* (London), 5 January.

Mercedes-Benz. 2004. "Mercedes-Benz Reinvents the Vision Grand Sports Tourer: Vision Grand Sports Tourer Hybrid On Display at 2004 Detroit Auto Show." Press release, 5 January. www.prnewswire.com/cgi-bin/micro_stories.pl?ACCT=638221&TICK=NAIAS&STORY=/www/story/01-05-2004/0002082937&EDATE=Jan+5,+2004

Mercedes-Benz. 2004a. "Mercedes-Benz SLR McLaren Makes North American Debut." Press release, 6 January. www.mbusa.com

Mercedes-Benz. Undated. "Mercedes-Benz USA Grand Vision Sports Tourer." Mbusa.com. www.mbusa.com/microsite/gst/index.jsp (downloaded 7 January 2004).

Metshies, G.P. 1999. *Fuel Prices and Taxation, with Comparative Tables for 160 Countries.* Eshborn, Germany: German Agency for Technical Cooperation (May). www.zietlow.com/gtz/fuel.pdf

Michaelis, L. 1997. *CO$_2$ EMISSIONS FROM ROAD VEHICLES, Annex I Expert Group on the United Nations Framework Convention on Climate Change, Working Paper No. 1.* OCDE/GD(**97**)69. Paris: OECD. www.virtualcentre.org/en/dec/toolbox/Indust/gd9769.pdf

Miel, R. 2003. "Carbon Fiber Slowly Goes Beyond High-End Vehicles." *Automotive News,* 22 September.

Moody-Stuart, M. 2002. "A Powerful Partnership." European Business Forum Debate, PriceWaterhouseCoopers (May). www.pwc-global.com/Extweb/NewCoAtWork.nsf/docid/D7577D4C04B66CFB85256CDA00691370

Moody-Stuart, M. 2003. "The Curse of Oil?" Annual Presidential Address, The Geological Society, London, May. www.friendsofeurope.org/download/News%20Extra/The%20Curse%20of%20Oil.pdf

Moore, B. 2000. "Prodigy Points Way to Ford's Future." *EV World,* June. www.evworld.com/archives/interviews2/bculver.html

Moore, J.L., C.E. Behrens, & J.E. Blodgett. 1997. "Oil Imports: An Overview and Update of Economic and Security Effects." CRS 98-1. Washington, DC: Congressional Research Service (12 December). www.ncseonline.org/nle/crsreports/energy/eng-53.cfm?&CFID=6471470&CFTOKEN=24377660#Military%20Costs%20and%20Imported%20Oil

Moore, T.C. & A.B. Lovins. 1995. "Vehicle Design Strategies to Meet and Exceed PNGV Goals." SAE 951906. SAE (Society of Automotive Engineers) Future Transportation Technology Conference, Costa Mesa, CA, 4 August. www.rmi.org/sitepages/pid175.php

Moran, J.R. (COL). 2000. "Abrams Tank System." Brief to Defense Science Board Task Force, August.

Morris, D. 1994. "Green Taxes." Washington, DC: Institute for Local Self-Reliance. www.ilsr.org/ecotax/greentax.html

Morrison, D. 2004. "Harvesting Hydrogen." *Inventing Tomorrow* (Summer): 8–11. www.itdean.umn.edu/news/inventing/2004_Summer/harvestinghydrogen.html

Motor Trend. 2003. "2003 Tokyo Motor Show." motortrend.com. www.motortrend.com/autoshows/coverage/112_0310_tokyo/index3.html#2

Motor Trend. 2003a. "*Motor Trend* Announces 2004 Car of the Year." Press release, 20 November. www.motortrend.com/features/news/112_031120_coy

Moy, R. 2003. "Liability and the Hydrogen Economy." *Science* **301** (4 July): 47.

MSNBC News. 2004. "Demand High for First Hybrid SUV." MSNBC online, 4 June. http://msnbc.msn.com/id/5136654

Mulcahy, P. 2004. "Paul Mulcahy's Pages." www.pmulcahy.com

Müller, R. 2000. "Automobil: Beim Zusammenstoß zwischen Goliath und David darf es keinen Verlierer geben—'Crash-Tech'—Tagung in München." *VDI Nachrichten,* 1 September. Found in Verkehrswerkstatt Pressearchiv 2000/II. www.bics.be.schule.de/son/verkehr/presse/2000_2/v4002_47.htm

Murawiec, L. 2002. Defense Policy Board brief, 10 July. Described at http://slate.msn.com/?id=2069119 and www.washingtonpost.com/ac2/wp-dyn/A47913-2002Aug5?language=printer

Muser, M., G. Krabbel, V. Prescher, A. Dragan, F. Walz, & P. Niederer. 1996. "Advanced Energy Absorbing Components for Improved Effectiveness of Low Mass Vehicle Restraint Systems." International Conference On the Biomechanics of Impact, Dublin, 11–13 September. www.ircobi.org

Naillon, H. 2004. "L'usine à GEZ no 3: Du carbone et des solutions." *Mail-hébdo d'Agir pour l'Environnement,* no. 105, 14 July. http://bellaciao.org/fr/article_txt.php3?id_article=8192

NAS/NAE (National Academies of Sciences/National Academy of Engineering). 1999. *Concerning Federally Sponsored Inducement Prizes in Engineering and Science.* Workshop to Assess the Potential for Promoting Technological Advance through Government-Sponsored Prizes and Contests, Washington, DC, 30 April. Washington, DC: National Academies Press (November). www.nap.edu/books/NI000221/html

NAS/NRC (National Academies of Sciences/National Research Council). 1992. *Automotive Fuel Economy: How Far Should We Go?* Washington, DC: National Academies Press. www.nap.edu/catalog/1806.html

NAS/NRC. 1999. *Biobased Industrial Products: Priorities for Research and Commercialization.* Washington, DC: National Academies Press. www.nap.edu/catalog/5295.html

NAS/NRC. 2001. *Effectiveness and Impact of Corporate Average Fuel Economy (CAFE) Standards.* Prepublication online edition. Washington, DC: National Academies Press (30 July). http://books.nap.edu/catalog/10172.html

NAS/NRC. 2001a. *Was It Worth It? Energy Efficiency and Fossil Energy Research 1978 to 2000.* Washington, DC: National Academies Press. http://books.nap.edu/books/0309074487/html/89.html#pagetop

NAS/NRC. 2002. "Technology and Economic Analysis in the Prepublication Version of the Report Effectiveness and Impact of Corporate Average Fuel Economy (CAFE) Standards: Letter Report." Washington, DC: National Academies Press (16 January). http://books.nap.edu/catalog/10284.html

NAS/NRC. 2002a. *Effectiveness and Impact of Corporate Average Fuel Economy (CAFE) Standards.* Washington, DC: National Academies Press. http://books.nap.edu/catalog/10172.html

NAS/NRC/CAE (National Academies of Sciences/National Research Council/Chinese Academy of Engineering). 2003. *Personal Cars and China.* Washington, DC: National Academies Press. www.nap.edu/catalog/10491.html

NAS/NRC/CETS (National Academies of Sciences/National Research Council/Commission on Engineering and Technical Systems). 1999. *Reducing the Logistics Burden for the Army After Next.* Washington, DC: National Academies Press. http://books.nap.edu/catalog/6402.html

National Energy Policy Development Group. 2001. *Reliable, Affordable, and Environmentally Sound Energy for America's Future: National Energy Policy.* Washington, DC: U.S. Government Printing Office (May). www.whitehouse.gov/energy

Navistar International Corporation. 2003. "Navistar Annual Report 2003," 19 December. http://biz.yahoo.com/e/031219/nav10-k.html

Navy Information Bureau 613. 2002. "Navy Energy Conservation Team Wins Presidential Award." Navy Information Bureau 613 Release, 1 November. www.i-encon.com/pr_11_01_02.htm

NCSL (National Conference of State Legislatures). Undated. "Marriage, Fatherhood and Family Formation." www.ncsl.org/statefed/welfare/familyform.htm (downloaded August 2004).

NEDRI (New England Demand Response Initiative). 2003. "Dimensions of Demand Response: Capturing Customer Based Resources in New England's Power Systems and Markets. Report and Recommendations of the New England Demand Response Initiative," 23 July. http://nedri.raabassociates.org/Articles/FinalNEDRIREPORTAug%2027.doc

Nelson.com. Undated. "Chapter 11 Aircraft Makers 'Bet the Company'." www.cyr.nelson.com/financial/chapter11.html

NEP (National Energy Policy) Initiative. 2002. *Expert Group Report.* NEP Initiative Workshop, Washington, DC, 1–3 February. http://nepinitiative.org/pdfs/NEPInit_Report.pdf

Newman, R.J. 2000. "After the Tank." *U.S. News & World Report,* 18 September. www.newamericancentury.org/def_natl_sec_019.htm

NHA (National Hydrogen Association). Undated. www.hydrogenus.org

NHTSA (National Highway Traffic Safety Administration). 1997. *2020 Report.* Washington, DC: NHTSA (September). www.nhtsa.dot.gov/nhtsa/whatis/planning/2020Report/2020report.html

NHTSA. 2004. "2004 Toyota Prius 4-DR." NCAP (New Car Assesment Program). www.nhtsa.dot.gov/NCAP/Cars/2971.html

NHTSA. Undated. "CAFE Overview—Frequently Asked Questions." Washington, DC: NHTSA. www.nhtsa.dot.gov/cars/rules/cafe/overview.htm (downloaded 26 July, 2004).

NIC (National Intelligence Council). 2000 (declassified 2001). *Global Trends 2015: A Dialogue About the Future with Nongovernment Experts.* Washington, DC: NIC (December). www.cia.gov/cia/reports/globaltrends2015

Nixon, R.M. 1971. *Special Message to the Congress on Energy Resources,* on 4 June. www.nixonfoundation.org/Research_Center/PublicPapers.cfm?BookSelected=1971#P584_18482

Norr, M. & D. Imbsweiler (DaimlerChrysler). 2001."Experience in Crash Simulation of Composite Materials." Workshop on Composite Material Modeling, Institut für Verbundwerkstoffe (Kaiserslautern), 22 February.

NPC (National Petroleum Council). 2003. *Balancing Natural Gas Policy: Fueling the Demands of a Growing Economy Volume II: Integrated Report.* Washington, DC: NPC (September). www.npc.org/reports/ng.html

Nunn, S., J. Schlesinger, R. Ebel & G. Caruso. 2000. *The Geopolitics of Energy into the 21st Century.* Washington, DC: Center for Strategic & International Studies. http://csis.org/pubs/geopoliticspub.html

O'Neill, B., W. Haddon, & H. Joksch. 1974. "Relationship Between Car Size, Car Weight, and Crash Injuries in Car-to-Car Crashes." In *3rd Intl. Congress Automotive Safety Conference Proceedings.* Arlington, VA: Insurance Institute for Highway Safety (July).

O'Neill, B. 1995. "The Physics of Car Crashes and the Role of Vehicle Size and Weight in Occupant Protection." Arlington, VA: Insurance Institute for Highway Safety.

Ogden, J.M., R.H. Williams, & E.D. Larson. 2004. "Societal Lifecycle Costs of Cars with Alternative Fuels/Engines." *En. Pol.* **32**: 7–27.

Olerup, B. 2001. "Technology Development in Market Networks." *En. Pol.* **29**(3): 169–178 (February).

ORNL (Oak Ridge National Laboratory). 2002. *Transportation Energy Data Book: Edition 22.* Oak Ridge, TN: ORNL (September). www-cta.ornl.gov/data/tedb22/Full_Doc_TEDB22.pdf

ORNL. 2003. *Transportation Energy Data Book: Edition 23.* Oak Ridge, TN: ORNL (October). www-cta.ornl.gov/data/Download23.html

ORNL. 2004. *Science and Technology Highlights* **1**: 3. Oak Ridge, TN: ORNL.

OTA (Office of Technology Assessment). 1995. *Advanced Automotive Technology.* OTA-ETI-638. Washington, DC: OTA (September). www.wws.princeton.edu/cgi-bin/byteserv.prl/~ota/disk1/1995/9514

PACCAR. 2001. "The Dynamics of Fuel Efficiency." www.kenworth.com/6600_pro_dyn_aer_rea.asp

PACCAR. 2002. "Kenworth's Own 'Private Fleet' Stays Busy Delivering Fuel Economy Results." Press release, 8 January. www.kenworth.com/6500_arc_pre_mor.asp?file=873

PACCAR. 2003. "PACCAR, Inc. 2003 Annual Report," 12 March. http://biz.yahoo.com/e/040312/pcar10-k.html

Painter, D.S. 2002. "Oil." In *Encyc. of American Foreign Policy* **3**: 1–20, A. DeConde, R.D. Burns, & F. Logevall, eds. New York: Chas. Scribner's Sons/Gale Group.

Paris Motor Show. 2002. "Opel Eco Speedster." www.gm.com/company/gm_exp_live/events/paris_2002/opel/ecospeedster/index.html

Parker, J. 2004. "Ford's Hybrid Escape May Show a Profit." *Detroit Free Press,* 6 January.

Parker, G. & Shirouzu, N. 2004. "Toyota Pushes Up Its Global Targets for Sales, Output." *Wall St. J.,* 21 July, p. A2.

Paster, M., J.L. Pellegrino, & T.M. Carole. 2003. *Industrial Bioproducts: Today and Tomorrow.* Prepared by Energetics, Inc. Washington, DC: U.S. Department of Energy, Office of Energy Efficiency and Renewable Energy, Office of the Biomass Program (July). www.bioproducts-bioenergy.gov/pdfs/BioProductsOpportunitiesReportFinal.pdf

Patel, M. 2004. "Plastics Production and Energy." *Encyc. of Energy* **5**: 81–91. San Diego: Elsevier.

Patterson, P. 1987. "Periodic Transportation Energy Report 1." DOE CE-15. Washington, DC: U.S. Department of Energy (16 November).

Patterson, P., E. Steiner, & M. Singh. 2002. "What Future Car MPG levels and Technology Will Be Necessary?" Future Car Congress, Arlington, VA, 4 June. www.ott.doe.gov/facts/pdfs/fccmpglevels.pdf

Patton, P. 2004. "Low-Fat Car Springs from a Diet High in Fiber." *N.Y. Times,* 9 February. www.globalcomposites.com/news/news_fiche.asp?id=1083&

Patton, K.J., A.M. Sullivan, R.B. Rask, & M.A. Theobald. 2002. "Aggregating Technologies for Reduced Fuel Consumption: A Review of the Technical Content in the 2002 National Research Council Report on CAFE." SAE 2002-01-0628. Presented at SAE World Congress and Exposition, Detroit, 4–7 March.

PCAST (President's Committee of Advisors on Science and Technology). 1997. *Report to the President on Federal Energy Research and Development for the Challenges of the Twenty-First Century.* Washington, DC: President's Committee of Advisors on Science and Technology, Panel on Energy Research and Development (September). www.ostp.gov/PCAST/pch0exez_all.htm

Pearce, F. & Boesch (UNEP). Undated. "Hydrogen: Fuel of the Future." *AAAS (American Association for the Advancement of Science) Atlas of Population and the Environment.* http://atlas.aaas.org/index.php?part=4&sec=hydro

Peckham, J. 2002. "Biodiesel Wins $1/gallon Subsidy in the U.S. Senate Energy Bill." *Biodiesel Fuel News,* 18 February. http://articles.findarticles.com/p/articles/mi_m0CYH/is_4_6/ai_83353436

Peeters, P., P. Rietveld, & Y. Schipper. 2001. "Environmental Effects of Hub and Spoke Networks in European Aviation." In *Regional Configurations, Land Consumption and Sustainable Growth,* eds. O. Atzema, P. Rietveld, & D. Shefer. Cheltenham: Edward Elgar Publishing, Inc. www.flygforsk.lu.se/files/Environmental_impacts.pdf

Peeters, P., K. van Goeverden, Y. Schipper, P. Rietveld, B . van de Kerke, B. Veldman, & W. Dijkstra. 1999. *Milieu en netwerkvorm in de luchtvaart; Pilotstudy.* Ede, Netherlands: Peeters Advies.

Pehlivan, H. 2000. "Incentivized Energy Conservation (ENCON)." 37th Annual Technical Symposium, Assn. of Scientists & Engineers, 10 May. www.navsea.navy.mil/ase/Publications/ASE%202000%20Symposium%20Papers/ASE2000%20ENCON%20Paper.doc

People's Daily (Beijing). 2004. "China's Auto Sales Shoot Up 77 Percent in January," 24 February. http://english.peopledaily.com.cn/200302/24/eng20030224_112172.shtml

Perez, C. 2002. *Technological Revolutions and Financial Capital: The Dynamics of Bubbles and Golden Ages.* Northampton, MA: Edward Elgar Publishing, Inc.

Periscope1.com. Undated. "M1 Abrams Main Battle Tank." www.periscope1.com/demo/weapons/gcv/tanks/w0003593.html

Perkins, S. 2002. "Recent Developments in Road Pricing Policies in Western Europe." ALP-NET Pricing Workshop, Berne, 12–13 September. www1.oecd.org/cem/online/speeches/Spbern02.pdf

Perrett, K. 2003. "Electronic HGV Charging in Europe." ATLANTIC (A Thematic Long-term Approach to Networking for the Telematics and ITS Community), 14 Jan.
www.atlantic.net/AtDocs/KPerrett_14-01-03_17-05-17.doc

Peter, J. 2003. "Hybrid Driven: Toyota Aims the 2004 Prius at a Mass-Market Audience and Gives Us a Glimpse of Things to Come." *Automotive Industries* (October). www.findarticles.com/cf_dls/m3012/10_183/109505549/p1/article.jhtml

Peters, R. 2002. "The Saudi Threat." *Wall St. J.,* 4 January. www.opinionjournal.com/editorial/feature.html?id=95001685

Petersen, J. D. Erickson, & H. Khan. 2003. *A Strategy: Moving America Away from Oil.* Arlington, VA: Arlington Institute (August). www.arlingtoninstitute.org/energy_movingamerica.htm

PETRAS (Policies for Ecological Tax Reform: Assessment of Social Responses). 2002. "Environmental Tax Reform: What Does Europe Think?" (March). www.wupperinst.org/download/EU-Policy-Brief.pdf

Pistonheads.com. 1998. "PistonHeads Gassing Station," 1 April. www.pistonheads.com/gassing/topic.asp?f=23&h=0&t=90655

PNNL (Pacific Northwest National Laboratory). 2003. "Technology Procurement: A Method for Speeding Technology Introduction." PNNL-SA-40225. Richland, WA: Pacific Northwest National Laboratory (November). www.pnl.gov/cfldownlights/pdfs/TP.pdf

Podhoretz, N. 2002. "How to Win World War IV." *Our Jerusalem,* 24 February. www.ourjerusalem.com/opinion/story/opinion20020424c.html

Pole, G. 2003. "Boeing Seeking Ways to Make the 7E7 Work." AINonline, June. www.ainonline.com/Publications/paris/paris_03/pd1boeingpg40.html

Pollack, J. 2002. "Saudi Arabia and the United States, 1931–2002." *Middle E. Review of Intl. Affairs* **6**(3): 77–102 (September). http://meria.idc.ac.il/journal/2002/issue3/pollack.pdf

Ponticel, P. 2003. "BMW Takes Carbon-Fiber Technology to Next Level." *Automotive Engineering Intl. Online/Material Innovations* (November). www.sae.org/automag/material/11-2003/1-111-11-54.pdf

Pope, H. 2004. "Iraq, Terrorism Strain Brittle Mideast Status Quo." *Wall St. J.,* 5 May, p. A12.

Pope, H. 2004a. "A Saudi Leadership Adrift." *Wall St. J.,* 30 June, p. A7.

Porretto, J. 2004. "Toyota Hopes to Sell 300,000 Hybrid Vehicles Globally by End of 2005." *Miami Herald/AP,* 4 August. www.miami.com/mld/miamiherald/business/9318978.htm?1c

Porsche Engineering Services, Inc. (PES). 2001. *ULSAB-AVC (Ultra-Light Steel Auto Body/Advanced Vehicle Concepts) Engineering Report.* Troy, Michigan: PES (October).

Porsche Engineering Services, Inc. (PES). 2002. *ULSAB-AVC Final Engineering Report.* Southfield, MI: American Iron and Steel Institute. www.autosteel.org/ulsab_avc/avc_eng_rpt_index.htm summarized at www.autosteel.org/ulsab_avc/index.htm

Power, S. & J. Wrighton. 2004. "In Europe, SUVs May Face Taxes Amid Drive to Penalize Emissions." *Wall St. J.,* 30 June, p. A2. http://online.wsj.com/article_print/0,,SB108854077783850640,00.html

Prahalad, C.K. 2004. *The Fortune at the Bottom of the Pyramid.* Philadelphia: Wharton School Publishing.

Priest, D. 2003. *The Mission: Waging War and Keeping Peace with America's Military.* New York: Norton.

Pryce-Jones, D. 2002. "Saudi Breakpoint." *National Review Online,* 1 February. (Reprint from *Wall St. J. Europe).* www.nationalreview.com/nr_comment/nr_comment020102.shtml

Public Citizen. 2003. "Key Deficiencies in the 1997 and 2003 Weight/Fatality NHTSA Studies: Initial Review." Washington, DC: Public Citizen (15 October). www.citizen.org/documents/kahane2_guide.pdf

Quartermaster Professional Bulletin. 2002. "From the Quartermaster General" (Spring). www.quartermaster.army.mil/oqmg/Professional_Bulletin/2002/Spring02/CG's%20Letter.htm

Raphael, S. & M. Stoll. 2001. "Can Boosting Minority Car-Ownership Rates Narrow Inter-Racial Employment Gaps?" *Brookings-Wharton Papers on Urban Economic Affairs* **2**: 99–145. Washington, DC: The Brookings Institute. http://urbanpolicy.berkeley.edu/pdf/RS2001PB.pdf

Rechtin, M. 2003. "EPA Mpg Test Doesn't Work for Hybrids." *Automotive News,* 24 November. http://forums.vwvortex.com/zerothread?id=1123844

Reed, S. 2004. "Oil Shortage?" *Bus. Wk.* (European cover story), 5 April. www.businessweek.com/print/magazine/content/04_14/b3877007.htm?mz

Reeves, A. 2003. "Wind Energy for Electric Power: A REPP Issue Brief." Washington, DC: Renewable Energy Policy Project (November update). www.repp.org/articles/static/1/binaries/wind%20issue%20brief_FINAL.pdf

Renewable Fuels Association (RFA). 2004. *Ethanol Industry Outlook 2004: Synergy in Energy.* Washington, DC: RFA (February). www.ethanolrfa.org/outlook2003.shtml

Repetto, R., R.C. Dower, R. Jenkins, & J. Geoghegan. 1992. *Green Fees: How a Tax Shift Can Work for the Environment and the Economy.* Washington, DC: World Resources Institute. http://business.wri.org/pubs_description.cfm?PubID=2561

Ricks, T.E. 2002. "Briefing Depicted Saudis as Enemies." *Wash. Post,* 6 August, p. A1. www.washingtonpost.com/ac2/wp-dyn/A47913-2002Aug5?language=printer

Ricks, T.E. 2002a. "Views Aired in Briefing On Saudis Disavowed." *Wash. Post,* 7 August, p. A14. www.washingtonpost.com/ac2/wp-dyn/A50595-2002Aug6?language=printer

Robbins, J.S. 1992. "How Capitalism Saved the Whales." *The Freeman: Ideas on Liberty* (August). www.fee.org/vnews.php?nid=2618

Roberts, P. 2001. "Bad Sports." *Harper's* (1 April). www.stayfreemagazine.org/suv/harpers.html

Roberts, P. 2004. *The End of Oil: On the Edge of a Perilous New World.* Boston/New York: Houghton Mifflin.

Roberts, P. 2004a. "The Undeclared Oil War." *Wash. Post,* 28 June, p. A21.

Romm, J.J. & W.D. Browning. 1994. *Greening the Building and the Bottom Line.* Snowmass, CO: Rocky Mountain Institute. www.rmi.org/images/other/GDS/D94-27_GBBL.pdf

Roodman, D.M. 1998. *The Natural Wealth of Nations.* Washington, DC: Worldwatch.

RosAeroSystems. Undated. www.rosaerosystems.pbo.ru

Ross, M. & T. Wenzel. 2001. "Losing Weight to Save Lives: A Review of the Role of Automobile Weight and Size in Traffic Fatalities." ACEEE-T013, LBL-48009. Washington, DC: ACEEE (American Council for an Energy-Efficient Economy) (July). www.aceee.org/pubs/t013.htm

RSportCars.com. Undated. "Toyota Alessandro Volta Concept." www.rsportscars.com/eng/cars/toyota_volta.asp

Rudman, M. 2003. "The California Energy Commission's Peak Load Reduction Program." Prepared for ACEEE Conf. on Energy Efficiency as a Resource, Berkeley, CA, 9–10 June. www.aceee.org/conf/03ee/Rudman-3w.pdf

Sachs, S. 2004. "Attacks in Mideast Raise Fear of More at Oil Installations." *N.Y. Times*, 8 May.

Salameh, M.G. 2004. "Oil Crises, Historical Perspective." *Encyc. of Energy* **4**: 633–648. San Diego: Elsevier

Sallie Mae. Undated. "History of the Sallie Mae Name." salliemae.com. www.salliemae.com/about/slma_name.html

Salyer, LTC R.F. (U.S. Army Research Lab., NASA Langley Res. Ctr.). 1999. "The Impact of Fuel Efficiency on the Army After Next." Brief to Defense Science Board panel, Institute for Defense Analyses, Alexandria, VA, 17 August.

San Joaquin Geological Society. 2002. "How the Oil Industry Saved the Whales." www.sjgs.com/history.html#whales

Savage, T. 2003. "Brack Gives First Interview Since Crash at Texas." *IndyRacing.com,* 4 November. www.indyracing.com/indycar/news/story.php?story_id=2115

Sawhill, I. 1999. "From Welfare to Work." *Brookings Review* **17**(4): 27–30 (Fall). www.brook.edu/dybdocroot/press/review/oldtoc.htm#FA99

Schachter, J.P., L. Jensen, & G.T. Cornwell. 1998. "Migration, Residential Mobility, and Poverty in Rural Pennsylvania." *Rural Development Perspectives* **13**(2): 40–45. www.ers.usda.gov/publications/rdp/rdp698/rdp698f.pdf

Schatz, A. & K. Lundegaard. 2004. "Safety Data Give SUVs Poor Grade in Rollover Tests." *Wall St. J.,* 10 August, p. A1.

Schindler, K.-P. (VW). 2002. "Advances in Diesel Engine Technologies for European Passenger Vehicles." 8th Ann. Diesel Engine Emission Reductions (DEER) Conference, San Diego, 25–29 August.

Schipper, L. 2004. "International Comparisons of Energy End Use: Benefits and Risks." *Encyc. of Energy* **3**: 529–555. San Diego: Elsevier.

Schlußbericht der Enquête-Kommission. 2002. "Nachhaltige Energieversorgung unter den Bedingungen der Globalisierung und der Liberalisierung." Deutscher Bundestag (Berlin). www.bundestag.de/parlament/kommissionen/archiv/ener/schlussbericht/index.htm

Schneider, G. 2004. "Fuel Sippers Gaining on Heavyweights." *Wash. Post,* 20 May.

Schröder, G. 2002. "Flüssige Formen." *Truck Magazin.* www.truckmagazin.de/oldarchiv/2002/14/html/news.html

Schumacher, L.G., J. Van Gerpen, & B. Adams. 2004. "Biodiesel Fuels." *Encyc. of Energy* **1**: 151–162. San Diego: Elsevier.

Schumpeter, J. 1943. *Capitalism, Socialism and Democracy.* London: George Allen & Unwin.

Schumpeter, J. 1997. "The Creative Response in Economic History." In *Essays on Entrepreneurs, Innovations, Business Cycles, and the Evolution of Capitalism,* ed. R.V. Clemence. New Brunswick, NJ: Transaction Publishers.

Schwartz, P. 1996. *The Art of the Long View.* New York: Doubleday.

Schwartz, P. & D. Randall. 2003. "An Abrupt Climate Change Scenario and Its Implications for United States National Security." Emeryville, CA: Global Business Network (October).

Sciolino, E. 2001. "Ally's Future: U.S. Pondering Saudis' Vulnerability." *N.Y. Times,* 4 November. www.iranexpert.com/saudi4november.htm

Sehgal, K. 2003. "Wagoner on Wheels." *The Dartmouth Online,* 9 May.

Serious Wheels. Undated. "2004 Toyota Alessandro Volta." Seriouswheels.com. www.seriouswheels.com/top-2004-Toyota-Alessandro-Volta-Concept.htm

Service, R.F. 2004. "The Hydrogen Backlash." *Science* **305** (13 August): 958–961.

Sesit, M.R. 2004. "High Oil Prices Cast a Shadow Over the World's Recovery." *Wall St. J.,* 2 June, C1 and C16.

Shaw, J. & R. Roth. 2002. "Achieving an Affordable Low Emission Steel Vehicle; An Economic Assessment of the ULSAB-AVC Program Design." SAE 2002-01-0361 (SP-1684). Warrendale PA: Society of Automotive Engineers.

Shell Australia Limited. 1999. *Annual Review: "Achievement Through Partnerships."* Shell Australia Limited. www.shell.com

Shell International. 2001. "Exploring the Future: Energy Needs, Possibilities and Scenarios." Shell Group Report. www.shell.com/static/royal-en/downloads/scenarios.pdf

Shuman, M. & H. Harvey. 1993. *Security Without War, 1990–93.* Oxford: Westview Press. www.rmi.org/images/other/Security/S93-23_SecurityWoutWar.pdf

Silverstein, K. 2004. "Hybrid Cars on Fast Track." Utilipoint, IssueAlert, 25 May. www.utilipoint.com/issuealert/article.asp?id=2133

Simmons, M.R. 2004. "The Saudi Arabian Oil Miracle." Presentation given at Center for Strategic and International Studies (CSIS), Washington, DC, 24 February. www.simmonsco-intl.com/files/CSIS.pdf

Small, K. & K. Van Dender. 2004. "The Effect of Improved Fuel Economy on Vehicle Miles Traveled and on Carbon Dioxide Emissions; Estimating the Rebound Effect Using U.S. State Data, 1966–2001." Association of Environmental and Resources Economists Sessions at the ASSA—Allied Social Science Associations Meeting, San Diego, 3 January. www.feem.it/Feem/Pub/Conferences/Programmes/CONP2004-01-03-01.htm

Smil, V. 2004. "War and Energy." *Encyc. of Energy* **6**: 363–371. San Diego: Elsevier.

Smith, M.T. & C. Eberle. 2003. "Heavy Vehicle Mass Reduction Goals and Manufacturing Challenges." Presentation at DOE Workshop, Tooling Technology for Low-Volume Vehicle Production, Seattle, 28 Oct. www.pnl.gov/energy/tooling/presentations/smith.pdf

Smith, S.J., M.A. Wise, G.M. Stokes, & J.T. Edmonds. 2004. "Near-Term US Biomass Potential: Economics, Land-Use, and Research Opportunities." Baltimore, MD: Battelle Memorial Institute, Joint Global Change Research Institute (January). www.energyfuturecoalition.org/files/pdf/Battelle%20studyv4.pdf

Sobel, D. 1995. *Longitude: The True Story of a Lone Genius Who Solved the Greatest Scientific Problem of His Time.* East Rutherford, NJ: Penguin.

Solomon, B.D. & A. Banerjee. 2004. "A Global Survey of Hydrogen Energy Research, Development & Policy." Duluth, MN: U.S. Society for Ecological Economics (21 July). www.ussee.org/working_papers/4wpssolomonhydrogen.pdf

Sovran, G. & D. Blaser. 2003. "A Contribution to Understanding Automotive Fuel Economy and Its Limits." SAE 2003-01-2070. Warrendale, PA: Society of Automotive Engineers.

Spitzer Silo-Fahrzeugwerke GmbH. Undated. "Spitzer Silo-Fahrzeugwerke GmbH." www.spitzer-silo.com

SSB (Schweizerische Bundesbahnen AG). 2003. Statistisches Vademecum: Die SSB in Zahlen 2003. Bern: SSB. http://212.254.205.131/geschaeftsbericht_2003/pdf/vademecum_d.pdf

Starbuck, A. 1878/1989. *History of the American Whale Fishery, from Its Earliest Inception to the Year 1876.* U.S. Commission on Fish and Fisheries Report, Part IV. Secaucus, NJ: Castle (reprinted 1989).

Stavins, R. 2001. "Lessons From the American Experiment With Market-Based Environmental Policies." Discussion Paper 01-53. Washington, DC: Resources For the Future (November). www.rff.org/Documents/RFF-DP-01-53.pdf

Steiner, E. 2003. *Consumer Views on Transportation and Energy.* NREL/TP-620-34468. Golden, CO: National Renewable Energy Laboratory (August). www.nrel.gov/docs/fy03osti/34468.pdf

Stelzer, I.M. 2004. "Sticker Shock." *The Weekly Standard,* 24 May. www.weeklystandard.com/Content/Public/Articles/000/000/004/128eccon.asp

Stern, P.C., E. Aronson, J.M. Darley, D.H. Hill, E. Hirst, W. Kempton, & T. Wilbanks. 1986. "The Effectiveness of Incentives for Residential Energy Conservation." *Evaluation Review* 10(2): 147–176 (April). Beverly Hills/London/New Delhi: Sage Publications.

Stipp, D. 2004. "Climate Collapse: The Pentagon's Weather Nightmare." *Fortune,* 26 January. www.fortune.com/fortune/technology/articles/0,15114,582584,00.html

Stommes, E.S. & D.M. Brown. 2002. "Transportation in Rural America: Issues for the 21st Century." *Rural America* 16(4): 2–10 (Winter). www.ers.usda.gov/publications/ruralamerica/ra164/ra164b.pdf

Suvilehto, H.-M. & E. Öfverholm. 1998. "Swedish Procurement and Market Activities—Different Design Solutions on Different Markets." In *ACEEE 1998 Summer Study on Energy Efficiency in Buildings,* Panel 7, "Market Transformation," pp. 311–23. http://aceee.org/conf/98ss/98sstoc7.pdf

Swisher, J.N. 1997. "Incremental Costs of Carbon Storage in Forestry, Bioenergy and Land-Use." *Critical Reviews in Environmental Science and Technology* 27 (Special): S335-S350.

Swisher, J.N. 2003. *Cleaner Energy, Greener Profits: Fuel Cells as Cost-Effective Distributed Energy Resources.* Snowmass, CO: Rocky Mountain Institute. www.rmi.org/images/other/Energy/U02-02_CleanerGreener.pdf

Swisher, J.N., K. Maracas, J.P. Moscarella & E. Hoyt. 1997. "Joint Implementation of a Land-Use Project without Trees: Dryland Restoration and Carbon Storage with Annual Cultivation of Halophytes." Prepared for the International Conference on Technologies for Joint Implementation, Vancouver, May.

Synlubes.com. 2004."Synlubes.com - Al Smith's Automotive Products." www.synlubes.com/basics.htm

TACOM (U.S. Army Tank-Automotive and Armaments Command). 2003. *Future Combat Systems: 2004.* TACOM brief, *2004 Briefing Book,* 9 September. www.boeing.com/defense-space/ic/fcs/bia/040428_2004flipbook.pdf

Tan, L. 2000. "Spending Patterns of Public Assisted Families." *Monthly Labor Review* 123(5): 29–35 (May). http://stats.bls.gov/opub/mlr/2000/05/art2full.pdf

Tarr, J.A. 1999. "Transforming An Energy System: The Evolution of the Manufactured Gas Industry and the Transition to Natural Gas." *The Governance of Large Technical Systems,* ed. O. Coutard, pp. 19–37. London/New York: Routledge.

Tarr, J.A. 2004. "Manufactured Gas, History Of." *Encyc. of Energy* 3: 733. San Diego: Elsevier.

Taxpayers for Common Sense. 2003. "A Hummer of a Tax Break," 12 December. www.taxpayer.net/TCS/whitepapers/SUVtaxbreak.htm

Taylor, J. & P. Van Doren. 2003. "Mighty Porking Power Rangers: Scanning the Energy Bill." Washington, DC: CATO Institute (19 November). www.cato.org/research/articles/doren-031119.html

Thomas, C.E. 2004. "An Affordable Hydrogen Entry Pathway." 15th Annual U.S. Hydrogen Conference and Hydrogen Expo USA, Los Angeles, 26–30 April.

Thomas, J. 2002. "Case History: International Truck and Engine Corporation Developing a High Performance Truck: 'Do's and Don'ts' of Product Development in a Traditional Industry." *Visions* (April). www.pdma.org/visions/apr02/trucks.html

Three Point Motors Ltd. 2003. "How Safe are Smart Cars?" www.three-pointmotors.com/smart/index.asp

Thucydides. 431 BCE. *The History of the Peloponnesian War.* Translated by R. Crawley. 1910. London: J.M. Dent; N.Y.: E.P. Dutton. www.perseus.tufts.edu/cgi-bin/ptext?lookup=Thuc.+1.141.1

Tirpak, J.A. 2004. "Saving the Galaxy" *Air Force* 87(1), January. www.afa.org/magazine/Jan2004/0104galaxy.asp

Tobias, A. 1993. *Auto Insurance Alert: Why the System Stinks, How to Fix It, and What to Do in the Meantime.* New York: Simon & Schuster. www.andrewtobias.com/insurance.html

Tolan, M. (Accenture). 2003. "The Art of the Possible: Potential for a Dramatic Energy Shift." International Utilities and Energy Conference, Aventure, FL, 23–26 March.

Totten, M. & N. Settina. 1993. "Feebates—Market Incentives for Fuel Efficiency." In *Energy Wise Options for State and Local Governments.* 2nd ed. Washington, DC: Center for Policy Alternatives. http://sol.crest.org/efficiency/energywise_options/ch2-3.html

Toyota. 2001. "Toyota Displays Earth-friendly ES3 Concept Car at International Frankfurt Motor Show 2001." Press release, 12 September. www.toyota.co.jp/en/news/01/0912.html

Toyota. 2003. "Toyota Prius Hybrid Production Increased by 31 Percent for U.S. Market." Press release, 8 December. www.toyota.com/about/news/product/2003/12/08-1-Prius-Production.html

Toyota. 2004. "Toyota Environmental Update" 25. Toyota.com, 1 April. http://pressroom.toyota.com/photo_library/display_release.html?id=2004AprEnvUpdate

Toyota. 2004a. "Cleaner, Leaner and Greener: Toyota Offers a Bevy of Higher-Mileage, Lower-Emission Vehicles." Press release, 29 July. http://pressroom.toyota.com/photo_library/display_release.html?id=20040728

Toyota. 2004b. "Model Selector." Toyota.com. www.toyota.com/vehicles/modelselector/index.html

Toyota. Undated (downloaded 6 January 2004). "Toyota.com: Vehicles: Future Vehicles." Toyota.com. www.toyota.com/vehicles/future/index.html

Toyota. Undated (downloaded 12 April 2004). "Toyota.com: Vehicles: Future Vehicles: Alessandro Volta." Toyota.com. www.toyota.com/vehicles/future/volta.html

Train, K. & C. Winston. 2004. *Vehicle Choice Behavior and Declining Market Share of U.S. Automakers.* Brookings Institution & University of California, Berkeley (January). www.ce.berkeley.edu/~jittichai/Seminar/Vehicle%20Choice.pdf

TransDecisions. 2003. "Object FX and TransDecisions Offer Transportation Industry Advanced Asset Management Tool." Press release, 19 May. www.transdecisions.com/press/pressrel/objectfx051903.html

Transparency International. 2003. *Global Corruption Report 2003.* Berlin, Germany: Transparency International. www.globalcorruptionreport.org

Transport Topics. 2003. "100 For-Hire and Private Carriers 2003." www.ttnews.com/tt100/2003/index.asp

Trottman, M. 2004. "Increased Oil Prices Jeopardize Recovery in U.S. Airline Industry." *Wall St. J.,* 20 May, p. A1. http://online.wsj.com/article/0,,SB108500386191516154,00.html?mod=todays_us_page_one

Truly, R.N. (Chairman VADM, USN Ret.). 2001. "Improving Fuel Efficiency of Weapons Platforms: An Analysis." Power Point presentation. www.nrel.gov/analysis/docs/truly_dsb_analysis.ppt

TTI (Texas Transportation Institute). 2003. *2003 Urban Mobility Study.* College Station, TX: Texas A&M University. http://mobility.tamu.edu/ums

Tully, S. 2004. "Airlines: Why the Big Boys Won't Come Back." *Fortune,* 14 June.

Turbokart.com. Undated. "Textron Lycoming AGT 1500 Turboshaft." http://turbokart.com/about_agt1500.htm

U.S. Bureau of Mines. 1993. "Copper Prices." *Metal Prices in the United States through 1991.* Washington, DC: U.S. Bureau of Mines.

U.S. Congress. Senate. 1975. *Standby Energy Authorities Act.* P.L. 94-163, 94th Cong. (7 February). http://thomas.loc.gov/cgi-bin/bdquery/z?d094:SN00622:@@@L|TOM:/bss/d094query.html

U.S. Supreme Court. 2004. "Engine Manufacturers Association et al. *v.* South Coast Air Quality Management District et al." (02-1323) 309 F.3d. 550. Argued 14 January, decided 28 April. http://a257.g.akamaitech.net/7/257/2422/28apr20041215/www.supremecourtus.gov/opinions/03pdf/02-1343.pdf

Uchitelle, L. 2004. "Controlling Energy Costs on the Factory Floor." *N.Y. Times,* 27 May, p. C1. www.nytimes.com/2004/05/27/business/27conserve.html

UNDP (United Nations Development Programme). 2002/3. *Arab Human Development Report 2002 and 2003.* New York: UNDP. www.undp.org/rbas/ahdr

University of Nebraska, Lincoln, Institute of Agriculture and Natural Resources. 1996. "NebGuide—Rug and Carpet Fibers: Selection and Care." http://ianrpubs.unl.edu/homefurnish/g1222.htm

Urbanchuk, J. 2001. "An Economic Analysis of Legislation for a Renewable Fuels Requirement for Highway Motor Fuels." Moorestown, NJ: AUS Consultants (7 November). www.eere.energy.gov/biomass/national_energy_security.html

Urbanchuk, J. 2003. "Economic Implication of an E-10 Policy." Economic analysis done for the presidential campaign of Howard Dean. Washington, DC: LECG Economics and Finance (26 September).

Urbanchuk, J. & J. Kapell. 2002. "Ethanol and the Local Community." AUS Consultants, SJH & Company. Washington, DC: Renewable Fuels Association (20 June). www.ethanolrfa.org/pubs.shtml#three

USCB (U.S. Census Bureau). 1975. *Historical Statistics of the United States, Colonial Times to 1970* 1:594. Washington, DC: U.S. Bureau of the Census.

USCB. 1997. *Plastics Material and Resin Manufacturing: 1997 Economic Census: Manufacturing: Industry Series.* Washington, DC: USCB (issued July 1999). www.census.gov/prod/ec97/97m3252a.pdf

USCB. 1999. *Heavy Duty Truck Manufacturing: 1997 Economic Census: Manufacturing: Industry Series.* Washington, DC: USCB (October). www.census.gov/prod/ec97/97m3361c.pdf

USDA (U.S. Department of Agriculture). 2004. *World Agriculture Supply and Demand Estimates Report.* Washington, DC: USDA (12 May). http://usda.mannlib.cornell.edu/usda/reports/waobr/wasde-bb/2004

USDA. 2004a. "USDA Releases 2002 Census of Agriculture." Press release. Washington, DC: USDA (3 June). www.usda.gov/Newsroom/0219.04.html

USDA. 2004b. "Fact Sheet: Conservation Reserve Program Haying and Grazing of Acreage." Washington, DC: USDA (June). www.fsa.usda.gov/pas/publications/facts/html/haygraze04.htm

USDA/NASS (U.S. Department of Agriculture/National Agricultural Statistics Service). 2002. *2002 Census of Agriculture.* www.nass.usda.gov/census

Van Creveld, M. 1977. *Supplying War: Logistics from Wallenstein to Patton.* London: Cambridge University Press.

van der Veer, J. (Chairman of the Committee of Managing Directors, Royal Dutch/Shell Group). 2004. "Securing the Promise of Natural Gas." Speech given at International Energy Business Forum, Amsterdam, 22 May. www.shell.com/static/media-en/downloads/speeches/jvdv_22052004.pdf

Viegas, J. 2002. "Tolling Heavy Goods Vehicles on European Roads: From a Diverse Set of Solutions to Interoperability?" Implementing Reform on Transport Pricing: Identifying Mode-Specific Issues, Brussels, 14–15 May. www.imprint-eu.org/public/Papers/imprint_viegas_final.pdf

Vincent, G.A. 2004. "Hydrogen and the Law." Presentation at George Washington University Law School, Washington, DC, 11 June. www.fuelcells.org/info/HydrogenandtheLaw.pdf

Virtualtourist.com. 2003. "Luigi Colani —He Even Designs Trucks!" 27 April. www.virtualtourist.com/m/3fa12/bdf4/9

Volk, M.J. 2004. "Tanker Aircraft Delivers 1 Billionth Pound of Fuel." *Air Force Link,* 22 April. www.af.mil/news/story.asp?storyID=123007539

Volkswagon AG. 2002. "TECABS (Technologies for Carbon Fibre Reinforced Modular Automotive Structures)," 31 March. www.bbw.admin.ch/html/pages/abstracts/html/fp/fp5/5gr99.0286-2.html

Volkswagen. Undated. "Die Zukunft ist da." www.volkswagen-umwelt.de/_content/wissen_303.asp

von Frankenberg, R. 1977. *Porsche: Double World Champions 1890–1977.* Somerset England: Haynes.

von Weizsäcker, E.U., A.B. Lovins, & L.H. Lovins. 1997. *Factor Four: Doubling Wealth, Halving Resources.* London: Earthscan Publications Limited.

Wagoner, R. 2003. Remarks at the North American International Auto Show, Detroit, MI, 6 January. Quoted at www.eere.energy.gov/hydrogenandfuelcells/news_about_hydrogen.html

Wahl, J. 1996. "Oil Slickers: How Petroleum Benefits at the Taxpayer's Expense." Minneapolis, MN: Institute for Local Self Reliance (August).

Wall St. J. 2002. "Panel of Researchers Trims Estimates For SUV, Light-Truck Fuel Efficiency." *Wall St. J.,* 17 January, p. A2.

Wall St. J. 2004. "Hybrid Vehicles Gain Popularity Among Americans." *Wall St. J.,* 22 April, p. D4.

Wall St. J. 2004a. "Commodities Futures Market Data." http://online.wsj.com/documents/mktindex.htm?fs-contract-set-frameset-m99cl2.html (downloaded Spring 2004).

Wallace, J. 2003. "Everett Called a Tough Sell for 7E7." *Seattle Post Intelligencer,* 6 December. http://seattlepi.nwsource.com/business/151368_everett06.html

Walsh, M.E., R.L. Perlack, A. Turhollow, D. de la Torre Ugarte, D.A. Becker, R.L. Graham, S.E. Slinsky, & D.E. Ray. 2000. "Biomass Feedstock Availability in the United States: 1999 State Level Analysis." Oak Ridge, TN: Oak Ridge National Laboratory (January).

Walsh, M.W. 2004. "Bailout Feared if Airlines Shed Their Pensions." *N.Y. Times,* 1 August.

Walsh, M.P. 2004. "Toyota Seen Selling Hybrid Camry in 2006." *Car Lines* 2: 32–33; 45–48. www.walshcarlines.com/pdf/nsl20042.pdf

Walsh, M.P. 2004a. "World's Hydrogen Fuel Stations Up By 33 Pct To 87." *Car Lines* 3 (June): 38.

Wang, M.Q. 1999. *GREET 1.5—Transportation Fuel Cycle Model.* ANL/ESD-39 1: 43 (August).

Ward's Auto World. 2002. "CTS Rollin' Out of Grand River." wardsauto.com, 1 February. http://waw.wardsauto.com/ar/auto_cts_rollin_grand/

WardsAuto.com. 2004. "Escape Hybrid Will Sticker Near $22,000," 20 April. www.evworld.com/view.cfm?section=communique&newsid=5506

Warren, S. 2004. "As Oil Prices Hit Stratosphere, Strategic Reserves Keep Rising." *Wall St. J.,* 17 May, p. A2.

Warrings, F. 2003. "Spardose am Start." *Stern* 27: 168.

WBCSD (World Business Council for Sustainable Development). 2004. *Mobility 2030: Meeting the Challenges to Sustainability.* Geneva: WBCSD. www.wbcsd.org/DocRoot/nfGx0tY87RjAQIIxqLAt/mobility-full.pdf

Weber, A. 2002. "Flexible Factory Reveals Future of GM." *Assembly Magazine,* 1 April. www.assemblymag.com/CDA/ArticleInformation/features/BNP__Features__Item/0,6493,98596,00.html

Weiss, M.A., J.B. Heywood, A. Schafer, & V.K. Natarajan. 2003. *Comparative Assessment of Fuel Cell Cars.* MIT LFEE 2003-001RP. Cambridge, MA: MIT Laboratory for Energy and the Environment (February). http://lfee.mit.edu/publications/PDF/LFEE_2003-001_RP.pdf

Welch, D. 2004. "Gentlemen, Start Your Hybrids." *Bus. Wk.,* 26 April. www.businessweek.com/magazine/content/04_17/b3880057.htm

Wene, C.-O. & H. Nilsson. 2003. "Creating Markets for Efficient Technologies by Establishment of Strategic Niche Markets." In *eceee 2003 Summer Study Proceedings* 2:30–46, Panel 4: "Building the Bridge from Lab to Customer." www.eceee.org/library_links/proceedings/2003/abstract/4030wene.lasso

Wenzel, T. & M. Ross. 2003. "Are SUVs Safer Than Cars? An Analysis of Risk by Vehicle Type and Model." 82nd Annual Meeting of Transportation Research Board, Washington, DC, 15 January.

Wernick, I.K., R. Herman, S. Govind, & J.H. Ausubel. 1996. "Materialization and Dematerialization: Measures and Trends." *Daedalus* **125**(3): 171–198 (Summer). http://phe.rockefeller.edu/Daedalus/Demat

White, J.B. 2004. "Bigger Discounts, Luxury Battles, Clamor for Crossover Lie Ahead." *Wall St. J. Online*, 19 July. http://online.wsj.com/search#SB108999238356365940

White, M.J. 2004. "The 'Arms Race' on American Roads: The Effect of Heavy Vehicles on Traffic Safety and the Failure of Liability Rules." NBER Working Paper 9302. Washington, DC: National Bureau of Economic Research. http://ideas.repec.org/p/nbr/nberwo/9302.html

The White House. 2002. *The National Security Strategy of the United States of America.* Washington, DC: The White House (September). www.whitehouse.gov/nsc/nss.html

Whitfield, K. 2004. "Can Carbon Fiber Compete?" *Automotive Design & Production* (August). http://autofieldguide.com/articles/080407.html

Williams, B.D., T.C. Moore, & A.B. Lovins. 1997. "Speeding the Transition: Designing a Fuel-Cell Hypercar." National Hydrogen Association 8th Annual Meeting, Alexandria, VA, 11–13 March. www.rmi.org/images/other/Trans/T97-09_SpeedingTrans.pdf

Wilson, A. 2003. "WORLD CONGRESS: Work Together, Stop Whining." *Automotive News*, 20 January. www.autonews.com/article.cms?articleId=42054

Wilson, J. 2004. "Weapons of the Insurgents." *Pop. Mech.*, March. http://popularmechanics.com/science/military/2004/3/weapons_of_insurgents

Wilson, D. & R. Purushothaman. 2003. "Dreaming with BRICs: The Path to 2050." Global Economics Paper No. 99. New York: Goldman Sachs (1 October). www.gs.com/insight/research/reports/99.pdf

Wiltsee, G. 1998. "Urban Waste Grease Resource Assessment." Golden, CO: National Renewable Energy Laboratory (November). www.nrel.gov/biomass/biobased_products.html

Wisby, G. 2004. "Environmentalist No Threat to Growth: Panelists." *Chicago Sun-Times*, 30 January.

Wolfgang. 1998. "Wolfgang's ML Page: Smart Crash Tests." www.whnet.com/4x4/Smart_crashtest.html

Womack J.P & D.T. Jones. Forthcoming. *The Solutions Economy.*

Wonacott, P. 2004. "Global Aims of China's Car Makers Put Existing Ties at Risk." *Wall St. J.*, 24 August, p. B1

Wonacott, P., J.B. White, & N. Shirouzu. 2004. "Car Companies Jockey for Slice of China Market." *Wall St. J.*, 8 June, p. A13.

Wood, R.M. 2004. "Impact of Advanced Aerodynamic Technology on Transportation Energy Consumption." SAE 2004-01-1306. Presented at SAE 2004 World Congress & Exhibition, Detroit, MI, March. Warrendale PA: Society of Automotive Engineers. www.sae.org

Woolsey, R.J. 2004. "Biomass Use in Energy Production: New Opportunities for Agriculture." Testimony to Committee on Agriculture, Nutrition and Forestry, U.S. Senate (6 May). http://agriculture.senate.gov/Hearings/hearings.cfm?hearingid=1161&witnessId=3315

Woolsey, R.J., A.B. Lovins, & L.H. Lovins. 2002. "Energy Security: It Takes More Than Drilling." *Christian Science Monitor*, 29 March. www.csmonitor.com/2002/0329/p11s02-coop.html

World Bank. 2002. "Can Vehicle Scrappage Programs Be Successful?" *Urban Air Pollution: South Asia Urban Air Quality Management Briefing Note No. 8.* Washington, DC: World Bank (August). http://lnweb18.worldbank.org/sar/sa.nsf/Attachments/Briefing8/$File/Briefing_Note_No_8.pdf

World Bank. 2003. *World Development Indicators 2003.* Washington, DC: World Bank (April). www.worldbank.org/data/wdi2003/

World Bank. 2003a. *Global Development Finance.* Washington, DC: World Bank. www.worldbank.org/prospects/gdf2003

Worrell, E., A.P. Faaij, G.J. Phylipsen, & K. Blok. 1995. "An Approach for Analyzing the Potential for Material Efficiency Improvement." *Resources, Conservation & Recycling* **13**: 215–232.

Worrell, E., B. Meuleman, & K. Blok. 1995. "Energy Savings by Efficient Application of Fertilizer." *Resources, Conservation and Recycling* **13**: 233-250.

Wrynn, V.D. 1993. *Detroit Goes to War: The American Auto Industry in World War II.* Osceola, WI: Motorbooks International.

www.colani.de. Undated. "Colani Truck." www.colani.de/html/truck.htm

www.fueleconomy.gov. Undated. "Tax Incentives for Hybrid Vehicles." www.fueleconomy.gov/feg/tax_hybrid.shtml

www.handwerk-ist-hightech.de. Undated. "Trierer Karosseriebaufirma TRIGEFA schneidert Colani-Truck." www.handwerk-ist-hightech.de/archiv/betriebe/trigefa.htm

www.theodora.com. 2003. "Chad Economy 2003." www.theodora.com/wfb2003/chad/chad_economy.html

Wyman, C. 2004. "Ethanol Fuel." *Encyc. of Energy* **2**: 541-555. San Diego: Elsevier.

Wyman, C.E., R.L. Bain, N.D. Hinman, & D.J. Sevens. 1993. "Ethanol and Methanol from Cellulosic Biomass." In *Renewable Energy*, ed., T.B. Johansson. Washington, DC: Island Press: 866-923.

Yergin, D. 1991. *The Prize: The Epic Quest for Oil, Money & Power.* New York: Simon & Schuster.

Zingale, N. 2002. "Environmental Analysis: Managing Used Oil Can Be Slippery." *Industrial Heating* (June). www.industrialheating.com/CDA/ArticleInformation/features/BNP__Features__Item/0,2832,78790,00.html